RUSSIAN LAW AND LEGAL INSTITUTIONS

Studies in Russian, East European, and Eurasian Law

William E. Butler (Series Editor)

Butler, W. E., *Russian Law and Legal Institutions*. 3d ed.; 2021. ISBN 13: 978-1-61619-648-6; 10: 1-61619-648-3

The Vinogradoff Institute • Dickinson Law • Pennsylvania State University

RUSSIAN LAW AND LEGAL INSTITUTIONS

THIRD EDITION

William E. Butler
John Edward Fowler Distinguished Professor of Law
Dickinson Law, Pennsylvania State University
Emeritus Professor of Comparative Law, University College London
Foreign Member, Russian Academy of Natural Sciences
Foreign Member, National Academy of Sciences of Ukraine and
National Academy of Legal Sciences of Ukraine

TALBOT
PUBLISHING
Clark, New Jersey

ISBN 9781616196486

TALBOT PUBLISHING
AN IMPRINT OF
The Lawbook Exchange, Ltd.
33 Terminal Avenue
Clark, New Jersey 07066-1323

Please seee our website for a selection of our other publications and fine facsimile reprints of classic works of legal history
www.lawbookexchange.com

Library of Congress Cataloging-in-Publication Data

Names: Butler, William Elliott, 1939- author. | Vinogradoff Institute (Dickinson School of Law), sponsoring body. | Russia (Federation). Konstitut͡sii͡a (1993). English.
Title: Russian law and legal institutions / William E. Butler, John Edward Fowler Distinguished Professor of Law, Dickinson Law, Pennsylvania State University, Emeritus Professor of Comparative Law, University College London, Foreign Member, Russian Academy of Natural Sciences Foreign Member, National Academy of Science of Ukraine and National Academy of Legal Sciences of Ukraine.
Description: Third edition. | Clark, NJ : Talbot Publishing, 2021. | Series: Studies in Russian, East European, and Eurasian law | "The Vinogradoff Institute, Dickinson Law, Pennsylvania State University." | Includes bibliographical references and index. | Summary: "An overview of the Russian legal system and its historical and theoretical sources"-- Provided by publisher.
Identifiers: LCCN 2021001316 | ISBN 9781616196486 (hardcover) | ISBN 1616196483
Subjects: LCSH: Law--Russia. | Law--Russia--History. | Law--Russia--Sources.
Classification: LCC KLB68 .B885 2021 | DDC 349.47--dc23
LC record available at https://lccn.loc.gov/2021001316

Printed in the United States of America on acid-free paper

CONTENTS

Annex: Constitution of the Russian Federation

PREFACE

The present volume is a revised and expanded version of the first and second editions, which appeared respectively in 2014 and 2018. The revisions are substantial and permeate the entire volume without changing its scope. The organization of the book follows the syllabus of the LL.M. External course "Russian Law and Legal Institutions" at the University of London and the J.D./LL.M. syllabus for the seminar "Russian Law" at Dickinson Law, Pennsylvania State University. It incorporates material, as appropriate, from my treatise *Russian Law*, published in three editions by the Oxford University Press and its predecessor, *Soviet Law*, published in two editions by Butterworths.

I am indebted as always to my students who over the years have been generous with their reactions to the course materials. Readers will find the several editions of *Russian Public Law* (London, Wildy, Simmonds & Hill) and the updated loose-leaf service *Russia & The Republics: Legal Materials* (Huntingdon, New York, Juris Publishers) helpful for access to many of the legislative acts referred to herein.

I am obliged to Maryann E. Gashi-Butler and to Elena Shelepchikova for comments and observations which have improved the text. Gratitude is expressed to Consultant Plus for making available a personal database that has facilitated the preparation of this volume.

Status juris: 1 January 2021

W. E. BUTLER

Newville, Pennsylvania

ABBREVIATIONS

CIS	Commonwealth of Independent States
comp.	compiler/compiled
ed.	edition/editor
FSB	Federal Security Service
FSKN	Federal Service for the Control of Narcotics
GPU	State Political Administration
KGB	Committee of State Security
M.	Moscow
MAK	Maritime Arbitration Commission
MID	Ministry of Foreign Affairs
MKAC	International Commercial Arbitration Court
MVD	Ministry of Internal Affairs
NEP	New Economic Policy
no.	number
RF	Russian Federation
RSFSR	Russian Soviet Federated Socialist Republic
САПП	Собрание актов Президента и Правительства Российской Федерации [Collection of Acts of the President and Government of the Russian Federation]
Spb	St. Petersburg
СЗ РФ	Собрание законодательства Российской Федерации [Collection of Legislation of the Russian Federation]
USSR	Union of Soviet Socialist Republics Ведомости Ведомости Съезда Народных Депутатов и Верховного Совета РФ (РСФСР) [Gazette of the Congress of People's Deputies and the Supreme Soviet of the Russian Federation (Russian Soviet Federative Socialist Republic]
ZAGS	Registry for Acts of Civil Status

1

RUSSIAN LAW IN COMPARATIVE LEGAL STUDIES

Russian law and the Russian legal system continue to seek an established place in the constellation of world legal systems. From the mid-eighteenth[1] and to the early twentieth centuries – the formative period of modern comparative law – Russia and her legal system were basically unknown to European comparatists and by default were commonly grouped together with the legal systems of continental Europe.

The dissolution of the former Soviet Union (1922-1991) and its legal system (1917-1991) and the re-emergence of the Russian State continue to offer another dimension to the debate among comparative lawyers generated by the 1917 Russian Revolutions. The Revolution of February 1917 brought an end to the Russian monarchy; the Revolution of October 1917 terminated the rule of the coalition Provisional Government that had supplanted the monarchy. Soviet law claimed, on the basis of ideological axioms, to be unique among all existing and preceding legal systems. Whereas most Bolsheviks accepted that "law" was a component of the Soviet public order, whatever its ultimate fate was postulated to be, this claim to uniqueness challenged the classical classifications of legal systems or families of legal systems.

Some considered the Soviet legal system to be merely a species of the European Romano-Germanic civil law system embellished with ideological encrustations.[2] Professor Albert Ehrenzweig (1906-1974) observed that if the Soviet legal system could validly be segregated as unique in the traditional realm of private law, he would be obliged "to abandon the philosophical pattern of two and one-half millennia and the comparative concern of a thousand years". Whatever innovations may have been wrought in public law, he believed that the "essentially civilian structure'" in the law of the family, property, succession, contract, and tort remained unchanged, and he perceived only minor changes in established European patterns of criminal law and procedure.[3]

[1] On a revisionist history of the origins of the science of comparative law, see O. V. Kresin, *Comparative Legal Studies: 1750-1835. Approaches to Conceptualization*, ed. & transl. W. E. Butler (London, 2019). 2 vols.

[2] See F. H. Lawson (1897-1983), cited in the preface to J. N. Hazard, W. E. Butler, and P. B. Maggs, *The Soviet Legal System* (3rd ed., 1977), p. vi.

[3] See Ehrenzweig's review of J. N. Hazard (1909-1996), *Communists and Their Law* (1969), in

Presumably those partial to this perception of Soviet law will have seen nothing novel in the post-Soviet period, merely a discarding of certain Soviet "forms"' of no substantive consequence and the preservation of a "legal mentality" formed during the decades of Soviet rule. Those who truly do know Soviet law will have found the 1990s and first two decades of the twenty-first century challenging, for the effort to "democratize" and to "marketize" the Soviet legal legacy has been a formidable task going far beyond the rejection or replacement of "forms" and the importation of "transplants". Three decades on, the transition is still in process.

Perceptions of uniqueness in the classification of foreign legal systems depend partly upon developments within our own. Those who in the interwar or early post-1945 era attributed significance when analyzing Soviet law to the differences in economic system between East and West found that by the mid-1980s the enlarged State sector and greater commitment to social welfare in Western economies and enhanced decentralization and recourse to economic accountability in socialist economies had reduced a distinction of principle to one of degree.[4] The transition instituted in 1986 by Mikhail Sergeevich Gorbachev to a socialist market economy in the former Soviet Union reduced and mutated the elements of distinction all the more. The accession of the Russian Federation to the Council of Europe and the World Trade Organization required yet more changes in order to approximate domestic Russian legislation to the requirements of those entities. The partial disengagement noticeable from 2013 of Russia from European institutions and reorientation towards the Far East and Southeast Asia has not altered significantly the continued pursuit in Russia of further market-oriented law reform.

In the course of comparison much depends on what one considers to be important when asserting or dismissing claims for uniqueness. All modern legal systems experience continuous change of greater or lesser moment, but few claim to be in "transition" from one developmental stage to another or even have an awareness of being at a particular developmental stage. Soviet law, however, was claimed to be in constant transition, moving towards the creation of a socialist and eventually a communist society. Russian law today purports to be in transition while dismantling the legacy of the Soviet era. In this sense Soviet and post-Soviet law have been avowedly "transitional" since February 1917.

California Law Review, LVIII (1970), p. 1007.

[4] René David was among those who altered his view with respect to these criteria for classifying legal systems. Compare his *Traité élémentaire de droit civil compare* (1950), p. 224, with his *Major Legal Systems in the World Today* (3d ed., 1985), as translated and revised by J. E. C. Brierley. Russian legal scholars continue to reappraise their own post-Soviet past. Sergei Sergeevich Alekseev (1924-2013) was among those who believed that the Soviet legal system qualified as a "totalitarian" legal system, which constituted a distinct family within the world family of legal systems. See S. S. Alekseev, Теория права [Theory of Law] (1993).

The Soviet law codes of the New Economic Policy (NEP) era (1921-1928) were modeled upon those of Germany, France, Switzerland, Austria, and the draft Russian codes under preparation in the twilight years of the Empire. In the NEP years the Soviet authorities pursued mixed economic and legal policies containing capitalist and socialist elements, both implemented in the legislation of those times. The more considered Soviet codifications of the 1960-1970s elevated the claims of uniqueness and novelty. Although certain codification statutes from the Soviet era remain in force, the codes in force in the Russian Federation from the Soviet era eventually were replaced; in some cases more than two decades were required for this to transpire.

The concept of "families of legal systems" is among the analytical categories extensively used in comparative law to differentiate legal systems, individually and collectively, from one another.[5] Although this concept matured early in the twentieth century (in the writings of, *inter alia*, John Wigmore),[6] it achieved popularity from the mid-twentieth century in the works of the French comparatist, René David (1906-1991). Because "families of legal systems" is an analytical concept, a kaleidoscope through which different facets of legal systems interplay and acquire different hues, a particular individual legal system may belong to two or more families of legal systems simultaneously.

The Russian science of comparative law – still greatly attracted by the concept of "families of legal systems"[7] – is divided as to whether Russian law (and presumably other CIS legal systems) remains outside the Romano-Germanic legal family. Many see Russian law as falling within the category of "transitional" legal systems whose ultimate destination, for comparative law classification purposes, remains as undetermined as it is uncharted.[8] General western studies of comparative law have not decided what to do with Russia. Karl Zweigert (1911-1996) and Hein Kötz deleted their chapter on socialist legal systems from recent editions. Some recognize that Russia

[5] See L. A. Luts, "Typologies of Modern Legal Systems of the World", in W. E. Butler, O. V. Kresin, and Iu. S. Shemshuchenko (eds.), *Foundations of Comparative Law: Methods and Typologies* (2011), pp. 36-52.

[6] See John Wigmore (1863-1943), *A Panorama of the World's Legal Systems* (1928; rev. ed., 1935); also see W. R. Roalfe, *John Henry Wigmore: Scholar and Reformer* (1977).

[7] For recent examples, see Veniamin Evgenevich Chirkin (1924-2019), Основы сравнительного правоведения [Foundations of Comparative Law] (2014); V. I. Vlasov, G. B. Vlasova, and S. V. Denisenko, Сравнительное правоведение [Comparative Law] (2014); M. V. Zakharova, Сравнительное правоведение [Comparative Jurisprudence] (Moscow, 2016).

[8] See the Uzbek jurist, A. Saidov, *Comparative Law*, transl. W. E. Butler (2003); on Russian writings, see Iu. A. Tikhomirov, Курс сравнительного правоведения [Course of Comparative Law] (1996); M. N. Marchenko, Сравнительное правоведение [Comparative Law] (2d ed.; 2011; reprinted annually between 2013 and 2018); id, Правовые системы мира [Legal Systems of the World] (2d ed.; 2008; reprinted 2009 and 2016).

and other CIS countries may become "hybrid" legal systems.[9] Glenn saw "force" as the overriding characteristic of Soviet law and gave but the most cursory attention to Russia at all.[10]

One may ask why jurists in post-Soviet legal systems place such emphasis upon the classification of national legal systems into legal families. The answer lies in their conception of law as one of the social sciences. One purpose of the scientific method is to isolate, describe, and categorize living and non-living things according to their generic characteristics, determine what is similar and what differs, why, and what follows from such an analysis. Law is deemed to be no exception; as a phenomenon, it should be subject to the same standards of classification as any others. Thus commences the challenge.[11]

A number of classifications exist, each of which emphasizes certain features of Russian law, legal history, and legal experience:[12]

Russian Legal System as Socialist. Insofar as Soviet law constituted a separate and distinct family of legal systems, Russian law was an integral part of that family during the period from approximately late 1917 until 1991. This view was universally accepted in Soviet legal doctrine. Given that some western comparatists did not regard Soviet law as something distinct from the Romano-Germanic legal family, they would have classified Russia as part of the Romano-Germanic family.

At one time thirteen countries with a total population exceeding two billion persons would have fallen into this family of legal systems; at present, five (or six) countries remain: Vietnam, China, Cuba, Laos, and North Korea, with Ethiopia considered by many to qualify.[13] The collective population

[9] P. de Cruz, *Comparative Law in a Changing World* (3d ed., 2007), p. 193.

[10] H. Patrick Glenn (1940-2014), *Legal Traditions of the World* (5th ed., Oxford, 2014), the first edition of 2004 was collectively reviewed in *Journal of Comparative Law*, I (2006), pp. 100-176 (Russia, reviewed by W. E. Butler, pp. 142-146). Russian law students have enjoyed access to several editions of René David since 1967 in the Russian language, as well as to Zweigert and Kötz.

[11] See W. E. Butler, "What Makes Socialist Legal Systems Socialist?", *Journal of Comparative Law*, XIII (2018), pp. 1-19,

[12] The analysis with respect to Belarus and Ukraine would be similar. With respect to Ukraine, see W. E. Butler, «Україна на юридичній карті світу» [Ukraine on the Legal Map of the World], in O. V. Petryshyn (ed.), Правова доктрина України [Legal Doctrine of Ukraine] (Kharkiv, 2013), I, pp. 250-263; translated in O. V. Petryshyn (ed.), *Ukrainian Legal Doctrine* (London, 2015), I, pp. 170-190. With respect to Belarus, see A. V. Egorov, Теоретико-методологическе основания сравнительного правоведения [Theoretical-Methodological Grounds of Comparative Jurisprudence] (Vitebsk, 2014); Egorov, Сравнительное правоведение [Comparative Jurisprudence] (Minsk, 2015).

[13] See S. G. Abebe, *The Last Post-Cold War Socialist Federation: Ethnicity, Ideology and Democracy in Ethiopia* (2014), p. 2: Ethiopia is "... fundamentally a socialist federal system based on the Stalinist notion of 'the right to self-determination of nationalities' and Marxist-Leninist organizational principles of the state". Subsequent changes in Ethiopia may constitute a

of these five States exceeds 1.6 billion persons. The fate of the other eight countries, insofar as the classification of legal systems is concerned, remains controversial. Some have joined or become associated with the European Union. Some fragmented into multi-States, and the Soviet Union itself dissolved into twelve independent States (the three Baltic countries seceded earlier). All have distanced themselves to some extent from the classical "socialist" model of legal system, but to varying extents.

Although comparatists share different views with regard to what the distinguishing indicia of a socialist legal system were/are with respect to Russia, the following would be singled out in the discussion:

(1) private ownership of the means of production leads to the exploitation of man by man and should be replaced by socialist, State, and social forms of ownership, usually achieved by the nationalization of private property and State predominance in the economy;

(2) capitalist anarchy in production and distribution relations is replaced by State economic planning and centralized distribution; five-year and one-year economic plans are issued in the form of a law;

(3) antagonistic class elements are eliminated or isolated through various means of legal discrimination (deprivation of some civil rights, class justice);

(4) the laboring masses comprise the people, and those who use hired labor for their personal enrichment do not fall within the concept of the "people";

(5) class struggle is the driving force of historical change, and class enemies may take the form of exploiters or enemies of the people;

(6) members of the working proletariat are accorded certain advantages in comparison with the peasantry and intelligentsia, at least in principle;

(7) the Communist Party played the role of vanguard in the Soviet State and enjoyed a monopoly of political power;

(8) social (that is, non-State) organizations must be under Party direction; religious organizations may be tolerated, but were not encouraged and experienced various levels of persecution;

(9) Marxism-Leninism, sometimes augmented by the writings or doctrines of other local revolutionary leaders, operated as the official State and Party ideology;

move away from this model.

(10) drawing upon the experience of the Paris Commune in the early 1870s, the foundation of the Soviet State system is the "soviets", or councils, which acted as agencies of State power (as distinct from agencies of State administration);

(11) the separation of powers is recognized, but not the principle of checks-and-balances;

(12) the principle of democratic centralism within the State system means that medium-level and local soviets are subordinate to superior soviets, and the principle of dual subordination means that executive committees of soviets are subordinate to their own soviet and to their superior executive committee;

(13) courts at the lowest levels are elected directly by citizens and at the higher levels by the respective soviets. The principle that judges may not be removed is not recognized in socialist legal culture;

(14) the exercise of rights and freedoms is subject to the cause of achieving socialism or communism and to the leading role of the Party;

(15) the distinction between public and private law is not recognized;

(16) unequal forms of ownership, discouragement of personal enrichment, cooperative marketing of goods; civil marriage; duty to rescue socialist property; greater emphasis given to crimes against the State and ideological crimes; discouragement or prohibition of strikes in labor relations; and many others.

Russian Legal System as Totalitarian. In the post-Soviet era some jurists have reclassified the Soviet legal system as a "totalitarian" system which was never truly "socialist" and which, in their view, belongs to a distinct family of legal systems. They would regard Russia as being within the totalitarian family.[14] This classification has not been widely accepted in comparative law circles because it is, in effect, a classification based principally upon political characterizations of leaders (Stalin, Hitler, Pol Pot, and so on) rather than legal principles and institutions.[15] Some have characterized this as an

[14] See, for example, Alekseev, note 3 above. Baglai regarded Soviet constitutional law from 25 October 1917 through the late 1980s as "totalitarian constitutional law". See M. V. Baglai, Конституционное право Российской Федерации [Constitutional Law of the Russian Federation] (13th ed.; 2018), p. 58.

[15] The term originated in the Italian as "totalitario" and first appeared in its English language guise in the translation of Luigi Sturzo (1871-1959), *Italy and Fascismo*, transl. Barbara Barclay Carter (1926). As a political characterization it received considerable purchase in the philosophical analysis by Hannah Arendt (1906-1975), *The Origins of Totalitarianism* (New York, 1951), originally published at London as Arendt, *The Burden of Our Time* (1951). Il'in introduced the term in his work on the essence of legal consciousness when he completed his final emendations to that work ca. 1953. The term did not appear, presumably because it

"ideological" classification. Yet others have collapsed two classifications into one and refer to the "legal system of totalitarian socialism".[16]

There is a substantial political science literature on the concept of "totalitarianism" and whether this concept was relevant or useful with respect to the former Soviet Union or Hitlerite Germany. A number of western specialists on Soviet law, with support from the Ford Foundation, attempted during the 1980s to identify the distinctive "Stalinist' or "totalitarian" component of Soviet law, without a great deal of success, in both private and public law.[17] The specific legal component(s) in a "totalitarian" State and its legal system could not be satisfactorily isolated and identified. In particular, it has been difficult to identify uniquely totalitarian elements of law and legal systems which cannot be otherwise described (authoritarian, dictatorial, and so on).

Although examples of "totalitarian" legal systems cited in the literature happen to be associated with a particular ideology, the presence or absence of an ideology does not appear to be decisive. The "seeds of totalitarianism" have been traced as far back to China in the years 210 to 258 BC.[18]

Russian Legal System as Technocratic. The observation has been and is being made in comparative-law circles that the legal systems of western countries, including Russia, are becoming increasingly "technocratic". For these purposes "technocracy" means that normative legal acts are being drafted more in the style of "technical documentation" than in the style of "legislation". The excessive detail means the enactments lose any link with reality, reflecting, as Lafitsky expressed the position, "the illusions of their compilers".[19] The more they are divorced from reality, the greater the reliance upon sentences and words that are meaningless.

did not exist, in the 1919 proofs of this work. One may reasonably assume that Il'in became aware of the term as part of its cold war currency and, indeed, may have been among the first Russian jurists to include the term in his doctrinal oeuvre. See Iu. T. Lisitsa (ed.), И. А. Ильин. Сочинения в двух томах [I. A. Il'in. Works in Two Volumes] (Moscow, 1993), I, p. 107; Il'in, *On the Essence of Legal Consciousness*, ed. W. E. Butler, P. T. Grier, and V. A. Tomsinov (2014).

[16] See Chirkin, note 7 above, pp. 315-330. For a more general use of this characterization, see V. I. Lafitsky, Сравнительное правоведение. Национальные правовые системы [Comparative Jurisprudence. National Legal Systems] (2012), I, p. 99: ".... There exist two communities of legal systems which are built on the denial of spiritual (ethical) values. These are the legal systems of totalitarian and technocratic communities".

[17] See D. D. Barry, G. Ginsburgs, and P. B. Maggs, *Soviet Law After Stalin* (1977-79). 3 vols.

[18] See V. I. Lafitsky, Сравнительное правоведение в образах права [Comparative Jurisprudence in the Images of Law] (2010-2011), II, p. 394. Also see Weitseng Chen and Hualing Fu (eds.), *Authoritarian Legality in Asia* (Cambridge, 2020) for application of the authoritarian analytical perspective to China, Singapore, Taiwan, Hong Kong, Japan, Vietnam, and South Korea. Authoritarian legality "falls between liberal rule of law ... and lawless autocracy". Ibid., p. 17.

[19] Lafitsky, note 18 above, II, p. 394.

In effect, a technocratic legal system moves away from setting out general principles of law in the texts of legislative acts and indulges in excessive legislative activity, "over-legislates". Partly this trend results from the absence of a clear doctrine and principle determining the spheres of social life in which it is inappropriate for the State to intervene. Legal theorists devise concepts of the "perfect legal system" to which ideal legislation should correspond, but fail to indicate those domains of human existence which the State in the broadest sense of the word should refrain from regulating. In practice, legislation becomes increasingly fragmentary as it explodes in quantity and more readily reflects the interests of special groups.

The language and terminology of legislation is no longer comprehensible by the average citizen in a technocratic legal system. Judicial practice tends to follow legislative patterns, and as a result in a technocratic legal system the issues confronting the courts move away from the application of legal principles towards the application of technicalities of construction that defy sound reason.

Measured by the standard of "technocracy", the Romano-Germanic, Common Law, and former socialist legal systems form a single family. One may conjecture about the extent to which elements of technocracy were accelerated by the introduction of national economic planning within the socialist legal tradition and continue to be reflected by the introduction of "administrative reglaments" and similar normative legal acts in the post-Soviet legal systems. Technology itself doubtless furthers "technocracy" by reducing the costs of publication and dissemination of the texts of normative legal acts.

Russia is doubtless among the technocratic legal systems of the world.

Russian Legal System as "Formalist". Modern legal systems may be characterized not only by the volume of normative legal acts which they adopt, but by the way in which those acts are interpreted and applied. Comparative lawyers, legal practitioners, and socio-legal specialists have noted the extent to which post-Soviet legal systems have preserved, some would say reinforced, the "extreme formalism" as a characteristic Russian pattern of thinking about what law is and how it should be understood. The origins of this phenomenon have yet to be fully investigated. Whether it originated in Soviet legal experience or existed previously and merely found a congenial context in national economic planning remains to be explored, not least in comparative studies of legal systems whose historical experience differs.

The formalist approach is embodied in Article 431 of the Civil Code of the Russian Federation, as amended 8 March 2015, which instructs courts when interpreting contracts to use "the literal meaning of the words and expressions contained therein" by means, in the event of ambiguity, of comparing the contract provisions with other provisions and the sense of the contract as a whole. Only if that approach fails may the court take into account the purpose of the contract, including preceding negotiations, practices between the parties, customs of business turnover, and subsequent conduct of the parties. This formulation, it should be stressed, is a post-Soviet formulation, but one which departs but little from the earlier Soviet civil codes.[20]

The plausibility and efficacy of a Planned Economy from a legal perspective depends upon the rationality of the planning "command system" of normative legal acts implementing the Plan and disciplining the discretion of actors within the system. There can be minimal scope, if any, for human volition, lest the symmetry of Plan relations be disturbed. A literal approach to the interpretation of contracts (and of legislation and treaties) is essential. There is a mental set in the Russian legal system and among Russian professionals that finds reflection in the general population:

> The manner in which law is interpreted is formalistic in the extreme; law in practice is expected to be equated with the letter of the law. In other words, the characteristic Russian vision of law does not allow space for interpretations that would give prominence not so much to what the law actually says, as to what its makers intended to bring about, with an appreciation that any given legal principle or stimulation should be adjusted to fit the circumstances. However, in extreme formalism, the legal space of law is restricted to the law as it is written down. It is assumed that if the law is a good law, it must be applicable to any relevant circumstances just as it is written; when the time comes to implement the law there can be no legitimate requirement for flexibility or adjustment. It follows that there is very limited provision for a judge to exercise discretion and adapt the content of the law to specific circumstances of a particular situation, as judges do in many other jurisdictions.[21]

[20] See W. E. Butler (ed. & transl.), *Civil Code of the Russian Federation* (2021), I, p. 351. In 2015 Article 431 was amended to provide that if the literal interpretation does not enable the content of the contract to be determined, the "true common will of the parties" is to be taken into account by eliciting all the respective circumstances. See Butler (ed. & transl.), *Civil Code of the Russian Federation* (2021), p. 351. Insofar as this formalism is a "Russian characteristic", it is nonetheless present in all the post-Soviet civil codes, having been carried over from Soviet legal experience.

[21] M. Kurkchiyan and A. Kubal (eds.), *A Sociology of Justice in Russia* (2018), p. 268. In ca. 1999 an associate justice of the United States Supreme Court and a senior appellate judge were sent to Russia in order to explain to Russian judges of all the court systems why and how in corporate cases it would be advisable for Russian courts to have regard to the interests of parties (for example, stockholders) who were not before the court but nonetheless might be affected by the outcome of litigation between the parties – an approach that would have required a modification of the principles set down in Article 431 of the Civil Code.

In the language of socio-legal studies, this would appear to be an example of where the "law in the books" and the "law in action" coincide, and the "law in the books" has an overriding impact on law in practice. Although Article 431 of the Civil Code addresses contract interpretation, it has been generally understood to extend to all interpretation, including statutory interpretation, and is an integral element of legal education in all post-Soviet law faculties. Formalism affects the interpretation and application of law by the courts. Legal formalism "prompts judges to think (mostly if not exclusively) about the wording of norms, not about substantive legal institutions, principles and concepts".[22] The "… mentality of Russian courts is (still) strongly imbued with formalism".[23]

Formalism in law is said to be systemically greater in Romano-Germanic than in Common Law legal systems, reflected in greater distrust of the judiciary, less honesty in the administrative system, and higher levels of corruption.[24]

Russian Legal System as Transitional. All modern legal systems experience legal change of greater or lesser moment, but few claim to be in "transition" from one developmental stage to another. Russian legal doctrine during the Soviet era claimed that Soviet law and the legal system were constantly in transition towards the creation of a socialist and, ultimately, a communist society. In the post-Soviet period, Russian law purports to be in transition while dismantling the legal norms and legacy of the Soviet era. In this sense, Russian law in the Soviet and post-Soviet periods has been avowedly "transitional" since 1917.

The question within comparative law is: "transition" from what to what, or from where to where? Modern Russia is plainly no longer part of the socialist family of legal systems. Some comparatists believe that Russia has returned to, or always been a part of, the Romano-Germanic family of legal systems. Although Russia is a member of the Council of Europe and in the process of attaining membership received elements or standards of European human rights law into the Russian legal system, and likewise has modified its legislation to accommodate membership in the World Trade Organization, that "approximation" or "harmonization" of the legal systems is far from completed.[25]

[22] S. Belov, "Russia: Foreign Transplants in the Russian Constitution and Invisible Foreign Precedents in Decisions of the Russian Constitutional Court", in T. Groppi and M-C. Ponthoreau (eds.), *The Use of Foreign Precedents by Constitutional Judges* (Oxford, 2013), p. 363.
[23] M. Mazza, "The Russian Constitutional Court and the Judicial Use of Comparative Law: A Problematic Relationship", in G. F. Ferrari (ed.), *Judicial Cosmopolitanism: The Use of Foreign Law in Contemporary Constitutional Systems* (Leiden/Boston, 2020), p. 542.
[24] See Gerrit de Geest, *American Law: Comparative Primer* (Cheltenham, 2020), p. 32.
[25] Both the Council of Europe and the World Trade Organization are international organizations established by treaty and subject to the law of treaties. Within their respective parameters, however, both are developing a body of law applicable to the legal relations

Russia has never officially declared an intention to become part of the Romano-Germanic family of legal systems in the non-EU sense of the word, and it remains unclear what the threshold criteria would be to qualify for classification in that family. Whatever the criteria may be, it is not simply a matter of "reversing", or "repealing", or "substituting" the legal changes from the Soviet era, as some comparatists have suggested.[26]

Modern post-Soviet Marxist thought in Russia, however, shares a different understanding of "transition" and believes that the transition underway has a particular destination in view: the reintroduction of capitalism, albeit in a new variant.[27]

Russian Legal System in the Family of Slavic Law. Russians are among the early Slavic peoples;[28] the Slavs of Belarus and Ukraine figure marginally, if at all, in most discussions[29] in comparative law circles with respect to the existence of a Slavonic family of legal systems. A "native, pure, and distinctive Slavic legal system" never came to pass, as Wigmore observed, yet he devoted nearly 80 pages of his treatise on the world's legal systems to those territories inhabited principally by Slavs.[30] The category of "Slavonic, or Slavic, law", as a term, poses some of the same conundrums that "comparative law" does. There is no country called "Slavonia" and therefore no positive law which purports to govern all peoples of Slavonic ethnic affinity or origin.

that arise under their respective treaties. To the extent that law is formulated, articulated, and enforced by Council of Europe and WTO institutions, it is not inappropriate within the framework of comparative legal analysis to refer to the constituents of those legal rules as members of the Council of Europe or WTO family. Russian jurists and legislators have reacted negatively to decisions of the Council of Europe and of the European Court of Human Rights which, in their view, are contrary to the supremacy of the Russian Constitution and introduced measures to restrict the application of such judicial decisions since 2015.

[26] See Glenn, note 10 above.

[27] These views are explored in M. N. Marchenko, Советское и постсоветское государство и право: сравнительно-правовое исследование [Soviet and Post-Soviet State and Law: Comparative-Legal Study] (2018).

[28] S. Plokhy, *The Origins of the Slavic Nations: Premodern Identities in Russia, Ukraine, and Belarus* (2006).

[29] A recent major multi-volume treatise on comparative law begins with the "legal systems of Eastern Europe" and, following introductory chapters on the history and subject-matter of comparative law, devotes chapters to the "national legal systems of the Slavonic world": Russia, Poland, Czech Republic, Bulgaria, and Croatia. Ukraine and Belarus are not given separate treatment. See V. I. Lafitsky (ed.), Сравнительное правоведение: национальные правовые системы [Comparative Law: National Legal Systems] (M., 2012), I, pp. 119-527. Of relevance is A. V. Seregin, Цивилизационный феномен средневекового многообразия форм Славянских государств [Civilization Phenomenon of the Medieval Diversity of Forms of Slavic States] (M., 2017).

[30] J. H. Wigmore, *Panorama of the World's Legal Systems* (Library ed., 1936), pp. 733-808. Others who singled out "Slavonic law" as a basis for classifying families of legal systems included Adhémar Esmein (1848-1913) and Adolf F. Schnitzer (1889-1989). See A. F. Schnitzer, *Vergleichende Rechtslehre* (2d ed.; 1963).

Instead we are dealing with an ethnos whose rulers formed sundry entities and allegedly gave expression in their positive-law enactments to Slavic mores, values, traditions, folkways, and the like. Slavic law, insofar as expressed in norms, is customary law, or is a body of values reflected in particular formulations of positive State legislation in countries where the Slavonic population is predominant, or is a sub-stratum of natural law founded on the religious principles of Christian Orthodoxy. For some comparatists the concept of a family of Slavonic legal systems falls within a larger classification of the "legal community of the Christian tradition of law", which includes Slavic, Romano-Germanic, Common Law, Scandinavian, and Latin American legal families. Jurists of this persuasion emphasize the Christian writings that determine the "spiritual heart", distinctive features, and, ultimately, the fates of the major legal systems of the world. The Christian roots of individual legal enactments are traced.[31]

Comparative research on Slavonic legal systems originated in the nineteenth century within. the Eastern European countries concerned and eventually became known to western European comparatists.[32] The pioneer in this field was the Polish legal scholar, Waclaw Aleksander Maciejowski (1793-1883), who published a four-volume history of Slavonic legislation between 1832 and 1835. The purpose of this work was to demonstrate that there existed in Europe, in addition to Roman and German law, legislation distinctive in its foundation and original in its development – Slavic legislation.[33] The immediate German translation of this work made it accessible to an all-European audience.

Within the Russian Empire, Russian and Ukrainian jurists elaborated his approach. Among these was Nikolai Dmitrievich Ivanishev (1811-

[31] See, for example, R. A. Papian, Христианские корни современного права [Christian Roots of Contemporary Law] (2002); Iu. A. Ziubanov, Христианские основы уголовного кодекса Российской Федерации [Christian Foundations of the Criminal Code of the Russian Federation] (2007). These themes are pursued in greater detail by V. F. Lafitsky, Практическое пособие по сравнительному правоведению: ступени познания зарубежного права для чиновников, предпринимателей и юристов [Practical Manual on Comparative Jurisprudence: Steps of the Cognition of Foreign Law for Officials, Entrepreneurs, and Jurists] (Moscow, 2019-2020). 2 vols.

[32] Among the western comparatists who drew attention to Slavic law was R. M. Dareste de la Chavanne (1824-1911), who published several articles during the 1880s and collected these in *Études d'histoire de droit* (1889; 2d ed., 1908), later published in Russian as R. Dareste, Исследования по истории права [Studies on the History of Law] (reprint ed.; 2012). One modern comparatist believes that the reception of Byzantine legal forms and norms was facilitated by the fact that "... in Byzantium itself they were drawn up under the influence of a Slavonic element". V. N. Siniukov, Российская правовая система: Введение в общую теорию [Russian Legal System: Introduction to General Theory] (2d ed.; 2010), p. 106.

[33] W. A. Maciejowski, *Historya prawodawstw słowiańskich* (Warsaw, 1832-35; 2d ed., Warsaw, 1856-65); a German translation was published at once. See Maciejowski, *Slavische Rechtsgeschichte*, transl. from the Polish by F. J. Buss and M. Navrocki (Stuttgart, 1835-39). 4 vols.

1874), who argued persuasively that Russian criminal legislation could only be understood against the background of Slavic legislation generally. A national school of Slavonic law emerged which led to the conviction that medieval Russian law should be studied by means of comparing it with the law of other Slavic peoples. Mikhail Flegontovich Vladimirskii-Budanov (1838-1916), Fedor Ivanovich Leontovich (1833-1911), Ivan Mikhailovich Sobestianskii (1856-1896), Baltazar Bogišić (1834-1908), Fedor Vasil'evich Taranovskii (1875-1936), and others became active proponents of the proposition that Slavic law should be studied comparatively and distinguished from other legal traditions.[34]

In his Ilchester Lectures at Cambridge University in 1900, Fedor Fedorovich Zigel (1845-1921), professor *ordinarius* at Warsaw University, suggested that Slavic law was the law of an agricultural people and, insofar as the Slavic peoples lived according to their old customs and usages preserved only by tradition, was perhaps nearer to English and American law than to the law of continental Europe. In his view the rules of Slavonic law were more independent of Roman and canon law than in Europe. The Slavs elaborated their legal rules themselves; the undoubted substantial influence of foreign ideas was confined to ideas and did not affect the legal rules themselves.[35]

The fundamental approach developed by Russian, Ukrainian, and other comparatists during the nineteenth century is shared by their modern colleagues who support the idea of a family of Slavonic law and legal systems. They believe that Slavonic law is where "Christian values find their fullest embodiment".[36] The Slavs, they observe, are the largest and probably the most ancient ethnos in Europe, today comprising about one-third of the inhabitants there. They believe that Slavonic law is developing during recent decades at the greatest rate, increasingly exerting more influence on other Christian legal families.

Specific features of Slavic law, including, in this view, Russian and Ukrainian law, are identified as: a distinctive relationship among the State, the law, and the citizenry which emphasizes (notwithstanding historical

[34] See, generally, M. A. Damirli, "Comparative-Legal Science in Ukraine: Theoretical-Methodological Traditions", *Journal of Comparative Law*, VIII (2013), pp. 1-44.

[35] See F. Sigel, *Lectures on Slavonic Law* (London, 1902). On Zigel, see K. P. Krakovskii, "Zigel, Fedor Fedorovich", in W. E. Butler and V. A. Tomsinov, *Russian Legal Biography* (2007), I, pp. 391-402.

[36] Lafitsky, note 16 above, I, p. 200. Also see Mykhaĭlo Iuriĭovych Riazanov, Слов'янське право в правовій спадщині України [Slavic Law in the Legal Heritage of Ukraine] (Odessa, 2015). But compare D. V. Lukianov, "Religious Legal Systems: Features and Classifications", in Butler, Kresin, and Shemshuchenko, note 5 above, pp. 304-317. Christian legal systems are classified as "canon law" systems and discussed at length in D. V. Lukianov, Релігійні правові системи в сучасному світі [Religious Legal Systems in the Contemporary World] (Kharkiv, 2015), together with Islamic, Jewish, and Hindu.

experience to the contrary) the depersonalization of authority, a non-class and non-estate organization of society, and an unusually strong sense of collectiveness and community. Economic development, in this view, has proceeded on the basis of collective forms of economic management expressed in the peasant community, artel, agricultural cooperative, labor democracy, traditions of local self-government, and others. The individual has a special type of social status in which collectivist elements predominate in legal consciousness and a sharp line is not drawn between the individual (and individualism) and the social State.

Russian Legal System in the Romano-Germanic Family. Those comparatists who regard the Russian legal system as an integral part of the Romano-Germanic family of legal systems emphasize the influence of continental European legal traditions, values, and rules upon the development of Russian law, the existence of Russia within continental historical experience and legal development, and the numerous similarities of Russian approaches to law and legal institutions with those of continental Europe.[37] For those comparatists who perceived the "socialist legal tradition" to be a development within the Romano-Germanic legal tradition, *a fortiori* Russia continues to be a part of that tradition. Many modern Russian comparatists describe the Russian legal system as "gravitating" towards the Romano-Germanic family.

While some observe that "the legal system of Russia has no distinctions of principle" when compared with the legal systems of continental Europe, nonetheless the "Russian legal system has still not become fixed in comparison with the leading legal systems of the family of continental law".[38] It is, in other words, a legal system still in transition from its socialist past to its undetermined future.

Russian Legal System as "Mixed" Legal System. There is no such thing as, and perhaps never has been, a "pure" legal system. All legal systems are "mixed" systems; the mere fact that an individual legal system is, for the purposes of classification, thrown together with others suggests an analytical "mixture", if nothing else. The term "mixed legal system" is used variously in doctrinal writings, sometimes to refer merely to legal systems combining elements of the "civil law" and "common law" traditions; sometimes to refer to a "third family" of legal systems having overlapping civil law and common law elements; sometimes to describe other combinations of legal traditions (religious, tribal, socialist, customary, civil, common, and so on). Although the subject of "mixed" legal systems has generated a substantial

[37] But for an analysis of European private law experience that distinguishes between the Eastern and Western European approaches, see E. O. Kharitonov and O. I. Kharitonova, "Classification of European Systems of Private Law", in Butler, Kresin, and Shemshuchenko, note 5 above, pp. 255-275.

[38] See Vlasov, et al., note 7 above, pp. 220, 221.

literature in recent times, Russia does not figure in these writings except for the most passing mention as a "transitional" legal system.[39]

The history of Russian law gives more than ample evidence of the multiple influences of other legal traditions throughout Russia, but not the classic juxtaposition of "civil law" and "common law" influences. If there is to be any serious trace of "common law" influence in Russia, this is a development of the period since 1991 and the outcome of individual law reform undertakings that deliberately drew upon Anglo-American legal experience or upon "common law" elements of European legal institutions and rules. Under any definition of a "mixed legal system", Russia would constitute one of the most complex (and interesting) examples.

Implications of classifications. The classification of legal systems can have practical consequences. In international treaties and arbitration clauses one finds references to the "principal legal systems of the world" as a criterion for representation on international judicial tribunals (see Article 9, Statute of the International Court of Justice; Article 2(2), Statute of the International Tribunal for the Law of the Sea; Article 36(8), Rome Statute of the International Criminal Court) or even arbitral tribunals. On the basis of these criteria, should Russia be considered part of the Romano-Germanic legal tradition and compete with other continental European jurisdictions, or even those of Latin America and Japan, for electing individuals to an international court? Or does "principal legal systems" have reference in practice to a combination of geographical representation and status as a great or influential power?

Classifications of legal systems have been used in judicial and arbitral proceedings to influence or determine the outcome of a proceeding. It has been suggested, for example, that an alleged "gap" in Russian law might be filled from another legal system by analogy. If an analogy were drawn, should one look to other post-socialist legal systems, or to Romano-Germanic legal systems, or to "technocratic" legal systems, or to "mixed" legal systems, to the law of the Council of Europe, or others?

TEACHING AND RESEARCH ON RUSSIAN LAW

Russian law was not taught as a distinct subject in European and American law schools prior to 1917, and the same was true of Soviet law throughout the inter-war era.[40] The rise of Soviet legal studies as a component of legal

[39] See Esin Örücü, "What is a Mixed Legal System? Exclusion or Expansion?", in Örücü (ed.), *Mixed Legal Systems at New Frontiers* (2010), p. 77.

[40] Although lectures may have been given on Soviet law in a general course on comparative law; for example, by T. A. Taracouzio (1896-1958) at the Harvard Law School during the mid-1930s. Moreover, both Imperial Russian law and Soviet law were taught by émigré Russian legal scholars in Berlin, Harbin, Paris, Prague, Sofia, and Uppsala within Russian or other law faculties abroad. Imperial Russian law remained in force after 1917 in the Baltic States,

education dates from the aftermath of the Second World War, when the international status of the Soviet Union changed abruptly from that of a medium power to a great power. Mention of Russian law in Anglo-American writings dated from the sixteenth century; serious research on the subject commenced from the nineteenth century, principally in England (Baron Alexander A. Heyking (1860-1930)), France (Ernest Lehr (1835-1919)) and Germany, and developed into Soviet legal studies promptly from 1918. In the interwar era Soviet law was examined principally as the legal system of a large country whose legislation and institutions were part of the corpus of foreign law and, for some, because the Soviet Union claimed to be charting new paths by using law for social change. Those who were supportive of changes occurring in what became the Soviet Union believed the legal reforms contained much of possible interest to like-minded individuals abroad.[41] Governments and commercial firms needed to know the rules applicable to transnational transactions. For most, language was a formidable barrier, but a small cadre of Russian *émigré* lawyers (including in England: Samuel Dobrin, Boris Elkin, Alexander Halperin, and Marc Wolff; in the United States: George C. Guins, Alexander N. Sack and Timothy A. Taracouzio; in Germany: Alexander N. Makarov; in France: Boris Mirkine-Guetzévich, Baron Boris Nolde, Alexander Pilenko, Alexander Stoyanovitch, Baron Mikhail A. Taube; in Germany and Switzerland: Ivan A. Il'in) kept pre-Soviet Russian legal traditions alive through to the 1950s. The number of Anglo-American law graduates suitably trained to engage in serious comparative study or legal practice was then and remains tiny.

The principal Western research center of consequence was founded as the Institut für Ostrecht in Germany under the direction of Heinrich Freund (1885-1946) at the University of Heidelberg from 1925. The Institute published an excellent journal, *Zeitschrift für Ostrecht*, which during the first decade of its existence included many Soviet jurists among its regular contributors.

Comparative legal studies in general prior to 1939 were dominated by the belief that a principal task of the discipline was to identify and develop general or common principles of law in at least the major extant legal systems. Harmonization and unification were cherished objectives,

eastern Poland, and areas controlled by the Far Eastern Railway in Manchuria until as late as 1939. See, *inter alia*, V. P. Ponomareva, "Legal Space in Harbin: The Russia Abroad", *Journal of Comparative Law*, VIII (2013), pp. 247-263. Also see G. S. Starodubtsev, Международно-правовая наука российской эмиграции (1918-1939) [International Legal Science of Russian Emigration (1918-1939)] (2000); W. E. Butler, "Russian International Lawyers in Emigration: The First Generation", *Journal of the History of International Law*, III (2001), pp. 235-241.

41 For the undoubted impact of the Soviet legal example on western society, see J. B. Quigley, Jr, *Soviet Legal Innovation and the Law of the Western World* (2007); P. B. Stephan, "The Impact of the Cold War on Soviet and US Law: Reconsidering the Legacy", in T. Borisova and W. B. Simons (eds.), *The Legal Dimension in Cold-War Interactions: Some Notes from the Field* (2012), pp. 149-158; the last reviewed in *Journal of Comparative Law*, VII (2012), pp. 334-341.

particularly in the minds of those who sought to reconstruct the world after the devastating carnage of the First World War. To those who regarded the Soviet legal system as a variant of the Romano-Germanic civilian tradition, the Revolutions of 1917 posed no insuperable barriers to unification and harmonization of law. Insofar, however, as Soviet claims to represent a qualitatively new and higher socio-economic, political, and legal order contained substance, the foundation for harmonization and codification even in the most congenial international political climates had narrowed considerably.

Following the Second World War, that narrow base appeared to have vanished as the Cold War unfolded. On one hand, the group of States where communist regimes were in control had enlarged from the Soviet Union, Mongolian People's Republic,[42] Chinese Soviet Republic,[43] and a brief episode with the Hungarian Soviet Republic to embrace Central and Eastern Europe, China, Vietnam, and Cuba, and arguably even portions of the Third World which had "legal systems of a socialist orientation".[44] The ensuing intense political hostility and confrontation, although they had the lamentable result of cutting off meaningful contacts, stimulated area and disciplinary studies of the region. Comparative studies were faced not merely with a different legal model, but one that was being received, transplanted, absorbed, assimilated into countries of widely varying legal cultures, languages, revolutionary experience, values, and traditions.

During the Cold War period, Soviet legal studies in the West were mostly a part of the "know thine enemy" syndrome: to comprehend how he lived, to facilitate means of understanding and communication so as to avoid miscalculation and minimize misperception in a nuclear age, to identify and clarify opposed positions and values. Professor Harold J. Berman (1918-2007) observed in the introduction to his interpretation of Soviet law: "a legal system expresses in a most vivid and real way what a society stands for. It represents both what is preached and what is practiced".[45] Meaningful harmonization and unification of law on a worldwide scale were inconceivable under these conditions, indeed ideologically rejected by the East, and so too was the prospect of identifying or developing general principles of municipal law common to the principal legal systems of the world.

This was a period in which Soviet legal studies as a field found its own place in the cosmos of comparative law, pointing up the need to study foreign and domestic law in the larger context of the basic philosophical, historical, sociological, economic, and political premises of the existing

42 See W. E. Butler, *The Mongolian Legal System* (1982).

43 W. E. Butler (ed.), *The Legal System of the Chinese Soviet Republic, 1931-34* (1983).

44 J. N. Hazard, *Communists and Their Law* (1969).

45 H. J. Berman, *Justice in the U.S.S.R.* (rev. ed., 1963), p. 3.

worldview, first in order to better comprehend them and second, in order better to comprehend our own. Architects of programs in Slavonic and East European studies were quick to appreciate that some knowledge of law and legal institutions would be essential to an understanding of Soviet society and the group of States called "socialist";[46] most who specialized in Soviet law maintained close links to Slavonic studies as part of the infrastructure of their area of concentration.

The final four decades of Soviet law under Soviet power were followed by Western students closely and with fascination: first the processes of de-Stalinization; then the rise and decline of structures intended to further a "socialist community law of economic integration", the postulation and then abandonment of policies aimed at eliminating law in a society building communism, the emergence of a Soviet legal profession able to pursue a long-term role for law in society, the stagnation of the economy and social system and the market-oriented measures designed to rectify the situation, and the ultimate dismantling of Soviet structures (although not necessarily of Soviet law). Access to materials improved beyond imagination, partly due to more democratic attitudes towards disclosure of normative documents, partly to the heavy demand for a knowledge of local law on the part of the foreign legal profession, and partly to the prodigious labors of Western legal specialists in translating Russian texts.[47] It continues to be the case that the Western law student or lawyer has more available to him in English translation concerning the Russian legal system than for any continental European jurisdiction, leaving aside mediocre computer translations.

The demise of the Soviet Union has altered in some measure the reasons commonly given for studying Soviet law, yet an improved knowledge and understanding of Russia remain as important today as was the case earlier with respect to the closed Soviet society. The ideological component of political tension and mistrust between East and West, although largely dissipated, is not entirely absent. Law remains a shared interest and a mechanism for resolving disputes between Russia and other States, and one which the Russian leadership has emphasized much more than its predecessors and the domestic and international levels. Indeed, law has an even larger role to play than in the past. As governments enlarge their domains of cooperation and foreign investors operate routinely within Russia, and Russian investors do so abroad, the need for a thorough command of legal rules and institutions is self-evident.

[46] The Hayter Report issued during 1968 in the United Kingdom led to Professor George Keeton (1902-1989) at University College London obtaining support for an Established Readership in Soviet Law, later renamed the Readership in Comparative Law.

[47] My own contributions in this respect are most extensively recorded in W. E. Butler, *International and Comparative Law: A Bibliography with Annotations and Notes of the Published Writings and Reports of William E. Butler* (2d ed., 2015).

Although the configuration of Russian law in the larger domain of comparative law has assuredly altered, Russian law continues to offer the same scope of comparative enquiry as other European systems together with fundamentally different and challenging approaches or views for the student's consideration. Russian law is a legal system within a single State and simultaneously within a federated system of "subjects of the Russian Federation", some of which are themselves recognized as sovereign States. Russian law continues to seek its identity within a cluster or family of legal systems. Although Marxism-Leninism has been discredited as an ideology, powerful forces of varying orientations offer substitutes which would differentiate Russia from the West. The transition from a planned economy to a market economy is one which no State has previously undertaken in human history; Russian law is the principal vehicle of this transition. No less absorbing is the transition from a single-Party authoritarianism to multi-party democracy based on a rule-of-law State, political pluralism, separation of powers, and checks and balances.

One may examine the impact of Revolution upon a pre-existing legal and social order in several societies, including the English, American, and French. But Russia offers the more immediate and compelling example in two respects: a Revolution against capitalism, and a second in 1991 against the socialist authoritarianism that followed. The dynamics and effects of both are best viewed through the legal system.

The tensions between revolutionary change and the need for order, stability, and predictability are manifest in the substance of law and law reform, in the nature and role of the legal profession, in the sources of law and schemes for its codification, systematization, and dissemination, and in the functions of State and non-State organizations created to "administer" or reinforce legality. Although Russian law eschews the explicit educational role of law associated with Marxism-Leninism and the concept of "Soviet Man", it continues to be accepted that law does and should influence character and personality formation, and consequently the law-maker needs to consider how legislation will affect social behavior.

In modern times Russian law, just as Soviet law did in the past, sees itself as having more than merely "national" significance, of being more than an oasis to be frequented when seeking to develop a comprehensive theory of law. In its Soviet costume, Russian law was an historical and contemporary model for other legal systems in the socialist and Third worlds; and Soviet and post-Soviet experience of the industrial and post-industrial ages[48] contains positive and negative lessons instructive for other advanced Western legal systems. In its guise as a transitional legal system during the post-Soviet era, the Russian legal system continues to exert

[48] J. N. Hazard, *Managing Change in the U.S.S.R.: The Politico-Legal Role of the Soviet Jurist* (1982).

enormous influence by example over the other independent states of the former Soviet Union and to shape the foundations of what may become the "law of the Commonwealth of Independent States" or the law of the Eurasian economic community.[49]

The legal aspects of the transition from a planned to a market economy continue to be of practical relevance to Western lawyers and investors throughout the CIS. Concepts of ownership, freedom of contract, intellectual property, State immunity, delict, juridical persons, and the proper distribution of legal regulation among civil, family, land, economic, environmental, and other branches of law are but some examples which contain difficult issues of reconciling the Soviet past with the Russian present and immediate future. In the domain of administrative law one encounters a range of offences and penalties which have no equivalent in Anglo/American law, whereas in the criminal law and procedure the equation of public and individual rights and the system of investigation and adjudication proceed, even in their post-Soviet form and even after substantial discussion with Western colleagues, from premises, considerations, and values quite different from Anglo/American legal systems.

Comparative issues of this magnitude and nature help us to rethink crucial social, economic, cultural, and legal questions which confront our own legal system, the reasons those issues arise, the historical foundations of our law, and the appropriate role(s) for law in society. Russian law, just as other legal systems, including the Soviet legal system, offers a convenient backdrop, an analytical screen, for approaching our own problems with a fresh and perhaps unique perspective.

For the legal practitioner these considerations take on a different dimension. One no longer speaks only of commercial transactions with Russia: one speaks of investment transactions under which the foreign investor operates within the Russian legal framework and Russian law is the applicable law. Most special Soviet institutions created as part of the State monopoly of foreign trade have been dismantled, but in their place arise modes of operation and thought deeply indebted to the Soviet past. The totality of the Russian legal order, including its immediate past, must be within the range of Western practitioners who offer services in or connected with Russia.

Moreover, the value of Russian legal studies, as in the case of the former Soviet Union, transcends the traditional realm of comparative law. Russian State practice in the form of foreign affairs legislation in the broadest sense contributes to the development or clarification of international law.[50]

[49] See the essays in the special issue "Legal Integration in Eurasia", *Russian Law Journal*. VII, no. 3 (2019), pp. 5-219.
[50] See Butler, *Russian Foreign Relations and Investment Law* (2006).

Although the ideological elements of hostility are now removed from the equation and Russia is gradually being absorbed into a vast spectrum of international engagements which previously were off limits, there is nonetheless emerging a sense of Russian statehood which will have its own impact upon the codification, reception, and application of international law. The essential components of Russian law will continue to be of fundamental importance to the education of the public international lawyer as part of his understanding of the principal legal systems of the world.[51]

It remains to be seen how rapidly the international legal vocabulary of Marxism-Leninism will disappear from the diplomatic lexicon of the Russian Federation, for Russia is officially the "legal continuer" and, under 2020 amendments to the Russian Constitution, in some instances the "legal successor" of the former Soviet Union and the international treaties to which it was a party. To the extent that this terminology is indebted to domestic legal institutions, it is likely to survive and affect international negotiations (for example, the foreign investment protection treaties concluded by the former Soviet Union with several Western States fail to take account of the repertoire of terms in the Russian language for various forms of "taking"). And there are nuances in Russian legal terminology which have nothing to do with the Soviet legacy but nonetheless can create awkward moments in international negotiations of a public or private nature.

The Russian international lawyer is himself a product of his municipal system of legal education, be it Soviet or post-Soviet. His concepts of law, the manner and style in which he reasons and expounds his views, his legal consciousness, are deeply indebted to his domestic legal milieu and his legal heritage. Also formed in his municipal legal context is the international lawyer's perception of what role(s) a lawyer has in giving counsel to his employer or client.

On a larger scale, the implementation of international legal arrangements can depend upon the effectiveness of, or obstacles within, national legal systems. The 1993 Russian Constitution is truly remarkable in its approach to making customary and treaty rules of international law an integral part of the Russian legal system (Article 15[4]). But this provision needs to be read together with changes introduced in the Russian Constitution (Articles 79 and 125) with effect from 4 July 2020.[52] Moreover, within Russia this situation is complicated by the federated structure of the Federation. Those who draft international arrangements must have regard not merely to the municipal formalities for approving international agreements but likewise to the municipal legal context in which they will operate. These are but a

[51] Butler, "Comparative Approaches to International Law", *Recueil des cours*, CXC (1985), pp. 9-89; Butler, "Comparative International Law", in W. E. Butler and O. V. Kresin (eds.), *The Interaction of Legal Systems: Post-Soviet Approaches* (2015), pp. 297-314.

[52] See Butler, *International Law in the Russian Legal System* (Oxford, 2020), pp. 226-227.

few of the concerns to which comparative legal studies, including Russian or CIS legal studies, can make an indispensable contribution to improving our understanding of the nature and effectiveness of international law.

COMPARATIVE LAW IN RUSSIA

The study of foreign law dates back to the earliest days of formal legal education in Russia, not least because the early professors were of foreign origin and had little, if any, command of the Russian language. The Byzantine and European origins of Russian legislation were explored by Russian historians of the eighteenth century; Roman law was taught at Moscow University from its founding in 1755 and included in the teaching syllabus at the Russian Academy of Sciences from 1725 (there were only a handful of students, the offspring of foreigners in Russia). A comparison of Russian and Roman law by Aleksei Artem'evich Artemev (c. 1740-1820), based on the lectures of Philip Heinrich Dilthey (1723-1781)[53] at Moscow University, may have rightful claim to being the first printed Russian work on comparative law.[54] Russian works on Chinese law were undertaken in the form of translations of Chinese legal texts.[55]

Foreign legislation, especially Swedish, Danish, Dutch, Prussian, English, French, Austrian, and Italian, was studied and adapted by Peter the Great.[56] Catherine II read Beccaria, Blackstone, and Montesquieu, among others and drew upon them when composing her celebrated Nakaz or Russian enactments. Their works were translated into the Russian language in furtherance of Catherine's legal reforms. Mikhail Mikhailovich Speranskii (1772-1839) and his associates were well-schooled in French and German law when they prepared their draft codes under Emperor Alexander I and sufficiently attracted by the ideas of Jeremy Bentham (1748-1832) to translate his major work on codification into Russian.[57]

[53] On Dilthey, see V. A. Tomsinov, "Dilthey, Philip Heinrich", in W. E. Butler and V. A. Tomsinov (eds.), *Russian Legal Biography* (London, 2007), I, pp. 189-193.

[54] A. A. Artemev, Краткое начертание римских и российских прав с показанием купно обоих равномерно как и чиноположения оных историй [Brief Outline of Roman and Russian Law Showing the Symmetries of Both and the Rituals of Their Histories] (1777), published by Moscow University in an octavo of 200 pages.

[55] See Aleksei Leontovich Leont'ev (1716-1786), Китайское уложение [Chinese Statute] (1779). 2 vols. 1200 ptd.; reviewed in Спб. Вестник [St. Petersburg Herald] (September 1779), IV, pp. 202-222. Also see Leont'ev, Тайцин гурунь в Ухери коли, то есть все законы и установления китайского (а ныне манжурскаго) правительства [Taitsin Gurun and Ukheri koli, that is, All Laws and Statutes of the Chinese (and now Manchurian) Government] (1781-1783). 3 vols. 1200 ptd. Vol. 1; 600 ptd. Vols. 2-3. Leont'ev was a councilor in the College of Foreign Affairs of the Russian Empire. Harvard and Yale Law School libraries hold both titles.

[56] W. E. Butler, "Peter the Great as a Comparative Lawyer", in J. M. Hartley and D. J. B. Shaw, *Magic, Texts and Travel: Homage to a Scholar, Will Ryan* (London, 2021), pp. 214-226.

[57] J. Bentham, Разсуждение о гражданском и уголовном законоположении: С предварительным изложением начал законоположения и всеобщаго начертания полной Книги законов, и с присовкуплением опыта о влиянии времени и места

A major bibliography of Russian law published in 1891 enumerated more than 200 titles devoted to the "Comparative-Historical Method Applied to the Study of the History of Russian Law".[58] Amongst the Russian and Ukrainian scholars who pioneered comparative legal studies were Nikolai Mikhailovich Korkunov (1853-1904),[59] Vasilii Ivanovich Sergeevich (1832-1910), Kronid Ivanovich Malyshev (1841-1907),[60] Nikolai Pavlovich Zagoskin (1851-1912), Maksim Maksimovich Kovalevskii (1851-1916), Sir Paul Gavril'ovich Vinogradoff (1854-1925), Sergei Andreevich Muromtsev (1850-1910), Gabriel' Feliksovich Shershenevich (1863-1912), and Fedor Vasil'evich Taranovskii (1875-1936). Kovalevskii in particular produced works on the usefulness of the comparative method in studying Russian law.[61] One comparatist observed that the comparative method had become so popular, so fashionable, that

> at present in Russia there is no textbook on procedure or any branch of law which does not give its due to the spirit of the time; even a manual of practical jurisprudence, making pretensions to comprehensiveness, encumbers the innocent reader with a mass of facts compiled without any conclusion and selected from all foreign legislation possible.[62]

Sir Paul Vinogradoff, who became the Corpus Professor at Oxford University in 1903 upon resigning his Chair at Moscow University, is

относительно законов [Discourse on Civil and Criminal Legal Provisions: With a Preliminary Account of the Principles of Legislation and General Sketch of a Complete Book of Laws, and with the Addition of Experience concerning the Influence of Time and Place Relative to Laws], transl. Mikhail Mikhailov (1805-1811). 3 vols.

58 N. P. Zagoskin, Наука истории русского права [Science of the History of Russian Law] (1891), pp. 13-34. A number of these individuals are of Ukrainian origin and justly claimed as being among the fathers of Ukrainian legal science and/or comparative legal studies. See M. Damirli, "Comparative Legal Science in Ukraine: A Historical Introduction", *Journal of Comparative Law*, VIII (2013), pp. 1-44.

59 See N. M. Korkunov, *General Theory of Law*, transl. W. G. Hastings (Boston, 1909).

60 See V. S. Ivanenko, "Kronid Malyshev and the Renaissance of Private International Law, *Jus Gentium: Journal of International Legal History*, III (2018), pp. 539-551; also see Ivanenko, "The Rising Generation of International Lawyers at St. Petersburg University: Zaremba and Spasovich", in ibid., III (2018), pp. 419-435.

61 M. M. Kovalevskii, Историко-сравнительный метод в юриспруденции и приемы изучения русского права [Historical-Comparative Method in Jurisprudence and Methods of Studying Russian Law] (1880); also see Kovalevskii, «Сравнительно-историческое правоведение и его отношение к социологии» [Comparative-Historical Jurisprudence and Its Relationship to Sociology], in Iu. S. Gambarov (ed.), Сборник по общественно-юридическим наукам [Collection on Socio-Legal Sciences] (1899). I, p. 9. Legal anthropology in the tradition of these scholars is enjoying a revival in the study of Russian law with special emphasis upon customary law. See A. I. Kovler, Антропология права [Anthropology of Law] (2002).

62 A. Bashmakov, in Юридический вестник [Legal Herald], XXII (1882), pp. 551-552.

regarded as having based virtually all of his works upon the comparative method.[63]

Ideological constraints severely limited comparative legal studies during the Soviet period. Several Soviet jurists produced interesting comparative works during the 1920s, but by the end of the decade comparative legal research was reduced either to ritualistic contrastive self-justification of Soviet law in contradistinction to "bourgeois" law or to purely descriptive, albeit often quite useful, accounts of foreign legal systems.

A more enlightened view emerged in the early 1960s. The comparative method was recognized to be useful in analyzing the Soviet legal system itself, the legislation of the fifteen union republics. Comparison also was essential to investigations of other socialist legal systems, the more so as the Council for Mutual Economic Assistance (Comecon) pursued measures requiring the harmonization or unification of law. The expanding international contacts of the former Soviet Union required a sound knowledge of foreign legal systems, including those of a "socialist orientation". Although some Soviet legal research institutions had impressive numbers of specialists on individual branches of law in foreign countries, neither the academies of sciences nor the universities formed sectors or chairs expressly devoted to comparative law. Even in the *perestroika* era progress was slow in comparative legal studies, although the term "comparative law" gradually appeared in the designations of certain sectors of research institutes and teaching institutions.

Applied comparative law took on a life of its own in Russia and elsewhere in the CIS with the opening of offices of foreign law firms and, in due course, the opening of law offices abroad by Russian law firms. Many younger Russian lawyers have obtained law degrees from foreign universities, whether in Russia or abroad, and a few western lawyers have qualified for Russian degrees. The impact of these measures is accumulating in the form of published comparative law dissertations, translations of important foreign codes or model legislative acts, collaborative works by Russian and foreign jurists, and translations of leading foreign treatises into Russian or of important Russian works into foreign languages. The Society of Comparative Law, founded in May 2000 at Moscow, has published a yearbook of comparative law at irregular intervals. Russian law students are required to master at least one foreign language as an integral part of their legal studies, and some undertake two. Foreign language materials are expected to be an integral part of the diploma thesis which each law student must produce as a condition of graduation; individuals writing dissertations are required to publish in foreign legal media as a condition of supplicating for the degree. The phenomenon of globalization and its

[63] On the jurist and a bibliography of his principal works, see "Vinogradoff, Pavel Gavrilovich", in Butler and Tomsinov, note 53 above, I, pp 368-386.

attendant awareness of the larger legal community are recognized as a driving force in Russian legal education.

Russian law, in the third decade of the third millennium, is beginning to configure its new presence in the community of world legal systems. It remains close, as before, to the continental European legal tradition, but not part of it, still detached, still uncommitted, still indebted to its twentieth-century legal heritage, still in "transition" to a destination undetermined.

SOCIO-LEGAL RESEARCH IN RUSSIA AND COMPARATIVE LAW

Probably everyone outside Russia who works in the field of Russian law, whether a legal scholar and/or legal practitioner, has encountered the question: "Russian (or Soviet) Law? Is there any"? When the question is not facetious, one wonders what the interlocutor has in mind: law [*jus*] or law [*lex*]. If the former, the question is a matter of jurisprudential consequence and a fair, even probing, query. If the latter, the question would betray astonishing unfamiliarity with how a legal system designed to serve a Planned Economy or a society transitioning away from a Planned Economy operates.

An awareness that a distinction should be drawn between "law in the books" and "law in action", originally an insight of significance, has become a banal truism. In the former Soviet Union, matters were not so simple and continue to be delicate. To empirically demonstrate that the law and legal institutions may not operate in practice as it would appear to read will sometimes be understood as political failure, an explicit or implied criticism of the existing regime. On the other hand, all regimes, however democratic or authoritarian, need feedback on what in the legal system actually seems to work, what does not, and why.

Feedback has no predetermined forms and is subject to the canons of sound research: opinion surveys, informed observations, interviews, questionnaires, sampling, analysis of official and gathering of unofficial statistics, letters to the editors of mass media or specialist publications, appearances on television, video, facebook, twitter, and other sources of information or opinion, recordings or verbatim transcripts of court and arbitral proceedings, access to doctrinal writings and normative legal acts, the publishing practices of State agencies, case reports and other materials of judicial and arbitral practice, among others. The feedback may be mundane or full of insight – much turns upon the analytical qualities of those who assembled the data, the representativeness of the material, and the accuracy of the sample.

That law mattered and matters in Imperial Russia, the Soviet Union, and Post-Soviet Independent States has never been doubted by most western comparative lawyers. Puzzling perhaps is that the question is even asked: Is there (was there) Russian or Soviet law? How many other legal system on the planet, past or present, have routinely confronted that question. For most of its history Rome was hardly a democracy – does one assume there was no Roman Law? The answer may lie in a traditionally Russian sardonic sense of humor and a misperception by foreigners of this quality among Russians.[64] The "politicization" of the justice system is a concern in Russia, and indeed elsewhere, although western specialists in Soviet law were well aware that even under the scale of terror in the Stalin era for most people, most of the time, most disputes were considered with no or limited outside interest or interference.[65]

Evidence of this on the basis of direct access to the Russian population was another matter; indeed, simply impossible, and efforts by other social scientists to take steps in this direction encountered suspicion and enforcement actions on the part of Soviet authorities. From the 1960s, however, the Soviet authorities, including the Communist Party, became interested in learning about the effectiveness of rules and institutions. To this end, empirical social science research was encouraged to some extent and the results evaluated; some was classified and to this day the outcomes and reactions to the outcomes remain out of public view.

In post-Soviet Russia the equation has changed with respect to the "politicization" of the justice system. There is no longer a single ruling Party, and the "private sector" has assumed a role to such an extent that individuals of wealth, power, and influence in Russia often prefer to have their disputes settled abroad (London being a favorite venue) rather than in Russian courts. One observer has noted:

> As a result of the relentless emphasis on high-profile cases in countries like Russia, a backhanded consensus has emerged that politicized justice is a cancer that, once present, will inevitably take over the organism. The belief lends credence to the popular image of Russia as lawless. Further buttressing this image is the sad reality

[64] This tendency reaches far back into Russian (Slavic?) legal culture. Hendley noted: "A comparative assessment of the actual data suggests that Russians are no more nihilistic when it comes to law than are others". See K. Hendley, "Who Are the Legal Nihilists in Russia?", *Post-Soviet Affairs*, XXVIII (2012), pp. 149-186. But they are more "formalist", which may contribute to an exaggerated impression of nihilism when formalism breaks down.

[65] This view was sustained through studies of Soviet case reports, interviews with Russian emigrés, and similar efforts to collect empirical material on the Soviet administration of justice under the most challenging conditions. See, for example, H. J. Berman (ed. & transl.), *Soviet Law in Action: The Recollected Cases of a Soviet Lawyer* (1951); a mimeographed edition, published two years later by Harvard University Press. Another specialist observed: "Then, as now, most cases had little political resonance, and hence, even during the worst of the Stalinist purges, law retained its relevance for mundane cases". See R. Sharlet, "Stalinism and Soviet Legal Culture", in R. C. Tucker (ed.), *Stalinism: Essays in Historical Interpretation* (1977), pp. 155-179.

> that predicting outside intervention is impossible … Focusing on this view of Russia as lawless fails to capture the full richness of Russians' experience of law. It leaves no room for the everyday reality … that Russians routinely negotiate resolutions to their problems with others in the shadow of the law or, when informal efforts prove futile, take their problems to the courts and have them resolved in accordance with the law.[66]

It might be argued that at this level of socio-legal verification, the discipline is merely confirming what has been believed about the Soviet and post-Soviet legal system for nearly nine decades, the proverbial "low-hanging fruit" of comparative legal analysis. Evidence of a legal system operating more or less routinely in most cases is news only to those whose ideological proclivities inclined them to suppose the opposite. Once that threshold is crossed, research into the actual operation of legal institutions becomes more detailed and interesting – and possibly sensitive insofar as such research demonstrates maladministration, misconceptualization of the system, inherent institutional shortcomings, bureaucratic incompetence, personnel failures, disenchantment with particular legal rules or institutions, and the like.

It remains the reality, moreover, that a considerable portion of socio-legal research is conducted by sociologists who have no knowledge of legislation or of legal practice; what seems, for example, to them to be a clever circumvention of the law may be nothing more than a routine professional response to legislative drafting and client interest. Neither corrupt nor close to the margin of illegality, it may be innovative, imaginative, and responsive to client interests. Similarly, some Russians have become so inured to what one observer called the "negative myth of the rule of law" that they are skeptical when empirical evidence suggests a positive impression of the quality of the justice system.[67]

The challenges for socio-legal studies, and their integration with comparative law in Russia and abroad, will intensify as the Russian social system become more amenable to this type of legal research.

[66] K. Hendley, *Everyday Law in Russia* (2017), pp. 3-4: "… official interference is very much the exception in ordinary cases" (p. 10).

[67] M. Kurkchiyan, "The Illegitimacy of Law in Post-Soviet Societies", in D. Galligan and M. Kurkchiyan, *Law and Informal Practices: The Post-Communist Experience* (2003), pp. 24-47. Also see Kurkchiyan and Kubal, note 21 above.

2

RUSSIAN LAW AND LEGAL TRANSLATION

For all practical purposes, "law" has no independent being or existence apart from "language": the signs (words) and symbols through and in which legal concepts and terminology are expressed. The transmission of legal concepts and terminology from one language to another in written form is called "translation" and in oral form, "interpreting".[1] There are few, if any, more daunting and challenging tasks confronting the legal professional than the "translation" of law in the broadest sense of the word from one language and legal system to another. Although some elements of the challenge are common to all languages, each language will confound the jurist with individual conundrums that need to be recognized in order to be addressed. Russian legal language is no exception.

Legal translation may be the proverbial iceberg in the larger world of translation, but not the tip. The ordinary consumer of translations – the layman, the ordinary reader – encounters translation in the domain of literature and poetry. The bookshops and the libraries are full of these and, quite frankly, these receive all the publicity – the prizes, the advertising, the conversation ("have you read ...?"), the assignments in schools and universities, and the mill that is called "literary criticism". What the layman does not and cannot see is the submerged portion of the translation iceberg. Legal translation – beyond doubt the most difficult and challenging of all and the essence of comparative law – comprises a vast volumetric portion of the iceberg:

> Legal texts are translated in vaster quantities than books and in more varied directions. Dreary as it may seem to all but legal eagles, the translation of law is a prerequisite for the construction and maintenance of a global society".[2]

[1] For a lively, gifted, and amusing account with respect to the Russian language, see Michele A. Berdy, *The Russian Word's Worth: A Humorous and Informative Guide to Russian Language, Culture, and Translation* (Moscow, 2013), esp. pp. 87-102.

[2] D. Bellos, *Is That a Fish in Your Ear?* (2011), p. 217. The "Fish" to which the title of the book refers is a literary reference to the "Babel fish" in D. Adams, *The Hitchhiker's Guide to the Galaxy* (1980). The "Babel fish" is an imaginary device that provides instant communication with all the peoples on earth, that is, "speaks" and "comprehends" all languages in the universe.

Legal translation is an inherently comparative exercise, indeed, the very foundation of comparative law.[3] Insofar as legal translation is accurate, the comparative description and analysis of law is, in principle, possible. To the extent that legal translation is transformed into something other than translation, that is, no longer is an accurate description of the legal phenomenon but rather an attempt to recharacterize or redress the terminology of one legal system into the guise of another, the description is inaccurate and, for scholarly and professional purposes, of limited utility and potentially devastating in result. One specialist put the issue more sharply and succinctly in the European context: "The language of Europe is translation".[4]

With respect to Russian legal language, we continue to be in an era of transition, discarding, redefining, or replacing the conceptual and terminological foundations of Soviet Law and accommodating the definitional innovations of a market-oriented legal system. We may be witnessing the third major revolution in Russian legal terminology: the first introduced by Peter the Great and accompanied by the introduction of civil script and the importation of European legal terminology;[5] the second by the Great October Revolution of 1917 and the deliberate systematic sovietization of legal terminology; and third, the absorption or invention of new terms and concepts associated with the legal infrastructure of a market economy. Some of the new terminology expresses institutions and concepts previously alien to Russian society; others embody the global process of the approximation, harmonization, and unification of national, regional, and supranational legal systems.

Traditional Russian terms, long forgotten, are being revived or redefined; terms previously associated with the State sector of the economy are being "privatized" and used now to denominate non-State transactions or hybrid institutions; and other Independent States that formerly were part of the Soviet Union and use the Russian language as their principal legal language are developing novel ways to describe their own developments in law.

The challenge for the law student and legal practitioner not proficient in Russian is to understand some of the canons and complexities of legal translation and to contain or reduce elements of legal risk associated with the use of translations.

[3] W. E. Butler, *Russian-English Legal Dictionary* (2001), p. vi.

[4] "La langue d'Europe, c'est la traduction". F. Ost, *Traduire : Défense et illustration du multilinguisme* (Paris, 2009), p. 12 ; quoted in J. Bengoetxea, "Multilingual and Multicultural Legal Reasoning: The European Court of Justice", in A. L. Kjaer and S. Adamo (eds.), *Linguistic Diversity and European Democracy* (2011), p. 120.

[5] See R. S. Wortman, *The Power of Language and Rhetoric in Russian Political History: Charismatic Words from the 18th to the 21st Centuries* (2018), pp. 7-13.

ON THE ROLES OF LANGUAGE

As will be explored in greater detail in chapters below, the origins of Russian law engage questions of language. With respect to the surviving treaties and legislative acts, one key issue is the extent to which those documents contain rules of law that originated with the Slavic peoples inhabiting the territory of Kievan Rus and antecedent communities or represent borrowings from other peoples. Depending upon the resolution of that issue is the determination of: who are the Rus? Where does their law come from? The etymological origins of legal vocabulary and the lexicological meanings of terms are central to the analysis. The language of these documents, in other words, is simultaneously evidence of "influence", or absence thereof, from elsewhere. The "elsewhere" may include Scandinavia, Germanic lands, Byzantium, other Slavic lands, Tatar, and other eastern tribal influences. Language thus can be evidence of the comparative legal transmission, or transplanting to use a modern concept, of legal rules and institutions from one civilization or community to another. This applies to the concepts originating in domestic legal systems and the concepts of the law of nations.

In coming to their conclusions of "borrowing" in one direction or the other, comparative and international legal historians will examine the legal vocabulary used in the documents, the roots and sequence of words, the structure of sentences, the employment of conjunctions, and similar elements. One would expect to find treaties to have greater indications of calques (or borrowings) than legislation simply because the treaty is an agreement between two different peoples or entities whose legal systems and legal terminology differ one from the other.[6] Or language can frustrate the transmission of concepts and rules. With respect to Byzantine influence on Slavic law, the observation has been made: "Byzantine law existed in Rus' in a Slavonic translation. The translation was not particularly good, so that it was impossible to understand a number of its provisions. One cannot apply a norm that one is unable to understand".[7]

An inquiry of this nature into the historical origins of Russian legal texts does not involve, in and of itself, their translation into another language. It focuses more on the architecture of language than the substantive meaning of the words themselves.

There are perhaps as many approaches to legal translation as there are translators; each has his or her own canons of style and substance and experience with legal texts. These introduce subjective elements into

[6] For an interesting analysis which demonstrates what factors should be weighed, see H. Birnbaum, "On Old Russian and Old Scandinavian Legal Language: Some Comparative Notes on Style and Syntax", *Scando-Slavica*, VIII (1963), pp. 115-140.

[7] V. Zhivov, "Once Again in Whether Byzantine Law Was Applied to the Administration of the Law in Medieval Rus'", in M. di Salvo, D. H. Kaiser, and V. A. Kivelson (eds.), *Word and Image in Russian History* (Boston, 2015), p. 33.

translation, which is probably why computer translations of legal materials have proved to be so unsuccessful. Legal translation is to a significant extent rather more an "art" than a "science", notwithstanding the requirements of rigor that comparative legal scholarship would wish to impose.

Broadly speaking, among the approaches to legal translation are the: (1) literary; (2) contextual; and (3) literal. The "literary" approach views legal texts as a species of literature, whether doctrinal writings, legislation, legal forms, case reports, treaties, and the like. The translator should, under the most extreme version of this approach, apply the same canons as translating a novel or poetry. The quality and elegance of the translation is paramount; the translator is at liberty under this approach to effectively "rewrite" the Russian legal material in excellent English, using where necessary Anglo-American legal terminology. To the untutored consumer of such a translation, Russian law looks *remarkably* like English or United States law – and no wonder, for the translator has in effect "anglicized" or "Americanized" the original text so as to make it unrecognizable in substance. It is precisely for these reasons that the "literary" approach, widely and effectively used to translate fiction and poetry, cannot be used to translate legal materials. For the lawyer, the legal risk in using translations of this nature is considerable.

The "contextual" approach likewise recognizes that both law and the languages of law are culturally and historically conditioned social phenomena; accordingly, there can be no absolute equivalence between any two languages. It would follow that no fully precise translation is attainable and one is left with, at best, identifying the closest possible equivalents. Linguists (but not necessarily lawyers) examine the contextual use of a word, by which they mean the parts of a written or spoken passage preceding or following a particular term or intimately associated with it. They also consider, under this approach, the extra-lingual aspects connected with the term, sometimes called "co-situation". Applied to institutions, this approach would seek to identify Russian legal institutions in the English language by applying analogy, seeking in both the Russian and English languages institutions that have a similar origin, purpose, and formal aspects.[8] The outcome can be misleading. For example, the Federal Assembly of the Russian Federation is the parliament of Russia in purpose and function. But it is not called the Parliament, and to translate "Federal Assembly" as parliament would be not a translation of the Russian words, but a description of the functions performed by that institution.

Another example arises from the terminology for the legal profession itself. In February 2014 the Council of Bars and Law Societies of Europe

[8] For an account of the double contextual approach in legal translation from the Polish, see B. Z. Kielar, "The Method of Double Context in Translation", *Studia Anglica Posnaniensia*, no. 3 (1970), pp. 89-93.

(CCBE) announced that the "Federal Chamber of Lawyers of the Russian Federation" had joined the CCBE as an observer member as of November 2013. The Russian entity which had actually joined the CCBE was the Federal Chamber of Advokats. To an American reader, the use of the term "lawyers" to describe Russian advokats would suggest that the Federal Chamber included in its membership all Russian jurists who had a degree in law (analogous to the American Bar Association); to the English reader, the use of the term "lawyers" would suggest the component of the English legal profession called "solicitors". There are in fact two "legal practitioners" in Russia: the advokat and the jurisconsult; the Federal Chamber of Advokats includes only one segment of the legal practitioners. The present writer for years translated the Russian "advokat" (transliterated) as "advocate", a literal translation but nonetheless potentially misleading in English because an "advocate" more generally is simply a proponent for something or someone, rather than a legal professional. Because the Russian advokat is a distinctive professional category and does not coincide in function or stature with counterparts outside the former socialist legal systems, the present writer abandoned the term "advocate" as a literal translation in favor of "advokat" as a literal transliteration in order to avoid confusion with the "lawyer', the "barrister", the "solicitor" the "attorney", or the "attorney-at-law".[9]

The contextual approach arises surprisingly frequently: falling back on a description of a legal concept, term, or institution rather than relying on the intelligence of the reader to make the mental linkage between a foreign appellation and a perception of the functions and purposes of that institution. In practice the outcome of a contextual approach can be beguilingly deceptive or misleading in the extreme. But this is not to minimize the larger importance of "context" and "culture" on terminology which cannot fail to affect choices of equivalents.

The literal approach seeks to convey the sense, cadence, and rhythm of the original text as much as possible, preserving the ambiguity or unwieldiness of the original without improving upon it. Russian legislative drafting carries over the Soviet traditions of directness and bluntness, usually at the expense of certainly elegance and sometimes subtlety. Often the Russian legislative acts are more specific than would ordinarily be expected in European-style systematizations and codifications – an approach that is reinforced by the exceptional volume of detailed regulatory material being produced in modern Russia. The Russian Federation is indeed among the "technocratic" legal systems of the world. The literal approach also reinforces consistency in choice of English-language equivalents. The aim is not to anglicize or Americanize the Russian versions, but to render them as accurately as possible and, having done so, approach the next

[9] See W. E. Butler, *The Russian Legal Practitioner* (2011), p. v.

level of comparative analysis by seeking to understand precisely what the differences and similarities may be with respect to other legal languages and legal systems. Such an approach draws the attention of the reader to the reality that something of note is present and the reader must take steps to properly understand the particular term or word. If the translation is wrong, the likelihood that the correct perception of the substance of the law is wrong will be much the greater.

The perils of departing from the literal approach are well illustrated by the Berman/Spindler translation of the 1960 RSFSR Criminal Code. The title of Article 191^2 of the Criminal Code in their translation read: "Infringing Life of Policeman or of People's Guard". A reviewer objected to the excessive literalness of the translation: "... why not say 'an attempt on the life of'?"[10] That would leave the legal issue: does "infringing the life of a policeman" mean "an attempt" or something else? By coincidence the Supreme Court of the USSR published one of its case reports whose headnote said: "By infringement of the life of a policeman or people's guard ... should be understood the homicide or attempted homicide of such persons".[11] Had the translators followed the non-literal approach, they would have arrogated the resolution of an unresolved legal issue and been unable to translate the headnote.

TRANSLATION CONUNDRUMS

Every comparative lawyer who undertakes legal translation has his or her own anecdotes about issues that arise seemingly in the guise of a translation matter but upon closer examination reveal substantive legal concerns. By way of illustration, we consider several below.

What is the rule of law? A trick question, for the true concern is what word represents "law" and what turns on the distinction. For legal translations, the issue is monumental and fundamental. Most of the world's principal tongues distinguish between two words for law. We cannot do this in English, as can the French, Germans, Italians, Russians, Spanish, and any speaker of Latin. In the Russian language, the distinction is between право and закон, or, to fall back on the Latin, between *jus* and *lex*. In most contexts the term "*jus*" refers to all law within a legal system, whether of natural and/or positive form, whereas "*lex*" normally encompasses positive forms of law: legislation, normative legal acts, and the like.

10 Y. A. Sdobnikov, "Translating the Criminal Code", *Anglo-Soviet Journal*, XXX, no. 1 (1969), p. 29.

11 See H. J. Berman and J. W. Spindler, *Soviet Criminal Law and Procedure: The RSFSR Codes* (2d rev. ed.; 1972), p. 116.

When one explores the concept of the rule of law, it matters whether one is referring to "*jus*" or "*lex*", to право or закон.[12] Indeed, one cannot enter into a learned discussion about the difference between the two without having two words available to conduct the discussion.

Who is the party to a transaction. In the legal chaos that followed the dissolution of the former Soviet Union on or about 25 December 1991, the Russian Federation moved expeditiously to address commodity shortages within the country by encouraging or directly entering into substantial contracts for the export of various raw materials. In retrospect it seems clear that the Western party in some instances insisted that the Russian party should be the "Government" [правительство] of Russia, or that the Russian "Government" should guarantee performance under the transaction. And, in English, especially American English, the contracts were drafted accordingly. The problem was that the Russian Government has no autonomous legal personality; that is, the Russian Government is a legal entity but is not a juridical person[13] and may only enter into transactions as a specifically duly authorized representative of the Russian State [государство], which under both Russian domestic and international law does have legal personality and capacity. As a matter of Russian law, unless the State authorized the Government of Russia to enter into a particular transaction, the Government had no autonomous power to do so.

A number of contracting parties at the time were unaware of the distinction because of a mistranslation and a misperception. The Russian word for "State" [государство] was incorrectly translated as "Government" [правительство]. The misperception carries over to other legal concerns. For example, in Russian law the reference is always to "State immunity" [государственный иммунитет] and never to "governmental immunity", for the latter is inconceivable. Similarly, the expression "State interference" [государственное вмешательство] is not "governmental regulation", but something far worse and substantially different.

Where are economic disputes settled? Until 2014, the Russian Federation had an autonomous system of "arbitrazh courts" [арбитражные суды];

[12] The difference between *jus* and *lex* bedeviled later perceptions of Lenin's position with regard to law. At one stage he declared: «Закон есть мера политическая. Есть политика» [In my version: "A Law is a political measure. There is policy"], but one can see what a difference another version would make. Lenin used the Russian equivalent word for "*lex*", but left open whether one should say "a *lex*" or "the *lex*", and whether he referred to a particular *lex* or in general to positive law enactments. The Russian language does not use articles and cannot readily distinguish between "a" and "the" law, which in a discussion such as this would require reformulating the sentences to clarify the position. The same applies to translating the word политика, which may be rendered as "politics" or as "policy". For reflections, see Jane E. Henderson, *The Constitution of the Russian Federation: A Contextual Analysis* (2011), p. 36.

[13] See W. E. Butler, "Legal Entities and Juridical Persons: Confusion of Concepts and Comparative Law", Государство и право [State and Law], no. 1 (2020), pp. 145-146.

these have now become part of the system of courts of general jurisdiction. Laymen routinely assume that the word "arbitrazh" must be an importation into the Russian language of "arbitration" for, after all, the two words sound alike. The mistake is endemic to the general literature on Russia and frequently appears in legal documents. Indeed, for some time the English-language website of the Supreme (or High) Arbitrazh Court of the Russian Federation described itself as the "Supreme Arbitration Court". Nothing could be further from the truth.

The arbitrazh courts were part of the Russian judicial system and specialized in resolving litigation in accordance with the Code of Arbitrazh Procedure of the Russian Federation. They were, in other words, the precise antithesis of arbitration, or arbitral, tribunals. The confusion led on all too many occasions to unfortunate consequences. A Russian and a foreign party would enter into a contract which contained a dispute resolution clause providing, in Russian, for the referral of disputes to an arbitrazh court and, in English, to an arbitration court. When a dispute arose over performance of the contract, the parties discovered that they had a second, and unsuspected, dispute: to whom did they intend to refer a dispute for resolution. The foreigner had preferred to be in an arbitration tribunal with agreed neutral arbitrators, whereas the Russian side preferred that disputes be settled in a Russian arbitrazh court where the judge, although he might lack commercial sophistication, would be familiar with Russian law.

Rationing the use of equivalents. In the ideal of all possible translation worlds, there would be a single Russian term and a single English term for the same idea, concept, institution, or relevant thing. Synonyms create difficulties for lawyers and raise issues of construction. Those who translate extensively from the legal Russian into English will seek to be as consistent as text and memory permit in their choice of terminology. This can mean that when choosing an English equivalent for a Russian legal term, one must bear in mind not merely what the appropriate equivalent should be, but also what other terms may arise and need to be factored into the choice.

To choose an example from Russian civil law: the Russian legal system has three principal equity interests in property: stock [акция], participatory share [доля], and share [пай]. Commonly the Russian word (here translated as "stock") in other works, especially in the mass media, is translated as "share" (this choice creates special difficulties for dealing with the Anglo-American expression "shares of stock"). It is not wrong to translate акция as share; but if one does so, there are no terms readily available to translate the other two Russian equity interests, and it is vital to draw the necessary distinctions among them. Indeed, in English it is necessary to fall back on "participatory share" for доля in order to ultimately use the word "share" in English for пай. This is a form of "defensive" translation, trying to anticipate what range of terms the legislator may deploy as part of his legal arsenal. The distinction is crucial for the foreign investor because the owners of "stock", "participatory shares", and "shares" have different rights and obligations; correct and consistent use of the terms usually will indicate what type of investment vehicle is involved on the Russian side.

For many decades the Russian word for police was милиция. A literal translation would produce the English word "militia", which simply was not appropriate because in Anglo-American parlance the "militia" are Army personnel and not law enforcement. When the Russian legislator several years ago decided to rename the "militia" in Russian "полиция", which is precisely "police", we had no words available to reflect the change.

An analogous problem arises with what in Russian is the joint-stock society [акционерное общество]. The problem is with the second word, "society", which is widely translated (incorrectly in this author's view) as "company". To put it otherwise, "company" is a correct description, but not a correct translation. The Republic Kazakhstan inadvertently illustrated the point by introducing into its legislation not only the "joint-stock society", but also the "joint-stock company" [акционерная компания]. In Kazakhstan the last term was used to designate a joint-stock society in which the State owned 25% or more of the stocks and therefore subject to different legislation. Those who had translated "joint-stock society" as "joint-stock company" were unable to cope with the newly-formed Kazakhstan entity. The literal approach to translation would have safeguarded the position.

During the Soviet era, especially in the post-Stalin era, considerable emphasis was placed in the legal system on the role of the "social organization" [общественная организация]; in modern legislation one also encounters the "social association" [общественное объединение]. Here there is a parting of the ways between the English and American languages. Some translators prefer "public" to "social", and indeed in other contexts, for example, "public order"[14] [общественный порядок], "public" would be the equivalent in both England and the United States. In Russian the term translated as "social" means "non-State" and is widely used in that context.

A case arose in the United States courts concerning the legal status of a Soviet media organization called "Novosti". Under Soviet law, Novosti was a "social organization". Novosti was sued in the State of New York by a former Soviet citizen for libel; in defense, Novosti pleaded State immunity. The court heard evidence which indicated, using the English (and not American) language, that Novosti was a "public" organization. The New

[14] But not to be confused with what appears at first glance to be "public order", but is in fact "public policy" or "ordre publique" [публичный порядок]. Constitutional amendments in force from 4 July 2020 introduce the term "public legal order" [публичный правопорядок] in place of "public policy", the latter term not being regarded as a proper Russian legal term.

York judge granted immunity. In New York "public" meant "State", whereas in England "public" meant non-State, or private.[15]

Translation conventions or canons. Comparative lawyers who translate extensively from the Russian commonly develop conventions or canons of translation and a consistent translation lexicon, familiarity with which can help the reader to appreciate some of the nuances of the Russian. The present writer, for example, is among those who, as a rule, translates Russian normative materials into the future imperative rather than following the original, which is almost invariably in the present tense. Anglo-American legislation is generally phrased in the future imperative: "shall". It is not inappropriate to translate Russian normative provisions into the future imperative in order to accentuate their value as law – but distinguishing, where one is able, clauses or formulations that are clearly programmatic and not normative provisions. The Soviet legislator was especially prone to write programmatic provisions – statements of non-normative future objectives or aims. For the translator this is an exercise of discretion. For the reader or consumer, this means that the interpretation of the clause should not turn upon the word "shall", which is pure translator convention.[16]

Translator discretion inevitably arises with respect to the use of articles, for the Russian language does not have them. Whether something is "a" or "the" can sometimes be determined from the subject-matter and context of the sentence; often, however, what was intended is ambiguous. In the field of law the distinction can be of immense consequence. Many translators will perforce minimize the use of articles where this is possible.

Imports of words from Russia. Some authentically Russian expressions have been absorbed into the English language. The Gorbachev era in Soviet history is known as "perestroika" [перестройка], a major feature of which was "glasnost" [гласность], or openness. These were bywords for the Gorbachev era policies of "restructuring" and "transparency", although in the Russian context they had specific meanings that do not carry over easily into Anglo-American terminology. They have in effect become English words to describe Soviet and post-Soviet domestic policies of their time, and their meaning in English is not always one that a Russian would find comprehensible.

So too do we understand that a "sputnik" is a space satellite and that a "cosmonaut" is an "astronaut"; both terms have entered the vocabulary of space law; and from 2020 "sputnik-V" refers to the Russian coronavirus vaccine.

[15] On the divisions of meaning created by sharing a common language, see M. Arnheim, *Anglo-American Law: A Comparison* (Clark, New Jersey, 2019).

[16] For a discussion of the controversy surrounding use of the future imperative in other translations of Soviet codes, see Berman and Spindler, note 10 above, pp. 117-118.

Foreign words become legal Russian. "Hooliganism" is a term known to England and the United States, although perhaps is more common in England, where the term is popularly associated with "soccer" or "football". It is accepted that the term in Russian, "hooliganism" [хулиганство], entered the Russian language sometime from the 1890s onward, possibly from the Irish surname "Houlighan" or from translations of the works of Charles Dickens into Russian. However, in the Soviet Union the word "hooliganism" metamorphosed into a specific offense in the 1960 Criminal Code of the RSFSR (Article 206) and has been retained in the 1996 Criminal Code of the Russian Federation (Article 213).

TRANSLATION DUE DILIGENCE

However well one may work in a foreign language, no one has a command of all languages and perforce must rely upon translations. For the legal practitioner, legal translations represent legal risk. Reliance upon an inaccurate translation may lead to an error in legal advice based upon a mistaken text. "Taking apart", or "parsing", a translation, investigating the original text upon which it was based, gaining an understanding of how the translator may have approached his or her task, knowledge of how translators work and what limitations they inherently encounter in their operations, and an awareness of who actually did the translation will contribute to a better understanding of the document. In an ideal world of translation a Russian-speaking reader familiar with the translator can "work backwards" and resurrect the original Russian text – a useful tool when the translation is ambiguous.

Sometimes the attentive translator will discover clues in the text that substantively affect a legal outcome – clues that a less meticulous or inexperienced translator would miss or dismiss as inconsequential. An expert on Russian law was retained some years ago to offer a view on a Polish legal document dating from the mid-1930s. The document was in the Polish language, quite brief, occupying less than half a page of typewritten text. An English translation was supplied together with the original; there was no indication of who did the translation or when it was done. The document itself purported to be a marriage certificate. A comparison of the Polish text and the English translation indicated that three Polish words in the upper right corner of the document did not appear on the English translation. The Russian legal expert was invited to comment on the document because the document originated in Eastern Poland, where Russian Imperial law continued to govern family relations during the interwar era.

What seemed at first to be a simple omission proved not to be so. Polish-English dictionaries consulted to translate the three Polish words did not contain those words (which presumably is why they were not translated). Eventually, an unusually obscure mimeographed Polish-English dictionary produced during the Second World War was obtained and did contain the mysterious three words. The missing words identified the source of the document (which proved to be London); consultations with London archives disclosed the circumstances of the marriage certificate and ultimately led to the discovery that a spouse believed to have died during the Nazi occupation of Eastern Poland was, in fact, still alive – a circumstance that rendered the marriage certified by the document invalid under canon law. The outcome affected the rights of the surviving individuals to obtain social security benefits.

Computer translations and online translations whose translator is not specified should be avoided. Commercial data banks do not always disclose whether they are marketing computer translations. In computer translations of certain languages (for example, Ukrainian to Russian or *vice versa*) the incidence of error is, in percentages, 1% or less; the translations follow the original so closely that errors are difficult to ascertain and often quite subtle, albeit material. These can be the most dangerous of all.

What constitutes a "reputable" translation? At the outset, at least, a reputable translator. However, in practice these days the commercial legal world operates with translations deliberately anonymous (produced within law firms by translation divisions or outsourced to translation agencies, or downloaded from the Internet). Firms, just as governments or international organizations, do not translate. People do. It is essential to know who? What qualifications do they have? Are they experienced legal practitioners or young graduates in languages? Who in the firm is qualified to assess the quality of the work being produced? Worse are the unattributed translations on the Internet or those offered by commercial data bases. In the CIS, where the quality and accuracy of the data bases may vary from one country to another, appropriate account must be taken of those data bases where computers are being used without disclosure (e.g., Ukraine); the English-language versions of this material can be nothing short of dreadful.

The same due diligence that lawyers routinely undertake when assessing the quality and veracity of evidence needs to be undertaken with respect to the accuracy of translation. Legal translation being the foundation of comparative law, translation is a matter for the experienced lawyer/linguist/comparatist. Monolingual arbitrators and judges work at their peril with translations whose origins are unknown. Monolingualism is not merely a self-imposed disability; it fractures the ability to place oneself within the mental set of another legal system and its signs, including to appreciate and anticipate the perplexities that may arise simply by virtue of multilingual situations.

OFFICIAL, STATE, AND AUTHENTIC LANGUAGE TEXTS

The 1993 Russian Constitution provides (Article 68) that the Russian language is the State language of the Russian Federation. Some authorities regard the concepts of "State" language and "official" language as synonymous and, indeed, go so far as to translate the phrase "State language" as "official language". Literal translation comes to the rescue here, for if one consistently translates the terminology and distinguishes between the words "official" and "State", one can at least have the discussion about whether they are the same or different. To collapse the terms together into one another destroys the possibility of the discussion.

Although the Russian language is the State language of the Russian Federation, Russia is a multilingual jurisdiction, with literally more than a hundred languages actively spoken in various parts of the country. In some sufficiently populous and wealthy subjects of the Russian Federation, legal enactments are produced in the local language together with Russian versions. As a rule, the working language nonetheless is Russian and the texts in other languages are usually translations rather than original texts.[17] That is no longer the case in some of the Independent States of the former Soviet Union: for example, in Armenia, Azerbaijan, Georgia, Tadjikistan, Turkmenistan, Ukraine, and Uzbekistan, among others, the legislator works in the primary State language of the republic and secondarily in Russian.[18] In a few independent States the Russian language remains the working language irrespective of what the State language may be. The Gazette of the Supreme Rada in Ukraine, for example, was published in Ukrainian and Russian, but the Russian language version was stated to be a translation from the Ukrainian and ceased appearing from 2016.

Sometimes the texts provided by the parties to a judicial or arbitral proceeding enjoy the status of an "official" translation produced within or for a government or a parliament – a status that involves its own problems. "Official" rubbish is rubbish nonetheless; attaching the word "official" to a

[17] Prior to the 1917 Russian revolutions, the Russian language served as the official language in Russian courts even in areas where the population had no native command of Russian. Interpreters were widely used, but insufficient in numbers to cope with the caseload. In some regions (Bessarabia, Eastern Poland, some Baltic provinces) local languages were allowed and appeals to St. Petersburg were summarized in Russian. In the regions of Kazan, Middle Volga, Crimea, and Central Asia local languages were extensively used in practice but not reflected in the official record of the proceedings, where Russian translations were supplied. See in general S. B. Kirmse, *The Lawful Empire: Legal Change and Cultural Diversity in Late Tsarist Russia* (2019).

[18] On some of the difficulties encountered by judicial and arbitral proceedings as a result of the new status of official and State languages in the post-Soviet independent States, see H. J. Berman, *Law and Language: Effective Symbols of Community*, ed. John Witte Jr. (2013), pp. 171-173.

translation does nothing to enhance the quality of the product. Governments do not translate; people do (or computers, which is a danger, as noted above, of an entirely different magnitude). Governments (or churches, in the case of Biblical texts) endorse the quality or accuracy of a translation at their peril; in doing so, they do not elevate the text to the level of legislation. Rather, they seek to quell a measure of dissonance over what the legislation adopted in one language means in another. In attempting to do so, they may create more problems than they resolve. Tempting as superficially the prospect may be, labeling a translation as "official+-" confers upon it an immutable and unassailable quality that in reality is undeserved.

The international legal system employs the "ostrich" theory of legal translation: produce a treaty text in multiple languages and provide that each text is "equally authentic". The European Union operates under the rule that all languages of the Union enjoy equal status. The rule itself is paradoxically ungrammatical: "a single original in Danish, Dutch, English ...". The implication is that within the European Union, just as in the case of the multilingual texts of international treaties, there are no translations (a practice and appropriate clause that often is carried over to many commercial civil-law contracts). Every language text is an original – that is, has the same legal force, the same authority, the same validity. Although this overlooks the reality that in almost all international forums, whether the European Union or international treaty-making conferences, or in multilingual national parliaments, the delegates worked in one or a few languages and generated a working document in a single or handful of languages, the fiction of equal authenticity is maintained even though the drafting history is otherwise. The authentic texts, thus, are routinely agreed once the final text is achieved in the single or handful of working languages of the conference or parliament. In other words, the act of translation actually did occur, and may indeed have resulted in the original working-language version being tweaked in order to address nuances that arose in the context of further discussion. The ostrich sees only the authentic text-outcomes of the process and ignores the means by which the texts were actually achieved.

TRANSLATION AND PROOF OF FOREIGN LAW

Where issues of the application of foreign law are involved that require recourse by a court or arbitration tribunal to the texts of foreign legislation, judicial practice, or doctrinal writings, the guidance offered by the legislator is helpful only to a point. The Civil Code of the Russian Federation is probably representative, at least generally, of the approach taken in many, if not most, countries of the world. A Russian court or arbitral tribunal is directed, when applying foreign law, to establish the content of norms of foreign law "... in accordance with their official interpretation, practice of application, and doctrine in the respective foreign State" (Article 1191(1),

Civil Code). The court or arbitral tribunal is at liberty to apply in the established procedure for assistance and explanation either to the Ministry of Justice of the Russian Federation and other competent agencies or organizations in Russia, or abroad, or to enlist experts for this purpose.[19]

Participants in a Russian proceeding may submit "documents" to the court or tribunal that confirm the content of norms of foreign law which are referred to either in substantiation of or by way of objection to demands being made or to otherwise assist the court or tribunal in establishing the content of these norms (Article 1191(2), Civil Code). Russian law is the default position if the content of norms of foreign law cannot be established, notwithstanding the measures taken pursuant to Article 1191.

What the legislator glides over in silence (and does so, virtually universally) is that legal translation will inevitably underlie establishing the "content of the norms of foreign legislation". No standards are prescribed for translations, and judicial practice can be astonishingly cavalier in its naiveté about the central role translation must play in determining what the rules of foreign law may be in a particular situation. Experts may be enlisted to assist the court (Article 1191(2), Russian Civil Code; §44.1, Federal Rules of Civil Procedure, United States), although the need to involve them is doubted in some circles. So-called "certified" translations in substance certify nothing at all are frequently are of no higher quality than those not "certified" under the relevant procedure. This is a charade considered below.

The parameters of the problem are well illustrated in a case in the United States Court of Appeals for the Seventh Circuit.[20] Unless the court reads the relevant foreign language, translations must be consulted, whether supplied by the parties or located by the court independently. Courts are circumspect about their capacity to work in foreign languages. Arbitrators may be less circumspect and often have a command of two or more languages without interpreters – a facility which may have contributed to their being chosen to arbitrate. Nonetheless, international arbitrations addressing foreign law situations widely use legal translations of foreign normative, judicial, and doctrinal material and will usually depend upon the parties to provide texts in support of their allegations or objections.

This has generated a number of subsidiary legal fictions (leaving aside the proposition that all law is a fiction – a proposition that flows from the

[19] But contrast the United States practice, which allows a federal court to undertake its own research and consider any relevant material found. The court may have better foreign law materials available than counsel or may reexamine and amplify material presented by counsel in partisan fashion or in insufficient detail. See the Note published in 1966 to Rule 44.1, Federal Rules of Civil Procedure.

[20] Bodum USA Inc., Plaintiff-Appellant, v. La Cafetiere, Inc., Defendant-Appellant, 621 F3d 624; 2010 U.S. App. LEXIS 18374; 96 U.S.P.Q.2D (BNA) 1689, 2 September 2010.

roots of law in symbols, or words).[21] These fictions surface in international arbitrations because such arbitrations are by definition "international", that is, more likely than ordinary domestic litigation, arbitration, or other forms of dispute settlement to engage two or more languages either in the proceeding or in the materials submitted by the parties and/or consulted by the arbitrators. We address several of these below, some based on experience, others on anecdote.

THE FICTION OF EQUIVALENCE

The self-enclosed nature of the terminology of law encourages the creation of an internally coherent set of signs that can never be successfully superimposed upon any other system. The seemingly abstract and neutral statement of that proposition is complicated immeasurably by the fact that the coherence of the system – being a human creation and part of the political process in any given society – is far from perfect and is reflective of cultural, historical, sociological, anthropological, and other extraneous elements that influence the choice and the meaning of the signs (words) chosen. Taken to an extreme, this state of affairs would suggest that legal translation is impossible. Even within a single language the signs vary, such that English law, American law, Australian law, Canadian law, despite a measure of shared signs, operate different distinctions with respect to the same legal terms. As Barros aptly observed, these are the reasons "... you can't translate legal language – except that you must".[22]

Can one teach legal terminology of a foreign language to law students without teaching the law itself? Or should, or must, one be legally trained in order to teach the legal terminology of a foreign language, together with all other aspects of the foreign language, to law students?

Possible corollaries fall into place rather quickly. Should one be legally trained in order to undertake legal translation or interpreting? Should international and comparative lawyers, as an integral part of their education, be required to produce a legal translation of quality using materials from the legal system(s) in which they propose to concentrate? Should international arbitrators be required to demonstrate proficiency in legal translation as part of their qualifications to serve on a panel of arbitrators?

It is easy to fall into the creation of "false standards" attempting to deal with the problems of translation. In fact, legal systems create false

[21] "Law is the very model of an untranslatable text, because the language of law is self-enclosed and refers to nothing outside of itself". Bellos, note 2 above, p. 217. Oddly enough, studies of comparative law classify families of legal systems on the basis of legal traditions, legal cultures, legal sovereignties (geography), and others, but not on the basis of languages. Are we overlooking the obvious?

[22] Bellos, note 2 above, p. 220: "... the terms they use are not interchangeable. Each one is truly *sui generis*, constituted exclusively by the particular distinctions it makes". Ibid.

standards routinely. It is a widely accepted axiom of court procedure and due process that a defendant or respondent has, or should have, the right to understand the proceeding in which he or she participates and to speak to the court in his or her own language. Interpreters are commonly used for this purpose. They are unlikely in practice to be legally trained and may themselves not understand what they are witnessing or being asked to interpret. The fiction is that because they have some knowledge of the languages involved, they are proficient to act. Courts on appeal will not be sympathetic to the complete absence of an interpreter, but are rarely well placed to address the consequences of poor interpreting.

International arbitrations confront the same issues. Interpreters will routinely be provided by the parties and the costs absorbed for this. But the search for individuals who are capable of simultaneous interpretation (a considerable skill quite different from translations done in the solitude of one's study or office) and who have a genuine command of the terminology is perhaps more difficult than for routine court cases. International arbitrations are by their nature sophisticated forms of litigation and the issues more nuanced – and therefore more difficult to translate.

Notaries are commonly requested or required under domestic procedural rules and international conventions to certify or attest the quality of the translations of documents being submitted from one legal system to the courts, officials, or institutions of another. Apostille is a simplified means of such certification. Yet the exercise itself, so far as translation is concerned, is pure charade. The notary invariably has absolutely no basis, skills, or even time to make such a determination.

Law is not literature. The legislator (how deceiving is the singular, when even in the most totalitarian systems legislation is the product of many hands) is about as far removed from producing texts of literary quality as can be. The legislator's inherent provincialism (preoccupation with his own legal system and its signs) means that he uses words in ways that create opportunities for the fashioning of transactions that in effect produce results not merely not intended, but actually in circumvention of what the legislator was seeking to achieve. This happens, for example, when the legislator, in seeking to prohibit certain outcomes, fails to take into account what exists in other legal systems to which parties may have recourse in their transactional activity.

Russian family law offers an example. All property acquired during marriage by spouses, under the Russian Family Code, is in their joint ownership, subject to certain exceptions, unless provided otherwise by a marriage contract. It did not occur to the Russian legislator that other legal systems might make available trust structures under which Russian spouses could arguably acquire property abroad and place it outside the spousal ownership regime. Had the Russian legislator done his homework in comparative law and been determined to close the door to any possible circumvention by recourse to institutes of foreign law, such closure might have been easily achieved. By failing to address himself to, in this example, well-known signs extant in other legal traditions, questions arise about the comprehensiveness of the Russian marital property regime.

LANGUAGE-PARITY

With respect to authentic texts of treaties, the principle at stake is "language-parity". Because every official European Union text or treaty text so designated is deemed to be original and authentic, issues of incorrect translation do not enter into the equation. Just as the Emperor has no clothes, so too every language in which the treaty is concluded is the original. Parallel authentic texts go back early into human history. A favorite example is the Rosetta stone (196 BC), which recorded a tax amnesty in Greek, Egyptian, and hieroglyphics. Other examples include the Treaty of Nerchinsk (1689), in which the Jesuits accompanying the Chinese delegation elaborated a text in Latin and then Russian and Chinese language versions were prepared,[23] or a privatization transaction in Kazakhstan in which parallel Russian and English language texts were negotiated and the text in the Kazakh language generated later. Or arbitral awards in which the arbitrators drafted a Russian-language version and then produced the English text as required (or *vice versa*), both texts of the award being equally authentic.

In a sense what the European Union is doing at quite a high level is developing its own self-enclosed system of legal language within the 24 languages that have official status. For all of its difficulties and denials, that system is capable of working and supporting the myths that it generates. It is strengthened in this mission by the fact that its translators at the level of the European Court of Justice are legal and language professionals who are involved in drafting exercises, or as Barros put it, "... the manipulation of the law as language and language as law".[24]

International commercial arbitrations operate in a far more decentralized environment with respect to translations and multiple languages, as indeed do most domestic courts. In American federal courts, the judges often see the issue with respect to languages as one which either requires the court to consult existing translations of foreign legislation, doctrine, and judicial practice, or to permit or encourage the parties to enlist the services of experts on foreign law: "But ... the law of most ... nations that engage in extensive international commerce, is widely available in English. Judges

[23] The Latin, Manchurian, and Russian language text are reproduced and accompanied by Russian translations from the Latin and from the Manchurian in S. L. Tikhvinskii (ed.), Русско-китайские отношения: Материалы и документы [Russian-Chinese Relations in the XVII Century: Materials and Documents] (1972), II, pp. 645-659.

[24] Bellos, note 2 above, p. 236.

can use not only accepted (sometimes official) translations of statutes and decisions but also ample secondary literature, such as treatises and scholarly commentary".[25] Arbitrators may say the same.

TRANSLATION LIABILITY

Legal risks extend beyond the consumer of translations to the producer. Lawyers neglecting to take reasonable steps when working with foreign language source material may incur liability to clients. But more far-reaching possibilities are conceivable. In the United States a translator/interpreter who translated a letter from an imprisoned Muslim cleric to his Egyptian lawyer was convicted of conspiracy to incite kidnappings and killings; in this case the translator was a court-appointed translator/interpreter working on the instructions of the defendant's lawyers.[26]

Incorrect translation can lead in Russia to criminal prosecution of the interpreter, as is the case in many legal systems. The court interpreter has procedural status under the Code of Criminal Procedure of the Russian Federation (Articles 59, 169).[27] Criminal prosecution may be instituted for an incorrect translation or for bribery to commit an incorrect translation (Articles 307, 309, Criminal Code).[28]

In the Russian Federation criminal proceedings are conducted in the Russian language and/or in the State languages of republics within the Russian Federation, except in the Supreme Court and in military courts, where Russian is the language of the proceeding. Participants in the proceeding are guaranteed the right to speak in court in their native language or other language of which they have a command or to take advantage of the services of an interpreter, which are provided without cost. Documents that under procedural law must be handed over to a suspect, accused, or other participants in a proceeding must be translated into the native language or language of which the participant has a command (Article 18).[29]

[25] Chief Judge Easterbrook, in Bodum, note 20 above.

[26] See M. Powell and M. Garcia, "Translator's Conviction Raises Legal Concerns", *The Washington Post*, 16 January 2006, pp. A1, A9.

[27] See W. E. Butler, *Russian Criminal Law and Procedure* (2011), pp. 295, 367.

[28] Ibid., pp. 212-214.

[29] Ibid., p. 254.

3

THE PRE-REVOLUTIONARY HERITAGE

The 1917 October Revolution proclaimed in the exuberance of its triumph a complete break with the Russian past. In 1918 there followed a formal repeal of Imperial legislation (although Soviet courts were allowed for some years to fill gaps in Soviet legislation by having recourse to pre-revolutionary legislation in certain circumstances). But law is not merely the statute book at any given moment of time; it represents an accumulation of experiences, values, terminology, attitudes constructed in the course of human affairs over many centuries, elements which the Revolution could not dispense with no matter how radical the policies it sought to introduce.

Neither was the study of Russian legal history entirely abandoned, although it experienced periods of comparative neglect and, when revived, suffered from the superimposition of ideological constraints. The demise of the Soviet Union removed those constraints and invited legal scholars to return to the legacy of the past in order to find lessons and solutions for the future development of Russian law.

Reconstructing the pre-revolutionary legal heritage is no easy task. Records for the early period are exceptionally sparse, and for later centuries, hardly touched by legal historians. Moreover, even within the frontiers of the Imperial Russian Empire and the present Russian Federation there were dozens of legal systems operating simultaneously: the customary law of various tribes, towns, regions, and peoples, Islamic law, Baltic law, canon law, Judaic law, and others, side by side with Russian law enacted by the central authorities. The development of Russian law itself was influenced by foreign law: Byzantine,[1] Roman, Tatar, Polish, Swedish, German, French, English, Italian, Dutch, Lithuanian, among others, sometimes by precept, more often perhaps by deliberate adaptation.

[1] Whether there was Byzantine influence and precisely what that influence may comprise has been debated for centuries. The treaties between Byzantium and Kievan Rus are conclusive evidence of international interaction between the two legal orders; more controversial is whether Byzantine law influenced Kievan Rus canon and secular law. The debate continues. For a concise account of twenty-first century views, see V. Zhivov, "Once Again on Whether Byzantine Law Was Applied to the Administration of the Law in Medieval Rus", in M. di Salvo, D. H. Kaiser, and V. A. Kivelson (eds.), *Word and Image in Russian History* (2015), pp. 33-42

KIEVAN RUS

The importance of legal materials for an understanding of early Russian history may be simply stated: virtually all of the few surviving documents from the Kievan period are legal texts of one kind or another. The earliest are in fact international legal documents, four peace or trade treaties concluded in or about the years 907 (860), 911, 944, and 971 between the Grand Prince of Kievan Rus and Byzantium. These offer insight into penal practices and judicial procedure, the status of foreigners, the law of shipwreck, and the ratification of treaties and legal status of envoys.[2] The first treaty is known through the chronicles; texts of the others have survived. Reference is made in them to pre-existing Russian law as an extant legal system.[3] The conversion of Kievan Rus to Christianity (c. 988) created a channel for the reception of canon law and perhaps the means for readily reducing to written form the enactments of the princes and the customary rules applied.

There is a strong supposition that the Slavic peoples inhabiting the lands of what became Kievan Rus had fashioned definite rules for interpersonal and interclan or intertribal behavior long before the Kievan princes consolidated their authority.[4] Whether the earliest surviving compilations

[2] For the texts of the treaties and a discussion of their historiography, see R. A. Khachaturov (ed.), Памятники права древней Руси [Monuments of the Law of Medieval Rus] (M., 2013), I, pp. 359-421. The likelihood is that the original texts of the treaties were in Greek. Slavonic language versions were probably produced later and translated from a Byzantine chronological collection of diplomatic documents. See S. Franklin, *Writing, Society and Culture in Early Rus, c. 950-1300* (2002), pp. 164-165. Feldbrugge observed: "… the invention of writing did so significantly improve the possibilities of communication between human beings from different places and times, that the world became a different place from that moment on". F. J. M. Feldbrugge, "The Earliest Law of Russia and its Sources", in Feldbrugge (ed.), *The Law's Beginnings* (2003), p. 92; also see Feldbrugge, *A History of Russian Law* (2017), pp. 85-100. For translations of the treaties, see D. H. Kaiser (transl. & ed.), *The Laws of Rus' – Tenth to Fifteenth Centuries* (1992), pp. 1-13, this version also reproduced in *Jus Gentium*, I (2016), 627-638. The treaties have been extensively discussed, recently in S. V. Kudin, "Treaties of Kievan Rus (X-XIII Centuries): Cognition of the 'Common' and the 'Different' in the Law of States", *Jus Gentium: Journal of the History of International Law*, I (2016), pp. 573-580. Also on the pre-treaty period, see V. G. Butkevych, "The International Legal Ideology of the Pre-Slavic Chiefdoms of the Ukrainian Ethnos", *Jus Gentium*, I (2016), 345-390; II (2017), pp. 7-66, 389-442; III (2018), pp. 7-62. Plausible arguments are made that the treaties should be dated to the years 860 or 866. More generally, see V. E. Rubanik, Государство, право и суд в Киевской Руси [State, Law, and Court in Kievan Rus] (2013).

[3] On the origin of the treaties, see S. Franklin and J. Shepard, *The Emergence of Rus 750-1200* (1996), pp. 103-107.

[4] For background, see R. Portal, *The Slavs: A Cultural and Historical Survey of the Slavonic Peoples* (1969); P. M. Barford, *The Early Slavs: Culture and Society in Early Medieval Eastern Europe* (2001). Barford's view was that "the Soviet state derived from the Tsarist Russian Empire, which in turn had its origin in the Duchy of Moscow in the late medieval period. There is only the most tenuous of links between this and the Kievan state of the tenth century" (p. ix). This is the perception of an archeologist, not a jurist. On the historiography of Kievan Rus, also see A. Wilson, *The Ukrainians: Unexpected Nation* (2000). On medieval criminal law, see E. V. Georgievskii, Формирование и развитие общих положений древнерусского

of Russian laws, the Правда Русская [*Pravda Russkaia,* as it is known in English], represented a creative codification of law or a reduction to writing of customary law continues to be debated.[5] So too does the extent to which the substance of the *Pravda Russkaia,* which contains striking parallels with aspects of Frankish and Anglo-Saxon law, was the result of mutual influence or of the independent development of peoples at a similar stage of societal development. The surviving versions pose internal obstacles to understanding. Their obsolete terminology and grammar have spawned interminable debates about the true meanings of terms.[6] The document was the more momentous as an example of East Slavic writing (as distinguished from the Cyrillic based on Greek), symptomatic of a transition to native uses of writing on a large scale.[7] East Slavic was the vernacular, whereas Church Slavonic was an imported written language developed specially

уголовного права [Forming and Development of General Provisions of Medieval Russian Criminal Law] (2013).

5 Hellie believed the Russkaia Pravda "... began as a court handbook to facilitate the protection of the people of Novgorod against mercenary Viking oppression. Accretions added around 1072 by Iaroslav's sons, probably based on estate codes, were motivated by an attempt to protect representatives of the princely administration and their property within sanctions of various fines for homicide or theft or destruction of princely property". See R. Hellie, "The Law", in M. Perrie (ed.), *The Cambridge History of Russia* (2006), p. 360. Nikolai Vasil'evich Kalachov (1819-1885) in his pioneering study considered that the *Russkaia Pravda* was a "collection compiled by private persons and at various times augmented in the same way". See N. V. Kalachov, Предварительные юридические сведения для полного объяснения Русской Правды [Preliminary Legal Information for a Full Explanation of the Russkaia Pravda] (1846), a dissertation for the degree of magister.

6 See the study and subsequent revision and retraction by V. M. Zhivov, «История русского права как лингвосемиотическая проблема» [History of Russian Law as a Lingua-Semiotic Problem and Postscriptum], in Zhivov, Разыскания в области истории и предыстории русской культуры [Quests in the Domain of History and Prehistory of Russian Culture] (2002), pp. 187-305. On the individual terminology, see S. G. Pushkarev (comp.), *Dictionary of Russian Historical Terms from the Eleventh Century to 1917* (1970); V. A. Rogov and V. V. Rogov, Древнерусская правовая терминология в отношении к теории права (очерки IX – середины XVII вв.) [Medieval Russian Legal Terminology with Respect to the Theory of Law (Surveys from the IX to Mid-XVII Centuries] (M., 2006); M. A. Isaev, Толковый словарь древнерусских юридических терминов от договоров с Византией до Соборного Уложения царя Алексея Михайловича (IX-XVII вв.) [Interpretative Dictionary of Medieval Russian Legal Terms from the Treaties with Byzantium to the Sobornoe Ulozhenie of Tsar Aleksei Mikhailovich (IX-XVII Centuries)] (2d ed.; Moscow, 2017). The various meanings of the term "pravda" are explored at length in R. S. Wortman, *The Power of Language and Rhetoric in Russian Political History: Charismatic Words from the 18th to the 21st Centuries* (2018), pp. 133-158: "... the boundaries of the word's meanings are vague and shifting, adapting to the needs of the speaker to lend legal, philosophical, political, even theological gravitas and uplift to his particular viewpoint ... *pravda* is the perfect charismatic word: its cloudy meanings are given to associations with higher authorities of any type on any occasion, evoking sacral overtones for its referent" (p. 133).

7 See Franklin and Shepard, note 3 above, p. 219: "Before the age of Iaroslav traces of any native uses of writing, though not entirely negligible, are barely visible; after the age of Iaroslav all forms of native writing ... steadily proliferate". On the origins of the Slavic languages, see A. M. Schenker, *The Dawn of Slavic: An Introduction to Slavic Philology* (1995), with illustrations of major lettering styles.

for the translation of the Scriptures from the Greek, the language of "high culture", as distinguished from the language of "civil administration".[8]

Most texts available for study were copied centuries after the original was allegedly composed; the Пространная Правда Русская [Expanded *Pravda Russkaia*], for example, attributed on the basis of internal evidence to the eleventh or twelfth centuries, survives in only three texts dating prior to the fifteenth century and 92 texts dating from the sixteenth to eighteenth centuries.[9] The Краткая Русская Правда [Short *Russkaia Pravda*], believed to antedate the Expanded version, is known to us only in manuscript versions that were transcribed after the earliest manuscripts of the Expanded version. Although the traditional approach has been to consider that three (original, Short, and Expanded) versions of a single law exist, it is possible that each version may comprise an autonomous enactment to be studied in tandem with the other collected legal texts with which the *Pravda Russkaia* appears.

The initial *Pravda Russkaia* is believed to have been composed in the reign of Iaroslav the Wise (1015-54).* The text began with the rules of the blood feud, which the Expanded version tells us was abolished by Iaroslav's sons and replaced by a system of monetary compositions; the latter contained provisions treating various forms of stealing, interest, keeping, suits for money, shipwreck, bee-keeping, succession, oaths, slavery, and ownership. The versions of the *Pravda Russkaia* suggest that the prince's court played a minor role in prosecution and litigation. The system relied upon party initiative; there were no permanent judges, merely officials who presided over the proceedings, and ultimate judgment was decided by kissing the cross or by ordeal, later augmented by numbers of witnesses. So far as is known, there was no possibility of appeal, no system of courts, no legal profession, no legal commentary on the princely legislation or judicial decisions. Nor can we judge with any certainty the territorial extent to which even within Kievan Rus the provisions of the Pravda were applied.

It does seem clear that the *Pravda Russkaia* did influence local legal texts in regions north and west of Kiev. International legal documents are

[8] Franklin and Shepard, note 3 above, p. 220. The implication is that, whatever foreign influences may have been reflected in the text of the *Pravda Russkaia*, the customs and procedures were of local origin "… without the merest hint of Byzantine-style window-dressing". Ibid., p. 221.

[9] D. H. Kaiser, *The Growth of Law in Medieval Russia* (1980), p. 18. Kaiser gives an excellent account of the manuscript sources and the problems they pose for the legal historian. See generally J. Martin, *Medieval Russia 980-1584* (2d ed., 2007). For a recent study and the Russian judicial system in general, see S. A. Koluntaev and V. M. Syrykh (eds.), История суда и правосудия в России [History of Court and the Administration of Justice in Russia] (Moscow, 2016-), an intended nine-volume work. The texts are examined in detail in M. B. Sverdlov, Латиноязычные источники по истории древней Руси IX-XIII вв. Правда Русская. История текста. Избранные статьи [Latin Language Sources for the History of Medieval Rus of the IX-XIII Centuries. Germany. "Pravda Russkaia". History of the Text. Selected Articles] (Spb., 2017), pp. 31-485.

a key: the treaty negotiated by Novgorod with Gotland (c. 1189-99) and the Smolensk treaty of 1229 in its Gotland and Riga versions.[10] Both texts contain provisions that can be traced to the Pravda concerning criminal law, commercial matters, and the legal status of foreigners.

The sources of legal rules in these early documents must have been several. Customary rules, princely decisions, borrowings from Byzantine, German, Scandinavian, Slavic, or other peoples – all are plausible candidates. But Christianity brought an incontestably imported body of canon law whose texts have survived principally in the form of the Book of the Pilot (Кормчая книга, also known in English as the *Kormchaia Kniga*), sometimes called the Book of the Rudder or the Book of the Helmsman.[11] The collections, varied in content, generally encompassed church canons, epistles, sermons, selections from Byzantine secular legislation, versions of the *Pravda Russkaia*, and princely statutes. Canon law was important throughout the entire pre-revolutionary era, for it was therein that provisions regarding marriage, divorce, and the family, for example, were to be found. In dispossessing the church of its powers in 1917, the Soviet Government was not merely eliminating a rival source of influence; it also was asserting for the first time in perhaps ten centuries secular authority over facets of interpersonal relations. In the Kievan period ecclesiastical courts came to exercise jurisdiction over certain classes of the populace.

The Book of the Pilot often included portions of Byzantine law, notably the *Ecloga* of the eighth century* and the *Procheiros Nomos* of the ninth. A Bulgarian compilation of Byzantine law, the Закон судный людем [*Court Law for the People*], was extensively disseminated in Kievan Rus; later manuscript versions sometimes incorporated the *Pravda Russkaia.* It is the Byzantine heritage in these forms which has led one observer to suggest that Roman law provided Russia and the West with a common legal vocabulary, a common set of legal distinctions, and a concept of legislation.[12]

[10] G. V. Vernadsky (transl.), *Medieval Russian Laws* (1947). A superior translation is D. H. Kaiser (transl. & ed.), *The Laws of Rus' – Tenth to Fifteenth Centuries* (1992). The fine study by A. A. Zimin, Правда Русская [*Pravda Russkaia*] (1999), completed in 1979, has been published posthumously, and the classic analysis by S. V. Iushkov, Русская Правда [*Russkaia Pravda*] (2002) reissued with an excellent biographical sketch of the author. For exhaustive commentary, see G. Baranowski, *Die* Russkaja Pravda – *ein mittelalterliches Rechtsdenkmal* (2005) and Feldbrugge, note 2 above (2017).

[11] Five thirteenth century copies survive in Riga and a sixth from the fourteenth century. Three derive from a version composed in Gotland and may have been translated from a Low German original. The others originate in a version drawn up in Riga and probably were translated from a Latin original. See Franklin, note 3 above, pp. 166-167. The texts are published in R. I. Avanesov (ed.), Смоленские грамоты XIII-XV веков [Smolensk Documents of the XIII-XIV Centuries] (1963).

[12] On the origins and status of the Book of the Pilot, see P. I. Žužek, *Kormčaia kniga* (1964) and Franklin, note 3 above, p. 138; E. V. Beliakova, L. V. Moshkova, and T. A. Oparina, Кормчая книга от рукописной традиции к первому печатную изданию [Kormchaia Kniga from the Manuscript Tradition to the First Printed Edition] (2017); and the monumental M. V.

MONGOL SUBJUGATION 1240-1480

In the mid-thirteenth century there thundered across the Eurasian steppes the most powerful armed adversary Europe had ever encountered. For nearly two and one-half centuries the Golden Horde exacted tribute from Russian communities and episodically laid waste to pockets of resistance. Kievan Rus, which in its prime had flourished as a center of civilization with familial and commercial links ranging from England and Scandinavia in the North, to Spain and France in the West, Byzantium, Persia, and India southward, and China to the East, was devastated by the Mongol advance, never to rise again.[13] The Mongol subjugation of Russia is unanimously, it would seem, regarded as the principal reason for Russia's failure to keep up with the pace and course of legal development in Western Europe. Had Kiev survived, in the course of time universities might have opened, law might have been systematically taught, commentaries compiled, a legal profession formed, and the Russian legal system might have come to resemble more closely others of the Romanist tradition.

The Mongols were not a sedentary people. It was not their practice to conquer and then permanently occupy territory.[14] They preferred to introduce a tributary structure, often relying upon local Russians who appeared to be loyal, and to exact horrible retribution when the tributary obligations were not fulfilled. So far as the conquered legal system was concerned, the Mongols were content that it should operate normally; but they imposed a style of autocracy and public administration which many observers believe left an indelible imprint on subsequent Russian styles of State leadership. Nor, it should be added, did the Mongols in principle oppose commercial or other intercourse between Russian cities or principalities and Western Europe. Why then could not law in Russia, or at least private law, have continued to develop under European stimulus?

There is no conclusive answer, but it may not be amiss to suggest that something other than the Mongol presence needs to be taken into account. It is incontestable, and paradoxical, that the number of manuscript copies of Russian legislation during the period of Mongol subjugation is much larger than for the earlier period and that several medieval Russian legal texts actually originated in the Mongol era, for example, the Charter of Dvina Land (c. 1397), the Charter of the City of Pskov (1397-1467), and the Charter of the City of Novgorod (1471).

Korogodina, Кормчие книги XIV – первой половины XVII века [Kormchie knigi of the XIV-First Half of the XVII Centuries] (Spb., 2017). 2 vols.

[13] The Ecloga, dated to the year 741, was a concise selection and restatement of Roman law chosen from Justinianic texts reworked by the *Antecessores*. See M. Humphreys (transl. & commentary), *The Laws of the Isaurian Era: The Ecloga and its Appendices* (2017), pp. 13-18. Also see M. T. G. Humphrey, *Law, Power, and Imperial Ideology in the Iconoclast Era c, 650-850* (2015).

[14] H. J. Berman, *Justice in the U.S.S.R.* (rev. ed., 1963), p. 189.

The Pskov Judicial Charter (Псковская Судная грамота), which survives in two versions, represents a Digest of Pskov duties and extracts from earlier Pskov legislation dating as far back as Alexander Nevskii.[15] Repeatedly reworked after 1397, the second and third versions are considered to have appeared in 1409-1424 and after 1462; it is likely to have influenced the I Lithuanian Statute. Although designed for a particular region, this document and others like it are believed to have been tantamount to a local *Pravda Russkaia* and are important for the insight they offer into the legal and social problems of urban and rural inhabitants. The Novgorod Charter (Новгородская Судная грамота), of which one late version survives, is indebted for some provisions to the *Pravda Russkaia* and contains articles devoted to judicial procedure and land disputes. Both the Pskov and Novgorod documents were drawn upon later when all-Russian legislation began to be prepared. The *Dvina Charter* (Двинская уставная грамота), which originated in the chancellery of a Grand Prince, is devoted to dividing the spheres of competence between central and local authorities and has been described as "the initial stage of forming the legislation of a unified Russian State".[16]

During the Mongol period, the Book of the Pilot continued to proliferate in versions which more fully reflected Russian legal rules. This period saw the appearance of another collection of legal texts called the *Just Measure* (Мерило Праведное); it too owed its origin to the Russian Orthodox Church and included secular and clerical texts. Sometimes incorporated in the *Kormchaia kniga*, the Just Measure is believed to have been used by judges, possibly the supreme ruler himself, primarily within church courts or more generally; surviving texts date from the late fourteenth century. The stages of amalgamation of these texts into successive manuscript collections remains controversial, but the process of consolidation and codification during this era is in evidence.[17] Nevertheless, the substance of these enactments had developed only marginally beyond the *Pravda Russkaia*.

MUSCOVITE LAW 1480-1648

Factional rivalries within the Mongol Empire led in due course to its decline and disintegration. In Central and Western Russia the Grand Duke of Muscovy gradually asserted his authority over neighboring appanage princes and fashioned a centralized State which ultimately threw off the surviving remnants of Tatar bondage and then militarily eliminated serious

[15] See D. Ostrowski, *Muscovy and the Mongols: Cross-Cultural Influences on the Steppe Frontier, 1304-1589* (1998).

[16] On steppe warfare, see T. May, *The Mongol Art of War* (2007).

[17] See S. V. Vasil'ev, Псковская Судная грамота и I Литовский Статут [Pskov Judicial Charter and the I Lithuanian Statute] (2011).

threats to Muscovite lands from that direction. As the Grand Prince's authority extended over newly acquired provinces, charters were issued to confirm the relationship to Muscovy or to grant special privileges to certain communities.[18] The most important surviving text of this nature is the White Lake Charter of 1488, which defined, *inter alia*, the powers of the Grand Prince's judges and laid down judicial procedures and penalties.[19]

The Charter was followed nine years later by what has been called the first national Russian Law Code, the *Sudebnik* [Судебник] of 1497. This and the *Sudebnik* of 1550[20] are the two major legal monuments of the period under consideration. Both *Sudebniki* concerned themselves primarily with the technicalities of judicial procedure and, to some extent, criminal law. The few articles devoted to civil law may reflect the inability of the compilers to consolidate satisfactorily the diversity of local rules on the subject. The extent to which they created new rules of procedure or reflected pre-existing patterns is much debated; the evidence of judgment charters prior to 1497 would seem to indicate that the transition to a vertical system of justice with a hierarchy of courts and judges was a gradual process rather than an innovation in 1497. Of the 68 articles in the 1497 version, 25 originate in the *Pravda Russkaia*, nine are linked with the Pskov Charter, and ten with other known charters. Some legal historians believe the *Sudebniki* also reflect customary law and judicial practice, and there are indications that the compilers consulted Byzantine texts anew. The 1550 *Sudebnik* is known only through 40 later copies, of which 13 are of the sixteenth century. The text was adopted with the participation of the Boyar Duma in 1550, and confirmed by the Stoglav Assembly in 1551, convoked at the initiative of the Tsar. Consisting of 99 or 100 articles, depending upon which copy is consulted, this document had no official title. Reflecting the enhanced stature of the Tsar and further centralization of power in Russia, this *Sudebnik* began to lay the foundations of a Russian administrative system at central and local levels.[21]

[18] See I. N. Danilevskii, in Danilevskii, V. V. Kabanoy, O. M. Medushevskaia, and M. F. Rumiantseva (eds), Источниковедение: теория, история, метод. Источники российской истории [The Study of Sources: Theory, History, Method. Sources of Russian History] (2000), p. 231.

[19] Kaiser, note 2 above, pp. 26-27.

[20] On the legal factors influencing these developments, including inter-princely treaties, see S. A. Mel'nikov, Историко-правовые факторы эволюции древнерусского государства IX-XV вв. [Historical-Legal Factors of the Evolution of the Medieval Russian State IX-XV Centuries] (2010), pp. 130-137; V. E. Rubanik and S. A. Rubanik, Суд и правосудие в древней Руси и Московском государстве в историко-правовой науке и юридической доктрине [Court and the Administration of Justice in Medieval Rus and the Muscovite State in Historical-Legal Science and Legal Doctrine] (2013).

[21] Translated in H. W. Dewey, *Muscovite Judicial Texts* 1488-1556 (1966), pp. 3-6; commentary in Dewey, "The White Lake Charter: A Medieval Russian Administrative Statute", *Speculum*, XXXII (1957), pp. 74-83; also see Feldbrugge, note 2 above (2017), pp. 188-190.

The Grand Prince had the right to act as judge in first instance or as final appellate instance in all cases, if he chose. The right to the personal justice of the ruler was an esteemed privilege in Muscovy which many subjects had secured to them by charters of grant. Certain categories of the populace – the clergy, servitors, and peasants of priests and monasteries, some categories of peasants, guild merchants, foreigners present in Muscovy as merchants or military personnel, among others – were exempted from the ordinary courts and were dealt with by departments [приказы] more responsive to the central authority. The majority of cases, however, were to be heard by regional vice-regents endowed with judicial powers in certain types of cases. Notwithstanding charters of grant and the usual judicial channels, subjects retained the right of direct petition to the Grand Prince to redress wrongs, which ultimately led to the creation of a department specially charged to handle these. The *Sudebniki* would appear to reflect a realization that the personal dispensation of justice by the Sovereign had become too complex; accordingly, a hierarchy of agents came to perform these functions. Some charters of grant even provided for this possibility. But the judgment charters contain no conclusive evidence of a fixed judicial hierarchy; on the contrary, some court officials appeared to have different degrees of authority and sat on the same case on appeal two or more times.[22]

Litigation in Muscovy seems to have been open to anyone, from princes to slaves, women, children, clergy, and bondsmen. Representation and substitution were allowed at trial, even among witnesses and on appeal. Witness testimony was the form of evidence most frequently used; documentary evidence was less common and of great variety, ranging from charters of grant, to purchase deeds, land exchange or property division instruments, marriage settlements, promissory notes, or rent receipts. Witnesses unable to appear are known to have sent depositions containing their testimony. Extracts from land registry books were employed, and some parties even submitted default judgments. Forgeries were not unknown, and especially in land cases the court would personally verify or authenticate the documentary evidence. Divine justice also might be invoked. An icon or piece of turf might be carried during the boundary inspections and the appropriate oath taken. Kissing the cross also appears on the judgment charters as a means of confirming evidence or independent means of proof. A judicial duel might be invoked, usually by one of the

[22] The first English translation of the *Sudebnik* survives in manuscript at the Bodleian Library, Oxford, and the McLennan Library, McGill University, Montreal in three related manuscripts prepared c. 1599, possibly by Dr. Mark Ridley. See Selden supra 50 and Selden supra 60 at the Bodleian; MS McLennan 477 at McGill; and related Selden superius 112 and Selden superius 113 at the Bodleian. See M. S. Arel, "'The Lawes of Russia Written': An English Manuscript on Muscovy at the End of the Sixteenth Century", *Oxford Slavonic Papers*, XXIII (N.S. 1990), pp. 13-38. Russian legal historians did not locate an original text of the 1497 *Sudebnik* until 1817, relying until then on excerpts translated in Sigismund Herberstein's account of his Embassy to Muscovy in 1549.

parties but sometimes by initiative of the judge. Yet another method of divine justice was the casting of lots. Foreign visitors to Muscovy have left two descriptions of judicial duel and one foreigner an account of his own involvement in a trial resolved by casting lots (overdue freight account).[23]

In many cases the Muscovite judge merely prepared a trial record (доклад) of the proceedings and submitted this to a higher instance, which read the record and then questioned both parties to the dispute. The trial record could be challenged for inaccuracies and further evidence submitted. The higher instance would then come to a decision and instruct the inferior judge accordingly. Precisely when and why this procedural device was used is not disclosed by legislation or the judgment charter.

On the whole, the Muscovite lawsuits of this period have impressed scholars as an adversary type proceeding in which the two parties had primary responsibility for initiating the case, presenting the evidence, and adducing the arguments. The courts rarely summoned witnesses; judges seemed to have refereed the proceedings by ensuring that each party had full opportunity to present its case. Occasionally the court would carry out on-the-spot views and seek the submission of additional evidence. On the other hand, litigants did not employ professional counsel. There is no evidence of a nascent legal profession.[24] The judge did ask questions, but the records suggest mainly to ensure that all the evidence had been presented. Cross-examination or interrogation evidently was not practiced.[25]

Judicial corruption was punishable under the 1497 and 1550 *Sudebniki*. Contemporary accounts by foreigners reported official corruption to be commonplace (although there may have been cultural elements at work here that were misperceived). Appeals could be lodged by litigants on the ground of deliberate miscarriage of justice, violation of procedural rules, bribery, and an unjust decision. Appeals on the grounds of corruption appear not to have been unduly frequent, however, and one Western scholar who has examined the *ratio decidendi* of judgment charters of the period has concluded that the judges did base their conclusions on the evidence.[26]

[23] See I. Ia. Froianov (ed.), Судебник Ивана III: Становление самодержавного государства на Руси [*Sudebnik of Ivan III: Origin of an Autocratic State in Rus*] (M., 2004). On later versions or drafts, see A. S. Smykalin, Русское законодательство конца XVI - начала XVII века. Судебник 1589 года. Судебник 1606-1607 годов [Russian Legislation of the End of the XVI and Beginning of the XVII Centuries: Sudebnik of 1589. Sudebnik of 1606-1607] (Ekaterinburg, 2005).

[24] The roles of judges and sundry authority they exercised are addressed in A. M. Kleimola, *Justice in Medieval Russia: Muscovite Judgment Charters (Pravye Gramoty) of the Fifteenth and Sixteenth Centuries* (1975), pp. 10-21.

[25] See Butler, 'Foreign Impressions of Russian Law to 1800: Some Reflections', in Butler, *Russia and the Law of Nations in Historical Perspective* (2009) pp. 102-128.

[26] Nonetheless, the concept of representation was known in the form of an aide (*пособник*), referred to in the Pskov Charter, with limitations on who could perform such functions. See Hellie, note 5 above, pp. 369-370.

In the realm of public law the impact of the Mongol heritage has remained speculative, but many observers believe the centralist autocracy which came to characterize Muscovite administration was the consequence of Mongol despotism. Ivan the Terrible destroyed the power of the hereditary nobility and abolished the right to pass in service from one lord to another without loss of patrimonial property. The nobility became bound to the Tsar by service, and in turn the peasants were bound to their landlords, gradually being prohibited from leaving their estates and likewise becoming indirectly the servitors of the Tsar. Toward the end of the sixteenth century other progress was to be noted. Trial by ordeal became uncommon, and trial by combat was formally abolished in 1556. But in criminal proceedings the investigation of allegations was by torture, a practice which endured well into the eighteenth century. Evidence and proofs collected in this manner were then sent to Moscow, where they were reviewed and, if the party was deemed guilty, punishment assigned.[27]

From Byzantium, Muscovy had received Christianity via Kievan Rus, and with the fall of Constantinople in 1453 and the marriage of the Tsar to Sophia, the niece and heiress of the last of the Byzantine Emperors, Muscovy assumed the mantle of the "Third Rome". The Mongol tradition of tolerance for religious faiths was supplanted in Russia by intolerance for the non-Orthodox. But the Tsar's dual role as head of State and Church contributed, many believe, to an attenuation of some of the harsher features of the Mongol autocratic tradition being adapted by the Muscovite rulers.

THE RUSSIAN EMPIRE 1649-1917

The period 1647 to 1650 was a watershed in Russian legal history, as consequential as the Peace of Westphalia was for European diplomacy and the law of nations. Within that four-year span in Russia, two major law codes, unprecedented in scope and size, were approved and printed for distribution (the first to be printed in all of Russian history) and a substantial German work on the art and laws of war (1615-1617) by Johannes Jacobi von Wallhausen was translated into Russian and printed in 1647. The last was the first printed work treating the law of nations in the Russian language.[28]

[27] On punishments, see Butler, note 25 above, pp. 81-85.

[28] Two copies of this book are to be found in England, both in the British Library. The first came from the collection of Sir Hans Sloane (1660-1753) and the second bears the super-libros of King George III (1738-1820), having previously been owned by the Russian geographer and politician, Ivan K. Kirilov (1689-1737). See R. Cleminson, C. Thomas, D. Radoslavova, and A. Voznesenskij (comps.), *Cyrillic Books Printed Before 1701 in British and Irish Collections* (2000), item 103. Apparently no copies are recorded in the United States. The Wallhausen was released by the printing house of 26 August 1647 at a production cost of 20.02 altyn and sold retail at one ruble; the print run was substantial at 1,200 copies. See I. B. Pozdeeva, Человек. Книга. История. Московская печать XVII века [Man. Book. History: Moscow Printing of the Seventeenth Century] (2016), p. 55. The Russian General Staff printed a facsimile edition in 200 copies (1904). Also see O. Rusakovskiy, "The Russian Edition of Johann Jacobi von

Although we have referred principally to the 1497 and 1550 *Sudebniki* for the Muscovite period, there were hundreds of supplemental enactments issued in the late sixteenth and early seventeenth centuries. By 1649 the morass of legislation required a new compilation. In just over two months during 1648 and early 1649 the Land Assembly (Земский соборъ, also known in English as the *Zemskii sobor*) prepared the most substantial and important achievement of medieval Russian Law: the *Sobornoe ulozhenie* [Соборное уложение] of 1649. Whatever doubt there may be about earlier Russian enactments constituting "codes", the *Ulozhenie* indisputably qualified. Consisting of 967 articles divided haphazardly into 25 chapters, the *Ulozhenie* consolidated provisions drawn from the *Pravda Russkaia*, the *Sudebniki*, the *Litovskii Statut* [Литовский статут] (1588) or Lithuanian Statute,[29] and sundry individual decrees, and introduced some new provisions. Widely regarded as the benchmark in the transition of Russia from feudalism to absolutism, the *Ulozhenie* in any event came to represent a distillation of the past and the point of departure for Imperial Russian codification. It was printed at once in the Russian language and promptly found a translator in the person of Baron Augustin Freiherr von Mayerburg (1612-1688), who provided a Latin text in the narrative of his diplomatic mission to Russia, published c. 1661.[30]

Legal historians debate to this day the extent to which the *Ulozhenie* represented a reception of Polish-Lithuanian and even Byzantine law in Russia. The scope of the *Ulozhenie* embraced sacrilege, deference due to the Tsar, the Tsar's household, forgery and counterfeiting, jewelers, goldsmiths, and coiners, legal procedure, trials of various classes of the populace, oaths, land law, succession, land tax, serfdom, robbery, capital crimes, the Cossacks, and liquor licensing. Criminal penalties, especially severe under the *Ulozhenie*, became the object of repeated comment in foreign

Wallhausen's "Kriegskunst zu Fuss" (1649): The History of a Failure?", *Militargeschichtliche Zeitschrift*, LXXIX (2020), pp. 1-25. The author dates the publication incorrectly to 1649 rather than 1647.

[29] There were three principal versions of this enactment. On the first, see S. Lazutka, I. Valikonyte, and E. Gudavicius, Первый литовский статут (1529 г.) [The First Lithuanian Statute (1529)] (Vilnius, 2004). All three Statutes have been published in mediaeval Russian, modern Ukrainian, and, for the 1529 version, also in a Latin text, with extensive commentary, bibliography, and glossary. See S. V. Kivalov, P. P. Muzychenko, and A. Pankov (eds), Статути Великого князества Литовского [Statutes of the Grand Duchy of Lithuania] (Odessa, 2002-2004). 3 vols in 4.

[30] A translation into Danish was made from the Russian in 1721 by Rasmus Ereboe. On the Danish manuscript and its importance, see L. P. Paulsen-Hansen, "Русский закон 'Соборное уложение' в переводе Расмуса Эребо", in Дания и Россия-500 лет (1996), pp. 153-174. Three copies (one of the first edition and two of the second edition) are recorded in England, one each at the British Library, University College London (SSEES), and the Bodleian Library, Oxford. See Cleminson et al, note 28 above, item 108. Both editions are to be found in the Harvard Law School Library and the Library of Congress. For an excellent English translation, see R. Hellie (transl. & ed.), *The Muscovite Law Code (Ulozhenie) of 1649: Part 1: Text and Translation* (1988).

observations about Russia. The gradual enserfment of the peasantry was confirmed and consolidated by the *Ulozhenie,* which forbade peasants to leave their landlords' estates for any reason.

Ecclesiastical jurisdiction remained virtually intact under the *Ulozhenie,* and the Church immediately set about producing a modern version of the Book of the Pilot. This was approved by an ecclesiastical council and printed in 1650 and, with revisions, again in 1653. For the remainder of the Imperial era, this ecclesiastical "code" continued in effect with minor modifications introduced in the late eighteenth century. Here were preserved tenets of Byzantine and early Russian Law. In 1656 the Patriarch Nikon, acting through the Novgorod ecclesiastical court, ruled on the extent to which a widow's dowry was liable for her late husband's debts by applying the relevant provisions of the *Ecloga* preserved in the Book of the Pilot.[31]

The systematization and codification of law accomplished so expeditiously from 1648 to 1650 in the reign of Tsar Aleksei Mikhailovich, father of Peter the Great, was part of the process of "Westernization" of Russian society accelerated under Peter.[32] To the extent that the 1649 *Ulozhenie* did draw significantly upon the Lithuanian Statute of 1588,[33] for example, this represented a reception of European law. Peter's modernization of the Russian State and elimination of the patriarchate as an alternative repository of power had implications for Russian administrative law, and indeed it was here that Peter's chief claim to law reform lay. He acknowledged the need for the continuous systematization of Russian legislation and appointed no less than three commissions between 1700 and 1720 to attend to the matter. None progressed very far.

Peter's reforms of the State apparatus and of military and naval law gave him claim to the title of law reformer.[34] Russian government was

[31] Cited in E. L. Johnson, *An Introduction to the Soviet Legal System* (1969), p. 13. English libraries hold one copy of each version, the Cambridge University Library having the earliest and the British Library the second. The English copies shed new light on the printing of the two versions. See Cleminson et al, note 28 above, item 114. The Harvard Law School Library and the Library of Congress hold copies of each version.

[32] The first three volumes of the Complete Collected Laws of the Russian Empire (1826-1917) contained 1,559 acts published between February 1649 and February 1696, of which 24 were printed in annexes to other acts. Of these, 146 were not normative; at least 45 legislative acts issued during this period are known not to have been included in the Collection. These concerned land relations and the urban and rural population. See A. G. Man'kov, Законодательство и право России второй половины XVII в. [Legislation and Law of Russia of the Second Half of the XVII Century] (Spb., 1998), p. 19. For the text with commentary on the 1649 Sobornoe ulozhenie, see V. A. Tomsinov (comp. & intro.), Соборное уложение 1649 года. Законодательство царя Алексея Михайловича [Sobornoe ulozhenie of 1649. Legislation of Tsar Aleksei Mikhailovich] (2011).

[33] One copy of the Lithuanian Statute of 1588 is recorded in England, at the Francis Skaryna Belarusian Library in London. See Cleminson et al, note 28 above, item 45.

[34] The best single collection of Petrine legislation in which the Emperor had a role is N. A. Voskresenskii, Законодательные акты Петра I [Legislative Acts of Peter I] (M., 1945-

reorganized with close account being taken of Swedish and Germanic practices. Archival research has disclosed that Peter sought and obtained data on both the law and practice of Swedish, Danish, Prussian, Dutch, English, Italian, and Austrian institutions even while at sword's point during the Northern War[35] as early as 1699. He modeled his collegial reform of 1718 on the Swedish approach. Foreigners were extensively recruited to operate the administrative system until Peter could produce sufficient Russian trained personnel. In 1722 Peter established the Procuracy, perhaps also adapting Swedish institutions, to act as the "eye of the Tsar" and watch over the conformity to law of the actions of local officials and agencies.[36] Military and naval law were fundamentally reformed by the enactment of a Military Statute (1716) and a Naval Statute (1720), both drawing upon European models and remaining in effect with minor modifications for more than a century. These enactments extended to certain civilian matters.[37]

These were natural areas of concentration for a ruler intent on modernization and at war constantly during his reign. Had he lived longer, one may speculate what changes might have been wrought in private law. In some senses Peter deserved to be classified as a comparativist: he personally drafted or revised many of his enactments; it was he personally who instructed that foreign laws and legal experience be assembled, and

2020). 3 vols. in 2. An attractive collection of Petrine legislation is A. A. Preobrazhenskii and T. E. Novitskaia (eds.), Законодательство Петра I [Legislation of Peter I] (M., 1997). Also see L. Hughes, *Russia in the Age of Peter the Great* (1998), pp. 92-134; L. M. Balakiereva, Судебная реформа Петра I. Юстиц-коллегия [Judicial Reform of Peter I. Justice-College] (Novosibirsk, 2003); D. Serov, Администрация Петра I [Administration of Peter I] (M., 2007).

35 C. Petersen, *Peter the Great's Administrative and Judicial Reforms* (1979); V. A. Tomsinov (ed. & intro.), Законодательство Петра I. 1696-1725 годы [Legislation of Peter I. 1696-1725] (M., 2014). A classic study is N. A. Voskresenskii, Петр Великий как законодатель [Peter the Great as Legislator], ed. D. O. Serov (M., 2017), finally published after completion in the 1940s.

36 See D. O. Serov, Прокуратура Петра I (1722-1725 гг.) [Procuracy of Peter I (1722-1725)] (Novosibirsk, 2002).

37 The origins of the 1720 Naval Statute date to 1669, when Captain D. Butler, a Dutchman in Russian service, wrote down from memory and had translated into Russian key articles from the Dutch naval disciplinary regulations of 17 September 1662. His version was retained in the Ambassadorial Department together with Russian translations of the 1688 Dutch regulations and English regulations of 1692. Peter the Great drew upon these virtually verbatim when crafting his regulations of 1706, 1710, and, finally, 1720. See P. A. Krotov, «Об использовании голландского военно-морского законодательства при разработке уставных положений российского флота во второй половине XVII-первой четверти XVIII века» [On the Use of Dutch Naval Legislation When Working Out Charter Provisions of the Russian Navy in the Second Half of the 17th and First Quarter of the 18th Centuries], in Источниковедение: поиски и находки [Source Material: Searches and Finds] (Voronezh, 2000), pp. 120-130. On the role of the Military Statute in regard to Russian witchcraft trials, see W. F. Ryan, "The Witchcraft Hysteria in Early Modern Europe: Was Russia an Exception?", *Slavonic and East European Review*, LXXVI (1998), pp. 49-84, who observes: "From the introduction of Peter's military law in 1716 onwards, we ... have in Russia what would now seem distinctly odd, a *church* court administering *military* law in cases of heresy, blasphemy and witchcraft" (p. 77).

it was he who read or had specially translated these materials for his own edification. Whatever reception of foreign law may have occurred at earlier stages of Russian history, Russia herself had never before reached so insistently and assertively for foreign legal experience.[38]

The central importance of law, legal documentation, and legal processes to Petrine reforms is evident at another level. Whereas during the first 140 years of printing in Russia from approximately the 1540s to about 1682 most items published were of a religious character, in Moscow and St. Petersburg the number of printed items published during the reign of Peter the Great was more than double that of all titles printed in Russia before 1682, but "more than 60 per cent of this new printing ... comprised State and legal documents".[39]

Peter late in his reign left another legacy long-since forgotten: a visual image of law and legal consciousness in the person of the Zertsalo, a trihedral object containing the text on each of its three sides of designated edicts issued between 1722 and 1724. The edicts were those of 17 April 1722 on preserving civil rights; of 21 January 1724 on offenses in courts; and of 22 January 1724 on State statutes and their importance. Atop the prism was placed the Russian crowned double-headed eagle, which apparently was removable in some instances. The presence of the Zertsalo was required if the court was formally in session; in the presence of the Zertsalo, the court officials were considered to be performing their official duties. There was no right to smoke or to carry on private or personal conversations. If the court adjourned to consider matters unofficially, or other discussions were held on the court premises, the Zertsalo was to be taken from the room or the double-headed eagle was to be removed and carried out of the room. Penalties were established if these strictures were violated, the guilty official being subject to a fine and, after 1840, a reprimand.[40]

It was in the Petrine era, although some believe there were earlier manifestations of this view, that written law [закон] began to be accorded priority over custom as a source of law. So important was this development that in the eyes of some Russian legal historians the periodization of Russian legal developments should turn on this. Vladimirskii-Budanov identified

[38] W. E. Butler, "Peter the Great as a Comparative Lawyer", in J. M. Hartley and D. J. B. Shaw (eds.), *Magic, Texts and Travel: Homage to a Scholar, Will Ryan* (2021), pp. 214-226.

[39] See James Raven and Goran Proot, "Renaissance and Reformation", in Raven (ed.), *The Oxford Illustrated History of the Book* (2020), p. 157. On the importance of printing for the formation and issuance of legal "template" documents (receipts, draft contracts, mortgages, pledges, court materials, and others), see S. Franklin, *The Russian Graphosphere 1450-1850* (2019). The same was true with respect to China. See Ting Zhang, *Circulating the Code: Print Media and Legal Knowledge in Qing China* (2020).

[40] See W. E. Butler, "On the Formation of a Russian Legal Consciousness: The Zertsalo", in Butler, note 25 above, pp. 91-101; J. B. Chadaga, "Mirror Writing: The Literary Traces of the Zertsalo", *The Russian Review*, LI (2002), pp. 73-93. Both sources contain illustrations.

ИМПЕРАТОРА

three periods in the history of Russian law: the "princely period" from the ninth to the thirteenth centuries, when customary rules dominated; the Muscovy period of the fourteenth to sixteenth centuries, when custom and written law enjoyed equal stature; and the Imperial period of the eighteenth and nineteenth centuries, when written law had priority over custom.[41]

Peter's immediate successors did not pursue his pace of reform;[42] within less than four decades, however, a foreigner came to the Russian throne whose enlightened attitude toward law and law reform rapidly earned her the title "the Great". Catherine II set about immediately to bring Russia up to the standard of eighteenth-century Europe.

Peter I had set in motion the measures required to found the Academy of Sciences in Russia, which opened shortly after his death in 1725. Law was among the sciences to be pursued, and the Academy of Sciences was to serve simultaneously as a research and a teaching institution, an Academy and a university. The first appointee in law, Johann Simon Beckenstein (1684-1742) from Germany, offered lectures on natural law and politics but attracted no Russian students and left in 1735.[43] Christian Friedrich Gross (1680-1742) lectured at the same time on moral philosophy, using the Russian translation (1726) of Samuel von Pufendorf (1632-1694), *De officio hominis et civis* made at Peter's behest. Beckenstein's successor appointed in 1738 was Friedrich Heinrich Strube de Piermont (1704-1790), who published at St.

41 See M. F. Vladimirskii-Budanov, Обзор истории русского права [Survey of the History of Russian Law] (Kiev, 1915). A modem authority writes: "The more radical changes were in the mode of operation of the newly formed institutions compared with the Duma and the chancelleries of earlier times. The earlier institutions of government were ... based to a large extent on custom rather than written procedure. They followed the Conciliar Law Code of 1649 and the many decrees of Tsar and Duma, but much of their operations were still in the realm of orally recorded custom. Peter insisted on written rules of operation as well as adherence to written law ... The careful records were not just a matter of bureaucratic thoroughness, they were part of the process of orderly and legal government which Peter had learned from observing Western practice". P. Bushkovitch, *Peter the Great: The Struggle for Power 1671-1725* (2001), p. 443.

42 For the principal enactments of the period between Peter the Great and Catherine the Great, see V. A. Tomsinov (comp. & intro.), Законодательство Екатерины I и Петра II [Legislation of Catherine I and Peter II] (2009); id, Законодательство императрицы Анны Иоанновны [Legislation of Empress Anna Ivanovna] (2009); Tomsinov, Законодательство императрицы Елизаветы Петровны [Legislation of Empress Elizabeth Petrovna] (2009). One observer commented with respect to Petrine judicial reforms: "Peter's immediate successors maintained some ... positive developments, such as oversight of the death penalty and a simplified hierarchy of judicial venues. But they ... eradicated the distinction between judicial and administrative, taking a significant step backward in the development of the rule of law and the creation of a professional legal stratum". N. S. Kollman, "Change and Continuity in the Law under Peter I", in R. Bartlett and G. Lehmann-Carli (eds.), *Eighteenth-Century Russia: Society, Culture, Economy* (2007), p. 391. Also see generally O. A. Omel'chenko, Традиции и наследие русского права [Traditions and the Legacy of Russian Law] (2006); reviewed in *Slavonic and East European Review*, LXXXVII (2009), 189-190.

43 V. A. Tomsinov, Российские правоведы: XVIII-XX веков. Очерки жизни и творчества [Russian Jurists XVIII-XX Centuries: Essays on Life and Creativity] (2d ed.; 2015), I, pp. 90-98.

Petersburg in 1740 a major study on the origins of natural law, in the French language; a revised edition issued at Amsterdam in 1744 was reprinted several times with emendations. Under the 1747 Statute on the Academy a sharp distinction was drawn between the academicians and the professors; the last offered lectures in the physical, mathematical, and humanitarian sciences, law falling within the last, and Strube was appointed to offer them. In 1756 Strube delivered a lecture treating the origins of Russian law that was published in both Russian and Latin.[44]

Three chairs of law were initially established within the Law Faculty of Moscow University founded in 1755; the notable professors were Philip Heinrich Dilthey (1723-1781),[45] Carl Heinrich Langer, Ivan Andreevich Tret'iakov (c. 1740-1779), and Semen Efimovich Desnitskii (c. 1740-1789). The last especially merits our attention. Desnitskii was the first Russian law professor. Born in Ukraine and sent abroad in 1761 to read law at Glasgow University, he and Tret'iakov completed the full course of study at what then was Britain's leading university. Elected Academician in 1785, Desnitskii published several works upon his return to Russia, acquainting his countrymen with the ideas of Adam Smith and John Millar, and at Catherine's instruction translated into Russian volume one of Sir William Blackstone's *Commentaries*, published at Moscow in three volumes in 1780-83. He offered courses on the history of Russian law, on Justinian's *Pandects*, on a comparison of Russian and Roman law, and on the English language.[46] Since he and Tret'iakov, also appointed at the University and a Glasgow graduate, could lecture in Russian, the number of law students increased appreciably. Z. A. Goriushkin (1748-1821) introduced the practice of teaching Russian law through mock trials and actual proceedings.[47]

Catherine II's own enduring contribution to Russian law occurred in 1767 when there was published a Nakaz composed by herself with extensive borrowings from leading Enlightenment thinkers, notably Cesare Beccaria (1738-1794), Charles de Montesquieu (1689-1755), and Voltaire (1694-1778). Although the Nakaz was never enacted, its translation into the major European tongues and issuance in more than 40 editions made it the single piece of Russian legislative material best known abroad. An English version appeared at London in 1768.[48] The Nakaz and perhaps

[44] See W. E. Butler, "F. G. Strube de Piermont and the Origins of Russian Legal History", in Butler, note 25 above, pp. 129-144; Tomsinov, note 45 above, I, pp. 99-113.

[45] Tomsinov, note 43 above, I, pp. 114-130; Tomsinov, "Dilthey, P.-H.", in W. E. Butler and V. A. Tomsinov, *Russian Legal Biography: Series 1: Russian Historical Legal Biography* (2007), I, 189-193.

[46] A. H. Brown, "The Father of Russian Jurisprudence: The Legal Thought of S. E. Desnitskii", in Butler, *Russian Law: Historical and Political Perspectives* (1977), pp. 117-121; Tomsinov, note 43 above, I, pp. 131-156.

[47] Tomsinov, note 43 above, I, pp. 187-202; Tomsinov, "Z. A. Goriushkin", in Butler and Tomsinov, note 45 above, I, pp. 223-233.

[48] For the texts of the Nakaz, including two contemporary English versions, and a

Catherine's administrative reforms of 1775 and 1780, also widely published in Europe, were her major legal achievements; she too appointed codification commissions, but to no effect. However, the intellectual climate and institutions which she fostered, despite her later apprehension about some of their implications, laid the base for an emergent Russian legal elite in the nineteenth century. Foreign perceptions of Russian law had altered dramatically. No longer the epitome of arbitrariness and cruelty, Russia was praised in print and in public law lectures abroad for having set inspired examples which other nations might profitably emulate in their law reforms.[49]

An indigenous legal literature began to complement translations into Russian of foreign works. Pufendorf and Blackstone have been mentioned: Jakob Friedrich von Bielfeld (1717-1770), Johann Heinrich Gottlob Justi (1702-1771), Daniel Nettelbladt (1719-1791), and Charles de Montesquieu, among others, were translated, as were extracts from Denis Diderot's *Encyclopedie* relating to law. Strube de Piermont, Dilthey, and Langer all left significant works. Vladimir Trofimovich Zolotnitskii (1741-after 1771) published the first original Russian work on natural law in 1764. Nikolai Ivanovich Novikov (1744-1818), Mikhail Dmitrievich Chulkov (1743-1792), and others began through their compilations to introduce the Russian public to original texts of their early legal heritage. By the end of the century collections of and indexes to Russian legislation began to appear, essential raw material for teaching Russian law to students.

Russia embarked upon the nineteenth century with a new Emperor, Alexander I (1777-1825), in a liberal frame of mind determined to modernize the State apparatus and bring order to the chaotic state of Russian legislation. In 1801 the tenth codification commission since Peter I was instituted. The Commission looked initially to Europe for ideas. The works of Jeremy Bentham (1748-1832) were translated into Russian (1805-1811) in three volumes and the Code Napoleon was closely followed in preparing the initial draft codifications. But imposing intellectual or foreign schemes for systematization did not find favor with Emperor Alexander I in the end; codification work fell into desuetude, to be revived in the 1820s in the spirit of the historical school of Friedrich Carl von Savigny (1779-1861): Russia

bibliography, see W. E. Butler and V. A. Tomsinov (eds.), *The Nakaz of Catherine the Great: Collected Texts* (2010).

[49] Butler, note 25 above. Key legislation from Catherine II's reign is collected in two volumes with extensive annotations and bibliography by O. N. Chistiakov and T. E. Novitskaia (eds.), Законодательство Екатерины II [Legislation of Catherine II] (M., 2000-01). Also see V. A. Tominsov (comp.), Законодательство императора Петра III 1761-1762 годы. Законодательство императрицы Екатерины II [Legislation of Emperor Peter III 1761-1762. Legislation of Empress Catherine II 1762-1782] (2011); Tomsinov, Законодательство императрицы Екатерины II 1783-1796 годы [Legislation of Empress Catherine II 1783-1796] (2011).

would look to her own historical experience and legislation to fashion a new code of law.

Alexander I introduced ministerial reforms to supplant the collegial model of Peter the Great. Based upon the French scheme, the administrative reform was accompanied by an expansion of the education system and a transition to a system of civil service recruitment which relied on examination performance rather than exclusively hereditary links. "Jurisprudence" was among the subjects examined; it encompassed natural law, Roman law, private law, criminal law, and the State economy. New universities were founded and faculties of law formed. Foreign law professors had to be recruited in the early decades, but preference was given to Russian candidates and in the course of time Russian graduates came to fill the majority of posts. Moscow University continued to offer legal training in both general law subjects and in the procedures and arts of advocacy in Russian tribunals.

With the accession of Nicholas I in 1825, codification work resumed at an accelerated pace. Drawing upon the talents of a small group of lawyers at St Petersburg University, Mikhail Andreevich Balugianskii (1769-1847), of Hungarian origin, and Mikhail Mikhailovich Speranskii (1772-1839) brought to completion the most ambitious and comprehensive systematization of legislation attempted in Europe. First to appear was the Полное собрание законов Российской империи (Complete Collected Laws of the Russian Empire), a chronological collection of Russian legislation (more than 30,000 enactments) commencing with the *Sobornoe ulozhenie* of 1649 to 1825.[50] Published in 48 massive tomes (1830), this collection formed the base for the next stage: the Свод законов Российской империи (Digest of Laws of the Russian Empire) published in 15 volumes in 1832. Both collections survived with continuations until the end of the Empire. A second series of the Complete Collected Laws was published annually from 1826 to 1881, and the third series, from 1881 to 1916. From time to time the Digest of Laws would be supplied with supplementary volumes and reissued at intervals in a complete revised edition.[51] This pattern of systematizing legislation was taken over by the Soviet Government and is continuing to be used by the Russian Federation.

Speranskii's account of preparing the collections offers much insight into the administration of law and justice in that time. Few enactments had been printed. No chancellery had a complete register of enactments, and

[50] The first series of the ПСЗ is being reissued in modern orthography, with the correction of obvious misprints, by Iuridicheskii-Tsentr Publishers in St. Petersburg (2010-). As of 2014, the first three volumes had appeared, but none thereafter as of 2021.

[51] See N. D. Renaud, "The Legal Force of the 1832 Svod Zakonov", *Sudebnik*, II (1997), pp. 83-124; V. N. Galuzo, Систематизация законодательства в России (1649-1913) [Systematization of Legislation in Russia (1649-1913)] (M., 2007).

those that existed were badly organized. A full record of the law did not exist. Much of what did exist was inaccessible, not to say unknowable, by official and citizen alike. Systematization, Speranskii wrote, was an absolute prerequisite for the development of a legal system:

> It is not therefore from the Roman Law, nor yet from the isolated efforts of our lawyers, that we can expect to construct a solid foundation for a systematic study of the laws. It must be based upon a body of laws, and will date its commencement from their publication. Until this is done, it would be useless to devise commentaries and prescriptions calculated to develop the science of national legislation.[52]

Although the model of the Digest appears to be inspired by the Justinian example, the precepts for its compilation were drawn from the writings of English jurists, Sir Francis Bacon (1561-1626) and Jeremy Bentham, especially the former, as Speranskii makes unequivocally clear.

Administrative reforms, the expansion and improvement of legal education, the publication of comprehensive law collections, a trained civil service – the gradual implementation of these measures in the nineteenth century contributed mightily to legal professionalization in Russia.[53] The precise origins of the legal profession, however, remain obscure. It is probable that litigation in medieval Russia was conducted by the parties themselves, although some contemporary accounts referred cryptically to "attorneys". In the eighteenth century it is evident that laymen experienced in the ways of the courts often interposed themselves between party and judge and acted as a kind of advocate on behalf of their client. Lord George Macartney (1737-1806) described them as "in general very sharp and expert ... they will undertake to spin out any cause for a term of years, on payment of a certain sum agreed on".[54] Judges depended for their livelihood upon a percentage of monetary compensation awarded; contemporary accounts provide conflicting evidence on the extent of judicial bribery and corruption in Russia, but there is ample evidence of public opinion, including the rulers of Russia – Peter I, Catherine II, Alexander I, and Nicholas I – being profoundly distrustful of judges and lawyers. By the third quarter of the nineteenth century legal professionalization and legal values were beginning to leave their imprint within the State administration and without. Many observers believe that these were among the factors which contributed to

52 M. M. Speranskii, *A Summary of Historical Sketches on the Formation of the Body of the Russian Laws*, transl. W. Wall (Spb., 1841), pp. 89-90.

53 R. S. Wortman, *The Development of a Russian Legal Consciousness* (1976); Wortman, "Russian Monarchy and the Rule of Law: New Considerations of the Court Reform of 1864", in Wortman, *Russian Monarchy: Representation and Rule* (2013), pp. 3-32. For the emergence of these values and their impact upon criminal punishment, see A. M. Schrader, *Languages of the Lash: Corporal Punishment and Identity in Imperial Russia* (2002).

54 G. Macartney, *An Account of Russia* (1767), p. 103.

the great nineteenth century reforms of Russian law: the emancipation of the serfs in 1861 and the judiciary reforms of 1864.[55]

The emancipation of the serfs, quite apart from ending an intolerable social injustice, set in motion reforms of land, family, and inheritance law that required several decades to gestate.[56] Reforms of local government in 1864 and the introduction of the *zemstvo* system in 1870 gave the peasants greater involvement in self-government. The judiciary reform, which originated within the councils of the Tsar, wholly restructured the court system and officially established an organized legal profession. English influence was to be seen, including the intellectual genius of Bentham. The judiciary was made independent of administrative officials, with rights of appeal, and judges not to be removed except for malfeasance in office. *Volost'* courts were retained for the peasants, but otherwise courts based on class were abolished. The "justice of the peace", adapted from English law and nominated by local *zemstvos*, was introduced to handle minor offenses. The complicated system of written pleadings characteristic of Russian procedure was replaced by oral proceedings and trials were to be open, again on the English model. Jury trial was available for serious criminal offenses. French influence was to be seen in the creation of two cassational instances in the Ruling Senate (civil and criminal) to review cases when appeal had been exhausted. But although many features of the common law had been adapted and although medieval Russian trial practice had been akin to an adversary-type proceeding, the continental type of inquisitorial proceeding in criminal cases was received, many aspects of which survive in modern Russian criminal procedure. A professional bar was instituted, and all parties to civil and criminal proceedings were accorded the right to professional representation.

The last half century of Imperial rule has been called the "Golden Age" of Russian law.[57] The Russian legal profession flowered, producing distinguished practitioners, judges, and legal scholars, successfully challenging in several celebrated jury trials an absolutist autocracy bent upon eradicating political dissent and pluralism. Even to the revolutionary, the legal profession in Russia had its attraction as a channel for effectuating political and social change. Lenin read law at Kazan and St Petersburg universities and passed the bar precisely for these reasons. In the course of time the reforms came to be attenuated by subsequent legislation.

[55] See V. A. Tomsinov (comp.), Крестьянская реформа 1861 года в России [The Peasant Reform of 1861 in Russia] (2012); Tomsinov, Законодательные акты судебной реформы 1864 года в России [Legislative Acts of the 1864 Judicial Reform in Russia] (2012); Alan P. Pollard (transl. & ed.), *The Laws of February 18-19, 1861 on the Emancipation of the Russian Peasants* (2008); S. F. Williams, *Liberal Reform in an Illiberal Regime: The Creation of Private Property in Russia, 1906-1915* (2006).

[56] See W. G. Wagner, *Marriage, Property and Law in Late Imperial Russia* (1994).

[57] S. Kucherov, *Courts, Lawyers and Trials Under the Last Three Tsars* (1953).

Judicial independence was circumscribed, the jurisdiction of class courts was somewhat enlarged, trial by jury was precluded in a growing number of instances, opportunities for imposing administrative sanctions were increased, the jurisdiction of justices of the peace was narrowed, the openness of trials was limited, and courts martial were used increasingly to try civilians.

Pressure for social and legal reform intensified early in the twentieth century. The Revolution of 1905 brought a constituent assembly, the State Duma, and a form of constitutional monarchy. Political parties became active; attempts at enacting far-reaching economic and social reforms were made. A serious but belated effort to reshape the Russian socio-economic and political order was commenced. Russian jurists were busy with civil and criminal law reform. A draft criminal code of 1903, based on several years of deliberations, was approved only in part, but as a whole it represented the most advanced statement of criminal jurisprudence in the world. A draft civil code compiled in 1910-13 achieved a similar standard of technical and substantive proficiency.[58] Both were drawn upon in the Soviet period and again in the post-Soviet era by those who crafted the RSFSR and then the Russian civil and criminal codes. The legal profession played an increasingly prominent role in Russian political life; many members of the State Duma were individuals with legal background or education, from all parties. But reform could not keep pace with the demands for societal change. In 1917 the Imperial order collapsed under the pressures of war and revolutions.

Imperial Russia always contained a multiplicity of legal orders operating simultaneously to govern the affairs of the more than 200 ethnic groups inhabiting its territories.[59] Even within the frontiers of the Russian Federation as presently constituted there are more than 100 ethnic minorities, the majority of whom are organized into administrative-territorial entities called "subjects of the Russian Federation". In areas conquered or annexed by Russia it was generally the practice to introduce the Russian administrative system, to eliminate some of the worst local practices (slavery, blood vengeance), and to allow local legislation or customary law to otherwise continue to operate.[60] The full introduction

[58] See A. F. Povorinskii, Систематический указатель русской литературы по гражданскому праву 1758-1904 гг. [Systematic Index of Russian Literature on Civil Law: 1758-1904], ed. O. Iu. Shilokhvost (3d ed.; 2001).

[59] S. V. Kodan and S. A. Fevralev, Местное право национальных регионов в Российской империи (вторая половина XVII – начало XX в.) [Local Law of National Regions in the Russian Empire (Second Half of the XVII – Beginning of the XX Century] (2014).

[60] See, for example, A. N. Abazov, Народы центрального Кавказа в судебной системе Российской империи в конце XVIII – начале XX в. [Peoples of the Central Caucasus in the Judicial System of the Russian Empire at the End of the XVIII – Beginning of the XX Century] (Nalchik, 2016); B. B. Suleimanov, Система публичного управления и право Дагестана во второй половине XIX века [System of Public Administration and Law of Dagestan in the

of Russian law would have required a political and military commitment to the russification of non-Russian minorities beyond the strength of the Empire. Tolerance of customary rules, however, was in the mainstream of Russian practice with respect to the Russian populace itself. Land relations and succession amongst the rural Russian populace were based chiefly upon local customary rules enforced by peasant courts. It was commonplace to speak of "peasant customary law".[61] Amongst the nomadic tribes of Siberia, Russian legislation came gradually to play a larger role, especially through the Code of Steppe Laws of the Nomadic Peoples of Eastern Siberia, but on the whole local customs remained the basic source of law of these peoples.[62]

CONTINUITY, CHANGE, AND CONTINUITY

What of the pre-revolutionary heritage endured after the October 1917 Revolution, consciously or unconsciously, has engaged the attention of dozens of observers, Russian and foreign. Bolshevism arrived in the initial expectation that it would spark a world revolution and rapidly found itself obliged to contend with the formidable natural limitations of the Russian Empire itself: its size, its vulnerability, its languages, its multi-ethnicity, its standard of industrialization, its illiteracy and poverty, its hunger for peace and land reform, its historical, religious, and political experience, and its economic order. The October 1917 Revolution having been engendered in Russian experience and expectations, it was unavoidable that many responses to problems would draw upon Russian patterns.

The forms of pre-revolutionary legislation were adopted at once. Decrees were cumulated into chronological collections which later served as the base for systematic compilations and digests. Whereas Decree No. 1 of the young Soviet Government was "On Peace", Decree No. 7 dealt with the publication of laws. Habits of neglecting systematization and codification, of allowing legislation to fall into an appallingly chaotic state of confusion and inaccessibility, likewise persisted throughout the Soviet era, despite attempts to eliminate those habits in the 1970-1980s. This pattern of behavior already plagues the post-Soviet Russian State, which must amalgamate its post-Soviet legislation with that which went before.

In the period since the demise of the Soviet Union, many Russian legal institutions continue to stress their roots in the Russian past which incorporates the Soviet period. In 2022 the Russian Procuracy will celebrate its 300th jubilee. The Russian legal publishing house, Iuridicheskaia literatura, marked its centenary in 2018. The system of arbitrazh courts (abolished in 2014) in 1997 traced its roots to the Trade Statute (Торговый

Second Half of the XIX Century] (M., 2012).

[61] R. Beermann, 'Pre-Revolutionary Russian Peasant Laws', in Butler, *Russian Law: Historical and Political Perspectives* (1977), p. 190.

[62] V. A. Riasanovskii, *Customary Law of the Nomadic Tribes of Siberia* (1938), pp. 61-62.

устав) of 1667. St. Petersburg University will celebrate its 300th anniversary in 2024. These are institutions which have experienced institutional transformations, changes of name and modifications of function, even reorganization without formal legal succession. Yet Russian they remain in contemporary eyes. The debate of the Soviet era regarding elements of continuity and discontinuity has for the present been resolved in favor of continuity: discontinuity never existed, or was never achieved; or, the Soviet claim to uniqueness, to non-Russianness, was never realized.

Modern Russia has inherited its burdens of the past, both Imperial and Soviet. Many believe the Imperial pattern of autocracy, intolerance, russification, bureaucratism, backwardness, and the absence of a modern legal tradition, however much the Revolutions of 1917 may have been directed at these evils and abuses, contributed in the Soviet era to resistance to political pluralism, religious freedom, disregard of the rule of law, a suspicion of legal rationalism, Stalinist arbitrariness, a reluctance to subject the political system to legal intervention, and a fetish with legal formalism. The post-Soviet Russian legal order must come to terms with the entire Russian historical legacy, and shows signs of a willingness and ability to do so.

Continuity and change in law is not a mechanical exercise in identifying what seem to be analogous institutions, rules, or practices. Context is of the utmost significance; nor should one lose sight of the fact that both eras of Russian experience relate to the larger Western and Eastern legal traditions. Some similarities and differences may owe their explanation or more plausible hypotheses to legal developments or traditions beyond the limits of Russia itself.

4

RUSSIAN LEGAL THEORY

For nearly three-quarters of a century the fundamentals of Marxism-Leninism comprised the starting point in the former Soviet Union for university and secondary-level studies in every discipline, including law. Courses in political economy, historical materialism, dialectical materialism, history of the Communist Party, and basic principles of Marxism-Leninism were required in the first and second years of higher education to create what the Soviet authorities considered to be the proper ideological and philosophical base for the further acquisition of knowledge.

With the demise of the Soviet Union, those ideological foundations were discredited and removed from the curriculum (although not instantaneously). There is nothing comparable to insert in their place, even though most Russian legal educators believe that students require an introduction to the philosophical and jurisprudential foundations of their chosen discipline and most, if not all, law faculties offer introductory surveys of legal and political doctrines, historical and contemporary. Russian legal theory accordingly has been set unexpectedly adrift to seek new moorings in the Russian past, in the Russian present, and in the world of legal theory at large. While there is discomfort associated with being adrift, there also has been an explosion of interest in Russian political and legal thinkers whose works were previously inaccessible and a certain interest in contemporary legal philosophers, whose works even in the post-Soviet era seem so alien to Russian values and Russian objectives. The Russian jurist of whatever generation and specialty in the law finds either his previous training in Marxism-Leninism to be irrelevant and unacceptable or his present training, eclectic and uncertain. In either case, his concepts of law, its origins, role, and purpose, and its future are a new intellectual challenge. We examine below the historical foundations to which the Russian jurist is being introduced and some of the contending jurisprudential concerns of post-Soviet Russia.[1]

[1] This chapter draws to a significant extent upon my introductory essay in W. E. Butler (ed.), *Russian Legal Theory* (1996), where substantial selections are reproduced from those few Russian legal philosophers whose works have been translated into English. Also see G. M. Hamburg, *Russia's Path Toward Enlightenment: Faith, Politics, and Reason, 1500-1801* (2016), where many of the legal philosophers discussed herein are treated.

RUSSIAN JURISPRUDENTIAL ROOTS

In the Russian perception legal theory is not an arid subject to be divorced from the "practical" subjects of legal study. One modern legal theorist has called his field "the methodological laboratory of political theory ... with a view to forecasting the ways and means of the further development and perfection of contemporary historical knowledge on State and Law".[2] The linkage between State and law, and between politics and law, is crucial in Russian thinking. The "legal succession of ideological structures as a whole and of politico-legal knowledge in particular is not merely an immutable condition for their further development, but also for perfecting the process of State-legal construction".[3] In other words, the past is part of a direct continuum to policy decisions of the present regarding the development of law and legal institutions.

To say that the depths of the history of Russian legal doctrine remain unplumbed is itself part of the legacy of the recent and remote past. Russian legal theory was in its infancy before the revolutions of 1917,[4] and the history of Russian legal theory even more so. Russian theorists looked principally to their contemporary European colleagues for inspiration, and to the classics of European political and legal thought in Russian translation. The highly regarded work by Boris Nikolaevich Chicherin (1828-1904) on political doctrines made no mention of Russian legal theory.[5] The Soviet Union had little use for political and legal doctrines of the Russian past, particularly those rooted in theological postulates, and consequently offered the most superficial of surveys in law school compulsory subjects. The considerable attention given to the so-called "revolutionary-democratic" Russian thinkers, while deserved, was unduly exaggerated by other ideological

[2] See V. S. Nersesiants, Политические учения и современность [Political Doctrines and Modern Times] (1976), p. 6.

[3] See I. A. Isaev and N. M. Zolotukhin, История политических и правовых учений России XI-XX вв. [History of Political and Legal Doctrines of Russia from the Eleventh to the Twentieth Centuries] (1995), p. 3. Analogous views are expressed in the magisterial work of V. S. Nersesiants (ed), История политических и правовых учений [History of Political and Legal Doctrines] (1995). Also see V. A. Tomsinov, История русской политической и правовой мысли. X-XVIII века [History of Russian Political and Legal Thought of the Tenth to Eighteenth Centuries] (2003). This chapter draws upon these studies and others of the post-socialist era; collectively they are the most objective and thorough introductions to Russian legal theory to appear in nearly a century in the Russian language.

[4] This will be deemed a harsh view by some Russian legal theorists, past and present. Nonetheless, in my perception, Russian legal theory remains profoundly particularistic, most especially those strands drawing upon Russian values and experience. The view expressed by V. D. Katkov in 1913 would be widely shared today: "The jurisprudence of the West is not on the right path and cannot serve us as a *general* example". See V. D. Katkov, *Jurisprudentiae novum organon* (Odessa, 1913), I, vi, quoted by V. A. Tomsinov, reviewing the first edition of Butler, *Russian Law* (1998), in Зерцало [Zertsalo] (2000), V, p. 123.

[5] See B. N. Chicherin, Политические учения [Political Doctrines] (1869-79). 5 vols. See G. M. Hamburg (ed. & transl.), *Liberty, Equality, and the Market: Essays by B. N. Chicherin* (1998).

constraints which prejudiced objectivity. A separate subject, ignored undeservedly in both East and West, is the contribution of the Russian *émigré* community in the twentieth century to legal and political theory.

LEGAL DOCTRINES OF THE XI-XIV CENTURIES

The emergence of the formal trappings of the Grand Princedom of Kievan Rus[6] was accompanied by a manuscript culture which included translations into Church Slavonic of texts by Aristotle, Plato, Plutarch, Homer, Zenon, Epicurus, Herodotus, Demosthenes, and others, together with legal texts from Byzantium and southern Slavdom. These contributed in turn to the tradition of Russian Chronicles that treated, *inter alia,* issues of law and politics and accounts of voyages by Russian travelers who described laws of the lands they visited. In the course of time these sources addressed the origin of Kievan Rus and the ruling dynasty, the unity and sovereignty of the Grand Prince and his officialdom, possible forms of limitation on the absolute power of the Grand Prince (consultative councils and advisors), legality, and the settlement of disputes. A legal terminology came into being, and concepts such as law (jus [право] and lex [закон]), truth, and justice were discussed.

Ilarion

Assuming that the texts of the documents and chronicles which have survived from the Kievan era or which are attributed to that era are contemporary and genuine – assumptions which are not beyond reproach – the early works of Russian legal theory are several. Perhaps the earliest is the Sermon on Law and Grace [Слово о Законе и благодати], believed to have been written c. 1037-50 by Ilarion, the Metropolitan of Kievan Rus, the first Russian to be elevated to that office, in 1051. Composed principally for theological instructional purposes and comprising a unique source of medieval Russian vocabulary, grammar, and literary style, the Sermon is treated by Russian historians as the "earliest surviving political treatise of Ancient Rus".[7]

The Sermon addressed three main issues: the relationship between law and grace, the significance of baptism for Kievan Rus, and the future development of the Kievan Rus State.[8] Ilarion did not distinguish sharply

[6] For an excellent account of those complicated times, see A. Wilson, *The Ukrainians: Unexpected Nation* (2000), pp. 1-39.

[7] See V. S. Pokrovskii, История политических учений [History of Political Doctrines] (1960), p. 134. There are indications that in 1048 Ilarion headed a Kievan Rus Embassy to Paris for negotiations concerning the marriage of Anna, daughter of Prince Iaroslav, to Henry I of France. The marriage took place in 1051.

[8] V. A. Tomsinov shares quite a different understanding of this text and its implications for the development of legal thought. In his view, the work is concerned principally with contrasting Judaism and Christianity in the "political meaning" of those religions. Judaism

between human and divine laws, nor offer any form of classification of legislation. Law amounted to the performance of an obligatory prescription, whether of divine origin or issued by the sovereign, and was contrasted with Truth, achieved as the result of realization of man's free will, informed by the moral and aesthetic teachings of the New Testament. The divine origins of law, modern Russian political theorists suggest, do not preclude law also being understood teleologically and juridically as external prescriptions regulating behavior of the individual in society by way of prohibitions.

In Ilarion's perception law and truth were not juxtaposed to one another. Truth was comprehended by man thanks to law, and not despite law; Jesus Christ was sent to this world not to violate law, but to perform, or execute, law. This, in turn, led to a terminological issue which continues to bedevil contemporary discussions of legal theory.[9] The issue turned on his use of the Russian terms "justice" [правда] and "lex, law" [закон]. The term "правда" is associated primarily with positive law codifications or systematizations: the *Sudebnik*, the *Pravda Russkaia*, the *Pravda Iaroslava*, the *Sborniki ulozhenii*, and others, with the power to judge, to chastise, to pardon. But the word also was used in a broader legal and philosophical sense to embrace "truth", "virtue", "justness", and the like, and in this case these elements inform the content of law. In a larger sense, Ilarion uses "правда" to describe both the content and the moral motivation of law, as a "legal formula" which "means consideration of a case according to Law irrespective of the final result". The approach is believed to have influenced the Teachings of Vladimir Monomakh and later legislative material.

Ilarion declared all Christian peoples to be equal, disputing in so doing Byzantium's claim to hegemony. As for the nature of political society itself, Ilarion treated the essence of the State as divine because it represented a realization of Divine Will. The bearer of supreme power is in communion with and a descendant of the heavenly Kingdom. The origin of power is by way of inherited succession, and Ilarion sought to establish the legitimacy of rules contemporary to him by tracing their lineage back to the "ancient Igor". While supporting the concept of rule whereby the Grand Prince

at the time, Tomsinov argues, was not a pure abstraction for Kievan Rus, but rather a power center represented by the Khazars and a potential choice for the official faith of Kievan Rus, together with Roman Catholicism and Byzantine Orthodoxy. Ilarion's principal message, Tomsinov believes, was that "Judaism is a religion which serves only Jews, whereas Christianity is a religion called upon to serve all peoples". As for State power, Ilarion's teachings, in Tomsinov's view, were directed towards emphasizing succession in dynastic rule and the benefits such would bring to the lands of Rus. See Tomsinov, in O. E. Leist (ed), История политических учений [History of Political and Legal Doctrines] (1999), pp. 127-136.

[9] See R. A. Romashov, "The Concepts of 'Jus' and 'Lex': Historical and Legal Linguistic Aspects", in W. E. Butler, O. V. Kresin, and Iu. S. Shemshuchenko (eds.), *Foundations of Comparative Law: Methods and Typologies* (2011), pp. 189-206. See especially R. S. Wortman, *The Power of Language and Rhetoric in Russian Political History* (2018).

was the sole and sovereign power within the lands subject to his rule, the Prince was not to be arbitrary and was to rule on the basis of law (which presumably meant law in both its positive and moral sense), mercy, generosity towards his subjects, and concern for orphans, the ill, widows, the church and monasteries.

Justice, he wrote, must be administered according to law and with mercy, setting out the moral criteria with which a Christian ruler should comply when dispensing punishment. These ideas were accepted almost entirely by Vladimir Monomakh in his Teachings and later developed by Daniil Zatochnik. Ilarion also posited the notion that a ruler was accountable to his subjects before God, a subject much discussed by later Russian writers.

Works of Vladimir Monomakh

In or about 1113 the grandson of Iaroslav the Wise, Vladimir Monomakh (1053-1125), came to the throne in Kievan Rus. To him are attributed three works: Teachings for Children [Поучение детям], Message to Oleg Chernigovskii [Послание Олегу Черниговскому], and an autobiographical sketch known as the Fragment [Отрывок]. These works touched upon the powers of the Grand Prince, the relations between Church and State, and the principles for administering justice. The Teachings give considerable attention to organizing and exercising supreme power. He advised future princes to rule with the advice of a council and not to permit unlawfulness and injustice in the lands. To be just means to adjudicate according to law. Judicial functions, Monomakh proposed, the ruler should exercise himself, not permitting a violation of the laws and dispensing mercy to his most defenseless subjects. Blood feud and capital punishment were rejected, including in inter-princely relations.

Monomakh elaborated Ilarion's notion of the ruler's accountability to his subjects. The military forces should not cause harm to the peasant villagers, and wherever possible internecine conflict should be avoided. The ruler and his princes should seek means to achieve peace, and disputes should be settled peacefully. As for Church and State, Monomakh accorded to the Church an honorable but subordinate place.

Daniil Zatochnik

Manuscripts attributed to Daniil Zatochnik of the late twelfth or early thirteenth century, by which time Kievan Rus had broken up into countless warring princedoms and was on the eve of being subjugated by the Mongols and Tatars from the East, counseled centralization of power in the interests of defending Rus against invaders. Whether the manuscripts were by one author or two, the Sermon [Слово] or Supplication [Моление] (titles vary from one manuscript to another), they posit an idealized Grand Prince who is physically attractive and merciful. He rules with strength, tempered by wisdom and justness. His State is a strong one, well-organized and orderly.

He rules with the assistance of advisors and counsellors and accepts their advice. His task is to select good and wise advisors, but not necessarily only the old and experienced. Wisdom is not only age and experience.

This account suggests that Daniil Zatochnik regarded Vladimir Monomakh as having represented the ideal form of power. The Grand Prince also must have good military forces capable of defending his lands against outside enemies. But peace is to be generally desired, as is the peaceful settlement of disputes. Daniil advises the Grand Prince to recruit foreigners to his service for the benefit of his country. Strong warnings are given against internal threats to the Grand Prince in the form of the arrogation of power by boyars, a commentary on the fractionalization of Rus into warring princedoms underway at the time. These were themes continued and enlarged upon in the manuscript culture that emerged after the celebrated Battle of Kulikovo in 1380, when the Muscovy Grand Prince Dmitrii Ivanovich (1350-1389) defeated the Mongol forces amassed against him.

LEGAL AND POLITICAL THEORY 1500-1613

In the period here considered the forces of decentralization in Muscovy had been overtaken by those of centralization. The Mongol hordes receded, gradually defeated in Russia and recalled by internal dissension at home, and the Grand Princes Ivan III (1462-1505) and Vasilii III (1505-1533) succeeded in uniting the appanage princes and their lands under the rule of the Grand Prince of Muscovy. With the fall of Constantinople in 1453 and the marriage of Ivan III to Sophia Zoe Paleologue (1455-1503), Princess of Byzantium, Muscovy laid claim to the two-headed eagle of the Eastern Roman Empire and to succession as the Defender of Orthodoxy, the Third Rome.

The principal themes of earlier works continued to be debated: the formation of a single sovereign political community, the type of monarchy which should emerge, the origins of the Russian State and the lineage of its princes, the organization of State administration, the relations of Church and State, and the administration of justice. The position of the Church itself began to be debated, now a center of wealth, land, and power.

The Russian clergy came to be conditionally divided into those who favored a reorganization of the Church under which the Church would renounce all wealth and lands and refrain from any interference in the affairs of the State, and those who preferred preserving the existing forms of church organization and its economic status.

Nil Sorskii

Idealizing the early Christian communities, Nil Sorskii (1433-1508) organized his own Nilo-Sorskii Hermitage in the Vologda Region. There he and his followers drew attention to those passages in the Gospels where Christ and his disciples renounced all worldly goods and counseled their fellow monks to follow that example. In relations between Church and State Nil Sorskii departed from the Byzantine tradition, where there had been a complex combination of the two, and suggested that each had its own domain of activity and therefore its own measures of dealing with problems confronting it.

These rather general propositions were elaborated by his friend and follower, Vassian Patrikeev (c. 1470-c.1531-45), who directly put the question of depriving monasteries of their wealth and even eliminating monasteries as such. He favored a sharp delineation in legislative acts of the spheres of operations of State and Church and the principle of non-interference in one another's affairs.

Maksim Grek

The ideals of Nil Sorskii were most fully elaborated by a theologian of Serbo-Croatian origin who came to Russia in 1518 by invitation of Grand Prince Vasilii III to translate theological works from the Greek language into Russian or to correct translations badly done. Born in Albania or Salonika (the sources differ), Maksim Grek (c. 1475-1556) studied in Paris, Florence, and Venice, where he had witnessed the movement and heard the teachings of Girolamo Savonarola (1452-1498), then returned in 1505 to a monastery on Mount Athos before accepting the invitation of the Grand Prince. His Russian years were not happy ones. He aroused opposition in senior circles of the Russian Orthodox Church; twice condemned by assemblies of the Church, he spent nearly 25 years in exile, where he continued to write.

Drawing upon his years of learning at the University of Paris, he advocated broadly based education in all disciplines and not merely the theological sciences. He elaborated Nil Sorskii's teaching on free will, laying the groundwork for natural law conceptions that were to follow. His political and legal views have been extensively investigated by Russian historians of political thought.

Maksim Grek argued that a legitimate ruler could come to the throne either by way of succession-descent or by way of election by a representative assembly, citing the example of Alexander of Macedonia. The principal task of the ruler or the State was to ensure the peaceful and quiet life of its subjects and a stable internal order. The preferred form of power was one in which the ruler relied upon wise and conscientious advisors, councils, and counsellors, which in Russian conditions meant not merely the boyars but also other representatives of the nobility – an interpretation of Maksim Grek which remains controversial.[10]

[10] For the view that Maksim Grek favored boyar-aristocratic rule, see S. A. Pokrovskii, «Из

The limitation of the ruler's power was to be achieved not only by advisors, but also by law and accepted moral criteria. He interlinked *jus*, *lex*, and legality in his concept of justice. Injustice he equated to a violation of law, a crime against law. Although his understanding of "justice" is broad, it takes on juridical forms in a number of instances, most notably court proceedings in which punishment must be meted out on the basis of law, without hypocrisy and with mercy. Maksim Grek is regarded as being the first in Russian politico-legal literature to develop a detailed doctrine for limiting the actions of a ruler by positive law, following divine teachings and law.

The quality of justice in Muscovy was remarked upon by virtually all writers of the period. Maksim Grek subjected the judicial system to scathing criticism, condemning the bribery of judges who "steal estates and property from widows and orphans". Such practices, he wrote, not only bring harm to subjects of the princedom, but also undermine the authority of the Tsar and the prestige of the State itself. He opposed the medieval practice of casting lots as inherently unjust, preferring witness testimony and oath in its stead.

Maksim Grek linked the application of the law with the extending of mercy. The unlimited power of the ruler would be limited through law by creating a just court system and eliminating extra-judicial types of arbitrariness on the part of the ruler himself and his officials. He held that the Tsar had no right to appropriate another's private ownership, or to take the things of his servitors. One limit on his power was the right of private ownership protected by law.

The duties of the ruler to his subjects were elaborated in a late work composed about 1545: Message to Tsar Ivan Vasilevich. There he enumerated the duties of the Tsar: he must rule with justice and reason, respect his officials, reward the military, listen to the advice of his wise counsellors and the clergy, protect orphans and the indigent, and in all order the life of his subjects on the basis of good laws.

Iosif Volotskii

The philosophical and jurisprudential protagonists of Nil Sorskii and Maksim Grek were those who identified with Iosif Volotskii (1439-1515). Volotskii's principal works were Messages to Various Persons [Послания

истории русской политической мысли XVI в.», [From the History of Russian Political Thought of the Sixteenth Century], Труды Всесоюзного юридического заочного института [Proceedings of the All-Union Juridical Correspondence Institute] (1971), pp. 5-7. This view was challenged in N. A. Kazakova, «Максим Грек в советской историографии», [Maxim Grek in Soviet Historiography], Вопросы истории [Questions of History], no. 5 (1973), p. 155; id, «Максим Грек и идея сословно-представительной монархии», [Maxim Grek and the Idea of an Estates Representative Monarchy] in Общество и к различным лицам] and a number of sermons directed against heretics, later collected under the title The Enlightener [Просветитель]. His political orientation in Muscovy changed several times; initially an opponent of the Grand Prince by reason of his secularization intentions, he came successfully to defend the monastery system for its good deeds – the building of monasteries and churches, provision for monks, assistance for the needy, and the like.

He differed from Nil Sorskii and Maksim Grek in his doctrine of power, distinguishing between the concept of power as being divine in origin from the actual fact of realizing power by an individual person acting as the Head of State. While the ruler attempts to achieve divine purposes, he relies in so doing upon ordinary mortals who inevitably cause harm to the realm. Consequently, the ruler and his princes are not guilty before God for all misfortune and misadventure that occurs. This distinction opened the possibility for the first time in Russian politico-legal literature for a discussion and critique of the merits and actions of the actual ruler and condemning those who proved to be bad rulers and against whom one might legitimately resist.

Iosif Volotskii also postulated the supremacy of spiritual power over secular. He adhered to the long-established Byzantine concept of the "symphony" of powers, an alliance of power under which the secular authority is obliged to assist the Church, to persecute enemies of the Church and heretics, and not to appropriate Church property, whereas the Church in turn is to support the authority and lawfulness of the secular ruler, provided however that the dominant role is accorded to the Church. Much attention was accorded by Iosif Volotskii to the issue of heresy. He undertook to prove that heresy was both a crime against religion and the Church, and also against the State, and as a political offence it should be persecuted (including investigation and punishment) by the State – a position which led Iosif Volotskii to come close to according primacy of place to the State. He drew parallels between ordinary criminal behavior and heresy which enabled him to justify the trial and punishment, including the death penalty, of heretics in ordinary State courts.

The "symphony" of powers led Iosif Volotskii to postulate a classification of laws which undertook to combine within a single system all the rules and norms by which man should be guided. Accordingly, he did not distinguish sharply between divine law and positive, man-made law. Divine will, in his view, was both a source of power for the ruler and a source of all legislation, especially as formulated in assemblies and councils of the Russian Orthodox Church. Free will had no place in his approach, and he drew no sharp line between law and morality.

After 1504 Iosif Volotskii and his followers became dominant in Muscovy and their ideas played an influential role in Russian legal and political thought throughout the sixteenth century.[11]

Filofei

"Moscow – the Third Rome" is a doctrine in its developed form traditionally associated with Filofei, also known as Philotheus of Pskov (1465-1542), a follower of Iosif Volotskii.[12] His social and educational background is uncertain, but he was undoubtedly of a pro-Muscovy orientation. His politico-legal views were formulated in a series of Messages addressed to the Pskov Namestnik Mikhail Grigorevich Misiur-Munekhin and to the Grand Princes of Muscovy, although precisely which one remains in dispute amongst scholars.

Filofei set out a doctrine of supreme power which stressed the legality of the origin of the Grand Princes, their succession, and their stature as God's representative on Earth. The Tsar was to be concerned for his subjects, and to be so his kingdom must be in awe of God, symbolized by the scepter in his hand and crowned with a laurel wreath. The image of the Tsar was dwelt upon at length. He was severe with all who depart from justice, but just with all of his subjects, being especially solicitous of the weak. His subjects in turn were to obey him without reservation.

Following many mediaeval thinkers, Filofei did not distinguish between morality and law [*jus*]. Accordingly, any immoral act was in his view unlawful whether it had a legal basis or not. His concept of justice also included moral principles.

The unification policies of Muscovy vis-a-vis its near neighbors convinced Filofei that the time had come for Russia to fulfill its historic mission, a mission that in his eyes was inseparable from the mission of Russian Orthodoxy. Russia was the sole remaining kingdom true to Orthodoxy, and consequently the sole successor to its predecessors: "two Romes have fallen, a third stands, and a fourth will not be". This historic role of grandeur for Russia was confirmed by her recent experience – fidelity to Orthodoxy, defeat of the Tatar-Mongols, successful defense of Russian frontiers, and a promising diplomacy. The might and glory of Byzantium and Rome had passed to Muscovy, to the Russian State. Whether the doctrine of the Third Rome is an expansionist, aggressive one continues to be much discussed, including comparisons with the Soviet era and, more recently, renewed Russian interest in other Slavic peoples.

[11] See D. M. Goldfrank, *The Monastic Rule of Iosif Volotsky* (1983).

[12] N. M. Zolotukhina, Политико-правовая мысль России XVI века: Филофей и «Филофеев цикл» [Politico-Legal Thought of Russia in the XVI Century: Filofei and the "Filofei Cycle"] (2015).

It followed that the center of Orthodoxy could only be a powerful sovereign State enjoying universal respect and being possessed of sufficient power to defend the faithful Orthodox wherever situated. This was a powerful impetus to those who supported a centralized Muscovite State, and figured as a central tenet of Russian foreign policies for centuries thereafter, at least in words: "There are sufficient grounds to assert that the political formula of Filofei was part of documents expressing the official ideology of the State and for a long time was a constituent part thereof".

Fedor Karpov

The emergence of Muscovy as a centralized grand duchy gave rise to a manuscript literature treating the changes in the form of rule and State structure. Fedor Karpov, publicist and diplomat, was among those who addressed these issues. Close to Maksim Grek and his followers, Karpov set out his views in a Message to the Metropolitan Daniil, ascribed to the 1530s. His political discourses and terminology have been studied extensively and variously construed. It is generally accepted that he favored a representative form of rule of the Grand Prince and his senior officials and accepted the Aristotelian position that every city and kingdom required a Tsar and his counsellors. As regards the categories of justness and law [*jus*], which he conflated into one, Karpov required that all laws must be just and directed attention to existing schemes for payment for labor. Earnings must be just and fair, and wealth fairly distributed. Subjects unfairly paid, including those in military service, might cease to listen to their Tsar. Compliance with law [*lex*] is both the moral base of social life and the foundation of the well-being of the State. Illegality is the consequence of a decline of morality.

Karpov offered an original interpretation of "groza" [гроза], widely translated in English as "terror" but having in fact a strong connotation of "awe". Many Russian political theorists held that the ruler should incorporate "awe" as a vital component of the exercise of power. Karpov held that "awe" was not an attribute of power, but rather an attribute of law [*lex*] itself. Order in a State created the necessary foundations for the element of "awe" in a law and thereby enabled the sovereign and his officials to rule effectively and protect their subjects against "evil" people. Laws [*lex*] and the State were human creations. Laws Karpov divided into three categories: natural, divine (the laws of Moses and the laws of Jesus Christ), and positive (State), the last being enacted on the basis of the former. He rejected justifications of any illegal actions, even if founded on such ethical categories as "patience" and "forgiveness".

In his capacity as a diplomat and public official, Karpov is credited with according greater attention to the interests of the State and the status of its citizens. His theory of law and politics is regarded as being close to that of Niccolo Machiavelli, although there is no evidence of Karpov being aware of Machiavelli's writings, of being a "material link" in the process of the formation of an autonomous juridical doctrine in Russia based on natural law and human reason. That process was evidence of Muscovy moving into a new stage of cultural and historical development closer to the thinkers of the Renaissance.[13]

Ivan Semenovich Peresvetov

The program of State and legal reforms associated with the name of Peresvetov (dates of birth and death unknown) may or may not have originated with him,[14] or with a group of individuals, or even, as some suspect, with Tsar Ivan IV himself. Whatever the case, the ideas associated with his name treated a number of principally legal matters, including the creation of a system of unified legislation applied by a centralized judicial system. Without being enmeshed in the religious disputes of the time, his writings elaborated and extended in substance many of the ideas advanced by Maksim Grek.

Judicial reforms favored by Peresvetov were directed above all towards eliminating the evils of localism. Judges should be appointed directly from the center and paid from the State treasury. Court costs and duties accordingly should be recovered to the State treasury and not to the judges, and the judges should rely only upon the law [*lex*] in administering justice. He would have endowed judges also with certain administrative and supervisory functions on behalf of the central authority. The great attention accorded in Peresvetov's writings to matters military was reflected in his proposal for a separate military court to be organized separately from the civil courts. The military court was to be local, expeditious, just, and without cost to those who appeared before it.

In matters of administering justice Peresvetov favored severe punishments, including the liberal application of the death penalty at least in principle in order to create the right climate of obedience to law. He too introduced the concept of "terror" or "awe" to instill respect for law, having in mind the scheme of strict punishments which might be applied to miscreants. Within the half century which elapsed after the period in which his writings originated, many of the reforms proposed were acted upon. With respect to legislation, the Sudebnik of 1550 was introduced.

[13] See A. K. Leontev, «Государственный строй, право и суд», [State System, Law, and Court] in Очерки русской культуры XVI века [Essays on Russian Culture of the Sixteenth Century] (1977), p. 74.

[14] Regarded as among the most "fascinating Muscovite political thinkers of the sixteenth century", he is described by Hamburg as a Russian-speaking nobleman from the Grand Duchy of Lithuania with Polish, Czech, and Hungarian military experience who came to Moscow ca. 1538 and who had been impressed by the military organization of Muslim adversaries. His full writings became known only in 1956. See Hamburg, note 1 above, pp. 61-62.

Ivan the Terrible

Foreign impressions of the less salubrious side of Russian medieval and subsequent politico-legal thought are invariably associated with the legacy of Ivan IV (1530-1584), known principally through two works attributed to him which may or may not be contemporary: his so-called "epistles" and a correspondence with Prince A. M. Kurbskii (see below).[15] The essence of those ideas reduced to absolute autocracy, terror, and a police State. Following the tradition of Russian political thought in tracing the origins of the Russian crown back to its historical roots, Ivan IV reputedly rejected the view that the legitimacy of the ruler depended in part upon his personal and moral qualities. The bearer of ultimate power was accountable solely to God in the hereafter, not on earth in any way to his subjects. And as for representative rule, the Tsar's sole counsel was God himself and no one else. Similarly, he rejected the combining of spiritual and secular power with the Patrichariate, favoring a sharp delineation between the two and rejecting any limitation on secular power by the spiritual authorities.

In the Tsar's view, the supreme ruler combined also the role of law-giver and judge. The type of punishment and precise penalty should be determined not by the law, but by the Tsar himself. The scale of severe punishments applicable was entirely arbitrary and derived principally from examples of various honorable rulers rather than from legislative material. Punishment might extend not merely to wrongful deeds, but to evil and dangerous thoughts.

Ivan the 'Terrible' (or 'Awesome') attached new meaning to the word which has come down in history linked with his name. The term no longer implied a concern about the safety of the realm against external enemies or good order for its own sake. "Terror" or "awe" was secured by the *oprichnina*, or special police created by the Tsar. "Awe" came to be associated with fear and the lawlessness associated with his arbitrariness: "from the beginning of Russian literature until the end of the sixteenth century not a single political doctrine is to be found which understood the power of the Tsar to be as absolute so as to be decisively unlimited"[16] except for the doctrine of Ivan IV.

Andrei Mikhailovich Kurbskii

A major source for the political thinking of Ivan IV is correspondence which reputedly passed between the Tsar and Prince Kurbskii (1528-1583), and which in any event proved to be a vehicle by which juxtaposed politico-

[15] For a useful recent collection, see Ivan IV, Сочинения [Works] (2000). The definitive biography is I. de Madariaga, *Ivan the Terrible: First Tsar of Russia* (2005). Also see A. A. Vasil'ev, Государственное учение Ивана IV Грозного [State Doctrine of Ivan IV the Terrible] (2014).

[16] See V. E. Valdenberg, Древнерусские учения о пределах царской власти [Medieval Russian Doctrines on the Limits of Tsarist Power] (1916), pp. 359-360.

legal approaches arising out of disagreements between the Tsar and senior officials in the late 1550s and early 1560s could be expressed. Those disagreements led to the disgrace of the senior officials concerned, mass repressions, and the flight into exile of Kurbskii himself.

In the writings attributed to him Kurbskii criticized the style of rule introduced by Ivan IV as tyrannical, comparing the Tsar with King Herod. Addressing matters of law and administration, he reiterated many of the criticisms levied against the courts by Maksim Grek, Otenskii, and Peresvetov, enlarging their comments to embrace legislation. He analyzed both the processes of creating legislation and applying it. Invoking the traditional Russian concepts of justness and law, Kurbskii asked whether a law [*lex*] adopted by the State should always be complied with if it failed to conform to those criteria which a good law satisfies? His reply, based to some extent upon the actual application of law, was that law [*jus*] and justness must coincide for a law [*lex*] to be considered to be lawful.

As for legislation, Kurbskii believed that a law [*lex*] must contain prescriptions which can actually be complied with; illegality he described as not only the failure to comply with a law, but also the adoption of cruel laws. The latter type of legislation Kurbskii labeled "criminal". In the view of Nersesiants, Kurbskii was the "first in the history of political and legal thought to put the question that justness and justice, and also the natural rights of man (natural laws), are a source of rights and freedom of the individual not subject to the arbitrariness of the legislator".[17]

Following Peresvetov, Kurbskii criticized the actual application of the law within and without the courts. The courts, he said, dispensed neither justice nor mercy. He singled out trials *in absentia* for special condemnation; a slandered individual had no opportunity to defend himself against his accusers – a fate experienced by those with whom Kurbskii was politically associated. The terrorist regime introduced by the *oprichnina,* Kurbskii argued, rendered judicial and representative organs useless. Accordingly, Kurbskii elaborated upon the theory posited by Iosif Volotskii concerning the right of a people to resist the ill-intentioned exercise of power.

Kurbskii favored a limited monarchy, a monarch advised by representatives of strata of the populace who took part in all the major decisions of State. A distinction was drawn between what might be loosely described as legislative powers, to be exercised by the Tsar together with a representative council, and administrative or executive powers, to be exercised by the Tsar together with councils of advisors chosen for their wisdom and experience.

17 See V. S. Nersesiants, Право и закон [Jus and Lex] (1983), p. 196.

Ivan Timofeev and the Time of Troubles

The turn of the sixteenth-seventeenth centuries in Muscovy found the realm in disarray as the Rurik dynasty came to be succeeded by the Romanovs. A substantial political and legal literature emerged addressing the issues of succession to the throne and the political organization of society, of which perhaps the most noted is a manuscript entitled *Vremennik* [Временник]. Discovered in 1834 and attributed to a senior official, Ivan Timofeev [Semenov], the *Vremennik* is regarded as the most significant and influential example of such literature in its day.

Addressed principally to political rather than legal issues, the manuscript treated the legitimate succession of Tsars traditionally, considering those to be legitimate who succeeded by way of inheritance or by way of lawful election. Illegal Tsars were those who seized or appropriated the throne, offending thereby human and divine will and, it would follow, subject to punishment for their misdeeds. A stern opponent of Boris Godunov (1551-1605), Timofeev regarded the False Dmitrii as being sent by God to punish Russia for allowing Boris Godunov to take the throne.

Timofeev supported a limited monarchy, basically following the reasoning of Maksim Grek, F. Karpov, Z. Otenskii, Ivan Peresvetov, and A. Kurbskii, but substantially elaborating the argumentation in favor of such a scheme. He advocated the formation of a Council of Cities of the Realm, which would recognize and confirm the authority of the Tsar and would take part in helping the Tsar exercise his functions.

The formulations advanced by Timofeev persuaded many later students of his manuscript to believe that Timofeev advocated more than a mere Council to assist the Tsar. Such a Council should express and reflect public opinion, which would lay the basis for resisting laws and acts of the Tsar that were considered to be unlawful or unjust. Given the tenor of the times, he strongly endorsed the thesis that subjects of an evil ruler had not only the right, but the duty to resist his reign.

Timofeev accepted the classifications of legislation advanced by Maksim Grek, Otenskii, and Kurbskii. He used the words "natural law" [*lex*] and distinguished it from "*ustavnoi zakon*" [*lex*], or positive law. Natural laws he sometimes called "reasonable", and he would appear to have accepted the view of Kurbskii that natural law categories emanate from divine will and express eternally just and reasonable principles. Positive law must conform to natural law. By "*ustavnoi zakon*" Timofeev meant all positive legislation in force from the earliest days of Kievan Rus. His concept of justice, however, went beyond the classical limits of law to embrace elements of faith and morality. Although an opponent of Boris Godunov, Timofeev praised his devotion to justice and to the eradication of injustice.

LEGAL THEORY AND ROMANOV ABSOLUTISM 1613-1800

The accession of the Romanovs to the Russian throne in 1613 led in the course of time to a decline in those Russian institutions which had contained elements of representative power – the assemblies (Zemskii sobor) giving way to the Boyar Duma and the *Osviashchennyi sobor*, both formed on a non-elective basis. By the mid-seventeenth century the Romanovs were firmly in place, and under Tsar Aleksei Mikhailovich (1629-1676) a series of major reforms commenced that in turn produced deep divisions in Russian society and new politico-legal theories. In 1649 law reform was introduced in the form of the *Sobornoe ulozhenie*, followed in 1650-51 by a similar systematization of canon law and in 1654 by sweeping church reforms. The last led to schisms within the Russian Orthodox Church, of which the group known as the Old Believers continued to adhere to liturgies and scriptural readings of the pre-reform era and to favor a different relationship between Church and State.

Simeon Polotskii

The consolidation of Romanov power led to politico-legal theories which justified various forms of absolute monarchy. Samuil Petrovskii Sitnianovich (1629-1680), born at Polotsk and known by his monastic name of Simeon, is associated with the doctrine of "enlightened absolute monarch" in Russian politico-legal theory.

Simeon first extolled the person of the Tsar, comparing the Tsar with the sun, introducing the formula into the Russian political language: "Tsar-Sun". He rejected comparisons between the Tsar as a human personage and his subjects. God and Tsar were of virtually equal greatness: "The Tsar – a celestial citizen – is the Father of all". In Simeon's view, the Tsar and the State were identical, and he accordingly gave much attention to the formation and education of the Tsar. The Tsar must above all be an educated individual who acquires knowledge and wisdom from books and from wise people. Books about history were of special importance, so that the ruler might master the historical experience of other countries and peoples and live by their example. Distinguishing between the Tsar and a tyrant, Simeon observed that to know the difference, one should read Aristotle.

An enlightened monarchy, Simeon taught, is one in which the State is based on laws: "All punishments must be suffered under the law". There was no exception, either for the Tsar himself, or his son, or any subjects. The courts must establish the truth and not be a source of retribution nor administer harsh sanctions. He urged the creation of a court before which all were equal and a unified judicial system without "red tape".

Iurii Krizhanich

Born in Croatia and educated at Zagreb and then Vienna, and resident in Rome for nearly two decades, Iurii Krizhanich (1618-1683) came to Russian service in 1659. Victim of a libelous denunciation in 1661, he was exiled to Tobolsk for 15 years. After two further years in Moscow, he left Russia in 1678 forever. While in Tobolsk, he devoted himself to composing reflections on government, best-known in history as his treatise on Politics [Политика].[18]

Krizhanich's European background and education and his command of Russian history and theology placed him in a special position among Russian politico-legal theorists. He criticized those Russian thinkers who endeavored to trace Russian Tsars back to the Caesars of Rome. Such kinship, he suggested, would be shameful rather than honorable. He also questioned the doctrine of Muscovy being the Third Rome, dismissing this view as merely one means of extolling Ivan the Terrible.

His treatise on politics ranged widely over many affairs of State. He accepted the divine origin of the ruler. All kings, he wrote, are placed by God and are themselves divine. The purpose of the State is to achieve the "common good" for all members of society. Krizhanich considered the best form of rule to be a perfected absolute monarchy which must be secured against transformation into tyranny by certain guarantees. Among the guarantees Krizhanich enumerated the presence on the throne of a philosopher-king, compliance with good laws which were in accord with divine and natural law, and the normative regulation of all estates and officials of society under which they would have defined rights and duties.

As an educated European, Krizhanich had been well-schooled in the Digest of Justinian. His writings frequently contain propositions derived from that source. Those who draft Russian laws, he counseled, should have a thorough command of all laws and customs of the country and, when necessary, study the laws of long-established States (including contemporary France) in order to draw upon their experience. All officials of State should strictly comply with the law in their activity. However, the philosopher-king he placed technically above the law; the King is himself the living law and not subject to other laws except divine law – here his writings repeat virtually verbatim the passages from the Digest of Justinian.

Krizhanich criticized Russian laws of his day as being excessively cruel and harsh: "By reason of such harsh laws all European nations with one voice call the Orthodox Kingdom tyrannical ... And moreover they say such tyranny is greatest here". Krizhanich offered certain proposals to improve the judicial system. He recommended that a Boyars' Court be instituted to

18 Iu. Krizhanich, Политика [Politics] (1997).

settle serious criminal cases by a majority vote and that lesser criminal and the civil cases be referred to one judge for settlement who would be chosen from among the boyars.

A. L. Ordin-Nashchokin

By the late seventeenth century Russia began to manifest mercantile protectionism in its legislation, usually accompanied by various projects and programs for economic transformation of Muscovy. One of the ablest Russian diplomats, Afanasii Lavrentevich Ordin-Nashchokin (1605-1680), proposed to encourage entrepreneurship partly by means of law reform.

He prepared the draft New Trade Statute [Новоторговый устав] (1667) which contained rules regulating foreign and domestic trade and gave Russian merchants the same legal status as accorded to foreign merchants and to others granted certain immunities. Partly the Statute was based on foreign practice and experience. However, it was to be more than a century before the politico-legal underpinnings of his program came to the forefront of the Russian agenda for reform.

I. T. Pososhkov

The trends toward absolute monarchy intensified under Peter the Great as a form of rule. In his legislation Peter proclaimed: 'His Majesty is an Autonomous Monarch Accountable to No One in the World'. The Senate and Synod declared Peter to be the Emperor of All the Russias, thereby transforming the Grand Duchy of Muscovy into the Russian Empire. The Duma of Boyars was replaced by the Ruling Senate; the administrative departments (приказы, also known in English as prikazy) became colleges operating under special Reglaments; the patriarchiate was abolished and a Synod created to administer the Church.

Among the noted political theorists of the Petrine era was Ivan Tikhonovich Pososhkov (1652-1726), who flourished in a variety of entrepreneurial/industrial capacities and travelled widely throughout Russia. In 1724 he prepared his "Book on Poverty and Wealth" addressed to the Emperor and set out his views on a number of matters which he believed should be the subject of urgent attention, among which was the system for the administration of justice.[19] The book was not published at the time and may have led to the author's arrest and death in prison. Whether Peter the Great ever saw the manuscript is unknown. It eventually was rediscovered in 1842 and published, although not without difficulties even then with Russian censorship.

[19] For an excellent English translation, see I. T. Pososhkov, *The Book of Poverty and Wealth*, ed. A. P. Vlasto and L. R. Lewitter (1987).

Pososhkov set himself the task of identifying why poverty and illegality were so widespread in Russia. The manuscript was mostly devoted to issues of organizing industry and trade. Merchants, he advised, should be given the right of free trade and internal commercial duties and taxes should be uniform throughout the realm. Pososhkov believed the State should ensure enterprises had a labor force, including if necessary by assigning prisoners for this task. Merchants in turn should trade honorably and in certain cases statutory prices should be introduced for goods. As regards serfdom, he recommended the enactment of a special law which would precisely define the extent of duties of peasants and the limits of labor based on forms of legal bondage. A progressive land tax was suggested as a source of revenue for the State, which should not permit use of land free of charge.

Considerable attention was given to the eradication of injustice. Pososhkov basically accepted the position of Peresvetov with respect to the relationship between justice and law [*lex*]. Illegality was injustice. He proposed a draft scheme for "direct justice", which would be effectuated by judge-bureaucrats of the State paid from the State treasury. The judges should come from the lower classes, as the nobility was too susceptible to bribery. For unjust activity Pososhkov proposed severe penalties, including capital punishment.

Court proceedings should be transcribed in writing according to rules laid down in law, and any State revenues from the trial should be paid into the State treasury directly. He also urged that judges should be informed at once about all detentions of suspects so that no one was unlawfully detained.

Codification he recommended on a large scale, to include all ancient and recent laws, to add whatever provisions were necessary, and to set out the entire body of legislation in precise detail. Both Russian and foreign legislation should be used as models, including Turkish examples. He recommended that a special commission be appointed to undertake codification which would include two to three persons from each province of the Empire and of all social strata, including peasants and soldiers. The entire commission would sign the final draft and submit it to the Tsar for confirmation, ensuring democratic participation in the drafting but leaving the final word for the Emperor.

V. N. Tatishchev

Known as an historian, diplomat, and distinguished military officer, Vasilii Nikitich Tatishchev (1686-1750) was assigned in 1717 by Peter the Great to compose a geographical description of Russia and to prepare a history of the country. This task he worked on episodically, eventually completing the work after 1745 when he fell into disgrace under the Empress Elizabeth. His views were based on natural law and a contractual theory of the origin of the State.

The State originated in a social contract amongst peoples who could not otherwise secure their safety and security against others and achieve the common good. Historically, he suggested, all known human communities first concluded contracts between spouses, then between parents and children, and ultimately between lords and servitors. As families became extended, entire societies emerged which required a head, who became the monarch and to whom all were subordinate just as children are subject to their father. The social contract was thus a series of contracts, and he regarded serfdom as one of such contracts which could not be dissolved at the instance of one of the parties without the agreement of the other.

Tatishchev devoted considerable attention to the forms of the State. The various forms of rule, he postulated, reflected the size of territory and degree of security from foreign threat. Peoples small in number who were not subject to attack could establish democratic forms of rule, whereas vulnerable and large states required a strong ruler. The worst of all forms of rule was tyranny, and the best, monarchy. In his view the best monarchy would rely upon a two-chambered elective organ, one a Senate composed of 21 representatives from the nobility and the second a consultative council composed of 100 persons elected on a representative basis. While the monarch was the supreme legislator, the laws he issued must correspond to natural law, justness, and the general benefit. And one individual could not perform the task of legislation alone; the monarch was a formal legislator who must rely upon his departments and elected institutions to prepare the draft laws. The task of the monarch was to sign the draft laws prepared.

Tatishchev urged the preparation of a new *Ulozhenie* to replace that of 1649. The new legislation should be written in precise accessible language comprehensible by all. Codification consisted of eliminating the contradictions and inconsistencies in the law. As regards court organization and procedure, Tatishchev advocated the professional training of judges, a view ultimately introduced in the 1864 judicial reforms.

S. E. Desnitskii

The first native-born professor of law in the Russian Empire, Semen Efimovich Desnitskii (c. 1740-1789), born in Ukraine, studied at the Theological Seminary at the Troitse-Sergiev Monastery and then the Petersburg Theological Academy before being sent by Catherine II to read law at Glasgow University in Scotland in the company of Ivan Tretiakov. There he came under the influence of Adam Smith (1723-1790) and John Millar (1735-1801); upon returning to Moscow, he translated Sir William Blackstone (1723-1780) into Russian at the request of Catherine II. He also published a number of works in which he set out rather radical proposals for the legal transformation of Russia.[20]

[20] See A. H. Brown, "The Father of Russian Jurisprudence: The Legal Thought of S.

Desnitskii did not accept the contractual theory of the origin of the State. He suggested that mankind had proceeded through historically successive "states": the first period of hunting; the second, herding; the third, cultivation; and the fourth, commercial. The collective possession of things predominated in the first two stages, whereas fully-fledged ownership arose in the third and fourth. The right of private ownership, following John Locke, originated in the expenditure of labor. The State was essential only in the fourth stage of societal development.

The purpose of the State was to achieve good for the greatest number of people. The best form of State was the constitutional monarchy founded on the separation of powers. The three principal powers were: legislative, judicial, and punitive. Legislative power would be exercised by the monarch together with a unicameral parliamentary organ called the Senate and consisting of 600 to 800 persons. Deputies from all social strata would be elected, including the intelligentsia. Senators would be equal irrespective of social origin.

His ideas relating to the courts included a number of proposals of a constitutional character. He believed the judiciary should be entirely separate from the administration and recommended the jury system, open trials, direct and continuous trials, and allowing the accused to defend himself. At the lower levels of the court system, however, he compromised on these principles and allowed links between the courts and local government.

Punitive power was within the jurisdiction of the Emperor and local officials, who were to be responsible for combatting crime, executing court judgments, prisons, and the collection of land duties. He classified law into State (the person and the State), civil (parents, children, spouses), criminal (crimes against society and the State) and judicial (relations between persons). In the domain of court proceedings he favored the introduction of democratic principles such as equality of all before the law, equal punishment for those who committed the same crimes, commensurate punishment for the gravity of crimes, and greater emphasis on crimes against the individual and private ownership instead of those against religion, the Church, and the State. The death penalty might be applied only for intentional homicide and treason, and must be humane rather than applied so cruelly as in his day.

E. Desnitskii", in W. E. Butler (ed), *Russian Law: Historical and Political Perspectives* (1977), pp. 117-142; I. S. Ross, *The Life of Adam Smith* (1995); V. V. Tomsinov, «Семен Ефимович Десницкий» [Semen Efimovich Desnitskii], in Tomsinov, Российские правоведы XVIII-XX веков: очерки жизни и творчества [Russian Jurists XVIII-XX Centuries: Essays on Life and Creativity] (2d ed.; 2015), I, pp. 131-156.

A. P. Radishchev

The efforts of Russian legal and political philosophers in the late eighteenth century to identify the most desirable form of law and government produced, in the case of Aleksandr Radishchev (1749-1802), a genuinely radical response. Born into a family of the nobility with large landholdings, he read law at Leipzig University and pursued a civil service career before turning to literary pursuits. His mission was to help to put an end to serfdom and autocracy, understanding by the latter term the concentration of unlimited power in the hands of a monarch. In his works autocracy was no longer a description of the sovereignty and independence of supreme power; it designated a form of rule, which in time came to be accepted as a characterization of the form of rule in Russia.

In Radishchev's eyes autocracy was a state of being contrary to human nature. All forms of monarchy, whether "enlightened" or otherwise, in his eyes were equally pernicious. An "enlightened" monarch had never been and could not be. He also criticized the bureaucracy which surrounded the throne and in Russia was notable for being divorced from both the monarch and the people.

Radishchev proceeded from the theory of natural human rights and the contractual origin of the State. The natural sociability of people was the reason for creating States. Following Jean-Jacques Rousseau (1712-1778), he attributed the formation of States to the emergence of private ownership and the attendant inequalities among people. The social contract was a tacit one, concluded for the purpose of ensuring a prosperous life to all and defending the weak and oppressed.

Positive legislation enacted by a State must be based on natural law; if legislation is contrary to natural law, it is invalid, a point of departure used by Radishchev to reject serfdom. Contradictions such as this between natural law and positive legislation led Radishchev to the revolutionary proposition that an oppressed people had a right to rise up against the State if their natural rights were flagrantly violated.

His social ideal was a society of free and equal owners of property. Land should be given to those who cultivate it. Social privileges should be abolished and the nobility made equal in rights to all other strata of society. The Russian Table of Ranks should be eliminated, and the bureaucracy reduced and made accountable to a representative body. He favored a Republic within Russia based on the model of the medieval city-States of Pskov and Novgorod.

Radishchev rejected the doctrine of the separation of powers on the principle that only the people are the true ruler. The State should secure to its people their sacred natural rights: freedom of thought, speech, action, self-defense when the law could not protect them, ownership, and to be judged by their equals. The administration of justice he would have placed in the hands of land courts elected by citizens of the Republic. The judicial system should be made up of Church, civil, military, and equity courts, and he urged the introduction of juries.

LEGAL AND POLITICAL THEORY 1800-1850

The Decembrists

The reformist spirit of the reign of Tsar Alexander I contributed to the emergence of tiny oppositionist organizations created by like-minded individuals who composed programs for altering the absolute Russian monarchy and abolishing serfdom. These secret societies ultimately contributed to the so-called Decembrist uprising in December 1825 in St. Petersburg, the perpetrators being severely punished by death and exile.

A key figure was Pavel Ivanovich Pestel (1793-1826), born in Moscow, educated at home and then in Germany; upon returning to Russia, he became the first graduate of the Corps of Pages. He spurned a promising military career in favor of joining the secret societies and later became the organizer and head of the Southern Society, for which he composed a *Russkaia Pravda* as a program for action.[21] He was executed in 1826 for his role in the December uprising.

Pestel was a materialist and an atheist philosophically. He believed in the natural equality of all individuals and their mutual aspiration to satisfy their requirements on the basis of a social organization through the division of labor. The State, he said, was to introduce legal order into society and to balance mutual rights and duties of the government and the people. The task of government was to choose the best means of achieving general prosperity for each and everyone. Pestel divided laws into three types: spiritual, natural, and civil. Spiritual laws are disclosed through the Holy Scripture; they link the spiritual and the natural worlds. Natural laws arise from the requirements of nature and natural needs; they are imprinted in our hearts. State or civil laws are decrees of the State whose aim is to secure general prosperity, and consequently they must be issued in full accordance with spiritual and natural laws. Such conformity, he said, was an absolute condition of the validity of State laws.

Pestel also believed that State laws must conform to social interests in the sense that the advantage of the whole must always prevail over the advantage of the particular. Consequently, civil laws should be so composed that the interests of an individual do not take precedence over

[21] P. I. Pestel, Русская Правда. Наказ временному Верховному правлению [Russkaia Pravda. Instruction to the Provisional Supreme Government], intro. P. Shchegolev (Spb., 1906).

the interests of all society. Any action contrary to the general prosperity should be deemed to be criminal. Every just society must be based on the absolute authority of law and not the personal predilections of the ruler.

Addressing the various differences which existed in the basic laws of various countries and peoples, Pestel argued that such differences arose principally from the various social and political institutes and institutions which existed in each State or society, rejecting Montesquieu's view that such differences originated in varying climates and geographic positions.

The Russian State, said Pestel, did not pursue the achievement of social prosperity and therefore represented an abuse of power which ultimately would lead to the State itself perishing. The flouting in Russia of natural, spiritual, and positive laws required, he suggested, "changes of the existing State order and the introduction in its place of that which would be based only on precise and just laws and decrees". In these propositions lay the right postulated by Pestel of the people to overthrow a government which violated spiritual, natural, and positive laws.

Pestel's *Russkaia Pravda* contained a scheme for social and political transformations in Russia and the means for achieving these ends, a scheme which was, in the true sense of the word, radical. It proposed the abolition of serfdom and the division of land amongst the peasants free of charge on the premise that land according to natural law is the weal of all of the people. Each individual holds a participatory share therein since land is the principal source for feeding mankind. However, he recognized that private ownership existed and was so deeply imbedded in the consciousness of people that eliminating ownership was impossible. Accordingly, Pestel's idea was not to eliminate land ownership, but to transform all Russians into land-owners.

Politically, Pestel described himself as a republican because in that form of rule he saw the greatest possibilities for prosperity in Russia. State power would be divided into legislative and executive; all male citizens of 20 years or more enjoyed the right of suffrage except those in service. The legislative branch would be a single-chamber parliament elected for five years, with the annual election of one-fifth of its membership by rotation. No one might dissolve parliament. Executive power would be lodged in five persons elected for a five-year term to a Derzhavnaia Duma; all ministries and governmental bodies would be subordinate to this executive organ. Supervisory power of the legislative and executive branches would be vested in an assembly, or sobor, consisting of 120 persons called boyars who would be appointed for life and might not take part in either legislative or executive life. Candidates would be nominated by the provinces. All laws would be sent to the assembly, which would not consider it in substance, but carefully verify that all necessary formalities had been complied with as a condition of the law entering into legal force.

The other supervisory functions of the assembly would be exercised through the appointment of one of its members to each ministry and to each region of the country. The sobor would appoint the supreme military command and could send for trial any official of any level who abused his power.

Pestel proposed that the Russian State operate under a Constitution, which he called the "State Testament". Under his scheme, Russia would be divided into a federation composed of ten regions and three udels; each region in turn would consist of five provinces or national areas, each province of uezds, and each uezd of volosts. He proposed to transfer the capital of Russia to Nizhnii Novgorod, which he regarded as the geographic center of Russia and the cradle of Russian freemen.

The best means of achieving these transformations in Russian life, Pestel counseled, was a military-revolutionary coup with immediate elimination of the monarchy and physical elimination of the members of the Imperial family in order to prevent restoration of the monarchy. The creation of a new order would require a provisional supreme ruler headed by a dictator for a period of ten to fifteen years. A constitutional order would come into being only when the existing order had ceased to exist and the memories of that order had been erased from the people's memory.

A second key figure in the Decembrist movement was Nikita Mikhailovich Muravev (1796-1843), who became head of the Northern Society. His intellectual development was shaped by the ideas of French Enlightenment doctrines, the Greek and Roman classics, and Russian writers and historians, of whom Karamzin was especially important. After the December uprising, he was sentenced to 20 years forced labor in Siberia.

Muravev composed three draft constitutions which contained the essence of his social and political program. The third draft, written while in prison at the behest of the investigative authorities, was the most radical. He was well grounded in the United States Constitution and the documents of Revolutionary France. Deeply religious, Muravev combined natural law doctrines with those of the New Testament and criticized absolute monarchy from these positions as being contrary to natural law. The Russian people, he wrote, are free and independent and may not belong to any person or family. The people are the source of power and have the exclusive right to make the basic provisions of such power for themselves.

The first step by way of transformation of the State, said Muravev, should be the abolition of serfdom and slavery. He considered the constitutional monarchy to be the best for Russia based on the principle of separation of powers. Legislative power would be placed in a two-chamber parliament. All individuals who had attained majority and who owned movable or immovable property, except those in private service, would have the right to vote. One chamber of parliament would be elected for six years, one-third of its membership being renewed every two years. Members of this chamber must be at least 30 years old and own property of a specified minimum amount. The other chamber would consist of 450 members and be elected for a term of two years, the chamber presupposing the creation of a federated Russian State. Laws would be adopted by majority vote; any member of parliament or a minister had the right of legislative initiative.

The monarch could not as the head of executive power change or repeal laws nor appropriate the functions of legislative power. But he was endowed with extensive powers in Muravev's scheme, including being the commander-in-chief of the armed forces and representing Russia in negotiations with foreign powers. The monarch could convoke both chambers of the parliament and change the time of sessions of the chambers, but not for more than two months. All power of the monarch would be supervised by the parliament, including even visits to other countries. His courtiers would enjoy no special rights or privileges and could not be elected or appointed to State offices. Women could not inherit the throne.

A Constitution would make provision for the competence of the chambers of the parliament and for local government on an elective basis. He proposed a rather complex judicial system which would have reinstated courts of equity originally introduced briefly under Catherine II. Amendments to the Constitution could only be introduced according to a special procedure; a people's assembly would be elected whose principal responsibility was to draft and submit major laws and constitutional amendments. The monarch would be required to take an oath to comply with the Constitution.

Muravev did not accept Pestel's version of social transformation which postulated a temporary dictatorship, for he apprehended this might lead to the creation of conditions encouraging arbitrariness and illegality.

Slavophiles and Westernizers

In the 1830-1840s two orientations in social and political thought emerged which dominated the next decades of Russian politico-legal discourse. The central theme of the dialogue was the historical fates of Russia, the place and role of Russians among other peoples, and the distinctiveness of Russia's political and legal experience against the background of European and Oriental experience.

Law and legal institutions were a passing component of this dialogue, but of interest nonetheless. The Slavophiles urged the need to reassess certain elements of earlier Russian experience, of which those of legal interest included the peasant community, local self-government, and the correlation of law and custom. The communities and customs of early Russia had given way to mercenary judges, vain boyars, and power-worship amongst the clergy. The extent of power wielded by the State had led to the destruction of regional rights and the stifling of local self-rule, and under Peter the Great, to a Westernization of Russia which was completely alien.[22]

The Westernizers responded that Russia should not be juxtaposed to European Russia, that Europe shared Christianity in common, and the differences between Russia and Europe lay in the special types of Christianity, in a special orientation towards Enlightenment, and in differences in private and personal life. A leading proponent of the Westernizers and one of the founders of the so-called "State school" in interpreting Russian history was Konstantin Dmitrievich Kavelin (1818-1885). This approach argued that the moving force in history was the struggle between the individual for freedom and the gradual changes of social forms from family to the State. Russia had traversed the same historical path as Europe in this regard, but more slowly and therefore, being behind, had to borrow the achievements of civilization where appropriate. The reforms of Peter the Great placed Russia on the path of Europeanization with respect to freedom and administration on the basis of modern acts and laws.

THE GOLDEN AGE 1850-1900

The year 1850 as a benchmark of periodization is purely arbitrary. The socio-legal reforms of 1861 linked with the emancipation of the serfs and the judicial reforms of 1864 gave new stimulus to legal theory, new varieties of political programs, and new groupings among those writing on the subject, which may be classified roughly into the reformers, the radicals, the liberals, and the conservatives.

The Reformers

The practicalities of land reform engaged the attention of legal theorists from the 1850s. Various drafts circulated in the government, the minimal position being granting peasants the right to acquire in ownership their peasant house and immediately adjacent land plot. Under this scheme, peasants would obtain only the right of use over other lands, with attendant duties, by proceeding from local circumstances and customs. Later drafts recognized that greater rights over land needed to be given, responding to a considerable public reaction that peasants should acquire land and freedom without obligatory duties to the land-owner or to the State. The so-called "narodnik" movement pressed this view, drawing upon earlier discussions of the role of the *obshchina* [община], or community, in Russian life and

[22] See N. Iu. Andreev, Государственно-правовой идеал славянофилов [State-Legal Ideal of the Slavophiles] (Moscow, 2014).

maintaining that as the community was liberated from the dual yoke of serfdom and bureaucratism, so would it take on its own natural life.

These views were shared to some extent by Aleksei Mikhailovich Unkovskii (1828-1893/94), a reformer from the ranks of the nobility who initiated the most radical draft regarding the peasant question. His draft, submitted to Tsar Alexander II as early as 1857 in the name of the nobility of Tver Province, recommended that peasants be accorded the right to acquire both their personal plot and field allotment immediately and compulsorily. Neither expectation was fully met by the reforms of 1861.

The Radicals

The 1860s also saw the emergence of new social movements advocating radical programs and radical social actions. Some Russian historians have called this period the formation of revolutionary utopian socialism in Russia, a combining of Russian utopian peasant socialism and the mass revolutionary movement among the Russian intelligentsia. Leading representatives of this movement were Alexander Herzen (1812-1870) and Nikolai Gavrilovich Cherynshevskii (1828-1889). Herzen placed great hopes in the revival of the Russian *obshchina*, a theme pursued in its legal aspects by Chernyshevskii.

Chernyshevskii believed that the existence of a high level of civilization as achieved in contemporary Europe did not preclude the concept of *obshchina* possession of property as the highest form of relations of man and land. This form of ownership in his view was much to be preferred to private ownership because it better secured the general prosperity by combining the owner, master, and worker into a single person. Contrasting intra-*obshchina* regulation with governmental regulation on the basis of legislation, he concluded that the former was preferable for the absence of the interference of any central and outside administration, which enhanced the freedom of the individual. Intra-*obshchina* regulation was inherently more reasonable than governmental as it was formed by generations on the basis of legal customs and agreement. Although private ownership in Western Europe had its virtues, in his eyes it led to excessive individualism and competition which in the end meant the strong triumphing over the weak and labor being the victim of capital. The way out was to create an alliance and brotherhood among people on the basis of the latter combining into a society sharing a common interest and using the forces of nature and science in common. In the domain of land ownership, this brotherhood was to be expressed in the transfer of land to *obshchina* use, whereas factories would become a company of all those working at the factory and also transferred as *obshchina* weal. When he became convinced that the existing State apparatus could not be reformed, he advocated peasant revolution and the formation of a society and State free from bureaucratism, local representative government and self-rule, an independent and just court, limitation of imperial power, and administration on the basis of laws.

Also among the radicals, Mikhail Aleksandrovich Bakunin (1814-1876) is associated with the ideas of collectivist anarchism, a species of ultra-revolutionary socialism. He cautioned against the uncritical acceptance of the Russian *obshchina,* criticizing the *obshchina* in Russian history for its humiliation of women, absolute denial of women's rights and honor, patriarchal absolutism and despotism, disrespect for the mir, and the lack of both legal rights and even elementary justness in decisions of the mir. Bakunin's treatment of the rights of the individual or duties of State officials was natural-law based; he rejected State laws and regulation as having been formed under the influence of negativist influences and inherently despotic. So-called political legislation was inevitably hostile to freedom and contrary to the natural laws of nature. The greatest guarantee of freedom in Bakunin's view was control over State power.

Another noted anarchist was Petr Alekseevich Kropotkin (1842-1921), who sought to combine the doctrine of anarchism with his studies of the science of nature and society. He linked the historical development of the State with the emergence of land ownership and the aspiration of one class to concentrate such ownership in its hands. The State, he said, in essence was a mutual insurance society composed of the land-owners, military, judges, and clerics each seeking to maintain their respective power over the people and to exploit the poor. The organization of State power was accordingly closely linked with law and the system of justice. The court administered legalized revenge called justice.

The Liberals

The liberals favored reforms of autocratic Russia and greater recognition of the worth of the individual. Respect for law was a central theme of liberal writings about legal subjects. Leading representatives of the liberal orientation included B. N. Chicherin and S. A. Muromtsev, N. M. Korkunov, and M. M. Kovalevskii.

Boris Nikolaevich Chicherin (1828-1904) wrote widely on the history of political and legal thought and the philosophy of law.[23] In his view the State in history was an alliance of the people who were linked by law in a single legal whole and administered by supreme power for the benefit of all. The aim of the State was not the good of the individual, but rather to ensure the safety of the person and create a moral order, defining and defending civil rights and freedoms (but not natural rights). The domain of natural law, as contrasted with positive law, is truth and justness: the

[23] See G. M. Hamburg, *Boris Chicherin & Early Russian Liberalism 1828-1866* (1992); Tomsinov, «Борис Николаевич Чичерин» [Boris Nikolaevich Chicherin], in Tomsinov, note 20 above, II, pp. 1-18.

system of general legal norms arising from human reason and obligations which serves as a standard and guide for positive legislation. Justness is the standard by which the domain of the freedom of individual persons is demarcated and the requirements of laws are established. The aim of socio-political development is to avoid the extremes of individualistic anarchism and mechanical statism, to know how to combine individual freedom harmoniously with the general law.

Law does not reduce, he said, to benefit or to interest; it is inextricably linked with freedom as an individualistic and *a priori* metaphysical principle. From this standpoint law is the external freedom of the individual, determined by external *lex*. *Lex* determines, defines, freedom and its limits or boundaries and the relations arising from them. In part Chicherin was influenced by the Hegelian proposition that law is a development of the idea of freedom, but was critical of its statist and anti-individualistic implications. Chicherin schematized freedom as: external (law), internal (morality), and social. Freedom as subjective morality becomes objectified and is combined with law as a norm of freedom in social linkages – the family, civil society, Church, State.

The essence of liberalism in Chicherin's perception was the essence of the individual as a free being who became part of society while preserving that status. Even when the individual voluntarily limited his freedom in the interests of the freedom of others and accepted civil duties and the authority of the State, he retained his human dignity and inherent right to develop his powers of reason. Freedom of conscience, freedom of thought – these are the divine sources of spiritual power that impart freedom to the individual.

Sergei Andreevich Muromtsev (1850-1910) contributed significantly in Russia to the study of law from a sociological perspective, directing attention to law as the existing legal order and justifying the creation of legal rules by judges.[24] He hoped the last would further the evolution in Russia of a more liberal regime: "There is no reason to fear arbitrariness on the part of judges", he wrote, for their high level of education and orderly progression in the ranks of the judiciary, and the very "corporation of jurists" reflected in their methods of selection, openness of proceedings, and stability of tenure in office, their adherence to law, custom, and legal doctrine, their social conscience, justness, and morality were all grounds for allowing them to participate in the law-creation process.

Muromtsev's originality lay in his concept that law is not merely the aggregate of legal norms, but rather the aggregate of legal relations, the legal order. This perception contributed in Russian jurisprudence to a more profound understanding of law as not merely the will of the ruler (Tsar,

[24] Tomsinov, «Сергей Андреевич Муромцев» [Sergei Andreevich Muromtsev], in Tomsinov, note 20 above, II, pp. 268-310.

parliament), but to the entire complex of legal relations in Russian society. A strong proponent of constitutional reforms, he was elected chairman of the I State Duma. When he died his students placed a wreath on his grave inscribed: "To the first Russian citizen – from future Citizens".

Nikolai Mikhailovich Korkunov (1853-1904) developed the ideas of Muromtsev and of Rudolf von Jhering (1818-1892). Society, said Korkunov, is an objective social order representing conflicting personal and social interests in the political, economic, and religious domains. These conflicts are coped with by imposing certain limitations on each subject of legal relations. Law both demarcates the interests and acts as an instrument for ensuring order in the process of the emergence and settlement of conflicts of interests.

Korkunov was influential in his day for his sociological and philosophical approaches to the study of law, contrasted to the formalistic orientation of dogmatic jurisprudence which dominated in university circles. The translation into English of his general theory of law established Korkunov in Western circles as the best-known Russian jurist of his generation.

Maksim Maksimovich Kovalevskii (1851-1916) was a jurist of many parts: legal theorist, comparative lawyer, publicist, publisher, and member of the State Duma. He spent considerable time in England, where he came to know the work of Sir Henry Maine (1822-1888); he pursued and developed Maine's comparative legal studies, combining the study of law with an analysis of its inter-linkages with State institutions. Kovalevskii also achieved, through his studies of customary law, considerable reputation as an ethnographer.

The Conservatives

As a group those legal theorists classified as "conservatives" were noteworthy for their patriotic cultural-nationalism and a growing distrust of the relevance of European political and legal experience for Russia. This meant a distrust of representative rule, of the idea of equality, and of respect for the rights and freedom of man and citizen.

Nikolai Iakovlevich Danilevskii (1822-1885), in a monumental work contrasting the cultural and political relations of Russia and Europe, developed a theory of the cultural-historical types of human civilization. Not a jurist, his views and approach, sometimes described as a species of comparative Russian culturology, nonetheless influenced many Russian legal theorists. In particular, he believed that the only special guarantees of political and civil rights which were possible were those which the supreme power in a society wished to grant to its people. He ridiculed the notion of a social Russian parliament, although unlike many other neo-slavophiles, he did value the freedom of speech as a natural right and not merely a privilege granted by the State.

Konstantin Nikolaevich Leontev (1831-1891) was a strong proponent of the terror of power personified in the status of the Tsar as supreme ruler. Developing the ideas of Danilevskii, Leontev believed that the future of various cultures and historical types of society were capable of being predicted, provided that a sufficient time-frame was taken into consideration – at least a half-century or century. State organisms proceeded through cycles, which Leontev calculated occurred every 1,200 years.

Leontev rejected the egalitarianism of liberalism, which he equated to a species of anarchism. Russian statehood and law, he believed, were derived partly from Byzantium and partly from Europe. The cycles of statehood led States to commence as aristocracies, develop into monarchies, and then decline and die as egalitarian and liberal democracies.

Vladimir Sergeevich Solovev (1853-1900) does not fit neatly into any of the preceding categories but nonetheless made his own contribution to Russian legal thought. A patriot and very much a Russian philosopher, he cautioned nonetheless against the "extra-European" and "anti-European" views in Russian society of his day as an "empty pretension". Among those ideas of Western Europe of which he approved was the rule-of-law State, which he saw as a step forward towards a more perfected variant of community. He gave considerable attention to theocracy in his published writings, and in later years to social Christianity. In his understanding of law Solovev endeavored to separate out the moral value of law and of legal institutes and principles. He defined law as the "lowest limit or certain minimum of morality binding equally upon all". Natural law for him was the formal idea of law rationally derived from the general principles of philosophy. For Solovev natural law and positive law were merely two aspects of the same thing. Natural law embodied the "rational essence of law" and positive law personified the historical phenomenon of law whose realization depended upon the State of moral consciousness in a particular society and on other historical conditions. Positive law constantly adds to natural law.

Natural law is an algebraic formula which comes down in essence to two factors: freedom and equality. Freedom is a necessary substratum, and equality the necessary formula thereof. The aim of a normal society and law is the common good, and not merely the collective good (the sum of individual purposes). This common good by its essence internally links everyone and everything through joint and several actions to achieve the common aim. Law endeavors to effectuate justness, but this aspiration is merely a general trend, the "logos" and idea of law. Positive law embodies and realizes, albeit not always fully, this common trend in specific forms.

Solovev's ideas about law influenced in some measure the legal views of Novgorodtsev, Trubetskoi, Bulgakov, and Berdyaev, among others.

As investigations into the history of legal theory from this period continue, there are other important figures whose contribution was real but remains relatively unknown. Among them is Konstantin P. Pobedonostsev (1827-1907),[25] whose reputation as a jurist has long been overshadowed by his reputation as an *eminence grise* behind the Russian throne.

THE TWILIGHT YEARS 1900-1917

Among the thinkers influential at the turn of the century was Georgii Valentinovich Plekhanov (1856-1918), sometimes styled the "father of Russian Marxism". Departing from the "*narodniki*", Plekhanov believed that Russia had to pass through a full phase of capitalist development, which meant not only the development of production forces but also the respective superstructure, including a constitution and parliamentary rule. The Great Mission of the working class of Russia was to complete the task commenced by Peter the Great: the Westernization of Russia. In August 1903 he advocated the slogan "The Good of the Revolution is the Highest Law", a phrase which on its face justified any means to the end, but also advocated the existence, adapting the English expression, of a "Long Parliament" and its rapid demise when necessary. Constitutional revolutionary law played a purely auxiliary role; the dictatorial power of the State was for him the highest law and not bound by constitutional requirements and prescriptions.

The mainstream of Russian legal philosophers were preoccupied in the early years of the twentieth century with constitutionalism. Sergei Aleksandrovich Kotliarevskii (1873-1939) wrote a major treatise on the rule-of-law State (1915) in which he observed:

> the idea of the rule-of-law State came into the practice of modern civilized States, in aggregate those expectations which turn a member of a State union into the leaders thereof. A rule-of-law State became one of the political tasks. The crisis of legal consciousness, the loss of faith in the majesty of law and institutions, has been noted many times ... the conviction that the State must take on the face of a rule-of-law State remains unshakeable.

Kotliarevskii believed that the principal purpose of a rule-of-law State is to be a State of justness, which presupposes that *lex* must always be just. The first requirement or first principle of a rule-of-law State, wrote Aleksandr Semenovich Alekseev (1851-1916),[26] is the inadmissibility of changing the legal order in a State without the participation of popular representation.

[25] See V. A. Tomsinov, «Констатнин Петрович Победоносцев» [Konstantin Petrovich Pobedonostsev], in Tomsinov, note 20 above, I, pp. 376-443.

[26] See Tomsinov, «Александр Семенович Алексеев» [A. S. Alekseev (1851-1916)], in note 20 above, II, pp. 311-321; Butler and Tomsinov, *Russian Legal Biography* (2007), I, pp. 21-27.

And the second requirement is the supremacy of *jus* (and not of *lex*): "It is not *lex* which gives force to *jus*, but *jus* which gives force to *lex*, and the legislator must not create, but must find *jus*, worked out in the consciousness of society".

Gabriel Feliksovich Shershenevich (1863-1912), a noted legal philosopher and specialist in civil law, combined a professional legal dogmatism with philosophical positivism, arguing that the State is the source of law because it represents power. Power is linked with the will and knowledge to oblige others to form their behavior so as to correspond to the will of the rulers. He supported the sociological concept of the State, which rests on the fact that it is difficult to build the concept of the State as power or as a legal relationship, but it is possible to imagine the State as a combination of power and will. State power in this sense is based on the autonomous will of some (those who rule) who subordinate others to their will (the ruled).

Bogdan Aleksandrovich Kistiakovskii (1868-1920) is credited with taking the initiative in posing the question of how a rule-of-law socialist State would be as part of the process of overcoming the imperfections of a bourgeois rule-of-law State. He criticized the Russian intelligentsia for neglecting law and for having an underdeveloped legal consciousness, especially those who linked their fate with revolutionary ideas and causes. He accused the Slavophiles of legal nihilism. The *narodniki*, he felt, exaggerated the so-called ethical preoccupation of the Russian people, and this inhibited the transition from custom to written legislation in the countryside. He was himself partial to a Kantian definition of law, which in terms contemporary to Kistiakovskii was defined as the "aggregate of norms establishing and delimiting the freedom of persons". From the sociological point of view, he accorded preference to treating law as the aggregate of norms creating a compromise among various demands.[27]

Evgenii Nikolaevich Trubetskoi (1863-1920) defined law as "external freedom granted and limited by a norm". He criticized definitions of law based on concepts such as "power"', "State", and "coercion" because they failed to appreciate that any State and any power must be conditioned themselves by "law" [*jus*]; they overlooked the fact that varieties of law exist independently of whether they may be recognized or not by a particular State, examples being canon law, international law, and certain legal customs. Trubetskoi sought to harmonize natural law and positive law; natural law was the moving principle in history. The very idea of natural law gave the individual the possibility to climb above his historical milieu and save him from being enslaved by that which existed.

[27] See S. Heuman, *Kistiakovsky: The Struggle for National and Constitutional Rights in the Last Years of Tsarism* (1998); Butler and Tomsinov, note 26 above, I, pp. 279-282.

Pavel Ivanovich Novgorodtsev (1866-1924) distinguished himself early as a legal historian and philosopher. A member of the Kadet political party, he was elected to the State Duma. After the Russian revolutions he emigrated to Prague, where he formed the Russian Law Faculty with the assistance of the Czech Government; recognized to be the leader of a school of reborn natural law, his pupils included Ivan A. Il'in, B. P. Vysheslavtsev, N. N. Alekseev, and A. S. Iashchenko.

Author of several noted works, most fundamental perhaps is his Introduction to the Philosophy of Law (1907-1917) published over a decade in three parts. The first treated the need for a renaissance of natural law, and the second, what he called the "crisis" in the use of ideals and values of the Enlightenment, including those of the rule-of-law State. In his last volume, on the "social ideal", he analyzed the ideals of socialism and anarchism. His own position was that there should be a break with the traditions of exclusive historicism and sociologism and a transition to a system of moral idealism:

> Natural law structures are an integral property of our spirit and evidence of its high calling. A society which has ceased to create ideal structures would be a dead society; each time these structures show a spirit is alive, that there is movement of moral feeling and consciousness.

RUSSIAN LEGAL THEORISTS IN EMIGRATION

In the aftermath of the Russian Revolutions, Russian legal theorists unsympathetic to Bolshevism found themselves in Harbin (Manchuria), Prague, Berlin, Paris, London, Sofia, and various cities in Yugoslavia. A detailed study of early Soviet legal experience by a collective of Russian jurists published at Prague in 1925 contained essays by Nikolai Nikolaevich Alekseev (1879-1964)[28] and Nikolai Sergeevich Timasheff (1886-1970). They observed that the constitution was not important in order to establish a dictatorship in Soviet Russia; a direct and multifarious political experiment was underway. The category of *lex* [закон] was irrelevant because in practice the distinction between *lex* and subordinate enactments, the existence of a hierarchy of legal norms, was inoperative. Alekseev observed that Soviet power rested on the fact that the seizure of power was effectuated by the oppressed, which he understood to mean that naked power had not created Soviet Russia, but a power equipped with the idea of a struggle for liberation. According to this logic, the proletarian State possessed a right of limited coercion, which presupposes the elimination of any coercion – propositions which Alekseev based on his interpretation of natural law.

[28] See Tomsinov, «Алексеѐв Николай Николаевич» [N. N. Alekseev (1879-1964)], note 20 above, III, pp. 236-251; Butler and Tomsinov, note 26 above, I, pp. 27-34.

Other noted Russian legal theorists in emigration included Pitirim Aleksandrovich Sorokin (1889-1968), who commenced his academic career at Petrograd University and then at the University of Minnesota and Harvard University. He had been the personal secretary of M. M. Kovalevskii. In 1919 he offered the first course of lectures on sociology. After the Russian Revolution he became the personal secretary of A. F. Kerensky (1881-1970). In 1922 he was exiled from Soviet Russia and took up his posts in Western institutions. Petr Berngardovich Struve (1870-1944) evolved philosophically from legal Marxism to State liberalism in the spirit of Kavelin and Chicherin and found himself after the Russian Revolutions in Belgrade and Berlin.

P. G. Vinogradoff

Although contemporary Russian treatises on the history of legal thought consign Sir Paul (Pavel Gavrilovich) Vinogradoff (1854-1925) to the category of Russian émigrés,[29] his was not the usual emigration and had nothing to do with the coming of the Bolsheviks to power in 1917. A fellow student at Oxford in the 1880s during the era of Sir Henry Maine (1822-1888) and a contemporary of Sir Frederick Pollock (1845-1937), he resigned his Chair at Moscow University in 1901 and accepted election to the Corpus Chair at Oxford University in 1903. He was elected Corresponding Member in 1892 and full Academician of the Imperial Russian Academy of Sciences in 1914, Fellow of the British Academy, and an Academician elsewhere.

Vinogradoff came to historical and jurisprudential studies at a time when social history had become fashionable. He was the first Russian legal scholar to choose English history as a field of research, having devoted considerable time to medieval Lombardy, and later expanded into the history of jurisprudence, which he viewed as the history of doctrines and institutions.

Legal history, in his perception, dealt with flows of doctrine and institutional activity which across many centuries and State frontiers pass from one historical formation into another. The archetype examples of such cultural succession were the reception of Roman law in medieval and modern Europe, or the linkages between Roman codifications and their Oriental predecessors.

His perception of law as a social phenomenon and a part of social experience caused him to range widely among the humanities and social sciences in his research. He gave considerable attention to the law of

[29] See Tomsinov, note 20 above, II, pp. 331-381; Butler and Tomsinov, note 26 above, I, pp. 368-386; V. G. Grafskii, in V. S. Nersesiants (eds.), История политических и правовых учений. XX в. [History of Political and Legal Doctrines. XX Century] (1995), pp. 27-30; O. Kaznina, Русские в Англии [Russians in England] (1997), pp. 87-89; W. E. Butler (ed.), *On the History of International Law and International Organization: Collected Papers of Sir Paul Vinogradoff* (2009).

ownership, maintaining that how society structures its law of ownership determines how that society establishes the status of the family, of women, of labor relationships, of crime and punishment, and of State structure and organization.

Political theory he believed was a constituent part of jurisprudence, part of the "literary development of State Law". The "various branches of State Law and the sundry norms of civil, criminal, and canon law stand together with State Law, covering it like a shield and dustwrapper".[30] Although Vinogradoff enjoys a kinship with those legal theorists preoccupied with the "law in action", his historical orientation, which he himself called a "synthetic" approach, led him always to examine the origins and evolution of law, and in this he also departed from the positivism of Jeremy Bentham and John Austin. The weakness of the analytical school, he counseled, was that it contained the danger of being preoccupied with abstract concepts and terms and losing sight of social realities. The "world of concepts" becomes an end in itself.

His late works were strongly interdisciplinary, exploring how the other branches of the social sciences and humanities might profitably use legal phenomena in their disciplines. His studies were always comparative in spirit if not in substance, and he remains one of the greatest Russian progenitors of comparative law. In the early 1920s his attention turned to the history and typologies of legal systems and law, a line of enquiry interrupted by his death. In Russia his collected papers have been published to some extent,[31] but in the minds of most Russians he is viewed as an historian, and not a jurist.

I. A. Il'in

Ivan Aleksandrovich Il'in (1883-1954) emerged in the 1990s as the Russian legal philosopher of greatest historical importance and interest for modern Russian legal thought. An individual of exceptional intellectual breadth, he devoted much of his legal writing to aspects of "legal consciousness". The science of law, he wrote, must be structured not merely as a "science concerning 'law', but as a science concerning 'law in a normal legal consciousness': since law is not *thought* about often, one must *experience* and *see* it".[32]

[30] See P. G. Vinogradoff, История правоведения (Курс для историков и юристов) [History of Jurisprudence (Course for Historians and Jurists)] (1908), p. 10.

[31] See P. G. Vinogradoff, Россия на распутье: Историко-публицистические статьи [Russia at the Turning Point: Historico-Publicist Articles], comp. A. V. Antoshchenko (2008)

[32] See I. A. Il'in, «Основные задачи правоведения в России» [Basic Tasks of Jurisprudence in Russia], Собрание сочинений в 10 томах [Collected Works in 10 Volumes] (1999), vol. 9-10, p. 221. By 2021, 31 volumes of his collected works had appeared in Russia, with at least thirteen awaiting publication. His personal archive and library were moved from Michigan State University to Moscow Lomonosov University in 2006. The term "legal consciousness"

Il'in's diagnosis of the shortcomings in the Russian legal consciousness and his proposals to redress the problem were unknown to Russians in his day except those few in the émigré community. He defended a two-volume dissertation on Hegel in May 1918 at Moscow University, having been released from police custody literally hours before the defense; his academic opponent, Professor Novgorodtsev, appeared for the occasion while the police were searching for him. The fact that Lenin was familiar with and held a reasonably positive opinion of the dissertation probably saved Il'in from execution and enabled him to flee abroad. The dissertation committee awarded Il'in the degree of magister for volume one and the doctorate of laws for volume two of the dissertation. Arrested again in September 1922, Il'in, given the choice of exile or execution, took passage on what became known as "The Philosophy Steamer".[33]

In Germany until Hitler forced him to emigrate again, and then in Switzerland for the remainder of his days, with occasional visits throughout Europe, Il'in devoted himself to lecturing and writing in French, German, and Russian. A ferocious polemicist and pamphleteer whose works, besides law, dealt with current international affairs, the situation within the Soviet Union, religion, philosophy in general, and matters of interest to the Russian émigré community at large, Il'in corresponded extensively with colleagues and friends and prepared his memoirs. His thinking has proved to be not merely a revelation of astute perceptiveness to the modern Russian reader, but positively prophetic in its appreciation of the crisis of values that has accompanied the downfall of communism in Russia and the quest for modern legal values or, as he would have it, a normal legal consciousness.

Il'in had begun to work on legal consciousness in 1917, but did not actually complete a version until two years later, when publication was impossible in Soviet Russia. The term "complete" is relative here, for actually Il'in never did conclude the work to his satisfaction. Instead he used his sundry versions for lectures in Europe, discussions at the Moscow Law Society, and private discussions with Russian docents and professors. Portions appeared in the German language during 1925-26, and this version was not published in the Russian language in the Russian Federation until 1998 as part of his collected works.[34] At a memorial service for Il'in in 1955, a colleague who knew of the work and its continuous polishing said: "This is

was used in the Law of 6 May 1991, No. 2211-1, "On the Constitutional Court of the RSFSR", but replaced on 21 July 1994 with the term omitted.

[33] There were in fact two chartered German ships, the *Oberbürgermeister Haken* and the *Preussen*, which sailed six weeks apart from one another. See L. Chamberlain, *The Philosophy Steamer: Lenin and the Exile of the Intelligentsia* (2006).

[34] The first fragments in English appeared in I. A. Il'in, "On the Essence of Legal Consciousness", *The Journal of Comparative Law*, VII (2012), pp. 88-107. For the complete text, see I. A. Il'in, *On the Essence of Legal Consciousness*, ed., intro., and transl. W. E. Butler, P. T. Grier, and V. A. Tomsinov (2014).

not merely a most important contribution to legal literature, but a genuinely new, living word on the spiritual atmosphere which law and the State need in order to flourish".[35]

THE SOVIET MARXIAN LEGACY

Marx and Engels had comparatively little to say about law in their writings, and what they did say appertained principally to their larger critique of the society contemporary to them and their explanation of societal change. Law in effect was explained away. Future society, it was supposed, would administer itself without need of legal rules. Those who came to power in October 1917, who confronted, as Marx and Engels had not, the need to govern nations, peoples, an economy, an army, found no specific blueprint in the writings of Marx and Engels. There commenced the process of developing and adapting theories of revolutionary change to cope with a real revolution, a process which continues to this day, by devising sub-stages through which a society was to pass in the course of the transition to socialism and communism. Those levels of societal development were closely linked to and dependent upon law and legal institutions. Intense and important debates about the role or purpose of law figured in Soviet policy dialogues on those issues at various periods of the Soviet era of legal theory; or more precisely, the theory of State and law contributed to those discussions within the Communist Party and without and, of course, duly reflected the ultimate decisions taken. Law was, *inter alia*, policy as well as politics, whether one spoke of law writ large (*jus*) or as a single legislative act (*lex*); it was the product of political processes, it recorded a policy judgment or decision, and it transmitted that decision to whosoever it was addressed in the form of a normative rule.

In his *Critique of the Gotha Programme* Karl Marx (1818-1883) spoke of a transition period between capitalist and communist society when the former would transmute into the latter. Politically the State during this period could be nothing, Marx said, other than the "revolutionary dictatorship of the proletariat". Lenin (1870-1924) developed the notion in his *State and Revolution* (1917), suggesting that a proletarian State would be essential in order to crush the bourgeoisie but would commence the dying out process at once. Much of Soviet Marxian legal theory thereafter was devoted to the relationship between those contradictory processes and the relative weight to be accorded to each.

[35] Quoted from Il'in, note 32 above, (1993), II, p. 416. The first Russian-language version eventually was published at Munich in 1956. The task of law, Il'in wrote, is "... to create in the soul of man a prayer for best behavior". For the application of Il'in's concepts to Russian legal history, see T. I. Demchenko, Правовое сознание в древнерусской и российской государственно-правовой жизни [Legal Consciousness in Medieval Russian and Russian State-Law Life] (Moscow, 2013).

Once power passed into their hands, the Soviet leadership fashioned a highly centralized form of government within a federated structure. Initial expectations that an untrained, often illiterate, proletariat and peasantry could simply step into a dismantled State apparatus proved illusory. Normative acts represented "proletarian commands" that were to be obeyed because they represented the will of the new ruling class. Philosophically, however, the Soviet leadership saw no long-term virtue in those legal rules and institutions governing the personal interests of citizens. Those were expected to disappear during the transition period. The classics of Marxism were explicit with respect to State and law of the old order: it was to be smashed; the power base of the old order was to be dismantled with all the legal institutions which supported it.

The dismantling and restructuring processes simultaneously at work during this early transition period were variously interpreted against the background of the New Economic Policy (NEP). Some viewed the legal history of 1917 to 1921 as an era primarily of dismantling the old Imperial order and experimenting *ad hoc* with the minimum legal measures required for transition.[36] To them the NEP represented an unfortunate but essential tactical reversal of this process, a restoration of capitalist elements whose doom otherwise was sealed by early proletarian legislation. Others viewed the NEP as a logical continuation and development of the revolutionary measures. The NEP codifications, according to this view, were a consolidation and systematization of revolutionary achievements and by no means a retreat or compromise; the NEP was a necessary next step in the class struggle to achieve socialism.

In one sense it is perfectly true to say that in the Soviet period the history of legal thought was a battleground in which various forms of Marxism-Leninism fought against what was perceived to be State and law in their non-communist sense, against a bourgeois world-view. Massive resources were dedicated to replacing systematically a history and ideology of law [*jus*] with one based on a proletarian, Bolshevist, Marxist-Leninist, communist ideology and a reinterpretation of the historical past into one which was congenial to the nature of Soviet institutions and a postulated withering away of State and law.

In the early years after the Russian Revolutions numerous discussions and dialogues addressed the fate of law under the new socio-political circumstances and alternative theories emerged. Law as an instrument of the dictatorship of the proletariat figured centrally in the writings of Dmitrii Ivanovich Kurskii (1874-1932), an early People's Commissar of Justice. Law under the dictatorship of the proletariat, he said, was an expression of the interests of the proletariat, and there was accordingly no place for

[36] See J. N. Hazard, "Soviet Law: The Bridge Years, 1917-1920", in W. E. Butler (ed.), *Russian Law: Historical and Political Perspectives* (1977), pp. 235-257.

recognition and defense of the rights and freedoms of the individual. He extolled the revolutionary people's courts as a new source of law-creation; their principal function being "criminal repression", he asserted the courts should be absolutely free and should be guided above all by their legal consciousness.

The new "proletarian communist law" was based on the Soviets, a family freely-formed and unburdened by oppressive ties to the land or an employer, and the ownership by the proletarian State of all the instruments of production. With the transition to the NEP Kurskii asserted that Soviet law had become a species of "rule-of-law" State, although the interests of the State always were postulated to prevail over competing personal rights of individual citizens.

Petr Ivanovich Stuchka (1865-1932) viewed law as a procedure for social relations. The basic principles for a new revolutionary-Marxist law Stuchka reduced to three: the class character of any law; the revolutionary-dialectical method (in substitution of formal legal logic); and material social relations as the basis for explaining and understanding the legal superstructure (instead of explaining legal relations by proceeding from a law and legal ideas).

In his role as a senior legal official Stuchka was positioned to pursue his ideas in the drafting of legislation. Writing about the preparation of the 1919 Guiding Principles of Criminal Law of the RSFSR, he said:

> When before us, in the collegium of the People's Commissariat of Justice, was the necessity to formulate our own, so to speak, 'Soviet understanding of law', we rested on the following formula: 'Law-is a system (or procedure) of social relations corresponding to the interests of the ruling class and protected by the organized power thereof'.

Much of what was written attempted to draw upon certain strands of European legal philosophy and criticism of them in the light of Soviet experience of Marxian tenets. In the absence of a cohesive Marxist theory of law for the dictatorship of the proletariat, it was easier to react against the ideas of others. Georg Jellinek (1851-1911), Leon Iosifovich Petrazhitskii (1867-1931), Leon Duguit (1859-1928), Karl Renner (1870-1950), and Hans Kelsen (1881-1973) were among those who had Marxist followers, albeit in a revisionist spirit, and whose pre- and post-revolutionary writings were subject to avid scrutiny in Soviet legal media. For all of the searching for a Marxist theory of State and law in the 1920s, however, no one seriously challenged the notion that law was expected to die away rapidly.[37] In the

[37] See on this period A. A. Plotnieks, Становление и развитие марксистско-ленинской общей теории права в СССР [Origin and Development of Marxist-Leninist General Theory of Law in the USSR] (1978).

interim, law was an instrument for revolutionary social change. Legalism was decried as a "bourgeois fetish".

The Soviet jurist who developed original notions of the role of law in a society building socialism and of the rapid withering away of law and who came to lead intellectually the legal policies associated with the transition from NEP to national economic planning and collectivization was Evgenii Bronislavovich Pashukanis (1891-1937). His ideas acquired considerable reputation in the West at the time through a German translation of his *General Theory* and enjoyed fresh consideration in the late 1970s. He rejected the concept of "proletarian law" because in his perception bourgeois law, the historically most developed type of law, was not to be followed by another, post-bourgeois law. He accordingly developed an "anti-law" position and offered instead the "commodity exchange theory" of law. Those who purchase and sell goods in the market-place rely on contract or other forms of transactions to define and enforce reciprocally their mutual economic relations. The participants identify themselves as juridical persons bearing particular rights and duties. The law of contract, to Pashukanis, is founded upon the intentional voluntary reciprocal conduct or consent of the parties giving effect, in this instance, to their economic relations, but the same consensual base underlies other branches of law: labor relations, between management and employee; family law, in the form of marriage and parent-child relationships; or even constitutional law, based on a social contract reflecting an alleged consensus to govern. All law consequently had an economic basis, in this case founded on commodity exchange.

Pashukanis believed he had accurately diagnosed the legal process in society, not law as an abstract ideal but as a genuine operational element in human relations. Although law was to be found in every level of societal development after primitive communalism, its inherent individualism and contractual or consensual base led naturally to its apogee of development under capitalism. The dictatorship of the proletariat would avail itself of bourgeois law only insofar as the transition to a socialist economy required. With the introduction of national economic planning (hereinafter "Plan") and the elimination of a commodity-exchange economy, the legal superstructure of bourgeois law would die away.

His Soviet critics accused Pashukanis of applying abstract characterizations of law which existed before and outside of socialism; these were not applicable to proletarian law. In the course of time Pashukanis was obliged to accept that a new post-revolutionary and post-bourgeois "Soviet law" did in fact exist, albeit with a very special and specific nature.

The psychological conception of class law is associated with Mikhail Andreevich Reisner (1868-1928), who even before the Russian Revolutions began to pursue these lines of enquiry under the influence of L. Knapp and L. Petrazhitskii. The idea of law as a form of social consciousness was developed by Isaak Petrovich Razumovskii (1893-1937). He offered a general definition of law: "The procedure of social relations, ultimately relations between classes, insofar as it is reflected in the social consciousness, is historically inevitably abstracted, differentiated for this consciousness from its material conditions and, objectified for it, receives further complex ideological development in systems of 'norms'". The dying out of bourgeois law Razumovskii described as the "death of law as an ideology".

From the late 1920s to the early 1930s there occurred what in Soviet legal history is known as the "struggle on the legal front". Soviet jurists of all orientations, influenced by the transition to a Planned Economy, collectivization of agriculture, and campaigns against various forms of ideological "deviations", adjusted their jurisprudential positions. This led to an increased politicization of legal science and greater direct influence of the Communist Party on the substance of legal doctrine. An address by Lazar Moiseevich Kaganovich (1893-1991) on 4 November 1929 to the Institute of Soviet Construction and Law of the Communist Academy was the signal for unleashing a campaign of Bolshevist criticism and self-criticism. Kaganovich accused communist legal theorists of being imprisoned by the "old bourgeois legal methodology", which led to such doctrines as State agencies being subordinate to the commands of the law: "We have our laws. Our laws determine the functions and ambit of activity of individual agencies of State power. But our laws are determined by revolutionary expediency at each particular moment".

The struggle on the legal front contributed to a polarization of the two principal positions in Soviet jurisprudence of the day: those of Pashukanis and Stuchka. Pashukanis subjected himself to self-criticism and began to recant his views in favor of considering law and policy (or politics) to be identical, interpreting law as one of the forms of policy or as a component of policy (or politics). Stuchka in turn acknowledged an excessive reliance on the bourgeois sociological school of law in his early writings. In 1931 the I All-Union Congress of Marxist specialists in the State and legal sciences attempted to form a single correct position and line. The Congress was dominated by adherents of Pashukanis, but in the end adopted an eclectic resolution which tried to save face for the various approaches.

In the early stages Pashukanis and his followers secured the upper hand and enjoyed an opportunity rarely open to legal theorists: to practice what they preached. The introduction of national economic planning in 1928 brought a revolutionary offensive against law. The day of law dying away was believed to have arrived, and the goals were not modest. Large-scale industrialization required the planned concentration and allocation of resources and investment. Part of the rural labor force had to be released for the factories, and this could be accomplished it was believed only by mechanizing agriculture on a large scale and eliminating the potential economic stranglehold of the middle and wealthy peasants over the nation's food supply. Moreover, the State intended to finance industrialization partly through the export of grain and raw materials, which also required that the State have full control over agricultural production. Survivals of capitalism were to be abolished. By the end of the Second Five-Year Plan antagonistic classes were to have disappeared.

The pace of change gave rise to vigorous debate about economic policy and the human capacity to effectuate short-term vast social change. Those who believed man was not fully capable of shaping his own destiny carried the day. A dynamic approach was preferred to the stability-mindededness of those who counselled caution. In the realm of law, Plan was expected to supplant the remnants of bourgeois law. The transition to socialism had accelerated; an adaptive socio-economic policy needed a flexible set of institutions and policies that would give effect to Plan not in terms of rights and duties but in terms of elastic revolutionary legality. As a means of social control, law would be superseded by Plan in economic relations. Codification and systematization of legislation, at an advanced stage in 1929-1930, were suspended for fear the forms of law would constrain socio-legal change. In the realm of interpersonal relations, civil law was relegated to a minor place in legal studies. Draft penal codes prepared by followers of Pashukanis consisted of broad principles and no Special Part (defining the constituent elements of individual crimes), for Pashukanis had regarded preexisting criminal law and its fixed penalties for offenses as a kind of contractual relationship between society and the individual.

By 1936 it was apparent that the pace of imposed change could not be sustained. On the other hand, it was felt that the necessary threshold had been crossed. The adoption of a new Constitution for the USSR in 1936 to mark the transition of the Soviet Union to a society building socialism required a new concept of law. Pashukanis in 1936 advanced the concept of "socialist law", abandoning his former characterization of all law as "bourgeois": "The Great Socialist October Revolution dealt a blow to capitalist private ownership and laid the principle of a new socialist system of law. Therein is that which is fundamental and principal for an understanding of Soviet law, its socialist essence as the law of a proletarian State".

The 1936 USSR Constitution declared the Soviet Union to be a socialist society. Antagonistic classes had been eliminated. Those who counseled restoration of stability of laws came to the forefront, and those responsible for earlier policies of rapid change were purged and in many cases, including Pashukanis, executed. The State under socialism would not wither away rapidly. Socialism existed only in one country (the USSR) and was being built in another (Mongolia), neighbors surrounded by hostile capitalist powers, and for self-defense the State would be maintained and strengthened. For the State ultimately to disappear, Stalin said, it must pass through the dialectically contradictory stage of becoming stronger.

The ideological underpinnings of these postulates culminated in 1938 with the Conference devoted to the science of Soviet law and State convoked by Andrei Ia. Vyshinskii (1883-1954). From 16-19 July 1938, 600 legal workers, teachers, and practitioners assembled in Moscow to attend the I Conference on Questions of the Science of the Soviet State and Law. The aim of the Conference was to lay down a single true Marxist-Leninist, Stalinist-Bolshevist general line in legal science and on the basis thereof to reorientate all approaches and conceptions posited by Soviet jurists of the earlier periods, most of which were rejected as "hostile" or "anti-Soviet". In his initial theses submitted to the Conference and in his oral address Vyshinskii defined law [*jus*] as:

> the aggregate of rules of conduct established by State power as the power of the ruling class in society, and also customs and rules of community life sanctioned by State power, effectuated in a compulsory procedure with the assistance of the State apparatus for the purpose of protecting, consolidating, and developing social relations and procedure advantageous and suitable for the ruling class.

This definition was altered as follows in the final written text of Vyshinskii's address and in theses approved by the Conference. Law [*jus*] is:

> the aggregate of rules of conduct expressing the will of the ruling class established in a legislative procedure, and also the customs and rules of community life sanctioned by State power, the application of which is ensured by the coercive power of the State for the purposes of the protection, consolidation, and development of social relations and procedures advantageous and suitable for the ruling class.

Together with this general definition of law the Conference also approved a definition of Soviet law:

> Soviet law is the aggregate of rules of conduct established in a legislative procedure by the power of the working people expressing their will and the application of which is ensured by the entire coercive power of the socialist State for the purpose of the defense, consolidation, and development of relations and procedures advantageous and suitable for the working people, the full and final destruction of capitalism and its survivals in the economy, domestic life, and consciousness of people, and the building of a communist society.

This definition dominated Soviet legal thought throughout the remainder of the Stalin era and beyond. The principal doctrinal writings on law repeated it verbatim. The thaw of the mid-1950s was accompanied in legal circles by some embryonic criticism of the Vyshinskii position, and its monopoly as the official line was sundered forever. Now styled a "narrow-normative" approach by its critics, it began to be supplanted by doctrines of law as a unity of legal norm and legal relations (Stepan Fedorovich Kechekian (1890-1967), Andrei Andreevich Piontkovskii (1898-1973)) or as a unity of legal norms, legal relations, and legal consciousness (Iakov Filippovich Mikolenko). The substance of these positions acknowledged the normativity of law as laid down in 1938 but attenuated such normativity by recognizing the importance of law-in-action.

Vyshinskii's "socialist legality" evolved into a standard by which excesses of the Stalinist era came to be condemned and legal reforms to be effectuated in the post-Stalin era. The initial law reforms of the post-Stalin period amounted to an attenuation of the harsher political terror and the introduction of greater substantive and procedural guarantees. Following the XX Congress of the CPSU, most of the jurists criticized during the Stalinist era were rehabilitated. The relaxation in the post-Stalin era likewise brought an extensive preoccupation with Western political and legal philosophy of all periods and orientations, both critiques and translations. The turning point in Soviet legal thought, however, dates from the XXI and XXII Congresses of the CPSU in 1959 and 1961 respectively. At the XXI Congress, Soviet society was said to have entered a higher phase of socialist development, the period of the "expanded construction of communism". A new Program of the CPSU adopted at the XXII Congress called for completion of the first phase of communist construction by 1980, a timetable that was quietly shelved when the economic prerequisites proved too ambitious.

For a brief period the transition to this new level of socialist development refueled the debate about the imminent withering away of the State. The 1961 Party Program declared the Soviet Union to be a "State of the whole people" or an "all people's State". The dictatorship of the proletariat had ceased to be necessary. The all-people's State would rely less on coercion and more on persuasion and would commence the process of divesting its functions to non-State bodies such as social organizations. The comrades' courts and people's guards were introduced as social agencies to assume law enforcement functions. Criminal law reforms placed greater emphasis upon social measures to reform first offenders who committed minor crimes. A constitutional revision commission appointed in 1962 was to prepare a new constitution reflective of the new level of societal development. It may have been intended to reduce the numbers of lawyers; reports persist of an unpublished Party resolution c. 1963-1964 calling for a reduction in the number of law students. Soviet jurists gave serious thought for the first time to mechanisms for social control in the first phase of communism as the State withered away. Customary law took on special interest in this connection and no longer was deemed to be inherently retrograde.

Vyshinskii's definition of law was deemed unsuitable for the new stage of societal development.

The change of leadership in 1964 brought a new style and slight reorientation to the debate. The new codifications of civil and criminal law had been completed. Attention concentrated on economic reforms and upon making the middle and lower levels of State power and administration more democratic, participatory, and responsive. The all-people's State emphasized less the immediate divestiture of its functions and more the greater involvement of citizens in its affairs. The comrades' courts and people's guards were retained as proven quasi-legal institutions but modified to introduce better procedural safeguards. Legislation on local government was reworked thoroughly for the first time since the 1930s. For reasons not wholly clear, the new Constitution was delayed until 1977. Its enactment signaled the full-fledged legislative acceptance of the all-people's State.

Soviet legal theory during this period was preoccupied with the "nuts and bolts" of legal development. As legislation became more detailed and comprehensive, the theorists were engaged with the minutiae of legal institutions and rules. Larger questions, to be sure, were of concern. Soviet jurists confronted the issue of distinguishing "good" laws from "bad". State command, it was widely recognized, was not always sufficient to establish the "legality" or the "justness" of legislation. Various efforts to measure legislation against the larger goals of a socialist society building communism, or against communist morality, or against laws of societal development or analogous basic standards brought Soviet jurisprudence close to some sort of natural law position in the minds of many Western legal philosophers.

Soviet jurists began publicly to question the identification of pravo [*jus*] and zakon [*lex*] which underlay Vyshinskii's theses. To distinguish between the two reflected in some measure a return to the thinking of Russian jurists of the past and involvement in the ratification of the 1966 covenants on human rights. The dialogue is one which has not been followed in detail by Western scholarship, but will repay study in due course, for in that dialogue lie in part the roots of *perestroika* and the eventual dissolution of the Soviet Union. The search for freedom, equality, and rule-of-law [jus] in the post-Soviet era has its roots in the jurisprudential legacy of Russia.

Perestroika itself in the late Soviet era and the developments in Russian law following the dissolution of the Soviet Union were neither foreseen nor shaped by legal theory. Nor has a single generally-accepted theory emerged to assist the legislator in pursuing democratic reforms. The Russian legal system remains a theory-minded system in search of a theory:

Without Marxist-Leninist ideology and communist notions about law and State, without the former conceptual foundation, worldview, conceptual apparatus, and vocabulary, the post-Soviet theory of law and State and legal science as a whole proved to be in an ill-defined state.

We refer in essence to the transition from the former communistically ideologized, coercive-command comprehension of law and worldview of the dying out of State and law to the new conception of jurisprudence orientated to that form (or variant) of juridical comprehension of law, recognition of the original legal sense, value, and inalienable character of human rights and freedoms, necessary legal foundations, and characteristics of the constitutional system, civil society, rule-of-law State, and lawful law.[38]

POST -SOVIET LEGAL THEORY

The search for a theory has seen several basic orientations emerge in Russian legal doctrine: the liberal-democratic, the modernized Marxist-Leninist, and the so-called traditional. Others categorize these orientations differently: normativist-statist, sociological jurisprudence, libertarian legal,[39] neo-liberal, or an amalgam essentially based on the capitalist legacy of theories.[40] The liberal-democratic or libertarian-liberal takes as its point of departure the 1993 Russian Constitution and the legal structures based on it;[41] the principal defect of this orientation in the view of some of its warmest proponents is its excessive preoccupation with bourgeois values and aspirations.[42] The more appropriate foundations for the liberal-democratic approach are, it is argued, a "civilitarian system" and a "civilitarian law". In place of the bourgeois emphasis upon formal legal equality, civilitarian law (accentuating the word "citizen", *civis* in Latin) stresses equal civil ownership, that is, an identical participatory share for everyone in all of the desocialized socialist ownership:

> This conceptual perspective of the movement from nonlegal socialism to civilitarianism and to a civilitarian law has important theoretical-criterial significance and enables one to adequately evaluate the history of the Soviet theory of law and Marxist doctrine

[38] V. S. Nersesiants, Общая теория права и государства [General Theory of Law and State] (2012), p. 185.

[39] A. V. Poliakov, Общая теория права [General Theory of Law] (2001), p. 124.

[40] M. N. Marchenko, Советское и постсоветское государство и право: сравнительно-правовое исследование [Soviet and Post-Soviet State and Law: Comparative-Legal Study] (Moscow, 2017).

[41] Works reflecting this approach include: V. A. Chetvernin, Понятие права и государства [Concept of Law and State] (1997); V. N. Khropaniuk, Теория государства и права [Theory of State and Law] (1995); V. V. Lazarev (ed), Общая теория права и государства [General Theory of Law and State] (1996); G. N. Manov (ed), Теория государства и права [Theory of State and Law] (1996).

[42] See V. S. Nersesiants, Юриспруденция [Jurisprudence] (1998), p. 156

on law as a whole in their correlation with the realities of nonlegal socialism and to determine the coordinates of post-socialist paths to law in the general bedrock of world-historical progress of freedom, equality, and law.[43]

The 1993 Constitution is based in this view on a legal (anti-legist, anti-statist) type of comprehension of law, which in turn determines the legal orientation and aims of Russian jurisprudence. The Constitution serves a society in transition from totalitarianism, anti-law socialism, to a post-socialist legal structure, the commencement of the formation of a civil society, a rule-of-law State, and a law [*lex*] which must accord with law in the highest sense [*jus*]. The core of the 1993 Constitution is the recognition, concretization, and defense of the rights and freedoms of man and citizen; these are deemed to be vital for a country with a totalitarian-socialist past whose jurisprudence reflected class-communist positions. The Constitution combines a "legal-axiomatic" approach (the rights and freedoms of man are the highest value) with a natural law view (the rights and freedoms of man are innate and not conferred by the State). The task of the civilitarian school is to measure the Constitution, its virtues and shortcomings, against the realities of Russian life and seek to identify and repair those domains where the Constitution falls short.[44]

The modernized Marxist school, on the other hand, seeks to adapt the precepts of the past to the society of the future. The foundations of the Soviet State, they observe, were to be found in the Marxist doctrine on State and law and severely criticized from all sides. But those doctrines were never fully applied, even in the former Soviet Union, for various "objective and subjective reasons"; instead, "surrogates, pseudo-Marxist" institutions were created. Marchenko singled out these basic postulates of the Marxist doctrine on the socialist State:

(1) socialist State and law originates not by way of evolution, but by socialist revolution, the seizure of power by the proletariat and transformation of the proletariat into the ruling class;

(2) a prerequisite of a socialist State and law is the destruction of the old State machine and bourgeois State apparatus;

(3) the essence of the new State operating in the transition from capitalism to socialism is the dictatorship of the proletariat, which means not only violence with respect to those classes resisting the power of the proletariat but also various economic, social, and other creations;

[43] Ibid., p. 156.

[44] On the role of "civilism" during the Putin era, see Nersesiants, *The Civilism Manifesto: The National Idea of Russia in the Historical Quest for Equality, Freedom, and Justness*, transl. W. E. Butler (2000).

(4) the origin and development of socialist State and law will pass through several stages of evolutionary change, hotly debated in Marxist circles, but in Marchenko's view reducible to the following: State of dictatorship of the proletariat, functioning of a socialist State proper; and State of the whole people – all introduced and affirmed in Soviet constitutional experience;

(5) the form of rule or government in a socialist State, which Marxism believes should be a republic and in the Marxist understanding should serve the interests of the toiling masses and contain socialist content. This meant in Soviet practice "all power to the soviets"; experience with a Presidential system is not evaluated positively. There is a strong preference for a unitary State based on the principle of democratic centralism. However, a federated, or federal, State system was not rejected;

(6) law is an integral and inextricable part of a socialist State, a means of resolving tasks confronting the State, and reflects the will and interests of the ruling class – initially the interests of the workers, peasants, and labor intelligentsia and at the stage of a developed socialist society, the interests of the whole people;

(7) State and law, in the Marxist understanding, are not eternal and immutable phenomena. As class society develops and classes gradually die out, so too do State and law.[45]

These elements, seen against the realities of historical Soviet experience, are perceived as "fragmentary" by reason of "objective circumstances connected with the radical changes which occurred in the social and other structures of Soviet society". Post-Soviet legal theory, likewise is seen as fragmentary, at least from a Marxist perspective, by reason of its "pluralism" – its theory of a rule-of-law and social State, theory of a civil society, theory of human rights, and – at least as seen by Marxist theoreticians – its theory of transition from socialism to capitalism. On this view, the contemporary Marxist theory of State and law does postulate a destination for legal changes underway: not to a destination undetermined, but to the restoration of a capitalist (as distinct from market) legal system.

To some Russian legal theorists this state of affairs has suggested a return to terminology and typologies first witnessed back nearly a century ago, in the 1920s – the "theory of State and law of the transition period". There are various formulations: transitional States and legal systems; transitional conditions of the State and legal systems, for example. Transition in this sense is another word for change, but for many Russian legal theorists, this means systemic or typological change, progress or regression, manipulated

[45] Here summarized. For details, see Marchenko, note 40 above, Chapter 4.

or inevitable change. Some refer to this as "inter-typal" change, which is inherently transitional, that is, represents a transition from one type of State and law to another, such as from "socialist" or "pseudo-socialist" to "capitalist". On this view the transitional State and law, in addition to the "classical" features of State and law, gives evidence of the following traits:

(1) all States and legal systems of the transitional types generally arise as a result of various social revolutions, wars, unsuccessful radical reforms, or coups d'état;

(2) the transitional condition of State, law, and society itself contain several variants of the further evolution of social and constitutional bedrocks or alternatives to the transition of State, law, and society from one type to another. These are pursued, and in Russia it is believed have been pursued, on pragmatic and on philosophical-theoretical levels. Embedded in these perceptions are larger conceptions of whether history unfolds in an upward spiral direction or in repetitive cycles;

(3) the transitional period is inevitably linked with sharp changes in the character and scale of traditional economic links, temporary disruptions of the economy, weakening of the material foundation of the State and legal systems, and a decline in the standard of living for a significant part of the population;

(4) transitional States and law experience a temporary weakening of their social and political foundations during conflicts between the old and new political elites;

(5) the transitional type of State and law, as a rule, is dominated by the principle of separation of powers;

(6) special characteristics to be found in each society expressed in the economy, ideology, political and social system, and others.

Factors and analyses such as the above lead Russian legal theorists to seek a model of transition and post-transition appropriate to Russian circumstances. One model which has been influential, albeit not entirely successful, has emphasized elements of liberalism and social democracy:

(1) the liberalization of political life, emphasizing the institutionalization of civil freedoms and a certain openness or transparency of government;

(2) the dismantling of old or obsolete political and economic institutions associated with the previous regime;

(3) the democratization of socio-political life; and

(4) the introduction of measures to "re-socialize" citizens, that is, persuade them to accept the new values and new politico-legal system.

Although this model, in the view of Russian legal theorists, has its attractions and virtues, neither liberalism in its Benthamite or other version or social democracy is capable of coping with the challenges of post-Soviet Russia. States with a federal or federated system are, in this view, especially vulnerable, incapable of responding to the tasks of reformation while undertaking the essential protective and defensive functions associated with social stability, economic growth, and the rule-of-law. Transitional States confront nationalism, extremism, and other disintegrating forces of considerable magnitude – some internal and some external. It continues to be a central element of post-Soviet Russian legal theory that legal theory is expected to explain and to offer a solution to these challenges. Legal theory remains central to the formation of the Russian jurist and, in the Russian view, to comprehending the forces at work within and without Russia and offering potential strategy and tactics for shaping, directing, and combatting them.

In some Russian legal and philosophical circles "post-Marxism" has emerged, distinguished from "neo-Marxism" as follows:

> Neo-Marxism included political and legal theories, aesthetic and culturological doctrines, sociology, psychology, futurology, and religious studies. Post-Marxism enters the ideas of Neo-Marxism in the context of post-contemporality – the globalizing informational or post-industrial society, the post-colonial system of world structure ... The ideas of Marx in the second half of the twentieth century do not simply retain their actuality, but become an important integral element of post-classical thought.[46]

A traditionalist approach, anti-Western in essence, survives in Russian legal theory and seeks to find the future of Russian jurisprudence in pre-revolutionary Russian legal theory with a Slavophile disposition. A revived Eurasianism is regarded as a variant of this approach.

As during the last five decades of Imperial Russian rule and even to a surprising extent during the Soviet era, Russian jurisprudence today gives evidence of a considerable range of innovative and imaginative legal theory, mostly indebted to the distinctively Russian conditions and circumstances. The importance of legal theory is expressed as follows to Russian law students:

[46] I. L. Chestnov, «Постмарксистская методология права: перспективы научной состоятельности» [Post-Marxist Methodology of Law: Perspectives for Scientific Well-Foundedness], in Проблемы постсоветской теории и философии права: сборник статей [Problems of Post-Soviet Theory and Philosophy of Law: Collection of Articles] (2016), p. 264.

The most significant contribution to the development of legal science is linked with theoretical studies orientated towards identifying the subject-matter of legal science in all of its wholeness and comprehensiveness; that is, in all of the wealth comprising its objective natural laws of the functioning and development of the State and law. Such a result may not be achieved at once, in the course of a single study, but gradually, by means of conducting a number of studies in which only part of the subject-matter of legal science or individual natural laws thereof is subjected to a special profound study …

Russian jurists carry on notorious disputes concerning the nature of law, the essence thereof, and the forms of expression. The most significant theoretical results were achieved by Russian jurists when investigating individual components of the legal system: the mechanism of legal regulation, law-making, the application of law, legal responsibility, the mechanism of the State, the political system of a civil society, and others.[47]

Whatever theory or theories come to achieve consensus in post-Soviet Russia, the role and importance of legal theory is deeply embedded in Russian legal culture and unlikely to give way to an alternative approach in which legal theory plays a lesser role.

[47] V. M. Syrykh, История и методология юридической науки [History and Methodology of Legal Science] (2012).

5

SOURCES OF LAW

During the Soviet era, Marxist-Leninist legal doctrine conventionally distinguished between two meanings of "sources of law". In their most "fundamental" sense the "sources of law" were said to be the socio-economic order of a particular society; it was that order which gave birth to and shaped the distinctive political, economic, and legal superstructure of a society. A socialist society, in this larger sense, formed and shaped the substance of its socialist law and legal system.

In their technical meaning, which is the aspect treated in this chapter, the "sources of law" are the rules or norms created, sanctioned, or recognized by the State or its agencies in a duly established manner. Not all acts fall within this definition; only those prescribing general rules of conduct, or *normative* legal acts,[1] as they are often called. Non-normative acts appertain to individual specific matters and are issued on the basis of legal norms. The distinction between normative and non-normative is more easily drawn in theory than in practice, and is one drawn in many different ways.

It also follows from this definition that not all sources of law originate in the State itself. The discussion of *jus* [право] in Chapter 3 turned entirely upon the proposition that *jus* is something above the State. "Customs" are also recognized as a subsidiary source of law emanating from non-State bodies, and many local normative acts are adopted by or within non-State entities.

Unlike the common law, which ascribes no special priority to the sources of law, the Russian legal system attaches significance to a formalistic hierarchy of the sources of law. The 1993 Russian Constitution has introduced an entirely new dimension to that hierarchy, whose implications continue to unfold.

[1] The legislator has never actually defined "normative legal act", although definitions appear in doctrinal writings and documents of agencies of State power. On 25 May 2000 the Plenum of the Supreme Court of the Russian Federation by Decree No. 19 explained that a normative legal act is an "act issued in the established procedure by a duly empowered agency of State power, agency of local self-government, or official establishing legal norms (or rules of behavior) binding upon an indefinite group of persons intended for repeated application and operating irrespective of whether specific legal relations provided for by the act have arisen or terminated". Decree No. 19 was repealed on 20 January 2003 by Decree No. 2 of the same Plenum in connection with the introduction into operation of the 2001 Code of Civil Procedure. The legal status of the preamble of a normative legal act is explored in V. M. Baranov, Преамбула нормативного правового акта [Preamble of a Normative Legal Act] (Moscow, 2014).

JUS [ПРАВО]

Russian law has incorporated from its earliest recorded days the concept of "*jus*", that is, of law which originates somewhere other than with the ruler of the day or the State. Whether its origins be the Will of God, or the natural order of the universe, or the laws of societal development, or the fabric of Russian (or Slavic) socio-cultural values, or otherwise continues to be the subject of lively discussion. In the post-Soviet era that debate is of crucial significance for the future of the rule-of-law in Russia. In some measure the Russian legal system has taken refuge in those elements of "*pravo*" incorporated in general principles of international law or in international treaties of the Russian Federation, most notably in human rights treaties. For the rest, proponents of *jus* [право] equate it with natural law, or a community-based unwritten law which takes precedence over all others. The Constitutional Court of the Russian Federation has yet to consider a case which juxtaposes a provision of the Constitution to some higher law, and much may depend, if such a case be instituted, upon the willingness of that Court to give formal recognition to the existence of Russian law in its most fundamental meaning. The modern Russian general theory of law recognizes that "law [*jus*] does not reduce itself to the aggregate of laws [*lex*]. It is considered that law [*jus*] stands by virtue of its own laws [*lex*]".[2]

The position has been eloquently expressed in a basic text on Russian constitutional law:

> Law can not be reduced only to the written part thereof, to positive law. This is the more so with respect to constitutional law, which is called upon to protect human freedom. In addition to positive legal regulation, always vulnerable to the danger of going too far and the temptations of authoritarian decisions, universal human concepts exist concerning freedom and justice that comprise the essence of law [*jus*].
>
> Natural law includes the aggregate of rights and freedoms historically recognized by mankind as inalienably inherent in every person from birth. These rights and freedoms do not depend upon the will of the State and are not a gift on its part. On the contrary, the State is bound by these primary moral and reasonable imperatives and obliged to recognize, comply with, and guarantee them. …
>
> Marxism resolutely rejected natural law, suggesting that there cannot be a law [*jus*] generated by nature and reason and that there may be only one law in a State created by this very State. It is understandable

[2] See A. A. Rubanov, «Понятие источника права как проявление метафоричности юридического сознания» [Concept of Source of Law as a Manifestation of a Metaphor of Legal Consciousness], in Судебная практика как источник права [Judicial Practice as a Source of Law] (1997), p. 47.

that such an interpretation eliminated the barrier on the path to the creation of a totalitarian State with its system of denying freedom and of arbitrariness.

> In Russia the idea of natural rights found reflection in the Declaration of Human Rights and Freedoms (adopted 5 September 1991) which spoke of "natural, inalienable, and indestructible rights and freedoms". The 1993 Constitution (Article 17) establishes that man and his rights and freedoms are the highest value (Article 2). …
>
> In the present Constitution of the Russian Federation, for example, all the basic natural rights have been precisely consolidated (to life, inviolability of the person, private ownership, freedom of speech, and others). This means that positive law is increasingly merged with natural law. …
>
> Natural law must remain the basis of the legal consciousness of citizens, legislators, bureaucrats, and judges, invisibly present in the process of applying positive law. …
>
> A truth must be contained in the flesh and blood of people's life: if a law [*lex*] is contrary to natural law [*jus*], it is void.[3]

GENERAL PRINCIPLES OF LAW

Although the 1993 Russian Constitution makes reference in Article 15 to "general principles of international law", there is no specific mention of general principles of Russian law. The Civil Code of the Russian Federation does mention individual general principles of law, and Russian legal doctrine identifies general principles of law peculiar to individual branches of law:

> By principles of civil law are understood basic principles of the civil-law regulation of social relations. Principles of civil law permeate all civil legislation, reflecting its most material properties. Therefore, a proper understanding and application of norms of civil legislation is possible only by taking into account general principles of civil law.[4]

The Constitutional Court of the Russian Federation has referred to general principles of law from time to time, as have arbitrazh courts. In a Decree of 8 June 2010, the Constitutional Court of the Russian Federation, when verifying the constitutionality of Article 292(4) of the Civil Code regulating the rights of minor family members to alienate a dwelling

[3] M. V. Baglai, Конституционное право Российской Федерации [Constitutional Law of the Russian Federation] (13th ed.; 2018), pp. 31-33.

[4] See N. D. Egorov, in A. P. Sergeev and Iu. K. Tolstoi (eds.), Гражданское право. Учебник [Civil Law. Textbook] (4th ed.; M., 1999), p. 22.

premise with the authorization of a trusteeship and guardianship agency, concluded that such a transaction might not arbitrarily be prohibited:

> ,,, the right of trusteeship and guardianship agencies to arbitrarily prohibit transactions relating to the alienation of property of minor children concluded by their parents does not arise from Article 28(1) and Article 37(2) and (3) of the Civil Code of the Russian Federation; on the contrary, in accordance with general principles of law and the requirements of Articles 2, 17, and 38(2) of the Constitution of the Russian Federation, and as judicial practice shows, decisions of trusteeship and guardianship agencies ... are subject to evaluation by a court by proceeding from the concrete circumstances of the case.[5]

In another case involving the inclusion of disputed immoveable property on a List of property to be considered to be in the ownership of the Republic Crimea, a court was determined not to be confined to merely the formal circumstances of a case, but also should apply the applicable "general principles of law".[6] Citing what it considered to be analogous holdings of the Constitutional Court, the Ninth Arbitrazh Appellate Court on 4 December 2018 invoked the principle of *lex posterior derogat priori* as a general principle of law unless legislation established a different rule for determining priority.[7] The same Appellate Court on 28 January 2020 interpreted the application of Article 55 of the 1993 Russian Constitution to the introduction of responsibility in general and establishment of a concrete sanction limiting a constitutional right; such responsibility and the sanction must, "proceeding from general principles of law", meet the requirements of justice.[8]

SOVIET LAW

Legislation of the former Soviet Union continues to play a significant part, albeit declining, in Russian legal affairs. Its history in the development and application of Russian law is brief but complex. When the RSFSR declared its State sovereignty on 12 June 1990, the First Congress of People's Deputies of the RSFSR established the "supremacy of the RSFSR Constitution and laws of the RSFSR throughout the territory of the RSFSR; the operation of acts of the USSR which are contrary to the sovereign rights of the RSFSR shall be suspended by the Republic on its territory".[9] The date of the Declaration, 12 June 1990, thereafter became a benchmark when assessing the applicability

[5] Decree of Constitutional Court of the Russian Federation, 8 June 2010, No. 13-П.
[6] Decree of Constitutional Court of the Russian Federation, 7 November 2017, No. 26-П.
[7] Decree of the Ninth Arbitrazh Appellate Court, 4 December 2018, No. 09АП-56165/2018.
[8] Decree of the Ninth Arbitrazh Appellate Court, 28 January 2020, No. 09АП-78205/2019.
[9] Ведомости СНД и ВС РСФСР (1990), no. 2, item 22; transl. in W. E. Butler, *Basic Legal Documents of the Russian Federation* (1992), pp. 35-37.

of USSR legislation, and indeed has been declared a State holiday celebrated as Russia Day.

On 24 October 1990 the RSFSR adopted the Law on the Operation of Acts of Agencies of the USSR on the Territory of the RSFSR. This Law recognized the operation of laws and other acts of the highest agencies of State power of the USSR, edicts and other acts of the President of the USSR, acts of the Council of Ministers, and of ministries and departments of the USSR only insofar as they were adopted within the powers transferred by the Russian Federation to the USSR in accordance with the Declaration of Sovereignty of 12 June 1990 and certain other enactments. If USSR enactments met this test, they were of direct application on the territory of the RSFSR; if they violated the sovereignty of the Russian Federation, they were subject to suspension by the RSFSR Supreme Soviet or the RSFSR Council of Ministers. If the USSR enactments did not satisfy the criteria set out above, they entered into force in the Russian Federation only after their ratification by the RSFSR Supreme Soviet, RSFSR Council of Ministers, or empowered State agencies of the RSFSR respectively. Acts of agencies of the USSR issued before 24 October 1990 operated on the territory of the RSFSR insofar as they had not been suspended by the RSFSR Supreme Soviet or the RSFSR Council of Ministers.[10]

On 31 October 1990 the RSFSR required that any acts of agencies of State power and administration of the USSR connected with the seizure of material, financial, currency, monetary valuables, and other property belonging to citizens, labor collectives, social organizations, and other owners were not subject to execution on the territory of the RSFSR unless so provided by legislation of the RSFSR, pursuant to the Law on Ensuring the Economic Foundations of the Sovereignty of the RSFSR.[11] Enterprises and organizations situated on the territory of the RSFSR or effectuating activity on that territory, even if of Union subordination, were required to be guided by RSFSR legislation and apply USSR enactments in accordance with the Law of 24 October 1990.[12]

On 12 December 1991 the RSFSR ratified the Agreement on the Creation of the Commonwealth of Independent States, providing in point 2 of the Decree on ratification:

> For the purposes of creating conditions necessary for the realization of Article 11 of the said Agreement, to establish that the norms of the former USSR shall apply on the territory of the RSFSR until the adoption of respective legislative acts of the RSFSR in that part

[10] Ведомости СНД и ВС РФ (1990), no. 21, item 237; transl. in Butler, note 9 above, pp. 49-50.

[11] Ведомости РСФСР (1990), no. 22, item 260; transl. in Butler, note 9 above, pp. 45-47.

[12] See the Edict on Ensuring the Economic Foundations of the Sovereignty of the RSFSR, 20 August 1991. Ведомости СНД и ВС РСФСР (1991), no. 34, item 1140; transl. in Butler, note 9 above, pp. 41-43. This Edict is still in force.

which is not contrary to the Constitution of the RSFSR, legislation of the RSFSR, and the present Agreement.[13]

The Agreement itself contained a rather baffling formulation of Article 11: "From the moment of signature of the present Agreement, the application of the norms of third States on the territories of the States which have signed it, including the former USSR, shall not be permitted".[14] On one reading, at least, Article 11 of the Agreement would appear to take away that which earlier Russian legislation had permitted, and if that interpretation were correct, being embodied in an international treaty Article 11 would override inconsistent Russian legislation. In practice the formulation of the Decree on ratification of 12 December 1991 has been applied.

Taking all the foregoing enactments together, the accepted position is that USSR legislation may apply on the territory of the Russian Federation unless it has been expressly repealed or suspended, unless it is contrary to the Constitution of the Russian Federation and other Russian legislation adopted after 12 June 1990, or unless it has become obsolete.[15] In some instances special provision has been made for the continued operation of USSR legislation even though Russian enactments have been adopted. The 1991 Fundamental Principles of Civil Legislation of the USSR and Republics, for example, were enacted by the former Soviet Union to enter into force on 1 January 1992. Since the USSR had been dissolved before the date of their entry into force, they did not become legally binding, but were specially introduced into force as from 3 August 1992 by the Russian Federation[16] insofar as they were not contrary to the Constitution of the

[13] ВВС РФ (1991), no. 51, item 1798; transl. in Butler, note 9 above, p. 51. See generally P. P. Kremnev, Распад СССР: международно-правовые проблемы [Dissolution of the USSR: International-Legal Problems] (2005); Kremnev, Распад СССР и правопреемство государств [Dissolution of the USSR and Legal Succession of States] (2012); B. M. Lazarev, Можно ли было сохранить СССР (правовое исследование) [Could the USSR Have Been Preserved (Legal Study)] (2002); D. Lukashevich, Юридический механизм разрушения СССР [Legal Mechanism of Destruction of the USSR] (2016); A. N. Lebedev, Прекращение существования СССР (1985-1991 гг.) (государственно-правовое исследование) [Termination of the Existence of the USSR (1985-1991) (State-Legal Study)] (2017).

[14] Signed at Minsk, 8 December 1991; transl. in Butler, note 9 above, pp. 3-6.

[15] As of 3 September 2020, the portal inaugurated by the Ministry of Justice of the Russian Federation, "Normative Legal Acts in the Russian Federation" contained on one site more than eleven million legislative acts, both federal and regional, of which 36,155 dated from the Soviet period and were in force. In February 2020 the intention was announced to formally repeal and/or replace enactments from the Soviet period and cleanse the statute book from unnecessary or obsolete normative legal acts.

[16] See the Decree of the Supreme Soviet of the Russian Federation on the Regulation of Civil Law Relations in the Period of Conducting Economic Reform, adopted 14 July 1992, as amended. ВВС РФ (1992), no. 30, item 1800; (1993), no. 11, item 393; (1996), no. 5, item 411; lost force with effect from 1 January 2008 with the entry into force of Part Four of the Civil Code; and the Decree on Certain Questions of the Application of Legislation of the USSR on the Territory of the Russian Federation, adopted 3 March 1993. ВВС РФ (1993), no. 11, item 393. The last Decree has been amended numerous times to reflect the enactment of various

Russian Federation and legislative acts of the Russian Federation adopted after 12 June 1990. The 1964 RSFSR Civil Code finally lost force as from 1 January 2008, when Part Four of the 1994-2006 Civil Code entered into force.

The Family Code of the Russian Federation recognizes legal relations established under pre-revolutionary and Soviet legislation, as well as according to international treaties of the Russian Empire, irrespective of whether those treaties remain in force.

LEGISLATION

Constitution of Russian Federation

The Russian Federation is founded on the principle of popular sovereignty. The 1993 Russian Constitution proclaims (Article 3) that the sole source of power is the multinational people of Russia. They exercise their power directly, by way of referendum, and through agencies of State power and agencies of local self-government. State power, in turn, is effectuated on the basis of separation into legislative, executive, and judicial powers (Article 10, Constitution). These principles are the antithesis of the late Soviet constitutional system, which emphatically rejected the checks and balances associated with western liberal approaches to separation of powers and its delegation of power to non-representative organs. "All power to the Soviets" had been one of the hallmarks of the 1917 October Revolution.

The Constitution of Russia, adopted by an all-people's vote on 12 December 1993, is by reason of the method of its enactment and of its substance the highest source of man-made law in the Russian Federation. The Constitution has "the highest legal force, direct effect", and other legal acts must not be contrary to the Constitution; all agencies of State power, local self-government, officials, citizens, and their associations must comply with the Constitution. In order to preserve the special stature of the Constitution *vis-à-vis* other types of legislation, Articles 1 to 16 (Chapter 1) are characterized as the "foundations of the constitutional system" and may not be changed except in the procedure established by the Constitution. Chapter 1 accordingly occupies a special place even within the Constitution itself, reflected in the formulation of Article 16(2) stipulating that no other provisions of the Constitution may be contrary to that Chapter.

The Constitution being the highest law, all other enactments are subordinate [подзаконный, literally, sub-law] legislation (note that the expression "delegated legislation" is avoided, for subordinate acts may be issued without delegation so long as they are "on the basis and in execution of" the acts of superior agencies or agencies at the same level as the issuing

Russian codes and remains in force as amended 18 December 2006. СЗ РФ (2006), no. 52(I), item 5497.

organ). This novel concept sits uneasily with the terminological legacy of pre-revolutionary Russia and the Soviet Union, for never before in Russian history has a constitution been placed above monarch and State.[17] In the Russian psyche, the Federal Assembly remains the source of *lex* [закон], the President as Head of State the source of edict [указ], and the government the source of decree [постановление]. The language of the sources of law lags behind the realities of the hierarchy embodied in the 1993 Constitution.

Although legislation is the paramount source of law in the Russian Federation, hierarchical relationships among subordinate acts containing legal rules (normative) are confused and confusing, a situation aggravated by the inconsistent and extensive use of more than 40 denominations for enactments.

Federal Assembly

Primacy of place is given to the constitution [конституция], of which there exist the Constitution of the Russian Federation and the constitutions of the 22 republics within Russia. The right to adopt laws [закон] remains with the legislative branch of the State, including at the Federation level, the Federal Assembly, and the respective legislative bodies of the republics within the Russian Federation, down to and including the legislative branch of the Cities of Moscow, Sevastopol, and St. Petersburg. A law also may be adopted by way of referendum.

The Constitution of Russia draws a distinction between two types of laws: federal constitutional laws and federal laws. A qualified majority is required to adopt the first, and a simple majority, the second. Amongst enactments which must take the form of a federal constitutional law are the laws on the Constitutional Court, the Supreme Court, and the judicial system. In the hierarchy of sources of law, federal constitutional laws are superior to federal laws.

In addition, the chambers of the Federal Assembly may adopt decrees [постановление] relegated specifically to their respective jurisdiction. The Soviet of the Federation adopts decrees to appoint judges of the Constitutional Court, Supreme Court, and others. The State Duma declares an amnesty or appoints the Chairman of the Central Bank by way of decree (see Articles 102, 103, Constitution). The Reglament (yet another type of normative act) of the State Duma provides that the decree shall be used for certain internal matters, for example, the disposition of draft laws after a first or second reading.[18]

[17] On the various constitutional projects in Russia, mostly directed towards establishing some form of constitutional monarchy, see V. A. Tomsinov, Конституционный вопрос в России в 60-х – начале 80-х годов XIX века [The Constitutional Question in Russia in the 1860s-Early 1880s] (2013).

[18] See, e.g., Article 93, Reglament of the State Duma of the Federal Assembly of the Russian

Finally, the Federal Assembly confirms, by way of federal laws, other normative acts: statute [положение], code [кодекс], and fundamental principles [основы]; from time to time the Federal Assembly may adopt an appeal [обращение], declaration [декларация], statement [заявление], resolution [резолюция], or message [послание] for transmission to other governments, parliaments, or peoples, especially in the domain of foreign policy. The Supreme Soviet of the Russian Federation used the form of the "Declaration" on 12 June 1990 to declare State sovereignty and once more on 25 October 1991 to regulate the languages of the peoples of Russia.

In quantitative terms the law-making activity of the Federal Assembly has changed beyond recognition in comparison with the parliaments of the Soviet era. Working in session from eight to ten months annually, the Federal Assembly has been generating hundreds of laws and thousands of decrees each year.

President of Russian Federation

The President of the Russian Federation issues enactments in the form of an edict [указ] and regulation [распоряжение] (Article 90, Constitution), which must not be contrary to either the Constitution or to federal laws. Both are a form of subordinate legislation, and the Constitution does not specify which type of act should be used for what purpose. Edicts in practice are used for the most important Presidential enactments; regulations for, as a rule, non-normative enactments addressed to individual administrative matters.

There exists a certain tension between the stature of federal laws and edicts, partly linked to the inherent rivalry of branches of State power and partly to ambiguities in the precise demarcation of legislative and presidential power.[19] In the period leading up to the adoption of the 1993 Constitution of Russia and following the attempted displacement of Presidential power in September 1993, edicts were used as a surrogate for laws in the absence of parliamentary authority. In the early days of radical economic reform, the Supreme Soviet of the RSFSR conferred additional powers on the President of the RSFSR by virtue of which the President could issue edicts which were contrary to and therefore could alter the operation of laws of the RSFSR. The additional powers were exercised principally in the domains of banking, stock exchange, currency control, foreign economic, investment, and customs activities, the budget, price formation, taxation, ownership, land reform, and employment. The Civil Code of the Russian Federation

Federation; transl. in W. E. Butler, *Russian Public Law* (3d ed.; 2013), pp. 275-384.

[19] Some Russian jurists and judges believe that President Eltsyn greatly abused the power to issue edicts on subject matter that should have been dealt with only by laws. See V. O. Luchin and A. V. Mazurov, "Presidential Edicts in Russia: General Characteristics", *Sudebnik*, V (2000), pp. 55-97. There has been no criticism of the Putin and Medvedev Administrations on this score.

goes to some lengths in an attempt to prevent presidential edicts from introducing rules departing from the Code. It follows from the separation of powers, however, that within their domain of competence edicts of the President enjoy the same stature as sources of law as do the enactments of the legislative branch of the State – a view reinforced by the absence in the Constitution of a formulation requiring that edicts be issued "on the basis of and in execution of" laws.

The Procedure for the Preparation and Submission of Draft Edicts and Regulations of the President of the Russian Federation, confirmed by Regulation of the President of the Russian Federation of 5 February 1993, as amended,[20] regulates the drafting of presidential enactments. Ordinarily a draft edict or regulation is circulated within the Government and Administration of the President for agreement and then referred for legal expert evaluation to the State Law Administration of the President of Russia, next to the Chancellery of the President for agreement with the respective aide of the President. After this process is completed, the draft is submitted directly to the Head of the Chancellery, who passes the draft to the Director of the Administration of the President.

The decision to submit a draft edict or regulation to the President for signature is taken by the Director of the Administration of the President of the Russian Federation. Edicts, regulations, and laws are signed by the President in his own hand; only exceptionally is a facsimile signature used, and then only with the personal authorization of the President himself (the facsimile is kept by the Head of the Chancellery of the President).[21] The failure to comply with this procedure for agreement and legal expert evaluation means that, if the President signs the document, it is issued only after the express instruction of the President to the Director of the Presidential Administration or Head of the Chancellery.

Government of Russian Federation

Executive power in the Russian Federation is the responsibility of the Government, which "on the basis of and in execution of" the Constitution, federal laws, edicts, regulations, and assignments of the President, issues enactments in the form of a decree [постановление] or regulation [распоряжение]. As a rule, decrees are normative, and regulations treat routine administrative matters. In practice the Government of Russia follows patterns of the past in enacting new legal rules which are within its jurisdiction and not contrary to law or edict. However, if decrees and regulations fail to conform to the Constitution, federal laws, or edicts and

[20] СЗ РФ (1996), no. 33, item 3982; the current text as amended 12 January 2010 appears in the legal database Consultant Plus.

[21] See M. V. Baglai, Конституционное право Российской Федерации [Constitutional Law of the Russian Federation] (13th ed.; 2018), pp. 505-506.

regulations of the President, the President of the Russian Federation has the power to repeal them (Article 115, Constitution). The Government has the right to adopt appeals, statements, and other acts not having a legal character,[22] and occasionally does so.

The procedure for the submission, preparation, and consideration of draft enactments by the Government is enormously complex and regulated in detail by the Reglament of the Government of the Russian Federation, confirmed by Decree of the Government of 1 June 2004, as amended.[23] Decrees and regulations of the Government are binding throughout the Russian Federation without further confirmation by the Federal Assembly or President and without further action by subjects of the Russian Federation. Thousands are issued each year. However, their importance within the general fabric of legislation has diminished because of the substantial volume of law-making undertaken by the Federal Assembly and the President.

Acts of the Government are superior to all others adopted by agencies of State administration and, paradoxically perhaps, even many decisions of subjects of the Russian Federation.

Ministries and departments

The names of enactments of ministries, State committees, and other departments and of ministers and similar officials are no longer a matter of constitutional regulation. In practice the denominations of ministry and ministerial enactments are determined by the statutes on the ministries or State committees, and the terminology of the past largely survives. The acts of ministries and State committees are sometimes called decrees, instructions, instructive regulations, and others. Ministers issue, as a rule, an order [приказ] or confirm an instruction [инструкция].

Russian Federation ministries and officials are empowered to issue, and frequently do, joint instructions and other normative acts. These acquire no greater force in the hierarchy of normative acts by reason of their joint issuance. The difference between an instruction [инструкция] and an instructional directive [указание] is unclear in theory and practice, except that one rarely encounters a joint instructional directive. As for orders and instructions, the first may be normative or non-normative, whereas the last are always normative because they elaborate a particular law, edict, or governmental decree. In recent years State agencies have confirmed various types of "administrative reglament" [административный регламент] in large quantities.

22 Article 23, Federal Constitutional Law on the Government of the Russian Federation, 17 December 1997, as amended. СЗ РФ (1997), no. 51, item 5712, as amended; transl. in Butler, *Russia & The Republics* (2006-).

23 СЗ РФ (2004), no 23, item 2313, as amended; transl. in Butler, note 18 above.

Other State agencies or officials occupying equivalent positions within the State system as ministries or federal services or ministers or heads of federal services promulgate enactments. These are sometimes designated as orders or instructions, but may bear other appellations. The Central Bank of the Russian Federation, for example, may issue an instruction or letter [письмо]. Ministries, federal services, and departments sometimes issue rules [правила] or a *nastavlenie* [наставление], which may extend to institutions and personnel or their own particular system or may be binding generally. In the latter case they are normative.

Subjects of the Federation

The constitutions of republics within the Russian Federation and the charters and other legislation governing the other subjects of the Federation contain analogous terminology with respect to normative acts and are, for the most part, also analogous in their internal State structures. They are required to comply with normative acts issued by Federal agencies within their jurisdiction. On 10 August 2000 the President of the Russian Federation introduced additional measures to ensure the unity of legal space of the Russian Federation, among which was the establishment of the Federal Register of Normative Legal Acts of Subjects of the Russian Federation to be maintained by the Ministry of Justice. The heads of the highest executive agencies of State power in the subjects of the Federation are required to send copies of normative legal acts within a 7-day period after their adoption and the official publications in which these acts are published for inclusion in the Register and so that legal expert evaluation can be undertaken to determine whether they are consistent with federal normative legal acts; electronic forms of the enactments are acceptable for this purpose.[24]

The Statute on the Procedure for Keeping the Federal Register of Normative Legal Acts of Subjects of the Russian Federation was confirmed by Decree of the Government of the Russian Federation of 29 November 2000, as amended.[25] The Federal Register includes the constitutions or charters of each subject, laws and other normative legal acts of agencies of legislative or representative power of subjects of the Federation, normative legal acts of the highest officials of subjects of the Federation, agencies of executive power of subjects of the Federation (including State councils, governments, cabinets of ministers, administrations, mayorates, ministries, and others) which affect the rights, freedoms, and duties of man and citizen, establish the legal status of organizations, or have an interdepartmental character. If as a result of legal evaluation undertaken by the Russian Ministry of Justice it is determined that the acts in whole or in part do not conform to the Constitution or a federal law, the expert opinions of

[24] СЗ РФ (2000), no 33, item 3345, as amended.

[25] СЗ РФ (2000), no 49, item 4826, as amended.

the Ministry of Justice are included in the federal register as additional information. The Federal Register includes a State registration number for each normative legal act, an indication of the type of act and name of the agency which adopted it, date of adoption or signature, and the number and heading thereof, the sources of official publication, the texts of the acts, and additional information, a list of which is determined by the Ministry of Justice. Access to such enactments and materials is available through the Internet portal of the Ministry of Justice of the Russian Federation.

By an Order of 20 August 2013, the Ministry of Justice confirmed and introduced into operation the "Explanations With Regard to the Application of the Statute on the Procedure for Keeping the Federal Register of Normative Legal Acts of Subjects of the Russian Federation". The Register is maintained in electronic and documentary forms.[26] The Procedure for the Provision of Information Contained in the Federal Register of Normative Legal Acts of Subjects of the Russian Federation was confirmed by Order of the Ministry of Justice on 20 December 2005, as amended, and entered into force from 27 January 2006;[27] the Procedure was replaced on 13 July 2018 by Order No. 150 of the Ministry of Justice.[28]

Local self-government

Agencies of "local self-government", which bear different names in different municipalities although the term "soviet" is still widely used, adopt decisions within the limits of the powers granted to them by legislation of the Russian Federation. In the City of Moscow an entirely new terminology has accompanied the creation of new urban structures. The Moscow City Duma adopts laws, the Mayorate, decrees, and the Mayor, decisions.

Other appellations for acts do arise in the practice of local self-government. A decision [решение] frequently confirms a statute [положение], provisional statute [временное положение], or model statute [примерное положение] of regulatory agencies attached to local government. Many local soviets have enacted reglaments to govern their own internal procedures.

Some decisions of local self-government concern matters within their exclusive jurisdiction, in which event the enactment is an act independently operative within the territorial jurisdiction of the local soviet. The decision must conform to enactments of superior subjects of the Federation and to superior agencies of federal power and administration. Other decisions are adopted on the basis of and in execution of acts of superior bodies.

26 Российская газета [Russian Newspaper], no. 202 (11 September 2013). Available on Consultant Plus.

27 БНА РФ, no. 3 (2006).

28 Available on Consultant Plus.

The acts of local self-government executive committees and of their departments, sections, and administrations are in all instances issued on the basis of and in execution of acts of superior agencies. Such acts may contain normative prescriptions, and the same is true of orders and regulations issued by the heads of departments and administrations of local self-government executive committees.

TREATIES OF THE FEDERATION

On 31 March 1992 the Russian Federation concluded a series of three treaties, collectively known as the Treaty of the Federation, as a step towards drafting a new Constitution of the Russian Federation. These documents delimit the subjects of jurisdiction and powers between federal agencies of State power and the agencies of power of the various subjects of the Federation and are expressly referred to in Section Two, Concluding and Transitional Provisions, of the 1993 Russian Constitution.[29] Thereafter the Russian Federation quietly concluded a series of bilateral treaties with individual subjects of the Federation on a vast scale. Five treaties and agreements with Tatarstan, for example, addressed banking, currency, oil refining, foreign economic relations, ownership, and related issues. The Republic Sakha concluded more than 15 treaties and agreements with the Russian Federation. Vitebsk Region in Belarus and Tver Region in Russia concluded a Treaty on Cooperation of 16 July 1997.[30] Since nearly all the subjects of the Federation followed this practice, nearly a thousand such treaties and agreements were in place. Beginning in November 2001, large numbers of these treaties were terminated by mutual agreement.

The texts of these treaties were not gazetted at the federal level, although some appeared as unnumbered annexes in the C3 PФ. Russian doctrine is unanimous that they are not "international treaties" of the Russian Federation. Their substance differs one from the other so that in reality the shared jurisdiction between the Federation and an individual subject of the Federation may vary considerably from that of others. Moreover, some subjects of the Federal concluded agreements between themselves without including the Russian Federation as a party.[31]

Russian doctrine is reticent on the subject of placing these internal documents in the hierarchy of sources of law. Depending upon their subject matter, they may be a source of rules of particular branches of law. There is a compelling argument that such treaties and agreements may override inconsistent provisions of federal laws. Since, however, the Federal

[29] The treaties are transl. in Butler, note 8 above, pp. 686-699.

[30] Российская газета [Russian Newspaper], 16 August 1997. The treaty is still in force.

[31] On 15 January 2020 the Republic Crimea and the City of Sevastopol concluded an Agreement clarifying and confirming the boundary between these subjects of the Russian Federation. For the text of the Agreement, see Butler, note 22 above.

Assembly is not as a rule involved in their conclusion or termination, there are conceptual problems with this view.

The pace of domestic treaty-making slowed after 20 May 2003.[32] Efforts were made to bring order to the process of concluding such treaties and agreements by the enactment on 24 June 1999 of the Federal Law on the Principles and Procedure for Delimitation of Subjects of Jurisdiction and Powers Between Agencies of State Power of the Russian Federation and Agencies of State Power of Subjects of the Russian Federation.[33] In a federal law of 4 July 2003 the decision was taken to phase out all remaining treaties on the delimitation of subjects of jurisdiction between federal agencies of State power and agencies of State power of subjects of the Federation. It was provided that any such treaties in force were subject to confirmation by a federal law within two years, and in the case of agreements concerning the transfer of the effectuation of powers, subject to confirmation by a decree of the Government of the Russian Federation within two years. Any treaties and agreements not so confirmed would terminate their operation upon the expiry of the two-year period, that is, as from 8 July 2005.

Treaty-making between subjects of the Russian Federation, however, continued. On 26 September 2018 the Republic Ingushetia and the Republic Chechnya signed the Agreement on the Establishment of the Boundary between the Republic Ingushetia and Chechen Republic. On 4 October 2018 the Republic Ingushetia adopted a Law to confirm the Agreement; the Law entered into force on 16 October 2018. On 30 October 2018 the Constitutional Court of Ingushetia adopted a Decree determining that adoption of the Law confirming the Agreement was contrary to the Constitution of Ingushetia because a referendum was not held to obtain the consent of the electorate to a change in the boundaries of the Republic. In a Decree of 6 December 2018, the Constitutional Court of the Russian Federation held that the Law of Ingushetia confirming the Agreement was not contrary to the 1993 Russian Constitution.[34]

[32] This is the date of the last treaty included in the Consultant Plus legal database, a Treaty between the Russian Federation and Murmansk Region to terminate the Treaty on the Delimitation of Subjects of Jurisdiction and Powers Between Agencies of State Power of the Russian Federation and Agencies of State Power of Murmansk Region, signed 30 October 1997. The 2003 treaty on termination entered into force on the day of official publication, 24 May 2003, in accordance with its provisions. Although the great majority of treaties have been terminated, it should be noted that termination also occurs by way of treaty, so that a significant number of treaties remain in force between the Federation and subjects of the Federation.

[33] СЗ РФ (1999), no. 26, item 3176. This Federal Law lost force on 8 July 2003.

[34] СЗ РФ (2018), no. 51, item 8095.

JUDICIAL AND ARBITRATION PRACTICE

The Heritage

The role of judicial practice in Russia prior to the nineteenth century has not been systematically investigated.[35] The Ruling Senate played an active role in deciding individual cases and in issuing various forms of guidance to Russian courts and judges. Its decisions were routinely incorporated into Russian commentaries on individual legislative acts and the Digest of Laws of the Russian Empire as a whole: "The rulings of the high court were widely known, specially among judicial personnel and legal practitioners ... in the wake of judicial reform there emerged a juridical infrastructure that granted the courts ... unprecedented influence over the development of imperial law".[36] The judiciary reforms of 1864 enhanced the position of the Ruling Senate and opened a dialogue in Russian legal doctrine that continues to echo in contemporary writings; among the protagonists were the civilists E. V. Vaskovskii (1866-1942), S. A. Muromtsev (1850-1910), and G. F. Shershenevich (1863-1912).

The introduction of "checks and balances" into the Russian constitutional order has contributed to a reappraisal of the role of judicial practice as a source of Russian law. During the Soviet era, the objections raised against the doctrine of "precedent" were several: it would diminish the role of legislation; it would give scope for judicial arbitrariness; it would encourage a mechanical concentration on analogous elements in cases to the detriment of their individual distinguishing features. In fact, judicial practice was not ignored in the Soviet legal system and at various periods of Soviet legal history played a creative and unusual role in the development of law.[37] Many appellate court rulings and judgments were reported in supreme court bulletins and other law journals. Practitioners routinely kept or made special card indexes containing the case headnotes of reported cases so that lawyers could review relevant judicial practice with respect to each article of the laws or codes concerned. Procurators, judges, investigators, advokats, and jurisconsults were counseled to read case reports in order

[35] But see K. V. Petrov, «'Прецедент' в средневековом русском праве (XVI-XVII вв.)» ['Precedent' in Mediaeval Russian Law (XVI-XVII Centuries)], Государство и право [State and Law], no. 4 (2005), pp. 78-83.

[36] See W. G. Wagner, "Civil Law in Late Imperial Russia", in P. H. Solomon (ed.), *Reforming Justice in Russia, 1964-1996: Power, Culture, and the Limits of Legal Order* (1997), p. 33. This article builds upon Wagner's magisterial study, *Marriage, Property and Law in Late Imperial Russia* (1994).

[37] "The actual existence of judicial precedent even in Soviet judicial practice cannot be denied since only on the basis thereof (at the initiative of the court which rendered a respective decision) and without a change of the 'letter' of a criminal law at times judicial practice seriously changed". A. V. Naumov, Российское уголовное право. Курс лекций [Russian Criminal Law. Course of Lectures] (3rd ed., 2004), I, p. 143.

to familiarize themselves with errors which higher courts rectify when reviewing judgments.

An Index to published judicial practice for the period 1938 to 1969 cautioned users against regarding "rulings and decrees of superior courts as a standard or model for deciding other analogous cases. This would be recognition of the practice of 'judicial precedent'".[38] In practice Soviet courts were required to fill "gaps" in the law, notably the legal rules governing obligations arising out of the causing of harm (delict, or tort, to the Anglo-American lawyer). The law of necessary defense and the duty to rescue owed much to judicial decisions and to guiding explanations of the Plenum of the USSR Supreme Court.[39]

Contemporary approaches

At one level the Russian Federation inherited entirely the legacy of the debate over judge-made law by the USSR and RSFSR supreme courts for the simple reason that the "guiding explanations" issued by those courts remain in force except insofar as repealed, suspended, or changed by the Supreme Court of the Russian Federation. Although for the most part these "explanations" interpret rather than create legal norms, the line is no less difficult to draw in Russian law than in other legal systems; many Russian jurists believe that in some instances the Plenum of the Russian Supreme Court has stepped across the line into law-creation. Normative acts in the form of explanations of the Plenum of the Supreme Court, and, when it existed, of the Supreme Arbitrazh Court, are binding upon all lower courts and therefore upon all who appear before those courts. Such explanations continue to be published cumulatively in book form and are repealed and amended as required.[40] The authority for giving such explanations is the 1993 Russian Constitution (Articles 126 and 127).

The position taken by Soviet jurists, it should be noted, was a doctrinal position. There was no rule of Soviet law which rejected judicial precedent. As a meeting held in April 1997 by the Institute of State and Law of the Russian Academy of Sciences and attended by senior representatives from the entire Russian legal profession, the doctrinal position regarding judicial practice as a source of law was re-examined and revised. One rapporteur declared: "In modern reality the decision in a specific case also may be a source [of

38 See S. V. Borodin (ed.), Вопросы уголовного права и процесса в практике верховных судов СССР и РСФСР (1938-1969) [Questions of Criminal Law and Procedure in the Practice of the Supreme Courts of the USSR and RSFSR (1938-1969)] (2nd ed., 1971), p. 5.

39 See W. E. Butler, "Judicial Precedent as a Source of Russian Law", in J. A. R. Nafziger and S. C. Symeonides (eds.), *Law and Justice in a Multistate World. Essays in Honor of Arthur T. von Mehren* (2002).

40 See, for example, V. M. Lebedev (ed.), Сборник постановлений Пленума Верховного Суда Российской Федерации 1967-2007 [Collection of Decrees of Plenum of Supreme Court of Russian Federation 1967-2007] (2008).

law]".[41] The reasons for the change in Russian legal doctrine were several: one was the new and central role of Russian courts in verifying the legality of normative acts. If such acts are found to be illegal or unconstitutional, those acts are vacated by the courts, which action "gives rise to new rights and duties of the participants of social relations, so that in essence such a decision is more norm-creative ... A judicial decision to vacate a particular normative act proves to be a source of law [jus]".[42] Another is the role of individual judicial decisions, when construing provisions of legislation, in changing "prevailing law". Judicial decisions also fill in gaps in the law and clarify the substance of legal norms otherwise ambiguous. It is accepted that only published judicial decisions can have precedential value, but the expansion of computer-based legal databases for home use has made judicial practice accessible on an unprecedented scale.

That "precedent" is an integral component of modern Russian law is contested by few. In a path-breaking study a Russian jurist has identified four categories of precedents in Russian law: (1) precedents of interpretation and gap-filling; (2) precedents arising out of judicial review; (3) precedents of discretion; and (4) law-finding precedents.[43] Precedents of interpretation are considered to be most common, although gap-filling is encountered with some frequency. Instances are known even from the Soviet era when the injustice of a result persuaded the court to find flexibility in legal rules.[44] Precedents of judicial review have been encountered in practice and seem to be expanding through the jurisprudence of the Constitutional Court. The exercise of judicial discretion is not binding as a precedent, but examples are sometimes publicized in the judicial media for other courts to be aware of. The finding of law by a court is believed to occur rarely. Rules enforced by courts which are not found either in primary or subordinate normative

[41] R. Z. Livshits, "Judicial Practice as a Source of Law in Russia", *Sudebnik* II (1997), p. 632. The issue also was debated by those who participated in the Conference charged with preparing the draft 1993 Russian Constitution, particularly with respect to guiding explanations. See the various volumes of Конституционное совещание. Стенограммы. Материалы. Документы 29 апреля-10 ноября 1993 г. [Constitutional Conference. Verbatim Transcripts. Materials. Documents. 29 April-10 November 1993] (1995). 20 vols.

[42] Livshits, note 41 above, p. 629. On the other hand, many Russian jurists believe the position with respect to precedent remains unresolved. See T. T. Aliev, «Механизмы прецедентного правового регулирования в Российской Федерации» [Mechanisms of Precedential Legal Regulation in the Russian Federation], Современное право [Contemporary Law], no. 1 (2018), pp. 75-80.

[43] A. Vereshchagin, *Judicial Law-Making in Post-Soviet Russia* (2007), p. 117. Another Russian jurist has written: "Officially ... [judicial precedents] are not recognized as a source of law in Russia. However, elements of precedent have actually been a part of Russian judicial activity for a long time ...". See S. Marochkin, "The Russian Federation", in A. Reinisch (ed.), *The Privileges and Immunities of International Organizations in Domestic Courts* (2014), p. 223.

[44] Examples are cited in A. Fedotov, «Возможно ли применение contra legum в демократическом правовом государстве» [Is the Application of Contra Legum Possible in a Democratic Rule-of-Law State], Журнал российского права [Journal of Russian Law], no. 8 (2002), pp. 92-99.

legal acts or in decrees or decisions of the highest courts of the judicial system have encouraged "the formation of a ... peculiar form of judge-made law as judicial custom (or 'usage')".[45]

Constitutional Court of Russian Federation. Evidence is accumulating that the Constitutional Court of the Russian Federation expects its previous decisions to be followed as *stare decisis*. It has on several occasions indicated that legal positions taken in previous decisions, decrees, rulings, and the like are to be treated as resolved as a matter of law unless and until the Court is persuaded to change them. In a Ruling of 7 December 2001 concerning the right of a defense counsel and a person under investigation to have an interpreter present without the investigator himself being privy to their conversation, for example, the Constitutional Court said:

> From the legal position set out by the Constitutional Court of the Russian Federation in a Decree of 25 October 2001 with regard to the case concerning the verification of the constitutionality of provisions contained in Articles 47 and 51 of the RSFSR Code of Criminal Procedure and Article 16, paragraph two, point (15) of the Federal Law 'On Confinement Under Guard of Suspects and Persons Accused of the Commission of a Crime' it follows that the fulfillment by an advocate having the order of a legal consultation office to conduct a criminal case of the procedural duties of a defender may not be made dependent upon the discretion of an official under whose proceedings the criminal case is situated based on circumstances not enumerated in criminal procedure law limiting the possibility of effectuating the powers of defense. Construing Article 17(4) and (5) and Article 18 of the Federal Law on Confinement Under Guard of Suspects and Persons Accused of the Commission of a Crime as enabling access of an interpreter to a meeting with the defender of an accused under guard who does not possess the language of the court proceeding to be refused is, in essence, contrary to criminal procedure law.[46]

Courts of general jurisdiction. The existence of guiding explanations issued by the Plenum of the Supreme Court of the Russian Federation has been regarded by some Russian jurists as a constraint upon the independence of judges. The legality of provisions of guiding explanations is not subject to review by the highest Russian courts. They do have normative effect and, notwithstanding doctrinal assertions to the contrary, are not confined merely to the application of legal rules or act purely as instructions or guidance to judges. Their status has been rightly characterized as a "grey zone" of uncertainty.[47]

45 Vereschchagin, note 43 above, pp. 117-121, 126-129.

46 See the Case of L. S. Islamov. C3 PФ (2002), no. 7, item 743.

47 Vereschchagin, note 43 above, p. 109.

The role of judicial practice in the criminal law has been singled out. Naumov observed that "one cannot do without judicial practice when classifying crimes … the criminal law is augmented by real content only through judicial practice in respect of concrete cases. Each new judicial decision enlarges … or narrows the law enforcer's concept of the content of a criminal-law norm".[48]

The classic position of the Soviet era, however, still commands support in some doctrinal writings, even with regard to the explanations of courts: "… it is considered that for all their significance neither judicial precedents nor decrees of the Plenums of the Supreme Court … of the Russian Federation may be regarded as sources of civil law. Judicial institutions do not possess norm-creative functions; they do not create norms of law, but merely interpret and apply them".[49]

Arbitrazh courts. Although arbitrazh courts no longer exist as a distinct system of courts and from 2014 were merged into the courts of general jurisdiction, the approach of the arbitrazh courts in their time probably influenced their ultimate demise. The arbitrazh courts were regarded as more manageable than the courts of general jurisdiction, and the arbitrazh judges were considered on average to possess better legal skills than judges of the general courts.[50] In the popular legal mind, at least, "the fact of the existence of judicial precedents in Russia was denied by arbitrazh courts".[51] Official recognition and strengthening of the precedential character of the decisions of the highest arbitrazh courts was considered to have transpired with the adoption by the Plenum of the Supreme Arbitrazh Court of Decree No. 17 on 14 February 2008 amending an earlier Decree issued by the same body on 12 March 2007 concerning the application of the Code of Arbitrazh Procedure when reviewing judicial acts which had entered into force with regard to newly-discovered circumstances. The Plenum in essence determined that the review of judicial acts when the possibility of review by way of supervision has been lost by reason of the expiry of the period of limitations is now impossible. One reason for introducing this position was to reduce the opportunities for destabilization of the positions of the parties when a significant lapse of time had occurred. The reform was calculated to

[48] Naumov, note 37 above, I, p. 144.

[49] V. V. Dolinskaia, in A. G. Kalpin and A. I. Masliaev (eds.), Гражданское право [*Civil Law*] (1997), I, 38; the author takes the same view in V. P. Mozolin and A. I. Masliaev (eds), Гражданское право [*Civil Law*] (2007), I, p. 56. By 2009 the same writer was more guarded and noted that the "discussion continued" as to whether judicial practice could be regarded as a source of law. See V. P. Mozolin and A. I. Masliaev (eds.), *Russian Civil and Commercial Law*, transl. W. E. Butler (2009), I, p. 36.

[50] Vereshchagin, note 43 above, p. 233.

[51] V. Zaripov, «Сила прецедента» [Force of Precedent], *Эж-юрист* [Weekly Jurist], no. 7 (February 2008), p. 1.

reduce the case load of the Supreme Arbitrazh Court and improve judicial efficiency.[52]

Arbitration courts. It has not been suggested that published arbitration awards by Russian arbitral tribunals have the value of precedent or even significance for the Russian legal system generally. To a greater extent perhaps than most other countries, however, Russian arbitral tribunals often do publish awards in the legal media or, in the case of the Russian Court of International Commercial Arbitration, in the form of commentaries or collections of awards. At a minimum these collections are invaluable guides to the reasoning of the arbitrators when applying the applicable law to disputes before them and may be said to represent a repertoire of arbitral practice in the Russian Federation. At a maximum Soviet and Russian arbitral awards in a few celebrated instances are considered to have influenced the development of the law of international arbitration (Lena Goldfields; Jordan Investments Ltd; JOC Oil).[53]

European Court of Human Rights. On 30 March 1998 the Russian Federation ratified the Convention for the Protection of Human Rights and Fundamental Freedoms, with the changes in the Convention made by Protocols 3 (6 May 1963), 5 (20 January 1966), and 8 (19 March 1985) and additions contained in Protocol No 2 (6 May 1963) and Protocols thereto Nos. 1 (20 March 1952), 4 (16 September 1963), 7 (22 November 1984), 9 (6 November 1990), 10 (25 March 1992), and 11 (11 May 1994). The Convention became binding upon Russia from 5 May 1998.

Russian jurists are preoccupied with the issue of the extent to which, if at all, the jurisprudence and judicial practice of the European Court on Human Rights (hereinafter: ECHR) may be binding upon the Russian Federation and may be a source of law in Russia. The Federal Law on the ratification of the 1950 European Convention provides: "The Russian Federation in accordance with Article 46 of the Convention recognizes *ipso facto* and without special agreement as binding with regard to questions of interpretation and application the Convention and Protocols Thereto in instances of a supposed violation by the Russian Federation of the provisions of these treaty acts when the supposed violation occurred after their entry into force with respect to the Russian Federation".[54] It is

[52] For a discussion of these events, see Aliev, note 42 above.

[53] V. V. Veeder, "1922: The Birth of the ICC Arbitration Clause and the Demise of the Anglo-Soviet Urquhart Concession", in *Global Reflections on International Law, Commerce and Dispute Resolution: Liber Amicorum in Honour of Robert Briner* (2005), pp. 881-901; Veeder, "Lloyd George, Lenin and Cannibals: The Harriman Arbitration", *Arbitration International,* XVI (2000), pp. 115-139; id, "The Lena Goldfields Arbitration: The Historical Roots of Three Ideas", *International and Comparative Law Quarterly,* XLVII (1998), pp. 747-792. Extracts from all three appear in T. E. Carbonneau, W. E. Butler, and H A. Blair, *International Litigation and Arbitration: Cases and Materials* (3d ed.; 2020), pp. 725-739.

[54] C3 PФ (1998), no 14, item 1514.

undoubted in Russian doctrine that the Russian Federation is bound by virtue of this language to comply with decisions of the ECHR concerning cases in which Russia is a party. This follows as a treaty obligation under the 1950 European Convention, and by virtue of Article 15(4) of the 1993 Russian Constitution the provisions of the said Convention are an integral part of the Russian legal system.

A number of residual issues remain, however. When acceding to the 1950 European Convention, did Russia also become bound by the jurisprudence and decisions of the ECHR which preceded Russian accession and is Russia bound by the decisions of the ECHR in cases that do not concern Russia as a party? Irrespective of whether the answer to the preceding questions is affirmative or negative, do decisions of the ECHR constitute a form of judicial precedent that is binding upon Russia and, indeed, part of the Russian legal system.

The Supreme Court of the Russian Federation has instructed the courts of general jurisdiction that "the application by courts of the ... Convention must be effectuated by taking into account the practice of the European Court for Human Rights in avoidance of any violation of the Convention on the Protection of Human Rights and Fundamental Freedoms".[55] No limitation is placed upon what "practice" of the ECHR should be considered. However, some Russian jurists doubt that such "practice" has the value of judicial precedent: "... one of the necessary indicia, properties, of a judicial precedent as a source of law is that such precedent (or decision of a court) should contain a legal norm, that is, generally-binding rule of behavior ensured by the compulsory power of the State (if we speak of national legal norms). Can one assert that decisions and/or judgments of the ECHR contain a legal norm? To this question it is necessary to give a negative answer".[56] Zimnenko takes the view that the ECHR does not create law, but merely applies the norms contained in the 1950 European Convention; to do otherwise would be contrary to the treaty empowering the ECHR: "... decisions and judgments of the ECHR are the result of law-application and not law-creative activity ... and therefore these judicial acts may not contain any legal norms. There is no substantiation for speaking about the existence of a law of precedent of the ECHR".[57] It would be admissible, though, to speak of "precedents of interpretation" by the ECHR, which form "legal positions" to assist the ECHR thereafter to more effectively and efficiently consider a case. A "legal position" developed by the ECHR is characterized as a "special form of subsequent practice of the States-parties connected

[55] Point 10, Decree on the Application by Courts of General Jurisdiction of Generally-Recognized Principles and Norms of International Law and International Treaties of the Russian Federation, of 10 October 2003; transl. in Butler, note 22 above.

[56] B. L. Zimnenko, *International Law and the Russian Legal System*, ed. & transl. W. E. Butler (2007), p. 257.

[57] Ibid., p. 258.

with the application" of the 1950 European Convention and subdivided into "material and procedural legal positions". Decisions and judgments of the ECHR are "a form of the existence of legal positions", but these are binding upon Russia only insofar as Russia is a party to the case concerned. As regards other cases not involving Russia, State agencies of the Russian Federation may be guided in their activities by these decisions and the legal positions consolidated in them, but they are not bound by them.[58]

Other Russian jurists take a different view: Russian legislation and judicial practice both under the 1950 European Convention and the 1993 Russian Constitution may not diverge from the provisions and standards of the Convention nor "… may Russian laws diverge from the case law created by the principal official interpreter of the European Convention – the European Court of Human Rights".[59]

The foregoing positions have been altered by a Decree of the Constitutional Court of 14 July 2015 which took the position that judgments of the European Court of Human Rights might not be enforced in Russia if those judgments were contrary to provisions of the 1993 Russian Constitution. In relevant part the Decree provided:

> a court of general jurisdiction or arbitrazh court when reviewing cases in the procedure established by procedural legislation in connection with the adoption of a decree by the European Court of Human Rights in which a violation is stated in the Russian Federation of human rights and freedoms when applying a law or individual provisions thereof, leading to the conclusion that the possibility of the application of a respective law may be decided only after confirmation of its conformity to the Constitution of the Russian Federation, requests the Constitutional Court of the Russian Federation for a verification of the constitutionality of this law; in any event the court of general jurisdiction or arbitrazh court effectuating a proceeding with regard to a review of a judicial act which has entered into legal force upon the application of a person whose appeal was accepted by the European Court of Human Rights, the decree stating the violation of the Convention of the Protection of Human Rights and Fundamental Freedoms by provisions of legislation of the Russian Federation applicable to the case of this person shall be obliged to suspend the proceedings and request the Constitutional

[58] Ibid., pp. 260-268.

[59] See P. A. Laptev and G. A. Gadzhiev, «Предисловие» [Preface], in Iu. Iu. Berestnev (ed.), Европейские правовые стандарты в постановлениях Конституционного Суда Российской Федерации [European Legal Standards in Decrees of the Constitutional Court of the Russian Federation] (2003), p. 7.

Court of the Russian Federation for a verification of the conformity thereof to the Constitution of the Russian Federation.[60]

The position of the Court has been the subject of public statements by the Chairman of the Constitutional Court, V. D. Zorkin:

> The participation of Russia in international agreements and conventions means merely that Russia voluntarily assumes the obligations enumerated in these international documents. And retains the sovereign right of final decisions in accordance with the Constitution of the Russian Federation in the event of controversial moments or legal conflicts.[61]

The substance of the Decree of the Constitutional Court of 14 July 2015 was transformed into amendments to the 1993 Constitution of the Russian Federation adopted 14 March 2020 and in force as of 4 July 2020. Article 79 was amended to read that "decisions of inter-State agencies adopted on the basis of provisions of international treaties of the Russian Federation in a construction thereof contrary to the Constitution of the Russian Federation shall not be subject to execution in the Russian Federation". This provision was reinforced by an amendment to Article 125 of the Constitution requiring that the Constitutional Court of the Russian Federation "settle the question" of whether a decision of an inter-State agency might be enforced in Russia in a "construing thereof" which is contrary to the Russian Constitution.[62] The formulation of the amendments, however, does leave open the question of whether the term "inter-State agency" encompasses a foreign or international court or arbitral tribunal.

CONCEPTIONS AND STRATEGIES

In a country with a history of national economic planning, it is hardly surprising to see vestiges or elements of "soft" planning or orientation documentation in post-Soviet legal systems. This is a legacy of the Planned Economy which has been adapted and survived. Documents of this nature appear under various designations: Strategy (including National Strategy, State Strategy); Conception; Doctrine; or Fundamental Principles. These, as a rule, undergo the same process as ordinary legislation; indeed, they are confirmed – depending at what level they are adopted – by laws, edicts, or

[60] The full text is translated in Butler, note 22 above.

[61] Remarks made in May 2015 at an International Legal Forum in St. Petersburg. Quoted in Ведомости [Gazette], 1 February 2018, p. 9. In May 2017 in a lecture at the VII Petersburg International Legal Forum Zorkin declared: "The defense of human rights should not undermine the moral pillars of society and destroy its religious identity. Ensuring the rights of citizens should not create a threat to State sovereignty. Finally, the defense of the dignity of a person should not lead to a rejection of those moral universals on which mankind sometime formed and which still enabled it to save itself from self-destruction". Ibid.

[62] Butler, *International Law in the Russian Legal System* (Oxford, 2020), pp. 226-227.

decrees and sometimes by lower-level subordinate acts. They have been characterized as "sources of law of a political-ideological character";[63] if acted upon, they are capable of influencing virtually all other elements of the Russian legal system.

Although in substance these enactments may be "policy" documents, they are couched in legal form and language and undergo the same legislative process as normative legal documents, irrespective of from what level they may emerge. They may themselves generate or call for legislation or serve as justification for a "line on the budget". They enter into force, but not always gazetted, and are repealed as legislative acts. Both Russian and Belarus jurists have singled out State conceptions, programs, strategies, basic orientations, and similar documents as an "autonomous source of law which may be called a policy-program document"; these documents are believed by some to be of a doctrinal nature.[64]

Leaving aside the Soviet era, the presidents and governments of Russia seem to have introduced, returned to, or accelerated recourse to policy-program documents from 1996 onwards. There are three main types: strategies (or national strategies, State strategies); conceptions; and doctrines. Related miscellaneous documents include: national plan; fundamental principles of State policy. Unlike general legislation, it is common for policy-program documents to be adopted for designated periods, after which they will either lapse or be renewed or replaced for another period. More than fifty have been adopted since 1996.[65] The foreign policy Conceptions, however, have been an exception: they are not adopted for designated periods of time. Of the five enacted since 1993, all but one originated under the leadership of President Putin; the earliest dates from the presidency of Boris Eltsyn. The conceptions seem to be replaced when senior foreign policy officials believe a new version is desirable, although the years correspond roughly to election cycles in Russia.

Policy dialogue as a category suggests discourse about policy alternatives and choices, a discussion about why and how certain paths should be pursued over others – influenced by perceptions of what is

[63] See M. A. Mushinskii, «Стратегии, концепции, доктрины в правовой системе Российской Федерации: проблемы статуса, юридической техники и соотношения друг с другом» [Strategies, Conceptions, and Doctrines in the Legal System of the Russian Federation: Problems of Status, Legal Technique, and Correlation with One Another], Юридическая техника [Legal Technique], no. 9 (2015), pp. 488-499.

[64] Ibid., p. 488, also citing N. V. Sil'chenko, «Концепция совершенствования законодательства: понятие, структура, содержание» [Conception of Improving Legislation: Concept, Structure, Content], Веснік Канстытуцыйнага Суда Рэспублікі Беларусь [Herald of the Constitutional Court of the Republic Belarus], no. 3 (2001), pp. 68-73.

[65] The figure comes from Mushinskii, but it is a low figure. He lists only those in force at the time he wrote and therefore omitted, for example, the Conceptions of Foreign Policy of 1993, 2000, and 2008. Had he attempted a List of all adopted after 1992, the List would have been considerably longer.

important in the subject-matter being considered, what trends are at work, and what desirable State policies may be to prevent or encourage certain outcomes.[66] While these are not absent in Russia, the fact that strategies, conceptions, doctrines, and the like are embodied in normative legal acts puts a significantly different spin on their relevance and importance. In the quarter century since foreign policy conceptions began to be produced in Russia, they have moved from being, it would seem, rapidly, even hastily, compiled statements of objectives and preferences to increasingly formal products of legislatively-mandated working groups clothed in normative-type documents (presidential edicts) and embodying formulations increasingly noteworthy for legislative technique.

CUSTOMS

Soviet attitudes toward customary law were ambivalent. During the Kievan Rus and Muscovy eras of Russian legal history, custom was the principal source of law. Written legislation began to achieve priority with respect to custom only from the late seventeenth century. In Imperial Russia customary rules had been widely applied in property, inheritance, family, and other legal relationships, and amongst non-Russian peoples to other legal domains as well. Native courts and customs were supplanted in the early 1920s by Soviet courts and written legislation. Customs deemed to be primitive and retrograde were made illegal in the Russian Federation. Chapter XI of the 1960 RSFSR Criminal Code, for example, contained articles punishing the payment and acceptance of bride price, compelling or obstructing the marriage of a woman, concluding a marital agreement with a person under marital age, and bigamy or polygamy when such acts are committed in republics within the Russian Federation or other localities where the acts constitute survivals of local customs.

The Civil Code of the Russian Federation introduced the concept of "customs of business turnover" (Article 5) as a source of civil law and on 30 December 2012 amended this Article to prefer the term "customs", deleting "of business turnover". As amended, these are the rules of behavior formed and extensively applied in any domain of entrepreneurial or other activity and have not been provided for by legislation, although they may have been crystallized in any document. They are not applicable if they are contrary to legislation or to a contract binding upon the parties to a respective relation; that is, they may not override legislation or contractual provisions agreed between the parties.

[66] See Butler, "Foreign Policy Discourses as Part of Understanding Russia and International Law", in S. Morris (ed.), *Russian Discourses on International Law: Sociological and Philosophical Phenomena* (2019), pp. 177-196.

Purely sources of "civil" law, they may exist in any sphere of life; they may be regional, local, national, international, or relate to branches of industry or activity or inter-branches.[67] In this sense customs relate primarily to the law of obligations, and not to the law of things (ownership). Russian jurists construe the term widely. Such customs not having been provided for by "legislation" is interpreted broadly to include subordinate normative acts: edicts of the President, decrees of the government, and departmental acts. The customs must be stable and generally recognized in the respective sphere of activity; they may be oral or written. Examples of customs include the conditions of model Russian contracts published in the press (Article 427, Civil Code), Incoterms, published collections of commercial seaport customs, and others. Proving their existence is a question of evidence. They are dispositive, and therefore the parties to a contract are at liberty to include contractual provisions which are contrary to customs.

The 1999 Merchant Shipping Code of the Russian Federation allows the use of "merchant shipping customs recognized in the Russian Federation" to help determine the law subject to application to relations arising from merchant shipping with the participation of foreign citizens or foreign juridical persons or complicated by a foreign element (Article 414(1)) and authorizes recourse to "other international merchant shipping customs" if the law applicable to general average is "incomplete" or the parties so agree (Article 285).[68] The 1993 Law on International Commercial Arbitration refers to "trade customs" (Article 28).[69]

NORMATIVE ACTS OF NON-STATE ENTITIES

Although the roles of trade unions, collective farms, consumer cooperatives, the Communist Party, and other "social organizations" have changed drastically in the transition to a market economy in the Russian Federation, Russian legal doctrine continues to regard certain non-State enterprises and organizations as being vested with the right to enact normative legal acts. These are called a "local" [локальный] act. Classic examples occur within the enterprise: collective labor contracts and other acts adopted by the executive of the organization with the participation of workers or their representatives, in the case of labor law. The authority for the right to enact local normative acts is the 2001 Labor Code of the Russian Federation: "Employers, except natural person-employers who are not individual

[67] See V. P. Mozolin, in T. E. Abova and A. Iu. Kabalkin (eds.), Комментарий к гражданскому кодексу Российской Федерации, части первой [Commentary to Civil Code of the Russian Federation, Part One] (2004), I, p. 34.

[68] СЗ РФ (1999), no. 18, item 2207, as amended. The formulation preceded but is consistent with Part Three of the Civil Code of the Russian Federation, and indeed is based on Article 5 of the Civil Code.

[69] Ведомости СНД и ВС РФ (1993), no. 32, item 1240, as amended; transl. in Butler, note 22 above.

entrepreneurs, shall adopt local normative acts containing norms of labor law (hereinafter: local normative acts) within the limits of their competence in accordance with labor legislation and other normative legal acts containing norms of labor law, collective contracts, and agreements" (Article 8, as amended 13 August 2020).[70] Such local normative acts extend to all workers of the enterprise or to individual categories of workers; they may be adopted for a determined or an indeterminate period, with or without the participation of the representative organ of workers as provided by the Labor Code or collective contract. In certain instances, however, the opinion of the representative organ of workers, when there is such, must be taken into account; local normative acts worsening the status of workers in comparison with labor legislation or other normative legal acts containing norms of labor law or the provisions of the collective contract or other agreement are not subject to application.

The procedure for adopting such acts depends upon the nature of the act. Collective contracts are negotiated between management and workers and then confirmed by the general meeting or conference of workers. Agreements concerning the protection of labor are concluded between the administration of the enterprise and the elective trade union agency of the enterprise. The rules of internal labor order are confirmed by the general meeting or conference of workers upon the recommendation of the administration. Most others are adopted by management after having agreed them with the trade union. There is no obligatory list of local normative acts nor requirements as to their substance, so long as they are not contrary to Russian legislation.[71]

Russian juridical persons confirm or are subject to other local normative acts. Many Russian jurists regard the charter of a juridical person as a local normative act, together with individual internal statutes regulating, for example, the management organs of the juridical person: statutes on the general meeting of stockholders, council of directors, management board, internal audit commission, and the like. In Russian doctrine local acts may be classified into two groups: (a) internal acts, and (b) charters and statutes of juridical persons sanctioned by the State. The "sanctioning" is expressed in State registration, confirmation, or joint adoption of the act.[72]

[70] СЗ РФ (2002), no. 1(I), item 3, as amended.

[71] For earlier practice see A. F. Nurtdinova, in Iu. P. Orlovskii (ed.)., Словарь по трудовому праву [Dictionary of Labor Law] (1998), pp. 172-174. In a sense the 2001 Labor Code has strengthened the rights of employers in this regard.

[72] See V. V. Dolinskaia, in V. P. Mozolin and A. I. Masliaev (eds.), note 49 above (2008), I, p. 49.

"SOFT LAW" RECOMMENDATORY INTERNATIONAL ACTS

The expression "soft law" has come to be used in Russian legal doctrine to discuss municipal recommendatory documents of various types and, more commonly, acts adopted by international organs, agencies, organizations, conferences, or bodies. This may be explained in substantial part by the reference in Article 15(4) of the 1993 Russian Constitution to generally-recognized principles and norms of international law: "the said constitutional principle is perceived by agencies of State power not only in the formal juridical sense. On the contrary, courts have elaborated its literal content and rely on virtually all elements of the international legal system – resolutions and recommendations of international organizations, decisions of international agencies, model acts, legal holdings and decisions of international judicial institutions".[73] In the view of some Russian jurists, the practice of national courts (not precedent in this instance) is charting the path towards the implementation of international law in domestic forums and not legal doctrine. There is taking place a "... gradual mixing of the focus on questions concerning the operation of recommendations in the domain of international relations with the subject-matter of municipal jurisdiction".[74]

The formalities of drafting and signing intergovernmental acts which are not treaties is regulated in Russia by the Statute on the Preparation and Signing of International Intergovernmental Acts Which are Not International Treaties of the Russian Federation, confirmed by Decree of the Government of the Russian Federation on 7 February 2003.[75] The Statute regulates how decisions within Russia are to be prepared and adopted with regard to signing international intergovernmental acts with the governments of foreign States or with international organizations, or organs thereof which do not fall into the category of international treaties. The Statute extends to international acts regardless of what they are called, but does not extend to international acts adopted by the international organizations acting autonomously. As a rule, the acts concerned will be called declarations,

[73] S. Iu. Marochkin, Действие и реализация норм международного права в правовой системе Российской Федерации [Operation and Realization of Norms of International Law in the Legal System of the Russian Federation] (2011), pp. 280-281. These views are expanded upon in Marochkin, *The Operation of International Law in the Russian Legal System: A Changing Approach* (2019), pp. 242-284.

[74] See R. M. Khalafian, «К вопросу о месте и роли международных рекомендательных актов в правовой системе Российской Федерации» [On the Question of the Place and Role of International Recommendatory Acts in the Legal System of the Russian Federation], in A. A. Petrov and R. M. Khalafian (eds.), Роль международных и внутригосударственных рекомендательных актов в правовой системе России [The Role of International and Municipal Recommendatory Acts in the Legal System of the Russian Federation] (Irkutsk, 2013), p. 141.

[75] Decree No. 79. СЗ РФ (2003), no. 7, item 647.

memoranda, joint statements, plans, programs for cooperation, and so on. Such acts may not contain binding provisions, although they may make reference to obligations assumed by the parties under treaties.

In the hierarchy of normative acts, because "soft law" recommendations are by definition not binding as such, they may not be contrary to the Russian Constitution, generally-recognized principles and norms of international law, international treaties of the Russian Federation, normative legal acts of the President or Government of Russia, or, most interestingly, international acts previously signed by Russia which do not enjoy the status of treaties. Federal agencies of the Russian Federation are required within the limits of their competence to take measures to fulfill such international acts and to issue respective normative or other legal acts to achieve this purpose.

Some federal agencies in Russia have elaborated at length instructions on the procedure for drafting international acts or treaties by way of implementation of the 1995 Federal Law on International Treaties of the Russian Federation.[76]

The Constitutional Court of the Russian Federation has on a number of occasions made reference in its decisions to "international and international legal acts", "international documents", and "international acts in the domain of human rights".[77] The Federal Law of the Russian Federation "On Communications" of 7 July 2003 requires the Government of Russia to determine procedures for the distribution and use of resources by taking into account the "recommendations of international organizations in which the Russian Federation is a participant ...".[78]

ACTS OF THE UNION STATE

On 8 December 1999 the Russian Federation and Belarus concluded the Treaty on the Creation of the Union State, which is in the process of formation. The Union State has its own organs: the High State Council, the Parliament of the Union State, the Council of Ministers, the Court of the Union State, and the Counting Chamber. The agencies of the Union State adopt within the limits of their competence normative legal acts provided for by the Treaty of 8 December 1999: laws, fundamental principles of legislation, decrets, decrees, directives, and resolutions, recommendations, and opinions.

[76] See, for example, the Order of the Federal Customs Service of 5 September 2016, No 1707, "On Confirmation of the Reglament of International Legal Work of the Federal Customs Service and Instruction on the Procedure for Elaborating Draft International Treaties". Таможенные ведомости [Customs Gazette], no. 12 (2016). Available on Consultant Plus. This Order repealed Order No. 1310 of 21 June 2011.

[77] See, among others, the Decree of the Constitutional Court of 4 April 1996, and the Ruling of the Constitutional Court of 19 February 2009. Available on Consultant Plus.

[78] Article 26. СЗ РФ (2003), no. 28, item 2895, as amended.

On matters within the exclusive jurisdiction of the Union State laws, decrets, decrees, and resolutions are adopted. Decrets and decrees are adopted by agencies of the Union State on the basis of the Treaty of 8 December 1999 and laws of the Union State. With regard to questions within the joint jurisdiction of the Union State and the states-participants, fundamental principles of legislation, directives, and resolutions are enacted. These are then to be realized by means of the adoption of national normative acts of the states-participants. Although the terminology is not used, it would appear that enactments of the Union State serve as the foundation for "subordinate" legislation by Russia and Belarus respectively.

Laws and decrets are intended for general application, are binding in all respects, and after their official publication are subject to direct application on the territory of Russia and Belarus. In the event of a conflict between a law or decret of the Union State and norms of internal law of Russia or Belarus, the norm of the law or decret of the Union State has preferential force, except that this rule does not apply in the event of a conflict with norms contained in the constitutions and constitutional acts of Russia or Belarus. Decrees are binding in all respects upon the states and the natural and juridical persons to whom they are addressed. Directives are binding upon each State to whom they are addressed, but the agencies of the respective State retain freedom of choice as to the forms and methods of action. Resolutions are acts by means of which the current activities of agencies of the Union State are ensured. Decisions of the Court of the Union State are binding and subject to official publication; only Russia, Belarus, and agencies of the Union State may transfer questions for the Court to consider which are connected with the interpretation and application of the Treaty of 8 December 1999 or with normative legal acts of the Union State.

DOCUMENTS OF THE COMMONWEALTH OF INDEPENDENT STATES

During its existence, the Commonwealth of Independent States has generated more than 15,000 normative documents. The forms are various: international treaties and agreements, decisions of CIS organs, protocols, and others. Their publication is irregular, although many matters which these documents address are of considerable legal interest and importance. Insofar as these documents are international treaties, they are pursuant to Article 15 of the 1993 Russian Constitution an integral part of the Russian legal system. The great majority are doubtless interdepartmental agreements.

INTERNATIONAL LAW

The status of international treaties, and of international law generally, in the Russian legal system has been transformed by the 1993 Russian

Constitution.[79] The 1993 Russian Constitution provides (Article 15(4)) that "generally-recognized principles and norms of international law and international treaties of the Russian Federation" are an integral part of the legal system of the Russian Federation. This is a formulation without precedent in Imperial Russian and Soviet law and legal practice insofar as it, first, accepts generally-recognized principles and norms of international law as part of Russian law and, second, places such norms and principles side by side with norms of municipal Russian law. This may imply that such norms and principles are incorporated into domestic Russian law and overridden by rules of Russian law later in time or *lex specialis*. It further follows that applicable law clauses in contracts which choose Russian law automatically incorporate the general rules of international law and the norms of international treaties of the Russian Federation.

There is no legislative definition in Russia of "generally-recognized principles and norms of international law". The Plenum of the Supreme Court of the Russian Federation, in its Decree No. 5 of 10 October 2003,[80] has instructed courts of general jurisdiction that such "generally-recognized principles" are the "basic imperative norms of international law adopted and recognized by the international community of States as a whole, deviation from which is inadmissible" (point 1). Although the term is not used, this definition is similar to the definition of *jus cogens* given in the Russian language text of the 1969 Vienna Convention on the Law of Treaties. The translation of *jus cogens* as "imperative norms", however, does not give full expression to the "cogens" nature of the norms; "imperative" norms in Russian municipal law are merely norms which the parties are not at liberty to change by agreement between themselves.

Examples of "imperative norms" given by the Plenum include universal respect for human rights and good-faith fulfillment of international obligations. The courts are instructed that the content of these principles may be elicited in documents of the United Nations and its specialized agencies, among other sources. Russian doctrinal writings in many instances equate such "generally-recognized principles" to customary international law. Russian courts have had recourse to these principles when deciding individual cases.

The expression "international treaties" embraces all interstate, intergovernmental, or interdepartmental documents irrespective of their form and appellation (treaty, agreement, convention, pact, covenant, protocol, exchange of letters, or notes) or other forms and appellations (see Article 1, 1995 Law on International Treaties of the Russian Federation).[81]

[79] One Russian jurist has characterized Article 15(4) as a "... quite radical provision ...". Marochkin, note 73 above, p. 222.

[80] Point 1, note 22 above, p. 48.

[81] СЗ РФ (1995), no 29, item 2757, as amended; transl. in Butler, note 22 above.

The Constitution gives priority to treaty norms over those of domestic law: "If other rules have been established by an international treaty of the Russian Federation than provided for by a law, the rules of the international treaty shall apply" (Article 15(4)). Whether, however, treaty provisions as interpreted by an international tribunal take precedence over the 1993 Russian Constitution was addressed by the Constitutional Court of the Russian Federation in a Decree of 14 July 2015. The said Decree was issued in response to a query initiated by deputies of the State Duma of the Russian Federation:

> ... the applicants do not subject to doubt either any provisions of the Convention on the Protection of Human Rights and Fundamental Freedoms as a multilateral international treaty of the Russian Federation or the Federal Law "On the Ratification of the Convention on the Protection of Human Rights and Fundamental Freedoms and Protocols Thereto" as the normative foundation of the inclusion thereof in the legal system of Russia in accordance with Article 15(4) of the Constitution of the Russian Federation.
>
> Moreover, the said Federal Law is in extricable normative unity with other provisions contested in the query of procedural legislation and the Federal Law "On International Treaties of the Russian Federation", forming with them the normative-legal base for the execution of decrees of the European Court of Human Rights rendered with respect to Russia on the basis of provisions of the Convention on the Protection of Human Rights and Fundamental Freedoms and their construction by the European Court of Human Rights in a concrete case.
>
> The deputies of the State Duma link the uncertainty which has arisen, as they suggest, on the question of whether these legal provisions correspond to the Constitution of the Russian Federation with the unconditional bindingness consolidated by them of decrees of the European Court of Human Rights rendered with respect to Russia in those instances when a conflict arises between the interpretation contained in such a decree of the Convention on the Protection of Human Rights and Fundamental Freedoms and the provisions of the Constitution of the Russian Federation.[82]

With respect to the correlation between an international treaty and the Russian Constitution (as distinct from "ordinary" legislation below the level of the constitution), the Constitutional Court determined that:

[82] The Decree is translated in Butler, note 22 above.

Insofar as the Convention of the Protection of Human Rights and Fundamental Freedoms as an international treaty of the Russian Federation is an integral part of its legal system, the State is obliged to execute a decree of the European Court of Human Rights rendered on the basis of the provisions of the Convention with regard to an appeal against Russia with respect to persons participating in the case and within the framework of the concrete subject-matter of the dispute. The realization of measures provided by a decree of the European Court of Human Rights of an individual and common character should be effectuated in accordance with Article 15(4) of the Constitution of the Russian Federation also on the principles of deeming such a decree to be an integral part of the Russian legal system.

As follows, however, from the Constitution of the Russian Federation, Articles 4(1), 15(1), and 79 consolidating the sovereignty of Russia and the supremacy and highest legal force of the Constitution of the Russian Federation and the inadmissibility of the implementation in the legal system of the State of international treaties, participation in which may entail a limitation of the rights and freedoms of man and citizen or permit any infringement on the foundations of the constitutional system of the Russian Federation and thereby violate constitutional prescriptions, neither the Convention of the Protection of Human Rights and Fundamental Freedoms as an international treaty of the Russian Federation or the legal positions based on it of the European Court of Human Rights containing an evaluation of national legislation or concerning the need for a change of the provisions thereof do not repeal for the Russian legal system the priority of the Constitution of the Russian Federation and therefore subject to realization within the framework of this system only on condition of recognition of the highest legal force of the Constitution of the Russian Federation.

Being a rule-of-law, democratic State, Russia as a member of the world community in which generally-recognized principles and norms of international law operates concluded international treaties and participates in inter-State associations, transferring to them part of its powers (Preamble; Article 1(1); Article 15(4), Article 17(1); and Article 79 of the Constitution of the Russian Federation), which, however, does not mean a renunciation of State sovereignty relating to the fundamental principles of the constitutional system and assumed supremacy independence, and autonomy of State power, and plenitude of legislative, executive, and judicial power of the State throughout all of its territory and independence in international communion, and also being a necessary qualitative indicator of the Russian Federation characterizing its constitutional-legal status

(Decree of the Constitutional Court of the Russian Federation of 7 July 2000, No. 10-П).

Proceeding from this in a situation when the very content of the decree of the European Court of Human Rights, including with respect to prescriptions applicable to a defendant State based on the provisions of the Convention of the Protection of Human Rights and Fundamental Freedoms interpreted by the European Court of Human Rights within the framework of a concrete case, unlawfully – from a constitutional legal point of view – derogates from the principles and norms of the Constitution of the Russian Federation, Russia may by way of exception depart from the fulfillment of obligations placed on it when such deviation is the sole possible means of avoiding a violation of the fundamental principles and norms of the Constitution of the Russian Federation.

This significant development in Russian jurisprudence was consolidated in the 1993 Russian Constitution by amendments of 14 March 2020. Article 179 was amended in relevant part as follows:

The Russian Federation may participate in inter-State associations and transfer to them part of its powers in accordance with international treaties of the Russian Federation if this does not entail a limitation of the rights and freedoms of man and citizen and is not contrary to the foundations of the constitutional system of the Russian Federation. Decisions of inter-State agencies adopted on the basis of provisions of international treaties of the Russian Federation in a construction thereof contrary to the Constitution of the Russian Federation shall not be subject to execution in the Russian Federation.

Point 5^1 was added to Article 125 of the Constitution directing the Constitutional Court of the Russian Federation as follows:

(b) in the procedure established by a federal constitutional law, settle the question concerning the possibility of the execution of decisions of inter-State agencies adopted on the basis of provisions of international treaties of the Russian Federation in a construing thereof which is contrary to the Constitution of the Russian Federation, and also the possibility of the execution of the decision of a foreign or international (or inter-State) court or foreign or international arbitration court imposing duties on the Russian Federation if this decision is contrary to the fundamental principles of public policy of the Russian Federation.

FOREIGN AND COMPARATIVE LAW

Two issues arise in connection with foreign and comparative law. The first is whether either may be regarded as a source of law in the Russian Federation; the second is whether Russian judges may or do draw upon foreign and/or comparative legal materials when formulating judicial decisions.

The response to the first issue is categorically negative. Foreign judicial practice is not binding in the Russian judicial system and would be considered to be superfluous; the Russian legal system is viewed as self-contained; Russian judges are taught to concentrate on the formulation of legal norms, construe them literally, and avoid aspects of legal policy, principles, and concepts. The reasons for a judicial decision are explained solely on the basis of Russian sources of law. Whether there is an express internal rule against citing foreign and comparative law cannot be determined, but this approach is embedded in Russian judicial practice. In this foreign and comparative law differ from international law, which as noted above is an integral part of the Russian legal system.

The response to the second issue is less than categorical. Russian judges have the right to issue a "special opinion" (особое мнение), which may be dissenting or concurring. At least eight instances are known of the Constitutional Court of the Russian Federation producing special opinions with reference to foreign law (out of over 20,000). In one example, foreign laws served as illustrations of the judicial practice concerning the right of a driver in an automobile accident not to testify against himself;[83] a Slovak Constitutional Court decision was cited for legislation unlawfully limiting the freedom of the mass media in an election campaign;[84] foreign practice of three countries was summarized citing examples of prohibitions against increasing sentences during appeals;[85] the British Commonwealth served as an example of a jurisdiction using legal terms differently in various branches of law;[86] the law of the United States[87] and the United Kingdom[88] was cited in two cases concerning election law; the German Constitutional Court judgment of 14 March 1963 was cited in connection with resolving

[83] Special Opinion of A. L. Kononov, Decree of Constitutional Court of the Russian Federation, 25 April 2001, No. 6-П. The practices of six countries were cited.

[84] Special Opinion of A. L. Kononov, Decree of the Constitutional Court of the Russian Federation, 30 October 2003, No. 15-П.

[85] Special Opinion of S. M. Kazantsev, Decree of Constitutional Court of the Russian Federation, 16 May 2007, No. 6-П.

[86] Special Opinion of G. A. Gadzhiev, Ruling of the Constitutional Court of the Russian Federation, 2 November 2006, No. 444-O.

[87] Special Opinion of G. A. Gadzhiev, Decree of the Constitutional Court of the Russian Federation, 14 November 2005, No. 10-П.

[88] Special Opinion of A. L. Kononov, Decree of the Constitutional Court of the Russian Federation, 16 June 2006, No. 7-П.

conflicts between legal certainty and the principle of material justice;[89] and Panamanian law was referred to in a case relating to fixing an age limit for sitting judges before the law had entered into force.[90] In none of these examples was foreign law referred to as a precedent, but rather as evidence of a similar approach or of a "parallel way of thinking".[91] The references, although deliberate, were casual in their details of the decision itself or the facts of the respective case.

As from 1 January 2021 Russian judges on the Constitutional Court of the Russian Federation are forbidden from disclosing the existence of, publishing, or referring publicly to the existence of Special Opinions. Whether the cloak of confidentiality will affect references to foreign or comparative materials in Russian judicial practice will become difficult to ascertain unless such references are made in the majority published opinions.

The Administration of International Relations and Generalization of Constitutional Control Practice of the Constitutional Court of the Russian Federation has the duty to collect and translate international and foreign court decisions, constitutions, and relevant normative legal acts. The members and personnel of the Court may and frequently do request assistance and reports from this Department, which is further evidence of the interest of the Court in matters of comparative law. Other factors militate against the explicit use of comparative legal materials in Russian adjudication. One specialist has suggested that a combination of "constitutional patriotism" and "Russian exceptionalism", reinforced by legal formalism, have dictated a species of Russian "national style" in constitutional matters.[92]

DOCTRINE

The teachings and writings of jurists have no formal place among the sources of Russian law. It is exceptional for Russian courts to cite the published works of jurists when issuing a decree or judgment, although such examples are known. On 29 May 2001 the Judicial Division for Civil Cases of the Supreme Court of the Russian Federation criticized the Briansk Regional Court for referring in its decision to the textbook on the theory of

[89] Special Opinion of G. A. Gadzhiev, Decree of the Constitutional Court of the Russian Federation, 14 July 2005, No. 9-П.

[90] Special Opinion of V. G. Iaroslavtsev, Ruling of the Constitutional Court of the Russian Federation, 15 February 2005, No. 1-O.

[91] See S. Belov, "Russia: Foreign Transplants in the Russian Constitution and Invisible Foreign Precedents in Decisions of the Russian Constitutional Court", in T. Groppi and M.-C. Ponthoreau (eds.), *The Use of Foreign Precedents by Constitutional Judges* (Oxford, 2013), p. 365, where these cases are discussed.

[92] M. Mazza, "The Russian Constitutional Court and the Judicial Use of Comparative Law: A Problematic Relationship", in G. F. Ferrari, *Judicial Cosmopolitanism: The Use of Foreign Law in Contemporary Constitutional Systems* (Leiden/Boston, 2020), p. 550.

State and law edited by S. S. Alekseev and to a commentary on the Code of Civil Procedure "because textbooks and commentaries on legislation are not sources of law and by virtue of Article 10 of the Code of Civil Procedure of the RSFSR may not be applied by a court directly as substantiation of a judicial decision".[93]

However, in a Decree of the Presidium of the Supreme Arbitrazh Court of the Russian Federation of 29 January 2013, No. 11524/12, Judge N. V. Pavlova in a dissenting opinion addressing the principle of proportionality in distributing the burden of proof between parties made reference to a leading Soviet work on the subject in support of her views.[94] Pre-revolutionary Russian jurists have been cited as authority.[95] Less common are references to foreign doctrinal sources, although such have occurred.[96]

As trained jurists, Russian judges are aware of doctrinal views and may be influenced by them. A survey was undertaken between 2003 and 2006 of 1,737 newly-appointed judges and judges undergoing continuing legal education courses. Nearly 50% were between ages 40 to 50; 33% of the total surveyed were men, and 67% women. Nearly 80% worked in courts of first instance; about 40% had 10 years judicial experience or more. When asked whether there were any works by jurists (doctrinal writings) that were absolutely primary or fundamental, 54% replied negatively. Unexpectedly, however, about 42% answered positively, and of these 9% named specific authors and 33% said there should be such works, but it was difficult to specify them.[97]

[93] See Ruling of 29 May 2001 in Case No. 83-Г01-08. Available on Consultant Plus. A similar position was taken by the Moscow City Court in a Ruling of 14 December 2011, in Case No. 33-41218, where a textbook on the securities market and a commentary on the Law on the Defense of Consumer Rights were cited: "the opinions of authors of a textbook are not legal norms, but are the positions of authors and bear the character of a theoretical discourse on the legal regulation of a bond loan". Available on Consultant Plus.

[94] See Decree of 29 January 2013, No. 11524/12. The work cited was A. F. Kleinman, Основные вопросы теории доказательств в советском гражданском процессе [Basic Questions of the Theory of Evidence in Soviet Civil Procedure] (1950). Available on Consultant Plus.

[95] See the Separate Opinion of Judge S. D. Kniazev in the Ruling of the Constitutional Court of the Russian Federation of 17 July 2012, No. 1286-O, who referred to V. V. Ivanovskii, Учебник административного права (Полицейское право. Право внутреннего управления) [Textbook of Administrative Law (Police Law, Law of Internal Management] (Kazan, 1911). Kniazev also cited a contemporary journal article by a Russian jurist. Available on Consultant Plus.

[96] See the Ruling of the Arbitrazh Court, City of Moscow, on the Enforcement of a Foreign Judicial Decision, of 21 December 2005, where English doctrinal writings are cited. The Ruling is translated in *Russian Law: Theory and Practice*, no 1 (2008), pp. 128-136. Dicey and Morris on *Conflicts of Law* is cited by the court.

[97] See S. V. Boshno, «Прецедент, закон и доктрина (опыт социолого-юридического исследования)» [Precedent, Law, and Doctrine (Attempt of Sociological-Legal Study)], Государство и право [State and Law], no 4 (2007), p. 76. Among Soviet and Russian jurists expressly mentioned were: S. S. Alekseev; B. V. Erofeev (on land law); M. I. Braginskii, V. V. Viatrinskii on contract law; I. B. Novitskii on Roman law; O. S. Ioffe (on the law of obligations);

On the other hand, when asked whether doctrinal works should be cited in judicial decisions, opinions were divided: 32% of respondents were in favor, and 40% were opposed. Most of the remaining respondents found it difficult to express a position on the issue. On the whole, the survey determined that about a third of the judges believed doctrinal literature could be the basis of a judicial decision as a form of law. Of the types of doctrinal writings, most popular among judges were collections of judicial practice (35%); commentaries less so; and articles, monographs, and textbooks enjoying the least popularity.[98]

The wisdom of the German philosopher, Georg Wilhelm Friedrich Hegel (1770-1831), has been cited from a work in 1821: "Justice triumphs so that the world does not perish".[99] The role of doctrine was emphasized in another respect: discussing the duty of a driver to render assistance to a victim in a road accident which he caused, whether a violation of this duty was subject to the Criminal Code the judge doubted because such a violation lacked "sufficient doctrinal substantiation" and had not been confirmed in practice.[100]

The surveys above were made with respect to judges of arbitrazh courts and courts of general jurisdiction. A further observation may be relevant with respect to judges of the Constitutional Court of the Russian Federation. Most have been or are University law professors with lower and/or higher doctorates. Some have published works that address foreign legal systems. The probability is high that they are familiar with the judicial practice and constitutional doctrines of one or several foreign countries and the use of comparative law argument and application of the comparative method – which may lead to implicit use of foreign legal doctrine and judicial practice.[101]

Russian advokats are at liberty to refer to doctrine and commentary in oral pleadings in court and in arbitration tribunals. It should be noted that Russian judges often serve as co-authors of commentaries on legislation.

PUBLICATION AND ENTRY INTO FORCE OF LEGISLATION

The publication and entry into force of normative legal acts usually are two closely interrelated processes. Publication is associated with the "presumption of knowledge of the law"; if a normative legal act has been

and V. F. Iakovlev (on law and market relations).

[98] Boshno, ibid., p. 76.

[99] Special Opinion of Judge V. G. Iaroslavtsev, Decree of the Constitutional Court of the Russian Federation, 14 July 2005, No. 9-П.

[100] See the Special Opinion of Judge A. L. Kononov, Decree of the Constitutional Court of the Russian Federation, 25 April 2001, No. 6-П.

[101] Mazza, note 92 above, p. 556.

brought to the information of the general public in a duly established procedure – ordinarily printing the act in a designated official gazette or on the portal of the Russian Government or Ministry of Justice – no one may plead ignorance of the law as a pretext for failure to comply with its provisions. Publication in printed form also may establish the official text of the enactment, provide a precise benchmark in time from which the normative legal act takes effect, and enable the legislator to communicate most efficiently with those to whom his enactments are addressed.

For the first time in Russian history the 1993 Constitution of the Russian Federation provides that laws are subject to official publication, that unpublished laws shall not be applied, and that any normative legal acts affecting the rights, freedoms, and duties of man and citizen may not be applied unless they have been published officially for general publication (Article 15(3)). In practice this principle has rested uneasily with long-established Russian administrative traditions; the result has been that access to Russian normative legal acts, although incommensurately improved in comparison with the Soviet period, nonetheless falls short of full disclosure. The Federal Law on State Secrecy of 21 July 1993, as amended, does not make specific provision for classifying normative legal acts or part thereof, but in enumerating (Article 5) in a general way the information comprising a State secret, it is evident that some information would inevitably be contained in normative acts issued by the President, by the Government, or by other agencies of executive power. On the basis of the Law, a List of Information relegated to a State secret was confirmed by Edict of the President of the Russian Federation on 30 November 1995, as amended. Included on the List is "information concerning the preparation, conclusion, ratification, preparation for denunciation, content, or fulfillment of treaties, conventions, or agreements with foreign States, the premature dissemination of which may cause damage to the security of the State" (point 71, as amended).[102]

Legislative acts

The Law on the Procedure for the Publication and Entry into Force of Federal Constitutional Laws, Federal Laws, and Acts of Chambers of the Federal Assembly of 14 June 1994, as amended,[103] provides that only those legislative acts which have been officially published shall be applied on the territory of the Russian Federation. Confusion can arise over the dates of adoption, approval, and signature of federal constitutional laws and federal laws. The 1994 Law provides that the "date of adoption" of a federal law is considered to be the date on which the State Duma adopted the law in

[102] СЗ РФ (1995), no 49, item 4775, as amended. Still useful is A. V. Kolomiets (comp.), Тайна. Коммерческая. Служебная. Государственная. Сборник нормативных правовых актов [Secrecy. Commercial. Employment. State. Collection of Normative Legal Acts of Russian Federation] (2001).

[103] СЗ РФ (1994), no 8, item 801, as amended; transl. in Butler, note 22 above.

its final version. In practice the "final version" of a federal law is actually in existence only after an editorial commission of the Federal Assembly incorporates the emendations required as a result of the final reading of the draft law; these emendations may be stylistic, or may record changes which the deputies accepted but left to be reduced to final wording by the editorial team. As for federal constitutional laws, the date of adoption is considered to be the day when it was approved by the chambers of the Federal Assembly in the procedure established by the Russian Constitution. The date, however, by which a federal law or federal constitutional law is commonly referred to is neither of the two dates mentioned above, but rather the date of signature by the President of the Russian Federation. This can lead to anomalies when the President succeeds in having adjustments made to the final text of a law and delays formal signature for an extended period. The legal data bases will routinely provide all of the dates concerned and draw attention to situations when it is impossible, or not easy, to determine when "first publication" occurred.

Official publication must occur in the case of federal constitutional laws or federal laws within seven days after signature by the President and within ten days, in the case of acts of the chambers of the Federal Assembly, after adoption. First official publication is considered to be the publication of the full text in Российская газета [*Russian Newspaper*], a newspaper published six days each week, the Собрание законодательства Российской Федерации [*Collected Legislation of the Russian Federation*], published weekly, some issues in multiple parts, but approximately ten days to three weeks after the cover date, or, from October 1999, Парламентская газета [*Parliamentary Newspaper*], a newspaper issued by the Federal Assembly, or from 21 October 2011, first placement or publication on the "Official Internet-Portal of Legal Information" (www.pravo.gov.ru). Additional publication in other printed media, television, radio, circulation internally to State agencies, officials, enterprises, institutions, or organizations, on-line, or in machine-readable form is acceptable. They also may be published as separate booklets, pamphlets, or brochures, and frequently are. Federal laws are subject to obligatory publication in a computer database prepared by the Scientific-Technical Centre for Legal Information, "Система" [System], whose machine-readable text has the stature of an official text, or inclusion of the full text on the official internet portal at www.pravo.gov.ru.[104]

Entry into force occurs simultaneously throughout the entire territory of the Russian Federation upon the expiration of ten days after official publication unless a different procedure for entry into force is established

[104] On-line publication is authorized by Edict of the President of the Russian Federation on the Procedure for the Publication and Entry into Force of Federal Laws, adopted 5 April 1994, as amended. СЗ РФ (1994), no 15, item 1173, as amended; transl. in Butler, note 22 above.

by the laws themselves or acts of the chambers. The practice varies widely: some laws or codes enter into force many months after signature. Certain portions of a law may enter into force on one date, and other articles or sections at a later date. Frequently a law enters into force on the date of official publication, in which case the date of first official publication becomes significant.

The Constitutional Court has ruled on the date of official publication of laws in connection with a case arising out of the adoption of the Federal Law of 7 March 1996 on Making Changes in the Law of the Russian Federation on Excises. This Law confirmed a new version of the Law on Excises which by its provisions entered into force from 1 February 1996 and introduced excise taxes on goods imported from CIS countries, whereas previously such goods had been exempt. On 15 March 1996 the State Customs Committee circulated the text of the law by teletype to the heads of regional customs administrations, instructing them to recover excise tax with respect to all affected goods as from 1 February 1996. Observing that this Law was retroactive and disadvantageous to the taxpayers concerned, the Constitutional Court held that it was in clear violation of Article 57 of the 1993 Russian Constitution. Invoking Article 4 of the 1994 Federal Law on the procedure for the publication of laws, the Court observed that it was to be determined whether first publication occurred in the СЗ РФ or in Российская газета [Russian Newspaper]. The relevant issue of the СЗ РФ was dated 11 March 1996, whereas Российская газета was dated 13 March 1996; however, the Court noted that the cover date of the СЗ РФ was the date on which the issue was signed to press and not the actual date of publication (which had to have been later and therefore the taxpayers to whom the law was addressed could not have had knowledge of the law on that date). Therefore the newspaper date was that of first publication, and the Law, not providing otherwise, could only enter into force no earlier than 24 March 1996, when ten days had elapsed from the moment of official publication.[105] Each issue of the gazette will bear scrutiny on this basis; the day on which they are signed to press, that is, officially approved for printing, can be days or weeks after the cover date.

Presidential, governmental, and departmental acts

According to the 1993 Russian Constitution, the President issues edicts and regulations (Article 90(1)), and the government issues decrees and regulations (Article 115). The publication of these is regulated by the Edict of the President of the Russian Federation on the Procedure for the Publication and Entry into Force of Acts of the President of the Russian Federation and of the Government of the Russian Federation and Normative Legal Acts of

[105] See T. G. Morshchakova (ed.), Конституционный Суд Российской Федерации: Постановления. Определения. 1992-1996 [Constitutional Court of the Russian Federation: Decrees. Rulings (1992-1996] (1997), pp. 459-465.

Federal Agencies of Executive Power, adopted 23 May 1996, as amended,[106] and by the 1997 Law on the Government of the Russian Federation, as amended. Whereas all federal laws are subject to publication without exception, accessibility to Presidential edicts, governmental decrees, and departmental acts is affected by the Law on State Secrecy. Accordingly, under the 1996 Edict, edicts and regulations of the President and decrees and regulations of the Government are subject to obligatory official publication except for those acts or parts thereof which contain information constituting a State secret or information of a confidential character. Publication takes place, when applicable, within ten days after their signature in the same organs as federal laws, noted above, including the computer database.

Acts of a normative character adopted by the President enter into force simultaneously throughout the territory of the Russian Federation upon the expiry of seven days after their first official publication. Other Presidential acts, including acts containing information constituting a State secret or information of a confidential character, enter into force on the date of their signature. However, all Presidential acts may enter into force on a different date as provided therein, commonly on the date of publication. Acts of the Government affecting the rights, freedoms, and duties of man and citizen or establishing the legal status of federal agencies of executive power or organizations enter into force seven days after their first date of official publication unless the acts provide otherwise. Other acts of the Government enter into force on the date of signature unless provided otherwise therein.

The greatest advances in the interests of a rule-of-law State with regard to publication of legislation have occurred with respect to departmental acts. Subject to exceptions (for example, certain acts of the Central Bank of the Russian Federation), departmental normative acts require registration with the Ministry of Justice of the Russian Federation as a condition of their validity. A departmental act will not be registered if in the view of Ministry of Justice specialists the act is contrary to law. Those departmental acts or parts thereof containing information constituting a State secret or information of a confidential character which have not undergone State registration, or those registered but not published in the established procedure, have no legal consequences on the grounds that they have not entered into legal force. Accordingly, they may not serve as grounds for regulating legal relations or applying sanctions to citizens, officials, or organizations for the failure to comply with the prescriptions contained therein; nor may they be referred to when settling disputes. Departmental acts enter into force simultaneously throughout Russian territory upon the expiry of ten days after the date of official publication unless a different period is specified therein, whereas those which by reason of State secrecy or the confidential information contained therein are not officially published enter into force

106 СЗ РФ (1996), no 22, item 2663, as amended; transl. in Butler, note 22 above.

from the date of their State registration and the conferment of a registration number on them, unless the acts themselves specify a later date.

The Rules for the Preparation of Normative Legal Acts of Federal Agencies of Executive Power and the State Registration Thereof were confirmed by Decree of the Government of the Russian Federation of 13 August 1997, as amended.[107] Normative legal acts are issued by federal agencies of executive power in the form of decrees, orders, regulations, rules, instructions, and statutes; the Rules expressly prohibit normative legal acts being issued in the form of letters and telegrams (this provision does not extend to the Russian Central Bank, which is not a federal agency of executive power).

Under the Rules of 13 August 1997, as amended, the Ministry of Justice registers not only normative legal acts affecting the rights, freedoms, and duties of man and citizen or those having an interdepartmental character, but also acts establishing the legal status of organizations (thereby giving effect to the Edict of the President of the Russian Federation of 23 May 1996, referred to above). Normative legal acts subject to State registration are submitted to the Ministry of Justice in a hard copy or as electronic documents. The Ministry sends the electronic copies to the federal State budgetary institution "Editorial Board of 'Russian Newspaper'" and to the Federal Protection Service of the Russian Federation. If the act contains information comprising a State secret or of a confidential character, only one original and one copy are submitted. The Ministry of Justice has up to 15 work days, with possible extensions for a further ten work days, to complete its expert legal evaluation of the draft normative legal act. If draft normative legal acts contain a violation of the established procedure for submission thereof or provisions contrary to law, they are returned to the issuing agency for rectification and possible resubmission. Non-normative acts, that is, acts not containing a legal norm, may proceed to issuance without State registration, a fact which also is confirmed by the Ministry of Justice and recorded in a separate published list.

A normative legal act deemed by the Ministry of Justice not to need State registration is subject to placement or publication on the "Official Internet-Portal of Legal Information" (www.pravo.gov.ru).

Nonetheless, there are numerous acts whose form is not mentioned in the 1997 Rules but which meet the definition of normative legal acts subject to State registration and official publication. Within this group are acts containing ecological, sanitary-epidemiological, hygienic, fire prevention, product safety, and analogous rules. In Russian legal doctrine these have been called "normative legal acts with technical content": State standards, construction norms and rules, State sanitary-epidemiological rules, and the

[107] СЗ РФ (1997), no 33, item 3895, as amended.

like. In practice some are registered and others are not. In a case which went to the Supreme Court of the Russian Federation a citizen alleged that certain provisions of an Order of the Ministry for Communications and Informatization on the procedure for introducing technical means to conduct operational and search operations were illegal because they violated his right to secrecy of telephone conversations. The claimant contended that the Ministry Order contained references to orders of certain ministries and departments that were unregistered and not officially published. The respondents averred that the unpublished orders were of a "technical" nature, non-normative, and did not require State registration. The Supreme Court accepted this distinction in rejecting the claimant's arguments.[108] The reasoning of the Supreme Court is not persuasive against the definition of a normative legal act set out in its now repealed Decree No. 19 of 25 May 2000.[109]

Departmental acts which are not subject to registration in the view of the Ministry of Justice may be published in designated departmental gazettes.[110]

The overall result is that Russian normative legal acts are more accessible than in the past, but nonetheless there remain secret, classified, and technical normative acts, particularly with respect to entrepreneurial matters, that make it impossible for lawyers who advise to eliminate elements of legal risk arising in this connection.

Enactments of Subjects of the Federation

Pursuant to an Edict of the President of the Russian Federation of 2 April 2014, as amended, laws and other legal acts adopted by subjects of the Russian Federation are published on the "Official Internet-Portal of Legal Information" of the Government of the Russian Federation (www.pravo.gov.ru) within ten days from the day of signature thereof. Publication on this Internet-Portal constitutes official publication of the enactment. If in accordance with legislation of the respective subject of the Federation the said enactments are subject to State registration, the placement or publication of the enactment of the Internet-Portal must be within ten days of the State registration thereof.[111]

The preparation of enactments of subjects of the Russian Federation in electronic form for inclusion in the Internet-Portal is governed by

[108] Бюллетень Верховного Суда РФ [Bulletin of the Supreme Court of the Russian Federation], no. 4 (2001), pp. 10-11.

[109] See Ia. Partsii, «О лицензировании отдельных видов деятельности» [On Licensing Individual Types of Activity], Хозяйство и право [*Economy and Law*], no. 1 (2002), pp. 31-40.

[110] An example is Regulation No СФ-13-р of 19 February 2002 issued by the Ministry of Transport of the Russian Federation. Ministry acts are subject to publication in the newspaper Транспорт России [Transport of Russia]. See Российская газета [Russian Newspaper], 16 March 2002.

[111] СЗ РФ (2014), no. 14, item 1612; transl. in Butler, note 22 above.

requirements established by the federal protection service of the Russian Federation; all subjects of the Federation are expected to comply with unified formats for laws and other legal acts.

International treaties

Under Article 15(4) of the 1993 Russian Constitution, international treaties of the Russian Federation are an integral part of the Russian legal system. The Federal Law on the Procedure for the Publication of Federal Laws of 14 June 1994 provides that "international treaties ratified by the Federal Assembly shall be published simultaneously with the federal laws concerning their ratification" (Article 3). This formulation does not specify that the treaties shall be published in the same gazette as the federal law ratifying the Convention, although the СЗ РФ does publish certain international treaties. In any event the requirement of "simultaneous" often is not complied with in practice. For example, the Federal Law on the Ratification of the Convention for the Protection of Human Rights and Fundamental Freedoms and the Protocols Thereto, of 30 March 1998, was published on 6 April 1998 with the emendation that the "Convention and Protocols thereto will be published upon their entry into force for the Russian Federation".[112] Similarly, the Agreement Among the States Parties to the North Atlantic Treaty and Other States Participating in the Partnership for Peace Regarding the Status of Their Forces of 19 June 1995, the Agreement between the Parties to the North Atlantic Treaty Regarding the Status of Their Forces of 19 June 1951, and the Additional Protocol of 19 June 1995 were ratified by the Russian Federation by a Federal Law of 7 June 2007, entered into force for Russia on 27 September 2007, and were published in the Russian official gazette bearing a cover date of 11 February 2008.[113]

Those treaties which have entered into legal force, except treaties of an interdepartmental character, are subject to official publication in the Бюллетень международных договоров [Bulletin of International Treaties] published monthly by the Administration of the President of the Russian Federation.[114] When necessary, they may also appear in Российская газета [Russian Newspaper], and in practice they frequently appear in the «Ведомственное приложение» [Departmental Annex] of the same newspaper, available weekly by special subscription. These requirements

[112] СЗ РФ (1998), no. 14, item 1514.

[113] СЗ РФ (2008), no. 6, item 445. The texts were published in English and in an official Russian translation.

[114] See Edict of the President of the Russian Federation on the Procedure for the Publication of International Treaties of the Russian Federation, adopted 11 January 1993, as amended 1 December 1995. СЗ РФ (1993), no. 3, item 182; (1995), no. 49, item 4777. Some believe the Edict de facto lost force with the entry into operation of the 1995 Federal Law on International Treaties of the Russian Federation, a position difficult to sustain in light of the fact that the Edict was amended after the entry of that law into force. Consultant Plus does not adhere to the view that the Edict has lost force.

apply to international treaties which were concluded or acceded to after 1 January 1992. By an amendment to the Federal Law of 14 June 1994 adopted on 25 December 2012, treaties in force for the Russian Federation or provisionally in force are published on the "Official Internet-Portal Legal Information" (www.pravo.gov.ru). Interdepartmental international treaties are often, but not always, published in the official organs of ministries or departments which concluded those treaties.

The amendments of 25 December 2012 regarding the publication of treaties provisionally in force were required by the Constitutional Court of the Russian Federation in its Decree concerning a suit brought by I. D. Ushakov against the State Customs Service objecting to the levy of customs duties on the basis of a treaty provisionally being applied but not yet officially in force and therefore not officially published. The Constitutional Court held that a treaty of the Russian Federation could not be provisionally applied unless and until the text was officially published and directed the Russian legislator to establish the procedure for the official publication of treaties subject to provisional application.[115]

Treaties concluded between the Russian Federation and subjects of the Federation find no mention in the legislation regulating the publication and entry into force of normative legal acts. The great majority appear to be unpublished, or if published, commonly in the newspapers of the subjects of the Federation concerned or in the departmental annex to Российская газета.

Official gazettes

The Собрание законодательства Российской Федерации [Collected Legislation of the Russian Federation] appears weekly as the official periodical publication in which are published:

> Federal constitutional laws, federal laws, acts of chambers of the Federal Assembly, edicts, and regulations of the President of the Russian Federation, decrees and regulations of the Government of the Russian Federation, decisions of the Constitutional Court of the Russian Federation concerning an interpretation of the Constitution of the Russian Federation and concerning the conformity to the Constitution of the Russian Federation of laws, normative acts of the President of the Russian Federation, Soviet of the Federation, State Duma, Government of the Russian Federation, or individual provisions of the enumerated acts.[116]

[115] See the Decree of the Constitutional Court of the Russian Federation, 27 March 2012, No. 8-П. СЗ РФ (2012), no. 15, item 1810. For a fuller discussion of the Ushakov case, see Butler, note 62 above, pp. 131-135.
[116] Article 7, 1994 Federal Law, note 103 above.

The internal structure of the gazette and the forms of citation and layout of normative acts are regulated by the 1994 Federal Law. The gazette is divided into five sections. Section One contains federal constitutional laws and federal laws and in practice also contains the texts of international treaties when they are published in this gazette. Section Two consists of the acts of the chambers of the Federal Assembly. In Section Three the edicts and regulations of the President of the Russian Federation appear. Section Four publishes the decrees and regulations of the Government of the Russian Federation. Section Five reproduces the decisions of the Constitutional Court subject to publication in this gazette.

Section Two is subdivided into two parts. The first contains decrees of the chambers of the Federal Assembly adopted with regard to questions relegated by Articles 102 and 103 of the 1993 Russian Constitution to the jurisdiction of the chambers. Part Two consists of other acts of the chambers of the Federal Assembly. Sections Three and Four also are subdivided into two parts; in each case Part One consists of normative acts, whereas Part Two contains acts of a non-normative character.

Acts placed within the gazette are given a consecutive item number; annexes to acts are placed under the same item number as the act itself. The full name of the federal constitutional law or federal law is given, the date of its adoption by the State Duma and the date of its approval by the Soviet of the Federation, the name of the official who signed it, the place and date of signature, and the registration number, which consists of the type of law and the number assigned; for example, No 5-ФЗ indicates Federal Law No. 5. The numeration commences anew each calendar year, so that the number of the law without a date is not helpful. International treaties are given an item number when published in the gazette but do not have a registration number as a federal law. Only the law on ratification of the treaty has a registration number.

When changes and additions are made to a federal constitutional law, federal law, or act of a chamber of the Federal Assembly, the new version may be published in an integrated text containing all the changes and additions, or a law instructing the changes and additions to be inserted may be adopted, as the Federal Assembly may choose. In practice both approaches are widely used.

The Federal Assembly of the Russian Federation published for many years two gazettes, one official and the other not. The Парламентская газета [Parliamentary Newspaper] since October 1999 has been recognized as an official gazette for federal constitutional laws, federal laws, and decrees of the chambers of the Federal Assembly whose publication is required by the parliament. The Ведомости Федерального Собрания Российской Федерации [Gazette of the Federal Assembly of the Russian Federation], issued weekly (but some weeks have multiple "parts" or subunits of weekly issues, numbered according; for example, No. 51(2), which is weekly issues No. 51 but published in at least two (or more) physical parts), contained the texts of federal constitutional laws and federal laws and decrees adopted by the chambers of the Federal Assembly. The texts, however, did not have the stature of official texts and publication ceased in 2004.

Normative legal acts of federal agencies of executive power were subject to official publication for many years in the newspaper Российские вести [Russian News] within ten days after their registration by the Ministry of Justice. That organ eventually disappeared, leaving as the principal printed source the Бюллетень нормативных актов федеральных органов исполнительной власти [Bulletin of Normative Acts of Federal Agencies of Executive Power], issued since 1996 at various intervals and from 1998, weekly; the Bulletin ceased to be an official source of publication as from 29 May 2017. The on-line versions of these acts are official. However, they appear on-line in the "Official Internet-Portal Legal Information" network (www.pravo.gov.ru) at the discretion of the federal agencies concerned.

Digest of Laws

Russia pioneered chronological and then systematic collections of legislation (see Chapter 3) in the nineteenth century. These efforts were renewed by the Soviet authorities in the 1920s and again from the 1960s to the 1980s.[117] They resulted in a looseleaf Свод законов [Digest of Laws] of the USSR and RSFSR (and all other union republics) and a more comprehensive Собрание действующего законодательства [Collection of Prevailing Legislation] in casebound format for the USSR and RSFSR (and other union republics).[118] The enactments in each case were an official text, although neither collection was close to being exhaustive.

Following the enactment of the 1993 Russian Constitution it was decided to revive the concept of the Свод законов Российской Федерации [Digest of Laws of the Russian Federation] organized according to subject and based on a chronological collection of all normative legal acts of the USSR, RSFSR, and Russian Federation in force on the territory of Russia. The chronological collection, reportedly completed, is maintained by the Chief State Law Administration of the President of the Russian Federation. The subject matter classifications have been developed and formally enacted by Edict of the President as the General Legal Classification System of Branches of Legislation on 15 March 2000, with later revisions published in the СЗ РФ.[119]

117 See W. E. Butler, "Toward a Svod Zakonov for the Union of Soviet Socialist Republics", in D. Barry, F. J. M. Feldbrugge, and D. Lasok (eds.), *Codification in the Communist World* (1975), pp. 89-111.

118 See K. Hendley, *The Soviet Sobranie of Laws: Problems of Codification and Non-Publication* (1991).

119 СЗ РФ (2000), no. 12, item 1260, as amended.

The advisability of introducing a Digest of Laws of the Russian Federation, whether in on-line and/or looseleaf form, is disputed by many Russian jurists, who stress the necessarily transitional and consequently imperfect state of Russian legislation for the foreseeable future.[120]

ACCESS TO JUDICIAL PRACTICE

Whatever the outcome of the debate in Russian legal circles over the nature and role of judicial precedent in the Russian Federation, it is beyond doubt that judicial practice plays a significant role in Russian legal processes. In the broad sense "judicial practice" here means not only judicial decisions of all types and varieties, but also the behavior of courts and judicial personnel in administering the judicial system. The technological revolution, creation of commercial and governmental legal databases, and imposition of legal requirements for freedom of access to judicial actions have collectively transformed the ability of Russian citizens, in comparison with the Soviet period, to know what their courts are doing.

The publication of judicial practice is governed by the Federal Law on Ensuring Access to Information on the Activity of Courts in the Russian Federation of 22 December 2008, as amended.[121] Internet access proves to be the key instrument, and all Russian courts are required to comply, of whatever level or nature.

The following must be placed on the "Internet":

(1) general information on the court:

(a) the name of the court, name of the court district to whose territory the jurisdiction of the court extends, postal address, e-mail address (when there is such), telephone number at which information of a reference character may be received;

(b) organizational structure of the court – plenum of the court, presidium of the court, chambers of the court, judicial divisions, permanent judicial offices, advisory and/or consultative organs (when there are such), and also the structural subdivisions of the apparatus of the court;

(c) powers of the court;

(d) list of laws regulating the activity of the court;

[120] For the debate and draft outlines of the Digest, see S. V. Polenina and N. P. Koldaeva, "On the Digest of Laws of the Russian Federation", *Sudebnik,* III (1998), pp. 28-81.

[121] C3 PΦ (2008), no. 52(I), item 6217, as amended; transl. in Butler, note 22 above.

(e) reglament of the court, instruction on clerical work on the court, and other acts regulating questions of the internal activity of the court;

(f) surnames, forenames, and patronymics of the chairman of the court, deputy chairman of the court, judges, executives of the apparatus of the court, and with the consent of the said persons – other information on them; grounds for endowing with power of the chairman of the court, deputy chairmen of the court, judges;

(g) lists of information systems and data banks within the jurisdiction of the court (when there are such);

(h) name of the mass media (journals, bulletins, gazettes, and others) founded by the court (when there are such);

(2) information connected with the consideration of the cases in the court:

(a) requirements for the form and content of documents used when having recourse to the court and/or samples of these documents and the procedure for the submission of the said documents to the court;

(b) information concerning the amount and procedure for the payment of State duty for the categories of cases subject to consideration in the court;

(c) information concerning the cases in the court: registration numbers of the cases, names thereof or subject-matter of the dispute, information concerning the participants in the judicial process, information concerning the passage of the cases in the court, and also information concerning the rendering of judicial acts with regard to the results of the consideration of the cases (designated for hearing with an indication of dates, time, and place of holding the judicial cession, considered, deferred, suspended, terminated, concluded amicable agreement, application left without consideration, and others, taking into account the peculiarities of the respective proceeding). Information concerning the participants shall be placed on the "Internet", subject to the requirements below;

(d) texts of judicial acts to be placed, information concerning the appeal thereof and the results of such appeal, and when judicial acts are published, information concerning the sources of their publication;

(e) procedure for appeal of judicial acts;

(f) explanations, generalizations, and surveys with regard to questions of judicial practice of the consideration of cases by courts;

(g) telephone numbers at which information of a reference character may be received, including on the passage of cases in court;

(h) information concerning extra-procedural resources received by judges with regard to cases in their proceedings, or the chairman of the court, deputy thereof, chairman of the bench, or chairman of a judicial division for cases in proceedings of the court, including the content of extra-procedural recourses and information concerning the subjects thereof;

(i) information concerning the broadcast of judicial sessions on the "Internet" with references to the name of the mass media or site on the "Internet" by means of which the broadcast was effectuated;

(3) texts of draft normative legal acts submitted by courts to legislative (or representative) agencies of State power (for courts which are subjects of the right of legislative initiative);

(4) forensic statistics to the extent established by the Constitutional Court of the Russian Federation, Supreme Court of the Russian Federation, and Judicial Department;

(5) information concerning personnel provision of the court:

(a) procedure for endowing judges with powers, requirements for candidates for the office of judge and procedure for the selection thereof;

(b) information concerning the vacant office of a judge and vacant offices of State service in the apparatus of the court;

(c) procedure for entry of citizens into State service in the apparatus of the court, qualifications requirements for candidates for the filling of vacant offices of State service in the apparatus of the court;

(d) conditions for conducting and the results of competitions to fill vacant offices of State service of State service in the apparatus of the court;

(e) telephone numbers at which information may be received with regard to questions of filling the vacant office of judge and vacant offices of State service in the apparatus of the court;

(6) information concerning the procedure and time for the reception of citizens (natural persons), including representatives of organizations (juridical persons), social associations, agencies of State power and agencies of local self-government, procedure for the consideration of their recourses with regard to questions of the organization of the activity of the court, appeals against actions (or failure to act) of a judge or workers of the apparatus of the court not connected with the consideration of concrete cases, appeal of judicial acts and procedural actions of judges, and also the telephone numbers at which information of a reference character may be received;

(7) information concerning the purchases of goods, work, and services for the needs of courts in accordance with legislation of the Russian Federation on the contract system in the sphere of purchases of goods, work, and services for ensuring State and municipal needs.

The Constitutional Court of the Russian Federation, together with the information specified above, must place on its official site the message of the Constitutional Court of the Russian Federation to the Federal Assembly of the Russian Federation concerning the state of constitutional legality in the Russian Federation.

The Supreme Court of the Russian Federation, together with the information specified above, must place on its official site information concerning the judicial system of the Russian Federation.

The Judicial Department must place on the "Internet":

(1) general information concerning the Judicial Department:

- (a) powers and structure of the Judicial Department, postal address, e-mail address, and telephone number at which information of a reference character may be received;
- (b) list of normative legal acts regulating the activity of the Judicial Department;
- (c) list of agencies of the Judicial Department, powers thereof, and also the postal addresses, e-mail addressed, and telephone numbers of references services of agencies of the Judicial Department;
- (d) surnames, forenames, and patronymics of the General Director of the Judicial Department attached to the Supreme Court of the Russian Federation, deputies of the General Director of the Judicial Department attached to the Supreme Court of the Russian Federation and executives of agencies of the Judicial Department and, with the consent of the said persons, other information concerning them;
- (e) federal targeted programs and other programs for the development of the judicial system of the Russian Federation (when there are such);
- (f) lists of information systems and data banks in the jurisdiction of the Judicial Department;

(2) information concerning agencies of the judge's commonwealth:

- (a) list of agencies of the judge's commonwealth operating on the territory of the Russian Federation, and the powers thereof;
- (b) list of normative legal acts regulating the activity of agencies of the judge's commonwealth;

(c) decisions of the High Qualifications Collegium of Judges of the Russian Federation concerning the suspension, renewal, or termination of the powers of judges of the respective courts, qualifications attestation of judges, and also information concerning the imposition of disciplinary sanctions on them.

The Judicial Department also must place on the "Internet":

(1) yearly reports of the General Director of the Judicial Department attached to the Supreme Court of the Russian Federation concerning the activity of the Judicial Department submitted to the Chairman of the Supreme Court of the Russian Federation, to the Council of Judges of the Russian Federation, and to the All-Russian Congress of Judges;

(2) surveys concerning the activity of courts, forensic statistics data published in the mass media in accordance with acts regulating the activity of the Judicial Department with regard to keeping forensic statistics;

(3) information concerning the purchases of goods, work, and services for the needs of courts in accordance with legislation of the Russian Federation on the contract system in the sphere of purchases of goods, work, and services for ensuring State and municipal needs.

An agency of the Judicial Department must place on the "Internet":

(1) general information on the agency of the Judicial Department:

(a) name, powers, and structure of the agency of the Judicial Department, postal address, e-mail address, telephone number of the reference service of the agency of the Judicial Department;

(b) list of normative legal acts which regulate the activity of the agency of the Judicial Department;

(c) surnames, forenames, and patronymic of the executive of the agency of the Judicial Department, deputy executives of the agency of the Judicial Department, and, with the consent of the said persons – other information concerning them;

(2) information concerning judges' community agencies operating on the territory of the respective subject of the Russian Federation:

(a) list of judges' community agencies and the powers thereof;

(b) list of normative legal acts regulating the activity of judges' community agencies;

(c) decisions of the qualifications collegium of judges of the respective subject of the Russian Federation concerning the suspension, renewal, or termination of the powers of judges of the respective courts, qualifications attestation of the judges, and also information concerning the imposition of disciplinary sanctions on them.

The balance between transparency in the judicial system by way of publication of details and the privacy of the parties or other participants in judicial proceedings or the protection of State secrecy has been adjusted more than once by way of amendments to the 2008 Federal Law. At present the balance is as follows:

The texts of judicial acts, except for judgments and judicial acts of arbitrazh courts, must be placed on the "Internet" within a reasonable period, but no later than one month after the day of their adoption in final form. The texts of judgments are placed no later than one month from the day of their entry into legal force. The texts of judicial acts of arbitrazh courts are placed on the "Internet" no later than the following day after the day of their adoption.

The texts of judicial acts subject in accordance with the law to publication, and also the texts of other judicial acts submitted by the Constitutional Court of the Russian Federation, constitutional (or charter) courts of subjects of the Russian Federation, and the Supreme Court of the Russian Federation, with regard to cases to be considered in accordance with arbitrazh procedure legislation, and by arbitrazh courts, except for secrecy issues, are placed on the "Internet" in full.

When placing on the "Internet" the texts of judicial acts adopted by courts of general jurisdiction or by the Supreme Court of the Russian Federation, except for the texts of judicial acts adopted by the Supreme Court of the Russian Federation in accordance with arbitrazh procedure legislation, for the purposes of ensuring the security of participants of a judicial proceeding and the defense of State and other secrecy protected by a law, personal data is excluded from these acts in certain instances. Instead of the excluded personal data, initials, pseudonyms, and other designations are used not enabling the participants of the judicial proceeding to be identified. The identification number of a taxpayer-individual entrepreneur, basic State registration number of an individual entrepreneur, surname, forename, and patronymic of a plaintiff, defendant, third person, civil plaintiff, civil defendant, administrative plaintiff, administrative defendant, interested person, person with respect to whom the proceeding in a case of an administrative violation is being held, surname, forename, and patronymic of a convicted person, acquitted person, secretary of the judicial session, judge(s) who considered the case, and also the procurator, advokat, and representative are not subject to exclusion. When placing texts on judicial acts on the "Internet" adopted by the Constitutional Court of the Russian Federation, constitutional (or charter) courts of subjects of the Russian Federation, certain personal data is excluded, except for the surnames, forenames, and patronymics of the applicants, representatives of the parties invited to the session by representatives of State agencies, experts, and specialists. In exceptional instances for the purposes of ensuring the security of the applicant and/or his representative, the Constitutional Court of the Russian Federation or constitutional (or charter) courts of a subject of the Russian Federation may upon the petition of the applicant or the representative thereof or at own initiative, adopt a decision to exclude their personal data and use instead of the excluded personal data the initials, pseudonyms, or other designations not enabling the applicant and/or representative thereof to be identified.

Personal data with regard to judicial acts is considered to be:

(1) surnames, forenames, and patronymics of participants of a judicial proceeding, date and place of birth, place of residence of sojourn, telephone numbers, requisites of passport or other document certifying identity, identification number of taxpayer-natural person, basic State registration number of individual entrepreneur, and insurance number of individual account;

(2) information concerning the location of a land plot, building, installation, dwelling house, apartment, means of transport, and other information concerning property and monetary means of participants of a judicial proceeding in banks or other credit institutions, if such information is relegated to the essence of the case.

Texts of judicial acts are not subject to placement on the "Internet" rendered with regard to cases concerning:

(1) the security of the State;

(2) family law relations, including cases concerning the adoption of a child and other cases affecting the rights and legal interests of minors;

(3) crimes against sexual inviolability and sexual freedom of the individual;

(4) limitation of the dispositive legal capacity of a citizen or deeming him to lack dispositive legal capacity;

(5) compulsory hospitalization of a citizen in a psychiatric in-patient institution and compulsory psychiatric certification;

(6) making corrections and changes in an entry of acts of civil status;

(7) the establishment of facts having legal significance to be considered by courts of general jurisdiction; or

(8) to be decided by way of Article 126 of the Code of Civil Procedure of the Russian Federation or by Article 123^{5} of the Code on Administrative Procedure of the Russian Federation.

In the event of the placement on the "Internet" of the texts of judicial acts providing for provisions which contain information comprising a State or other secret protected by a law, these provisions shall be excluded from the texts of judicial acts

These are far-reaching provisions because, although they determine the parameters of access to judicial practice, they determine the style and limits of case reports by the courts and by commercial providers of legal databases. Courts which do not fall within the operation of the 2008 Federal Law will have their own regulations governing access to judicial practice.

6

LEGAL PROFESSION AND LEGAL EDUCATION

The expression "jurist" [юрист] in the Russian language can be understood in the broad sense to encompass all who have a legal education and all who work in a legal specialty, whether as academician, professor, judge, procurator, arbitrator, notary, investigator, advokat, jurisconsult, ZAGS personnel, paralegal, or whatever. In this chapter we examine two types of jurist who most closely approximate the narrower Anglo-American concept of the lawyer, solicitor, barrister, or attorney-at-law, that is, those who principally advise citizens and juridical persons or appear in court on their behalf. These in the Russian legal system are the advokat and the jurisconsult.

Advokats and foreign lawyers who "effectuate advokat activity on the territory of the Russian Federation" are required to undergo, as of 1 July 2002, registration in a special register, the procedure for keeping which is implemented by the Ministry of Justice of the Russian Federation. The requirement of licensing, introduced by the President of the Russian Federation in 1991 and implemented by the Government of the Russian Federation from 15 April 1995,[1] was effectively abolished when the long-awaited Federal Law on the Licensing of Individual Types of Activity, of 25 September 1998, as amended, failed to include legal services on the list of activities subject to licensing.[2] This had the effect of restoring the long-established practice of regarding Soviet law graduates as immediately qualified in principle to practice upon receiving their first degree in law from an institution of higher education. When the 1998 law was replaced on 8 August 2001 by another federal law bearing the same name, legal services were omitted again from the list of those requiring a license, as they were in the federal law of 4 May 2011, also bearing the same title.[3] However, the Federal Law on Advokat Activity and the Advokatura of 31 May 2002 introduced the special register mentioned above.

[1] СЗ РФ (1995), no. 17, item 1550; repealed by Decree of the Government, No 548, of 20 May 1999. СЗ РФ (1999), no. 21, item 2637.

[2] СЗ РФ (1998), no. 48, item 5853, as amended; lost force 8 August 2001.

[3] СЗ РФ (2001), no. 33, item 3430, as amended; transl. in W E Butler, *Russia & The Republics: Legal Materials* (looseleaf service, 2006-); СЗ РФ (2011), no. 19, item 2716. For a discussion of the reform of the Advokatura leading up to the 2002 Federal Law on the Advokatura, see L. V. Liashenko, Развитие адвокатской деятельности в условиях проведения судебной реформы в Российской Федарации [Development of Advokat Activity in Conditions of Conducting the Judicial Reform in the Russian Federation] (Moscow, 2014).

It is common for auditors in Russia to have a degree in law, although degrees in economics and certain other disciplines are deemed to be acceptable for this profession. Under the Federal Law on Auditor Activity of 30 December 2008, as amended, auditing organizations and individual auditors may render "legal assistance in fields connected with auditor activity" (Article 1(7)(5)).[4] The last includes consultations on legal questions, representation of interests of the principal in a civil and administrative proceeding, in tax and customs law relations, and in agencies of State power and agencies of local self-government; an auditor's license is sufficient to sanction the rendering of such services without any additional licenses.

ORIGINS OF LEGAL REPRESENTATION

Legal representation, that is, the right and/or practice to have another individual appear to speak on one's behalf and to act in one's interest in a court of law, has a venerable history in Muscovy and Imperial Russia. Whether individuals who acted in this capacity with frequency or routinely may collectively be described as a legal profession or even the antecedents of the legal profession is more problematic, although not to be dismissed completely.

The periodization of the history of the legal profession in Russia has concentrated upon the Advokatura and its precursors to the detriment of the jurisconsult. A standard approach identifies four periods: (1) the pre-Advokatura times prior to the judicial reforms of 1864; (2) the classical Russian Advokatura (1864-1917); (3) the Soviet Advokatura (1917-1991); and (4) the modern Russian Advokatura (post-1991).[5] The surviving documents from Kievan Rus do not mention the institution of representation in any form. The presupposition is that personal appearance in court was expected and required.[6]

The "pre-Advokatura" period in its early stages is the history of legal representation as such rather than the emergence of a group of professionals specializing in such representation. The Novgorod Judicial Charter made provision in several places for a "representative" (ответщик) to act on

[4] СЗ РФ (2009), no. 1, item 15, as amended, replacing the Federal Law of identical name of 7 August 2001. СЗ РФ (2001), no. 33, item 3430, as amended.

[5] See A. V. Klevtsov, «Периодизация истории российской адвокатуры» [Periodization of the History of the Russian Advokatura], Адвокатская Палата [Advokat Chamber], no. 6 (2006), p. 4; also see A. V. Vorobev, A. V. Poliakov, and Iu. V. Tikhonravov, Теория адвокатуры [Theory of the Advokatura] (2002), pp. 444-447. Among the weaknesses of this periodization are not merely overlooking the jurisconsult and minimizing gradations in the role of the *striapchii*, but also linking the history of the institution to changes in political regime rather than, for example, the legislation on the legal profession.

[6] See T. M. Shamba and V. N. Kokin, Адвокатура в Российской Федерации [Advokatura in the Russian Federation] (3d ed.; 2010), p. 26.

behalf of a party. There were no limitations on who could so act. In the Kaiser translation:

> 5. And at court [there should be no more than] two men. If someone selects someone [else to represent him in court], then he must allow him [his representative] to conduct the case. …
>
> 15. If a representative from some plaintiff presents himself at court, and the complainant will not have kissed the cross [to be faithful] to this charter, then the complainant is to kiss the cross alone, and the defendant in his place answers [the charge]; but [if] he does not kiss the cross, then he loses [the case].
>
> 18. If they summon a boyar or man of middling means or merchant to his land, or to [his] wife's land, then he [himself] is to answer [them] or send a representative in his place and in [his] wife's [place], [and] kiss the cross on that.
>
> 19. And the representative [whom the defendant nominated] and a character witness are to kiss the cross at the hearing. ….
>
> 32. If a representative be in someone's place [and he] received a postponement, but before [the expiration] of that postponement the replacement died, then at the [expiration of the] postponement the litigant himself must appear [in court] or [he must nominate] some other representative [to appear in his place]; if he himself does not appear or if he does not nominate another representative [to appear in court in his place], then he loses the case.[7]

The text of the Novgorod Judicial Charter is incomplete, dates from about the 1470s, and incorporates elements reflecting the Muscovy presence in that principality. The extent to which these factors corrupt a pure Novgorodian account of legal representation can only be the subject of speculation. It is noteworthy that these texts are believed to record the existence of customary practices rather than to newly create and introduce the concept of representation.

Legal representation under the Pskov Judicial Charter (point 58) was permitted in a more limited way to women, children, monks, nuns, or any person who is old or deaf; they might have a "helper" (пособник).[8]

[7] See D. H. Kaiser (transl. & ed.), *The Laws of Rus' – Tenth to Fifteenth Centuries* (1992), pp. 79, 81, 84. I have modified the translation of point 15, as the translation plainly contains a typing error there. Also on the Charter, see F. J. M. Feldbrugge, *A History of Russian Law* (2018), pp. 184-187, where no mention is made of the provisions on representation.

[8] Kaiser, note 7 above, p. 97. The Pskov Judicial Charter is believed to date from 1397 to 1467 and to incorporate norms from a variety of sources, among them the Russkaia Pravda, decrees of the veche, a form of popular assembly, princely charters of Alexander (1327-1330) and Constantine (1404-1417), decisions of the ruling council, and rules of customary law. See R. Hellie, in Kaiser, note 7 above, p. xxiii. In describing this period, modern Russian historians

Officials were excluded from acting as a representative in order to avoid undue influence upon the court. Vladimirskii-Budanov doubted that "hired attorneys" were possible in this period: "this is evident from the fact that the Pskov Judicial Charter (point 71) prohibited the same attorney from conducting two cases on the same day".[9]

The possibility of the plaintiff or defendant not appearing in court was provided for by the 1497 Sudebnik (Article 36),[10] in which event they might send a representative to replace them. In the 1550 version of the Sudebnik (Article 13) the parties might have representatives in the form of *striapchie* and *poruchniki* in the event of a judicial duel. Whether these should be likened to legal representatives or to "seconds" is ambiguous,[11] nor do the materials definitively disclose whether persons acting in these capacities were "retained" or "hired" for these roles.[12] By the end of the sixteenth century the judicial duel had disappeared from Muscovite legal proceedings and the passages of the 1550 Sudebnik were eliminated or revised accordingly.[13]

The 1649 *Sobornoe ulozhenie* (Chapter 10, points 108 and 109) reinforced the right of a party to be represented by another under specified circumstances:

> But if a plaintiff or defendant becomes incapacitated prior to that continuance date, and because of illness he is unable to come to the chancellery by any means: he shall send on the appointed

of the advokatura use the term poverennyi (attorney) to describe the type of representation available. It should be noted that the original sources do not use that word and its aptness is subject to doubt.

[9] M. F. Vladimirskii-Budanov, Очерки истории русского права [Survey of the History of Russian Law] (6th ed.; Spb.-Kiev, 1909), p. 616. Also see Iu. G. Alekseev, Псковская Судная грамота и ее время. Развитие феодальных отношений на Руси XIV-XV вв. [Pskov Judicial Charter and Its Time: Development of Feudal Relations in Rus XIV-XV Centuries] (1980).

[10] See the translation by H. W. Dewey, *Muscovite Judicial Texts 1488-1556* (1966), p. 15. The text is suitably vague, referring merely to "someone" to act as the substitute in order to request a postponement.

[11] For a translation of the 1550 Sudebnik, see Dewey, ibid., pp. 49-50. Dewey translated the term *striapchii* as "backer" or "second". Ibid., p. 93.

[12] O. I. Chistiakov (ed.), Российское законодательство X-XX веков [Russian Legislation X-XX Centuries] (1985), II, pp. 58, 99. A legacy of the Soviet era is that the Commentary to these articles makes no reference to their implications for legal representation in Russia. For the assumption that these officials were remunerated for their services and constituted "hired attorneys", see A. G. Kucherena, Адвокатура в условиях судебно-правовой реформы в России [Advokatura in Conditions of Judicial and Legal Reform in Russia] (2009), p. 10. Also see S. Kucherov, *Courts, Lawyers and Trials Under the Last Three Tsars* (1953), p. 109: "Subsequent codes – the *Sudebniki* of Ivan III and Ivan IV, as well as the *Ulozheniye Tsarya Alekseya Mikhailovicha* – speak of hired representatives in court as of a well-established institution" (pp. 107-108).

[13] See A. S. Smykalin, Русское законодательство конца XVI -- начала XVII века [Russian Legislation at the End of the Sixteenth and Early Seventeenth Centuries] (2005), p. 61. The 1589 Sudebnik had eliminated reference to the judicial duel and, accordingly, to the *striapchie* in this connection.

date someone whom he trusts in his stead to pursue the suit or the defense. If someone fails to send someone in this stead on that mutually agreed date to pursue the suit or defense: direct the verdict against him in that case for that reason … [point 108]

If that plaintiff on the appointed date or after the date proceeds to send in his stead for the trial his son, or kinsman, or anyone else; and he himself at that time is unable to go to trial because of illness or for any other reason: order that person whom he sends to trial in his stead to pursue the suit in his stead.[14]

Whether such representatives were retained or hired is not disclosed by the texts of the legislation. In short, the institute of representation was established by Muscovite legislation, but the extent to which such representation could be said to constitute the embryo of an organized legal profession is obscure.[15]

The *striapchii, poruchnik,*[16] "helper", and others described as representatives throughout the medieval period of Rus and Muscovy in various forms of documents are not discrete classifications. Of the terms that endured into the Enlightenment, the *striapchii* is best known in a variety of meanings. Pushkarev confirmed that in Muscovite legal documents the *striapchii* was an aide, second, or representative of litigants and later came in the eighteenth and nineteenth centuries to designate persons who acted as "private solicitors" in the commercial courts. However, during the seventeenth century the *striapchie* collectively comprised a group and rank of men in service numbering perhaps as many as 800.[17] In the hierarchy of ranks they followed the *stol'niki.*[18] Some usages appear to confirm that the *striapchii* undertook to represent litigants before courts, whether remunerated or not; it is the mixing or confusion of roles that remains in doubt (i.e., did they act in the interests of the litigant represented or actually

[14] R. Hellie (transl. & ed.), *The Muscovite Law Code (Ulozhenie) of 1649* (1988), I, p. 38.

[15] Nonetheless, modern Russian advokats suggest that these legislative enactments indicate that the "institute of hired attorneys" existed. See Kucherena, note 12 above, p. 10.

[16] The term *poruchnik* suggests an individual acting more as a second, or a guarantor, than a representative, although representation functions are implicit in those roles. The term is used in the 1497 Sudebnik.

[17] See M. T. Poe, *The Russian Elite in the Seventeenth Century: A Quantitative Analysis of the "Duma Ranks" 1613-1713* (2004). 2 vols.

[18] S. G. Pushkarev (comp.), *Dictionary of Russian Historical Terms from the Eleventh Century to 1917* (1970), p. 150. See the various examples of usage given in V. B. Krysko (ed.), Словарь русского языка XI-XVII вв. [Dictionary of the Russian Language XI-XVII Centuries] (2008), XXVIII, p. 203. In its legal usage the *striapchii* is equated to the *khodatai*; the term is traced in written sources to the 1497 Sudebnik. See M. A. Isaev, Толковый словарь древнерусских юридических терминов [Interpretative Dictionary of Medieval Russian Legal Terminology] (2d ed.; 2017), p. 183; Poe placed the *striapchii* just after the *zhiltsy* and two beneath the Dvoriane Moskovskie and *stol'niki* with the category of "Sub-Duma" court ranks. See Poe, note 17 above, II, p. 24.

operate as court officials on behalf of the "State"). The term "poverennyi" (attorney) traces back to the 1690s, but without specific juridical usage.[19]

The term "advokat" dates from the Petrine period, ca. 1713.[20] In the "Concise Depiction of Trials or Judicial Litigation of 1715", Chapter 5 of which was entitled "On Advokats and Empowered Persons", litigants who were unable to appear in person in court were allowed to use advokats and other persons.[21] Although this is the first legislative use of the term "advokat", the advokat in this instance was a representative and did not differ in status from the terms used for a "representative" in earlier Russian legislation.[22] That is, the advokat replaced or substituted for the plaintiff or defendant and did not appear side by side with him to defend his interests.

Pursuant to an Edict of 5 November 1723, civil cases were prepared for hearing not by the *striapchii*, but by State officials. The parties need merely submit their requests, documents, and evidence, after which the court considered the matter. Procedural periods for considering cases were not established by legislation, which gave officials the opportunity to delay consideration arbitrarily without informing the parties as to where the case stood. This became an occasion for bribery and for seeking the assistance of others to determine at what stage the proceeding was.

Whether such views were just or otherwise, modern Russian advokats see the role of the *striapchii* becoming one in which his formal role was to collect and draw up documents, to confuse matters, to drag out and delay consideration of the case; individuals retained the services of the *striapchii* precisely to this end and evaluated the quality of services rendered against these criteria.[23] A modern critique recites that the "principal distinctive feature of the status of the *striapchii* lies in the fact that he was not linked either by control on the part of a professional corporation or by self-control

[19] G. A. Bogatova (ed.), Словарь русского языка XI-XVII вв. [Dictionary of the Russian Language XI-XVII Centuries] (1989), XXV, p. 148.

[20] Iu. S. Sorokin (ed.), Словарь русского языка XVIII века [Dictionary of the Russian Language XVIII Century] (1984), I, p. 25. The term "advokat" was initially introduced in Russian to describe the western European institution of the advokat.

[21] This document may have been composed and published as early as 1712 but assuredly appeared as a separate book in March 1715. A month later it was published in a single volume together with the Military Statute, with which it is often confused. Some believe that Ernst Friedrich Krompen prepared the first draft, which may explain the introduction of the European term. Peter the Great is believed to personally have edited and added to the draft.

[22] See O. I. Chistiakov, in A. G. Mankov (ed.), Российское законодательство X-XX веков [Russian Legislation X-XX Centuries] (1986), IV, pp. 404-405.

[23] See Kucherena, note 12 above, p. 11. The qualities of the *striapchie* figured in European perceptions at the time of their own legal personnel: "[Jurists] … were regarded as a boon to the rich, who could pay for their services and so prolong legal proceedings indefinitely, but as a bane to the poor, who could often afford to be represented only by half-trained but glib impostors, falsely claiming to be learned jurists. As a class, jurists were seen as unscrupulous and bad Christians … and there were many popular stories of how St. Peter waited in vain at the gate of heaven for a jurist to appear". P. Stein, *Roman Law in European History* (1999), p. 92.

in complying with professional standards. The *striapchii* was in principle unable to be in an estate and his essence was contrary to being organized in any way and to social solidarity".[24]

Perhaps reflecting his Scottish legal education, the first Russian professor of law in the Russian Empire, the Ukrainian S. E. Desnitskii (c. 1740-1789),[25] used the term "advokat" in his understanding of the "general-advokat". In his conception the "general advokat" would be a State prosecutor or plaintiff who would by his presence in the civil and criminal courts determine that "everything in detail may be judged according to the decrees" and perform certain pre- and post-conviction functions.[26]

On 7 November 1775 Empress Catherine II elaborated a reform of State territorial-administrative division introduced by Peter the Great in 1708 and divided Russia into forty *guberniya*, or governates.[27] Pursuant to the reform, the *striapchii* became an aide to the procurator and the protector of treasury interests.[28] However, these governate *striapchie* could not bring suit in court other than with the prior approval of the *namestnik* governing body, having presented their evidence to that body first. These roles were enhanced in further administrative-territorial reforms introduced in 1785. In the Charter on the Rights, Freedoms, and Privileges of the Well-Born Russian Nobility, dated 21 April 1785, the *striapchii* was assigned the function of overseeing that the Assembly of the Nobility did not impose requirements in violation of legislation (point 49) and of defending the Assembly of the Nobility in court (point 56). The same tasks were placed on the *striapchii* serving towns under the Charter on the Rights and Benefits for the Towns of the Russian Empire, also issued on 21 April 1785 (points 37, 44, 45) and was included in the unpromulgated State Charter to the State Peasants (points 14, 21).[29]

Who might be appointed to act as *striapchii* is not indicated. There were no requirements of age, education, moral qualities, or experience. Whether graduates of the Law Faculty at Moscow University entered service as a *striapchii* remains to be investigated.

[24] Vorobev, note 5 above, p. 59.

[25] See the biographical account in V. A. Tomsinov, Российские правоведы XVIII-XX веков [Russian Jurists of the XVIII-XX Centuries] (2007), I, pp. 131-156.

[26] For a translation of the Desnitskii proposal, see P. Dukes, *Russia Under Catherine the Great* (1978), I, pp. 52-53.

[27] ПСЗ, XX (1st ser.), No. 14,392, pp. 229-304.

[28] In his summary account of this enactment Dukes called the *striapchii* an "attorney". See Dukes, note 26 above, I, p. 144.

[29] See D. Griffiths and G. E. Munro (transl. & eds.), *Catherine II's Charters of 1785 to the Nobility and the Towns* (1991). See the references under Provincial Solicitor and Solicitor. These usages of the term *striapchii* contrast sharply with the usage in point 92(16) of the Charter on the nobility, where reference is made to the hierarchy of ranks.

PRECURSORS OF THE RUSSIAN LEGAL PROFESSION

In the western provinces of the Russian Empire the situation differed. The Lithuanian Statute of 1529 made reference (in the English translation) to the "advocate", providing that "On matters concerning estates, damages, [or] violence, no foreigner may speak as an advocate concerning that [matter] neither before us, the sovereign, nor in a land trial, but only one who is landed in the Grand Principality".[30] The principle of legal representation of one person in place of another was replicated in the 1529 Lithuanian Statute, subject to certain documentary formalities, in much the same version as the 1497 and 1550 Sudebniks.

A form of advokatura existed in the nine governates (six Belorussian and Lithuanian and three Ukrainian) of Russia comprising the Western Territory which became part of the Empire in the late eighteenth century as a result of the Partition of Poland. The advokatura was organized and operated under the Lithuanian Statute and the Polish constitutions of 1726 and 1764 and was attached to the governate and lower (uezd and city) courts, including canon law courts.

A Report of the Ruling Senate confirmed by the Emperor on 14 December 1797 on the situation in the Lithuanian province observed that abuses were occurring by people who had knowledge of the laws and rights of litigants and who stirred up litigation, increasing the caseload of the courts. To redress the situation it was decided to increase the requirements for becoming an "advokat" in the province. An advokat should be a noble, have his own estate villages in, at least, the province, know the laws, comply with his oath, and be of good character. Those who acted as a *striapchii* might be excluded from this status if that person appeared in court while intoxicated or neglected a case by reason of drunkenness or was discovered to be gambling.[31]

[30] See Karl von Loewe, *The Lithuanian Statute of 1529* (1976), p. 63. The Cyrillic texts form the basis of von Loewe's translation; the word translated as "advocate" was "procurator" in the original, defined in the glossary as the "representative of a litigant in court" (p. 194). The versions of the Lithuanian Statute of 1566 and 1588 contained similar norms. See I. N. Kuznetsov and V. A. Shelkoplias, История государства и права Беларуси [History of State and Law of Belarus] (Minsk, 2004), pp. 48-60. A recent Russian translation used the expression "entrusted person" (доверенное лицо) rather than "advokat" to translate "procurator", noting that this term and institution was a new phenomenon in Lithuanian law. The usage of the term gives grounds "... to speak about the 'procurator' as a specialist actually hired and highly-paid, that is, an advokat in the contemporary understanding". But the term "advokat" in the early sixteenth century meant a "governor-general" in court cases in the Grand Principality of Lithuania "as in the countries of Europe at that time". See S. Lazutka, I. Valikonyte, and E. Gudavicius, Первый Литовский статут (1529 г.) [First Lithuanian Statute (1529)] (Vilnius, 2004), pp. 283, 378.

[31] Summarized in Kucherena, note 12 above, p. 12.

Young people who wished to become advokats were called "applicants" (pupils) and prepared to qualify for the title of advokat by studying with experienced advokats called "patrons". The patrons assumed responsibility for their pupils before the court and law and could be accompanied by the pupils in court. In certain instances the patrons could send their pupils to act in court in place of themselves but under their responsibility.

By an Edict of 25 June 1840, the operation of Russian civil and procedural legislation was extended to the Western Territory and the advokats there were replaced by the attorney (*poverennyi*), common throughout the Russian Empire.

Russian legislation made provision for certain categories of the clergy and military, merchants, and others accused of a crime, that is, individuals whose rank or title attached them to a particular department of the State, to be represented by "deputies" from those departments. Landowners might be deputies of their peasants. Interrogations and investigative actions were to be carried out in the presence of these deputies except for (1) initial investigative actions; (2) investigation of an incident on the basis of "hot pursuit". These deputies were subdivided into the categories of "permanent" and "temporary".

The permanent deputies were individuals from the clergy, petty bourgeoisie, and merchants assigned to this task. The others were temporarily assigned to a particular investigation only. The permanent deputies were summoned to duty on the basis of a writ issued by the investigators; temporary deputies were assigned by the leadership of the departments to which they were affiliated. If for any reason an investigator arrived to perform his duties and there was no deputy, the local head of the *volost* or the *starshina* was summoned to remain until the investigation was completed or the deputy arrived.

The rights and duties of permanent and temporary deputies were regulated by legislation. They watched over the correctness and completeness of the investigation and by their signature so certified. If they disagreed with any action or failure to act by the investigator, they might set out their own view, which was attached to the file of the case. Deputies might be present as well during civil matters. They were, in substance and concept, acting more in the role of a verifier of the investigation than a defender of the person under investigation.

On 14 May 1832 the institute of the sworn *striapchii* was introduced by legislation in the commercial courts first established in St. Petersburg and Moscow and later in Odessa, Warsaw, and elsewhere. The sworn *striapchii* duly registered enjoyed a monopoly on the right of audience in the commercial courts in cases between private individuals. The list of persons who might engage in practice in the commercial courts included those who submitted attestations, service lists, or other evidence of their rank and behavior. It was left to the commercial court at its discretion to include the applicant on the list or to decline to do so orally without giving reasons. A person admitted to the ranks of the sworn *striapchii* took an oath. The courts were instructed to admit a sufficient number of sworn *striapchie* so that litigants could make a choice readily among possible individuals; however, the institute was so devised that the *striapchii* was dependent entirely upon the judge. A *striapchii* could be excluded from the list without reasons given. Nonetheless, despite the limitations and restrictions, the sworn *striapchii* was remunerated by the principal in the case on the basis of a contract.

There also existed the so-called "underground" or "street" advokatura composed of individuals who were well acquainted with the court system and officials and sought to influence the course or outcome of cases through the manipulation of legal technicalities or other forms of influence. They literally often gave their "consultations" to clients in pubs and were in the public mind during the eighteenth and nineteenth centuries associated with false accusations. As a rule, they had no formal legal education or knowledge of the law. Rather than prohibit their activities, the State sought to regulate them in rudimentary form. Under a Law of 15 October 1809, all persons in Moscow and St. Petersburg acting as *striapchie* were required to register with the police at the Address Office and to leave their internal passport or residence permit; they were thereupon issued with a residence document that served simultaneously as a residence permit and a certificate of approval to engage in their professional activity.[32]

Most of these "solicitors" remained unregulated; their presence and their activities were cited as being among the factors that led to the introduction of the judicial reforms in 1864.

THE ADVOKAT

Formation of the Russian Advokatura: 1864-1917

Few contest the characterization of the years 1864 to 1917 as the "Golden Age" of the Russian legal profession. The issues are rather: why and how did the Golden Age come to pass? Was it the immediate and spontaneous consequence of the enactment of legislation on judicial reform and the establishment of the Advokatura? Or was it part of the culmination of decades of increasing legal professionalization within the Russian State: that is, was it not the result rather than the commencement of legal modernization processes at work in Russian society. The case is compelling that the latter offers a better explanation.[33]

[32] Russian doctrinal writings disagree as to whether the registration requirement extended only to solicitors in commercial cases (ходатай по делам) or to all *striapchie* in the communities concerned.

[33] Most modern Russian historians of the Advokatura accept the "spontaneity" approach,

Although the point has been well made that in some measure, at least, the westernization processes instituted by Tsar Aleksei Mikhailovich and accelerated by Peter the Great represented in the field of law the development of a western legal consciousness in Russia,[34] there were Russian sources of strength to draw upon, not least the elements of a Russian legal consciousness already in place. Although Peter the Great identified "legality" (законность) with his commands expressed in legislation, hardly surprising given his view of autocracy and the fact that his realm was at war for most of his reign, the emphasis upon compliance with the written (and now printed) text represented a dramatic change for most Russians, symbolically embodied in the zertsalo whose presence was required throughout the country in Russian courts (see Chapter 3 above).[35]

Although the teaching of law was initially left in the hands of foreign jurists appointed to the Academy of Sciences and Moscow University, young Russians sent to Scotland for study and research in law returned to take up appointments at Moscow University and enrich the discipline of law with publications influenced by the thinking of Adam Smith and his followers.[36] Moot courts were introduced into Russian legal education by Ivan Tret'iakov and S. E. Desnitskii at Moscow University.

The ministerial reforms introduced by Alexander I in 1802 led to the formation of a single body of officials possessing specialized training in law, appointed more on the basis of ability and education than ancestral lineage and rank, and sharing a commitment to justice and even to the rule of law. They gradually replaced an elder generation comprising an "isolated caste without a sense of its own importance or dignity", as Wortman so aptly expressed the position.

By 1833 Russia had achieved the nucleus of a trained professoriate in law, a considerable number of law graduates appointed to civil service positions, an impressive expansion of higher legal education, and a systematization and codification of legislation unrivalled elsewhere in the world. By the

as did Kucherena, note 12 above. For the contrary view which emphasized the lengthy gestation period during which the forces of legal modernization gathered momentum, see R. S. Wortman, *The Development of a Russian Legal Consciousness* (1976); and reviews thereof in *The American Journal of Legal History*, XXI (1977), pp. 342-346 (H. J. Berman); *Journal of Modern History* (March 1978), pp. 178-183 (Marc Szeftel); *The Slavonic and East European Review*, LVII (1979), pp. 296-297 (W. E. Butler).

[34] See H. J. Berman, *The American Journal of Legal History*, XXI (1977), p. 344.

[35] See "On the Formation of a Russian Legal Consciousness: The Zertsalo", in W. E. Butler, *Russia and the Law of Nations in Historical Perspective* (2009), pp. 91-101.

[36] Among those who influenced the choice of Glasgow was Théodore Tronchin (1709-1781), a Geneva physician close to Voltaire and the French royal family, whose son studied at Glasgow. Desnitskii and Tret'iakov took Adam Smith's courses in ethics and jurisprudence and studied civil law with John Millar. "Both became dedicated Smithians who devoted their subsequent careers to propagating and adapting his ethics and jurisprudence for Russian purposes". See N. Phillipson, *Adam Smith: An Enlightened Life* (2010), p. 170.

1840s the legal staffs of Russian administrative and judicial agencies were manned primarily by law graduates. As these individuals rose in seniority and position, they encouraged the introduction of an independent judiciary, trial by jury, and adversarial legal procedures. By the early 1860s they succeeded in overcoming the reluctance of the ministers and the suspicion of the Tsar. The outcome was emancipation of the serfs in 1861 and the introduction of the judicial reforms of 20 November 1864. There occurred, in Wortman's expression, "an emancipation of legal expertise" essential in an industrializing, modernizing social system and increasingly complex and extended State administrative structure.

The innovations of 1864 should not be idealized or exaggerated. Those reforms introduced the "sworn attorney" (присяжный поверенный) into the Russian legal system, who operated together with the sworn *striapchii* in the commercial courts, the private attorney later introduced, the jurisconsult, and junior attorneys whose role will be addressed below.

The sworn attorney and the advokatura with which he was associated represented the highest echelon of the Russian legal practitioner. The Statute on Sworn Attorneys was first published for discussion and comment on 30 September 1862. More than 400 comments were submitted from throughout the realm; these were published in six volumes. A commission made up of thirty officials from the State Chancellery, Ministry of Justice, Ministry of Internal Affairs, Ruling Senate, governate judicial institutions, and others considered all the comments, summarized them, and then incorporated them as appropriate into a draft Statute which in turn was to be inserted into the Digest of Laws of the Russian Empire.

The judicial reforms entered into force on 17 April 1866. On that day the newly-created courts were solemnly opened and 27 sworn attorneys admitted to practice, among them future luminaries such as Anatolii Fedorovich Koni (1844-1927),[37] Dmitrii Vasilevich Stasov (1824-1906) and Konstantin Konstantinovich Arsenev (1837-1919).[38] By 1913 the number of sworn attorneys had reached about 6,000. Some became household names even down to the present day: Vladimir Danilovich Spasovich (1829-1907),[39] Aleksandr Ivanovich Urusov (1843-1900),[40] Petr Akimovich Aleksandrov (1838-1893), Sergei Arkadevich Andreevskii (1847-1919),[41] Fedor

[37] The literature by and about Koni is massive. A useful anthology is I.V. Potapchuk (comp.), А. Ф. Кони: Избранные труды и речи [A. F. Koni: Selected Works and Speeches] (Tula, 2000).

[38] Potapchuk (comp.), К. К. Арсеньев: Заметки о русской адвокатуре [K. K. Arsenev: Notes on the Russian Advokatura] (Tula, 2001).

[39] Potapchuk (comp.), В. Д. Спасович: Избранные труды и речи [V. D. Spasovich: Selected Works and Speeches] (Tula, 2000).

[40] Potapchuk (comp.), А. И. Урусов: Первосоздатель русской судебной защиты [A. I. Urusov: Creator of Russian Judicial Defense] (Tula, 2001).

[41] Potapchuk (comp.), С. А. Андреевский: Избранные труды и речи [S. A. Andreevskii:

Nikiforovich Plevako (1842-1908/09),[42] Aleksandr Iakovlevich Passover (1840-1910), Nikolai Platonovich Karabchevskii (1851-1925),[43] among them.

The structure and organization of the Advokatura established in 1864 has been discussed at length in Russian and western legal scholarship.[44] We dwell here merely on certain salient features which help better understand the contemporary Advokatura.

The qualifications required to be a sworn attorney were sufficiently high to elevate those admitted to their ranks immediately to the elite of legal professionals. Candidates were expected to have a diploma from a university or other institution of higher education in law or to have passed the examinations in law as an external student and have worked for no less than five years in a judicial department in posts enabling practical skills in judicial proceedings to have been acquired; or aides to sworn attorneys who were training to become fully-fledged advokats for no less than five years. The Ministry of Justice, pursuant to the Statute on the Introduction of the Judicial Statutes into Operation, exercised its power to waive the educational requirement during the first five years of the existence of the Advokatura in favor of those who had stipulated minimums of legal or judicial experience. Among the initial candidates for admission were a doctor of legal sciences, a former sworn *striapchii* in the commercial court, and judges or other officials from State institutions.

Excluded from membership in the Advokatura were persons under the age of 25, foreigners, persons declared to be insolvent or debtors, persons in government service or holding elective office, persons deprived of or limited in status under court judgments, including clergy, persons under investigation for crimes or with prior convictions, persons of poor moral character, and those prohibited from acting on behalf of another or expelled from the ranks of sworn attorneys. In 1889 limitations were introduced on the admission of sworn and private attorneys who were not of the Christian faith, such admissions being not otherwise than with the authorization of the Minister of Justice.[45]

Selected Works and Speeches] (Tula, 2000).

42 Potapchuk (comp.), Ф. П. Плевако: Избранные речи [F. P. Plevako: Selected Speeches] (Tula, 2000).

43 Potapchuk (comp.), Н. П. Карабчевский: Около правосудия: Статьи, речи, очерки [N. P. Karabchevckii: About Justice: Articles, Speeches, Essays] (Tula, 2001).

44 The best work in both its English version and later Russian translation is Eugene Huskey, *Russian Lawyers and the Soviet State: The Origins and Development of the Soviet Bar, 1917-1939* (1986), pp. 11-33. Also see E. V. Vaskovskii, Организация адвокатуры [Organization of the Advokatura] (Spb., 1893); Kucherena, note 12 above; Wortman, note 33 above; I. Gessen and M. Gernet, История русской адвокатуры [History of the Russian Advokatura] (1914-1916) in three volumes; N. V. Cherkasova, Формирование и развитие адвокатуры в России: 60-80 годы XIX в. [Formation and Development of the Advokatura in Russia: 1860-1880s] (1987).

45 A. P. Galoganov, Российская адвокатура: история и современность [Russian Advokatura: History and Modern Times] (2003), p. 18. "In 1889 the Government limited the

The Russian Advokatura was decentralized, self-governing, and, within the confines of legislation, self-regulating. By the end of the Imperial period, associations of sworn attorneys had been formed in all fourteen judicial districts of the Russian Empire in a loose relationship with the courts in each judicial district known as "chambers of justice". Each was responsible for its own admissions. An applicant filed a request to be admitted to the council of sworn attorneys specifying the necessary information and appending the documents confirming his education, work experience, and other data. The council, having considered the materials submitted and taken under advisement all information which it deemed to be necessary, adopted a decree to either accept or to reject the applicant. If the applicant was accepted, an oath was administered according to the profession of faith of the applicant. Then the applicant was entered on the list of sworn attorneys and a certificate issued to him. It was routine to publish admissions in the local media. The candidacy was then confirmed (or not) by the Minister of Justice, whose decision, if negative, might be appealed to the Ruling Senate.

In addition to accepting new members, the council of sworn attorneys in each district decided disciplinary cases and adopted decisions on other issues of common concern to the advokats. The actions of the council were reviewed at general meetings of the sworn attorneys, which also elected the council. The chambers of justice had the power to overturn decisions of the councils, but in practice this was uncommon.

Sworn attorneys had the right to accept criminal and civil cases in all courts of the district of the judicial chamber in which they were registered. At the request of his client, the sworn attorney might also operate outside of his district, in which event he was subject to the council of sworn attorneys of that court where the case was being heard. In criminal cases the sworn attorney was either retained by the client or appointed by the chairman of the court. An appointment could not be declined without justifiable reasons. Civil cases were accepted under a power of attorney issued by the client, or a declaration filed by the litigant in a court, or by appointment of the council of sworn attorneys at the request of a litigant, or by appointment of the chairman of a court. The client had the right to indicate whether he was retaining the sworn attorney to conduct the case to the very end or only to carry on certain actions. A client might have several sworn attorneys acting for him if he so wished. Payment for legal services was agreed by the parties in written form. If agreement was not reached or disagreements arose of the amount, payment was made on the basis of a fee schedule.

There were a number of limitations on the sworn attorney, none of which are surprising. A sworn attorney could not act in court for his

entry of Jews into the colleges of advokats, and they might thus practice only as an aide to a private attorney or *striapchii*". M. Iu. Barshchevskii, Организация и деятельность адвокатуры в России [Organization and Activity of the Advokatura in Russia] (1997), p. 12.

parents, spouse, children, brothers, sisters, uncles, and other kin. Nor could he act for both parties in a case, nor change sides. He was prohibited from purchasing or otherwise acquiring the rights of his clients with regard to their litigation either in his own name or under the pretext of acquiring them for other persons; all such transaction would be deemed to be invalid and the attorney subjected to disciplinary responsibility.

The sworn attorney was required not to divulge the secrets of his client not only during the case proceedings, but also upon their completion. Every sworn attorney was required to maintain a list of cases assigned to him and to submit this list to the council upon request.

For infractions a sworn attorney was subject, depending upon the offense, to criminal, civil, and disciplinary responsibility. The last was administered by the council of sworn attorneys or, in the absence thereof, by the local court. Four categories of disciplinary sanction existed: (1) warning; (2) reprimand; (3) prohibition to perform duties of a sworn attorney for a period determined by the council, but not more than one year; and (4) expulsion as a sworn attorney. Russian legislation required that certain procedures be complied with in disciplinary proceedings, including the submission of explanations by the person concerned, his appearance at the session of the council, the presence of a quorum at the council session, and the possibility to appeal against the decree of the council.

A council of sworn attorneys was formed when at least twenty such attorneys had been admitted in a judicial district and they petitioned for recognition. The council was elected annually by the general meeting and was required to report on the previous year's activities to the general meeting.

As time passed, the numbers of aides to advokats, or junior attorneys, eligible to become fully-fledged advokats increased markedly. Having registered with a sworn attorney, some practiced on their own while undergoing their apprenticeship or pupilage. In the later years of the Advokatura, about two-thirds of sworn attorneys admitted had served as aides to advokats and the balance were former judges or civil servants.[46]

The underground attorney continued to exist and flourish until the Russian revolutions of 1917.[47] Many who had engaged in this profession prior to 1864 were simply unable to meet the high qualifications imposed to become a sworn attorney, and others who might have done so were unwilling to assume the other duties that accompanied being a sworn attorney or the

[46] See Huskey, note 44 above, p. 14.

[47] Huskey noted that a "few private law firms were formed in the aftermath ..." of the 1864 Judicial Reform by *striapchie* in an effort to compete with the sworn attorneys. He considered it likely that these firms were disbanded when the private attorney was brought under State regulation in 1874. Huskey, ibid., p. 16, n. 17.

extent of supervision imposed by the organs of the Advokatura. In effect, anyone who wanted to become an underground attorney in Russia could do so unless he fell into the category of a person who was prohibited by law from acting in this capacity. An Explanation of the Ruling Senate elucidated which persons could not act in criminal proceedings as a defender: (1) notaries, except for defending close members of their families; (2) persons deprived of all rights of status or all special rights and privileges by judgment of a court; (3) persons who were prohibited from petitioning with regard to a court judgment, excommunicated from church, expelled from service by a court or from a religious department for moral offenses; (4) persons expelled as sworn attorneys; (5) persons excluded from being private attorneys by order of the Minister of Justice or by a judicial ruling; (6) persons removed from the ranks of private attorneys by *uezd* congresses; (7) private or sworn attorneys prohibited from engaging in professional activity as a disciplinary sanction; (8) and persons interrogated at a preliminary investigation as a witness if they were summoned to court by the opposing side. To these eight categories should be added persons who were prohibited from being attorneys in criminal cases in justice of the peace courts: (1) secretaries of justice of the peace congress or bailiffs; (2) clerks of a justice of the peace who considered the case; and (3) local justice of the peace and deputies of a procurator in the justice of the peace institutions of the judicial district concerned.

The underground attorney flourished primarily in the rural areas of Russia where there were few sworn or private attorneys.

Once the opportunity presented itself, many underground attorneys became private attorneys under the Rules on Persons Having the Right to be Attorneys with Regard to Court Cases, confirmed on 25 May 1874 in the form of amendments to the 1864 judicial reform legislation. Under the 1874 Rules persons who had received special certificates for the right to petition with regard to other cases could act as attorneys in both the general and in the justice of the peace courts. The forms of the certificates were established by the Ministry of Justice. The certificates were issued by the conferences of justice of the peace, district courts, and chambers of justice and gave the right to petition only in that court by which they were issued except for instances when an attorney who had accepted a case for proceedings in a justice of the peace court, district, or chamber of justice at the wish of the litigants or the person on trial submitted a petition with regard to this same case to the cassational departments of the Ruling Senate.

Those who wished to be a private attorney filed a request at the respective court, appending the necessary documents certifying his identity and affirming that there were no impediments to his becoming a private attorney. If it subsequently determined that there were such impediments, the certificate was withdrawn and this person was subject to criminal prosecution. If the court refused to issue a certificate, the refusal might be appealed to the superior judicial instance.

The court which issued a certificate informed the Minister of Justice thereof and published the names of private attorneys in the local media.

The courts exercised disciplinary responsibility over the persons to whom they issued certificates. The sanctions for "incorrect and reprehensible actions" by private attorneys were: (1) a warning or caution; (2) reprimand; (3) prohibition to perform the duties of a private attorney for a period exceeding one year; and (4) exclusion from the rank of private attorneys.

The 1874 Rules also granted the right to persons who had no certificate (that is, were not private attorneys) to act in cases before justices of the peace, but not more than three cases during the year within the justice of the peace district. Individuals acting in this capacity were asked by the justice of the peace whether they had acted during the year in another's case in the justice of the peace district, and if so, how many times. False testimony would engage criminal responsibility.

The market had its own impact on the private attorney as time passed. Gradually the private attorney gravitated towards those areas where there were few sworn attorneys, primarily in the provinces and away from the principal urban centers where the courts were located. By 1914 the cities of Moscow, Petersburg, Kiev, and Warsaw had about fifty percent of all sworn attorneys but only 11.2% of the private attorneys. Over half the private attorneys were in smaller provincial towns, whereas only 6.2% of the sworn attorneys were to be found there. Competition between the two segments of the legal profession was most intense in the district courts, where they were more or less evenly represented.[48]

The superimposition of the Advokatura upon the previously existing components of the legal profession – jurisconsult, sworn *striapchii* in commercial courts, private attorney, and underground attorney – apparently had no perceptible impact upon the last. Indeed, all the jurists of these categories together were not of sufficient number to satisfy the requirements for legal services in Russia.

The Soviet Advokatura: 1918-1991

The periodization of the development of the Soviet Advokatura is traditionally seen to fall into the following periods: (1) 1917-1922; (2) 1922-1939; (3) 1939-1961; and (4) 1961-1991.[49] A more nuanced analysis of the first two periods suggests a different breakdown: (1) 1917-1921; (2) 1922-1927; (3) 1928-1932; (4) 1933-1939 – and a caution against over-simplification:

[48] Gessen and Gernet, note 44 above, II, pp. 3-5, 57.

[49] See D. P. Baranov and M. B. Smolenskii, Адвокатское право [Advokat Law] (3d ed.; 2009), p. 59.

... [A] reperiodization of Soviet legal development ... shows that the shift toward the stability of law began as early as 1932 and not, as widely believed, in 1936, the year that witnessed both the enactment of the Stalin Constitution and the launching of the Great Purges. In general, the periods of early Soviet legal development ... swing back and forth from legal nihilism to legal revival. But they do not respect the divisions between the years of Leninist and Stalinist rule. The picture of Soviet legal development ... illustrates that the juxtaposition of a benign legal system under Lenin with a harsh and repressive Stalinist legal order is unjustified.[50]

The survival of a group of professional people in the Soviet Union who could be retained privately on a fee basis by individual citizens and State and social organizations came as a surprise to many in the West who imagined that the provision of services by one citizen to another was no longer possible. The initial reaction of the Bolsheviks to the Advokatura, or "Bar" as it is sometimes misleadingly styled, in Russia was antipathetic; the pre-revolutionary Russian Advokatura was dissolved on 24 November 1917 in Decree No. 1 "On Courts". The Petrograd and later the Moscow advokaturas refused to recognize the legality of the dissolution and continued to function for nearly a year.

Lenin himself had been a trainee advokat in the 1890s. Expelled from his law studies at Kazan University, he completed them externally at St Petersburg University, was admitted to legal practice, and actually appeared in court in several cases before devoting himself wholly to the revolutionary movement. He took a dim view in some of his writings about aspects of the Russian legal profession, but was never opposed to the legal profession in principle. It was Lenin who personally inserted clauses on defenders in the early draft enactments on criminal procedure.

Decree No. 1 "On Courts" allowed every citizen who enjoyed civil rights to act as defense counsel.[51] Under this proviso many advokats of the Tsarist era continued to practice their profession. Although this right was retained in Decree No. 2 "On Courts", adopted 15 February 1918, Lenin modified the draft to allow "colleges" of individuals to be formed and attached to local soviets; college members might act for remuneration either as prosecutors or defense counsel.[52] The link between prosecution and defense proved to be incompatible and was abolished in May 1918. There followed a period of constant reorganizations of the provision of legal services for some four years. As a rule, regulation of advokats was left to local soviets. Initially a fee system operated on the basis of a schedule fixed by councils within the colleges of defenders; then the colleges were reorganized and defense

[50] Huskey, note 44 above, p. 8.
[51] СУ РСФСР (1917-18), no. 4, item 50.
[52] СУ РСФСР (1918), no. 26, item 240.

counsel became salaried employees just as judges and procurators. Into the new scheme of colleges passed many members of the Tsarist Bar in November 1918 when they resolved to liquidate their former organizations.

In 1920 a dramatic new experiment was tried; local soviets were obliged to confirm twice-yearly lists of individuals who were capable of acting as defenders in court. They were paid *per diem* from State funds. Individuals on the list found themselves pressed into the role of defender whether they wished to act or not. The system proved unworkable, and in the majority of instances defenders were appointed from among officials of local justice agencies attached to the respective local soviets.

The introduction of the NEP brought a fully-fledged Statute on the Advokatura, adopted 26 May 1922.[53] Under the Statute, colleges of defenders for civil and criminal cases were formed and attached to the provincial justice sections. College members were confirmed by the Presidium of the provincial executive committee, but new members could now be admitted by the college itself with subsequent notification of the Committee. Members were precluded from holding posts simultaneously in State institutions and enterprises except for elective offices and law teaching positions. Defenders were free to negotiate their fees with the client except with workers of State and private enterprises or employees of soviet institutions and enterprises, for whom fees were regulated by the People's Commissariat of Justice. Indigents were exempted from legal fees by court decree. The defenders then paid a stipulated percentage of their remuneration to the College for overhead expenses. Defenders did not enjoy a monopoly position. Close relatives of an accused or a victim and authorized representatives of certain State and social organizations also might appear in court as a defender. Other individuals, however, required the special authorization of the court.

The influence of lawyers from the *ancien regime* in local advokaturas evidently troubled many local Party organizations. As late as early 1923, about 25% of the 2,800 advocates in the RSFSR were from the pre-revolutionary era. Should communists be allowed to join? The Central Committee of the Party on 2 November 1922 counselled affirmatively in a circular to all regional and provincial Party organizations; otherwise, the Committee said, all colleges would be taken over by elements hostile to Soviet power. But limitations were imposed. A communist was required to have the advance approval of a senior Party organization before joining the college; communist advokats must not accept cases, especially civil cases, involving the defense of "bourgeois interests" in disputes against workers or State enterprises, nor in criminal cases defend clearly counter-revolutionary

[53] СУ РСФСР (1922), no. 36, item 425. Although entitled as a separate Statute, the enactment was in fact an amendment to Articles 43-49 of the Statute on People's Courts, adopted 21 October 1920.

or other impure elements.[54] Throughout most of the NEP period advokats worked as private practitioners, the fee arrangements being attenuated by legal consultation centers at factories or public places where workers might obtain legal advice free of charge. During the era of forced collectivization in 1929-31, advokats in most places found themselves pressured to merge into voluntary "collectives" of advokats. The arrangements varied from locality to locality; as a rule, clients contracted for services with a collective and fees were paid to the collective. Advokats were then remunerated on the basis of quantity and quality of work performed.

Somewhat greater guidance over the legal profession ensued with the creation of a Legal Defense Section within the RSFSR People's Commissariat of Justice by legislation of 20 July 1930. On 27 February 1932 the RSFSR People's Commissariat of Justice adopted a Statute on Collectives of Members of Colleges of Defenders, confirming that the notion of collectives in this realm was on the whole regarded as a positive development. The collectives worked under the direct guidance of the presidium of colleges of advokats, whereas the colleges received their "general policy guidance and supervision" from the territorial, regional, and higher courts. Clients selected their own defenders from those available; fees varied depending on the qualifications, socio-legal work, and workload of the advokat but were levied at rates worked out by the Presidium of the College and confirmed by the court.[55]

The 1932 Statute was enacted at a time when the need for a legal profession at all was being seriously questioned by the Pashukanis school. In the event, the importance of defense counsel was staunchly defended. Following the adoption of the 1936 USSR Constitution, the system of court organization was remodeled and for the first time all-union legislation on the Advokatura was approved, on 16 August 1939, by the USSR Council of People's Commissars.[56] The 1939 Law changed the terminology from "defenders" to "advokats" and provided that colleges of advokats were to be created in autonomous republics, territories, and regions as voluntary professional associations. The management organs of the colleges were the general meeting of advokats, the presidium, and the internal audit commission. General direction over the advokatura was exercised by the USSR and union republic people's commissariats of justice, on whom the advokatura was dependent.

[54] The Circular was published in Еженедельник советской юстиции [Weekly of Soviet Justice], no. 1 (1923), p. 24; signed by V. M. Molotov.

[55] See M. V. Kozhevnikov, История советского суда 1917-1956 годы [History of the Soviet Court 1917-1956] (1957), p. 237.

[56] СП СССР (1939), no. 49, item 394.

The Secret Advokatura

Whatever Stalin may have known from Soviet intelligence sources about progress in the United States in developing an atomic bomb, historians of the Advokatura suggest that President Harry S. Truman's friendly disclosure to Stalin at the Potsdam Conference in 1945 that the United States had created an atomic bomb triggered a series of events that also affected the Soviet legal profession. Stalin is said to have made immediate urgent inquiries of his own security and scientific personnel and by 20 August 1945 to have created the "atomic industry" as a new branch of Soviet economic administration. The scientific research institutes and State enterprises merged into or created within this branch of industry were mostly located outside existing population centers on territories closed to outsiders. Phantom cities were formed one after the other without names and undisclosed on Soviet maps. Postal addresses took the form of fictitious designations: Arzamas-16, Penza-19, Tomsk-7, and so on. Nearly a decade later some of the "science cities" were given real names without indicating what kind of urban centers they were.

The closed cities rapidly grew in population, ranging from 50,000 to 100,000 persons, and naturally required the full range of urban services that any other city would require. This meant legal infrastructure – courts, procuracy, notariat, registries for acts of civil status, law enforcement, and advokats.

By an Edict of 27 June 1947 the Presidium of the Supreme Soviet of the USSR created a special Advokatura in the so-called "closed territories",[57] each territory having its own courts, procuracy, police, notariat, and Advokatura. These legal institutions had no special powers in comparison with those outside the closed territories. The designation "special" (abbreviated) was applied to them. Everything relating to their existence was classified, including the affiliation of individuals with these closed territories, their passport stamp, the judgment of any court in the said territories, including when and where it was proclaimed. The provision of the 1936 USSR Constitution allowing justice to be administered by, *inter alia*, "special" courts was construed to encompass military tribunals, transport and camp courts, and these courts on closed territories.

The lines of administration essential to organize these infrastructures appeared within the relevant ministries. The Ministry of Internal Affairs, the Ministry of Justice, and the Procuracy of the USSR formed special administrations within each of their structures. The judicial system created sub-units to handle appeals from the closed territory courts up to

[57] The Edict remains unpublished, and was not included in the Собрание действующего законодательства СССР [Collection of Legislation in Force of the Union of Soviet Socialist Republics].

and including the USSR Supreme Court. Because there was no all-union Advokatura, the selection of advokats to serve in the closed territories was passed to the chairmen of the special courts that had been formed there. Events moved so rapidly that advokats were already in place before the end of 1947 with "credentials" issued by the local courts. Advokats were present in seven closed cities and later at so-called "special-regime" objects in Moscow, Leningrad, Kaliningrad (near Moscow), the Far East, Kazakhstan (Baikonur), Kyrgyzia, Ukraine, and elsewhere.

Security considerations imposed unusual constraints upon advokat activity. Cases could be conducted only in special courts, which meant that the advokats were often underemployed. The crime rate was much lower in closed territories than elsewhere in the country. The special courts in closed territories had nothing in common with the "special boards" or "troikas" that carried out the Stalinist purges. The "special Advokatura engaged in ordinary advokat practice".[58]

The USSR Ministry of Justice itself began to appoint advokats at regime objects beginning on 12 November 1955. The camp and transport special courts had been abolished respectively in 1953 and 1956. When the USSR Ministry of Justice was itself abolished, the USSR Supreme Court assumed responsibility for directing the Special Advokatura. In due course the Special Advokatura was moved on to the RSFSR Ministry of Justice, and after its dissolution, to the RSFSR Supreme Court. It says something about the status of advokats that only in 1966, on the basis of a Decree of the USSR Council of Ministers, were the directors of regime enterprises required to provide the special courts and law enforcement agencies, and the advokats, with premises and their personnel with housing and medical services equal to that of the workers of the enterprises themselves.

On 24 July 1956 the first twenty-five legal consultation offices were created at regime objects and in closed territorial formations; their advokats served the special courts. The names of the legal consultation offices also were given classified names, which in 1971 were changed to classified numbers, for example Legal Consultation Office No. 9, 10, 19, 20, 25, 33, and others.

The 1979 USSR Law on the Advokatura permitted the creation of inter-territorial advokaturas. In 1982 at the initiative of the Minister of Justice of the USSR, Vladimir Ivanovich Terebilov (1916-2004), the Inter-Republic College of Advokats was formed on the base of 134 legal consultation offices located in these regime areas. During this period, responsibility for the work of the special advokatura was placed on various agencies, including

[58] N. N. Klen (ed.), Межреспубликанская коллегия адвокатов. 60 лет деятельности [Inter-Republic College of Advokats. 60 Years of Activity] (2009), p. 12.

the USSR Ministry of Justice, the Supreme Court of the USSR, the RSFSR Ministry of Justice, and the RSFSR Supreme Court.[59]

Post-Stalin Reforms of the Advokatura

Changes commenced with the accession to power of Nikita Sergeevich Khrushchev (1894-1971). In an address to the Supreme Soviet of the USSR in 1957 Khrushchev called upon advokats "to assist strengthening socialist legality and the administration of justice". The 1958 Fundamental Principles of Criminal Procedure of the USSR and Union Republics gave advokats greater possibilities to take part at earlier stages in certain categories of criminal cases or with certain categories of persons under investigation (Article 22).

The "decentralization" of legislation in the form of sets of "all-union fundamental principles" and "union republic codes" extended to the Advokatura. The 1958 Fundamental Principles of Court Organization of the USSR and Union Republics returned responsibility for the Advokatura to the union republics. The 1939 USSR Statute was replaced in the union republics between 1961 and 1963 by union republic statutes – in the case of the RSFSR by the Statute on the Advokatura of 25 July 1962.[60] Looking back, some saw in this Statute the first attempt since the 1917 October Revolution to return to the Advokatura "its former independence".[61]

In continuation of the reforms of the 1960s, the RSFSR Ministry of Justice confirmed an Instruction on the Procedure for the Payment of Legal Assistance Rendered by Advokats to Citizens, Enterprises, Institutions, State Farms, Collective Farms, and Other Organizations.[62]

Although the economic reforms of the mid-1960s chiefly enhanced the role and numbers of jurisconsults in the national economy, they also affected advokats. The joint decree of the Central Committee of the Communist Party of the Soviet Union and USSR Council of Ministers "On the Improvement of Legal Work in the National Economy" made provision for advokats to provide legal services at those enterprises which did not have jurisconsults permanently on staff. On 8 December 1972 the USSR Ministry of Justice confirmed a Standard Contract "On Rendering Legal Services at Enterprises, Institutes, and Other Organizations (Except Collective Farms) by Legal Consultations Offices attached to Colleges of Advokats", and a

[59] For names and biographies of early advokats who practiced in these areas, see Klen, ibid.

[60] Ведомости Верховного Совета РСФСР (1962), no. 29, item 450; transl. in H. J. Berman and J. B. Quigley, Jr., *Basic Laws on the Structure of the Soviet State* (1968). See L. M. Friedman and Z. L. Zile, "Soviet Legal Profession: Recent Developments in Law and Practice", *Wisconsin Law Review* (1964), pp. 32-77; K. F. Gutsenko, "New Legislation in the Union Republics with Respect to the Legal Profession", *Soviet Law and Government*, I, no. 2 (1962), pp. 57-64.

[61] Kucherena, note 12 above, p. 38. Also see D. D. Barry and H. J. Berman, "The Soviet Legal Profession", *Harvard Law Review*, LXXXII (1968), pp. 1-41.

[62] СП РСФСР (1966), no. 3, item 22.

year later confirmed a separate standard contract for advokats to provide legal services to collective farms. Russian advokats who viewed their role as being primarily one of advocacy in court did not greet this expansion of function positively; for them it was an additional burden of representation and a further "statization" of their role in society.[63]

Some central direction over the Advokatura, as time passed, was felt to be desirable, and in 1976 work commenced on drafting an all-union enactment. The 1977 USSR Constitution (Article 161) provided for a new pattern of regulation – USSR and union republic legislation – and elevated the college of advokats to organizations of constitutional stature for the first time in Soviet history. On 30 November 1979 the USSR Supreme Soviet adopted the Law on the Advokatura of the USSR. On the basis of that Law, the RSFSR Supreme Soviet adopted the Statute on the Advokatura of the RSFSR on 20 November 1980, which remained in force until 30 June 2002.[64]

The 1980 Statute retained essentially the same structure for the Advokatura internally but, in the eyes of many, consolidated the dependence of the Advokatura upon the USSR and RSFSR ministries of justice in ways consistent with the ideological precepts of the day. However, the Statute (and the 1979 USSR Law) did not contain a definition of "advokatura" or of "advokat activity". As the processes of perestroika advanced, the Advokatura in the Russian Federation experienced between 1986 and 1988 the "boom of cooperatives", as did so many other sectors of the Soviet economy. Legal cooperatives were formed for the provision of legal services, but most did not survive for long.

Some changes brought by the 1980 Statute were undoubtedly positive. All advokats were required to have a higher legal education. Greater emphasis began to be placed on the adversarial dimension of accusation and defense in criminal proceedings. The right of advokats to obtain documents or copies thereof from organizations was strengthened, which made it easier for them to perform their roles with respect to the collection of evidence. But as their rights expanded under criminal procedure legislation, so too did resistance grow to their presence in investigations. In 1988 advokats appeared in court in 70% of criminal cases, but were present at only about one-third of the preliminary investigations. Statistics released by the USSR Ministry of Justice show that during the 1970s more than 70% of petitions and applications submitted by advokats of the RSFSR were rejected by investigators.[65]

[63] For all of Russian history the relationship between the jurist and the State has been a major concern and preoccupation. For a useful summary, see I. S. Iartykh, Адвокатура и власть [The Advokatura and the Authorities] (2003).

[64] V. I. Sergeev, Комментарий а положению об адвокатуре [Commentary to the Statute on the Advokatura] (2001).

[65] See M. A. Gofshtein, «Обзор ходатайств и заявлений адвокатов РСФСР» [Survey of

Beginning in the late 1980s, a number of regional colleges of advokats combined into various social organizations for the purpose of defending the interests of the advokats as a profession and also to practice law. The aspiration of advokats to create an Advokatura truly independent from the State generated serious resistance from the Communist Party of the Soviet Union. The Ministry of Justice of the USSR, under instruction from the Central Committee of the CPSU, was directed not to permit the creation of an independent Union of Advokats of the USSR. When it became clear that the process was irreversible, by a secret decision of the Politburo adopted on 2 December 1988, No. 143, the Ministry of Justice was directed to "head the work for the creation of an Association of Advokats of the USSR ... by democratic means to allot to the organization committee advokats who properly understand the tasks of the Advokatura at the contemporary stage ...".[66]

CURRENT LEGISLATION

Federal Chamber of Advokats of Russian Federation

In 1991 an All-Union Congress of Advokats was held in the Soviet Union. The Congress created a Union of Advokats, elected the executive organs thereof, and adopted a Charter. Upon the dissolution of the Soviet Union, several associations of advokats were created within the Russian Federation: the Union of Advokats of Russia, founded in 1990, became the Federal Union of Advocates based in Moscow at the Founding Congress of 12-13 September 1994; the Regional Association of Russian Advokats, headquartered in Saratov, was established in 1994 and combined 13 colleges of advokats; the Guild of Advokats of Russia, based in Moscow, was formed on 27 January 1995 and combined more than forty so-called "parallel" colleges of advokats organized during the early 1990s; and the Union of Advokats of the USSR, founded in 1989, which became after the demise of the Soviet Union, the International Union (or Commonwealth) of Advokats, in Moscow, brought together advokats and their colleges on the territories of Belarus, Uzbekistan, and other CIS States and a number of Russian regions; it was formed in 1994 and re-registered in 1998. These associations neither rendered legal services nor directed the operations of their member colleges of advokats or individual members.[67]

Petitions and Applications of Advokats of the RSFSR], Советская юстиция [Soviet Justice], no. 21 (1989), p. 31.

66 Quoted in D. N. Kozak (ed.), Научно-практический комментарий к Федеральному закону «Об адвокатской деятельности и адвокатуре в Российской Федерации» [Scientific-Practical Commentary to Federal Law "On Advokat Activity and the Advokatura in the Russian Federation] (2003), p. 24.

67 For an informal but informed account of the early days of these rival groupings, see Iu. F. Lubshev, Адвокатура в России [The Advokatura in Russia] (2001).

Although the tasks of each association varied one from the other, the Federal Union of Advokats of Russia was not untypical. Under its Charter, the Federal Union was dedicated to strengthening an independent and strong Advokatura, defending the rights of advokats and their honor and dignity, promoting the training of specialists for advokatura work, publishing, strengthening links with academic lawyers, participation in drafting legislation, representing the interests of the Advokatura in State agencies and social organizations, and developing international links of Russian advokats.

These associations were supported by membership dues, publishing revenues, donations, and other private-sector assistance. Much of their role has been lost, however, for the 2002 Federal Law on Advokat Activity and the Advokatura in the Russian Federation succeeded in accomplishing a "centralization" of Russian advokats within a national framework that the various legal associations had frustrated for so long. They may continue to exist so long as they do not perform the functions reserved by Russian legislation to the chambers of advokats.

Under the 2002 law, the Federal Chamber of Advokats of the Russian Federation has been formed as an all-Russian, non-State, non-commercial organization in which membership is compulsory for chambers of advokats formed at the level of subjects of the Russian Federation. The aim of the Federal Chamber of Advokats is to represent and defend the interests of advokats in agencies of State power and local self-government and ensure a high level of legal assistance to clients. It is empowered to represent the interests of advokats and chambers of advokats of subjects of the Federation in relations with federal agencies of State power when questions are being resolved affecting the interests of the community of advokats, including the appropriations from the federal budget to pay the fees of advokats who act in criminal proceedings as defenders by assignment of agencies of inquiry, preliminary investigation or a court. The Federal Chamber is a juridical person which is formed by the All-Russian Congress of Advokats; however, the Federal Chamber is not subject to reorganization and may be liquidated only on the basis of a federal law. The existence of rival organizations is prohibited if they have functions and powers analogous to those of the Federal Chamber of Advokats. The Charter of the Federal Chamber of Advokats is adopted by the All-Russian Congress of Advokats and is subject to registration in the same procedure as applies to other juridical persons. Decisions of the Federal Chamber are binding upon all chambers of advokats and individual advokats.

The All-Russian Congress of Advokats meets at least once every two years and is quorate if not less than two-thirds of the delegates to the Congress take part. The Congress also, in addition to the charter, adopts the professional ethics code for advokats, confirms the uniform norms for representation at the Congress, forms the Council of the Federal Chamber, determines the deductions from chambers of advokats for the common needs of the Federal Chamber and confirms the estimates of expenditures, elects the internal audit commission, confirms the reglament of the Congress, personnel establishment, and performs other functions stipulated by the charter.

In intervals between congresses, the affairs of the Federal Chamber are conducted by its collegial executive organ, the Council, which elects the President of the Federal Chamber for a term of four years and, upon his recommendation, one or several vice-presidents for a term of two years.

A chamber of advokats exists in each subject of the Russian Federation also as a non-State, non-commercial organization. Membership of advokats in the chamber is obligatory. These chambers operate on the basis of the Civil Code of the Russian Federation[68] and general statutes for organizations of this type. They are created to ensure that qualified legal assistance is rendered and accessible throughout the territory of the particular subject of the Federation in which they are formed, that such assistance is free of charge when required or necessary, to represent and defend the interests of advokats in agencies of State power and local self-government and other organizations, supervise the professional training of persons admitted to effectuate advokat activity and compliance with the advokats' code of professional ethics. The chamber is formed by a constitutive meeting or conference of advokats. Each chamber is a juridical person and responsible for the obligations of the chamber. Each chamber is subject to State registration in the procedure established for the registration of juridical persons. There may be only one chamber in each subject of the Federation. No branches, representations, or subdivisions on the territory of other subjects of the Federation are permitted, and inter-regional or other inter-territory formations are prohibited. A chamber may not engage in advokat activity in its own name, nor engage in entrepreneurial activity. Reorganization is not a possibility for a chamber of advokats; however, if a new subject of the Federation is formed in accordance with relevant federal legislation – which has occurred several times – the chamber of advokats affected may be liquidated.

Advokat formations

As of 1 January 2021 there were more than 81,612 advokats in the Russian Federation, of whom one was a full Academician of the Russian Academy of Sciences, 187 were doctors of legal sciences, and 1,648 were candidates of legal sciences. The advokats were organized into 26,719 advokat formations, subdivided into 85 chambers of advokats (one for each subject of the Federation), 3,077 colleges of advokats, 880 bureaus, 22,675 cabinets,

[68] See Article 123$^{16-1}$, in W. E. Butler, *Civil Code of the Russian Federation* (2021), I, p. 122. The Article was introduced on 13 July 2015.

and 87 legal consultation offices. Even though the number of advokats has increased significantly in the post-Soviet era, the per capita ratio of advokats to the population continues to be lower than in other developed legal systems. However, because the Russian jurisconsult is part of the equation, the per capita ratio is better than first appears to be the case.

Under Article 72(k) of the 1993 Russian Constitution, the advokatura is the subject of joint jurisdiction of the Russian Federation and its subjects. Accordingly, the Federation may issue federal laws on the advokatura, and so too may the subjects of the Federation in elaboration of and in compliance with the Civil Code of the Russian Federation[69] and the 2002 Federal Law on Advokat Activity and the Advokatura in the Russian Federation and other federal legislation.

Advokats were, prior to 1 July 2002, organized into "colleges of advokats", which were independent, self-governing professional associations.[70] Under the 2002 Federal Law on Advokat Activity, so-called "advokat formations" may take one of four forms: the advokat cabinet, college of advokats, advokat bureau or office, and legal consultation office. It is for the individual advokat to decide the form and place of his (58.3% of advokats are male) or her (41.7% are female) preference, and to notify the council of the chamber of advokats of that choice in the established procedure. In January 2021 12.4% of advokats were under the age of thirty; 15.8% were age sixty or older. 4.7% had advokat experience of one year or less; 18.2% had from one to five years of experience as an advokat; 38.0% had from five to fifteen years experience as an advokat; and 39.1% had more than fifteen years of experience as an advokat.

An advokat who prefers to operate as a sole practitioner and who has no less than three years' experience of advokat activity has the right to form an advokat cabinet, having informed his chamber of advokats by registered letter the requisite information about himself, address of the cabinet, and telephone, cable, postal, and other addresses. An advokat cabinet is not a juridical person. Agreements with clients are concluded between the advokat and the client and registered in the documentation of the cabinet. If the advokat wishes, he may work from home. For accounting purposes, the advokat who chooses this model is equated to an individual entrepreneur.

Two or more advokats, of which two must have no less than three years of experience in advokat activity, have the right to form a college of advokats, which is a non-commercial organization based on membership and operating on the basis of a charter confirmed by its founders. This is

69 See Article 123$^{16-2}$, ibid., pp. 122-123.

70 The foundation documents of a number of colleges are reproduced in V. M. Anufriev and S. N. Gavrilov, Организация и деятельность адвокатуры в России [Organization and Activity of the Advokatura in Russia] (2001).

the most popular form of advokat formation; in 2019, 63.6% of all advokats were associated with a college of advokats. The founders and members of the college must be advokats, information concerning which is contained only in one regional register. The founders conclude among themselves a contract to found the college of advokats, their joint activity relating to the founding, and the conditions for the transfer of their property to the college. In the charter the founders determine the name and location of the college of advokats, the procedure and conditions for admitting new members, the rights and duties of each, and the procedure and conditions for withdrawal, management procedures, information concerning any branches, procedures for reorganization and liquidation, including the distribution of any property, and the procedure for making changes in and additions to the charter. The charter must contain information established in federal legislation, and the same procedure for notifying the formation of the college of advokats to the chamber of advokats applies as in the case of sole practitioners.

The college of advokats is a juridical person and may create branches anywhere in the Russian Federation or abroad, but within Russia must also register in the regional register of the relevant subject of the Federation and, if a foreign branch is created, this must be registered in the regional register where they were founded and information provided about the advokats serving in this foreign branch. Property contributed by the founders of a college of advokats belongs to the last by right of ownership. A college of advokats has limited responsibility: members of a college of advokats are not liable for its obligations, and the college of advokats is not liable for obligations of its members. However, agreements to render legal assistance in a college of advokats are concluded between the advokat and the client and are registered in the documentation of the college of advokats. A college of advokats may not be transformed into a commercial organization or into any other non-commercial organization (except into an advokat office, under certain conditions). The rules of the non-commercial partnership apply to a college of advokats insofar as they are not inconsistent with the 2002 Federal Law on Advokat Activity.

Two or more advokats may choose to form an advokat bureau or office, which requires the conclusion of a partnership contract. Under the partnership contract the advokat-partners are obliged to combine their efforts to render legal services in the name of all the partners. The contract is considered to be a document which contains confidential information and is not provided for State registration of the office. The contract must make provision for its period of operation, the procedure for taking of decisions by the partners, the procedure for electing the managing partner and the competence thereof, the procedure for admitting, suspending, or expelling partners, the distribution of remuneration, and any other conditions. Under this structure, agreements with clients are concluded by any partner in the name of all the partners on the basis of powers of attorney issued by them. The power of attorney must set out all limitations on the competence of a partner who is concluding agreements with clients and third persons.

The partnership terminates when the partnership contract expires, or is dissolved at the demand of one partner unless the contract provides otherwise, or a partner dies, is deemed to lack dispositive legal capacity or be limited therein, or declared to be missing, insolvent, or bankrupt unless the partnership contract provides otherwise.

A legal consultation office is formed by the chamber of advokats in a subject of the Federation in which the total number of advokats in all advokat formations on the territory of a judicial district comprises less than two per federal judge. This happens upon the recommendation of the agency of executive power of the respective subject of the Federation. The legal consultation office, a non-commercial organization, is regulated by the Civil Code and the Federal Law on Non-Commercial Organizations. The conditions for operating the legal consultation office are determined by legislation of the respective subject of the Federation.

Advokats

An advokat, as defined in the 2002 Federal Law on Advokat Activity, is a person who has received the "status of an advokat" in the established procedure and the right to effectuate advocate activity. He is an independent advisor on legal questions and does not have the right to engage in other paid activity except for scholarly, teaching, and other creative activities. In rendering legal assistance the advokat, according to legislation: (1) gives advice on and memoranda on legal questions in oral or written form; (2) draws up applications, appeals, petitions, and other documents of a legal character; (3) represents the interests of the client in constitutional court proceedings; (4) participates as a representative or defender of the client in a civil, criminal, or administrative proceeding; (5) participates as a representative of the client in an arbitration court, international commercial arbitration, and other agencies for the settlement of disputes; (6) represents the interest of the client in agencies of State power, agencies of social associations, social associations, and other organizations, courts, agencies of State power, courts, and law enforcement agencies of foreign States, and non-State agencies of foreign States; (8) represents the client in execution proceedings and tax relations; and may render other legal assistance not prohibited by a federal law.

The status of an advokat may be acquired by natural persons who have a higher legal education received in an accredited institution of higher professional education or a learned degree in a legal specialization. The individual must have either two years' work experience in a legal specialty or undergo a traineeship or apprenticeship. Persons who lack dispositive legal capacity, or who have a record of a criminal conviction may not be advokats. The decision to confer the status of advokat is taken by the qualifications commission attached to the chamber of advocates of the subject of the Russian Federation concerned after a qualifications examination is completed. In a significant change from previous practice, foreign citizens and stateless persons who have received the status of advokat in the procedure established by the 2002 Federal Law on Advokat Activity may engage in advokat activity throughout the entire territory of the Russian Federation.

The status of advokat is conferred for an indefinite period and is not linked in any way with age. An advokat is required to swear an oath as follows: "I solemnly swear to perform the duties of advokat honorably and conscientiously and to defend the rights, freedoms, and interests of clients being guided by the Constitution of the Russian Federation, law, and code of professional ethics of an advokat".

Advokat Activity

"Advokat activity" is a defined concept in the 2002 Federal Law on Advokat Activity: "qualified legal assistance rendered on a professional basis by persons who have received the status of advokat in the procedure established ... to natural and juridical persons ... for the purposes of defense of their rights, freedoms, and interests, and also ensuring access to justice" (Article 1). This sweeping definition is attenuated by certain exclusions, namely legal assistance rendered by workers of legal services of juridical persons, and also by workers of agencies of State power and agencies of local self-government, and participants and workers of organizations rendering legal services, as well as by individual entrepreneurs; and by notaries, patent attorneys (the last subject to certain exceptions). There is a limitation on certain terms associated with advocates. The expression "advokatura", "advokat activity", "advokat", "chamber of advokats", "advokat formation", and "legal consultation office" in their Russian-language versions, or word combinations thereof, are reserved exclusively for advokat formations.

There are no political constraints on advokats. They are free to join any political party. Indeed, the Guild of Advokats registered itself as a political party and nominated candidates for the 1999 parliamentary elections, some of whom were successful.

An advokat has the right to remuneration for his work provided that if all or any part of such remuneration is received in circumvention of the cashier in the legal consultation office, this is regarded as tax evasion, a violation of advokatura rules, and a disciplinary offense. Except for legal aid assignments which are compulsory and duty rosters in the legal consultation office, the advokat is at liberty to determine his own professional workload. Some advokats give the greater portion of their time to teaching, research, law enforcement activities, or legislative advice.

Most advokats spend the greater part of their time giving legal advice and drafting documents. As a rule, it is the advokat himself who gathers evidence or other data for submission to an investigator or to a court in a criminal or civil case or who retains a private detective to do so. An advokat has the right to represent the interests of a client in all State and social organizations: the courts, procuracy, Ministry of Internal Affairs, Federal Security Service, and others. On 27 March 1996 the Constitutional Court of the Russian Federation held that the participation of an advokat in a criminal case could not depend upon whether the advokat had clearance for access to State secrets. Article 21 of the Law on State Secrecy, the Court ruled, did not extend to advokats participating as defenders in a criminal proceeding. Construing Article 47 of the 1960 RSFSR Code of Criminal Procedure to exclude privately-practicing jurists who are not members of a college of advokats from participating in the preliminary investigation was held to be unconstitutional by the Constitutional Court in a Decree issued 28 January 1997.[71]

Legal Fees

Fees are determined by the contract with the client and may be based on an hourly rate or a specific fee for certain documents or transactions; transactions with juridical persons comprise the majority. The difference between Russian and foreign legal fees has narrowed considerably in the transition to a market economy. Certain categories of legal assistance are rendered free of charge to citizens who have resources below the living minimum, for example: for recovery of alimony, compensation of harm caused by injury or other impairment of health or death of a breadwinner connected with work, application for pensions or benefits, and questions connected with rehabilitation for those who suffered political repression.

Legal advice is given on the basis of a simple written agreement between the advokat and the client. The agreement is a civil-law contract classified under Chapter 39 of the Civil Code as a contract for the compensated rendering of services. The material conditions of the agreement are: (1) an indication of the advokat(s) who have accepted to perform the assignment as an attorney and their affiliation to an advokat formation and chamber of advokats; (2) the subject-matter of the assignment; (3) the conditions of

[71] The question turned partly upon who could act as a defender and be eligible for payment at State expense when acting in this capacity. The Statute on the Procedure for the Payment of Labor of Advokats at the Expense of the State was confirmed by the Minister of Justice on 27 January 1994 and circulated as a Letter of 31 January 1994, No 09-09/19-94. The text appeared in G. L. Pipilenko (comp), Адвокатура [Advokatura] (1998), pp. 69-71. The Letter was regarded as being in force by Consultant Plus legal database but then was apparently removed; the Supreme Court of the Russian Federation in a decision of 14 November 2000 declared the Statute to be illegal and not subject to application. The 2001 Code of Criminal Procedure (Article 49) permits "defenders" to act in criminal proceedings, and these may be close relatives of an accused or other persons whom the accused desires, as well as advokats.

remuneration; (4) the procedure and amount of contributory compensation for expenses connected with performance of the assignment; (5) the amount and character of responsibility of the advokat who has assumed performance of the assignment. The right to remuneration and expenses may not be reassigned to third persons without the special consent of the client.

The request of an investigator, inquiry official, or court for an advokat to be appointed was mandatory in the past for the presidium of the college of advokats and the managers of legal consultation offices[72] and remains binding upon advokat formations. They were obliged to make an appointment within a 24-hour period after receiving the request. In 2018, 43,000 advokats were assigned to assist clients in a criminal proceeding by agencies of inquiry, preliminary investigation, or a court. The average monthly fees for an advokat assigned to cases was 9,600 rubles. About 8,223 advokats represented the interests of natural persons in civil proceedings by appointment of courts, and 3,829 advokats acted in administrative proceedings.

If the financial status of the accused does not enable him to pay the costs of the advokat appointed, the investigator, inquiry official, or court has the right to exempt him from the payment of legal fees. Under scales introduced from 1 January 2021, an advokat participating in a criminal proceeding as a defender at the assignment of an agency of inquiry or preliminary investigation or a court, depending upon the complexity of the matter, receives payment on a per diem basis of not less than 1500 nor more than 2150 rubles per day, and if he works on a holiday, day off, or at night, not less than 1775 rubles nor more than 3350 rubles per day.[73]

The transition to a market economy has removed ceilings on the earnings of advokats. Those engaged in commercial work are likely to achieve earnings superior to those who concentrate upon family, housing,

[72] The Russian Supreme Court has held that substituting during the preliminary investigation a lawyer from a law firm who was not a member of a college of advokats for an advokat who was on holiday in order to avoid a two-day delay in the proceedings was an error which required the case to be returned for further investigation. See Бюллетень Верховного Суда Российской Федерации [Bulletin of the Supreme Court of the Russian Federation], no 3 (1998), p. 15. In this case the person under investigation objected to the substitution.

[73] The amounts of payment made to advokats were regulated by the Decree of the Government of the Russian Federation of 4 July 2003 "On the Amount of Payment for Labor of an Advokat Participating as a Defender in a Criminal Proceeding at the Designation of Agencies of Inquiry, Agencies of Preliminary Investigation, or Court". СЗ РФ (2003), no. 28, item 2925, as amended. This Decree lost force pursuant to the Decree of the Government of the Russian Federation of 1 December 2012, No. 1240, which confirmed the Statute on Compensation of Procedural Costs Connected with the Proceedings in a Criminal Case, Costs in Connection with the Consideration of a Civil Case, and also Expenses in Connection with the Fulfillment of Requirements of the Constitutional Court of the Russian Federation. СЗ РФ (2012), no. 50(VI), item 7048, as amended. This Decree entered into force from 1 January 2013.

or labor relations. The practice of contingency fees has met with legal problems; Russian courts have viewed the "contingency fee" as being unrelated to the services performed and the "result" obtained. For the most part contracts for legal services based on a contingency arrangement have been unenforceable under Russian law. However, since 1 March 2020 contingency fees dependent on the outcome of legal assistance provided may be negotiated, with the exception of criminal cases and cases concerning administrative violations. The right to remuneration for fees and expenses may not be assigned by an advokat to third persons without the special agreement of the client.

Legal Ethics

Awkward ethical and moral conundrums can arise for Russian advokats no less than other professionals. In 1925 the Moscow College of Defenders published a volume recounting presidium decisions relating to legal ethics.[74] The practice appears to have been infrequent.[75] Over the years several draft codes, statutes, or rules of ethics for Russian advokats were prepared and engendered lively discussion.[76] Not until 2003 did Russian advokats have a comprehensive set of regulations on the subject of general application.

The 2002 Law on Advokat Activity relegates to the Federal Chamber of Advokats the adoption of a code of professional ethics (Article 7). That Law, however, contains certain requirements of an ethical nature which have been incorporated and elaborated in Code of Professional Ethics of an Advokat, adopted 31 January 2003 by the First All-Russian Congress of Advokats and in force as amended. As a matter of Russian legislation, an advokat does not have the right to render legal assistance to a person as a client if the advokat has an autonomous interest with regard to the subject of agreement with the client which differs from that of the client, or if the advokat participated as a judge, arbitrator, mediator, procurator, investigator, inquiry official, expert, specialist, interpreter in a case or is a witness or victim, or if he was an official within whose competence it was to take a decision with regard to the interests of the client, or if the advokat is a relative or in family relations with an official who took part or who is

[74] See J. N. Hazard, *Settling Disputes in Soviet Society* (1960), pp. 281-291.

[75] See I. I. Skliarskii, Дисциплинарная практика Московской городской и областной коллегий адвокатов (Методическое пособие для адвокатов) [Disciplinary Practice of Moscow City and Regional Colleges of Advokats (Methods Manual for Advokats)] (1971), published by the Moscow City and Moscow Regional colleges of advokats.

[76] A draft Code of advokat ethics and draft Rules of professional ethics of Russian advokats were published in M. Iu. Barshchevkii, Организация и деятельность адвокатуры в России [Organization and Activity of the Advokatura in Russia] (1997), pp. 291-308; the Rules of Professional Advokat Ethics confirmed by the General Meeting of the Astrakhan Inter-Territory Specialized College of Advokats on 15 January 1998 were published in K. K. Lebedev, Правовое обслуживание бизнеса (корпоративный юрист) [Legal Servicing of Business (Corporate Jurists)] (2001), pp. 402-408.

taking part in investigating or considering the case with regard to the client, or if his interests are contrary to those of his client. Moreover, an advokat may not take a position contrary to the will of his client except in special situations, nor divulge information communicated to him by the client or connection with legal assistance rendered unless the client so consents, nor resign from a defense undertaken. Advokats are prohibited from rendering nontransparent cooperation to agencies engaged in operational search activity.

The duties of an advokat likewise are reflective of certain ethical principles. An advokat must honorably, reasonably, and in good faith insist upon the rights and legal interests of his client using all means not prohibited by Russian legislation. And he must comply with the code of professional ethics of an advokat and execute decisions of organs of the chamber of advokats and Federal Chamber of Advokats. The 2003 Code of Professional Ethics expressly "augments the rules established by legislation" on advokat activity (Article 1).[77] When legislation and the Code of ethics do not regulate a particular ethical issue, the advokat is obliged to "comply with the customs and traditions which have formed in the advokatura corresponding to the general principles of morality in society" (Article 4).

It is worthy of note that what in the west is routinely referred to as "client confidentiality" in the Russian Federation is labeled "advokat secrecy". Nonetheless, any information connected with the rendering of legal assistance by an advokat to his client is classified as "advokat secrecy". An advokat may not be summoned and interrogated as a witness concerning circumstances which became known to him in connection with the application of a client for legal assistance or the actual rendering of such assistance. An advokat's office or dwelling premises may be searched only on the basis of a court decision. However, advokat premises may nonetheless be searched, and confidentiality on the part of an advokat arises out of the contract with the client and not by virtue of the status of an advokat.

The Federal Chamber of Advokats monitors violations of the independence of advokats and issues annual reports concerning the state of affairs in this respect. In 2018 the Federal Chamber of Advokats recorded 589 violations of the professional rights of advokats – a reduction of 14.9% in comparison with the prior year. These included the murder of one advokat and six advokats sustaining impairment of health in the form of personal injuries. Illegal searches of the dwelling or office premises of advokats arose from thirty-four to forty, and illegal operational-search measures decreased from twenty-six to fourteen. Refusals of investigative agencies to admit

[77] Transl. in W. E. Butler, *Russian Public Law* (3d ed.; 2013), pp. 923-936. See Iu. S. Pilipenko, Научно-практический комментарий к кодексу профессиональной этики адвоката [Scientific-Practical Commentary to the Code of Professional Ethics of an Advokat] (2d ed.; 2013).

advokats to participate in procedural actions decreased from seventy-four to sixty three; advokat requests for documents and information were rejected 78 times, a decrease of 85% over the prior year.

Advokats filed 3,212 appeals and complaints with law enforcement agencies concerning violations of their professional rights in 2018, of which 758 were filed with the Procuracy agencies; 2,134 with investigative agencies, and 320 with courts.

In 2016 the Federal Law on the Advokatura was amended to make provision for the introduction of the Commission for Ethics and Standards as a collegial organ of the Federal Chamber of Advokats. The said Commission works out standards for rendering qualified legal assistance and other standards of advokat activity, gives explanations binding on all chambers of advokats and advokats with regard to questions of the application of the Code of Professional Ethics, and also exercises other powers in accordance with the Code of Professional Ethics of an Advokat and the Reglament of the Commission for Ethics and Standards.

The Commission consists of sixteen members who serve terms of four years chosen as follows:

- from advokats – the President of the Federal Chamber of Advokats, and also nine advokats elected by the All-Russian Congress of Advokats upon the recommendation of the Council of the Federal Chamber of Advokats;
- from the federal agency of justice – two representatives;
- from the State Duma of the Federal Assembly of the Russian Federation – two representatives;
- from the Soviet of the Federation of the Russian Federation – two representatives.

Disciplinary Practice

Complaints by clients or by State agencies against the conduct of advokats are considered by the qualifications commissions of chambers of advokats. In 2018, 24,432 complaints were received, of which 5,001 led to disciplinary proceedings. Of these, 40% were terminated and 60% resulted in a finding that the advokat concerned had violated legislation on advokat activity or the Code of Professional Ethics of an Advokat. Recommendations submitted by territorial agencies of the Ministry of Justice of Russia led to 53 advokats losing the status of advokat – the equivalent of being struck off or disbarred; complaints directly to chambers of advokats resulted in 693 advokats losing the status of advokat, of whom 205 were disciplined for a violation of professional ethics and 357 for the failure to comply with a decision of organs of a chamber of advokats. 87 were excluded from the advokatura for the commission of an intentional crime.

Foreign Lawyers and Legal Services

During the Soviet period, the Moscow City College of Advokats maintained from 1937 a special legal consultation office to handle, principally, civil cases for foreign citizens and organizations or foreign legal matters for Soviet citizens. It was one of two such institutions empowered to give legal advice throughout the entire former Soviet Union. Called "Iniurkollegia", it is still in existence, having been transformed into a specialized advokat bureau. Specializing as before in inheritance, property, insurance, intellectual property, and related matters, it has more than 50 advokats and operates a branch office in St Petersburg. Its fees have historically been approximate to those charged by leading Anglo-American law firms.

Since 1988 foreign law firms have established various forms of presence in the Russian Federation, ranging from a hotel-room office, to a representation office, to a Russian juridical person. Foreigners may apply to them for legal services or to any Russian legal consultation office, law firm, college, bureau, cabinet, or private practitioner. The hourly rates charged by foreign law firms are similar to those in London and New York; Russian law firms as a rule are less expensive than foreign firms but their rates for foreign clients can be more expensive than they would charge Russian citizens or juridical persons.

Under a Statute on Keeping the Register of Advokats of Foreign States Effectuating Advokat Activity on the Territory of the Russian Federation, confirmed by Decree of the Government of the Russian Federation on 19 September 2003, as amended, the Federal Registration Service registered advokats of a foreign State practicing in Russia.[78] Foreign jurists who meet the standards laid down by the 2002 Law on Advokat Activity may become Russian advokats. This Statute was replaced by the Administrative Reglament for the Provision by the Ministry of Justice of the Russian Federation of State Service with Respect to Keeping the Register of Advokats of Foreign States Effectuating Advokat Activity on the Territory of the Russian Federation, confirmed by Order of the Ministry of Justice of 31 July 2012, No. 151;[79] the Decree of 19 September 2003 was deemed to have lost force by Decree of the Government of the Russian Federation of 28 September 2015, No. 1028.[80]

In 2018 there were more than 100 foreign law firms who claimed a presence somewhere in the Russian Federation, principally Moscow and St Petersburg. They ranged in size from one to more than 100 lawyers. Many remain without Russian-speaking partners, and most concentrated

[78] СЗ РФ (2003), no. 39, item 3768, as amended; transl. in Butler, note 3 above.

[79] Российская газета [Russian Newspaper], 22 August 2012; available on Consultant Plus.

[80] СЗ РФ (2015), no. 40, item 5565. The Administrative Reglament entered into force from the day on which the Decree of 19 September 2003 lost force.

upon serving foreign clients investing in Russia, although increasingly they have as clients Russians seeking to invest beyond the limits of the Russian Federation.

THE JURISCONSULT

A thorough study of the jurisconsult in pre-revolutionary Russia has yet to be undertaken. It is evident that the term and position of jurisconsult existed in nineteenth century Russia and that the term itself dates back to at least Petrine Russia to refer more generally to a jurist or lawyer. Prior to the judicial reforms of 1864 in Russia, the term "jurisconsult" was ordinarily reserved for individuals who engaged in private practice in the capacity of what later came to be known as an "advokat". The term was used, nonetheless, also to designate jurists who held an official position in State service or at an enterprise.

It has been suggested that prior to 1917 the person closest to the jurisconsult by nature of occupation was the *prikazchik* [приказчик], a term used in various meanings from at least the sixteenth century and understood to refer, *inter alia,* to a person who entered into legal relations with third persons as an empowered representative of his principal to perform an assignment on the basis of legislation and the customs of business turnover.[81]

Historical Origins

The Statute on the Post of Jurisconsult of Imperial Plants of 7 November 1858 established the post of jurisconsult "in order to guard the rights of ownership of Imperial plants in instances when they are the subject-matter of an investigative, police, or judicial proceeding". The duties of a jurisconsult included offering advice at the request of plant management on the claims of a plant department against other departments and persons or on claims filed against the employer, watching over cases arising in various State agencies with regard to suits by the plant department against outsiders and suits against the department itself, and defense of the rights of the imperial plants in the event of an investigation.

It was customary for a jurisconsult to hold other posts together with that in the department of imperial plants. The plant management determined the amount of his salary. The number of places where a jurisconsult might work simultaneously was not limited by legislation.

Jurisconsults appeared at once in the Soviet people's commissariats and other State agencies after the October Revolution and survived in

[81] A. N. Chashin, Юридическая служба в Российской Федерации [Legal Service in the Russian Federation] (2005), p. 6. The *prikazchik* in some instances bore civil and criminal responsibility for the failure to perform the assignment properly.

a few of the large enterprises, where despite the early expectations of an administered economy and society, their skills were provisionally required. In the categories of Soviet workers established in 1918 for wage scales, jurisconsults were included in category 1 of Group I, the highest classification.[82] By 1920 the need for legally-trained personnel had become desperate. On 11 May 1920 the Council of People's Commissars ordered all individuals with a higher legal education to register so that "proper use of [their] specialized knowledge" might be made.[83] One week later the same agency created "consultation subsections of justice" to be staffed by jurisconsults in the "people's commissariats and all central institutions of the RSFSR".[84] The Moscow College of Defenders in 1922 requested the Moscow City Soviet to authorize members of the college to jointly hold the post of jurisconsult and practice in the College, which was approved on 23 July 1922.[85]

The establishment of the Procuracy in 1922 led to a reorganization of the regulation of the jurisconsult. Supervision over the jurisconsult previously vested in the People's Commissariat of Justice in May 1920 was transferred to the Procuracy in 1923, which was to register the jurisconsults and to oversee their activities in justice agencies. Outside that commissariat, the regulation of jurisconsults became largely a matter for the organization employing them. In industry an all-union conference of jurisconsults was convoked at the initiative of the USSR Supreme Economic Council. On 7 June 1925 the Statute on Jurisconsults of State Enterprises Subordinate to the USSR Supreme Economic Council was confirmed by Order No. 955.[86]

The 1925 Statute outlined the principal duties of a jurisconsult. They included the consideration and, when necessary, participation in drawing up draft contracts and various other acts of a legal nature and correcting them from a legal standpoint; and giving explanations of legal provisions and administrative regulations at the requests of the executive organ of the enterprise or sections thereof; giving oral and written opinions on all legal matters put by the executives of the enterprise; participation to give opinions in sessions of executive organs of the enterprise or in commissions and meetings convened by the enterprise; drawing up opinions at the request of the executive organ concerning the indicia and classification of illegal actions of workers and employees; and conducting cases of the enterprise in judicial, administrative, and social institutions.

[82] СУ РСФСР (1918), no. 48, item 567.

[83] СУ РСФСР (1920), no. 47, item 211.

[84] СУ РСФСР (1920), no. 51, item 221.

[85] Yu. Luryi, "Jurisconsults in the Soviet Economy", in D. Barry, et al. (eds.), *Soviet Law After Stalin* (1979), II, pp. 170-171.

[86] Бюллетень финансового и хозяйственного законодательства [Bulletin of Financial and Economic Legislation], no. 6 (1925), p. 18.

This document also prohibited placing on jurisconsults administrative functions and especially the combining of jurisconsult duties with administrative posts. The opinion of a jurisconsult had the significance of a view with regard to the application and interpretation of laws and was not binding upon the enterprise management. If management disagreed with an oral opinion given by a jurisconsult, the last was required to set out his view in writing. A jurisconsult advising on a transaction was responsible solely for the transaction conforming to legislation and bore no responsibility for the economic necessity or advisability of entering into the transaction, nor for the choice of contracting party.

On 30 March 1927 the RSFSR Council of People's Commissars enacted a Decree "On Jurisconsults of State Institutions and Enterprises and Cooperative Organizations and the Supervision of Their Activity".[87] The decree confirmed the supervisory role of the Procuracy over the jurisconsult, which was broadened by subsequent legislation. Throughout the late 1920s conferences of jurisconsults were held on an all-union or lesser scale to exchange work experience, hear reports, and even adopt resolutions about organizing and supervising the profession.

Unlike the advokats in Russia, however, jurisconsults during the pre-revolutionary and Soviet eras never formed a professional body that transcended ministerial or departmental lines. The transition from the NEP to the planned economy posed an initial threat to the jurisconsult insofar as law was expected to rapidly wither away and be supplanted by Plan. The 1927 legislation on jurisconsults had become obsolete; in most branches of industry the 1927 decree was superseded *de facto* by commissariat statutes on jurisconsults from 1932 to 1939. In many people's commissariats and State enterprises there were no legal sections or jurisconsults at all. When they were present, they were commonly incorporated into the chancellery of people's commissariats, where they visaed draft internal normative acts, or at enterprises were part of other sections, such as bookkeeping or sales, and basically occupied themselves with the work of those sections.

The supervisory role of the Procuracy diminished accordingly. The 1939 Statute on the Advokatura prohibited advokats from serving simultaneously as jurisconsults, but in 1941 enterprises which did not have the post of jurisconsult included in their personnel establishment were allowed to retain an advokat's services by agreement.

In 1957 N. S. Khrushchev initiated a major reorganization and decentralization of the administration of the national economy. These reforms were followed by local legislation on the jurisconsult endowing the post with widely varying duties and status. At the union republic level "model statutes" on the jurisconsult were enacted to aid enterprises and

[87] СУ РСФСР (1927), no. 36, item 238.

organizations in fashioning their own. The Ukrainian SSR approved a model statute in 1959 and the RSFSR on 29 March 1963,[88] among others. Despite these reforms, the great mass of enterprises was subordinated to union ministries and departments and the model statutes did not extend to them.[89]

Current Legislation

Although the transition to a market economy in Russia has enlarged the employment opportunities of the jurisconsult, his current status remains deeply indebted to the 1965 and 1987 economic reforms in the Soviet Union which gave State enterprises greater responsibility for their contractual relations with other enterprises and expanded the scope of economic accountability (still an element of post-Soviet Russian civil law). The enlarged discretion accorded to enterprise management required disciplining; law and contract were the chosen instruments and, in the Soviet era, the system of State Arbitrazh was initially the principal forum.

A massive increase in legal personnel was required together with improvements in the law, both on a scale reminiscent of the reforms of Emperors Alexander I and Nicholas I. Several tentative measures were introduced, but the key document for the jurisconsult was the Decree of 23 December 1970 "On the Improvement of Legal Work in the National Economy". The Decree, *inter alia,* required the enactment of a General Statute on the jurisconsult, the formation or strengthening of legal departments in the central apparatus and at all levels of economic administration, local government, collective and State farms; the USSR Ministry of Justice was reinforced in its role of exercising methods direction over legal work in the national economy and improving the substance and systematization of Soviet legislation; admissions to law faculties were greatly increased and measures introduced to raise the qualifications of jurisconsults already in post.[90]

On 22 June 1972 the USSR Council of Ministers confirmed the General Statute on the Legal Section (or Office), Chief (or Senior) Jurisconsult, and Jurisconsult of a Ministry, Department, Executive Committee of a Soviet of People's Deputies, Enterprise, Organization, or Institution.[91] On the basis

[88] See the Model Statute on the Legal (or Contract-Law) Section, Chief (or Senior) Jurisconsult, and Jurisconsult of an Enterprise, Institution, and Organization, confirmed by Decree of the RSFSR Council of Ministers of 29 March 1963, No. 386. СП РСФСР (1963), no. 7, item 44.

[89] See B. I. Puginskii and O. G. Neverov, Правовая работа [Legal Work] (2004), p. 26.

[90] J. Giddings [Henderson], "The Jurisconsult in the USSR", *Review of Socialist Law,* I (1975), pp. 171-211. The number of jurists working in the national economy in 1970 was about 30,000, which increased by 1978 to 60,000, in 1981 to 64,000; and on 1 January 1992, to 75,000 jurists. Puginskii and Neverov, Правовая работа [Legal Work] (2004), p. 26.

[91] Transl. in W. E. Butler, *The Soviet Legal System: Legislation and Documentation* (1978), pp. 311-318.

of this General Statute, ministries and departments drafted and confirmed their own statutes for their respective legal offices or legal personnel. Social organizations were recommended to use this General Statute as a model when establishing a procedure for carrying on legal work within their organizations. Collective farms and inter-collective farm enterprises and organizations arranged their legal services on the basis of an Instruction confirmed jointly by the ministers of agriculture and justice on 3 January 1973.

The 1972 General Statute, although dating from the Soviet era, remains in force in the Russian Federation as amended on 4 December 1980, 1 December 1987, and 21 December 1990, subject to a decision of the Supreme Court of the Russian Federation of 27 December 2000, No. ГКПИ 2000-1409.[92]

Status of jurisconsult. In the Russian market economy the jurisconsult remains, unlike the advokat, a salaried employee in the establishment where he works. This includes not only State institutions, enterprises, organizations, State farms, and collective farms, but also house counsel in private companies, banks, and foreign law firms operating in Russia.

The term "jurisconsult" has been criticized in post-Soviet Russia as being not very "appropriate", unable to escape associations of the past with "work of little interest in State enterprises".[93] In some instances the term itself has been corrupted and become "juristconsult" or "juristconsultant". Officially, however, the correct appellation is "jurisconsult" as confirmed by the Ministry of Labor of the Russian Federation in the "Unified Nomenclature for Posts of Employees".

Numerically, jurisconsults are beyond doubt the largest component of the Russian legal profession, even though, in the absence of an all-inclusive professional organization or of any collective registration requirements, it is impossible to say how many there are. Certainly, there are several hun-

92 СП СССР (1972), no. 13, item 70. Entered into force 22 June 1972. Point 4, paragraph 4, of the General Statute provided that the head of a legal section or the jurisconsult of an enterprise, organization, or institution is appointed to and relieved from office by the executive of the enterprise, organization, or institution with subsequent confirmation by a superior agency. This provision was originally intended to protect jurisconsults against arbitrariness, pressure, and reprisal from the enterprise director. It was declared to be contrary to subsequent legislation, namely, Part One of the Civil Code of the Russian Federation. The Civil Code provides that the rights of a juridical person may be limited only by a law, whereas the General Statute is a subordinate normative act. The Supreme Court also noted that the General Statute continued *de facto* to be applied. Consultant Plus records the General Statute as being in force. See Бюллетень Верховного Суда Российской Федерации [Bulletin of the Supreme Court of the Russian Federation], no. 10 (2001).

93 A. E. Zhilinskii, Профессиональная деятельность юриста: Введение в специальность [Professional Activity of the Jurist: Introduction to the Specialty] (1997), p. 142.

dred thousand.[94] On 8 May 2001 the President of the Russian Federation adopted an Edict on Certain Measures to Strengthen the Legal Services of State Agencies.[95] In addition to introducing substantial increases in salaries and benefits for jurisconsults, the Edict directed the Government of the Russian Federation to confirm a "Model Statute on the Legal Service of a Federal Agency of Executive Power", duly confirmed by Decree of 2 April 2002, No. 207.[96] Under the Model Statute, a legal service is to be organized as an autonomous structural subdivision of the central apparatus of the federal agency of executive power and to be headed by an executive who is appointed to and relieved from office by the head of the federal agency. The Model Statute applied, of course, only to State agencies, although it is widely used as a model in the Russian private sector.

Functions of jurisconsult. The duties of a jurisconsult vary depending upon whether the jurisconsult is employed by a ministry, State enterprise, private company, local soviet, agricultural organization or large farm, or a Russian or foreign law firm. Within the State sector and even for Russian companies, the jurisconsult has responsibility for verifying and certifying personally that draft legal enactments confirm to legislation in force. The jurisconsult supervises the conformity to law of similar enactments in structural subdivisions of his employer and prepares amendments for enactments. When necessary, the jurisconsult may be involved in helping to draft collective labor contracts or other measures to strengthen labor discipline. As a rule he will be extensively involved in drafting, evaluating, or even "visaing" contracts and other transactions. He will represent the employer in litigation, including arbitration and the arbitrazh courts and courts of ordinary jurisdiction. He may be involved, and in State enterprises will assuredly be involved, in the procedures for accepting goods and products. He will supervise claims procedures and prepare materials relating to wastage, thefts, and shortages for transfer to investigative agencies or the courts.

The jurisconsult may be called upon to advise other organizations within the employer, including the local trade union committee. His office will most probably operate as the control center for receiving and filing all internal normative and non-normative acts issued by the employer, informing others about them, and in general drawing the attention of fellow personnel to new relevant legislation.

[94] Aizin and Tikhomirov observed that the profession of jurisconsult has become a "mass profession" because of the new legal space opened to enterprises as a result of the transition to a market economy and reforms in legal education that enabled technical and other nonspecialist educational institutions to produce graduates in the field of law. See S. M. Aizin and M. Iu. Tikhomirov, Юридическая служба на предприятии: Настольная книга юрисконсульта [Legal Service at the Enterprise: Manual for the Jurisconsult] (2001), p. 3.

[95] СЗ РФ (2001), no. 20, item 2000.

[96] СЗ РФ (2002), no. 14, item 1307.

Within the State administrative sector there have not been dramatic changes in the role of the jurisconsult. The ministerial jurisconsult has less responsibility for direct economic operations and more involving legislation, administration, and supervision of inferior structural subdivision or enterprises. In some ministries the jurisconsult may be heavily engaged in issues of foreign law or of public and private international law. The ministries dealing with foreign trade, fisheries, civil aviation, shipping, and foreign relations are examples. The jurisconsult of a local soviet deals extensively with the legality of draft normative materials and gives legal advice not only to the local soviet and its executive committee, but even to the permanent commissions or individual deputies of the local soviet.

The career structure and remuneration of a jurisconsult in the State sector will depend upon what level he achieves within the personnel establishment. The following categories exist, as set out in Decree No. 37 of 21 August 1998, as amended, which confirmed the Qualifications Manual of Posts of Executives, Specialists, and Other Employees:[97]

(1) jurisconsult: higher legal education but without work experience – Tier 6;

(2) jurisconsult of II category: higher legal education and work experience as a jurisconsult of not less than three years – Tiers 7 and 8;

(3) jurisconsult of I category: higher legal education and work experience as a II category jurisconsult of not less than three years – Tiers 8 and 9;

(4) leading jurisconsult: higher legal education and work experience in post of jurisconsult for not less than three years – 10 and 11 Tiers;

(5) jurisconsult of II or I categories or leading: head of legal administration, section, or bureau – higher legal education and work experience in specialty of not less than five years – 8 to 12 Tiers, depending upon to which group for payment of labor the executives have relegated the particular organization.

Many Russian commercial organizations also follow this pattern, although it is accepted that the nomenclature may vary from one company to another and entries in the labor books of the jurisconsults accordingly. One encounters appellations such as "general director for legal questions", or "director of the legal directorate", and others.[98]

97 Available on Consultant Plus.

98 See K. K. Lebedev, Правовое обслуживание бизнеса (корпоративный юрист) [Legal Servicing of Business (Corporate Jurist)] (2001), p. 17.

Russian jurists employed by foreign law firms are advised in monographs published specially for them to expect a probation period and, if they are hired, a different life style. "Law firms with foreign participation", as they are sometimes styled, advise many "solid" clients who are foreign corporations that sell products or goods in Russia or invest in various projects in Russia. The work in law firms with foreign participation is "highly paid", being "much higher than the average level of earnings of practicing jurists" and is prestigious and interesting. Transnational "legal companies" systematically rotate personnel with their consent and allow Russians to undergo training in other offices of the law firm. But, there is another side to the experience: the foreign firms are "demanding"; there is "constant competition with other personnel of the firm, a tense work rhythm dictated by the client workload, and the "administration of the firm is far from always guided by norms of labor legislation concerning work time and leisure time".[99]

Methods Assistance. During the Soviet era, the USSR and union republic ministries of justice issued methods recommendations to jurisconsults. These related to major policy matters, such as the procedures for drafting normative acts of ministries or departments, for using legal means to ensure the issuance of high quality products, or for registering and keeping normative acts. The last function has nearly disappeared with the development of commercial legal data bases, but would continue to be vital for internal, or local, normative acts which may or may not find their way into external data bases. Insofar as departmental jurisconsults continue to be involved in drafting or evaluating interdepartmental normative legal acts, such methods guidance would be useful.

The jurisconsult survived throughout the entire Soviet era, albeit in unorganized form. The renaissance of the jurisconsult in 1970 represented at the time a concern for legality within a less centralized system of economic management of the national economy. Compliance with Soviet economic legislation was supposed to produce economic dividends measured by improved efficiency and "profit" as defined by the Planned Economy. State enterprises and collective farms were given a variety of incentives to employ jurisconsults, including through media campaigns which emphasized the role of the jurisconsult in reducing fines and penalties or enforcing claims successfully in court.

The role of the jurisconsult has assuredly survived the dissolution of the Soviet Union; indeed, that role has expanded as the private sector in the Russian Federation has created a greater demand for legal services from in-house counsel. Legal training and experience have in the rising generation been useful to those seeking careers in State service at the highest levels.

[99] Lebedev, ibid., pp. 47-48.

Three of the last four Presidents of the USSR and Russian Federation have a higher legal education and experience as jurisconsults (Presidents M. S. Gorbachev, V. V. Putin, and D. A. Medvedev).

STATE LEGAL BUREAUS

On 22 August 2005 the Government of the Russian Federation adopted Decree No. 534 "On Conducting an Experiment with Regard to the Creation of the State System of Rendering Legal Assistance Free of Charge to Indigent Citizens".[100] The stated aim of the experiment was to develop an optimal mechanism for the realization of State policy in the domain of rendering legal assistance free of charge to indigent citizens. The experiment was to be conducted for the calendar year 2006 (later extended to encompass 2007) in ten subjects of the Russian Federation (Republics Karelia and Chechnia, and the Volgograd, Irkutsk, Magadan, Moscow, Samara, Sverdlovsk, Tomsk, and Ulianovsk Regions). Each State legal bureau was created in the form of a federal State institution; each was allotted a personnel establishment of 15 jurists.

The agency responsible for organizing the experiment and setting up the State legal bureaus was the Federal Registration Service. Organizing the experiment included confirmation of the charters of the State legal bureaus, the internal structure and personnel establishment thereof, and ensuring the State registration of the charters.

On 25 December 2008 by Decree No. 1029 "On State Legal Bureaus" the Government of Russia extended the life of the legal bureaus and expanded the categories of citizens who might qualify for legal assistance free of charge.[101] The existing State legal bureaus were moved to the jurisdiction of the Ministry of Justice of the Russian Federation. A new Statute on Rendering Legal Assistance Free of Charge by State Legal Bureaus was confirmed by Decree No. 1029 to replace the Statute of 2005. By Decree No. 991 of 3 December 2009,[102] the Government of the Russian Federation extended the scheme to calendar year 2010.

The entire system of State legal bureaus was made permanent under the Federal Law on Legal Assistance Free of Charge in the Russian Federation of 21 November 2011.[103] The State legal bureaus, however, are regarded as a link, or more precisely as participants, within the "State system of legal assistance free of charge". This system consists of federal agencies

[100] СЗ РФ (2005), no. 35, item 3612, as amended. The Decree also confirmed the Statute on Rendering Legal Assistance Free of Charge to Indigent Citizens.

[101] СЗ РФ (2009), no. 2, item 229.

[102] СЗ РФ (2009), no. 50, item 6099. The various decrees regulating the experimental State legal bureaus were deemed to have lost force by Decree of the Government of the Russian Federation, No. 71, dated 31 January 2013. СЗ РФ (2013), no. 5, item 410.

[103] СЗ РФ (2011), no. 48, item 6725, as amended.

of executive power and institutions within their jurisdiction; agencies of executive power of subjects of the Russian Federation and institutions within their jurisdiction; management organs of State extrabudgetary funds; State legal bureaus; and advokats, notaries, and other entities rendering legal assistance free of charge who are endowed with the right to take part in the State system of legal assistance free of charge pursuant to Russian legislation.

Although the State legal bureaus have been characterized by some as an "alternative Advokatura",[104] they are in fact staffed by jurisconsults, a characterization confirmed by the personnel establishment of each legal bureau. A State legal bureau under the 2011 Federal Law is a juridical person created in the form of a treasury institution of subjects of the Russian Federation.

The State legal bureaus provide legal assistance to three general categories of persons: (1) natural and juridical persons who are participants of the State system of legal assistance free of charge; (2) natural and juridical persons who are participants of the non-State system of legal assistance free of charge; and (3) other persons who have the right to legal assistance free of charge under federal laws or laws of subjects of the Russian Federation. For the most part these three categories encompass: (1) those considered to be indigent under Russian legislation; and (2) designated categories of disabled persons, World War II veterans, unemployed pensioners receiving an old-age pension, disabled and orphaned children of various categories, adoptive parents, and a number of other categories.

The State legal bureaus give three types of legal assistance: (1) consultations in oral or written form; (2) drawing up applications, appeals, petitions, and other documents of a legal character; and (3) representation of the interests of citizens in a civil proceeding, execution proceeding relating to civil cases, and in State agencies and agencies of local self-government, social associations, and other organizations. Because legal assistance is rendered free of charge to low-income and needy persons, evidence of their income or lack thereof must be submitted in accordance with legislation of the subject of the Federation where the legal bureau is located. Except for oral consultations, legal advice is rendered under an agreement between the State legal bureau and the client according to a form confirmed by the Ministry of Justice.

Advokats may become involved in the advice rendered by a State legal bureau if their Chamber of Advokats has concluded a contract, usually on an annual basis specifying the precise advokats who will render legal advice, with the bureau providing that such advice will be rendered free of charge to citizens on a permanent basis or to a specific citizen. The names

[104] Kucherena, note 12 above, p. 184.

of those advokats who are available to give legal advice free of charge is published in the mass media and on the Internet. A citizen who applies for legal advice free of charge has the right to receive such advice unless he fails to submit the requisite documents, or his income does not fall within the range provided, or he seeks legal advice on matters not provided for by the relevant legislation. A refusal by the State legal bureau to provide advice may be appealed by the citizen concerned to the territorial agency of the Ministry of Justice in the subject of the Russian Federation; such appeals must be considered within 10 working days. If the refusal is supported by the territorial agency, the citizen concerned may appeal to a court.

In 2018 advokats were the principal participants in the State system of *pro bono* legal assistance in sixty subjects of the Russian Federation; in sixteen subjects of the Russian Federation advokats and State legal bureaus provided legal assistance free of charge, and in eight subjects of the Russian Federation such advice was provided only by a State legal bureau. 11,163, or 15% of the advokats in Russia participated in the State system of free legal assistance, advising 49,272 socially indigent individuals.

The internal organization of State legal bureaus is determined by legislation at the level within whose State system the legal bureaus are created, level here usually meaning subject of the Russian Federation. Those in existence generally follow the patterns established during the experimental era.

Legal personnel of a State legal bureau are required to have a higher legal education from a State-accredited educational institution, no conflict of interests with the interests of the citizen who has applied for legal advice, not participated as a judge, arbitrator, mediator, procurator, investigator, inquiry official, expert, specialist, or interpreter in considering or deciding a matter related to that brought in by the citizen, not have been an official within whose competence was the adoption of decisions in the interests of this citizen, or not have rendered legal assistance to another person whose interests are contrary to the interests of the citizen who applied for legal assistance. The said personnel also may not divulge information communicated by the citizen in connection with rendering legal assistance unless the citizen consents to such divulgence.

The system of State legal bureaus was adapted from that existing in Finland. Initially strongly resisted by the Federal Chamber of Advokats, the experiment was modified to meet the major objections of the advokats. The objections were various. Some observed that under Article 48(2) of the 1993 Russian Constitution, legal assistance might be rendered free of charge in instances provided by a law. The decrees of the Government establishing the experiment of State legal bureaus are subordinate normative acts, not laws – and arguably unconstitutional. Moreover, although the recipient of legal assistance might not pay, the labor of advokats in supplying such assistance should be paid for by the State. The financial duty to pay advokats for giving legal assistance free of charge has been placed on the subjects of the Federation, many of whom made no such financial provision. Others who did make budgetary appropriations for this purpose massively underfunded the need for such services. Now the federal budget was stepping in to finance the State legal bureaus and bypassing the advokats in so doing.

The State legal bureaus, it was argued, represented the State seeking to defend people against itself. Those jurisconsults who staffed the State legal bureaus were civil servants, bureaucrats, whereas the essence of the Advokatura was acting in a civil society as an institution independent of the State. Many doubted the qualifications and experience of the jurisconsults to be hired in the State legal bureaus. It was also felt that the bureaus would be inundated with work – about 20% of the Russian population qualified as indigent. And the program ignored the role of nongovernmental legal defense organizations which already gave legal assistance to Russian citizens free of charge within the scope of their interests and specializations.[105]

The State legal bureaus should be seen as a realization on the part of the State that the Advokatura was unlikely to be able to meet the demand for legal assistance to indigent Russian citizens. Perhaps some of the difficulties were inherent in the Russian federative system, which delegated these matters primarily to the jurisdiction of the subjects of the Federation. Most subjects of the Federation did little to meet the massive latent needs for legal advice among the low-income segments of the Russian population. Those that made efforts in this direction offered derisory financial support. Remarkable is the fact that the advokats were bypassed in the original initiative. The State legal bureaus are a prime example of "advokat activity" being directly and expressly performed by jurisconsults.

The State legal bureaus, it should be noted, are supplemented by a non-State system of legal assistance pursuant to which, in 2018, 3,759 advokats provided free legal assistance to 17,197 natural persons on the premises of legal assistance bureaus. In addition, on their own premises advokats gave free legal advice to 173,155 individuals.

To the activities of State legal bureaus in providing legal assistance free of charge should be added the contributions of legal clinics formed at several law faculties in the Russian Federation (see below).

[105] These concerns and others are summarized in Kucherena, ibid., pp. 173-203.

FOREIGN JURISTS IN RUSSIA

Historical Background

Foreigners were prohibited from being members of the Advokatura in the Russian Empire. They were not prohibited from holding positions in State service, however, and many did, including legal posts.

During the Soviet era, foreign citizens were prohibited from being advokats in the USSR. That prohibition was not removed until the present Law on the Advokatura entered into legal force, as from 1 July 2003. There was no explicit prohibition with respect to jurisconsults.

Foreign citizens received legal advice on matters of Soviet law through special legal consultation offices maintained by several colleges of advokats. These legal consultation offices chiefly handled civil cases for foreign citizens or organizations or represented Soviet citizens and organizations in foreign legal matters. The best-known legal consultation office was "Iniurkollegia", attached to the Moscow City College of Advokats. Iuiurkollegia specialized in inheritance, property, insurance, patent, trademark, and related matters. That organization would bring suit in the USSR or abroad on behalf of its clients. The fee schedule approximated the fees charged by leading Anglo-American law firms.

Foreigners could apply on the same basis as Soviet citizens to any legal consultation office for advice. The advantage of Iniurkollegia was special expertise not readily available elsewhere insofar as foreign law matters were involved and a *de facto* monopoly in serving foreigners.[106]

Foreign Advokats in Russia

The numbers of foreign citizens and stateless persons who have acquired the status of advokat in Russia is not known. The figure is believed to be a low one, and most probably comprises principally individuals who are citizens of other countries of the CIS.

On 22 April 2004 the Council of the Federal Chamber of Advokats issued an "Explanation" which took the view that:

> ... advokats of foreign States may effectuate advokat activity only with regard to questions of the law of the State of which they are a citizen with obligatory registration in a special register. Acquisition of the status of advokat of the Russian Federation by a person who

[106] See E. S. Shugrina, «Некоторые особенности оказания юридических услуг иностранному бизнесу в России» [Certain Peculiarities of Rendering Legal Services to Foreign Business in Russia], Адвокатская практика [Advokat Practice], no. 3 (2012). Available on Consultant Plus. The specialized college of advokats "Iniurkollegia" was transformed into the Advokat Bureau "Iniurkollegia" and continues to operate.

simultaneously is an advokat of a foreign State is not provided for by prevailing legislation.

Foreign citizens and stateless persons have the right to acquire the status of advokat in the established procedure if they in so doing are not advokats of other States.

The difficulties raised by the phrase "advokat of a foreign State" are considerable. The Explanation issued by the Federal Chamber would, but for the confusion inherent in the terminology of the legislation, preclude foreign "advokats", whatever that may mean, from acquiring the status of advokat in Russia or, to put it otherwise, multiple professional qualifications. There would be no reason for the legislator to address the issue of whether an "advokat of a foreign State" may become a Russian advokat; if that is not prohibited, it is permitted.

This construction of Russian legislation by the Federal Chamber is profoundly anti-competitive and not consistent with the legal status of foreign citizens and stateless persons under Russian law.[107]

As noted above, foreigners may become Russian advokats. The Federal Chamber of Advokats received in 2017 inquiries from individuals in twelve foreign States seeking information on whether and how a foreigner might become a Russian advokat. Such inquiries were reported from Azerbaidzhan, Armenia, Belarus, India, Kyrgyzia, Latvia, Dnistrian Republic, Uzbekistan, Ukraine, France, and the Donetsk and Lugansk republics.

Foreign jurists who do not wish to become members of the Russian Advokatura and acquire the status of advokat may engage in advokat activity on the territory of the Russian Federation by registering with the Ministry of Justice of the Russian Federation. Without such registration, engaging in advokat activity is prohibited in Russia. However, although a close reading of the Administrative Reglament requiring registration suggests that registration is not an authorization or a license to practice, the Administrative Reglament read against Article 6(2) of the Federal Law on the Advokatura suggests that the fact of registration and the issuance of a certificate confirming registration amount to a special authorization for advokats of a foreign State to carry on advokat activity in Russia.[108] The registration is a confirmation that the individual concerned has been included in the Register of advokats of foreign States.

[107] The most thoughtful analysis by a Russian advokat of the issues involved is A. I. Muranov, Российское регулирование отношений с иностранными элементами: некоторые аспекты правового статуса и деятельности иностранных адвокатов [Russian Regulation of Relations with Foreign Elements: Certain Aspects of the Legal Status and Activity of Foreign Advokats] (2006), pp. 50-52.

[108] Ibid., p. 80.

The 2012 Administrative Reglament[109] provides that the following documents must be submitted by an advokat of a foreign State for the purposes of registration: (a) completion of an application and questionnaire in the Russian language; (b) a document confirming the status of advokat of a foreign State, which must be translated into Russian and legalized unless provided otherwise by international treaties of the Russian Federation; (c) an identity document with a notarized translation into Russian; (d) documents confirming the legality of sojourn on the territory of the Russian Federation; and (e) two photographs of the prescribed dimensions.

These documents must be submitted in the original and copies translated into the Russian language, and any translations must be notarially certified or the genuineness of the translation attested if the notary does not have a command of the relevant foreign language. The failure to submit the necessary documents or the submission of unreliable information is grounds for refusing registration.

The Ministry of Justice of the Russian Federation has strictly determined periods within which the verification of documents must be completed pursuant to the Administrative Reglament. If all is satisfactory, the Ministry issues a Regulation to register the applicant.

On the basis of that registration, the advokat of a foreign State is issued a numbered certificate of registration. The registration number may not be conferred on any other person, even if the certificate were later to be annulled (although a duplicate certificate would be issued if the original were lost). An issued certificate is subject to annulment by the Ministry of Justice in the event of: (a) establishing the unreliability of documents submitted for registration; (b) deportation of the advokat from Russia in the established procedure; or (c) entry into legal force of the judgment of a court deeming the advokat to be guilty of the commission of a crime. If a certificate is annulled, the advokat concerned must return it to the Ministry.

Information contained in the register held by the Ministry of Justice may be provided to others upon the payment of an established fee, except for agencies of State power and agencies of local self-government, who may obtain the information free of charge. Such information was provided in the form of extracts relating to individual jurists under the Order on Confirmation of the Form and Procedure for the Provision of an Extract from the Register of Advokats of Foreign States Effectuating Advokat Activity on the Territory of the Russian Federation, issued on 12 January 2004, No. 2, as amended by Orders of 1 March 2006, No. 32, and 30 September 2008. No. 218.[110] The information is now available in accordance with the 2012 Administrative Reglament.

109 Available on Consultant Plus.

110 Available on Consultant Plus. The document lost force from the date of the Decree of

What are the risks for a foreign jurist who fails to register? Possibilities include administrative responsibility under an expansive interpretation of the Code of the Russian Federation on Administrative Violations (Article 19.20(2)), failure to pay which could lead to difficulties for the foreign jurist concerned in entering or leaving the Russian Federation. Another risk is that the contract for legal services entered into by the foreign jurist may be deemed to be invalid or void under the Russian Civil Code.[111] No Russian administrative or judicial practice is known in this connection.

Foreign jurists in the Russian Federation are regulated under the general regime for the legal status of foreigners and stateless persons.[112] If they have the language skills and pass the qualifications examination, they may qualify for the status of a fully-fledged Russian advokat. Foreign jurists may be appointed to academic positions in Russian law schools, obtain a diploma in law, magister degree, or the candidate or doctor of legal sciences, or serve on the International Court of Commercial Arbitration attached to the Chamber of Commerce and Industry of the Russian Federation, or on other arbitration tribunals in Russia.

Most commonly they are employed as partners or associates in foreign law firms (and exceptionally, Russian law firms), where they are regarded as jurisconsults. A very few have founded their own law firms as Russian juridical persons which are not related to a foreign legal entity or juridical person. Whether they actually advise on Russian law turns upon their language abilities and the extent to which they are prepared to assume the professional risks concerned. Some foreign jurists find positions with auditing companies in tax and legal sections or as house counsel for large corporations which have a Russian presence. It is estimated that upwards of 100 foreign law firms have a presence in Russia, principally in Moscow, secondarily in St. Petersburg, and less commonly in other Russian cities.

LEGAL EDUCATION

The education or "formation" of the legal profession in Russia is of crucial importance to an understanding of the Russian legal system. It is in the law schools that the knowledge, skills, and values of the jurist are initially inculcated, often to be followed by a period of further training or "apprenticeship" in a law office, enterprise, or legal agency.

To understand a lawyer from a foreign legal system, how he conceptualizes law and reasons in juristic categories, one must have some

the Government of the Russian Federation of 19 September 2004, No. 583, was deemed to have lost force; Decree No. 583 lost force in connection with the issuance of Decree of the Government of the Russian Federation of 28 September 2015, No. 1028. СЗ РФ (2015), no. 40, item 5565.

111 Muranov, note 105 above, pp. 77-82.

112 See W. E. Butler, *Russian Foreign Relations and Investment Law* (2006).

familiarity with the way he has been educated to perform legal or other roles in society. The teaching of law in turn is influenced by considerations of the kinds of lawyer which educational institutions seek to produce and the values and skills they undertake to impart. As Russia has integrated into the world market economy, the private sector of legal practice has been re-created after four generations of neglect and suppression, the Russian jurist integrated into international law firms, and Russian domestic and international law firms established.

And as Russia integrates into the various European communities, the rule of law must be thoroughly absorbed into the entire Russian legal fabric.

Historical Background

Ideas about legal education were in turmoil during the early years following the 1917 October Revolution. Throughout 1918 university law courses continued to be taught essentially as they had been before the Revolution, presumably taking due account of the new government's dismantling of the Tsarist courts, laws, and legal order. The extent to which expectations of a rapid "dying out" or "withering away" of law may have affected early attitudes toward legal education is debatable, but there was no doubt in the minds of educational policy-makers that the instructional plans extant at the universities were obsolete and non-Marxian.[113] In August 1918 the Soviet authorities altered admission requirements to make university learning accessible to everyone, irrespective of their social status. For students of proletarian origin the reform was inadequate because most were ill-prepared to undertake university work. By early 1919 it was decided to train legal personnel elsewhere for employment in Soviet universities. The university law faculties were formally abolished and replaced by faculties of social sciences (FON), which offered, *inter alia,* courses for judicial and administrative personnel on Soviet law. The early teaching syllabi for the FON were prepared by the politico-legal section of the Socialist Academy of Social Sciences, founded in 1918. The Academy itself offered advanced lectures in law during 1918-1919 to some 400 evening students, of whom 50 were regular attendees.[114] In many places "Workers' Faculties" (рабфак) were formed in 1919-1920 to provide secondary-level education on a Marxist basis for students of proletarian background who aspired to higher education. In Autumn 1921 legislation was enacted to give children of proletarian origin preference in admission to educational institutions.

[113] Some were openly hostile to legal education per se. M. N. Pokrovskii commented, when the law faculties were abolished: "the science of law was an attractive jacket which concealed the enslavement of hundreds of millions by tens of thousands ... of course, for socialist Russia all such 'sciences' are completely useless". See Народное просвещение [*People's Enlightenment*], nos. 23-25 (1918), p. 31.

[114] A. A. Plotnieks, Становление и развитие марксистско-ленинской общей теории права в СССР [*Origin and Development of Marxist-Leninist General Theory of Law in the USSR*] (1978), p. 114.

The FON offered courses on the history of State and law, the development of political and legal thought, State law of the Soviet Republic, social law, criminal sociology and policy, labor law and social policy, the history of international law and international relations, and social hygiene and sanitation. The introduction of the NEP in 1921 brought a partial restoration and adaptation of legal institutions previously known in Imperial Russia, such as the Procuracy, further stabilization of the court system, and an urgent need for codifying and systematizing legislation. As the demand for trained legal cadres within the State apparatus intensified, the Workers' Faculties and FON were supplemented by the widespread use of short-term (usually four to six months) courses on the basic principles of new Soviet legislation and codes.[115] The FON were officially abolished in 1924 (although some continued to operate until 1926) and their legal sections were superseded by Faculties of Soviet Law formed at the I Moscow University, Saratov, Irkutsk, eventually Leningrad, and later elsewhere in the country.[116]

The university law faculties offered a four-year course of study, including lectures on the basic principles of the Soviet constitutions, criminal law, economic law, land law, administrative law, court organization, criminal procedure, international law, and the cooperative and trade union movement. By 1928 there were some 15,000 Soviet jurists with a higher or secondary legal education.

At the end of the 1920s, Soviet legal education had been profoundly affected by contending approaches to the Marxist theory of State and law. Those of the university teaching staff most antipathetic to the revolutionary order had left in 1918-1919, and many other progressive but non-Marxian figures were screened out when the law faculties were reopened in 1924-26. There remained nonetheless a diverse, creative, and often original community of Soviet legal scholars excited by the prospect of revolutionary social engineering through law who represented a considerable range of non-Marxian, quasi-Marxian, and Marxian thought.[117] Among those, a pre-eminent role on the "theoretical front" was played by E. B. Pashukanis (see Chapter 4). By the end of the 1920s Pashukanis and his adherents exercised a predominant influence over legal education by virtue of control over the drafting of teaching syllabi, the placement of teaching personnel, and the implications of his commodity exchange theory for the legal system itself.

115 See E. I. Kelman, О системе юридического образования [*On the System of Legal Education*] (1926).

116 M. M. Isaev, «О высшем юридическим образовании РСФСР» [On Higher Legal Education of the RSFSR], Советское право [*Soviet Law*], no. 6 (1927), pp. 116-118.

117 An excellent selection of writings from this period is to be found in M. Jaworskyj, *Soviet Political Thought* (1967).

The preparation of syllabi for law courses had been concentrated by 1929 in the Institute of Soviet Construction and Law of the Communist Academy, directed by Pashukanis. The new syllabi amounted to a fundamental and far-reaching reworking of earlier eclectic approaches to course syllabi, introducing the terminology and conceptual apparatus of the commodity exchange theory. There was an intense campaign against 'bourgeois' legal scholarship, an appraisal of the principal bourgeois legal institutions, and an examination of the theory of State and law as laid down in the works of Karl Marx, Friedrich Engels, and V. I. Lenin. The syllabi on the "Doctrine of the Soviet State", which stressed the political rather than the legal dimension of the Soviet State, and on "economic and administrative law", which contemplated the abolition of the civil law, especially reflected the notions of the Pashukanis school. The first-year law course on the general theory of law became, in effect, an exposition of the commodity exchange theory, and students studying law externally through correspondence courses, including Party activists, offered by the Institute of Red Professors (of which Pashukanis was Rector), similarly were imbued with this approach.[118]

While law students were absorbing the lessons of the commodity exchange school, the larger implications of Pashukanis' views were becoming noticeable in legal education. The imminent dying out of law boded ill for legal careers. Study of the purely "legal infrastructure" – the constitution and State system – was being phased out of the curriculum, and law school enrollments dropped dramatically. In 1930-1931 Pashukanis and his associates were obliged to modify their position that the State would rapidly die out, but throughout the early 1930s they continued to emphasize the "flexible" and "expedient" dimensions of the law as an instrument of revolutionary policy rather than its stabilizing role.

The adoption of the 1936 USSR Constitution heralded a transition to a policy of "stability of laws", which in the realm of legal education meant a restoration and expansion of university-level law teaching and a substantial increase in numbers of law students. Pashukanis himself disappeared from the scene in January 1937 during the purges, to be succeeded in the leadership of the legal profession by A. Ia. Vyshinskii. Almost immediately after Pashukanis' execution, civil law was restored to the law curriculum in place of economic law and a massive effort undertaken to revise course syllabi and prepare new textbooks.[119]

118 For details see R. Sharlet, "Pashukanis and the Withering Away of Law in the USSR", in S. Fitzpatrick (ed.), *Cultural Revolution in Russia, 1928-1931* (1978), pp. 169-188; id, "Pashukanis and the Rise of Soviet Marxist Jurisprudence, 1924-1930", *Soviet Union* (1974), I, pp. 103-121.

119 An American student perspective on Soviet legal education from 1934 to 1937 is recorded in contemporary correspondence and lecture notes, reproduced in W. E. Butler (intro), *Law Student Life in Moscow: The Letters and Course Notes of John N Hazard, 1934-1939* (1978); excerpts from the letters are reproduced in D. Barry, W. E. Butler, and G. Ginsburgs (eds),

In 1936 the system of legal education was reorganized. The USSR People's Commissariat of Justice assumed principal responsibility for providing legal education, appointing the directors of law schools, and preparing the syllabi and textbooks for courses to be taught.[120] Four-year courses of legal studies were offered in juridical institutes and university law faculties. Special short-term courses of from six months to one year were established in outlying areas of the country to raise the proficiency of legal personnel in post. In addition, correspondence schools and three-month courses to train what today might be called paralegal and auxiliary legal personnel were introduced, and an advanced two-year course in law for higher-level legal personnel at the All-Union Legal Academy.[121]

Except for the early war years, legal education expanded from the late 1930s for nearly two decades. The course of law studies in universities was extended to five years in the mid-1940s, and pursuant to a Decree of the Central Committee of the CPSU adopted on 5 October 1946 and a joint Party-Government Decree of 30 August 1954, a number of steps were taken to improve the quality of legal studies. By the late 1950s, however, perhaps influenced by the transition of Soviet society to the stage of the building of communism and a concomitant emphasis on transferring State functions to non-State bodies, sharp reductions in law school enrolments were imposed. Between 1956 and 1963 the number of law graduates in full time study declined by more than 50 per cent (although night school and correspondence courses kept the total number of law graduates in 1963 at a higher level than in 1956). In the summer of 1964 a decree of the Central Committee of the CPSU (unpublished) reasserted the need for better jurists and an expansion and improvement of legal education, a need more keenly felt after the economic reforms of 1965. The economic reforms, inter alia, gave greater discretion and independence to economic units in concluding economic contracts, foreseeing at the same time that economic units would exercise their discretion within the constraints of the applicable law. It followed, of course, that economic units would require more and better advice in these matters from qualified legal personnel. A similar devotion of responsibility within the lower levels of local government also was accompanied by a substantial increase in the number of jurisconsults employed.

The veritable explosion in the number of Soviet law graduates had a dramatic impact upon the qualifications and quality of the corpus of legal personnel as a whole. In 1936, when the reversal of Pashukanis' theories

Contemporary Soviet Law (1974).

[120] For the period 1938 to 1945, see E. A. Prianishnikov, Страницы истории института законодательства и сравнительного правоведения [Pages of History of the Institute of Legislation and Comparative Law] (2000), pp. 64-80.

[121] See J. N. Hazard, "Legal Education in the Soviet Union", *Wisconsin Law Review* (1938), pp. 562-579.

commenced in earnest, less than 6.7% of Soviet judges had any formal higher legal education and more than 50% had no legal education at all.[122] By 1980 virtually all judges and procurators had a higher legal education. Today it is impossible to enter any branch of the legal profession without an educational qualification of this level.

Modern Legal Education

The dissolution of the Soviet Union and the transition to democratic institutions and a market-oriented economy brought a certain reform of higher legal education, but not initially a fundamental transformation. Marxism-Leninism disappeared promptly from the syllabus, as one would expect; new legislation brought new courses (taxation, commercial law, entrepreneurial law, and others) or a thorough reworking of traditional staples in the light of new codes (civil law, criminal law, family law, procedural law, and others). Dozens of educational institutions added law faculties or departments (sometimes existing law faculties even opened additional law schools) and the private sector founded new law schools or faculties. The Institute of State and Law of the Russian Academy of Sciences established the Academy University of Law for undergraduate and postgraduate training; the Academy of National Economy attached to the Government of the Russian Federation created the M. M. Speranskii Law Faculty for undergraduate training; an Anglo-Russian institution, the Moscow Higher School of Social and Economic Sciences, introduced an LLM degree with the University of Manchester and a PhD degree with Essex University; Moscow State University added a college of law to its own law faculty; analogous schools were founded in St Petersburg and other cities.

In 2020 some 512 State higher educational institutions offered a degree in law, twenty of which incorporated the word "legal" in their official names. The number of non-State higher educational institutions offering a degree in law was 597;[123] more than 51 operated within the system of Ministry of Internal Affairs plus several concerned with continuing legal education, four within the Federal Security Service, and two serving the military. The State Penal Service operated fourteen such institutions, and the Federal Protection Service, one. These figures are approximately stable compared with 2014; as standards become more demanding, there may be further attrition in the numbers of law schools and faculties.

The system of university and postgraduate education, including legal education, in the Russian Federation is regulated by the Federal Law on Education in the Russian Federation, adopted 29 December 2012, as

[122] Data published in Ia. Berman, «О правовом образовании» [On Legal Education], Советское государство и право [Soviet State and Law], no. 5 (1936), p. 115.
[123] academica.ru: date consulted, 1 January 2021.

amended.[124] The 2012 Law replaced the Federal Laws on Education of 10 July 1992, as amended,[125] and on Higher and Postgraduate Vocational Education of 22 August 1996, as amended.[126]

These laws determined the principles of State education policies, among which are the humanistic character of education, the priority of universal human values, the free development of the individual, nurturing respect for human rights and freedoms, love for the environment, the Motherland, and the family, general accessibility to education, the secular character of education in State and municipal institutions, freedom and pluralism in education, and others. Although there is substantial continuity between the values promoted by the 1992/1996 legislation and that of 2012, fundamental and far-reaching educational reforms were introduced between 2010 and 2012 which are continuing. For jurists the new legislation represents an abandonment of the concept of the "legal specialist" dating back to the Soviet era and produced in a five-year degree program. The four-year baccalaureate does not pretend to create a "legal specialist", but rather to lay the basis for specialization to be obtained through the two-year magister degree.

Whether this scheme will endure is for the future to determine. There is considerable skepticism in branches of the legal profession, notably the judiciary, the Advokatura, and the Procuracy as to whether individuals with merely a baccalaureate in law should be allowed or encouraged to proceed to take up positions in the profession. Some may require the magister degree as a condition of entrance; others may require special examinations or apprenticeships.

The principles and standards of legal education are now articulated through the establishment of Federal State Educational Standards of Higher Professional Education (hereinafter: "FGOS VPO") adopted in 2010 and replaced in 2016.[127] These lay down an obligatory minimum for the content of educational programs, the maximum instructional load for students, and requirements for the training of graduates. An accredited educational institution which trains graduates of poor quality can be sued by the State

[124] СЗ РФ (2012), no. 53(I), item 7598, as amended.

[125] СЗ РФ (1996), no. 3, item 150 (1996 redaction), as amended. This Law lost force from 1 September 2013.

[126] СЗ РФ (1996), no. 35, item 4135, as amended. This Law lost force from 1 September 2013.

[127] See the Order of the Ministry of Education and Science of the Russian Federation, 4 May 2010, No. 464, "On Confirmation and Introduction into Operation of the Federal State Educational Standard of Higher Vocational Education for the Orientation of Training 030900 Jurisprudence (Qualification (or Degree) "Baccalaureate"). Available on Consultant Plus. The same Ministry adopted the FGOS VPO for the magister degree on 14 December 2010, Order No. 1763. Order No. 464 lost force from 1 September 2017 pursuant to the Order of 1 December 2016, No. 1511, confirming the Federal State Educational Standard of Higher Education with Regard to the Orientation of Training 40.04.01 Jurisprudence (Level of Baccalaureata).

in court for compensation of additional expenditures needed to retrain the graduates in other educational institutions.

Although law is offered to some extent at the level of secondary vocational education, jurists are trained at the standard of higher vocational and postgraduate professional education. FGOS VPO 40.04.01 (jurisprudence) lays down the requirements for training a jurist at baccalaureate and magister levels. The training may take the form of full-time day, evening, or correspondence education. Citizens of the Russian Federation have the right to receive higher vocational and postgraduate education in State or municipal educational institutions within the limits of the FGOS VPO on a competitive basis. For those entering University, with certain exceptions specified in legislation, the school-leaving State examinations will qualify an individual for admission. Moscow Lomonosov State University, St. Petersburg State University, and a few others are permitted by legislation to require additional special entrance examinations.[128]

The aim of Russian higher legal education as set out in FGOS VPO 40.03.01 is to train jurists in the course of four years of full-time undergraduate study, for which the baccalaureate degree is conferred. Whether graduates choose to continue in an academic career, become a judge, or work as a legal practitioner (jurisconsult or advokat) or procurator, all are expected to undergo the same general training in the foundation subjects of Russian law. The general requirements for a jurist are that he or she is aware of the social importance of their future profession, possesses an adequate level of professional legal consciousness, is capable of performing professional duties in good faith and complies with the ethical principles of a jurist, is capable of generalizing, analyzing, and perceiving information, is capable of confronting tasks and finding ways to solve them, is ready to collaborate with colleagues and to work in a collective, is intolerant of corruption, respects the law, is capable of analyzing socially significant problems and processes, is computer literate, can communicate in a foreign language, among others.

The jurist is a person of principle and independence in ensuring the protecting the rights, freedoms, and legal interests of the individual. He has the requisite will and insistence to execute legal decisions made. He should be acquainted with the basic teachings in the humanities and socio-economic sciences, capable of analyzing scientifically socially significant problems and processes, and know how to use the methods of these sciences in various types of professional and social activities. Ethical and legal norms regulating the relations of individuals and of society and of the environment must be part of his make-up, and he must know how to take

[128] See the Federal Law on Moscow State Lomonosov State University and St. Petersburg State University of 10 November 2009, No. 259-ФЗ. СЗ РФ (2009), no. 46, item 5418, as amended.

them into account when working out ecological and social projects. The jurist should have an integral understanding of the processes and phenomena which originate in nature, living and non-living, and comprehend these at a standard needed to resolve tasks which arise in the course of performing vocational functions.

By training, if not ability, the jurist should be capable of continuing his education at the level of postgraduate studies, or the magistratura, and be able to carry on vocational activities in a "foreign language milieu". He should have scientific knowledge about a healthy way of life and the skills for physical self-improvement, possess the culture of thought and art of logical analysis, know the general laws thereof, and be able to express himself in writing and orally both correctly and logically. The jurist organizes his labor of a scientific basis and possesses the full range of computer skills applicable to his vocational activities. In an era when science is developing and social policy is changing, the jurist is capable of re-evaluating accumulated experience, analyzing his opportunities, knows how to acquire new knowledge, and uses modern information educational technologies. He appreciates the essence and social significance of his future profession, the basic problems of his discipline, and sees their interconnection with the integral system of knowledge. Capable of professionally building and using models to describe and predict various phenomena, he can undertake the quantitative and qualitative analysis of these. He can formulate the tasks connected with performing his vocational functions and can use the methods of the legal and other sciences to realize them.

The foregoing general requirements are linked in the FGOS VPO with knowledge and skills arising from the study of philosophy, logic, psychology, pedagogy, culturology, history, philology, mathematics, and physical culture. In the field of language, for example, the jurist should, in addition to the Russian language, have a minimum command of 1,500-2,000 words and word combinations in a foreign language and be able to use them correctly in oral and written discourse, be able to translate texts with a dictionary, work without a dictionary when searching for information, and prepare annotations and abstracts in a foreign language.

The educational values and aims which shape the jurist are expected to be achieved through the so-called "obligatory minimum" of academic subjects. These form the core curriculum for higher vocational education accredited by the State. The foundation humanities, socio-economic, and mathematical subjects include: philosophy, foreign language, culturology, Russian history, sociology, politology, psychology, economic theory, sport, mathematics and informatics, conceptions of the modern natural sciences, and certain elective subjects which, it is recommended, might include logic, Latin, and rhetoric.

The courses in law build upon these foundations. The obligatory minimum includes: theory of State and law, history of political and legal doctrines, history of Russian State and law, history of the State and law of foreign countries, Russian constitutional law, the constitutional law of foreign countries, civil law, civil procedure, administrative law, labor law, criminal law, criminal procedure, criminalistics, international law, ecological law, land law, tax law, social security law, entrepreneurial law, private international law, and financial law, plus elective subjects offered by each individual faculty of law. These are followed by special subjects: Russian municipal law, commercial law, family law, criminology, penal law, law enforcement agencies, and procuracy supervision, together with other specialist courses which the faculty may offer. Each student also spends several weeks in a so-called "practice", usually a form of internship with legal agencies or law firms, and prepares a written diploma work.

Within the above criteria, each individual law faculty may alter the required number of hours for each discipline within certain parameters provided that the weekly workload for students is not increased and the minimum content of the syllabus for each subject is maintained. The hours of instruction include time allocated to prepare essays and other course work.

The experimentation of the early 1990s has given way to the reintroduction of State-imposed standards and curriculum rigidity. Smaller seminars continue to be typical of the last year of study, with a substantial diploma work. Attention is given to information and computer skills. At least three major computer banks of Russian legislation compete for the market. All Russian law graduates know how to use them. Interpersonal skills receive less attention. Advocacy and other team skills are rarely part of the curriculum, although many Russian law schools take part in international mooting competitions such as the Jessup and the Vis. Purely Russian mooting competitions operate as well. Interdisciplinary training, on the other hand, is part of the curriculum. Both the pre-revolutionary Russian educational tradition and Marxism-Leninism in their own ways accentuated the importance of the social, economic, political, and historical sciences for a comprehension of law. Comparative law plays a minor role, the Socratic method rarely utilized, practical workshops and clinics normally shunned.

Legal clinics have been integrated into Russian legal education in several universities. St. Petersburg University led the way in 1998. During the 2018/2019 academic year, 1,765 applications of assistance were received; 571 documents were prepared, and 477 draft documents in collaboration with the Procuracy. Some matters are addressed through the Internet. About 40% of the inquiries relate to civil law cases, and the rest to housing, family, land, civil procedure, and administrative law and social security. The clinic operates during term about four months of the year. The students do not appear in court. The clientele of the clinic includes pensioners, unemployed, disabled persons, minors, students and personnel of educational institutions, and indigent individuals.

Moscow State Lomonosov University has operated a legal clinic since 2003. From 2017 to 1 July 2019, the clinic received 1,236 visitors by appointment only. Advice is offered in all branches of law and clinic students may appear in court. The Kutafin Moscow State Law University has operated a clinic "Pro Bono" for more than two decades and deals with 200 to 300 matters per year. Representation in court is not offered. Operations are suspended during examination periods and summer vacations. The National Research University "Higher School of Economics" and, since 2009, the Russian State University of Justice attached to the Ministry of Justice operate clinics as an integral part of the educational program.

Within the law faculties, headed by a dean, the key structural units are the chairs of law created for particular branches or subjects of law. A chair is usually headed by a professor, around whom are grouped senior and junior university staff of a similar specialization and the students who have chosen to concentrate on that area of law. Each chair has an office where students may meet the teaching and research staff, diploma theses may be defended, and the affairs of the chair conducted. The number of chairs varies from one university to another, depending upon the number of students and the quality and importance of the teaching staff; in new law faculties more modest physical facilities are requiring adjustments to the accoutrements of the classic chair.

Admission

An applicant for the study of law in an institution of higher education is required to have completed the full program of secondary education and successfully complete State-wide school-leaving examinations. The applicant must pass the following written Unified State Examinations (usually an essay is required): Russian language, social science (обществознание – a complex of philosophy, law, sociology and economics), history (depending on the university), foreign language (depending on the university). Interest in studying law continues to be exceptionally high, and the best institutions have more candidates than places. Ability to pay is a significant consideration.

Course of study

The full-time course of study in law now requires four years, the baccalaureate degree having become the norm. Evening programs or correspondence degrees require five or six years. Students who are willing to undertake self-study and sit the examinations when they consider themselves ready can sometimes shorten the degree course by as much as two years. The programs at Moscow State University illustrate the full range of possible programs.

The Law Faculty offers on a full-time day-study basis the specialty jurisprudence (правоведение, sometimes called in other universities юриспруденция) over a four-year term. Students may specialize in State law, civil law, or criminal law in the fourth year. There is an evening division which requires six years to complete. Upon completion of the course of study, graduates are awarded the qualification of "jurist" (but no longer of "specialist"). Foreign students who have a bachelor of law degree may be admitted to the faculty for a two-year course of study resulting in the magister of legal sciences and the qualification of "jurist". The courses offered closely approximate those in the obligatory minimum described above.

Within the Law Faculty of Moscow University, founded in 1755, a legal college was founded in 1992 as a higher legal educational institution. It offers a bachelor's degree in law after four years of full-time study or five years in the evening division. For those who already have a university degree in a discipline other than law, the bachelor's degree may be obtained in two years of full-time study or three years in the evening division.

Teaching and assessment

The basic method of instruction is the magisterial lecture. Russian full-time law students attend as many as 26 hours of lectures per week, tapering off in the last two years. These are augmented by small seminars, study groups or circles, and the like, to analyze and discuss matters or problems treated in the lectures. During the fourth year the special subjects often take the form of seminars since the numbers of students involved are smaller. Many subjects require students to present short essays or oral reports on selected topics. Although the case method is not used following the American model, Russian judicial practice is increasingly important and plays a larger role in the curriculum than previously.

Assessment is based on oral examinations administered by the teaching staff. Questions are drafted by persons designated within each chair and approved by the chair as a whole. The questions are then typed on individual slips of paper. When the student appears at the designated hour for the examination, he or she draws the questions by lot and then may sit for a quarter-hour or so to collect thoughts on the answer. He is then summoned to a small table opposite the instructor where he gives a discourse on the question. The instructor may ask supplementary questions to ascertain the depths of the student's mastery. Failures are not common and resits are readily granted. The diploma paper in the final year is submitted in writing and formally defended, usually before the members of the chair to which the student is attached.

Career placement

In the Soviet era graduates could expect to accept employment assigned by the State for a period of up to three years and then move on within the planned economy to a more satisfactory position. With the transition to a market economy guaranteed employment has disappeared, and the graduate finds himself in the employment market immediately upon graduation. Demand for law graduates is substantial in fact, with opportunities in private practice as advokats or as jurisconsults especially lucrative. Those willing to subsist on civil service salaries find ready employment in State agencies, the procuracy, or the courts. Law is increasingly accepted as excellent training for other professions and is a recognized qualification for becoming an auditor or a tax consultant.

Postgraduate studies

There are three postgraduate programs in Russian universities and a scheme of continuing legal education. The magister under the new system is a two-year full-time course of study. For those who wish to acquire a European master's degree, the English LLM is offered in Moscow by the University of Manchester through the Moscow Higher School of Social and Economic Sciences as a one-year program after the four-year degree at a Russian institution of higher education or equivalent elsewhere.

The postgraduate degrees in law of candidate of legal sciences and doctor of legal sciences remain essentially unchanged after being stripped of their ideological components from the Soviet period. Equivalents with the Anglo-American systems of legal education are not easy to identify, particularly in the United States, Canada, and Australia where the first degree in law is a postgraduate degree; nonetheless, taking into account the respective national systems of education *as a whole*, the candidate of legal sciences degree would correspond roughly to the British PhD degree and the American MA obtained by thesis. The Russian doctor of legal sciences would correspond to the highest degrees in Britain and the United States in the field of law, respectively the LLD in Britain and the PhD or SJD in the United States; this may vary, however, as many doctoral programs in law in the United States are in fact operated at near the candidate level and the European *habilitation* is rarely seen.

Entry to postgraduate study in the Russian Federation is open on a competitive basis to individuals who have completed their baccalaureate and magister degrees. Unlike Britain and the United States, postgraduate studies are supervised not only at universities but also within the academies of sciences and other research establishments or even enterprises which have been duly accredited for this purpose.

Postgraduate studies may be either full-time or part-time. Those pursuing the degree of candidate of legal sciences must take certain examinations, the so-called candidate minimum: Russian language, philosophy, and a third subject depending upon the specialty. Having completed these, the individual then prepares and defends the candidate dissertation. The candidate dissertation is the principal result of study for the candidate degree. Russian normative acts require that the dissertation be a scholarly work which contains the "resolution of a task" having significance for the respective branch of knowledge or which sets out new scientifically substantiated technical, technological, or other solutions and findings having material significance for the development of Russia.

The doctoral dissertation must be a scholarly work based on the author's research which elaborates theoretical propositions, the aggregate of which may be classified as a scientific achievement in the development of the respective branch of scholarship or which solves a scientific problem having important political, socio-economic, cultural, economic significance, or which sets out scientifically-substantiated technical, economic, or technological solutions, the introduction of which makes a significant contribution to the development of Russia. The work will ordinarily have been published in book or article form before submission.[129] An approved list of peer-reviewed scientific publications in which the principal scientific results of candidate or doctoral dissertations should be published with effect from 1 January 2014 was confirmed by the Ministry of Education and Science of the Russian Federation in late 2013.[130]

It remains possible in the Russian Federation to submit a classified dissertation 'for official use', in which event special procedures apply to the submission and defense.[131]

The procedures for writing and defending the candidate dissertation and doctoral dissertation and for conferring the respective degree are determined not by the supervisory university or institution, but by the

129 The author of the dissertation includes a bibliography which indicates all sources that have published articles and/or books on which the dissertation is based. In the field of law, the author will have been expected to have published at least three articles for a candidate dissertation and fifteen for a doctoral dissertation. Some of these must have been published in foreign publications included on the Scopus or Web of Science data bases.

130 Available on Consultant Plus. Peer members of the editorial review board, whether foreign or Russian, are required to maintain on the journal website relevant biographical and contact details.

131 These are now governed by the Statute on the Special Council for the Defense of a Dissertation Containing Information Comprising a State Secret for the Supplicant of the Learned Degree Candidate of Sciences and for the Supplicant of the Learned Degree Doctor of Sciences, confirmed by Order of the Ministry of Education and Science of the Russian Federation on 30 December 2015, No. 1388, which replaced the Instruction on the Procedure for the Consideration and Defense of Dissertations with the Cypher "For Official Use", confirmed by Order of the Ministry of Education and Science of the Russian Federation of 7 June 2007, No. 169. See БНА РФ, no. 28 (2007). For the text of Order No. 1388, see Consultant Plus; it entered into force on 30 March 2016.

Statute on the Awarding of Learned Degrees, confirmed on 24 September 2013 by Decree of the Government of the Russian Federation, No. 842.[132] It is the State which continues through the Supreme Attestation Commission (VAK) to award the degree or which has the right to verify the awarding of such. On 30 April 1998 the State Attestation Commission was abolished and its functions transferred to the Ministry of Education of the Russian Federation. The Supreme Attestation Commission operates on the basis of the Statute confirmed by the Government of the Russian Federation on 26 March 2016, No. 237.[133] However, on 15 May 2018 the Ministry of Education and Science was transformed into the Ministry of Enlightenment of the Russian Federation and the Ministry of Science and Higher Education of the Russian Federation; this involved a transfer of functions that will affect matters addressed in the present Chapter.[134]

Within each State-accredited university or institution authorized to supervise postgraduate study a "dissertation council" is created on the basis of the Statute on the Council for the Defense of Dissertations for a Supplicant of the Learned Degree Candidate of Sciences and Supplicant of the Learned Degree Doctor of Sciences.[135] Only these councils may accept candidate and doctoral dissertations for defense within their respective specialties. When the dissertation is ready for submission, the author prepares an abstract which is printed and circulated, commonly in 100 copies. In the case of law, the abstract would be sent to several law faculties and leading authorities. Two official opponents are appointed to read the dissertation in full; a law faculty or legal institution may be chosen to submit detailed written comments on the thesis.

The defense is a public occasion, often advertised in the press. Members of the specialized council hear the author outline his principal contentions and the views of the official opponents, to which the author may reply. Written comments submitted are read aloud to the dissertation council. When the defense is concluded, the dissertation council decides by secret ballot whether the dissertation conforms to the standard of the degree. The ultimate decision to award the degree rests with VAK,[136] which receives

[132] C3 PΦ (2013), no. 40(III), item 5074, as amended.

[133] C3 PΦ (2016), no. 14, item 1996; replacing a Statute of 23 September 2013. See C3 PΦ (2013), no. 40(III), item 5072, as amended.

[134] See the Edict of the President of the Russian Federation on the Structure of Federal Agencies of Executive Power, No. 215. C3 PΦ (2018), no. 21, item 2981.

[135] Confirmed by Order of the Ministry of Education and Science of the Russian Federation, 10 November 2017, No. 1093. This Order replaced the Order of 13 January 2014, No. 7, which in turn superseded the Statute on the Council for the Defense of Dissertations for the Learned Degree of Candidate of Sciences and for the Learned Degree of Doctor of Sciences, confirmed by Order of the Ministry of Education and Science of the Russian Federation, 12 December 2011, No. 2817. All are available on Consultant Plus.

[136] With effect from 1 September 2016, the Moscow Lomonosov State University and St. Petersburg State University received the right to autonomously create dissertation councils

a copy of the dissertation, the opinion and petition of the dissertation commission, and the other relevant documents. Although as a rule a dissertation is submitted in the Russian language, a dissertation council has the right to request that the dissertation be submitted in another language, in which case certain materials associated with the dissertation are translated into Russian. The defense also may occur in a language other than Russian.

The role of VAK in verifying dissertations is to ensure compliance with the unified standards for scholarship. Each dissertation is reviewed by an expert council, which has up to four months in the case of a candidate dissertation and eight months in the case of a doctoral dissertation to complete its work. Detailed procedures apply if the expert council and the dissertation council differ in their conclusions.

Other Types of Legal Education

Knowledge of law or of particular branches of law is regarded as essential for many non-legal professions and for every Russian pupil. An elementary course on the basic principles of Russian law is a part of many secondary school curriculums. Special training is organized for persons serving as people's assessors or as jurors in Russian courts. In higher education Russian law is a required component of the syllabus for economists, engineers, medical personnel, social workers, journalists, transport personnel, and others.

More advanced specialist law courses or subjects are offered at dozens of institutions, for example, the Moscow State Institute of International Relations (MGIMO), the Diplomatic Academy, the Ministry of Internal Affairs, the Academy of the Federal Security Service, the Ministry of Transport, and various of the military services. Auditors, bookkeepers, and tax personnel are routinely trained in law as part of their professional education; many have a degree in law. Many law faculties or colleges offer "preparatory courses" for those who have a higher education in a discipline other than law and require foundation courses before proceeding on to a shortened law degree program. Combined law and business programs are widespread throughout Russia.

Individuals already holding a law degree from the Soviet era are encouraged to enhance their marketability through various continuing legal education ("raising legal qualifications") schemes. These may take the form of a fully-fledged post-graduate degree, but more commonly are a continuing legal education certificate attested and recognized by State agencies.

and determine the procedure for conferring learned degrees. This right has since been extended to several other Russian institutions of higher education.

LEGAL RESEARCH

In the Soviet era legal research enjoyed significant State financial support and was closely linked to themes singled out for priority at the congresses and in the programs of the Communist Party and in the State five-year plans for economic and social development. The numbers of lawyers engaged in full-time research has diminished drastically, partly because remuneration in the private sector is more attractive and partly because of retrenchment in research establishment posts. Russian university teaching staff members also undertake legal research, although economic pressures require many to hold multiple teaching positions in order to make ends meet.

The most important and prestigious scientific research institution in the field of law is the Institute of State and Law of the Russian Academy of Sciences. The roots of the Institute as the first autonomous legal research body in the former Soviet Union date to 1925 with the formation of the Institute of Soviet Construction within the Communist Academy. The Institute was merged in 1929 with the Section for the General Theory of State and Law of the Communist Academy and renamed the Institute of Soviet Construction and Law. Several months later, in March 1930, the Institute absorbed the Russian Association for Scientific Research in the Social Sciences (RANION), which had functioned since 1920 attached to Moscow University. Other changes of name occurred from time to time, the present dating from 1960. The Institute has created the Academy University of Law as a direct adjunct institution which offers undergraduate and postgraduate degrees, including the Magister of Russian Law (LLM).

Attached to the Government of the Russian Federation is the Institute of Legislation and Comparative Law, formed on the base of the All-Union Scientific Research Institute of Soviet Legislation (VNIISZ), created in 1963 as a consequence of the reorganization in the All-Union Institute of Legal Sciences. The Institute is principally concerned with law reform and carries out studies of Russian and foreign legal experience to that end.

The All-Russian Scientific Research Institute of State Patent Expert Examination evaluates patent applications. The Institute of Justice of the Russian Legal Academy assists with the training of judges. The Centre of Private Law also is concerned with law reform and offers a postgraduate degree program concentrating upon civil and entrepreneurial law, being closely linked with the Scientific-Consultative Center for Private Law of the Commonwealth of Independent States.

The Ministry of Internal Affairs has its own all-Russian scientific research institute and a network of regional branches linked to the Russian Institute for Raising Qualifications. Attached to the General Procuracy of the Russian Federation is the Institute for Raising Qualifications of Procuracy-Investigative Workers and a second Institute for Raising the Qualifications of Executive Personnel of the General Procuracy, as well as the Scientific Research Institute for Problems of Strengthening Legality and Legal Order.

The Ministry of Justice system includes the Scientific Center for Legal Information, which concentrates upon legislative computer databases, and the Scientific Research Institute of Law Creation and Problems of Law Enforcement. Forensic expertise is within the responsibility of the Russian Federal Centre of Forensic Expert Examination.

Since about 2012 Russian jurists have been caught up in sundry "research assessment exercises" which impose penalties upon legal scholars who do not publish frequently or in the preferred places (for example, Scopus or Web of Science journals) or which offer attractive bonuses, including salary increments, to those who publish research abroad or in preferred places. This has positively influenced the international ratings of major Russian universities, including law faculties.

LEGAL PUBLISHING

Although a number of publishing houses issued legal materials in the Soviet era, the principal specialist legal publisher, "Legal Literature" [Юридическая литература], celebrated its centenary in 2017. It functions as a shadow of its former self, having undergone several cycles of internal reorganization, while continuing to be an important source for presidential and governmental materials. The advent of *perestroika* in the late 1980s brought the possibility of legitimate "Samizdat", which a number of lawyers took advantage of to publish their own monographs at their own risk, and non-State publishing houses eager to respond to a remarkable demand for legal and business literature: treatises, collections of legislation, individual codes and laws, commentaries, and monographs. The opportunity for publishing joint ventures was explored in the field of law by a hardy few: C. H. Beck, the distinguished German publisher, had an initial spectacular success by becoming the quality publisher of legal textbooks, manuals, commentaries, and looseleaf series but eventually succumbing to tax difficulties and being taken over by Wolters Kluwer in Russia. Others, such as Interlist (London), had a brief but inspired role that never matured into a true joint venture. The Soros Foundation through its sundry subfunds and societies included law to some extent within its translation programs and contributed importantly at a critical moment to foreign legal classics becoming accessible to a Russian readership.

Russian legal scholars, lawyers, and law firms founded their own publishing houses. Зерцало [Zertsalo], under the leadership of Professor V. A. Tomsinov, has played an outstanding role in the field of Russian legal history and produced excellent treatises, textbooks, and commentaries; the Law Firm Контракт [Contract] at one time published an excellent looseleaf set of Russian legislation, legal encyclopedias, treatises, and dictionaries.

The Pepeliaev Group has published extensively in the field of corporate and tax law and has supported important cultural-legal studies.[9] Other law firms issue important guides for the layman on key aspects of Russian law. Russian banks have supported significant publications on financial and banking law. The community of Russian international lawyers in Moscow and St Petersburg is indebted to commercial sponsors and a Russian foundation for the publication of journals, yearbooks, and bibliographies.

Legal literature became such a phenomenon that in the mid-1990s the weekly review of books published regular bestseller lists. The market for law books remains traditional: advokats, jurisconsults, judicial and procuracy personnel, arbitrators, law enforcement personnel (the majority have law degrees), military lawyers, tax and customs personnel, law students and legal scholars, auditors and bookkeepers, insurance personnel, foreign law firms and lawyers, and the law libraries of the greatly expanded number of law schools and faculties. Demand has since leveled off; substantial price increases have made legal books less of an attraction.

7

THE ADMINISTRATION OF LEGALITY

The expression "administration of legality" is used in a special sense in this chapter to refer both to State and non-State bodies directly concerned in the Russian Federation with the application and enforcement of the law, excluding the advokats and jurisconsults, who have been discussed previously (see Chapter 6).

MINISTRIES OF JUSTICE

History

The Russian ministries of justice in their present or past forms have no precise analogy in Britain or North America. The first RSFSR People's Commissariat of Justice created the day after the 1917 October Revolution included among its functions the investigation of offenses, the administration of prisons and camps, the administration of the separation of Church from State, and the codification of legislation, among others. In 1921 these functions were broadened to include supreme judicial control and in 1922 to embrace the Procuracy. The repeated reorganizations of the ministries of justice need not detain us here, except to note that from 1963 to 1970 they were abolished completely and their functions dispersed among other agencies. On 31 August 1970 the USSR Ministry of Justice was formed as a union-republic ministry and the Statute on the Ministry confirmed on 21 March 1972.

The Ministry underwent several reorganizations throughout the Soviet era, in time becoming responsible for the organizational direction of the courts, summarizing judicial practice, gathering forensic statistics, preparing the Digest of Laws of the USSR, developing methods guidance for legal work in the national economy, helping to distribute law graduates, supporting its own legal research institutions, and exercising State guidance over the Advokatura, the Notariat, and the ZAGS offices.

Since the USSR Ministry of Justice was a union-republic ministry, the dissolution of the former USSR left the Ministry of Justice of the Russian Federation to assume responsibility for the full range of ministerial functions. Republics within the Federation have their own ministries of justice; other subjects of the Federation have justice sections.

Current legislation

The legal status of the Ministry of Justice is determined principally by the 1993 Russian Constitution, the 2020 Law on the Government of the Russian Federation,[1] the Statute on the Ministry of Justice of the Russian Federation confirmed by Edict of the President of Russia on 13 October 2004, as amended,[2] and certain decrees addressed to individual Ministry functions or programs. Among the last is the Decree of the Government of the Russian Federation on Confirmation of the Conception of Reforming Justice Agencies and Institutions of the Russian Federation, adopted 7 October 1996.[3] The Ministry is the federal agency of executive power engaged in working out and realizing State policy and normative-legal regulation in the sphere of criminal punishments, advokatura, notariat, ensuring the activity of courts and execution of judicial acts, the registration of acts of civil status, and the registration of noncommercial organizations, social associations, political parties, and religious organizations. The principal tasks of the Ministry are to: work out the general strategy of State policy in the sphere of justice activity; normative-legal regulation in the sphere of justice activity; ensuring within the limits of its powers the defense of the rights and freedoms of man and citizen; and ensuring the activity of the Plenipotentiary of the Russian Federation attached to the European Court for Human Rights (who is a deputy minister of justice).

Pursuant to these tasks, the Statute on the Ministry enumerates more than 90 powers and 15 rights. Amongst them is the provision of support for what is called "norm-creation activity" of federal agencies of executive power. This involves offering expert advice on draft legislative and other normative acts submitted by federal agencies of executive power, as well as normative legal acts adopted by the subjects of the Russian Federation, from the standpoint of their constitutionality and conformity to federal laws, taking part in the legal expert evaluation of draft conceptions and technical planning assignments for preparing draft federal laws proposed for inclusion in plans for draft law activity of the Government of Russia, effectuating control over the correctness and timeliness of publication of normative legal acts registered by the Ministry, systematizing Russian legislation, maintaining the databank of Russian normative acts on computer, participating in the preparation of the Digest of Laws of the Russian Federation, and making proposals to bring existing legislation into conformity with newly-enacted laws, the Constitution, and international treaties.

[1] СЗ РФ (2020), no. 45, item 7061.

[2] СЗ РФ (2004), no. 42, item 4108, as amended; transl. in W. E. Butler, *Russia & The Republics: Legal Materials* (loose-leaf service; 2006-).

[3] СЗ РФ (1996), no. 42, item 4806.

In May 2018 the Ministry was assigned the duty to ensure the representation and defense of the interests of the Russian Federation in foreign courts and international arbitral tribunals, including the European Court for Human Rights and the Court of the Eurasian Economic Union. This will include instructing and liaison with foreign law firms retained to advise and assist the Russian Federation in individual court cases or international arbitrations.

The Ministry operates a system of State registration for normative legal acts of federal agencies of executive power and other agencies, records the normative legal acts of subjects of the Russian Federation, organizes the State registration of charters of municipal formations and municipal legal acts making changes in such charters, keeps the State register of municipal formations of the Russian Federation, and effectuates the State registration of agreements concerning the international and foreign economic links of subjects of the Russian Federation concluded by agencies of State power of subjects of the Russian Federation. When registers are maintained by other agencies or organizations, the Ministry in stipulated instances confirms the forms of such registers, among these being the form of registers for notarial actions and certificates or the form for keeping registers of advocates in subjects of the Federation, or the form of an order to perform an assignment issued by an advokatura.

A number of the various registration functions of the Ministry had been relegated to the federal agency of executive power effectuating functions in the sphere of State registration of rights to immoveable property and transactions therewith, registration of noncommercial organizations, including divisions of international organizations and foreign noncommercial nongovernmental organizations, social associations, political parties, and religious organizations, keeping the unified State register of self-regulating organizations of arbitrazh managers, the register of arbitrazh managers, and the unified State register of self-regulating organizations of valuers, law-application functions, and functions with regard to control and supervision in the sphere of the advokatura, notariat, State registration of acts of civil status, together with supervision and control functions over self-regulating organizations of arbitrazh managers and valuers. This agency was called the Federal Registration Service, widely known by the official acronym "Rosregistratsia", later "Rosreestr".[4] The Federal Registration Service was within the jurisdiction of the Ministry of Justice. It was transferred with effect from 1 October 2008 to the Ministry of Economic Development of the Russian Federation.[5]

[4] For the Statute on the Federal Registration Service confirmed by Edict of the President of the Russian Federation, 13 October 2004, see СЗ РФ (2004), no. 42, item 4110, as amended.
[5] СЗ РФ (2008), no. 20, item 2290.

The Unified State Registry of Juridical Persons, established pursuant to the Federal Law on the State Registration of Juridical Persons of 8 August 2001, as amended, is no longer the responsibility of the Ministry of Justice. The Ministry does issue registration certificates to noncommercial organizations entered in the said Unified State Registry, including divisions of international organizations and foreign noncommercial, nongovernmental organizations, social associations, and political parties.

Pursuant to a number of treaties, the Ministry of Justice is designated as the "competent agency" to which other parties to the treaty must have recourse if an issue arises. These include the 2001 Convention of the Shanghai Cooperation Organization on Counteracting Extremism with respect to rendering legal assistance concerning the transfer of persons sentenced to deprivation of freedom; the 2017 Protocol on the Procedure for the Transfer of Narcotics insofar as courts of general jurisdiction of the Russian Federation may be involved; the 1993 Minsk Convention on legal assistance and 1997 Protocol thereto regarding legal assistance in criminal, civil, and family cases;[6] and the agency which applies to institute proceedings for the Russian Federation in the Court of the Eurasian Economic Union under the 2014 Treaty on the Eurasian Economic Union,[7] among others. Insofar as the placing of apostilles on official documents is not relegated to other empowered competent Russian agencies, the Ministry of Justice performs that function.

The Ministry of Justice plays a key role in developing legal information systems within the Russian Federation, developing legislative databanks to be used for exchanging materials with subjects of the Federation and foreign States.

The reforms of the Ministry of Justice continue to be implemented in pursuance of the "Conception of Reforming Justice Agencies and Institutions of the Russian Federation", confirmed by Decree of the Government on 7 October 1996, as noted above. On 24 July 1997 the Government of the Russian Federation adopted Decree No. 930 entitled "Questions of the Ministry of Justice of the Russian Federation", parts of which were classified.[8] In furtherance of the Conception, the traditional functions of the Ministry in support of court organization were transferred, in the interests of separation of powers, to the Judicial Department attached to the Supreme Court of the Russian Federation in accordance with the Federal Law on the said

[6] W. E. Butler, *International Civil Procedure in Post-Soviet Space: The Participation of Foreigners* (London, 2020), pp. 116-128.

[7] T. Neshataeva and P. Myslivskiy, "Court of the Eurasian Economic Union: The Beginning", in W. E. Butler (ed.), *Russian Law Journal: Special Issue: Legal Integration in Eurasia*, VII, no. 3 (2019), pp. 134-154.

[8] СЗ РФ (1997), no. 30, item 3663, as amended. The Decree remains in force.

Department of 8 January 1998, as amended.[9] Not mentioned in the Conception but pursuant to obligations arising out of membership in the Council of Europe, on 8 October 1997 the President of the Russian Federation issued an Edict on reforming the system for the execution of criminal punishments; a principal element of the reform consisted of transferring in stages the entire system of penal institutions from the Ministry of Internal Affairs to the Ministry of Justice.[10] Penal institutions are administered by the Federal Service for the Execution of Punishments, which is within the jurisdiction of the Ministry of Justice.[11]

JUDICIAL SYSTEM

History

The Bolsheviks came to power determined to completely reshape the pre-existing judicial order. Revolutionary tribunals sprang up immediately, without legislative sanction, under various names. Cases were judged not on the basis of Imperial law, but according to revolutionary legal consciousness; judgments were not subject to appeal. The first official legislative act creating courts was Decret No. 1 "On Courts" enacted 24 November 1917.[12] In place of the old court system the Decret created "people's courts" presided over by a judge directly elected and two assessors, the latter being laymen who served on a part-time basis. Their jurisdiction was limited to civil cases of up to 3,000 rubles and criminal cases in which the punishment could not exceed two years' deprivation of freedom. Judgments could not be appealed but were sometimes subject to review by cassation. As a separate system of courts Decret No. 1 established revolutionary tribunals consisting of seven persons elected by provincial or city local soviets. These tribunals heard cases involving serious crimes or counter-revolutionary acts; their judgments were not subject to appeal, and they administered what came to be known as the "Red Terror".

This relatively simple judicial structure was elaborated by Decret No. 2 "On Courts" adopted 15 February 1918. Intermediate-level courts were organized in some provinces and a Supreme Judicial Control organ authorized but never actually instituted. The functions of people's assessors

9 СЗ РФ (1998), no. 2, item 223, as amended; transl. in Butler, note 2 above.

10 СЗ РФ (1997), no. 41, item 4683.

11 For the Statute on the Federal Service for the Execution of Punishments confirmed by Edict of the President of Russia on 13 October 2004, as amended, see СЗ РФ (2004), no. 42, item 4109, as amended.

12 The draft of Decret No. 1 usually is associated with P. I. Stuchka, correctly, but he was not at the time the People's Commissar of Justice. The true people's commissar, G. I. Oppokov (who used the pseudonym Lomov) (1888-1937), jurist, economist, theatre critic, and publicist, was never mentioned in the unclassified Soviet press until 1977. See A. Smykalin, «Создание советской судебной системы» [Creation of the Soviet Judicial System], Российская юстиция [Russian Justice], no. 2 (2002), p. 41.

were given in greater detail, and the courts were officially authorized to allow persons to speak their native tongue in court. The powers of cassational instances were enlarged.

Decret No. 2 said nothing of the revolutionary tribunals. These continued to be the object of special legislation; their numbers were reduced but their jurisdiction was broadened. The All-Russian Extraordinary Commission for the Struggle Against Counter-Revolution and Sabotage (VChKa) worked closely with the revolutionary tribunals as an investigative agency, possessing for some time the power to punish summarily without trial. New statutes on revolutionary tribunals were enacted on 12 April 1919 and 18 March 1920. The last was viewed as a kind of unification act for the tribunals; measures of repression had to be based on legislation. Outside this system there operated revolutionary military tribunals and revolutionary military railway tribunals on the basis of slightly different principles and their own legislation. In mid-1921 the entire scheme of tribunals was unified; the Supreme Tribunals attached to the All-Russian Central Executive Committee became the sole cassational and supervisory organ for the entire system and a court of first instance for especially important cases.

The people's courts likewise underwent modifications. They had jurisdiction over all civil and criminal cases except those within the competence of the revolutionary tribunals. Most cases were heard by a judge and two people's assessors; especially grave crimes were heard by a college of the court consisting of the judge and six assessors.

At the outset of 1921 moves were underway to set up a single center of judicial supervision for people's courts and revolutionary tribunals in the person of a body called Supreme Judicial Control; instead the People's Commissariat of Justice was given judicial supervisory powers, but only partial ones. The introduction of the NEP brought further changes for the judiciary: the All-Russian Extraordinary Committee was reorganized into the GPU; the Procuracy was founded; and criminal, civil, labor, civil and criminal procedure codes were enacted. The "judicial reform of 1922" in the RSFSR instituted a uniform system of judicial institutions consisting of the people's court (in two guises), the provincial court, and the RSFSR Supreme Court, broadened the right of people's assessors somewhat further, and clarified the competence of each level in the system. These reforms were hardly in motion before they were overtaken by the formation of the USSR (by Treaty of the Union, 30 December 1922) and the creation in July 1923 of the USSR Supreme Court.

The details of the USSR Supreme Court of this period are beyond the scope of this study except to note a few distinctive features. The Court exercised several types of supervisory power: general supervision, constitutional supervision, and judicial supervision, as well as trying important cases at first instance. It issued guiding explanations to inferior courts on all-union legislation. The Procuracy was linked to the Supreme Court in the person of the 'Procurator of the USSR Supreme Court' until 1933, when the two were separated and the Court lost its responsibilities for general supervision over legality.

Several reorganizations of the judiciary ensued. On 29 October 1924 the USSR enacted Fundamental Principles of Court Organization, followed on 19 November 1926 by the RSFSR Statute on Court Organization. Military courts were separately regulated by a Statute of 20 August 1926 on Military Tribunals and the Military Procuracy, but were considered to be part of the judicial system; the USSR Supreme Court exercised general guidance over them. Nevertheless, there persisted an inclination to create specialized tribunals. In 1930 "line courts for railway transport" were formed, followed in 1934 by analogous courts for water transport; both were served by the Supreme Court as a cassational instance.

In 1934 a separate body was formed outside the judicial system, the Special Board (Особое совещание) attached to the USSR People's Commissariat of Internal Affairs. The Special Board was authorized to apply to persons deemed "socially dangerous": (a) exile for up to five years under public supervision in localities listed by the Commissar; (b) banishment for up to five years under public supervision and a prohibition to reside in capitals, large cities, and industrial centers of the USSR; (c) confinement in correctional-labor camps for a term of up to five years; (d) banishment of socially dangerous foreign subjects beyond the limits of the Soviet Union. The Procurator might protest decisions of the Board, but no judicial review was possible under the Decree.[13] The Board was apparently free to decide who was "socially dangerous" on any basis it chose without regard to substantive or procedural law. The Board's operations were augmented by special legislation, including a Decree adopted by the Presidium of the Central Executive Committee of the USSR on 1 December 1934 concerning cases relating to the preparation or commission of terrorist acts. This type of case was to be considered within ten days, the conclusion to indict being handed to the accused 24 hours before the trial, the case was considered without a procurator or an advocate, cassational appeal and pardon were not allowed, and the death penalty, if assigned, was subject to immediate implementation. An analogous procedure was established on 14 September 1937 for cases concerning wrecking, sabotage, and smuggling. Countless Soviet citizens fell victim to this institution and legislation. The enactments of 1934 and 1937 were repealed by Edict of the Presidium of the USSR Supreme Soviet on 19 April 1956, but presumably ceased to function after Stalin's death in March 1953.[14]

[13] СЗ СССР (1935), I, no. 11, item 84.

[14] Details have emerged concerning so-called "courts of honor" created after the Second World War within Communist Party agencies, including the Central Committee, at the behest

The ordinary court system evidently functioned throughout this period in the normal way. The 1936 USSR Constitution transformed a number of established elements of judicial administration – electivity of judges, participation of people's assessors, national language in court proceedings – to the status of constitutional principles. The 1936 USSR Constitution also "federalized" a number of areas that had been shared between the central and union republic authorities. On 16 August 1938 the USSR Supreme Soviet adopted the Law on Court Organization to replace the 1924 Fundamental Principles. The 1936 USSR Constitution having proclaimed the disappearance of antagonistic classes in the Soviet Union, the 1938 Law made provision for the equality of citizens before the court. The concentration of judicial supervision in the Supreme Court, however, while it contributed to uniformity of judgments and perhaps in some areas (the law of delict) to judicial innovation in the law, did complicate and prolong the judicial process. During the war, military tribunals assumed jurisdiction in areas proclaimed to be in a military situation; in areas under siege, the ordinary courts were simply transformed into military tribunals.

In 1957 the USSR Constitution was amended to return responsibility for court organization to the union republics to be exercised in accordance with all-union Fundamental Principles of Legislation. The Fundamental Principles of Legislation were enacted on 25 December 1958, replacing the 1938 Law, and the union republics approved their own laws on court organization between 1959 and 1961. Those laws continued in force with slight amendments arising out of the 1977-78 USSR and RSFSR constitutions, the RSFSR Law on Court Organization in the version of 1981 remaining in force as amended to 7 February 2011.[15]

Current Legislation

The Russian judicial system is presently regulated by the 1993 Russian Constitution (especially Chapter 7, as amended in 2014 and 2020), the Federal Constitutional Law on the Judicial System of the Russian Federation of 31 December 1996, which entered into force from 1 January 1997, as amended,[16] and the 2002 Federal Law on Judges' Community Agencies of the Russian Federation, as amended.[17] These enactments require, *inter alia*, that judicial power be effectuated only by courts, that the courts be independent of legislative and executive power, and that extraordinary

of Stalin. These were used on occasion, if not always, for the purposes of political reprisal and punishment. Although they had certain analogies with the comrades' courts, apparently they were quite a separate and unrelated phenomenon. See V. D. Esakov and E. S. Levina, Дело КР. Суды чести в идеологии и послевоенного сталинизма [The KR Case. Courts of Honor in the Ideology and Practice of Postwar Stalinism] (2001).

15 Ведомости Верховного Совета РСФСР (1981), no. 28, item 976, as amended.

16 СЗ РФ (1997), no. 1, item 1, as amended; transl. in Butler, note 2 above.

17 СЗ РФ (2002), no. 11, item 1022, as amended; transl. in Butler, note 2 above.

courts and courts not provided for by the Constitution or by the 1996 Law on the judicial system are not permitted.

The judicial system comprises according to the 1993 Russian Constitution as amended in 2020: the Constitutional Court of the Russian Federation, the Supreme Court of the Russian Federation, federal courts of general jurisdiction, arbitrazh courts, and justices of the peace of subjects of the Russian Federation. Military courts fall within the federal courts of general jurisdiction, as do arbitrazh courts and the justices of the peace. All are conceived as being part of a unified judicial system, the unity of which is ensured by the shared origin of Russian courts in the Constitution and the 1996 Law on the judicial system, the concept of the "judges' community agencies", compliance by all courts with the rules of procedure established by federal laws, the application by all courts of the Russian Constitution, federal laws, generally-recognized principles and norms of international law and international treaties of the Russian Federation, recognition that judicial decrees which have entered into legal force are binding throughout the Russian Federation, the unity of the status of judges, and the financing of federal courts and justices of the peace from the federal budget.

In addition there are the courts of the subjects of the Russian Federation. These comprise the constitutional or charter courts of each subject and the justices of the peace, who are the judges of general jurisdiction in subjects of the Federation where they have been actually established. In all there were expected to be, as of 1 January 2020, 29,926 federal judges (including arbitrazh judges) in the Russian Federation (based on budget data).[18] However, the caseload is such that there should have been at least 35,700 judges, a figure still impossible to meet. Under the 2001 Code of Criminal Procedure a judge with 12 jurors or three professional judges hear cases under stipulated situations (Article 30).

The "judges' community" comprises judges of federal courts of all types and levels together with judges of courts of subjects of the Russian Federation comprising the judicial system of Russia. A judge becomes a member of the community from the moment he takes his oath of office and remains such until the decision terminating his powers as judge enters into legal force. The purpose of the judicial community is to express the interests of judges as the bearers of judicial power. The organs or agencies of the judges' community consist of: the All-Russian Congress of Judges, the conference of judges of subjects of the Russian Federation, the Council of Judges of the Russian Federation, the councils of judges of subjects of the Russian Federation, general meetings of judges of courts, the Supreme Qualifications College of Judges of the Russian Federation, and the qualifications colleges of judges of subjects of the Russian Federation. The principal tasks of the judicial

[18] See the Draft Law "On the Federal Budget in 2020 and Planning Period of 2021 and 2022", as of 25 September 2019, available on Consultant Plus.

community of judges are to facilitate the improvement of the judicial system and court proceedings, defend the rights and legal interests of judges, participate in the organizational, personnel, and resource provision for judicial activity, and affirm the authority of judicial power.

CONSTITUTIONAL COURT OF RUSSIAN FEDERATION

History

In the early years after the formation of the USSR by the Treaty of the Union on 30 December 1922 there was a certain interest in constitutional control. The 1924 USSR Constitution placed this responsibility on the USSR Supreme Court (Articles 30, 46, and 46(6)) as a subsidiary one,[19] but left most powers in this connection to the Central Executive Committee of the USSR. By the early 1930s the USSR Supreme Court ceased to play any meaningful role in constitutional control. The 1936 and 1977 USSR Constitutions, and all union and autonomous republic constitutions based thereon, placed constitutional supervision in the hands of the highest agencies of State power (the supreme soviets) and, during the intervals between sessions, in their presidiums.

On 1 December 1988, Article 125 of the USSR Constitution was amended and renumbered to Article 124 in order to make provision for the Committee of Constitutional Supervision of the USSR. The establishment of the Committee encountered considerable resistance; the Law on the Committee was not adopted until 23 December 1989 and the full Committee not elected until 26 April 1990. The Committee's ability to function effectively was further hamstrung by a provision in the legislation creating it which required that the provisions of the Law "affecting supervision over the conformity to the USSR Constitution and laws of the USSR of the constitutions and laws of the union republics enter into force simultaneously with changes in and additions to the Section of the USSR Constitution on national-State structure". In fact that section of the USSR Constitution was never amended, and constitutional control over those questions rested with the President of the USSR. The Committee on Constitutional Supervision of the USSR, however, did enjoy some successes during its brief existence, including declaring void unpublished legislation which affected the rights and legal interests of citizens. The Committee, of course, was not a court and its opinions could be overridden by a qualified majority of the USSR Congress of People's Deputies. Its intended RSFSR counterpart, authorized by amendments to the RSFSR Constitution of 27 October 1989 (Article 119), was never actually created.

[19] See V. K. Diablo, Судебная охрана конституций в буржуазных странах и в СССР [Judicial Protection of Constitutions in Bourgeois Countries and in the USSR] (1928), p. 94.

As the Russian Federation moved from 1989 to 1991 towards a Presidential system and separation of powers with checks and balances, the RSFSR Constitution was amended to create a Constitutional Court which functioned on the basis of the Law on the Constitutional Court adopted 12 July 1991.[20] During its period of operation from 1992 to 1993 the Constitutional Court considered 27 cases, of which 19 related to verifying the constitutionality of legal acts and eight concerned individual appeals by citizens. The Court declared unconstitutional two decrees of the Congress of People's Deputies of the Russian Federation in whole or in part, six laws and decrees of the Supreme Soviet of the RSFSR, two decrees of the Presidium of the RSFSR Supreme Soviet, eight edicts of the President of the Russian Federation, two decrees of the Government of the RSFSR, and four acts of the highest agencies of State power of republics within the Russian Federation. Two opinions also were given on the actions or decisions of the President of Russia. A full seven months was devoted by the Court to the constitutionality of the President's ban of the Communist Party of the Soviet Union and collateral issues of the constitutionality of the Party itself.

In Russia of those years the Constitutional Court was drawn into the sharp confrontation between the President and the legislative branch, the Court endeavoring to play the role of mediator and in the end aligning itself publicly with particular factions. Its decisions became politicized, or were perceived to be so; some judges of the Court appeared in the mass media in a clearly partisan role. After 20 March 1993, the politicization of the Court grew markedly, ultimately culminating in the "suspension" of the Constitutional Court by an Edict of the President of the Russian Federation adopted 21 September 1993 "until the commencement of work of the Federal Assembly of the Russian Federation".[21]

Current Legislation

The present Constitutional Court of the Russian Federation was established on the basis of the 1993 Russian Constitution and the Federal Constitutional Law on the Constitutional Court of the Russian Federation of 21 July 1994, as amended.[22] Until May 2008 the seat of the Court was Moscow; it is presently situated in St Petersburg, where the majority of Court support personnel are graduates of St. Petersburg State University. The Court consists of 11 judges, including the Chairman and Deputy Chairman, appointed to office

[20] Ведомости СНД и ВС РСФСР (1991), no. 19, item 621, as amended. The Law was deemed to have lost force by Edict of the President of the Russian Federation dated 24 December 1993, No. 2288, and entered into force 25 December 1993. Other sources suggest that the Edict "suspended" the Law and ultimately lost force on 21 July 1994. See САПП РФ (1993), no. 52, item 5086; СЗ РФ (1994), no. 13, item 1447.

[21] САПП РФ (1993), no. 39, item 3597, as amended. The Edict lost force on 24 December 1993. On the history of the Court, see A. Trochev, *Judging Russia: Constitutional Court in Russian Politics 1990-2006* (2008).

[22] СЗ РФ (1994), no. 13, item 1447, as amended; transl. in Butler, note 2 above.

by the Soviet of the Federation upon the recommendation of the President of the Russian Federation for an indeterminate term, the compulsory age of retirement being 70 years of age.[23] A judge may not be removed from office, although under certain circumstances his powers may be suspended or terminated. The powers of the Court itself are not limited by a determined period.

The jurisdiction of the Constitutional Court is complex and may not be changed other than by way of making changes to the Federal Constitutional Law which established the Court. With respect to conformity to the 1993 Russian Constitution the Constitutional Court may examine: (a) federal constitutional laws, federal laws, normative acts of the President of the Russian Federation, the Soviet of the Federation, the State Duma, and the Government of the Russian Federation; (b) the constitutions or charters, laws, and other normative acts of the subjects of the Russian Federation issued with regard to questions relegated to the jurisdiction of agencies of State power of the Russian Federation and to the joint jurisdiction of agencies of State power of the Russian Federation and agencies of State power of subjects of the Russian Federation; (c) treaties between agencies of State power of the Russian Federation and agencies of State power of subjects of the Russian Federation, and treaties between agencies of State power of subjects of the Russian Federation; (d) international treaties of the Russian Federation which have not entered into force.

The second domain of jurisdiction of the Constitutional Court appertains to disputes concerning competence: (a) between federal agencies of State power; (b) between agencies of State power of the Russian Federation and agencies of State power of subjects of the Russian Federation; (c) between the highest State agencies of subjects of the Russian Federation.

The Constitutional Court also considers in response to appeals against a violation of the constitutional rights and freedoms of citizens the constitutionality of laws and other normative acts that have been applied in a concrete case if all other municipal means of judicial defense have been exhausted, and inquiries from courts to verify the constitutionality of a law being applied or subject to application in a particular case; gives interpretations of the Constitution; and exercises other powers granted to the Court by the 1993 Russian Constitution, the Treaty of the Russian Federation, federal constitutional laws; and treaties delimiting the powers

[23] Except for the Chairman of the Court, for whom the age limit was removed in 2010. On 31 January 2018 the Soviet of the Federation reappointed Valerii Zorkin to his sixth term in that post. He served as Chairman from 1991 to 1993, was an ordinary judge until 2003, and then has been reappointed to, initially, three-year terms and when the Federal Constitutional Law on the Constitutional Court was amended to allow five-year terms without no maximum age limit, elected consecutively until his sixth term in 2018. In 2003, 2006, 2009, he was elected to this position by the judges on the Court; thereafter, by the Soviet of the Federation in 2012 and 2018.

among subjects of the Russian Federation. The Court has the right of legislative initiative with regard to questions of its jurisdiction.

In the event of an attempt to impeach the President of the Russian Federation, at the request of the Soviet of the Federation the Court gives an opinion concerning compliance with the established procedure for putting forward of an accusation against the President of the Russian Federation or President of the Russian Federation whose term of office has ended of treason against the State or commission of another grave crime.

Under amendments introduced in March 2020, the Court may with regard to a query of the President of the Russian Federation verify the constitutionality of draft laws of the Russian Federation concerning an amendment to the Constitution of the Russian Federation, draft federal constitutional laws and federal laws, and also laws before their signature by the President of the Russian Federation; in the procedure established by a federal constitutional law, settle the question concerning the possibility of the execution of decisions of inter-State agencies adopted on the basis of provisions of international treaties of the Russian Federation in a construing thereof which is contrary to the Constitution of the Russian Federation, and also the possibility of the execution of the decision of a foreign or international (or inter-State) court or foreign or international arbitration court imposing duties on the Russian Federation if this decision is contrary to the fundamental principles of public policy of the Russian Federation; and with regard to a query of the President of the Russian Federation in the procedure established by a federal constitutional law, verify the constitutionality of laws of subjects of the Russian Federation before their promulgation by the high official of a subject of the Russian Federation (or executive of the high executive agency of State power of a subject of the Russian Federation).

Acts or individual provisions thereof deemed to be unconstitutional lose force; international treaties of the Russian Federation which do not conform to the Constitution of the Russian Federation are not be subject to introduction into operation and application. Acts or individual provisions thereof deemed to be unconstitutional in a construction given by the Constitutional Court of the Russian Federation are not subject to application in another interpretation.

The Court acts in plenary session and is divided into two chambers containing respectively ten and nine judges of the Court. Which judge serves in which chamber is determined by lot. The chairman and deputy chairman of the Court may not be within the same chamber, and the individual composition of the chambers must be changed at least every three years. In plenary session the Court exclusively settles cases concerning the constitutionality of the constitutions and charters of the subjects of the Federation, interprets the 1993 Russian Constitution, gives an opinion regarding impeachment proceedings against the President, decides whether to exercise legislative initiative, and adopts messages to be issued by the Court, elects the chairman, deputy chairman, and secretary of the Court, determines whether to suspend or terminate the powers of a judge of the court or the term of office of the chairman, deputy chairman, or secretary of the Court. Matters not within the exclusive jurisdiction of the plenary session of the Court may be considered in sessions of the chambers of the Court.

The principles of a constitutional court proceeding are the:

- ·independence of the judges, which requires that judges of the Court be guided exclusively by the law, not represent any State or social agencies, political parties or movements, State, social, or other enterprises, institutions, or organizations, officials, State and territorial formations, or social groups, and adopt decisions under circumstances precluding outside influence or interference;
- ·collegiality, which demands that a decision be adopted only by those judges who participated in the consideration of the case in a judicial session with the requisite quorum of three-quarters of the membership of the chamber or two-thirds of the composition of the plenary session;
- ·*glasnost*, which means cases are considered openly unless the Law on the Court provides otherwise, and requires that decisions are proclaimed publicly;
- ·orality, which requires the Court to hear the explanations of the parties, testimony of experts, witnesses, and to read out available documents;
- ·language, being in this instance the Russian language with the right to use of an interpreter if participants in the case do not have a command of Russian;
- ·uninterruptedness, which mandates that the Court commence and complete a case except for time allotted for leisure or to enable the participants to prepare for further proceedings;
- ·adversariality and equality of parties, which gives the parties equal rights to support their position in a session of the Court.

The rules of procedure of the Constitutional Court are contained in the Law on the Court and in the Reglament of the Court adopted 1 March 1995,[24] as amended 10 October 2017. Recourse to the Court takes the form

[24] The Reglament was unpublished but available on Consultant Plus; transl. in Butler, *Russian Public Law* (2d ed.; 2009), pp. 556-577. The new version is available on Consultant Plus.

of an inquiry, petition, or appeal. The Court is required to reply to each recourse in writing, giving grounds for acceptance or rejection and, where possible, directing the person having recourse to other competent agencies or officials if the matter is not within the jurisdiction of the Constitutional Court. Between 1992 and 1995 the Constitutional Court received 41,633 instances of recourse by citizens, State agencies, and social associations, 52,068 between 1995 and 1999. There were 321,034 recourses between 2000 and the first half of 2020.

The Constitutional Court adopts four types of document, depending upon the nature of the matter under consideration. A decision adopted in a plenary session or the session of a chamber of the Court is called a decision (решение) of the Constitutional Court of the Russian Federation. With regard to most matters within its jurisdiction (Article 3(1)-(4), Law on the Constitutional Court), the final decision of the Court is called a decree (постановление); if the matter deals with impeachment of the President, it is called an opinion (заключение); all other decisions of the Court concerning a Constitutional Court proceeding are called a ruling (определение). A decision is adopted in an open vote, each judge being polled by name and the person presiding voting last. A majority of judges who participate in the voting is sufficient to adopt a decision unless expressly provided otherwise by the Law on the Constitutional Court. A tie vote in a case concerning the constitutionality of a normative act or treaty is considered to be in favor of the constitutionality of the act under consideration. Disputes concerning competence must be decided by a majority vote. A decision concerning an interpretation of the Constitution requires a majority of two-thirds of the total number of judges. There is no right of abstention.

During the initial period of its existence (January 1992 to ca. October 1993) the Constitutional Court considered 27 cases, 19 of which were petitions to verify the constitutionality of legal acts and eight of which related to individual appeals by citizens. More than half dealt with human rights questions, and a quarter with issues of State organization and structure. Following the adoption of the 1993 Russian Constitution (from 1995), as of 30 September 2020 the Constitutional Court had issued 642 decrees and for the years 1995 to 2020, 643 rulings (excluding rulings to refuse to accept recourses for consideration or with regard to reject recourses).

The form and style of a decision of the Constitutional Court is regulated by the Law on the Constitutional Court (Article 75). Special opinions are possible and may take the form of what in the United States would be called a concurring or a dissenting opinion. The decision of the Court is proclaimed in full in open court immediately after being signed by all judges who participated in the voting. Within a two-week period after signature decrees are circulated according to a list set out in the Law on the Constitutional Court and are subject to official publication in the Собрание законодательства Российской Федерации [Collection of

Legislation of the Russian Federation], the newspaper Российская газета [Russian Newspaper], and the official organ of the Court itself, Вестник Конституционного Суда Российской Федерации [Herald of the Constitutional Court of the Russian Federation]. With effect from 1 January 2021, a judge of the Constitutional Court does not have the right to issue a special opinion or opinion in any form or to refer to it publicly. A special opinion is attached to the protocol of the session and kept together with the protocol. Previously a special opinion was published together with the decision in the Herald of the Court and then placed on the website of the Court in the same file with the decision. That practice is now forbidden.

Court decisions have been collected in individual volumes edited by judges of the Court, sometimes with commentary. The decision is final, not subject to appeal, and enters into force immediately after promulgation. Although publication of the decision is mandatory, the legal force of the decision is not dependent upon nor connected with publication. No confirmation by other agencies or officials is required in respect of a Court decision; it has immediate direct effect and is subject to execution at once.

The Constitutional Court resolves cases of constitutionality in the form of so-called "abstract" norm-control and "concrete" norm-control. The former engages the right of recourse to the Constitutional Court with a "query" as to whether normative acts, treaties, or international treaties are constitutional and a request for verification thereof. Such a request is not linked with a concrete case, and the agencies which may submit a "query" are exhaustively enumerated: the President of the Russian Federation, Soviet of the Federation, State Duma, one-fifth of the members of the Soviet of the Federation or deputies of the State Duma, Government of the Russian Federation, agencies of legislative and executive power of subjects of the Russian Federation.

When performing this function, the Constitutional Court renders a Decree as to whether the normative act or treaty is constitutional or unconstitutional. This procedure was followed when the Republic Crimea and Sevastopol were accepted as subjects of the Russian Federation, for example.

Concrete norm-control occurs when natural persons or associations thereof file a complaint in the Constitutional Court. In practice, however, the constitutionality of laws and other normative legal acts was raised before courts of ordinary jurisdiction or arbitrazh courts. On 16 June 1998, in response to a "query" submitted by the Legislative Assembly of the Republic Karelia and another by the Republic Komi, the Constitutional Court adopted a Decree relating to the interpretation of individual provisions of Articles 125, 126, and 127 of the Russian Constitution. The Constitutional Court determined that the 1993 Russian Constitution placed the powers to verify the constitutionality of normative acts on a special organ – the

Constitutional Court – and did not endow other judicial agencies with such powers. Verifying constitutionality is a specific form of administering justice, in accordance with special procedures, and with particular legal consequences. Other courts are not so regulated at the constitutional level. Consequently, the Russian Constitution does not assume that such courts would verify the constitutionality of normative acts enumerated in Article 125 of the Constitution. If a court doubts the constitutionality of a normative legal act, it is obliged to submit a query to the Constitutional Court of the Russian Federation. A refusal to apply a law by reason of its supposed unconstitutionality without submitting a query to the Constitutional Court would be a violation of the Constitution.

An appeal against an alleged violation of constitutional rights and freedoms may be filed if the remaining municipal judicial remedies have been exhausted – which means that a cassational appeal has been filed at the highest court for the particular category of cases or a supervisory appeal if a judicial act which has entered into force may only be contested by way of supervision – and such recourse has been unsuccessful. The Constitutional Court may deem municipal remedies to be exhausted if judicial practice shows that the normative act was applied just the way it was done or officially interpreted by the highest court for the particular category of cases. Prior to 2021 a condition for the admissibility of an appeal was that a law was applied in a concrete case, the consideration of which had been completed; the criterion of "completion" was never determined. The new approach extends to a normative act, and not merely a law.

The judges of the Constitutional Court are served by a Secretariat which arranges the full organizational and informational support of the Court, receives visitors, considers recourses to the Court in a preliminary way, weeding out those not within the jurisdiction of the Court, assists the judges in preparing cases, and monitors the activity of State agencies in executing decisions of the Court. The Statute on the Secretariat is confirmed by the Constitutional Court itself; the text is an internal document and not available in the commercial databases. The Court sat in Moscow through April 2008 and, as a rule, sits in St Petersburg thereafter, but may conduct sessions in another place when the Court considers this to be necessary.

Judges wear gowns when the Court is in session. Designed by E. N. Korotkova, the gowns and caps were intended to bear the State Arms of the Russian Federation. The design was approved by the Presidium of the Supreme Soviet of the Russian Federation on 18 May 1992 but never submitted for confirmation of the full Supreme Soviet. In practice, therefore, judges wore the gown without the headgear and without the State symbols. The situation changed following the adoption of the Federal Constitutional Law on the State Arms of the Russian Federation of 25 December 2000, as amended.[25] The Court has developed its own internal protocol and forms of address during judicial sessions. The Court is addressed as the "High Court", or "Respected Court"; the judges as "Your Honor" or "Respected Judge"; and participants in the proceeding as the "Respected Party"; "Respected Expert"; "Respected Witness"; and the like, adding the surname of the individual if necessary.

COURTS OF GENERAL JURISDICTION OF THE RUSSIAN FEDERATION

The courts of general jurisdiction are headed by the Supreme Court of the Russian Federation, which is the highest judicial agency for civil cases, cases regarding the settlement of economic disputes, criminal, administrative, and other cases within the jurisdiction of the courts of general jurisdiction and arbitrazh courts. It is the directly superior instance to the supreme courts of the Republics within the Federation, territory or regional courts, courts of cities of federal significance, courts of the autonomous region and autonomous national areas, military courts of military districts, fleets, and types and groups of forces. The lowest tier of this system is the district court, which acts as a court of first instance, and with respect to the justices of the peace, as the court of second instance. The 1996 Federal Constitutional Law on the Judicial System of the Russian Federation made provision for a federal constitutional law to be adopted with respect to the Supreme Court and all inferior courts. Until that happened, these courts continued to be governed by the 1981 RSFSR Law on Court Organization, as amended. The Federal Constitutional Law on the Supreme Court of the Russian Federation ultimately appeared on 5 February 2014.[26]

The 1993 Russian Constitution (Article 126) establishes the place of the Supreme Court in the judicial system and confers on it the right of legislative initiative (Article 104). Under the 1996 Law on the Judicial System, the Supreme Court effectuates judicial supervision in the procedural forms provided for by a federal law over the activity of courts of general jurisdiction, including military and specialized federal courts, within its competence considers cases as a court of second instance, by way of supervision, and under newly discovered circumstances, and may act as a court of first instance under certain circumstances, and gives explanations with regard to questions of judicial practice. In 2005, for example, the Russian Supreme Court completed proceedings in five criminal cases at first instance, one case being returned to the procurator and four resulting in judgments. Two persons were acquitted, one of them by a jury. Five individuals were convicted, of whom three were sentenced to actual

[25] СЗ РФ (2000), no. 52(I), item 5021, as amended.

[26] СЗ РФ (2014), no. 6, item 550, as amended; transl. in Butler, note 2 above.

deprivation of freedom. One case was terminated by reason of the period of limitations having expired.

The Supreme Court consists of 170 judges appointed by the Soviet of the Federation upon the recommendation of the President of the Russian Federation, which in turn is based upon a recommendation of the Chairman of the Supreme Court and the opinion of the qualifications collegium of the Court. There is no limitation on the term of office of judges, but they must retire at age 70. People's assessors serve for a term of five years. In cases heard at first instance the case is heard by a bench composed of a single judge (with a jury if the accused so requests), although a court of three professional judges also is permitted. Cases heard by way of cassation in regard to appeal and protests are considered by three professional judges in one of the three judicial divisions of the Court: civil, criminal, or military. The same applies to cases heard by way of supervision or with regard to newly discovered circumstances. When the Presidium of the Supreme Court considers a case, a majority of its members must be present.

The Plenum of the Supreme Court, which is convoked at least quarterly, consists of the Chairman, first deputy chairman, deputy chairmen, and judges. The Chairman of the Constitutional Court, Procurator General, Minister of Justice, their deputies, and other judges are among those who may be invited to attend sessions of the Plenum. The Plenum adopts decisions by simple majority vote and requires two-thirds of the membership to be present for a quorum. It is the Plenum which issues Decrees and Guiding Explanations on judicial practice (see Chapter 5).

The 2014 Law on the Supreme Court contains a lengthy enumeration of the functions of the Plenum. Among them are: considering materials that analyze and summarize judicial practice and issuing explanations in the interests of uniformity of judicial practice; exercising the constitutional right of legislative initiative on behalf of the Supreme Court, submitting queries to the Constitutional Court of the Russian Federation, electing the secretary of the Plenum for a three-year term, confirming the benches of the various judicial divisions of the Court, electing the Appellate Division of the Supreme Court and the Disciplinary Division, confirming the membership of the Scientific-Advisory Council attached to the Supreme Court and the Statute thereof, and confirming the Reglament of the Supreme Court.

The Presidium of the Court is the highest judicial instance in the Russian Federation with regard to cases within the jurisdiction of courts of general jurisdiction. The Soviet of the Federation confirms the judges who sit on the Presidium upon the recommendation of the President of the Russian Federation. The functions of the Presidium are substantial and include deciding cases heard by way of supervision and for new or newly-discovered circumstances, making application to the Constitutional Court of the Russian Federation with a query on the constitutionality of a law subject to being applied in a specific case, ensuring the coordination of the activity of the judicial divisions, benches of those divisions, and apparatus of the Court, confirming the procedure for verifying the reliability and completeness of information concerning revenues, expenses, property, and obligations of a property character of judges of the Supreme Court and all lower courts, including their spouses and minor children, confirming the Statute on the Apparatus of the Supreme Court, its structure, and personnel establishment, considering individual issues of judicial practice, and others. Sessions of the Presidium are held at least monthly. Individual cases are reported upon by members of the Presidium or other judges; the Procurator General or his deputy participates to either support a procuracy protest or to comment on protests brought by the Chairman of the Supreme Court or his deputies. Decrees are adopted by simple majority open vote.

The greater portion of work in the Supreme Court is performed within its judicial divisions, of which there are five (administrative, civil, criminal, economic, and military serviceman cases), plus the Appellate Division and the Disciplinary Division. The five substantive divisions consider cases at first instance, by way of cassation, by way of supervision, and on the grounds of new or newly-discovered circumstances. The judicial divisions each are divided into benches composed of six to eight judges, one of whom acts as chairman to preside at judicial sessions and ensure the preparation of cases for consideration by way of cassation or supervision. Each bench is allocated lower administrative-territorial subdivisions from whose courts cases flow to it. It is felt that such allocation enables the judges to come to know the lower courts in detail, the kinds of errors they are likely to make, and the professional qualities of individual judges.

The rules governing whether cases are dealt with by way of cassation or supervision are complex. In general judicial supervision is exercised by considering appeals and protests against judgments and other decisions of inferior courts which have not entered into legal force, or those which have entered into legal force provided that they were not considered by way of cassation, special appeal, or special protest. It should be borne in mind, when tracing the progress of a particular case, that the presidium of each court and, at higher levels, also the plenum are places of resort for the parties or their lawyers. A particularly difficult case can pass through dozens of procedural stages and instances.

As a court of first instance the Supreme Court can take jurisdiction over virtually any case, as well as try those relegated specifically to its jurisdiction. In practice the Supreme Court tries criminal cases where important State interests are involved, or in which the crimes committed involve several administrative-territorial divisions, entail grave consequences, or are of unusual complexity. During election periods, the Supreme Court hears appeals against the decisions of the Central Electoral Commission of the Russian Federation not to register candidates for elective office.

The role of the Supreme Court in issuing guiding explanations is discussed in Chapter 5. Decisions, judgments, rulings, and decrees of the Supreme Court and other courts of ordinary jurisdiction are published in the monthly Бюллетень Верховного Суда Российской Федерации [Bulletin of the Supreme Court of the Russian Federation].

In the past organizational provision for the courts of general jurisdiction was made by the Ministry of Justice of the Russian Federation, a proximity to and dependence upon the Government that in the eyes of many compromised the independence of the courts. The 1996 Law on the Judicial System made provision for a Judicial Department attached to the Supreme Court of the Russian Federation, regulated by the Federal Law of 8 January 1998, as amended.[27] Although attached to the Supreme Court, the Judicial Department is a federal State agency whose responsibility is to organize the activity of the entire system of courts (except the Supreme Court itself, which has its own apparatus) of general jurisdiction, including specialized courts, and the financing of the justices of the peace. "Organize" for these purposes means personnel, finance, material-technical, and other measures which enable the courts to function independently and efficiently. The Judicial Department therefore constitutes a system having agencies and institutions at every level of State administration where there are courts. It is headed by a General Director who is appointed to and removed from office by the Chairman of the Supreme Court with the consent of the Council of Judges of the Russian Federation.

In effect an entire professional group of court administrators has been created by the 1998 Law on the Judicial Department. Its powers are immense: organizing the activity of all courts below the Supreme Court, assisting with the drafting of federal laws and other normative acts relating to questions within its jurisdiction, working out proposals to finance the courts and justices of the peace, making proposals to improve the organization of the courts, submitting proposals to create or abolish courts, monitoring personnel requirements of the courts, conducting work relating to the selection and training of candidate judges, interacting with educational institutions, training and raising the qualifications of judges and workers of the court apparatus, developing normative standards for the caseload of judges, helping reassign judges to courts with vacancies, keeping forensic statistics and court archives, organizing the construction and repair of court buildings, and others.

The training of future judges and continuing legal education for sitting judges also is the responsibility of the Russian Academy of Justice, founded by the Supreme Court and the Supreme Arbitrazh Court of the Russian Federation on the basis of the Edict of the President of the Russian Federation

[27] СЗ РФ (1998), no. 2, item 223, as amended; transl. in Butler, note 2 above.

of 11 May 1998, as amended.[28] The Academy undertakes fundamental and applied research on the organization and activities of the courts.

Attached to the Supreme Court is a scientific advisory council, which operates on the basis of a Statute confirmed by the Plenum of the Supreme Court on 11 December 1968.[29] This is a consultative body whose responsibility is to make recommendations on questions of principle which arise with respect to judicial practice in the form of draft explanations of the Plenum, draft submissions relating to legislation and interpretations of laws, draft instructions and other documents prepared by the Supreme Court, and legal issues arising out of individual court cases. Similar councils attached to lower courts may receive assistance from the Council attached to the Supreme Court. Members of the Council are confirmed for a term of three years.

The courts of general jurisdiction below the Supreme Court of the Russian Federation correspond to the administrative-territorial subdivisions of the Federation. All have equal powers and are commonly called for the sake of convenience "territory (or regional) courts and courts equated thereto". All hear cases at first instance, and all act at second instance with respect to the courts below them. At second instance, therefore, they exercise judicial powers by way of cassation and supervision. Collectively they comprise the middle link between the Supreme Court and the principal court of the Russian Federation: the district court. Until 1 July 2002 each court consisted of judges and people's assessors; however, from 1993 criminal cases were considered at first instance by juries in a number of territory and regional courts on an experimental basis. The jury system has since been introduced throughout the country. Courtrooms have been refurnished to accommodate juries; it is anticipated that juries may considered up to 15,000 cases annually in 2,300 district courtrooms.[30] When a jury is used, the case is heard by one professional judge and 12 jurors, plus two jurors in reserve. At second instance cases are heard by three professional judges. Each court contains a presidium and is divided into judicial divisions for civil and criminal cases, each division chaired by a deputy chairman of the court.

Although part of the middle link, the republic supreme courts also are the highest judicial instance in the respective republic, exercise judicial

[28] СЗ РФ (1998), no. 19, item 2110, as amended.

[29] The Statute was amended 20 December 1983, 21 December 1993, 25 October 1996, and 6 February 2007. In 2014 it was replaced by a new Statute confirmed by Decree of the Supreme Court of 7 August 2014, No. 8; although the old Statute remains in force, it is no longer applied. The text is available on Consultant Plus.

[30] See V. Kulikov, «Людей попросят рассудить» [They Seek to Judge People], Российская газета [Russian Newspaper], 25 January 2018, pp. 1, 3.

supervision over district courts, and have the right of legislative initiative in their republic.

The court which acted exclusively at first instance was the district court, formerly the "people's courts" but renamed under the 1996 Federal Law on the Judicial System. When justices of the peace were installed, the district court became an appeal court with respect to their decisions. The number of judges varies from one court to another; in remote areas there is but one judge, whereas in large urban concentrations there are several.

Complaints have persisted for years that Russian judges in the courts of ordinary jurisdiction are seriously overburdened with cases. A study undertaken by the Higher School of Economics in Moscow during 2017 of 1,700 judges and 4,500 court personnel examined how each spent the work day; that is, how much time was expended on hearing cases and performing other judicial tasks. A model was developed which demonstrated how many hours, for example, were required to consider a criminal case, depending upon its complexity and gravity. The time scale ranged from 30.8 hours for the consideration of a case involving an infringement on the life of a natural person to crimes connected with narcotics (12.9 hours); the study incorporated data from 1996 and 2008 and showed minimal changes in the number of hours required. In the courts of ordinary jurisdiction during 2016 judicial personnel numbering 25,405 considered 12,440,000 cases.[31]

MILITARY COURTS

Previously known as military tribunals until 1992, when they were renamed military courts, these institutions have survived in peacetime apparently on the premise that military life has special features which require adjudication in courts composed of military personnel. Russian military courts fall within the system of courts of general jurisdiction headed by the Supreme Court. They operated on the basis of a Statute confirmed on 25 December 1958,[32] as amended 25 June 1980, which applied insofar as not overridden by subsequent general legislation on court organization and the judicial system, and on the armed forces. The Federal Constitutional Law on Military Courts of 23 June 1999, as amended,[33] replaced the 1958 Statute.

The number of military courts and military judges is determined by the Supreme Court of the Russian Federation. Protests against decisions, judgments, rulings, and decrees of the Military Division of the Supreme Court and military courts which have entered into force are heard by the

[31] See Margarita Alekhina, Исследование ВШЭ зафиксировало перегрузку 62% российских судей [Study of the Higher School of Economics Determined the Overload of 62% of Russian Judges], РБК, 17 April 2017. Available online.

[32] Transl. in W. E. Butler, *Soviet Legal System: Legislation and Documentation* (1978), pp. 229-234.

[33] СЗ РФ (1999), no. 26, item 3170, as amended; transl. in Butler, note 2 above.

Presidium of the Supreme Court. Appeals and protests are decided by the Appellate Division of the Supreme Court. The judicial activities of military courts are taken into account just as those of other courts when summaries of judicial practice are prepared.

A military judge must be at least 25 years of age and a Russian citizen, have a higher legal education and work experience of at least five years as a lawyer, have committed no offenses, have passed a qualification examination and been recommended by the qualifications division of military court judges, be a military officer, and have concluded a contract to perform military service.[34]

JUSTICES OF THE PEACE

So-called justice of the peace courts were introduced in Russia by the celebrated Judicial Reforms of 1864, adapted in part from English law and practice. The courts were actually formed in St Petersburg, Moscow, Kharkov, and ten central Russian provinces, gradually expanding until 1889, when as part of a conservative backlash against liberal institutions they were abolished in 37 internal and six western Russian provinces and replaced by judicial-administrative agencies. In those areas where they were not abolished, they continued to operate until November 1917, when the Soviet authorities put an end to them.

Provision was made for justices of the peace in the Conception of Judicial Reform approved on 24 October 1991 by the Supreme Soviet of the RSFSR.[35] They were accordingly included in the 1996 Federal Constitutional Law on the Judicial System and expressly authorized by the Federal Law on Justices of the Peace in the Russian Federation of 17 December 1998, as amended.[36] Financial considerations delayed their introduction, however, although certain regions did undertake to finance their creation. Their existence has significantly reduced the workload of the district courts.[37]

Justices of the peace are judges of general jurisdiction and part of the unified judicial system of the Russian Federation. They issue decrees when deciding cases, and these, together with other documents issued by them, are binding throughout Russia upon all to whom they are directed. Justices of the peace enjoy the same protections and guarantees as other judges. Their competence at first instance extends to criminal cases concerning crimes for

[34] V. M. Lebedev and N. A. Petukhov (eds.), Комментарий к федеральному конституционному закону «О военных судах Российской Федерации» [Commentary on Federal Constitutional Law on Military Courts of the Russian Federation] (2000), p. 58.

[35] Ведомости Верховного Совета РСФСР (1991), no. 44, item 1435.

[36] СЗ РФ (1998), no. 51, item 6270, as amended; transl. in Butler, note 2 above.

[37] The overall caseload of civil, criminal, and administrative cases in 2010 exceeded 20 million cases for justices of the peace. See K. Hendley, "Too Much of a Good Thing? Assessing Access to Civil Justice in Russia", *Slavic Review*, LXXII (2013), p. 807

whose commission the maximum punishment that may be assigned does not exceed three years deprivation of freedom;[38] cases concerning the issuance of a judicial order; cases concerning dissolution of marriage if there is no dispute concerning the children between the spouses; cases concerning the division of jointly-acquired property between spouses; other cases arising from family law relations except those with regard to the establishment or contesting of paternity or motherhood; deprivation of parental rights; and adoption; cases concerning property disputes when the value of the suit does not exceed five hundred minimum amounts of payment for labor; cases arising from labor relations, except reinstatement at work; cases concerning determination of the procedure for use of land plots, structures, and other immoveable property; cases concerning administrative violations relegated to the competence of justices by the 2001 Code on Administrative Violations; and other cases that may by federal laws be relegated to the jurisdiction of a justice of the peace.

Justices of the peace act alone; there are no people's assessors or jurors to assist them. They operate within territorial units called judicial precincts. The total number of justices and number of judicial precincts is determined with a subject of the Russian Federation by a federal law to be introduced through the legislative initiative of the subject of the Federation concerned, agreed with the Russian Supreme Court, or vice versa.[39] Judicial precincts are to contain from 15,000 to 23,000 persons, and if there are less than 15,000 persons in the relevant administrative-territorial formation, only one justice of the peace operates. As of 1 January 2018 there were approximately 7,654 justices of the peace in Russia.[40]

A justice of the peace must be a Russian citizen aged 25 or more having a higher legal education and work experience as a lawyer for not less than five years, have committed no offenses, and have passed the qualifications examination and been recommended by the college of judges in the respective subject of the Russian Federation. Federal court judges

[38] Justices of the peace hear criminal cases in accordance with the 2001 Code of Criminal Procedure of the Russian Federation, Articles 318 to 323 inclusive laying down special provisions for criminal cases decided by a justice of the peace. In 2010 justices of the peace in Russia heard 1,065,200 criminal cases, a decrease of 20% in comparison with the year 2000. Hendley, ibid. In 2016 it was estimated that justices of the peace considered ten to fifteen cases per day. See «Как разгрузить российские суды» [How to Unburden Russian Courts], Ведомости [Gazette], 14 September 2017. Even though half these cases involved the adoption of judicial orders and similar procedural matters, judges often lack the time to carefully read the materials of the case.

[39] These numbers are then reflected in the Federal Law on the Total Number of Justices of the Peace and Number of Judicial Precincts in Subjects of the Russian Federation of 29 December 1999, as amended to 3 April 2018; the original version is transl. in Butler, *Russian Public Law* (2005), p. 529. СЗ РФ (2000), no. 1(I), item 1, as amended.

[40] For insight into how the justices of the peace operate in Russia under current legislation, see K. Hendley, *Everyday Law in Russia* (2016), pp. 134-221.

with more than five years experience as a federal judge are exempt from the examination. They are appointed or elected to office by the legislative agency of State power of the subject of the Russian Federation or elected directly by the population in the judicial precinct as established by a law of the subject of the Russian Federation. The term of office may not exceed five years and is determined by local legislation. Subsequent elections or appointments are possible for up to five-year terms, provided, however, that a justice of the peace must retire at age 70 irrespective of whether his term has been completed or not. Financing of salaries and expenses is from the federal budget; salaries are fixed at 60% of the salary of the Chairman of the Supreme Court of the Russian Federation, except in cities of federal significance, where the coefficient is 64%.

ARBITRAZH COURTS

Depending upon one's point of view, the arbitrazh courts were either "liquidated" in 2014 or "merged" into the system of courts of general jurisdiction. Although they no longer exist as originally constituted under the 1993 Russian Constitution, their history continues to be worthy of attention because their roots lie in the twentieth century Soviet planned economy. They played in their time an important role in the Russian conception of the administration of justice. The process of transition to full implementation of the 2014 judicial reforms will require some years to fully realize.

History

The conviction that commercial or economic disputes required special expertise to resolve, and perhaps special procedures, surfaced early in Soviet legal history. Even during the NEP, State arbitration commissions were established for this purpose, by a Statute of 21 September 1922. They functioned in each province, and in Moscow a Supreme Arbitration Commission was formed to decide appeals filed against awards of provincial commissions and hear certain disputes at first instance. In 1924 the USSR Supreme Arbitration Commission was created to take jurisdiction over disputes involving enterprises of all-union stature or enterprises from different union republics. The introduction of national economic planning rendered NEP-style arbitration obsolete. On 4 March 1931 the arbitration commissions were abolished; pending and future litigation between enterprises was to be transferred to the ordinary courts, which would assign two people's assessors employed in economic agencies to hear the case with a judge. For a brief spell unification was achieved in the Soviet judicial system, but it was short-lived. The ordinary courts at the time proved to be wholly unsuited to handle this type of dispute. On 3 May 1931 a system of State arbitrazh was created as an integral system attached to each administrative-territorial level from region upwards.

Introduced at a time when the Pashukanis school of economic law was ascendant, State arbitrazh initially represented a kind of hybrid between arbitration and adjudication. Reconciliation of the parties was to be the primary object; the enterprise managers themselves often appeared around the table to arrange a settlement. Failing that, arbitrazh was to resolve the dispute on the basis of prevailing economic plans and regulations, having regard to economic policy and expediency. Civil Code provisions were but useful guidelines and not binding; for a time even jurisconsults were barred from the proceedings. On 19 December 1933 arbitrazh jurisdiction was extended to pre-contractual disputes between socialist organizations; by the mid-1930s the restoration of "stability of laws" had left its imprint; arbitrazh was to apply relevant Soviet legislation to disputes, jurisconsults appeared on behalf of their management, civil procedure codes were used when relevant, and the arbitrator was required to produce a reasoned opinion based on an accurate account of the proceedings. Economic expediency had become a supplementary consideration to be invoked when legislation or the contract itself did not dispose of all the relevant issues.

The 1931 decree was replaced on 17 August 1960 by a statute which broadened the scope of arbitrazh activity, enlarged arbitrazh control over the terms of economic contracts, and elaborated the rules of arbitrazh procedure. The 1960 Statute was replaced on 18 January 1974. The 1977 USSR Constitution elevated State arbitrazh to an agency of constitutional stature, a status consolidated in the Law on State Arbitrazh in the USSR adopted 30 November 1979 and amended extensively in 1987 to reflect *perestroika* policies and move the arbitrazh system closer to that of a court.

The decision to abandon the system of State arbitrazh, so deeply linked with the Planned Economy, and to introduce arbitrazh courts as part of the judicial system was taken by the Russian Federation in the form of the Law on the Arbitrazh Court adopted 4 July 1991.[41] The Code of Arbitrazh Procedure was adopted 5 March 1992 and entered into force on 15 April 1992.[42] The 1993 Russian Constitution (Article 127) confirmed the arbitrazh courts as a branch of the federal judicial system and required the enactment of the Federal Constitutional Law on Arbitrazh Courts in the Russian Federation of 28 April 1995, as amended, in force from 1 July 1995.[43] On 5 April 1995 the Code of Arbitrazh Procedure was enacted to replace the 1992

[41] Ведомости СНД и ВС РСФСР (1991), no. 30, item 1013, as amended 24 June 1992.

[42] Ведомости СНД и ВС РСФСР (1992), no. 16, item 836; the Code was amended on 7 July 1993.

[43] СЗ РФ (1995), no. 18, item 1589, as amended; transl. in Butler, note 2 above.

version,[44] and on 24 July 2002, with effect from 1 September 2002, the third Code of Arbitrazh Procedure was adopted.[45]

The system of arbitrazh courts comprised the Supreme Arbitrazh Court of the Russian Federation, the federal arbitrazh courts of precincts (of which there are ten), and the arbitrazh courts of the subjects of the Federation.

In autumn 1996 fourteen arbitrazh courts began to experiment with arbitrazh assessors, individual non-lawyers at least 25 years of age, Russian citizens with experience in entrepreneurial or economic activity but who were not judges. Although the results of the experiment were reportedly mixed, the scheme evidently was successful and led to the adoption of the Federal Law on Arbitrazh Assessors of Arbitrazh Courts of Subjects of the Russian Federation, of 30 May 2001, as amended.[46] Such assessors must be citizens of the Russian Federation who have attained 25 years of age, with an irreproachable reputation, have a higher vocational education and work experience of not less than five years in the sphere of economic, financial, legal, management, or entrepreneurial activity. Upon taking office they are required to swear an oath. Candidacies for appointment are recommended by chambers of commerce and industry and associations of entrepreneurs or other professional associations, the Lists being subject to confirmation by the Plenum of the Supreme Arbitrazh Court of the Russian Federation and the names published in the official publication of that Court. There were to be no less than two arbitrazh assessors for each arbitrazh judge who considers cases at first instance. Arbitrazh assessors serve for two years and are subject to reappointment. Remuneration is based on a formula that takes into account the number of days worked and local levels of remuneration.

All arbitrazh courts are federal courts, even those organized at the level of subjects of the Russian Federation. Accordingly, all judicial appointments to arbitrazh courts are regulated by federal laws and not by legislation of the subjects of the Federation. The Chairman of the Supreme Arbitrazh Court was appointed to office by the Soviet of the Federation upon the recommendation of the President of the Russian Federation. The same procedure applied to the deputy chairmen and other judges of the Supreme Arbitrazh Court, except that in this instance the Chairman of the Supreme Court makes recommendations for appointment to the President of Russia. The other arbitrazh court judges are appointed in accordance with the 1996 Law on the Judicial System.

[44] СЗ РФ (1995), no. 19, item 1709, as amended. Changes were made in the 1995 Code by Decree of the Constitutional Court of the Russian Federation, 3 February 1998 and Ruling of the same Court of 14 January 2000. See respectively СЗ РФ (1998), no. 6, item 784; (2000), no. 10, item 1165.

[45] СЗ РФ (2002), no 30, item 3012, as amended; transl. in W. E. Butler, *Russian Civil and Arbitrazh Procedure* (2012), pp. 1-400.

[46] СЗ РФ (2001), no. 23, item 2288, as amended; transl. in Butler, note 2 above.

An arbitrazh court considered cases within its jurisdiction in which Russian citizens or organizations are parties, and also foreign organizations, organizations with foreign investments, international organizations, foreign citizens or stateless persons who are effectuating entrepreneurial activity, unless provided otherwise by an international treaty of the Russian Federation. Although commonly called "commercial" or "economic" courts in foreign language doctrinal writings because a considerable measure of their activity arose out of entrepreneurial relations, the arbitrazh courts had jurisdiction over matters which goes far beyond the ordinary understanding of "commercial". The jurisdiction of the courts set out in the 2002 Code of Arbitrazh Procedure (Article 27) speaks of "economic disputes". Examples of such are: disagreements relating to a contract which according to a law must be concluded or with regard to which the parties have agreed to submit to an arbitrazh court; the change of the conditions or dissolution of contracts; failure to perform or improper performance of obligations, recognition of the right of ownership, vindication suits, compensation of losses, defense of honor, dignity, and business reputation, deeming 'non-normative' acts of State agencies, local self-government, and other agencies to be invalid if they are contrary to laws and other normative legal acts and violate the rights and legal interests of citizens, deeming a writ of execution or other document to be not subject to execution in an uncontested proceeding; appeals against a refusal of State registration or evasion thereof, or against the recovery of fines, the establishment of legal facts having significance for the arising, change, or termination of the rights of organizations and citizens in the sphere of entrepreneurial and other economic activity, and others. In certain instances the arbitrazh courts may hear cases of formations which are not juridical persons and natural persons who are not entrepreneurs. The Code of Arbitrazh Procedure must be read together with decrees of the Plenum of the Supreme Arbitrazh Court construing its application.

The principles upon which the arbitrazh courts function are legality, independence of judges, equality of organizations and citizens before the law, adversarialness and equality of the parties, and openness of the examination of cases (Article 6, 1995 Law on Arbitrazh Courts). To these the 2002 Code of Arbitrazh Procedure adds directness (Article 10), glasnost (Article 11), and national language of court proceeding (Article 12).

The principle of collegiality operated differently in the arbitrazh courts. Cases at first instance were heard by a single judge except those involving bankruptcy, or declaring the acts of State agencies or agencies of local self-government to be invalid, or cases returned for new consideration or within the jurisdiction of the Supreme Arbitrazh Court, in which event three judges hear the case. By choice of the parties a judge and two arbitrazh assessors may hear a case. Openness means that persons present in the courtroom may take notes, keep a verbatim transcript, or record the proceedings on tape without the permission of the court. Permission is required for making videos, cinema films, and broadcast of the proceedings by radio or television.

The internal structure of the arbitrazh courts is similar in key respects with that of the courts of ordinary jurisdiction. The Supreme Arbitrazh Court consists of the Plenum, the Presidium, and two judicial divisions, one for disputes arising from civil and other legal relations and the second for disputes arising from administrative legal relations. The Plenum consists of the Chairman, deputy chairmen, and all judges of the Supreme Arbitrazh Court. Deputies from the Federal Assembly, the chairmen of the Constitutional Court and the Supreme Court, the Procurator General, the Minister of Justice, judges of arbitrazh courts, legal scholars, and others may be invited to take part in Plenum sessions. The Plenum is concerned principally with organizational matters, legislative initiative, referral of questions to the Constitutional Court, choosing members of the judicial divisions, confirming the Reglament of arbitrazh courts and the permanent sites of federal arbitrazh courts, and the like.

The Presidium of the Supreme Arbitrazh Court consisted of the Chairman, deputy chairman, and chairmen of the judicial divisions, together with individual judges who may be elected by the Plenum. It is the Presidium which considered cases by way of supervision upon protests against judicial acts of arbitrazh courts which had entered into legal force. The judicial divisions consider cases at first instance, study and generalize judicial practice, make proposals to improve legislation, analyze forensic statistics, among other functions. Within each judicial division so-called benches of judges were organized to hear cases. A Council of the Chairmen of Arbitrazh Courts, consisting of the chairmen of all arbitrazh courts in the Russian Federation, acted as a consultative organ to advise on organizational, personnel, and financial matters. There was also a Scientific-Consultative Council composed of leading legal scholars and practitioners attached to the Supreme Arbitrazh Court. In 1997 the Supreme Arbitrazh Court organized a sector of private international law to analyze systematically the consideration of cases with the participation of foreign persons; this sector played a key role in persuading the Russian Federation to ratify the Hague civil procedural conventions.

The ten federal arbitrazh courts of precincts had no plenums but did have a presidium and the same judicial divisions as the Supreme Arbitrazh Court. The term "precinct" in this instance referred to administrative-territorial combinations formed for the sole purposes of the arbitrazh courts; each "precinct" incorporated a number of geographic administrative-territorial divisions of the Russian Federation. They acted purely as a cassational instance and sat collegially with an uneven number of judges.

The remaining arbitrazh courts were organized along analogous lines, having regard to the number of judges in each. The Reglament adopted by the Supreme Arbitrazh Court governed internal organizational matters of the entire court system and relationships among the courts.

The Supreme Arbitrazh Court issued decrees based on summaries of judicial practice which were and remain binding upon lower arbitrazh courts until they are replaced or repealed. In exceptional instances these were issued jointly with the Supreme Court of the Russian Federation. The monthly Вестник Высшего арбитражного суда Российской Федерации [Herald of Supreme Arbitrazh Court of Russian Federation] was widely regarded as the best of all court gazettes, containing not merely relevant legislation, court decrees, and judicial decisions, but also comparative materials from other CIS jurisdictions and learned articles.

Current Legislation

Under the 2014 Law on the Supreme Court of the Russian Federation, cases previously heard by the arbitrazh courts fall within the jurisdiction of the courts of general jurisdiction, as reformed under the 2014 Law, and rise up, when necessary, to the Judicial Division for Economic Disputes of the Supreme Court. Judges within the systems of courts of arbitrazh courts and courts of general jurisdiction at the time of the reforms between 15 February 2014 and 1 September 2014 were entitled to seek reappointment within the newly unified system, or take early retirement. In the case of reappointment, each individual judge was required to pass through the qualifications commissions and, in effect, be reattested for judicial office.

In 2016 arbitrazh court judges considered on average 67.88 cases per month. In that same year 4,319 arbitrazh court judges considered 3,008,000 cases. Some Russian critics have called this "conveyor justice"; judges cope by becoming more productive and reducing the time needed to consider a case. For the calendar year 2019, arbitrazh courts of subjects of the Russian Federation received 2,124,000 petitions to sue, an increase of 1.2% over 2018. The greatest share related to disputes arising out of civil law relations (59.4%); those relating to administrative and other public law relations fell by 5.8% in comparison with 2018. Bankruptcy proceedings were up by 52.6% in 2019 over the preceding year, with debtors seeking relief in notable numbers.[47]

Court for Intellectual Rights. On 6 December 2011 Russian legislation was amended to authorize the establishment of a Court for Intellectual Rights as a specialized arbitrazh court,[48] which was to commence operations no later than 1 February 2013. The principal rationale for creating a specialized court within the specialized arbitrazh court system was the complexity and

47 See Обзор судебной статистики о деятельности федеральных арбитражных судов в 2019 году [Survey of Judicial Statistics on the Activity of Federal Arbitrazh Courts in 2019] (Moscow, 2020).

48 For the amending legislation, see СЗ РФ (2011), no. 50, item 7334.

technical nature of intellectual property cases and the need for specialist judges to consider them.

Foreign experience with such courts was examined; the principal models were Germany and Japan. Nonetheless, Russian specialists consider the court ultimately structured to be "… unique, without world analogies".[49] Judges on this court must be at least 30 years of age and have at least seven years work experience; applications for judgeships were opened on 13 July 2012. 33 individuals applied, of which 21 were selected – 19 as judges and two as personnel of the apparatus of the Court. A separate competition was held for the Chairman of the Court, to which L. A. Noveselova was appointed.

The Court has an unusual legal status. It is simultaneously a court of first instance and a cassational instance. As a court of cassation, it considers cases decided by its judges at first instance as well as cases considered by arbitrazh courts of subjects of the Russian Federation and arbitrazh appellate courts. Cases heard at first instance include:

(1) cases contesting normative legal acts of federal agencies of executive power affecting the rights and legal interests of the application in the domain of the legal protection of the results of intellectual activity and means of individualization, including patent rights and rights to selection achievements, topologies of integral microcircuits, rights to production secrets (know-how), rights to the means of individualization of juridical persons, goods, work, services, and enterprises, and the right to use the results of intellectual activity within a single technology;

(2) cases concerning the granting or termination of legal protection to the results of intellectual activity and means of individualization equated thereto of juridical persons, goods, work, services, and enterprises, excluding objects of author's and neighboring rights, and topologies of microcircuits, with a non-exhaustive enumeration of examples given. Some Russian jurists believe the jurisdiction of the Court for Intellectual Rights should be set out in an exhaustive formulation, but that view has so far been rejected.

The Code of the Russian Federation on Administrative Violations also gives the Court for Intellectual Rights jurisdiction over certain matters.

Cases are decided by a collegial bench of judges at first instance. Proposals to invited intellectual property "specialists" to participate in deciding cases would have required a constitutional amendment and were therefore rejected as inadvisable. However, the Court may submit queries to

[49] S. S. Popova, «Проблемы становления Суда по интеллектуальным правам в России» [Problems of the Development of the Court for Intellectual Rights in Russia], Имущественные отношения в РФ [Property Relations in the Russian Federation], no. 6 (2013), p. 97.

specialists with a view to obtaining explanations or advice from individual or institutions having special knowledge. Such queries are binding upon all to whom they are addressed.

In 2019 at first instance the Court for Intellectual Rights considered 791 economic disputes and other cases arising out of civil-law, administrative, and other public-law relations. Of these, 21.4% were considered with the participation of foreign persons. 96.1% of the cases concerned the granting or termination of the legal protection of intellectual activity and means of individualization (excluding author's and neighboring rights and topologies of integral microsystems), and of these, 38.9% concerned the termination of a trademark for failure to use.

By way of cassation the Court for Intellectual Rights considered 1,700 cases, of which 75.7% were appeals against judicial acts adopted by courts of subjects of the Russian Federation and arbitrazh appellate courts, and 24.3% against judicial acts adopted by the Court for Intellectual Rights at first instance or cassational rulings adopted by the Court. In all 332 judicial acts were vacated, of which 263 emanated from cases considered at first instance by the Court.

OTHER TRIBUNALS

For some brief months in 1993 an Arbitral Information Court was formed on an experimental basis to consider disputes arising out of access to or reports published in the mass media during the election campaign of that year. The mandate of the Court expired on 31 December 1993. In its place the Judicial Chamber for Information Disputes was created and existed from 1994 to 1996, issuing 103 decisions, nine recommendations, 20 expert opinions, 15 statements, and one ruling.[50]

PROCURACY

History

The Procuracy is a Russian institution whose precise origins await definitive study. Peter the Great created the office of 'fiskal' on 2 March 1711 with supervisory functions in treasury matters and is known to have studied carefully French and Swedish institutions analogous in nature. It is, however, to the classical Petrine model of procurator established by an Edict of 12 January 1722[51] to which the modern Russian Procuracy traces its direct origins. The Russian Procuracy marked its 275th anniversary in

[50] For details, see Butler, *Russian Law* (2d ed., 2003), pp. 171-172.

[51] For the text, see K. A. Sofronenko (ed.), Памятники русского права [Monuments of Russian Law] (1961), VII, pp. 172-174. To commemorate this date the President of the Russian Federation by an Edict of 7 June 1996 declared 12 January to be "Procurator's Day" in Russia. СЗ РФ (1996), no. 24, item 2876.

1997 with the publication of a monumental jubilee volume containing the biographies of the principal procurators from the beginning to 1917.[52]

In Peter the Great's concept, the procurator was an official independent of local influence who acted as the "eye of the Tsar"[53] in supervising the conformity to law of the actions of all State departments, officials, and courts, including the Ruling Senate itself. Subordinate procurators were authorized to submit "proposals" to local officials who violated the law and to present "protests and reports" regarding violations to superior procurators. In the three years or so of operations until the death of Peter the Great in 1725, the institutions reportedly enjoyed some success.[54] Peter's successors reduced its importance; Catherine II revived the Procuracy in modified form, transforming it into an administrative office rather than a supervisory one. Alexander I in his governmental reorganization of 1802 combined the Procurator General with the Minister of Justice and removed most supervisory powers over State administration. The 1864 judiciary reforms ultimately eliminated these and required procurators to confine their activities to the judicial department. Nevertheless, in the last half-century of Imperial government the procurators did participate as members of certain provincial committees, but without the right of supervision or protest. Prosecution of cases had become their principal function.

The pre-revolutionary Procuracy was abolished by Decree No. 1 "On Courts" of 24 November 1917. The prosecution function was passed initially to the public-spirited or aggrieved citizen. A college of "accusers and defenders" was formed by Decree No. 2 "On Courts", and revolutionary tribunals relied on their own colleges of accusers, to consist of at least three persons for each tribunal selected by the local soviets directly or upon the recommendation of its tribunal or the People's Commissariat of Justice. But these makeshift measures in the end proved to be unworkable. The supervisory functions of the pre-revolutionary Procuracy over justice matters was dispersed to organs of local soviets. One archival source of the period (1918) disclosed that the "Commissar of justice is the representative of central authority in the provinces, replacing the former procurators". Supervisory functions also were exercised by ancillary bodies, the People's Commissariat for State Control and later the People's Commissariat of the Workers'-Peasants' Inspectorate. These too were inadequate, and at Lenin's

[52] See A. G. Zviagintsev and Iu. G. Orlov, Призванные отечеством. Российские прокуроры 1722-1917 [Called by the Fatherland. Russian Procurators 1722-1917] (1997). The same authors have produced seven volumes examining in detail each era of the Procuracy through 1991 inclusive.

[53] This notion has been adapted in a series of six (to date) novels by Paul Watkins, writing under the pseudonym of Sam Eastland, in which Investigator Pekkala is appointed the "Emerald Eye" by Tsar Nicholas II and later Joseph Stalin with unlimited investigative authority.

[54] See D. O. Serov, Прокуратура Петра I (1722-1725 гг.) [Procuracy of Peter I (1722-1725)] (2002).

behest on 28 May 1922, following prolonged debate, the RSFSR instituted the State Procuracy.[55] The original model combined elements of the Petrine and Alexandrine versions: Peter's notions that the Procuracy was to be independent of all local authorities and that it would supervise the legality of acts of all State agencies, enterprises, and citizens through its powers of protest, proposal, and prosecution; Alexander's policy of placing the Procuracy within the People's Commissariat of Justice and making the Commissar simultaneously the Procurator of the Republic. The Procurator appointed all inferior procurators from candidates put forward by central and local agencies; a separate system of military procurators also was subordinate to the Procurator.

Under the 1924 USSR Constitution, an all-union Procuracy was created within the USSR Supreme Court with powers of constitutional, general, and judicial supervision; its powers were elaborated in a Statute of 24 July 1929.[56] In 1933 the Procuracy was reorganized; its role in constitutional supervision was abolished and it was separated from the USSR Supreme Court, but there remained the dual system of the USSR Procuracy and union republic people's commissars of justice acting simultaneously as procurators. The latter found themselves in a position of dual subordination: to the USSR Procurator and to the council of people's commissars of their respective republic. Ultimate centralization of the Procuracy came in 1936 with the formation of the USSR People's Commissariat of Justice and separation of union republic procuracies from that commissariat at all levels. Curiously, this centralization was not followed by new unified legislation. Articles 113 to 117 of the 1936 USSR Constitution became the principal legislative definition of Procuracy powers and functions together with the 1933 Statute. Specialized procuracies for water transport and the railway underwent episodic restructuring in the 1930s, and on 5 November 1936 the structural subdivisions of the Procuracy were reorganized. On 19 March 1946 the Procurator of the USSR was renamed the Procurator General of the USSR. After Stalin's death in 1953 and the abolition of the special boards, it was decided to reinforce rather than to abandon the supervisory role of the Procuracy.

On 12 April 1955 an editorial in *Pravda* called upon the Procuracy to eliminate "serious shortcomings" in its work and criticized the institution for having been "insufficiently principled", not fully taking advantage of the "rights granted to it by the USSR Constitution", not uncovering violations of law at the time, and not stopping the "anti-State activities of individual officials".

[55] СУ РСФСР (1922), no. 36, item 424.

[56] СЗ СССР (1929), no. 50, item 445. On the debates over the revival and powers of the procuracy, see J. N. Hazard, *Settling Disputes in Soviet Society* (1960); G. Morgan, *Soviet Administrative Legality* (1962); S. Kucherov, *The Organs of Soviet Administrative of Justice: Their History and Operation* (1970), pp. 404-447.

The extent to which the Procuracy was a willing collaborator or pawn in Special Board proceedings (Procuracy participation was compulsory under the decree establishing the Boards) has yet to be studied, but it is doubtful that in the political climate of the time that the Procuracy could have effectively altered the course of events when the Communist Party itself was unable, if not unwilling, to do so.[57] On 24 May 1955 the Procuracy received its first comprehensive legislation in the form of the Statute on Procuracy Supervision in the USSR. The Statute enlarged the scope of general supervision by the Procuracy, empowered procurators to demand and obtain data and documents from officials, and elaborated the procurators' powers to make proposals, representations, and protests.

Following the adoption of the 1977 USSR Constitution, legislation on the Procuracy was elevated to the status of a fully-fledged Law on the Procuracy of the USSR, enacted in 1979. The 1979 Law strengthened the qualifications required of those aspiring to be a procurator, enlarged the role of collegial decision-making within Procuracy institutions, and expanded the group of State agencies and institutions who were subject to Procuracy supervision. Amendments to the 1979 Law introduced in 1987 conferred on procurators the right to issue a written instruction and a caution in addition to their usual armory of recommendations, protests, and other means of recourse.

During the late years of *perestroika* in the Soviet Union, the Procuracy experienced further transformation, mostly linked to the transition to a market economy and taking the form of international reorganization. For a brief period from 1991 to 1992 the prospect of a CIS Procuracy was entertained, the idea being to transform the Procuracy of the USSR into the Procuracy of the Union of Sovereign States, an inter-republic Procuracy supervision agency which would function on the basis of all-union and republic legislation on the Procuracy. To this end a federal collegium headed by the Procurator General of the CIS was formed; the deputies of the USSR Procurator General and the procurators general of the republics were

[57] Insofar as the institutional foundations are concerned, the evidence is conflicting. The 1933 Statute on the Procuracy contained not a single word about the duty of the Procuracy to defend the rights and legal interests of citizens. A secret Decree of the Council of People's Commissars and Central Committee of the All-Russian Communist Party (Bolshevik) dated 15 June 1935 "On the Procedure for Agreeing Arrests", approved two days later by the Politburo of the Central Committee, provided that all agencies of the People's Commissariat of Internal Affairs (NKVD) without exception could perform arrests only with the sanction of a procurator, and when it was necessary to perform an arrest at the site of the crime, immediately to notify the procurator thereof for confirmation of the arrest. Arrests of senior union republic officials required that the NKVD and the Procuracy obtain the prior authorization of the chairman of the Central Executive Committee of the USSR or chairmen of the union republic central executive committee respectively. The Decree is published, together with others which cast further light on the Procuracy in this era, in V. M. Kuritsyn, История государства и права России 1929-1940 [History of State and Law of Russia 1929-1940] (1998), pp. 116-126.

members of the collegium. Many supervision functions previously handled by specialized procuracies or by the USSR Procuracy were transferred to the republics. These schemes came to naught when the USSR Procuracy ceased to exist upon the dissolution of the Soviet Union on or about 25 December 1991.[58]

Current Legislation

In the Russian Federation the decision to create a unified Russian Procuracy was taken on 15 November 1991 pursuant to the Declaration on State Sovereignty of the RSFSR and Articles 176 and 179 of the 1978 RSFSR Constitution. The Procurator General of the RSFSR accepted jurisdiction over all Procuracy agencies on Russian territory and all institutions formerly associated with the USSR Procuracy, including scientific research institutions. A period of dual subordination commenced in which Procuracy agencies were subordinate to the Procurator General of the republic and to the highest agencies of State power. The Procuracy experienced significant resignations from service, the Procurator General of the RSFSR reporting that his institution was short 1,200 persons on 1 January 1992, and a commensurate decline in prestige and authority.

On 17 January 1992 the RSFSR Supreme Soviet adopted the Law on the Procuracy of the Russian Federation, which, as amended, remains in force.[59]

Structure

True to its Petrine model, the Procuracy is a unified, federal, centralized system of Procuracy agencies and organizations comprising the General Procuracy of the Russian Federation, the procuracies of the 85 subjects of the Russian Federation, the military, transport, nature protection, and other specialized procuracies. Basically there are procuracies at each administrative-territorial level of the Russian Federation, with certain adjustments and terminological variations. The Buriat Republic, for example, has adat procuracies instead of district procuracies, and in Moscow the medium-level link is the procuracies of administrative precincts. Some subjects of the Federation have created "inter-district" procuracies whose jurisdiction extends to two districts. Although the 1993 Russian Constitution and the 1992 Law on the Procuracy emphasize the centralized, federal, and unified nature of the Procuracy, that principle is attenuated by the fact that procurators are appointed to office by the President of the Russian Federation upon the recommendation of the Procurator General of the Russian Federation "agreed with the subjects of the Russian Federation"

[58] On this episode see V. I. Baskov, Курс прокурорского надзора [Course on Procuracy Supervision] (1998), pp. 34-35.

[59] Ведомости СНД РФ и ВС РФ (1992), no. 8, item 366, as amended; transl. in Butler, note 1 above.

in the procedure established by the subject of the Russian Federation and are accountable in some measure to them.

The Investigative Committee attached to the Procuracy of the Russian Federation, introduced in 2007, was spun off into a separate and autonomous agency in 2010 (see below).

The General Procuracy of the Russian Federation is headed by the Procurator General of the Russian Federation who is appointed to office for a five-year term by the President of the Federation after consultations with the Soviet of the Russian Federation. The Procurator must be at least 35 years of age, have a higher legal education from a duly accredited educational organization in the specialty "Jurisprudence", not have foreign citizenship or be deemed by a court to lack dispositive legal capacity or have limited dispositive legal capacity, have or had a record of conviction, or suffer from an illness stipulated in the law, or be in kinship to a stipulated degree with other procuracy personnel and there are relations of subordination involved. The Procurator General has a first deputy procurator and several deputies, all of whom are members of a Collegium, together with other Procuracy personnel appointed by the Procurator General.

The structure of the apparatus of the General Procuracy has been subject to several reorganizations in recent years in connection with changes in the system of federal administration on the territory of the Russian Federation. In the year 2000 administrations of the General Procuracy were formed in seven federal districts, transformed into sections in 2002, and returned to the status of administrations in 2006. There are also support subsections concerned with such matters as correspondence, reception, secretariat, information centers, civil defense, security, and the like. There is a Scientific Advisory Council to assist with questions of the organization and activity of procuracy agencies; its Statute is confirmed by the Procurator General. In 2006 the Scientific Advisory Council included representatives of the Social Chamber of the Russian Federation, Union of Journalists, deputies of the State Duma, representatives of the judicial system, and leading scholars, among others.

The Procurator General directs the activity of Procuracy agencies and supervises their work. He issues four distinct types of subordinate normative act which are binding throughout the Procuracy system: the order (приказ), through which the strategic line for exercising powers of supervision over the execution of laws or other activities of Procuracy agencies is determined; the instructive directive (указание), which elaborates orders of the Procurator General; the regulation (распоряжение), intended to ensure the fulfillment of particular actions by a procurator or investigator; and the instruction (инструкция), which contains directions for the performance of procedural or operational actions, such as statistical reports or the registration of criminal offenses. Within budgetary and personnel establishment limits, he determines the personnel requirements and structure of the General Procuracy and of the procuracies and Procuracy institutions subordinate to him. In particular, he appoints and dismisses all personnel of the General Procuracy and all procurators throughout the entire system (subject to the duty to secure agreement to the appointment of procurators of subjects of the Federation).

The procurators of subjects of the Federation and procurators equated thereto direct the activities of city and district procuracies and other procuracies equated to them and operate on the basis of laws of the Russian Federation and normative acts of the Procurator General. Within their budgets and personnel establishments fixed by the Procurator General, they may make changes in their staffing. The procuracies of subjects of the Federation also have collegiums which consider the activities of Procuracy agencies, fulfill normative acts of the Procurator General relating to powers of supervision, hear reports of the heads of administrations and sections and of inferior procurators, and discuss personnel matters.

Until 2007 several institutions of a research or instructional nature were attached to the General Procuracy. The Scientific-Research Institute for Problems of Strengthening Legality and Legal Order (Moscow) deals with problems of organizing the struggle against crime by exploring the causes of crime and preventative measures. This is the principal institution in Russia concerned with criminology and Procuracy supervision and is a corporate member of the International Criminal Law Association. Procuracy personnel are required to undergo periodic attestation and courses to improve their skills. Such advanced training is conducted principally by the Institute for Raising the Qualifications of Executive Personnel of the General Procuracy of the Russian Federation (Moscow), the Institute for Raising the Qualifications of Procuracy Workers of the General Procuracy (Irkutsk), and the Juridical Institute of the General Procuracy (St Petersburg). Although the Procurator General of the Russian Federation appoints and relieves the directors of these institutions and confirms their statutes or charters, by Regulation of the Government of the Russian Federation of 24 March 2007, No. 345-p, all these institutions have been placed under the unified Academy of the General Procuracy of the Russian Federation.[60] In 2018 the Academy was renamed and became the University of the General Procuracy of the Russian Federation.

The Procuracy publishes its own monthly journal, Законность [Legality], formerly called Социалистическая законность [Socialist Legality].

60 СЗ РФ (2007), no. 14, item 1711.

Procurators

Citizens of the Russian Federation who have a higher legal education and the requisite professional and moral qualities and sound health may be procurators. A probation period of six months is required. Aides of procurators and certain investigative personnel in exceptional cases at city and district level may be persons studying law in institutions of higher vocational education. Age requirements depend upon the level of appointment in the Procuracy system. The minimum is 25 years of age to be appointed procurator of a city or district and at least three years of experience as a procurator or investigator. Procurators of subjects of the Federation must be at least 30 years old. Ranks – there are 11 in all – are conferred on procurators in accordance with the Statute on Class Ranks of Procuracy Workers, confirmed by the President of the Russian Federation. In an effort to attract and retain new recruits and existing personnel, the Law on the Procuracy includes a number of provisions intended to make the career of a procurator more attractive: paid tuition while obtaining a law degree, improved social and housing benefits, special protections against threats to his person or family, and other forms of incentive.

Procuracy workers may not be members of social organizations which pursue political purposes, nor may such organizations be formed within Procuracy agencies and institutions. Nor, recalling the close relationship in the Soviet era between the Communist Party and the Procuracy, may procurators and investigators be bound in their official activities by the decisions of social associations.

Branches of Procuracy Supervision

The supervisory functions of the Procuracy are multifarious and collectively comprise that institution's claim to uniqueness among bodies with analogous objectives in other families of legal systems. The Law on the Procuracy divides the supervision functions into four principal orientations. The first and most important is the Procuracy's power of "general supervision" over the execution of laws by federal ministries, State committees, services, and other federal agencies of executive power, representative (or legislative) and executive agencies of subjects of the Russian Federation, agencies of local self-government, military administration agencies, control agencies, officials thereof, and also over the conformity to laws of legal acts issued by the aforesaid agencies and officials. Acts adopted or issued by these agencies must correspond to the constitutions and other enactments of superior legislative and State agencies and be precisely and uniformly executed by officials and citizens. This formulation makes it clear that the Procuracy is not the supreme guardian of the law; it has no supervisory authority over acts of the Government of the Russian Federation, nor the Federal Assembly, nor the President of the Russian Federation. However, its supervisory authority does extend to the parliamentary and governmental agencies of the subjects of the Russian Federation. Its concern is to ensure that the Russian bureaucracy and citizenry adhere to law and not that the highest agencies of Federation power and administration do so.

The powers of the Procuracy to give effect to general supervision are several. They may personally visit the premises of the objects of supervision to inspect the state of affairs, they have access to materials and documents, and may require the directors and other officials to submit necessary documents, materials, statistical information, and the like, verify materials and appeals submitted to the Procuracy, and conduct an internal audit of the activity or organizations within the control or jurisdiction of the agencies being investigated. If necessary, officials and citizens may be summoned to the Procuracy to offer explanations regarding the violation of laws.

Once a violation of law is established, a procurator may react by submitting a recommendation to eliminate the violation, bring a protest against a legal act which is contrary to a law, or apply to a court to demand that a legal act be deemed to be invalid. If material harm was caused by a violation of law, the procurator may initiate civil proceedings for recovery. A criminal prosecution may be instituted if a crime has been committed, or an administrative proceeding if there was an administrative offense. A person illegally subjected to administrative detention on the basis of a decision of a non-judicial agency may be released upon the decree of a procurator.

In the domain of general supervision a procurator may bring a protest against a legal act which is contrary to a law. The protest is sent to the agency or official which issued the act and is subject to obligatory consideration within ten days from the moment of receipt; if the protest is against the decision of a representative or legislative agency of a subject of the Federation or agency of local self-government, the protest is to be considered at the next session thereof. Under exceptional circumstances requiring the immediate elimination of the violation of a law, the procurator may fix a shorter period for consideration of the protest. The filing of a protest does not mean the agency which issued the act must necessarily accept the protest. Its obligation is to consider the protest and the reasons for it; if it disagrees with the protest, the protest may be rejected, in which event the procurator may pursue the matter by carrying his protest to the next level of the Procuracy. Whether the protest is accepted or not, the results of the protest must be communicated to the procurator at once in written form. If the protest is considered by a collegial agency, the procurator who brought the protest must be informed about the date of the session and has the right to be present. A protest may be recalled by the person who brought it before consideration of the protest commences.

Although the Procuracy may not protest decrees of the Government or laws of the Federal Assembly which are contrary to the Russian Constitution, the Procurator General does have the right to bring such inconsistencies to the attention of the President of the Russian Federation. If a violation of law justifies the initiation of a criminal or administrative proceeding, the procurator's decree must be considered by the relevant agency or official within the period established by legislation and the results of the consideration communicated in written form.

New to the Procuracy is the category of supervision over compliance with the rights and freedoms of man and citizen. In exercising this function the procurator considers and verifies applications, appeals, and other communications concerning a violation of such rights, explains to victims the procedure for defending those rights and freedoms, takes measures to prevent or suppress such violations, and initiates proceedings against persons who have violated the law in this connection and seeks compensation for damage caused. If a criminal act has been committed, the Procuracy may institute a criminal proceeding, and if an administrative offense, either institute an administrative proceeding or bring the materials of the verification to the agency or official empowered to consider an administrative proceeding.

If a violation of the rights of man or citizen requires defense in a civil proceeding and the victim by reason of health, age, or other reasons cannot personally defend those rights in a court, or if the rights and freedoms of a significant number of citizens have been violated or for other reasons such violation takes on great social importance, the procurator has standing to bring a civil suit in a court of general jurisdiction in the interests of the victims. A protest may be brought by a procurator or his deputy against an act violating the rights of man and citizen to the agency or official which issued it. A recommendation to eliminate violations of rights and freedoms may be submitted by the procurator or his deputy to the agency or official empowered to eliminate the violation. All other procuratorial powers are available, as appropriate, which procurators possess when exercising general supervision.

The third branch of Procuracy supervision relates to execution of the laws by agencies effectuating operational search activities, inquiry, or, to a lesser extent in the light of reforms introduced in 2007, preliminary investigation. The Procuracy's powers are considerable in the domain of operational search and inquiry activities, significantly reduced with respect to the preliminary investigation because of the creation in 2007 of the Investigative Committee referred to above, and virtually eliminated with the formation in 2010 of the Investigative Committee as an autonomous entity.

The Procuracy's powers with regard to operational-search activities are narrower. A procurator may demand to see documents relating to such operations and may give instructions to operational-search agencies about taking measures relating to cases under investigative proceedings. He also may demand the termination of illegal or unsubstantiated operational-search measures or repeal related decrees which he considers not to correspond to legislation. A number of his powers available under general supervision may be used in connection with operational-search measures: protest, recommendations, initiating administrative and criminal proceedings, and others.

The fourth branch of Procuracy supervision concerns institutions where individuals may be confined or detained, ranging from preliminary confinement to imprisonment or compulsory medical treatment. The procurator is to ensure that legislation regarding the treatment of confined persons is complied with by visiting places of confinement systematically and at any time, familiarize himself with relevant documentation, release immediately persons illegally confined, questions detained or confined persons, and verify the conformity to law of orders, regulations, and decrees issued by the administrations of places of confinement.

The plurality of roles which the Procuracy faces can raise conflicts of interests, especially when the procurator must act as accuser on behalf of the State yet initiate objections to procedural or substantive violations by the court. To some extent conflicts are avoided or reduced by depersonalizing the conflict. Different committees, administrations, or sections of the Procuracy are concerned with different types of supervision, or investigation, or other activities. The essence of the Procuracy function is to persuade agencies to correct their own errors; except in certain aspects of inquiries and preliminary investigations, the Procuracy itself has no administrative power to set affairs in order by itself.

In addition to supervision, the Procuracy performs a number of other functions. The best known is that associated with the very name of the institution: acting on behalf of the State to prosecute criminal cases in Russian courts. The 2001 Code of Criminal Procedure introduced the term "criminal prosecution", which may, depending upon the character and gravity of the crime committed, be pursued in a public, private-public, or private procedure. The procurator now appears in the most serious cases, as enumerated in the Code of Criminal Procedure, at the trial stage in the role of State accuser. In civil cases the procurator may appear to defend the rights of citizens and interests of the State and society, and in so doing may familiarize himself with the materials of the file of the case, take part in investigating evidence, submit evidence, and offer opinions to the court regarding the substance of the case. Appearances in civil proceedings are uncommon, however, and usually confined to special circumstances.

If after the court considers a case the procurator comes to the view that judicial error has occurred, he is obliged to take measures to eliminate such error by bringing a cassational or private protest to the next higher court.

Most significantly, a procurator has the right to demand and obtain the file of any case from a court, or any category of cases, and to bring a protest by way of supervision against a decision, judgment, ruling, or decree which has entered into legal force and in the view of the procurator is contrary to law. The decision of a judge in an administrative proceeding also may be protested by the procurator. Exceptionally, the Procuracy has protested judicial decisions relating to the enforcement of arbitration awards.

The Law on the Procuracy expressly provides for the right of the Procurator General of the Russian Federation to have recourse to the Constitutional Court of the Russian Federation in connection with a violation of the constitutional rights and freedoms of citizens by a law being applied or subject to application in a specific case. The Federal Constitutional Law on the Constitutional Court of the Russian Federation makes no mention of the right of the Procuracy to apply to it, although in a Decree of 18 July 2003 the Constitutional Court did affirm the power of the Procurator General to apply to the Court with a query concerning a verification of the conformity of constitutions and charters of subjects of the Russian Federation to the 1993 Russian Constitution.

As of 2018 constitutional or charter courts were functioning in most subjects of the Russian Federation. Not all had made provision for procurators to take part in a constitutional or charter court proceeding. Many observers continue to believe that on the whole "procuracy agencies still rarely use the extensive possibilities granted to them by regional legislation to influence the quality of forming regional legal space and the legality and effectiveness of law-application".[61]

Specialized Procuracies

There exist two types of specialized procuracies in the Russian Federation which act with the rights of regional or district procuracies. The first type comprises military and transport procuracies or procuracies of military units. These perform the full range of functions in the respective spheres of legal relations which are placed on the procuracy. The second type consists of nature protection procuracies and procuracies for supervision over the execution of laws in correctional institutions. Neither type is intended to replace the activities of territorially-based procuracies as the principal element of the procuracy system.

[61] V. P. Riabtsev, in A. Ia. Sukharev (ed.), Прокурорский надзор [Procuracy Supervision] (2d ed.; 2008), p. 407.

Supervision over the precise and uniform execution of the laws in the Armed Forces of Russia is effectuated by military procuracies. The Military Procuracy constitutes a separate integral system, the highest organ of which is the Chief Military Procuracy within the General Procuracy of the Russian Federation. The Chief Military Procurator is a deputy of the Procurator General. The hierarchical structure of the Military Procuracy corresponds to the system of organizing the Armed Forces themselves and includes: Chief Military Procurator, military procuracies of military districts, fleets, strategic missile forces, border service of the Federal Security Service, Moscow City Military Procuracy, and other military procuracies equated to procuracies of subjects of the Russian Federation, and so on. The lowest level is the procuracies of garrisons and formations.

The Military Procuracy is governed by the Law on the Procuracy and by the Statute on the Military Procuracy confirmed by Edict of the Presidium of the USSR Supreme Soviet of 4 August 1981.[62] Its basic functions include taking measures to prevent violations of law, to enhance military discipline, combat readiness, and State security, to ensure that Russian legislation is correctly and uniformly applied, to protect the rights and legal interests of military servicemen and their families, workers and employees of the Armed Forces, and other citizens or military units, institutions, enterprises, and organizations. The supervisory powers of the Military Procuracy extend to ensuring that all military personnel execute the law when performing their duties; that military courts comply with legality when considering civil and criminal cases; and that legality is observed in guardhouses and disciplinary battalions. The ability of military procurators to demand data and information is more limited than their civilian counterparts, but they may obtain orders, instructions, and other acts to verify their conformity to law, conduct on-the-spot verifications, but only in connection with applications, appeals, or other information concerning violations, and demand explanations from officials, military servicemen, and other citizens.

The Transport Procuracy first appeared in the former Soviet Union during the 1920s; they were abolished in 1960 and revived in 1977, being subordinate directly to the union republic procurators. In 1980 the system was strengthened and extended to railway, air, and water transport. Severely criticized in 1987 for being sensitive to local interests, they nonetheless were retained and found their role in the post-Soviet period. In 2001 the

[62] Ведомости ВС СССР (1981), no. 32, item 956. The 1981 Statute occupies an unusual place in Russian legislation. Technically it has not lost force, but cannot be applied because confirmation of the Statute arose from Article 12 of the Law on the Procuracy of the USSR, which has lost force. See A. Iu. Vinokurov, «Привлечение прокурором специалиста при проведении проверки исполнения закона: история вопроса» [Enlistment by a Procurator of a Specialist When Conducting a Verification of the Execution of a Law: History of the Question], Административное и муниципальное право [Administrative and Municipal Law], no. 9 (2017), pp. 50-63.

centralized system of transport procuracies was abolished, and they functioned with the rights of inter-district procuracies, being subordinate to the procurator of the subject of the Russian Federation where located. Starting in December 2006 the process of reinstating the previous system was undertaken. The transport procuracies are concerned with supervision over the execution of laws on a particular railway line or sector thereof, or port, or air terminal.

Nature protection procuracies are of two types: those with the rights of procuracies of subjects of the Russian Federation and operating throughout a particular object of nature protection; and nature protection procuracies in subjects of the Federation with the rights of inter-district procuracies. They concentrate upon ecological violations: pollution, waste of natural resources, and the like. Their powers of supervision concentrate upon the protection of the natural environment, the activities of nature protection agencies, enterprises, institutions, organizations, and officials. An example of the first type is the Volga Nature Protection Procuracy. The objects under the supervisory jurisdiction of the Volga Procuracy are agreed with the procuracies of the republic and regions through which the Volga River flows. The Volga Nature Protection Procuracy is concerned with the execution of laws throughout the entire Volga River Basin and has 15 inter-district procuracies within it.

The reference to "other" procuracies found in many Russian textbooks includes the so-called procuracies of the "Second Administration of the General Procuracy". These originated in the Edict of the Presidium of the Supreme Soviet of the USSR, adopted 1 June 1979, "On Courts, Procuracy, Advokatura, Notariat, and Internal Affairs Agencies Operating at Special Regime Objects".[63] These procuracies were formed in order to protect State secrecy of and ensure the established regime of secrecy in special regime objects, a list of which was established by the Government of the former Soviet Union. The legal status of such procuracies was equated to procurators of cities or districts, and they were directly subordinate to the Procurator General of the Russian Federation. In 2001 the centralized system of procuracies of force systems which operated at special defense objects, basically in closed administrative-territorial formations, was abolished and the procuracies concerned transferred directly to the jurisdiction of procurators of subjects of the Russian Federation.

[63] The Edict was classified at the time of enactment, but published during perestroika by reason of the Opinion of the Constitutional Supervision Committee of the USSR "On Rules Permitting the Application of Unpublished Normative Acts on the Rights and Freedoms of Citizens", issued 29 November 1990. See Ведомости СНД и ВС СССР (1991), no. 10 for the 1979 Edict, which remains in force. For the Opinion of the Constitutional Supervision Committee, see ibid. (1990), no. 50, item 1080.

Procuracies created for supervision over the execution of laws in correctional institutions first appeared in 1983. They act with the rights of district procuracies and may extend their jurisdiction to a territory occupied by several institutions for deprivation of freedom. They are subordinate to the procurators of the respective subjects of the Russian Federation.

It is prohibited to create procuracies which are not within the unified system of the General Procuracy of the Russian Federation. The competence of territorial, military, and other specialized procuracies is delimited in detail, sometimes with reference to individually named specialized procuracies, in the Order of the General Procuracy of the Russian Federation of 7 May 2008, No. 84, "On Delimitation of the Competence of Procurators of Territorial, Military, and Other Specialized Procuracies", as amended.[64]

NOTARIAT

History

In mediaeval Russia notarial functions were performed by the senior clerks [подьячие]. The 1649 *Sobornoe Ulozhenie* permitted only minor transactions to be concluded without notarial recording: in particular, transactions transferring immoveable property were drawn up and entered in special books by these officials and a State duty recovered for the service. Peter the Great placed this function on special scribes who were attached to the chancelleries of governors and justice colleges. In 1866 the Statute on the Notariat was adopted; it attached notaries to the courts, determined their competence, and laid down the procedures for performing notarial actions. It was the Statute of 1866 which was overtaken by the 1917 October Revolution.

The Decree No 1 "On Courts" of 24 November 1917 omitted to mention the Notariat among the Imperial legal institutions being abolished. The Moscow Council of People's Commissars repealed on 23 March 1918 the "presently prevailing Statute on the Notarial Office" and municipalized all notarial offices. Local practices varied, but the general pattern was initially for local city soviets to open notarial offices. A Circular of the RSFSR People's Commissariat to eliminate these and distribute their functions among other agencies was not implemented; instead notarial "tables" operated in some cities attached to the judicial-investigative subsections of provincial justice sections or local people's courts. The exigencies of the NEP required some offices to certify legal transactions and verify their conformity to law. Despite some reluctance within the People's Commissariat of Justice, "Theses on the Notariat" were published for discussion early in 1922, and on 4 October 1922 the RSFSR Statute on the State Notariat was enacted, superseded on 7 July 1923 by a new version incorporating elements introduced by the

[64] Unpublished, but available on Consultant Plus.

1923 RSFSR Code of Civil Procedure. Divergences among the legislation of several union republics on the subject contributed to the adoption on 14 May 1926 of an all-union decree "On the Basic Principles of Organizing the State Notariat". On 4 October 1926 the RSFSR introduced a new Statute on the State Notariat of the RSFSR, succeeded successively by statutes of 20 July 1930, 31 December 1947, 30 September 1965, and 2 August 1974, as amended. The last Statute operated on the basis of the USSR Law on the State Notariat adopted 19 July 1973, which lost force when the Soviet Union was dissolved.

Current Legislation

The 1993 Russian Constitution (Article 72(k)) placed the Notariat within the joint jurisdiction of the Federation and the subjects of the Federation. On 11 February 1993 the Russian Federation adopted the Fundamental Principles of Legislation of the Russian Federation on the Notariat, introducing significant reforms reflecting the transition to a market economy.[65] These reforms are best expressed by the simple removal of the word "State" from the title of Russian legislation regulating the Notariat. The 1993 reforms introduced two notariats: the private notarial office and the State notarial office. Their functions are now identical as from 1 January 2015. The principal difference between them was that State notaries are salaried by the State and transfer the entire duties and fees for performing notarial actions to the State budget, whereas the private notary recovers the notarial tariff fee for his or her services which remains entirely with the notary, less deductions for taxes, other obligatory payments, and all overhead expenses for operating the private notarial practice. Where notarial action is obligatory, both State and private notaries charge the same tariff fixed by the State; otherwise, the fee is charged in accordance with a scale laid down in the Fundamental Principles. The private notary often being able to give more efficient and expeditious service than the State notarial office.[66]

The Fundamental Principles expressly contemplate that subjects of the Federation may enact their own laws on the Notariat, which must be consistent with the Fundamental Principles. In addition to the Fundamental Principles, notaries also are guided by a body of other legislative acts and by Instructions issued by the Russian Ministry of Justice. Among the major documents of this nature is the Instruction on the Procedure for Performing Notarial Actions by Heads of Local Administrations of Settlements and

[65] Ведомости СНД и ВС РФ (1993), no. 10, item 357, as amended; transl. in Butler, note 2 above.

[66] This remains controversial in Russian legal doctrine. Some deplore competition amongst notaries in private practice, arguing that all notaries are officials who perform notarial actions in the name of the State. See V. N. Argunov, in V. P. Bozhev (ed.)., Правоохранительные органы Российской Федерации. Учебник [Law Enforcement Agencies of the Russian Federation. Textbook] (2nd ed.; 1997), p. 327. This position is not consistent with the view that notaries act solely in the interests of their clients.

Specially-Empowered Officials of Local Self-Government of Settlements, Heads of Local Administrations of Municipal Districts, and Specially-Empowered Officials of Local Self-Government of Municipal Districts, confirmed 6 June 2017, No. 97, and in force from 27 June 2017,[67] and the Methods Recommendations With Regard to the Performance of Individual Types of Notarial Actions by Notaries of the Russian Federation, confirmed by Order of the Ministry of Justice of the Russian Federation No. 91, on 15 March 2000.[68]

The City of Moscow, in its capacity as a subject of the Federation, abolished the State Notariat in 1999; all notaries came to be called notaries of the city of Moscow without being divided into those working in State notarial offices and notaries engaging in private practice. As of 1 October 2020, there were about 1003 notaries in Moscow, all combined into the Moscow City Chamber. In Russia as a whole there are more than 12,149 private notaries and nine State notaries. The great majority continue to be women.

Citizens of the Russian Federation who have a higher legal education from an educational institution of higher education duly accredited by the State and who have no less than five years experience in a legal specialty, who are at least 25 years of age and no older than 70 years, and who have passed a qualifications examination may be notaries. A notary engaging in private practice must be a member of the notarial chamber in the subject of the Russian Federation where notarial activity is engaged in by this individual.[69]

A private notary not only has the right, but has the positive duty to maintain a notarial office. The office must be a premise in a non-housing fund and may be either owned or leased by the notary. It must contain a waiting room, a room for the secretary of the notary, and a notary's office. These minimum requirements are considered essential to maintain the confidentiality of notarial actions. The private notary may not form a juridical person, but also being prohibited from engaging in entrepreneurial activity, is not registered as an entrepreneur. Nonetheless, a private notary has the right to open settlement, deposit, current, hard currency, and other accounts. Accounts with clients may be settled in cash or non-cash remittance. The deposit account is a client account in which the monies are held to be transferred as the client instructs. Private notaries are required

[67] Российская газета [Russian Newspaper], no. 133 (2017).

[68] Available on Consultant Plus.

[69] Compulsory membership in such notarial chambers was challenged in the Constitutional Court of the Russian Federation by notaries who wished to form parallel chambers. The Court determined that compulsory membership was a legitimate exercise of legislative power in establishing professional notarial qualifications. See Decree of the Constitutional Court of the Russian Federation, 19 May 1998, No. 15-П.

to carry insurance to cover professional negligence; policies are arranged through the notarial chamber. If the insured amount is insufficient to cover the damage caused, recourse must be against the notary him or herself in court under the usual procedures. Russian law does not consider notaries to be fiduciaries, that concept in its Anglo-American meaning being absent in Russian law.

A private notary may conclude labor contracts with workers, while withholding income tax and making all necessary obligatory payments for pensions, medical insurance, and the like. It is estimated that the introduction of private notaries has created more than 30,000 jobs in the Russian Federation.

Notaries were initially licensed in the Russian Federation and required to undergo an apprenticeship. The procedure for issuing licenses to notaries was established by the Ministry of Justice of the Russian Federation. The Federal Registration Service issued licenses to newly-qualified notaries after the candidate passed the qualifications examination on the basis of the decision of the qualifications commission. The Administrative Reglament of the Ministry of Justice of the Russian Federation for the Provision of State Service with Regard to the Issuance of a License for the Right of Notarial Activity, confirmed by Order of the Ministry of Justice of the Russian Federation, on 29 November 2011, governed the procedure for issuing licenses until its repeal.[70]

The apprenticeship has been redesigned to prepare a law graduate to sit the qualification examination. The procedure for the apprenticeship is determined by the Ministry of Justice jointly with the Federal Notarial Chamber, as is the number of apprentices to be accepted annually. The apprenticeship lasts for one calendar year with a notary who has a private practice and at least three years experience as a notary. By way of exception, the period of apprenticeship may be reduced to six months.

Since 1 July 2015 the arrangements for the qualification examinations have been altered. Russian consular and local administrative officials who act as notaries are not required to sit the notarial examination. The examination is given online anonymously with anonymous verification of the results. The questions which may appear on the examination are placed in advance of the website of the Federal Notarial Chamber. Individuals who are successful on the examination have three years to find employment as a notary and may be required to resit the examination if they fail to do so.

[70] Российская газета [Russian Newspaper], 28 December 2011. Available on Consultant Plus. This document was repealed by Order of the Ministry of Justice on 29 June 2015, No. 154, and extends to legal relations which arose after its entry into force on 11 July 2015. The Administrative Reglament has apparently not been replaced.

The qualification examinations are administered by a qualification commission attached to the territorial justice agency. Decisions relating to the examination by a qualification commission may be appealed to an appeals commission. The appeals commission is formed and attached to the Ministry of Justice jointly with the Federal Notarial Chamber; the decision of the commission may be appealed to a court within a month from its being rendered.

The numbers of notaries are regulated by taking into account a variety of factors. The Ministry of Justice and the Federal Notarial Chamber jointly determine whether to institute or eliminate the post of notary and the number of notaries in each notarial precinct. Once the decision has been taken with respect to numbers, an open competition is held amongst individuals to fill the available positions. The notarial precincts correspond more or less to the administrative-territorial structure of the Russian Federation. Although a notary is not required to reside in her notarial precinct, her office must be opened in the precinct designated. A private notary may resign or be deprived of the powers to be a notary by decision of a court because of being convicted of an intentional crime, or being held to lack or to be limited in dispositive legal capacity, upon the petition of a notarial chamber for repeated disciplinary offences, a violation of legislation, or being unable by reason of health to perform her professional duties. A State notary may be dismissed in accordance with labor legislation of the Russian Federation.

State notarial offices are opened or abolished in the procedure determined by the Ministry of Justice jointly with the Federal Notarial Chamber. As a rule, there used to be a State notarial office in each city, and in large cities, in each district thereof. These are now far and few between; some State notarial offices were actually unmanned in 2020. The private sector of notarial practice has almost taken over completely.

Notaries in the Russian Federation perform many functions which in the Anglo-American legal system would be undertaken by lawyers or solicitors and commissioners for oaths. Since notaries are concerned with routine aspects of legal life, Anglo-American lawyers involved in Russian legal matters are certain to encounter them. Notaries are not necessarily concerned exclusively with the private affairs of their clients. Russian legislation requires that a notary refuse to perform a notarial action which is not in accordance with Russian legislation or international treaties. The Tax Code of the Russian Federation (Article 85(6)) requires that a notary in private practice or agencies empowered to perform notarial actions is obliged to inform the tax agencies within five days about the issuance of a certificate concerning the right to an inheritance and the notarial certification of a contract of gift.

A notary is obliged to maintain the confidentiality of information which became known to him or her in connection with professional activity;

however, a court may relieve the notary from this duty of confidentiality if a criminal case is instituted against her in connection with the performance of a notarial action. Information about such activities and documents is issued only to those on whose behalf or with regard to whom they were performed. Wills, however, are protected until the testator's death. The duty of confidentiality extends to all personnel of the notarial office who become aware of notarial activities in connection with their official duties, including the typist. Criminal penalties apply to unlawful disclosure under the Russian Criminal Code.

A notary is required to perform the notarial actions provided for by legislation for any person who applies to her unless the place where the notarial action must be performed is stipulated by legislation or by an international treaty, and assuming that a period of limitation has not elapsed.

Notarial activities fall into three basic categories.[71] The first concerns the certification of the authenticity of copies of documents. Although legislation requires the submission of notarially certified copies of documents in a number of cases, in practice virtually all ministries and departments so require. A notary must decline to certify the trueness of copies if their content is contrary to Russian legislation or if they have no legal significance. If the notary is doubtful about the document, she is obliged to submit it for expert examination.

The second category encompasses the certification of transactions, such as contracts, wills, powers of attorney, decisions of management organs of juridical persons, lists of shareholders in limited responsibility societies, mediation agreements, the equivalent significance of electronic documents, and others. Russian law requires many transactions to be notarially certified before they may become legally valid, and the notary will not do so if the contract or other document is contrary to law. A purchase-sale contract for a dwelling house or dacha, for example, must be notarially certified. The notary acts as the guardian of legality in transactions between private citizens, refusing to allow unlawful transactions to proceed. A certified contract, on the other hand, constitutes *prima facie* evidence of the facts recited in the document and the identity and legal capacity of the parties. The notarial office also keeps one copy of the contract and can supply replacements if the others are lost or destroyed.

[71] The transition to a market economy and the 1994 Civil Code have occasioned a tremendous increase in the number of notarial actions performed annually. Between 1998 and 1999 the number of notarial actions in the City of Moscow alone went up by about three million. Particularly large increases were recorded for certificates of inheritance and property transactions. See L. A. Steshenko and T. M. Shamba, Нотариат в Российской Федерации [Notariat in the Russian Federation], p. xi. The trend continues. In 2016 Russian notaries performed 57,542,629 notarial actions, of which more than three million involved the issuance of certificates of the right to inherit.

Russian notaries have been known to be reluctant to certify translations of documents because they do not know the language concerned or prefer to use their own, often inadequate, translations or to certify contracts containing applicable law provisions, they being proficient only in Russian law.

The Notariat also offers another service arising out of contractual relations when one party has not discharged his indebtedness. If there is no dispute between the parties as to responsibility for the debt and no issue requiring judicial settlement, and the contract falls among the list of documents subject to notarial execution, the creditor can secure a notice to pay from the notary which, if not contested or answered, can be followed by a notarial endorsement of documents of execution. These documents will be given to a court bailiff for execution in the same procedure as a civil court judgment. As a simplified procedure for execution, this method is extensively used to recover sums due for rates, utilities, and other local taxes. The debtor has recourse to the courts against any notarial action if he has any defence against the failure to pay.

Inheritance is a third major category of notarial activity.[72] Wills to be valid must be notarially certified, with certain exceptions provided for by law. Standard forms are widely used. The notary must verify the legal capacity of the testator, his identity and residence, and explain to him the relevant provisions of Russian civil legislation.

There is an inheritance tax in the Russian Federation. Administrators or executors of estates may be designated by a testator to manage property or oversee that testamentary dispositions are correctly effectuated. When evidence of the right to inherit is necessary, it is obtained through a certificate concerning the right to an inheritance issued by the notary; such a certificate may be necessary, for example, to claim monies due under an insurance policy, recover debts, establish heirs, divide property amongst heirs, or settle with the tax agencies. Notaries in such instances explain to the heirs their rights and duties and may help to decide disputes between them, although the right to appeal to the court is always available against the notary's determinations.

The Fundamental Principles contain a lengthy enumeration of other types of notarial activities.[73] These include taking measures to protect inheritance property, certifying rights of common ownership, certifying translations,

[72] See in general W. E. Butler, *Russian Inheritance Law* (2015).

[73] The Procedure for Keeping the Register of Notaries and Persons Who Have Taken the Qualifications Examination was confirmed by Order of the Ministry of Justice on 29 June 2015, No. 147, repealing the Procedure for Keeping the Register of State Notarial Offices and Offices of Notaries Engaging in Private Practice confirmed by Order of the Ministry of Justice of the Russian Federation, 2 December 2003, No. 306, as amended. БНА РФ, no. 3 (2004); no. 41 (2015).

certifying that a person is alive or in a particular place, accepting money, securities, or documents for deposit or safekeeping, performing maritime protests, and others.

Notaries give a great deal of legal advice and assistance. They routinely draft transaction documents and are required by law to explain not merely the rights and duties of the parties to a transaction but also to anticipate the consequences of notarial activities so that the lack of legal information or literacy cannot work to the prejudice of those seeking advice. Some advice is offered *pro bono* as part of the State program of legal assistance to low-income strata of the population.

Foreign natural and juridical persons have the right to apply to notarial offices, other agencies which perform notarial activities, or Russian consular institutions.[74] If it is within their competence, Russian notarial offices will also execute assignments on behalf of foreign justice agencies.

Notarial Chamber

Private notaries are members of a professional association called the notarial chamber. Individuals who have passed the notarial examination may be members of a chamber even though they are not notaries. A non-commercial organization in which membership of private notaries is obligatory, the chamber is a juridical person formed in each subject of the Federation. Its activities are carried on in accordance with Russian legislation and its own charter. Although non-commercial, the chambers may engage in entrepreneurial activity insofar as is necessary to fulfil their charter tasks. They are exempt from the tax on property of enterprises. Their principal tasks are to represent and defend the interests of notaries and further the development of private notarial practice; organize the training of persons who wish to become notaries and improve the skills of notaries, ensure compensation for expenditures for expert examination assigned by a court in regard to cases connected with notarial activity, and arrange professional insurance for private notaries. A notary pays dues to maintain the chamber and submits information and documents to the chamber required by legislation. Self-governing in principle, the highest organ of the chambers is the meeting of notaries of the chamber; daily activities of the chamber are managed by the president and his staff.

All notarial chambers are members of the Federal Notarial Chamber, which has its own charter and is supported by dues of members. In May 1998 the I Congress of Notaries was held at Moscow for the first time in Russian history.

[74] See the Consular Statute of the Russian Federation, of 5 July 2010, as amended; transl. in Butler, note 2 above.

In population centers where there are no State or private notaries, notarial actions are fulfilled by empowered officials of agencies of executive power. In isolated areas this is a convenience to citizens who otherwise would have to travel vast distances in order to obtain notarial services.

Absent from present Russian legislation on the notary is the duty of the notary to inform the Procuracy about violations of legality discovered in the actions of officials or citizens. This omission might be thought to reflect, in a market economy, the transition of the notary from being a Soviet State official, the humble guardian of socialist legality, to being an impartial neutral force serving his or her client. Russian doctrinal writings, however, suggest that the duty to inform the Procuracy continues to exist, being based on the "general sense of legislation on the notariat" and in particular on the formulation in Article 1 of the Fundamental Principles calling upon the notary to defend the rights and legal interests of citizens and juridical persons. In practice notaries report violations of legality to their notarial chambers, as a rule, forged documents and the theft of notarial documents.

The Russian notarial profession continues to consider whether to request a return to the pre-revolutionary system whereby notaries were linked with the courts. Under this scheme the court would supervise the work of the Notariat, minimizing the opportunities for extraneous influences to affect notaries in the performance of their duties.

Digitization of the Russian economy is contributing to a reconceptualization of notarial functions. The wider use of electronic documents is reducing the need for notaries to certify copies of documents; in 2018 the number of such notarial actions declined by 22% over the preceding year. By working through a so-called "single digital window", a notary is able to certify the genuineness of a signature once and submit the same to several agencies simultaneously. There are advanced services for arranging powers of attorney and digital registers of inheritance cases which include the details of the notary administering an inheritance. Even though certain transactions with immoveable property do not necessarily require notarization, natural persons increasingly are turning to notaries voluntarily for the notarization of housing transactions.

REGISTRY FOR ACTS OF CIVIL STATUS (ZAGS)

History

In pre-revolutionary Russia vital statistics concerning birth, marriage, divorce, death, or adoption were kept principally by the ecclesiastical authorities. By Decree of 18 December 1917 these functions were entrusted to the local administrative authorities, many of whom formed special sections for the registration of acts of civil status (ZAGS).The activities of ZAGS agencies were governed principally by the 1918 RSFSR Family Code and those family codes which supplanted it. In the post-Soviet period the regulation of ZAGS activities has been removed from the Family Code and become the subject of independent regulation in the form of a federal law.

Current Legislation

Vital statistics are registered in the Russian Federation at ZAGS offices formed by agencies of State power of subjects of the Russian Federation and, beyond the limits of Russia, by consular institutions of the Russian Federation. The Federal Law on Acts of Civil Status of 15 November 1997, as amended,[75] provides that State registration of acts of civil status is established for the purpose of protecting the property and personal non-property rights of citizens and only secondarily in the interests of the State. Seven acts of civil status are recognized: birth, marriage, dissolution of marriage, adoption, paternity, change of name, and death. The Law acknowledged that in certain respects the criteria for recognizing acts of civil status may vary from one subject of the Federation to another, for example, the age of marriage. Acts of civil status performed as part of religious rites are recognized only insofar as agencies for the registry of acts of civil status had not been formed or reinstated on the territory concerned. In this event they are equated to acts of civil status duly registered by the State in conformity with the legislation which was in force at the time the acts were performed and do not require subsequent State registration. This provision would affect acts of civil status on territories incorporated into the former Soviet Union from 1939 to 1944 and places such as Chechnia in the 1990s or Crimea after March 2014.

The registry books exist in two examples, known as the first example and the second example. Each is sewn, numbered, sealed, and kept in the agency for the registry of acts of civil status where the acts were registered. The so-called second examples, also sewn, numbered, and sealed, are kept in the agency of executive power of the subject of the Federation concerned together with metric books compiled before the registry was formed or reinstated. After 75 years the first examples are sent to the State archives, and the second examples are subject to being destroyed.

Under recent reforms, an entry of an act of civil status is drawn up in the Russian language as an electronic document and also in a hard copy format. This information is contained in the Unified State Register of Entries of Acts of Civil Status, which constitutes a systematized digest of documentary information in electronic form obtained through the State registration on acts of civil status and the performance of other legally significant actions by agencies for the registry of acts of civil status. The Unified State Register includes information concerning documents issued by competent agencies

[75] СЗ РФ (1997), no. 47, item 5340, as amended; transl. in Butler, note 2 above.

of foreign States certifying acts of civil status performed outside the Russian Federation with respect to Russian citizens.

Each entry in the Unified State Register and the information concerning documents issued by foreign agencies is identified by an unchangeable, non-repeatable identification number. This material is kept permanently, never subject to destruction or removal. Even if the entry is changed, the original entry is retained. The operator of this Federal Information System is the Federal Tax Service of the Russian Federation.[76]

Individual subjects of the Russian Federation have enacted legislation regulating certain aspects of civil status, for example, the age of marriage.[77]

ADMINISTRATIVE COMMISSIONS

Illegal or unlawful conduct in the Anglo-American legal systems is punishable in accordance with criminal law. Under Russian legislation anti-social behavior may be criminal or it may fall into a category unknown to the Anglo-American legal world: administrative offences. The 1993 Constitution of the Russian Federation relegates administrative violations and administrative procedure legislation to the joint jurisdiction of the Russian Federation and the subjects of the Russian Federation. For many years the principal Law regulating administrative offences was the Code of the RSFSR on Administrative Violations adopted 20 June 1984 and in force, as amended, from 1 January 1985. It was replaced by the Code of the Russian Federation on Administrative Violations of 28 December 2001, as amended.[78]

The number of agencies and officials empowered to levy administrative sanctions is difficult to calculate because most are named generically rather than specifically; that is, "agencies and institutions of the criminal executory system". It is estimated that more than 30 million persons are brought to administrative responsibility in the Russian Federation each year.

An administrative offense is an unlawful, guilty action (or failure to act) of a natural or juridical person for which administrative responsibility has been established by the 2001 Code on Administrative Violations or by laws of subjects of the Russian Federation on administrative violations (Article 2.1, Code on Administrative Violations). The subjects of the Russian Federation and local government adopt their own enactments providing

[76] The legal foundation of the Federal Information System is set out in two laws: The Federal Law of 27 July 2006, No. 149-ФЗ, "On Information, Information Technologies, and Defense of Information", as amended, and the Federal Law of the same date, No. 152-ФЗ, "On Personal Data", as amended.

[77] The relevant laws of subjects of the Federation are collected on Consultant Plus.

[78] СЗ РФ (2002), no. 1(I), item 1, as amended; substantial extracts are translated in Butler, *Russian Public Law* (3d ed.; 2013), pp. 1037-1060.

administrative responsibility, for example, for environmental, construction, and traffic offences. An administrative violation may be committed intentionally or through negligence, and the minimum legal age for the commission of such offences is age 16. Defenses of extreme necessity and imputability are recognized. Administrative sanctions which may be applied under the 2001 Code on Administrative Violations include a warning, an administrative fine, seizure with compensation or confiscation of articles and implements used to commit administrative violations, deprivation of a special right granted to a natural person (right to hunt, to drive, etc), administrative arrest for a term of up to 15 days, as a rule, and exceptionally up to 30 days. For foreigners and stateless persons there is the possibility of administrative deportation beyond the limits of the Russian Federation. The 2001 Code on Administrative Violations introduced "disqualification" as a sanction, which includes depriving a natural person of the right to hold executive offices in an executive management organ of a juridical person, to be a member of a council of directors or supervisory council, to effectuate entrepreneurial activity with regard to management of a juridical person. In 2005 the sanction of "administrative suspension of activity" was added to the said Code (Article 3.2.1.9), which entails the temporary termination of the activity of individual entrepreneurs, juridical persons, branches, representations, structural subdivisions, production sectors, and even the operation of assemblies, objects, buildings, or installations, in designated instances for a period of up to 90 days as determined by a judge. In 2012 "obligatory tasks" were added as a sanction, and in 2013, "administrative prohibition to visit places of holding official sport competitions on the day of holding them" – an attempt to combat football and other hooliganism. Juridical persons may be subjected to certain administrative sanctions.

The agencies which may consider cases of administrative violations are diverse, ranging from judges of courts of ordinary jurisdiction, arbitrazh courts, internal affairs agencies of State inspectorates, justices of the peace, and other agencies and officials duly empowered by law. A great number are heard by administrative commissions attached to agencies of local self-government or by commissions for cases of minors.

Judges, justices of the peace, and officials, together with administrative commissions which exist purely to dispose of cases concerning administrative violations, consider administrative cases as designated by the 2001 Code on Administrative Violations. Some local governments have several administrative commissions. Unless the administrative offence is subject to a fine levied on-the-spot (failing to pay public transport fare, for example), a protocol of the violation is drawn up and signed by the alleged offender and the apprehending person. The protocol usually follows a standard form of a page or two containing the date, place, data on the apprehending person, full name of the offender, year and place of birth, place of residence and telephone, place of work and position, amount of earnings, pension, or stipend, marital status and dependants, previous administrative sanctions, including details as to who imposed the sanction and when, the Article of the Code on Administrative Violations, identity document (passport data), the Article number, subpoint, and name of the normative act providing administrative responsibility for the act committed, details of any witnesses or victim, and an indication that the rights and duties of the natural or juridical person under the 2001 Code on Administrative Violations have been explained to the offender. There is space for the offender to give his explanations and any additional information, any relevant documents or materials being appended, and signatures by the offender, witnesses, and victim, and the person drawing up the Protocol. Under the 2001 Code on Administrative Violations there are more than 80 categories of officials empowered to draw up protocols.

The judge, justice of the peace, agency, or official hears the case on the basis of the protocol. The alleged offender has the right to familiarize himself with the materials of the case, give explanations, present evidence, make petitions, be represented by an advocate or defender, and appeal the decree in the case. If necessary, there may be an investigation and experts may be summoned. The case must be considered by the commission in the presence of the alleged offender, or in absentia if he fails to appear after timely notification. The case is considered in open session, and the commission is obliged to ascertain when the violation was committed, whether the particular person committed it, whether he is subject to administrative responsibility, whether there are aggravating or mitigating circumstances, whether property damage was caused, and any other relevant considerations, including possible challenges to those who are considering the case. The commission (or other agency considering the case) renders its judgment in the form of a decree, which may be appealed as laid down in legislation; the decree itself should state the period within which the decree may be appealed (ten days); the appeal is lodged with the judge, justice of the peace, agency, or official which rendered the decree, who then has three days within which to forward the appeal onwards to the relevant appellate instance. A procurator may protest a decree, which has the effect of suspending execution until the protest is considered. If the offender does not pay the administrative fine imposed, the administrative commission may issue a notice to the local court to levy execution against the earnings or the personal property of the offender. In the case of an employed offender, the notice may be issued to the employer with instructions to withhold the amount of the fine from earnings. The court also may issue a proposal to enterprises and agencies concerning elimination of the causes of the offence (for example, failure to take proper security measures in order to deter petty theft). The period of limitations for execution of a decree is one year from the day of entry into legal force thereof.

Although administrative violations are often petty transgressions, the sanctions imposed are intended to be more than perfunctory. The 'tasks' of legislation on administrative violations are the "defense of the individual, protection of the rights and freedoms of man and citizen, protection of the health of citizens, sanitary-epidemiological well-being of the population, defense of public morality, protection of the environment and the established procedure for effectuating State power, public order, and public security, ownership, defense of legal economic interests of natural and juridical persons, society, and the State against administrative violations, and also the prevention of administrative violations" (Article 1.2, Code on Administrative Violations). The principles of equality before the law and presumption of innocence both operate with respect to administrative violations.

The more serious categories of administrative violations (for example, petty stealing) are considered by judges in the courts of ordinary jurisdiction or justices of the peace or, in the case of a traffic violation, by the State Motor Vehicle Inspectorate, or by policy agencies of inspectorates. The procedures for considering the violation are the same, but the penalties can be far more severe, including administrative arrest, in the instance of petty stealing, for a period of up to 15 days (petty stealing on a small scale is the stealing of articles not exceeding 1000 rubles in value (twelve pounds sterling), or obligatory tasks for a term of up to fifty hours); petty stealing on a larger scale entails more severe penalties.

An administrative offense is not a crime, and an offender who commits what otherwise would be a criminal act but is subjected to administrative responsibility does not acquire a criminal record. Even the record of an administrative offense is expunged within a year if a second is not committed. Although an offender does not have the full protection of the Code of Criminal Procedure in administrative proceedings, the 2001 Code on Administrative Violations does considerably tighten due process elements of an administrative proceeding to bring them much closer to those of the criminal justice system.

Commissions for Cases of Minors operate in many respects just as the administrative commissions. They are created by the highest executive agencies of State power of subjects of the Russian Federation or, when so empowered by a law of the particular subject of the Russian Federation, may be created by agencies of local self-government. They are governed by the Federal Law on the Fundamental Principles of the System for the Prevention of Neglect and Violations of Minors of 24 June 1999.[79] Although Article 11 of the said Federal Law made provision for the adoption of a Model Statute on Commissions for Cases of Minors and Defense of the

[79] СЗ РФ (1999), no. 26, item 3177, as amended.

Rights Thereof, the Model Statute was not confirmed until 6 November 2013 by Decree of the Government of the Russian Federation, No. 995.[80] Until then, the Commissions operated under the Statute on Commissions for Cases of Minors confirmed by Edict of the Presidium of the Supreme Soviet of the RSFSR on 3 June 1967, as amended to 25 February 1993.[81] The commissions are concerned with juvenile delinquency, child neglect or abuse, school-leavers, orphans, foster parents, child labor, adoption, guardianship, protection of children's rights and interests, leisure time, education, and various kinds of reform schools. There is almost no aspect of a child's being that is not within a commission's purview. The commission also may consider administrative violations committed by a minor and impose the sanctions provided for by legislation.

LAW ENFORCEMENT AGENCIES

Police functions are vested principally in two agencies: the Federal Security Service of the Russian Federation (FSB) and the Ministry of Internal Affairs (MVD). These agencies and the various functions they perform have been the subject of special legislation intended to make them more transparent and accountable.

The expression "special services" is increasingly being used to describe agencies engaging in external policing, investigative, and protective functions, including counter-terrorism, both State and private. In this larger sense one would speak of the Foreign Intelligence Service of the Russian Federation (SVR Russia), the FSB, the Federal Service for the Protection of the Russian Federation, the foreign intelligence agency of the Ministry of Defense of the Russian Federation, the Ministry for Extraordinary Situations of the Russian Federation, the courier services; the passport-visa service of internal affairs agencies, private security companies, and private detective agencies, amongst others. These agencies have been subject to repeated reorganization during the past fifteen years; the recent trend has been towards consolidation and many federal services have been abolished or merged into larger structures.

Security Council of Russian Federation

The Security Council of the Russian Federation is a constitutional consultative agency charged with effectuating the preparation of decisions of the President of the Russian Federation with regard to issues of the developmental strategy of Russia, ensuring the security of vitally important interests of the individual, society, and the State against internal and

[80] СЗ РФ (2013), no. 45, item 5829, as amended.

[81] Ведомости Верховного Совета РСФСР (1967), no. 23, item 536; Российская газета [Russian Newspaper], 19 March 1993. The Edict was repealed by Federal Law of 27 June 2018, No. 170-ФЗ. СЗ РФ (2018), no. 27, item 3953.

external threats, and implementing a unified State policy in the domain of ensuring national security.

The Council adopts decisions by simple majority vote of the total permanent membership; these enter into force after confirmation by the Chairman of the Security Council. The President of Russia is the Chairman of the Security Council. The key official, however, is the Secretary of the Security Council, who is appointed by and directly accountable to the President of the Russian Federation. The present Statute on the Security Council was confirmed by Edict of the President of the Russian Federation adopted 7 March 2020, as amended.[82]

Federal Security Service (FSB)

The FSB is a unified centralized system of federal security service agencies effectuating tasks within the limits of its power relating to ensuring the security of the Russian Federation. It is under the direction of the President of the Russian Federation and is the legal successor to the Federal Counter-Intelligence Service of the Russian Federation. Its activities are governed by the Federal Law on Federal Securities Service Agencies in the Russian Federation, adopted 3 April 1995 and in force as from 12 April 1995, as amended.[83] The FSB consists of a complex of agencies with administrations or sections at the levels of regions and subjects of the Russian Federation and in military units and its own system of enterprises, educational institutions, scientific-research, expert and military-medical institutions and subdivisions, military construction subdivisions, special training centers, and special-purpose subdivisions, together with administrations, sections, and detachments of the federal agency of executive power in the domain of ensuring security for the border service. The "creation of Federal security service agencies not provided for" by the Federal Law is not permitted, and nor may organizational structures or political parties operate, or mass social movements pursuing political purposes, pre-election campaigns, or political agitation exist within the FSB (Article 2). Neither the subjects of the Russian Federation nor local self-governing agencies may adopt normative acts affecting the FSB or its activities.

The Statute on the FSB was confirmed by Edict of the President of the Russian Federation on 23 June 1995, as amended; replaced on 6 July 1998,

[82] СЗ РФ (2020), no. 10, item 1323, as amended. This Statute replaced earlier enactments of 10 July 1996, 2 August 1999, 7 June 2004 and 6 May 2011. See СЗ РФ (1996), no. 29, item 3479; (1999), no. 32, item 4041; (2004), no. 24, item 2392; (2011), no. 19, item 2721, each as amended. The Edict confirmed also the Statute on the Apparatus of the Security Council of the Russian Federation.

[83] СЗ РФ (1995), no. 15, item 1269, as amended. Many foundation documents of the Soviet security services previously classified are published in V. V. Korovin, История отечественных органов безопасности [History of Fatherland Security Agencies] (1998), pp. 103-247.

as amended; and replaced again on 11 August 2003, as amended.[84] Other enactments directing activities of the FSB include the Edict on Measures Relating to Ensuring Coordinated Actions of Agencies of State Power in the Struggle Against Fascism and Other Forms of Political Extremism in the Russian Federation, adopted 23 March 1995, as amended;[85] the Rules for Relegating Information Constituting a State Secret to Various Degrees of Secrecy, confirmed by Decree of the Government on 4 September 1995, as amended;[86] the List of Information Relegated to a State Secret, confirmed by Edict of the President of 30 November 1995, as amended;[87] the Federal Law of the Russian Federation on Counteracting Terrorism of 6 March 2006,[88] and relevant international treaties of the Russian Federation.

The FSB also is regulated by and gives effect to the Federal Law on State Protection, adopted 27 May 1996, as amended;[89] the Law on the State Boundary of the Russian Federation, adopted 1 April 1993, as amended;[90] and the Law of the Russian Federation on Security of 28 December 2010.[91] The Law on State Secrecy of 21 July 1993, as amended,[92] and the Federal Law on the Procedure for Exit from the Russian Federation and Entry into the Russian Federation of 15 August 1996, as amended,[93] are major concerns of the FSB.

In provisions which are unprecedented in Russian history, the State "guarantees compliance with the rights and freedoms of man and citizen" by the FSB agencies. A person who believes that FSB agencies or officials have violated his rights and freedoms has the right to appeal against the actions of the agencies or officials to the superior FSB agency, to the Procuracy, or to a court. State agencies, enterprises, organizations, social associations, and natural persons have the right to request explanations and information from FSB agencies if their rights and freedoms are limited and to seek material and moral compensation for damages caused by FSB agencies and officials (Article 6, 1995 Federal Law).

The FSB combines intelligence and police functions, "intelligence" encompassing both counter-intelligence and intelligence. The Law on the

[84] СЗ РФ (1995), no. 26, item 2453, as amended; СЗ РФ (1998), no. 28, item 3320, as amended; СЗ РФ (2003), no. 33, item 3254, as amended; transl. in Butler, note 2 above, pp. 980-996.

[85] СЗ РФ (1995), no. 13, item 1127; (2004), no. 45, item 4414. Also see the Federal Law on Counteracting Extremist Activity of 25 July 2002, as amended.

[86] СЗ РФ (1995), no. 37, item 3619, as amended 15 January 2008.

[87] СЗ РФ (1995), no. 49, item 4775, as amended.

[88] СЗ РФ (2006), no. 11, item 1146; no. 31(I), item 3452; this Law replaced the Law on the Struggle Against Terrorism of 25 July 1998, as amended.

[89] СЗ РФ (1996), no. 22, item 2594, as amended.

[90] Ведомости СНД и ВС РФ (1993), no. 17, item 594, as amended.

[91] СЗ РФ (2011), no. 1, item 2.

[92] СЗ РФ (1997), no. 41, pp. 8220-8235, as amended; Российская газета [Russian Newspaper], 21 September 1993.

[93] СЗ РФ (1996), no. 34, item 4029, as amended.

FSB gives great prominence to the intelligence function: to inform the President, the Chairman of the Government, and on their behalf federal agencies of State power and agencies of State power of subjects of the Federation about threats to the security of the Russian Federation, elicit, prevent, and suppress intelligence and other activity of special services and organizations of foreign States and also of individual persons directed towards inflicting damage on the security of the Russian Federation, and extracting intelligence information in the interests of ensuring the security of Russia and increasing its economic, scientific-technical, and defense potential. The FSB is designated in the Law on Foreign Intelligence of 10 January 1996, as amended, as one of the agencies "of foreign intelligence of Russia".[94]

Police functions are directed towards eliciting, preventing, and suppressing crimes, the inquiry and preliminary investigation of which is relegated primarily by criminal procedure legislation to the FSB and to search for individuals suspected of committing them, to combat terrorism, and to collaborate with other State agencies in working out and implementing measures against corruption, illegal circulation of weapons and narcotics, smuggling, illegal armed formations, criminal groups, and individuals or social associations whose purpose is forcibly to change the constitutional system of the Russian Federation.

The FSB is subject to Procuracy supervision, except, however, that information concerning persons rendering or who have rendered assistance to FSB agencies on a confidential basis and concerning the organization, tactics, methods, and means of effectuating activity are not subject to Procuracy supervision.

The number of federal laws regulating the Russian special services has become sufficiently complex to justify, in the opinion of some Russian jurists, a Code of the Russian Federation on the Special Services of Russia.[95]

Internal Affairs Agencies

The ordinary day-to-day functions of protecting public order and crime prevention fall principally upon the Ministry of Internal Affairs (MVD) and its various substructures. The principal tasks of the MVD are set out in the Statute on the Ministry of Internal Affairs of the Russian Federation and Model Statute on the Territorial Agency of the Ministry of Internal Affairs of the Russian Federation for a Subject of the Russian Federation, confirmed by Edict of the President of the Russian Federation on 21 December 2016, as amended.[96] The Ministry system consists of structural links at all levels

[94] СЗ РФ (1996), no. 3, item 143, as amended.

[95] For a draft outline of such a Code, see A. Iu. Shumilov, Спецслужбы России: Законы и комментарий [Special Services of Russia: Laws and Commentary] (1997), pp. 319-321.

[96] СЗ РФ (2016), no. 52(V), item 7614. This Edict repealed the Edict and Statute of 1 March

of all subjects of the Russian Federation, administrations or sections on railway, air, and water transport, closed administrative-territorial formations, so-called "especially important" and "regime objects", and regional administrations for the struggle against organized crime.

The Ministry also has material-technical supply and military supply administrations, a vast network of educational and training institutions, scientific-research institutes, and special subdivisions, units, enterprises, institutions, and organizations formed for special tasks.

The MVD has its own internal forces to perform designated tasks. The Ministry organizes the search on Russian territory for missing persons, individuals who have escaped from custody or investigation, or stolen property, the identification of unidentified corpses, the administration of passport-visa and other authorization systems, issues licenses for citizens to have weapons, exercises control over private detective activity in Russia, and establishes the rules for the entry, exit, sojourn, and transit through the territory of the Russian Federation of foreign citizens and stateless persons. The Ministry also organizes the State registration of fingerprints. The MVD drafts and confirms rules for traffic safety, organizes the registration and recording of means of transport, issues driver's licenses, and is responsible for the State Road Traffic Safety Inspectorate (legal successor of GAI), whose Statute was confirmed 15 June 1998, as amended.[97]

The police within the MVD are governed by the Law on the Police adopted 7 February 2011, as amended,[98] and replacing the Law of the same name (in English) of 18 April 1991, as amended.[99] This 1991 Law was the first to regulate police agencies comprehensively, an event described by Russian jurists as part of the "processes of democratization which led, finally, to the broad awareness of the position long recognized by the international community in accordance with which officials who guard the Law must be free in their activity from political partiality, being 'politically neutral' under all conditions and serving only the Law and the people".[100] The principles of police activity are compliance with and respect for the rights and freedoms of man and citizen, legality, impartiality, openness and publicness, public confidence and support of citizens, interaction and cooperation, and the use

2011. See СЗ РФ (2011), no. 10, item 1334, as amended. This Statute replaced those confirmed on 18 July 1996, as amended, and 19 July 2004, as amended.

97 СЗ РФ (1998), no. 25, item 2897, as amended.

98 СЗ РФ (2011), no. 7, item 900, as amended. The title of the two laws is identical in Russian but for two letters of the alphabet. In 2011 the legislator preferred the word полиция instead of милиция; in order to avoid confusion with the "militia", both terms had long since been translated in English as "police".

99 Ведомости СНД и ВС РФ (1991), no. 16, item 503, as amended.

100 See B. P. Kondrashov, Iu. P. Solovei, and V. V. Chernikov, Российский закон о милиции [Russian Law on the Police] (1992), p. 22.

of modern technologies. The duties of the police occupy a lengthy list of 43 subpoints, most of which enumerate multiple duties

Service in the Ministry of Internal Affairs is regulated by the Federal Law on Service in Internal Affairs Agencies of 30 November 2011, as amended.[101] These provisions are subject to the general requirements for being employed as a civil servant set out in federal legislation on the State civil service and labor legislation.

Under the Federal Law on Forces of the National Guard of the Russian Federation of 3 July 2016, as amended,[102] the National Guard is a State military organization designed to ensure State and public security and the defense of the rights and freedoms of man and citizen. Its units assist in the protection of public order and security, protect important State objects and special cargoes, installations, and communications, participate in the territorial defense of the Russian Federation, combat terrorism, render assistance to the border agencies of the FSB in protecting the State boundary, and exercise control or supervision over compliance with Russian legislation regulating the turnover of weapons, private protection and detective activity, ensure the safety of objects of the fuel and energy complex and over the activity of protection subdivisions of juridical persons having special tasks and the subdivisions of departmental protection services; the protection of especially important or regime objects pursuant to a list confirmed by the Government of the Russian Federation or the protection of the property of juridical or natural persons, and ensure the security, by decision of the President of the Russian Federation, of senior officials of subjects of the Russian Federation and other persons. The activity of the National Guard is directed by the President of the Russian Federation. Members of the National Guard have limited powers to detain individuals, open means of transport, penetrate or enter dwelling premises and other premises on land plots and territories, including aquatories, cordon off or block sectors of a locality or aquatory, dwelling and other premises, structures, and other objects, form and keep databanks on citizens, and use physical force, special equipment, weapons, combat, and other technologies, among others. The Procurator General of the Russian Federation and subordinate procurators effectuate supervision over compliance with the law by the National Guard.

Police Functions with Respect to Narcotics

As a result of sweeping reforms in governmental structure introduced in spring 2004, responsibility for law enforcement functions in the domain of

[101] СЗ РФ (2011), no. 49(I), item 7020, as amended.

[102] СЗ РФ (2016), no. 27(I), item 4159. The 2016 Federal Law replaced the Federal Law on Internal Forces of the Ministry of Internal Affairs of the Russian Federation of 6 February 1997, as amended. СЗ РФ (1997), no. 6, item 711, as amended. The Federal Service of Forces of the National Guard were formed under the Edict of the President of the Russian Federation of 5 April 2016, No. 157. СЗ РФ (2016), no. 15, item 2072.

narcotics was placed on the Federal Service of the Russian Federation for Control Over Turnover of Narcotic Means and Psychotropic Substances, also known by its Russian acronym "FSKN Rossii". The Federal Service was charged with concentrating upon the elimination of the foundations of the narcotics business and overseeing the legal turnover and production of narcotics to be used for medical and other purposes and taking part in programs to prevent narcotics addiction.

FSKN commenced operations with a personnel establishment amounting to about 40,000 persons, nearly three-quarters of whom were transferred from the abolished Federal Tax Police Service and the balance mostly individuals who had prior experience with narcotics matters in the MVD. The enumeration of FSKN functions occupied several pages in the Statute on the agency,[103] which in turn were reflected in the structural elements of the central apparatus of FSKN Russia: the Chief Operational Administration; the Chief Administration for Control over the Legal Turnover of Narcotic Means and Psychotropic Substances, the Chief Organizational-Analytical Administration, the Chief Investigative Administration, the Administration of Own Security; the Administration of International Cooperation; the Administration of Special Designation; and others.

The functions of FSKN encompassed: ensuring the execution of Russian legislation on narcotic means, psychotropic substances, and precursors; preparing and submitting reports to the President or the Government of Russia concerning the improvement of State policies in the domain of the turnover and counteracting illegal turnover of narcotic means, participating in working out and realizing federal special-purpose programs in the field of narcotics, effectuating prophylactic activities with regard to preventing the illegal consumption of narcotics, effectuating operational-search activity, including organization and conducting the search for persons who are accused or suspected of committing crimes within the jurisdiction of FSKN Russia, performing inquiries and preliminary investigations with regard to criminal cases relating to its investigative jurisdiction, conducting proceedings with regard to administrative violations, effectuating control over the activity of juridical persons and individual entrepreneurs in the domain of turnover of narcotics, presenting demands in court to liquidate juridical persons which have been connected with the commission of narcotics crimes, be responsible for controlling the keeping, carriage, and destruction of confiscated or seized narcotics, among others. FSKN Russia is the principal partner under interdepartmental treaties with foreign agencies and departments concerned with the enforcement of legislation against illegal activities involving narcotics.[104]

[103] СЗ РФ (2004), no. 31, item 3234, as amended; transl. in Butler, note 2 above.

[104] See generally W. E. Butler, *Narcotics and HIV/AIDS in Russia: Harm Reduction Policies Under Russian Law* (2005).

By Edict of the President of the Russian Federation of 5 April 2016, No. 156, the FSKN was abolished and its functions, personnel, and powers transferred to the MVD, which is the legal successor of the FSKN.[105]

Other Law Enforcement Agencies

The traditional functions of the MVD in overseeing the execution of punishments were transferred during the late 1990s to the Ministry of Justice of the Russian Federation.

The State Fire Prevention Service is part of the system of the Ministry of Russian Federation for Civil Defense, Extraordinary Situations, and Liquidation of the Consequences of Natural Disasters. It is governed in its work by the Federal Law on Fire Safety, adopted 21 December 1994, as amended.[106]

Integration of Crime Prevention Functions

On 23 June 2016 the Russian Federation adopted a Federal Law on the Fundamental Principles for the Prevention of Violations in the Russian Federation.[107] This Federal Law seeks to address the issue of "social relations arising in the sphere of violations in the Russian Federation" as a phenomenon cutting across all the institutions involved in the prevention of violations: (1) federal agencies of executive power; (2) procuracy agencies; (3) investigative agencies of the Investigative Committee; (4) agencies of State power of subject of the Russian Federation; and (5) agencies of local self-government. A violation for these purposes is a crime or an administrative violation constituting an unlawful act (or action, failure to act) entailing criminal or administrative responsibility. Prevention is the aggregate of social, legal, organizational, informational, and other measures directed towards the identification and elimination of the causes and conditions facilitating the commission of violations and the exerting of an educational impact on persons with a view to not permitting the commission of crimes or anti-social behavior. The legislation also is directed against "anti-social behavior", defined as actions of a natural person which do not engage administrative or criminal responsibility but violate generally-accepted norms of behavior and morality and the rights and legal interests of other persons.

The principal orientations of preventive (prophylactic) measures are to: (1) defend the individual, society, and the State against unlawful infringements; (2) prevent violations; (3) develop a system of prophylactic

[105] СЗ РФ (2016), no. 15, item 2071, as amended. The legislation establishing the FSKN was repealed only in part and in individual measures separately adopted.
[106] СЗ РФ (1994), no. 35, item 3649, as amended. See the Statute on the Federal Fire Prevention Service, confirmed by Decree of the Government of the Russian Federation, 20 June 2005. СЗ РФ (2005), no. 26, item 2649.
[107] СЗ РФ (2016), no. no. 26(I), item 3851; transl. in Butler, note 2 above.

recording of persons inclined to commit violations; (4) protect public order, including at sport, entertainment, and other large public occasions; (5) ensure public safety, including road traffic and transport; (6) counteract illegal migration; (7) prevent the neglect, homelessness, violations, and anti-social actions of minors; (8) counteract terrorism and extremist activity and defend potential objects of terrorist infringements; (9) counteract the illegal turnover of narcotics and psychotropic substances; (10) ensure the defense and protection of private, State, municipal, and other forms of ownership; (11) ensure economic security; (12) counteract corruption and identity its causes and conditions; (13) ensure ecological security and environmental protection; (14) ensure fire safety; (15) prevent, eliminate, and/or minimize the consequences of extraordinary situations; and (16) raise the level of legal literacy and develop the legal consciousness of citizens. State and municipal programs are to be introduced to the above ends.

The general prevention of violations under this Federal Law is to be achieved through the identification and elimination of the causes generating violations and the conditions facilitating the commission of violations or easing the commission thereof, and by raising the level of legal literacy and development of the legal consciousness of citizens. The Federal Law authorizes a court to consider the application of the following measures in an effort to further the cause of prevention:

(1) legal enlightenment and legal informing;

(2) prevention conversation;

(3) announcement of official caution (or caution) concerning the impermissibility of actions creating conditions for the commission of violations, or the impermissibility of continuing anti-social behavior;

(4) preventive recording;

(5) making of submission concerning the elimination of the causes and conditions facilitating the commission of a violation;

(6) prevention supervision;

(7) social adaptation;

(8) re-socialization;

(9) social rehabilitation;

(10) assistance to persons who suffered from violations or are susceptible to the risk of becoming such.

PRELIMINARY INVESTIGATION AGENCIES

History

The "preliminary investigation" and an "investigative apparatus" to conduct such have their own history in Russia. Peter the Great is credited with first acting on the idea of establishing a special investigative department to operate separately and independently from other agencies of State power and to distinguish between the stages in a criminal case of "preliminary investigation" and "judicial consideration". To this end in 1713 Peter the Great created so-called "large", "senior", or, more literally, "major" investigative chancelleries; these pursuant to the "Major Nakaz" of 9 December 1717 were made subordinate directly to the Tsar and charged with investigating the "major" crimes of corruption by officials. Eleven of 23 Russian senators were at one time investigated by these chancelleries during the Petrine era. Peter the Great's successors abandoned this "extradepartmental" model of a preliminary investigation in favor of an "administrative model" pursuant to which investigations were performed by various non-specialized agencies together with other functions placed on them.

Prior to 1860 in Russia investigative functions were performed largely by various components of the Russian police. Quarter overseers commonly acted as investigators, and in large cities the post of investigative bailiff existed for civil and criminal cases. By an Edict of 8 June 1860 the investigative function was removed from the police and placed on the office of judicial investigator, created in 44 provinces of the Empire within the system of the Ministry of Justice. At the same time two nakaz were issued which laid down the procedure for a preliminary investigation and determined the relations between judicial investigators, on one hand, and the police and the courts, on the other. Judicial investigators carried the rank equivalent to the judge of an uezd court. They were appointed to and dismissed from office by the Minister of Justice upon the recommendation of the governor and with the consent of the procurator of the province. This procedure immediately created difficulties, for although formally appointed by the Minister of Justice, each judicial investigator was in fact dependent upon the local governor. By the Statute on Criminal Procedure of 20 November 1864 it was provided that judicial investigators would perform the preliminary investigation concerning crimes and offences which were within the jurisdiction of okrug courts with the assistance of the police. In the absence of an investigator, the Statute required the police to perform an inquiry and then turn over the materials collected to the investigator.

Over the years the system was expanded. In 1867 the post of temporary investigators for especially important cases was instituted to investigate forged State credit notes. The post of judicial investigator for important cases was established in 1870, and in 1875, attached to okrug courts, the permanent post of investigators for especially important cases was created; these investigators were allowed to sit in individual cases as a judge provided they had not been involved in investigating the particular case and there were no other judges available.

The office of judicial investigator was abolished in November 1917 by Decree No 1, "On the Court", together with most other institutional survivals of the Imperial legal system and the investigative function placed on the local judges themselves. There followed a period of rapid changes of policy. The judges could not cope with the investigative burden, which was passed mostly to the investigative commissions of the Military-Revolutionary Committee. Analogous commissions to investigate counter-revolutionary crimes were formed and attached to local soviets. Then investigative commissions for grave crimes (homicide, rape, banditry, etc) were established and attached to the okrug courts.[108] The Statute on the People's Court of the RSFSR placed investigative responsibilities on investigative commissions, on the police (in the form of an inquiry), and sometimes on the judges.[109] The All-Russian Extraordinary Committee, formed 20 December 1917, investigated certain crimes against the State. The Statute on the Court of the RSFSR, confirmed in October 1920, introduced the post of people's investigator; these were to be elected by the provincial executive committees of soviets and attached to councils of people's judges. At the same time the office of investigator for especially important cases was attached to the provincial justice sections and to the People's Commissariat of Justice of the RSFSR.[110] The first Code of Criminal Procedure of the RSFSR, confirmed 25 May 1922, defined the term investigator as encompassing the people's investigators, investigators attached to provincial courts, investigators of military tribunals, and investigators for important cases attached to the People's Commissariat of Justice.[111] Only a very general definition of preliminary investigation agencies was offered by the 1924 Fundamental Principles of Court Proceedings of the USSR and Union Republics.[112] Thus by the mid-1920s Soviet legislation had laid the foundations for the preliminary investigation and designated certain agencies to conduct these.

Thereafter it was legislation on the Procuracy which addressed the preliminary investigation. The Statute on Procuracy Supervision confirmed 28 May 1922 placed on that institution, *inter alia,* the duty to supervise the investigation of criminal cases, which until 1928 continued to be carried out by investigative units that remained within the administrative jurisdiction of the courts. Amendments made in September 1928 to the Statute on Court

[108] See Decrees 1, 2, and 3 'On the Court'. СУ РСФСР (1917), no. 4, item 50; (1918), no. 26, item 420; no. 52, item 589.

[109] СУ РСФСР (1918), no. 85, item 889.

[110] СУ РСФСР (1920), no. 83, item 407.

[111] Article 23(5). СУ РСФСР (1922), no. 20-21, item 230.

[112] СЗ СССР (1924), no. 24, item 206.

Organization of the RSFSR removed the investigators from the courts to procurators.[113] In 1936 the investigative apparatus was removed from the justice system and placed within an independent Procuracy, formed in 1933. Throughout the 1930s the inquiry functions of police agencies were greatly enlarged for the great majority of crimes; in 1940 an investigative apparatus was formed within the Chief Police Administration of the USSR People's Commissariat of Internal Affairs (NKVD), and retained throughout the 1940-50s, having principal responsibility for investigating most ordinary crimes.

The adoption of the 1958 Fundamental Principles of Criminal Procedure of the USSR and Union Republics and attendant 1960 RSFSR Code of Criminal Procedure resulted in the abolition of the investigative apparatus within the Ministry of Internal Affairs (although specialized agencies of inquiry continued to investigate many crimes) and the transfer of preliminary investigation functions to the Procuracy and to State security agencies (KGB). The system was unsuccessful, as the Procuracy could not cope with the caseload. On 6 April 1963 the internal affairs agencies (then called the Ministry for the Protection of Public Order) were given back the right to perform preliminary investigations and the police retained the right to conduct inquiries in a substantial number of cases.[114] In the 1990s the federal tax police agencies and State Customs Committee agencies were authorized to act as agencies of inquiry; in 1995 an investigative apparatus was created in the Federal Tax Police Service and re-created in the Federal Security Service.

On 5 June 2007 the Law on the Procuracy and the Code of Criminal Procedure were amended to introduce far-reaching reforms of the investigative functions of the Procuracy. The Investigative Committee attached to the Procuracy of the Russian Federation was created to consist of: the Chief Investigative Administration of the said Investigative Committee, investigative administrations of the said Investigative Committee for the subjects of the Russian Federation and specialized investigative administrations equated to them, including military investigative administrations. This new system of agencies within the Procuracy implemented federal legislation on criminal proceedings at the investigative stage. The Chairman of the Investigative Committee was a first deputy of the Procurator General of the Russian Federation but was appointed to office by the Soviet of the Federation upon the recommendation of the President of the Russian Federation. Moreover, the first deputy and deputy chairmen

[113] I. I. Kolesnikov argued that the change of jurisdiction was purely nominal because investigators continued to be under the control of the People's Commissariat of Justice and local soviets and the Procuracy remained within the structure of the People's Commissariat of Justice. See Bozhev, note 60 above, p. 272.

[114] Ведомости СССР (1963), no. 16, item 181. The investigative apparatus formed under the NKVD Order of 1940 was in force until 1958.

of the Investigative Committee were appointed to and relieved from office by the President of the Russian Federation upon the recommendation of the Chairman of the Investigative Committee.

The Chairman of the Investigative Committee confirmed the structure and personnel establishment, as well as the powers, of structural subdivisions within the overall personnel establishment and wage funds fixed for the Investigative Committee. The workers of the Investigative Committee were considered to be Procuracy workers. The Statute on the Investigative Committee attached to the Procuracy of the Russian Federation was confirmed by Edict of the President of the Russian Federation on 1 August 2007 and replaced by the Edict of 14 January 2011, No. 38, which confirmed a new Statute.[115]

Current Legislation

By Edict of the President of the Russian Federation of 27 September 2010,[116] the Investigative Committee was separated from the Procuracy and transformed into an autonomous agency but operated as the legal successor of the Investigative Committee attached to the Procuracy of the Russian Federation. The legal status, competence, and powers of the Investigative Committee are regulated by the Federal Law on the Investigative Committee of the Russian Federation of 28 December 2010, as amended.[117]

The principal tasks of the Investigative Committee include the operational investigation of crimes pursuant to Russian legislation on criminal procedure allocating responsibility for the investigation of particular crimes; receiving reports of crimes allegedly committed, instituting criminal cases, performing the preliminary investigation, exercising procedural control over investigative agencies and officials, keeping statistics reports, and the like.

The Investigative Committee has a central apparatus in Moscow, chief investigative administrations and investigative administrations for subjects of the Russian Federation, specialized (including military) investigative administrations, and particular sections equated thereto. The Investigative Committee is headed by a Chairman appointed to and relieved from office by the President of the Russian Federation and is now no longer subordinate to the Procurator General. Investigative personnel have their own ranks, titles, oath of office, procedure for appointment and attestation, scales of remuneration, disciplinary procedures, and the like. Within the Armed Forces of the Russian Federation military investigative agencies operate which are accountable to the Chairman of the Investigative Committee.

115 СЗ РФ (2007), no. 32, item 4122; (2011), no. 4, item 572.

116 СЗ РФ (2010), no. 40, item 5043; transl. in Butler, note 2 above.

117 СЗ РФ (2011), no. 1, item 15, as amended; transl. in Butler, note 2 above.

Although now independent of the Procuracy, the Investigative Committee is subject to Procuracy supervision over the execution of laws just as any other State agency or officials.

Investigative Functions

Reference has been made above on several occasions to the preliminary investigative functions of a number of State agencies, including the Procuracy, Investigative Committee, internal affairs agencies, and narcotics police agencies. These functions have become sufficiently differentiated within each institution and characteristic of the general approach of Russian law to imposing responsibility for offences to justify independent treatment in this chapter.

Investigators are officials empowered by the State to establish in accordance with law the event of a crime, to engage in a search for and unmasking of the person(s) guilty of committing the crime (if one is determined to have been committed), to take measures for compensation of damage caused by the crime, eliminate the causes and conditions which led to the crime being committed, and to prevent the commission of new criminal acts. The 2001 Code of Criminal Procedure of the Russian Federation is the principal source for the rights and duties of investigators. The competence of Investigative Committee investigators extends to the gravest crimes against life, sexual crimes, official crimes, crimes committed by judges, procurators, investigators, and officials of internal affairs agencies, and customs agencies, and cases concerning crimes with respect to the said persons in connection with the performance of their official duties. Military investigators of the Investigative Committee investigate crimes committed by military servicemen, persons called up for military exercises, military builders, and persons equated to military servicemen of the Armed Forces, the Federal Security Service, the Foreign Intelligence Service, and others. The investigators of the internal affairs agencies investigate crimes in accordance with Article 151 of the 2001 Code of Criminal Procedure, as do the investigative agencies of the Federal Security Service.

All of the investigators are empowered to consider applications and communications concerning crimes, the Investigative Committee personnel having somewhat broader powers than the others.

The basic link in the apparatus of the Investigative Committee remains the city, district, and interdistrict subdivisions of the Investigative Committee, who are appointed to, transferred, and removed from office by the investigator of the superior investigative unit. Investigators at these levels sometimes work on a zonal principle, whereas those in large cities are likely to specialize in certain types of criminal cases. At the levels of the Russian Federation itself, republic, territories, and regions there are investigative entities within the Investigative Committee that are staffed by investigators for especially important cases, senior investigators, and aides thereof. Similar posts exist within the specialized investigative committees. The entire system is headed by the Investigative Committee of the Russian Federation. The Investigative Committee has military investigators, senior military investigators, and military investigators for especially important cases, and equivalent ranks within the Federal Security Service and internal affairs agencies.

The initial work of gathering evidence concerning a possible crime and conducting operational search activities to apprehend the culprit is performed by agencies of inquiry. These under Article 40 of the 2001 Russian Criminal Code are enumerated as the internal affairs agencies and "other agencies of executive power" endowed in accordance with a federal law with powers to effectuate operational-search activity, the Chief Judicial Bailiff of the Russian Federation and various officials subordinate to or connected with him, the commanders of military units, the heads of military institutions or garrisons, the masters of sea-going vessels, and others. The Federal Security Service agencies, the heads of correctional-labor institutions, State fire supervision agencies, operations agencies of the Federal Border Service of the Russian Federation, the investigators of the Investigative Committee of the Russian Federation and customs agencies are among the agencies of executive power so endowed. The specific jurisdiction of each agency is established, with distinctions drawn between cases in which a preliminary investigation is obligatory and those in which such investigation is not obligatory.

When the preliminary investigation is obligatory, the inquiry is directed towards an inspection of the site of the crime, performance of searches, seizures, the detention and interrogation of suspects, interrogation of the victim and witnesses, and similar urgent investigative actions. Under the second form of inquiry, the investigation of the case is performed by the agency of inquiry in full, up to and including a conclusion to indict or to termination of the proceedings in the case.

ARBITRATION

Informal dispute settlement, or to use modern parlance, alternative dispute resolution, has a venerable history in Russia. During the late nineteenth century, Russian jurists wrote major treatises as contributions to the emerging dialogue about the creation of permanent international institutions to settle interstate disputes. L. A. Kamarovskii's treatise on an international court was translated into French,[118] and F. F. Martens is an acknowledged father of the Hague arbitral tribunal and court.[119]

[118] L. A. Kamarovskii, *Le tribunal international,* transl. S. de Westman (1887); reissued in Russian with an Introduction by W. E. Butler: See Kamarovskii, Международный суд [International Court] (2007).

[119] See V. V. Pustogarov, *Our Martens: F. F. Martens. International Lawyer and Architect of Peace,*

For many years Russian legislation on arbitration was in a chaotic state, no less than three federal laws regulating arbitration: Annex 3 to the 1964 RSFSR Code of Civil Procedure; the Provisional Statute on the Arbitration Court for the Settlement of Economic Disputes, confirmed by Decree of the Supreme Soviet of the Russian Federation on 24 June 1992, as amended,[120] and the 1993 Law on International Commercial Arbitration.[121] On 24 July 2002 the first two, dealing with domestic arbitration, were replaced by the Federal Law on Arbitration Courts in the Russian Federation,[122] which in turn has been replaced by the Federal Law on Arbitration (Arbitral Consideration) in the Russian Federation of 29 December 2015.[123]

As a matter of Russian law, however, arbitration is not part of the judicial system. The Civil Code (Article 11) does refer to arbitration in connection with the "judicial defense of civil rights", and the 2002 Code of Civil Procedure of the Russian Federation makes provision for the "transfer by the parties for the consideration of an arbitration court" of a dispute (Article 3). A Russian court of ordinary jurisdiction will under the Code of Civil Procedure return a petition to sue if an arbitration court proceeding is already underway with regard to a dispute between the same parties, on the same subject, and on the same grounds (Article 135) or refuse to accept a petition to sue if an arbitration award has been rendered under the same circumstances, subject to a stipulated exception (Article 134).

There are several possible alternatives to arbitration under Russian law: *ad hoc* arbitration, recourse to various tribunals which have been or may be organized under Russian law, recourse to specialist arbitration tribunals, recourse to two permanent Russian arbitration courts, recourse to international arbitration.

Chambers of commerce, stock exchanges, unions of jurists, and even networks of enterprises and organizations have formed permanently operating arbitration courts which are now governed by the 2015 Federal Law on Arbitration. The Law on Chambers of Commerce and Industry in the Russian Federation of 7 July 1993, as amended,[124] empowers chambers of commerce to promote the settlement of disputes arising between subjects

transl W. E. Butler (2000), pp. 195-216.

120 Ведомости СНД и ВС РФ (1993), no. 30, item 1790; СЗ РФ (1997), no. 47, item 5341; (1999), no. 28, item 3493.

121 Ведомости СНД и ВС РФ (1993), no. 32, item 1240, as amended; transl. in Butler, note 2 above. For commentary on the law, see A. S. Komarov, S. N. Lebedev, and V. A. Musin (eds.), Международный коммерческий суд. Комментарий законодательства [International Commercial Arbitration. Commentary on Legislation] (Spb., 2007).

122 СЗ РФ (2002), no. 30, item 3019, as amended; transl. in Butler, note 2 above. This Law continues to apply to an arbitration begun but not completed before the entry of the 2015 Federal Law into force.

123 СЗ РФ (2016), no. 1(I), item 2.

124 Ведомости СНД и ВС РФ (1993), no. 33, item 1309, as amended.

of entrepreneurial activity (Article 3) and grants them the right to form arbitration courts and to confirm statutes on them and on the procedure for the consideration of disputes by the arbitration courts, lists of arbitrators, and recommend model arbitration clauses and agreements (Article 12). Subjects of the Russian Federation (for example, Bashkortostan on 14 October 1994) have adopted analogous legislation. Each permanently-operating arbitration court adopts its own rules (which may be known by various names: statute, charter, reglament, and others) laying down the procedures for the consideration of cases, in each instance any matters not regulated by the said rules being governed by the 2015 Federal Law on Arbitration. That law requires that there be an odd number of arbitrators, that any natural person possessing dispositive legal capacity and consenting to act may serve as an arbitrator (a formulation which includes the possibility of foreign arbitrators) on condition that the chairman or sole arbitrator must have a higher legal education, that the parties may by *compromis* agree the procedure for forming the court, in the absence of which three arbitrators shall be appointed; and that the arbitration court itself shall decide whether an arbitration agreement exists and whether it is valid. If the answer to the last is negative, the dispute is referred to an arbitrazh court for settlement.

The Federal Law on Organized Public Sales of 21 November 2011, as amended,[125] permits rules for organized public sales to provide that disputes between participants of a public sale or between parties to contracts concluded at organized public sales be settled by a permanently operating arbitration court (Article 24).

The Association of Russian Banks, the International Union of Jurists, and the Moscow Interbank Currency Exchange are among the associations that have formed specialized arbitration courts.

Those who were successful in the competitions conducted to receive stocks in federal ownership on pledge were required to accept as an obligatory condition of the credit contract an arbitration clause which referred disputes, if a party was a foreign juridical person or an enterprise with foreign investments, to the International Commercial Arbitration Court attached to the Russian Chamber of Commerce and Industry, and if a party was a juridical person registered in one of the Independent States or was a Russian juridical person without foreign participation, to the (now abolished) Arbitration Court for the Settlement of Economic Disputes attached to the Chamber of Commerce and Industry of the Russian Federation. Analogous clauses were required for the contract of pledge and commission agency arising out of such competitions.[126]

[125] СЗ РФ (2011), no. 48, item 6726, as amended. This Federal Law replaced an earlier version dating from 1992. Ведомости СНД и ВС РФ (1992), no. 18, item 961, as amended.

[126] See the Edict of the President of the Russian Federation, No. 889, adopted 31 August 1995, as amended, setting out the Rules for Conducting Auctions for the Right to Conclude

The Federal Law on Production Sharing Agreements of 30 December 1995, as amended,[127] allows disputes between the State and the investor connected with the use, termination, and invalidity of production sharing agreements to be settled in accordance with the conditions of the agreement in a court, arbitrazh court, or arbitration court, including institutes of international arbitration (Article 22). Analogous provisions have been imposed on Russian and Belarus parties who conclude contracts pursuant to the Agreement between the Governments of the Russian Federation and Belarus on Cooperation in the Development of the Oil and Gas Industry of Russia, concluded 2 March 1993 (Article 15).[128]

Ad hoc arbitration as a component of conciliation procedures to settle collective labor disputes is an available stage before workers have the right to strike against an employer. The 2001 Labor Code of the Russian Federation (Article 404), as amended,[129] makes provision for the formation of an *ad hoc* tribunal consisting of three persons who do not represent the parties to the dispute. The parties may choose the arbitrators by agreement or from those recommended by the State agency for the settlement of collective labor disputes. They have from three to five work days to consider the dispute from the moment of their appointment; however, their recommendations are binding only if the parties have so stipulated in advance in writing. These tribunals are called "labor arbitration tribunals"; even though they may only issue recommendations, the Russian word used is "*arbitrazhnyi*" [арбитражный], rather than, as one would expect, "*treteiskii*" [третейский].

International Commercial Arbitration

Reference has been made above to the unhappy choice of terminology in the Russian language to characterize the system of State arbitrazh courts. This confusion is perpetuated and exacerbated by the 1993 Law on International Commercial Arbitration, adopted to establish the framework for international commercial arbitration of all types in the Russian Federation. Here the Russian word "*arbitrazhnyi*" is used to mean "*treteiskii*", which is genuine voluntary third-party arbitration. It is common in commercial practice to see genuine arbitration confused with the State arbitrazh courts, the parties sometimes never ultimately understanding what type of dispute settlement they had in view. One consequence is certain from the confusion: a State arbitrazh court decision is not enforceable under the 1958 New York Convention on the Recognition and Enforcement of Arbitral Awards.

Contracts of Credit, the Pledge of Stocks in Federal Ownership, and Commission Agency. Model contract provisions for each transaction are appended to the Edict. C3 РФ (1995), no. 36, item 3527, as amended.

[127] C3 РФ (1996), no 1, item 18, as amended; transl. in Butler, *Foreign Investment Law in the Commonwealth of Independent States* (2002), pp. 634-655.

[128] See БНД, no. 5 (1994), pp. 25-28. Analogous provisions are found in Russian treaties with Armenia and Slovenia.

[129] C3 РФ (2002), no. 1(I), item 3, as amended; transl. in Butler, note 2 above.

The Law on International Commercial Arbitration encompasses any arbitration irrespective of whether it is formed *ad hoc* or effectuated by a permanently-operating arbitration institution. Specifically named are two such: the International Commercial Arbitration Court and the Maritime Arbitration Commission, both attached to the Chamber of Commerce and Industry of the Russian Federation. With insignificant changes, the 1993 Law on International Commercial Arbitration introduced into Russian Law the 1985 UNCITRAL Model Law on international commercial arbitration and thereby brought the Russian Federation into the forefront of the select number of European capitals who compete for the stature of being capitals for alternative dispute resolution.

The International Commercial Arbitration Court, known by its Russian acronym MKAC, is the legal successor to the Foreign Trade Arbitration Commission, founded in 1932 and attached to the USSR Chamber of Commerce and Industry.[130] Its Statute as amended comprises Annex 1 to the 1993 Law. The Reglament of the Court was confirmed by Order of the Chamber of Commerce and Industry on 18 October 2005 and entered into force from 1 March 2006[131] (replacing the Reglament of 8 December 1994). The 2005 Reglament was, in turn, replaced on 11 January 2017 with the Statute on the Organizational Foundations of the Activity of the International Commercial Arbitration Court attached to the Chamber of Commerce and Industry of the Russian Federation, in effect for cases commenced after 27 January 2017. This Statute and concomitant documents were issued as an Annex to Order No. 6 of the Chamber of Commerce and Industry. The panel of arbitrators of MKAC, which consisted solely of Soviet jurists prior to 1995, includes more than 100 experienced Western arbitrators proficient in the Russian language.

Between 1933 and 2011 inclusive, MKAC considered 7,847 cases. Of the 213 cases in the calendar year 2011, nearly half (103) related to contracts or delivery or purchase-sale; 28 to construction independent-work contracts; ten to the rendering of services; seven to international finance leasing contracts; seven to a contract of loan; one to a transport expediting contract; four to a contract of suretyship; seven to a contract of lease, and five to a license contract. The plaintiff succeeded in 48% of the cases (102) fully and partially in 24% of the cases (53).[132]

[130] A major virtue of MKAC is the repertoire of awards collected and commented upon in M. G. Rozenberg (1924-2012) (comp.), Практика международного коммерческого арбитражного суда: научно-практический комментарий [Practice of the International Commercial Arbitration Court: Scientific-Practical Commentary] (1997-).

[131] See A. S. Komarov (ed.), Регламент Международного коммерческого арбитражного суда при Торгово-промышленной палате Российской Федерации [Reglament of the International Commercial Arbitration Court attached to the Chamber of Commerce and Industry of the Russian Federation] (2012). These Rules continue to apply to cases commenced before 27 January 2017.

[132] The figures are drawn from A. I. Muranov (comp. & ed.), Международный

MKAC on average considered 300 cases per year from 2006 to 2011 inclusive. The majority involved parties from other countries of the Commonwealth of Independent States. In 2008, 63 cases involved a party from the European Union. About 22% of the claims fell within the range of US$10,000 to $50,000. The caseload has been analogous since then. 363 cases (including internal disputes) in 2017; 454 in 2018; and 522 in 2019. The largest component of the caseload in 2019 involved cases (34%) from the western hemisphere.[133]

The Maritime Arbitration attached to the Chamber of Commerce and Industry of the Russian Federation, known as MAK, is the legal successor to the Maritime Arbitration Commission founded in 1930; its Statute as amended comprises Annex 2 to the 1993 Law. It continues to operate substantially as before in accordance with the 1993 Law. MAK operates according to the Statute on the Organizational Foundations of the Activity of the Maritime Arbitration Commission attached to the Chamber of Commerce and Industry of the Russian Federation, in force from 27 January 2017. The Statute and four additional statutes, rules, and reglament were confirmed by Order No. 5 of the Chamber of Commerce and Industry on 11 January 2018.

Between 1932 and 2010, MAK decided 4,387 cases. Of these, 1,396 were concerned with the carriage of goods by sea; 1,034 with the rescue of ships; 741 with marine insurance; 635 with the chartering of ships, and 201 with the collision of ships. Of the 663 cases decided by MAK between 1991 and 2010, 328 involved Russian persons only; 49 cases involved foreigners on both sides; 115 involved a foreign person only as a plaintiff; 171 involved a foreign person only as a defendant.[134] The caseload thereafter is analogous. By 2020 the total number of cases decided reached 4,553.

коммерческий арбитраж: опыт отечественного регулирования/саморегулирования. 80 лет МКАС при ТПП РФ: 1932-2012 [International Commercial Arbitration: Experience of Fatherland Regulation/Self-Regulation. 80 Years of MKAC attached to the Chamber of Commerce and Industry of the Russian Federation 1932-2012] (2012), I, pp. 64-69.

[133] See in general T. E. Carbonneau, W. E. Butler, and H. Blair, *International Litigation and Arbitration: Cases and Materials* (3d ed.; 2020), Chapter 11.

[134] See Muranov, Международный коммерческий арбитраж: опыт отечественного регулирования. 80 лет МАК при ТПП СССР/ТПП РФ [International Commercial Arbitration: Experience of Fatherland Regulation. 80 Years of MAK attached to the Chamber of Commerce and Industry of the USSR/Chamber of Commerce and Industry of the Russian Federation. 1930-2010] (2011), pp. 3-7.

Enforcement of Arbitration Awards and Judicial Decisions

The autonomy of the arbitration clause is no longer doubted in Russian legal doctrine and legislation, but the juridical nature of the arbitration clause continues to be the subject of debate and can, depending upon its characterization, affect enforcement.[135] Some Russian jurists consider the arbitration clause to be a civil-law transaction; others believe such a clause to be fundamentally a procedural measure; and yet others are of the view that an arbitration clause is a provision *sui generis*. Those who favor the *sui generis* approach point in particular to the combination of contractual and procedural elements inherent in an arbitration clause as making it unique, sometimes called a 'civil law transaction of a special type'.

The "autonomy of the arbitration clause" carries the further implication that the legal regime of the clause is regulated first by arbitration legislation and only secondarily by the general provisions of civil legislation; that is, the 1993 Law on International Commercial Arbitration, although earlier in time, takes precedence over the Civil Code of the Russian Federation as *lex specialis*. It would follow that, in the absence in a contract or arbitration clause of special provisions to the contrary, rules of civil and company legislation providing for special requirements to conclude a valid civil law transaction (large-scale transaction, interested transaction, for example) are not applicable to arbitration agreements or clauses.

Russian international arbitration practice is consistent with this view. Credit and pledge agreements, for example, have been found invalid for failure to comply with Russian legislation and the requirements of charters of joint-stock societies. Jurisdiction over the dispute was assumed on the basis that even though the principal and derivative contracts were not valid, the arbitration clause contained therein survived that invalidity and conferred jurisdiction on the tribunal. It is presumed by the commentators that the legislative and charter provisions that rendered the principal civil-law transactions invalid did not taint the arbitration clause by reason of its special status, not merely its autonomy.

It was long a principle of Soviet law that the awards of foreign arbitration courts and decisions of foreign judicial instances were subject to recognition and enforcement in the former USSR if an international treaty of the USSR so provided. The position was elaborated last in the Soviet era in an Edict of the Presidium of the Supreme Soviet of the USSR adopted 21 June 1988.[136] That Edict remains in force in the Russian Federation (as do

135 V. A. Musin and O. Iu. Skvortsov (eds.), Международный коммерческий арбитраж: учебник [International Commercial Arbitration: Textbook] (2012), pp. 148-149; B. R. Karabelnikov, Международный коммерческий арбитраж: учебник [International Commercial Arbitration: Textbook] (2012), pp. 80-89.

136 See Ведомости СССР (1988), no 29, item 427; transl. in W. E. Butler, *Arbitration in the Soviet Union* (1989), pp. 16-21. Also see the Letter of the USSR Ministry of Justice of 9 March

the international treaties of the USSR containing relevant clauses), and the principle has been incorporated in the Federal Constitutional Law on the Judicial System of the Russian Federation of 31 December 1996, as amended (Article 6).The formalities of an enforcement proceeding are laid down in the Federal Law on an Execution Proceeding of 2 October 2007[137] and in the 2003 Code of Civil Procedure.[138]

Russian courts have found reciprocity in principle with the courts of England and Wales and granted recognition to and enforced English court judgments on this basis: "Judicial decisions rendered in Russia and other States of the CIS, and also judicial decisions rendered by courts of the United States, Central and South America, China, and Japan are subject to enforcement in England if they satisfy the requirements of the Common Law" even in the absence of a treaty.[139]

Although treaties regulating the mutual recognition and enforcement of judicial decisions were concluded with all of the Central and East European countries and with the Independent States of the former Soviet Union, there are but a tiny handful with the rest of the world (among them, Greece, Italy, Spain) and none with the leading investment countries. As a result, the 1958 New York Convention,[140] to which the USSR was and the Russian Federation therefore is a party, assumes special significance for most foreign investors and gives arbitration a far more prominent role than it would otherwise have in a normal investment climate.

ROLE OF NON-STATE ENTITIES

Comrades' courts are an institution of the Soviet era whose foundation legislation was deemed to have lost force in the Russian Federation by the enactment of the 1995 Federal Law on Social Associations, as amended

1972 and the Instruction of the same Ministry on legal assistance to foreign States by courts and the notariat of 28 February 1972, as amended 26 June 1985. Закон [Law], no. 8 (1998), pp. 40-45. The Instruction was declared not to apply on the territory of the Russian Federation by an Order of the Ministry of Justice of the Russian Federation of 24 May 2001, No. 160. The Letter of 9 March 1972 was included on a List of Normative Acts of the Ministry of Justice of the USSR Deemed Not to Operate on the Territory of the Russian Federation, pursuant to the Order of the Ministry of Justice of the Russian Federation of 19 February 2002, No. 52. Both are available on Consultant Plus.

137 СЗ РФ (2007), no. 41, item 4849; transl. in Butler, note 2 above.

138 Transl. in Butler, note 45 above.

139 Case No. A40-53839/05-8-388, 21 December 2005, Arbitrazh Court, City of Moscow; transl. together with the appeal against the decision, which affirmed the lower court, in *Russian Law: Theory and Practice*, no. 1 (2008), pp. 128-136.

140 B. R. Karabelnikov, Исполнение решений международных коммерческих арбитражей: Комментарий к Нью-Йоркской конвенции 1958 г. и главам 30 и 31 АПК РФ 2002 г. [Execution of Awards of International Commercial Arbitral Tribunals: Commentary to the 1958 New York Convention and Chapters 30 and 31 of the 2002 Code of Arbitrazh Procedure of the Russian Federation] (2d ed., 2003).

(Article 49).[141] The legislative acts regulating the people's guards were deemed not to operate on the territory of the Russian Federation by the same enactment. According to press reports, however, comrades' courts continued to be used in some communities, including in parts of Moscow, and the people's guards were revised after 1997 under various names to help cope with the incidence of street crime and threats of terrorism in individual cities.[142]

Both comrades' courts and people's guards represented a community response to law enforcement. A market response has been the emergence of private detective and bodyguard services pursuant to the Law on Private Detective and Protection Activity in the Russian Federation, adopted 11 March 1992, as amended.[143] Under this Law, specially licensed juridical persons or individual entrepreneurs may offer investigative and personal protection services on a contractual basis to natural and juridical persons. The rising crime rate experienced, especially contract assassinations, kidnappings, and armed robberies, created considerable demand for private sector provision of such protection. Investigative services include background checks on potential business partners, bodyguard services, search for lost or stolen property, data on unfair competition, information on business reputation, and the like. Licenses are issued by internal affairs agencies.

A private detective or protector must be a Russian citizen who has reached at least 21 years of age, has a law degree, or has special training of not less than three years in operational or investigative subdivisions of law enforcement agencies, internal affairs agencies, or the FSB. Individuals with a record of mental illness, alcoholism, narcotics addiction, criminal record for committing an intentional crime, or dismissed from State service under compromising circumstances, are not eligible to receive a license. The license to be a detective does not in and of itself make one a detective. There must follow a labor contract with an enterprise or the registration of an "individual private detective enterprise". A list of the types of special means which detectives and protectors are authorized to use in their work was confirmed by Decree of the Government of the Russian Federation No 587, adopted 14 August 1992, as amended.[144]

141 СЗ РФ (1995), no 21, item 1930, as amended.

142 The city of Moscow adopted on 26 June 2002 the Law on the Moscow City People's Guard as a State-social association created to render assistance to agencies of State power of the City of Moscow and law enforcement agencies in ensuring public order. See Ведомости Московской городской Думы [Gazette of the Moscow City Duma] (2002), no. 8, item 162, as amended 7 October 2015. Available on Consultant Plus.

143 Ведомости СНД и ВС РФ (1992), no 17, item 888, as amended; transl. in Butler, note 2 above.

144 САПП РФ (1992), no 8, item 506, as amended.

On 2 April 2014, however, the Russian Federation adopted the Federal Law on the Participation of Citizens in the Protection of Public Order.[145] Participation for these purposes is defined as rendering of assistance by citizens to internal affairs agencies (or police) and other law enforcement agencies for the purposes of the defense of human life, health, honor, and dignity, ownership, interest of society and the State against criminal and other unlawful infringements committed in public places and helping to search for missing persons whose life or health may be threatened by danger or with respect to whom unlawful acts may be committed. All participation is voluntary, and members of the people's guard – citizens of Russia who are members of a social association participating in the protection of public order in interaction with internal affairs agencies (or police) and other law enforcement agencies, agencies of State power, and agencies of local self-government – are singled out for special encouragement, although they are not the only means by which citizens may become involved in protection public order.

People's guard units or associations are created at the initiative of citizens of the Russian Federation who have expressed the wish to participate in the protection of public order in the form of a social organization with notification of agencies of local self-government of the respective municipal formation (in subjects of the Russian Federation which are cities of federal significance, Moscow, St. Petersburg, and Sevastopol, agencies of State power of the respective subject of the Russian Federation unless the need to inform agencies of local self-government of intra-city municipal formations has been established by a law of the respective subject of the Russian Federation) and territorial agency of the federal agency of executive power in the sphere of internal affairs.

The boundaries of the territory on which people's guards may be created are established by the representative agency of the respective municipal formation (in subjects of the Russian Federation which are cities of federal significance, Moscow, St. Petersburg, and Sevastopol, by agencies of State power of the respective subject of the Russian Federation unless this is relegated to the powers of the representative agencies of intra-city municipal formations by a law of the respective subject of the Russian Federation). Only one people's guard association may, as a rule, be created on a single territory.

People's guards may participate in the protection of public order only after the entry thereof in the regional register.[146]

[145] СЗ РФ (2014), no. 14, item 1536, as amended; transl. in Butler, note 2 above.

[146] The Procedure for Forming and Keeping the Regional Register of People's Guards and Social Associations of a Law Enforcement Orientation was confirmed by Order of the Ministry of Internal Affairs of the Russian Federation on 21 July 2014, No. 599. The Registers are kept by territorial agencies of the MVD and formed on the basis of information provided

The principal activities of people's guards are:

(1) assistance to internal affairs agencies (or police) and other law enforcement agencies in the protection of public order;

(2) participation in the prevention and suppression of violations on the territory at the place where the people's guards are formed;

(3) participation in the protection of public order in instances of extraordinary situations;

(4) dissemination of legal knowledge and explanation of norms of behavior in public places.

The creation, reorganization, and/or liquidation of social associations of a law enforcement orientation are determined by the Federal Law of 19 May 1995, No. 82-Ф3, "On Social Associations", taking into account the provisions of the Federal Law on the participation of citizens in the protection of public order.

There may not be founders of people's guards Russian citizens who:

(1) have an unremoved or uncancelled record of conviction;

(2) are being criminally prosecuted;

(3) were previously convicted for intentional crimes;

(4) are included on a list of organizations and natural persons with respect to whom there is information concerning their involvement in extremist activity or terrorism;

(5) are subject to a court decision establishing that their actions contained the indicia of extremist activity and which has entered into legal force;

(6) suffer from mental distress or are ill with narcotics addiction or alcoholism;

(7) are deemed to lack dispositive legal capacity or to have limited dispositive legal capacity by decision of a court which has entered into legal force;

(8) have been subjected repeatedly during the year preceding the day of creation of the people's guard unit to administrative punishment in a judicial proceeding for the administrative violations;

(9) are citizens or subjects of a foreign State.

at the district level.

The creation of people's guard units attached to political parties, religious associations, and also the creation and activity of political parties and religious associations in people's guards, are prohibited.

Commanders of people's guards elected by members of the people's guards direct these units by agreement with the agencies of local self-government of the respective municipal formation and the territorial internal affairs agency.

The return to people's guard units is a revival and adaptation, on this occasion with the avowed purpose of assisting State law enforcement agencies, of a Soviet institution originally conceived to represent a transfer of State functions to non-State bodies. Still in its formative stages at the level of national regulation, this initiative represents a potentially substantial involvement of non-State social associations in reinforcing the operations of State institutions.

LAW ENFORCEMENT COORDINATION IN THE CIS

Within the framework of the CIS a number of law enforcement coordination groups and councils have been created to encourage cooperation in law enforcement, training, research, and joint measures, when necessary, against particular threats. These bodies include the Coordination Council of Procurators General, the Council of Ministers of Internal Affairs, the Council of Heads of Security Agencies and Special Services, the Council of Those Commanding Border Forces, the Council of Heads of Customs Services, and analogous bodies for the campaign against narcotics. The priorities for cooperation have been joint efforts against organized crime, revision of the 1993 Minsk Convention on mutual legal assistance with regard to civil, family, and criminal cases, and the preparation of model codes, including on questions of narcotics.

8

CONSTITUTIONAL LAW

The enactment for the first time in Russian history of a genuinely democratic Constitution has given a new dimension to the branch of legal science devoted to State structures. Soviet legal doctrine traditionally preferred the term "State law" [государственное право], partly a legacy of the German *Staatsrecht* and partly a legacy of the Statist orientation of the Soviet legal era; in some quarters the term still finds favor in Russia. The great majority of Russian jurists now prefer the term "constitutional law" [конституционное право], partly as a break with the past and partly to reflect the new relationship between the individual and the State.[1]

In conformity with its federative structure, the Russian Federation is a country of many constitutions and constitutive documents – one for the Federation itself and one for each subject of the Federation, plus three treaties of the Federation (sometimes collectively referred to in the singular as the Treaty of the Federation), and a supplementary network of individual treaties concluded between the Federation and certain subjects of the Federation. During the late Soviet era, the sundry entities making up the Union of Soviet Socialist Republics spawned nearly one hundred constitutions, of which 36 were in force on Soviet territory when the Soviet Union was dissolved. The Russian Federation alone has exceeded that target.

CONCEPT OF FEDERATIONISM

The "federation" is a form of Russian statehood that originated in Leninist doctrines directed towards coping with the nationality problem of Russia. "Federated in form, but socialist in substance" was the formula often posited by Soviet legal textbooks. Federation also was a structure which the early Bolsheviks believed might be adapted to a world in which socialism had triumphed. The Russian Federation as such was proclaimed in the guise of the Russian Soviet Federated Socialist Republic (RSFSR) at the III All-Russian Congress of Soviets in January 1918. At first it was intended to encompass all of what became the former Soviet Union and not merely what falls within the boundaries of the contemporary Russian Federation. That vision of the future did not happen; the Grand Duchy of

1 "After 1917 the name 'State law' became more widespread mostly because of the little significance and formal role of socialist constitutions and the total statization of social life". See M. V. Baglai, Конституционное право Российской Федерации [Constitutional Law of the Russian Federation] (13th ed.; 2018), p. 21.

Finland, Russian Poland, the Baltic States, Ukraine, Tatarstan, and Tuva each declared independence, and Belorussia, Turkestan, and the Caucasian republics, also declared to be independent, entered into negotiations with the RSFSR about treaty relationships. Various formations came into being with sundry denominations on the territory of the present Russian Federation, complicated by the absence of well-defined pre-existing boundaries or frontiers and the lack of a clear distinction, for example, between an autonomous republic or a region. Other entities which had acquired some sort of administrative-territorial identity under the Russian Empire retained this, often with an elevated status. In 1923 the RSFSR consisted of 11 autonomous republics, 14 autonomous regions, and 63 provinces and regions.

The formation of the Union of Soviet Socialist Republics by the Treaty of the Union on 30 December 1922 superimposed, from the Russian perspective, another type of federation upon the RSFSR, which itself became a member of the new confederated Union. There remained throughout the existence of the Soviet Union a tension between the desirability of preserving nationality identification at various levels and strong pressures in favor of the centralization of economic management and unitary administration of the State. Throughout all, however, the federative principle was retained, and there is a compelling argument that its persistent existence considerably facilitated the dismantling of the Soviet Union in 1991 without violence.

Throughout the sunset years of the RSFSR, the Constitution in force dated from 1978. During the *perestroika* era from 1986 to 1991, more than 200 changes and additions were introduced, including the post of President, the Constitutional Court, eliminating of the leading role of the Communist Party of the Soviet Union, a revised parliamentary structure, a more democratic chapter on the rights and freedoms of man and citizen, and the restructuring of the Federation in accordance with the 1992 Treaty of the Federation. The resultant amalgam was pure "scissors and paste". The rivalries between the parliament and the President contributed to a number of attempts to shackle Presidential authority.

In December 1992 the VII Congress of People's Deputies incorporated Article 126^{6} into the RSFSR Constitution, which provided that in the event of the dissolution or suspension of the activity of any legally elected agencies of State power, the powers of the President would be subject to immediate termination. Preparations were openly made to impeach the President by using Article 126^{10} of the RSFSR Constitution. Relations worsened between the President and the Supreme Soviet of the RSFSR. On 20 March 1993 the President signed an edict introducing a special procedure for governing until the crisis of power was overcome, whereupon the next day the Supreme Soviet condemned the edict and on the day following the Constitutional Court of Russia (nine judges of 12), having nothing in their hands except a television account of the edict, decreed that the edict was contrary to the Constitution in at least nine respects. On 24 March 1993 the President signed an edict authorizing a referendum vote of confidence in the President, fixing the date of 25 April 1993 for the ballot. The referendum was held (although the questions put were altered by the Congress of People's Deputies), and 60.5% of those voting expressed confidence in the President and favored new elections of the parliament. The existing RSFSR Constitution was unable to cope with these conflicts.

It had been recognized in 1990 as soon as Russia had declared her State sovereignty that a new Constitution would be required. The I Congress of People's Deputies (22 June 1990) formed a Constitutional Commission under the chairmanship of Boris Eltsin (then a deputy of the Supreme Soviet of the RSFSR) containing 102 members from throughout the Federation. Within four months the Commission had produced a draft for public discussion, which was countered immediately by alternative drafts emanating from various circles or by proposals for amendments. The draft was considered in October 1991 by the V Congress of People's Deputies, reworked and again published for discussion. In April 1992 the VI Congress of People's Deputies approved the general conception of the draft. The Supreme Soviet and the Constitutional Commission were directed to revise the draft for the next session of the Congress.

The VII (December 1992), VIII (March 1993), and IX (April 1993) Congresses of People's Deputies did not consider the draft further, although the VII Congress had voted to submit the basic provisions of the draft to a national referendum, a decision that was repealed by the VIII Congress. When in May 1993 the draft version approved by the Supreme Soviet was published, it was proposed to convoke the Congress of People's Deputies on 17 November 1993 to consider and adopt the Constitution; it was this same Supreme Soviet which planned to impeach the President at the next Congress.

The President in the meantime pursued his own course of action. On 12 May 1993 he issued an Edict on Measures Relating to Completion of the Preparation of a New Constitution of the Russian Federation,[2] pursuant to which a Constitutional Assembly was convened in Moscow on 5 June 1993 widely representative of the entire country. On 24 June 1993 the Supreme Soviet refused cooperation with the Constitutional Assembly on the grounds that some of its coordinators and organizers were corrupt. The President of the Russian Federation submitted his draft Constitution to the Assembly for consideration, but encouraged the Commission to find compromises between his draft and its own. On 23 July 1993 the Constitutional Assembly completed its work and by a majority vote approved the draft which it had produced.[3]

[2] САПП РФ (1993), no. 20, item 1757.

[3] For an annotated text of the 1978 RSFSR Constitution in all of its versions and the draft

The crisis deepened in autumn 1993. Both the President and the Supreme Soviet had their own versions of the Constitution, and neither wished to compromise. On 21 September 1993 the President issued an Edict on the Step by Step Constitutional Reform of the Russian Federation which terminated the powers of the people's deputies, introduced a transition period for governing based on the draft new Constitution approved by the Constitutional Assembly, fixed elections to the State Duma for 11-12 December 1993, and an all-people's vote on 12 December 1993 to consider the adoption of the new Constitution.[4] On the same day the Presidium of the Supreme Soviet, citing Article 121[6] of the RSFSR Constitution, terminated the powers of the President of the Russian Federation and transferred the powers of the President to the Vice President of Russia, Aleksandr Vladimirovich Rutskoi. In the view of the Supreme Soviet, the President had perpetrated a *coup d'état*; the Constitutional Court declared the Presidential edict to be unconstitutional and called for his impeachment.[5] Appointments were made to the so-called "power" ministries, and the Criminal Code of the RSFSR was amended to introduce the crime of anti-constitutional activity, a capital offense. The opposition rested on an existing RSFSR Constitution out of step with democratic change, and the President relied upon the electorate and the subjects of the Federation.

The dramatic confrontation at the White House in Moscow led to Presidential rule. On 7 October 1993 the President issued an Edict on Legal Regulation in the Period of Step by Step Constitutional Reform in the Russian Federation.[6] This edict confirmed the operation throughout the territory of Russia of all laws and decrees adopted by the Supreme Soviet and by the Congress of People's Deputies before 21 September 1993. It further provided that legal regulation usually within parliamentary competence would during the transition period be effectuated by edicts of the President. The Constitutional Court was suspended until the new Constitution was adopted. The Chairman of the Constitutional Court resigned, and the Vice President of Russia, although directly elected by the people, was removed from office by the President of Russia.

Constitution produced by the Constitutional Assembly, see S. A. Avak'ian, Конституция России: природа, эволюция, современность [Constitution of Russia: Nature, Evolution, Contemporaneity] (1997). The verbatim proceedings of the Constitutional Assembly were published in 21 volumes. A six-volume history (in ten) of the Constitutional Assembly appeared to supplement the official documentation.

[4] САПП РФ (1993), no. 39, item 3597; no. 41, item 3907; no. 42, item 3993; no. 52, item 5086; (1994), no. 6, item 437. The "all-people's vote", the expression used in these normative acts, may have been chosen to distinguish this exercise from a routine referendum, where the thresholds of minimum participation and approval differed.

[5] Ultimately these events led to abortive attempts to actually pursue impeachment, thoroughly reviewed in Kaj Høber, *The Impeachment of President Yeltsin* (2004).

[6] САПП РФ (1993), no. 41. The Edict lost force on 24 December 1993. САПП РФ (1993), no. 52, item 5086.

The President terminated, by an Edict of 9 October 1993,[7] the powers of soviets of people's deputies and by an Edict of 27 October 1993 confirmed Basic Provisions on elections to representative agencies of State power in the regions.[8] This last edict effectively eliminated the last remnants of authority originating in the Soviet system. The draft Constitution to be considered at the all-people's vote was published on 10 November 1993. In the all-people's vote held on 12 December 1993, 54.8% of registered voters participated, and of those, 58.4% voted in favor of the new Constitution.

During 1990-1991, most autonomous republics and a number of autonomous regions in the RSFSR proclaimed themselves to be sovereign States within the RSFSR. In a few, separatist sentiments were strongly expressed (Chechnia, Tatarstan). The IV Congress of People's Deputies of the RSFSR voted to exclude the word "autonomous" from the designation of autonomous republics, which became "republics within the Russian Federation". These forces led to the conclusion of the Treaty of the Federation on 31 March 1992 and the formal incorporation of that Treaty into the 1978 RSFSR Constitution on 10 April 1992 (and subsequently into the 1993 Russian Constitution). In greater detail than any preceding Russian or Soviet constitutional document, the Treaty of the Federation delimited the areas of jurisdiction between the Russian Federation and the (then) 89 subjects of the Federation. The resulting State structure is paradoxical in that the Russian nation has no separate administrative-territorial entity as such but rather sees its interests best expressed in a multinational State formation, that the republics within the Russian Federation are far from homogeneous in nationality, and that the name "Russia", which identifies the predominant nationality within the frontiers of the Russian Federation, is chosen for what the Constitution described as a multinational State.

The foundation elements of the Federation are the provision of the Constitution stipulating that the Russian Federation is a State (Article 1) made up of the subjects of the Federation (Article 65). Subjects of the Federation have no right of unilateral secession; withdrawal from the Federation is possible only by mutual consent of the Russian Federation and the subject of the Federation in accordance with a federal constitutional law.[9] The number of subjects of the Federation may be enlarged, although the numbers of indigenous peoples and tribes inhabiting the Russian Federation are so fractionated that it is unlikely they will be accorded the

[7] САПП РФ (1993), no. 41, item 3924. Lost force by Edict of the President of the Russian Federation, 17 June 2000. СЗ РФ (2000), no. 25, item 2678.

[8] САПП РФ (1993), no. 44, item 4189; no. 45, item 4192. Lost force by Edict of the President of the Russian Federation, 17 June 2000. СЗ РФ (2000), no. 25, item 2678.

[9] See T. Ia. Khabrieva, Современные проблемы самоопределения этносов: Сравнительно-правовое исследование [Modern Problems of Self-Determination of Ethnic Groups: Comparative Law Research] (2010); reviewed in *The Journal of Comparative Law*, VIII (2013), pp. 297-304.

status of a subject of the Federation. Their rights are guaranteed separately in Article 69 of the 1993 Russian Constitution "in accordance with generally-recognized principles and norms of international law and international treaties of the Russian Federation", and their status is elaborated in the Federal Law "On Guarantees of the Rights of Native Small Peoples of the Russian Federation" of 30 April 1999, as amended.[10] The Russian Federation is a party to the Framework Convention for the Protection of National Minorities, signed at Strasbourg on 1 February 1995 and ratified by Russia on 18 June 1998.

The Constitution establishes the territory of the Russian Federation,[11] the Russian language as the State language, a uniform customs, monetary, and tax system, a delimitation of jurisdiction under which the Russian Federation possesses exclusive and joint jurisdiction with respect to the subjects of the Federation, and the subjects retain residual jurisdiction over matters not otherwise relegated. There is a complex structure for arranging executive and legislative power, but a unified judicial system and procuracy. Under circumstances determined by the 1993 Russian Constitution, the federal authorities have authorization to interfere in the affairs of the subjects of the Federation.

The status of the Russian language as the "State" language means that it is studied in all educational institutions, that official documents are issued in Russian, and that State legislative, executive, judicial, and other agencies work in the Russian language. The Law "On Languages of Peoples of the Russian Federation" of 25 October 1991, as amended,[12] provides that citizens who do not know Russian may use their native language in State agencies, organizations, and institutions and on some occasions will be provided with an interpreter (in courts). The Cyrillic alphabet is specially protected; both Russian and the alphabets of State languages of the republics within Russia must be based graphically on Cyrillic, although federal laws may establish exceptions. These provisions concerning Cyrillic

[10] СЗ РФ (1999), no. 18, item 2208, as amended.

[11] Russian territory comprises the territories of the subject of the Federation, internal waters and territorial sea, superjacent airspace, and what the 2020 amendments describe as "federal territories", which remain to be defined and created. The 2020 amendments further provided that actions (except for delimitation, demarcation, and re-demarcation of the State boundary of the Russian Federation with neighboring States) directed towards the alienation of part of the territory of the Russian Federation, and also appeals for such actions, are not permitted

[12] Ведомости СНД и ВС РСФСР (1991), no. 50, item 1740, as amended. On the same day the RSFSR Supreme Soviet also adopted the Declaration on the Languages of the Peoples of Russia as an Appendix to the Decree of the RSFSR Supreme Soviet of 25 October 1991, No. 1808-1, which provided that certain provisions of the said Law would enter into force between 1 July 1992, 1 June 1993, and 1 June 1995. Ibid., (1991), no. 50, items 1741 and 1742. In the 2020 amendments to the Constitution the Russian language was elevated in status to the "language of the State-forming people within the multinational union of equal peoples of the Russian Federation" (Article 68).

were challenged in the Constitutional Court of the Russian Federation and upheld as constitutional by the Court in a Decree of 16 November 2004,[13] with the observations that:

> ... a change of the graphic foundation of an alphabet is admissible only if it pursues constitutionally significant purposes, meets historico-cultural, social, and political realities, and also the interests of the multinational people of the Russian Federation. Resolution of this question by a republic unilaterally, without taking into account the requirements and guarantees in the language sphere arising from the Constitution of the Russian Federation, could lead not only to a weakening of federative unity and a violation of the powers of the Russian Federation in the language sphere, but also to a limitation of the constitutional rights and freedoms of citizens, including those residing beyond the limits of the republic for whom the particular language is native, on the use of the native language, the free choice of a language of communion, nurturing, teaching, and creativity, participation in cultural life, access to cultural valuables, many of which were created on the basis of the writing historically formed.

The design of the State symbols of the Russian Federation has been controversial. Under the Constitution they are the State flag, Arms, and anthem, the design or wording of which is determined by a federal constitutional law devoted respectively to each of them of 25 December 2000, as amended.[14] Those constitutional laws replaced temporary subordinate legislation: the Statute on the State Flag and Statute on the State Anthem, confirmed by Edicts of the President of the Russian Federation on 11 December 1993,[15] and the State Arms, by an Edict of 30 November 1993.[16]

The capital of the Russian Federation is the City of Moscow (Article 70(2), 1993 Russian Constitution), which is a subject of the Russian Federation whose status as capital is defined by the Federal Law on the Status of the Capital of the Russian Federation, of 15 April 1993, as amended.[17]

The March 2020 amendments to the Constitution address for the first time at the constitutional level the relationship between the former Soviet Union and the present Russian Federation. When the Soviet Union was dissolved as of 25 December 1991, the Russian Federation notified other

[13] СЗ РФ (2004), no. 47, item 4691.

[14] On the State Flag, State Arms, and the State Anthem respectively, see СЗ РФ (2000), no. 52(I), items 5020, 5021, and 5022; (2002), no. 28, items 2780-82.

[15] САПП РФ (1993), no. 51, items 4928 and 4929.

[16] САПП РФ (1993), no. 49, item 4761.

[17] Ведомости СНД и ВС РФ (1993), no. 19, item 685, as amended. Although Moscow is the capital city of Russia, it does not follow that all federal agencies are necessarily located there. The Constitutional Court moved to St. Petersburg in March 2008. Article 70 of the Constitution was amended in 2020 to provide that the permanent location of individual federal agencies may be in other cities.

States, the United Nations, and other international organizations that Russia was the "legal continuer" and the other eleven union republics were "legal successors" of the Soviet Union. The newly-created term "legal continuer" was understood to mean that the principles of legal succession were not relevant to Russia and that, for all practical purposes, the Russian Federation assumed the mantle of the Soviet Union. The 2020 amendments added Article 67[1] to the Constitution providing that:

> The Russian Federation shall be the legal successor of the USSR on its territory, and also the legal successor (or legal continuer) of the USSR with respect to membership in international organizations, organs thereof, participation in international treaties, and also with respect to obligations and assets of the USSR provided for by international treaties beyond the limits of the territory of the Russian Federation.

The formulation appears to contemplate a dual situation. Russia is said to be the legal successor of the Soviet Union on Russian territory, that is domestically, but enjoys a dual status at the international level with respect to participation in international organizations and treaties and to obligations and assets of the USSR outside Russia. The formulation in the present writer's translation distinguishes between legal continuer and legal successors; they are not synonyms. The historical continuity between Russia back to its earliest roots, including the adoption of Christianity ca. 988, is emphasized in the same Article: "The Russian Federation, united by a thousand-year history, preserving the memory of ancestors and the ideals and faith in God passed on to us, and also succession in the development of the Russian State, shall be deemed a historically-formed State unity". In this clause the use of the term "succession" is puzzling and may not have the same meaning as in the preceding point.

SUBJECTS OF THE FEDERATION

The subjects of the Federation are enumerated in alphabetical order and category by the 1993 Russian Constitution (Article 65). Originally there were 89; mergers amongst them and accessions have reduced the total to 85. Although one associates the Russian Federation with the nationality principle, the great majority of the subjects of the Federation are based purely on territorial considerations, and the remaining subjects are far from homogeneous nationality entities. The senior category is the republic within the Federation, followed by the territory, the region, the cities of federal significance (Moscow, St Petersburg, Sevastopol), the one autonomous region, and the national areas. Each has its own constitution, charter, law, or other constitutive document. Although their names are embodied in the Russian Constitution, each retains the right to change its name, such changes to date being incorporated without amendment of the Constitution by edict of the President of the Russian Federation.[18]

The republics within the Russian Federation have the stature of independent States, even though they have surrendered their right of unilateral secession. The hierarchy among the other subjects of the Russian Federation, except for the sequence of enumeration in the Constitution, is obscure. The Constitution speaks of subjects of the Federation changing their status (Article 66(5)), but why they should do so if each has equal rights is unclear. In matters of shared jurisdiction they are identical, as too are they equal in representation in the Soviet of the Federation. As noted elsewhere (Chapter 5), the subjects of the Federation went through a period from 1993 to 2001 when they quietly concluded treaties clarifying the sharing of jurisdiction with the Federation. In some cases the powers of the subject of the Federation were enlarged. No longer could it be said that each enjoyed necessarily the same powers as other subjects of the Federation.[19] On 12 March 1996 the President confirmed by Edict, as amended, the Statute on the Procedure for Work Relating to Delimitation of the Subjects of Jurisdiction and Powers Between Federal Agencies of State Power and Agencies of State Power of the Subjects of the Russian Federation and on the Mutual Transfer of the Effectuation of Part of Their Powers by Federal Agencies of Executive Power and Agencies of Executive Power of the Subject of the Federation.[20] A Commission attached to the President of the Russian Federation worked with the draft treaties and agreements. The principles guiding the Commission include: the principles of delimitation of the subjects of jurisdiction and powers are established by federal laws; a treaty may not establish or change the constitutional status of a subject of the Federation; the treaty may not allow an exception or redistribution of subjects of jurisdiction of the Russian Federation or subjects of joint jurisdiction established in accordance with Articles 71 and 72 of the 1993 Russian Constitution, and powers may not be transferred to a subject of the Federation which relate to guaranteeing the foundations of the constitutional system, the equality of rights and freedoms of citizens, or otherwise which

[18] See, for example, Edicts of the President of the Russian Federation of 9 January 1996, 10 February 1996, 9 June 2001, and 25 July 2003. C3 PФ (1996), no. 3, item 152; no. 7, item 676; (2001), no. 24, item 2421; (2003), no. 30, item 3051.

[19] This process ceased in the late Eltsin years. From June 1998 few, if any, treaties or agreements were concluded between the center and the subjects of the Federation and no existing treaties renewed or extended, although agreements were concluded in November 2001 between Far Eastern subjects of the Federation and the Russian Ministry of Justice on bringing regional legislation into conformity with federal laws. See J. Kahn, *Federalism, Democratization and the Rule of Law in Russia* (2002), p. 237. Commencing in November 2001 treaties began to be concluded between the federal government and subjects of the Federation which terminated the earlier treaties on the grounds that they had served their purpose. See, for example, C3 PФ (2002), no. 12, items 3277-3280.

[20] C3 PФ (1996), no. 12, item 1058; no. 49, item 5534. Lost force by Edict of 28 May 2004, No. 701. C3 PФ (2004), no. 22, item 2148.

would violate the territorial integrity of Russia or the supremacy of the Constitution and federal laws throughout the Russian Federation. The Edict of 12 March 1996 was replaced by the Federal Law of 6 October 2003 "On General Principles of the Organization of Local Self-Government in the Russian Federation"[21] and the Edict of the President of the Russian Federation of 27 November 2003 "On Measures for the Development of Federal Relations and Local Self-Government in the Russian Federation".[22]

Subjects of the Russian Federation have their own legal systems emanating from their own constitutive documents, laws, and subordinate legal acts. While each therefore has its own constitutional law, it must form part of an integral and non-contradictory whole with the legal system of the Russian Federation. The creation of free economic zones on the territory of subjects of the Federation has the effect of enlarging the rights of the subject of the Federation over customs, taxes, the investment regime, and entrepreneurial activity.

In practice many subjects of the Russian Federation abused their rights either by failing to introduce constitutional and other legislation where they should have done so or by adopting legislation which was contrary to the 1993 Russian Constitution or otherwise in violation of the delimitation of jurisdiction. The Commission for the Interaction of Federal Agencies of State Power and Agencies of State Power of Subjects of the Russian Federation when Conducting Constitutional Law Reform in Subjects of the Russian Federation attached to the President of the Russian Federation pursuant to an Edict of 25 January 1996 was abolished in August 2001. In a few instances the President of the Russian Federation has exercised his right to suspend the operation of acts of executive power of subjects of the Russian Federation which are contrary to the Constitution, federal laws, or international treaties of the Russian Federation. The Constitutional Court of the Russian Federation has held unconstitutional a number of enactments of subjects of the Russian Federation on the grounds that those enactments exceeded the powers of the subjects to adopt. Sakha, for example, repealed provisions in its Basic Law which provided that federal laws would enter into force on its territory only after ratification by the republic parliament and in 2009 removed provisions on sovereignty and on Sakha citizenship. In 2009 the Republic Tuva repealed a provision in its Constitution concerning the right to secede from the Russian Federation.

Subjects of the Russian Federation have the right to enter into international and foreign economic links of a limited character. They may not seek diplomatic recognition or open embassies abroad. However, they may – and many have done so – conclude trade, economic, and financial agreements with foreign States, assume debt obligations, including debt

[21] СЗ РФ (2003), no. 40, item 3822, as amended.

[22] СЗ РФ (2003), no. 48, item 4660, as amended.

restructurings. Whether these agreements are international treaties or merely commercial arrangements may depend upon their content. In any event, such agreements must be coordinated with federal agencies of executive power under the Federal Law on the Coordination of International and Foreign Economic Links of Subjects of the Russian Federation of 4 January 1999, as amended.[23] Such agreements must be registered by the Ministry of Justice of the Russian Federation as a condition of their entry into force for the subject of the Russian Federation.[24]

In the year 2000 the President of Russia introduced measures of Presidential control over the subjects of the Federation. An Edict of 13 May 2000, as amended, on the Plenipotentiary Representative of the President in a Federal District [округ] and accompanying statute divided the Russian Federation into seven federal districts whose boundaries coincided with existing military districts.[25] The seven plenipotentiary representatives appointed to head each district replaced the presidential representatives in each of the subjects of the Federation (established by an Edict of 9 July 1997, as amended).[26] Part of their mandate is to further the creation of unified legal space in the Russian Federation. The President of Russia intensified his use of his own edicts to suspend legislation in subjects of the Federation which was contrary to federal legislation. A variety of lesser measures were taken to assert Presidential vertical control directly over the subjects of the Federation and individual agencies thereof.

There remain on the statute books certain legacies pre-dating the 1993 Russian Constitution. Tatarstan, Sakha (Iakutia), Bashkortostan, Tuva, and others had proclaimed themselves to be not only sovereign States, but also subjects of international law. Tatarstan also declared itself to be "associated with" the Russian Federation rather than a part thereof.

> *Tatarstan.* The Republic Tatarstan is the direct descendant of one of the most powerful Empires ever to exist on this planet. In modern history what is regarded as the first State in the region was formed in the ninth and tenth centuries as the Khanate of the Volga Bulgars, who converted to Islam in the tenth century. This Khanate was overrun by the Mongols, who completed their conquest in 1236 and incorporated the Khanate into the Golden Horde; by about the 1420s the Khanate of Kazan liberated itself from the Golden Horde but

[23] СЗ РФ (1999), no. 2, item 231, as amended.

[24] СЗ РФ (2000), no. 31, item 3293, as amended. The Rules for the State Registration of Agreements on the Effectuation of International and Foreign Economic Links Concluded by Agencies of State Power of Subjects of the Russian Federation were confirmed by Decree of the Government of the Russian Federation on 24 July 2000, No. 552. Explanations on the application of the said Rules were confirmed by Order of the Ministry of Justice on 5 July 2011, No. 257. Российская газета [Russian Newspaper], 29 July 2011.

[25] СЗ РФ (2000), no. 20, item 2112, as amended.

[26] СЗ РФ (1997), no. 28, item 3421, as amended.

continued to raid Muscovy. For centuries the princes of Muscovy paid tribute to the Tatars. In 1552 the fortunes of Muscovy reversed, and the Khanate of Kazan was absorbed as an integral part into what became in due course the Russian Empire.

During the late nineteenth and earlier twentieth centuries, a latent Tatar national consciousness revived in various forms, including movements supporting Pan-Islamism. When the Russian Empire collapsed in 1917, Tatarstan formed its own parliament, government, State council, and military council as a functionally independent entity. Tatars fought on both sides of the those contesting for power after the Russian revolutions; an Idel-Ural State had a brief existence, followed by the entity which existed throughout the Soviet period: the Tatar Autonomous Soviet Socialist Republic.

The Tatar authorities pursued Tatarstan statehood vigorously from 1990 onwards. On 30 August 1990 Tatarstan declared State sovereignty in the form of the Declaration on State Sovereignty of the Tatarstan Soviet Socialist Republic, renamed two years later the Republic Tatarstan.[27] Tatarstan's Declaration on State Sovereignty was the first such to be enacted by an entity within the RSFSR. On 24 October 1990 the Tatar Soviet Socialist Republic declared its independence from the Russian Soviet Federated Socialist Republic through the Decree of the Supreme Soviet of the Tatar Soviet Socialist Republic on the Act of State Independence; that is, claimed full and equal status with the other union republics of the then Soviet Union.[28] The Preamble to the Constitution of Tatarstan was amended on 18 April 1991 to remove provisions stipulating that Tatarstan was part of the Russian Federation and that federal laws took precedence over Tatarstan legislation. This was followed on 24 October 1991 by the Decree of the Supreme Soviet of the Tatarstan SSR "On the Act of State Independence of the Republic Tatarstan", which reaffirmed the principles set out in the Declaration on State Sovereignty and, as a "sovereign State", objected to the treatment of its status by the USSR. On 26 December 1991 Tatarstan ratified the Almaty Agreement on the creation of the Commonwealth of Independent States (CIS).[29]

[27] See B. L. Khamidullin, «Татарстан» [Tatarstan], Большая Российская энциклопедия [Great Russian Encyclopedia] (Moscow, 2016), XXXI, pp. 689-691.

[28] The relevant clause of the Preamble provided: "noting the failure of the status of an autonomous republic to conform to the interests of the further political, economic, social, and spiritual development of its multinational people".

[29] The fate of that ratification is unknown, but there has never been, so far as can be determined, any confirmation that the CIS accepted such ratifications or has treated the Republic Tatarstan as a member. And indeed there is doubt as to whether Tatarstan, in its "Declaration" on joining the CIS, dated 26 December 1991, actually ratified the Almaty Agreement. This would depend upon whether the Declaration was tantamount to ratification – Tatarstan did not use the language of the law of treaties to this end.

Relations with the Russian Federation were addressed through bilateral international treaties. Tatarstan refused to sign the relevant Treaty of the Federation that the Russian Federation concluded on 31 March 1992 with all the other subjects of the Federation but two: Tatarstan and Chechnia.

Notwithstanding an adverse ruling of the Russian Constitutional Court, a referendum was held in Tatarstan which confirmed that Tatarstan was a sovereign State and a subject of international law. In keeping with the positive result of the referendum, the Constitution of Tatarstan was adopted in November 1992 that incorporated the Declaration of Sovereignty and asserted that Tatarstan was associated with Russia on the basis of a Treaty concerning a mutual delimitation of powers. More than a year of further negotiations was required to finalize the text of such a Treaty, eventually achieved on 15 February 1994.[30] The extent to which Tatarstan is a subject of international law and has separate citizenship was left open (in October 1997 Tatarstan rejected the use of Russian internal passports on the ground that there was no space for the entry of "nationality"). In 2002 further arrangements were reached between Russia and Tatarstan which brought the Constitution of Tatarstan into conformity with the 1993 Constitution of the Russian Federation. Tatarstan is therefore a fully-fledged subject of the Russian Federation that has surrendered a significant portion of its sovereign statehood in the process of becoming a constituent entity of the Russian Federation.

A border dispute between Northern Osetia and Ingushetia remains unresolved, although on 16 March 1996 a State Commission was appointed to consider the matter by the Government of the Russian Federation (the Statute on the Commission was repealed by Decree of the Government on 26 July 2004, No. 380).[31] Some subjects of the Federation have advanced excessive claims to ownership over the land, subsoil, and natural wealth, whereas others assert the priority of their local laws over federal. The republics within the Federation vary widely in regulating the status of languages. In only six of the 21 republics within the Russian Federation does the nationality named in the title of the republic actually constitute a

[30] See the Treaty of the Russian Federation and Republic Tatarstan "On Delimiting the Subjects of Jurisdiction and Mutual Delegation of Powers between Agencies of State Power of the Russian Federation and Agencies of State Power of the Republic Tatarstan", translated in W. E. Butler, *Russian Legal Texts: The Foundations of a Rule-of-Law State and a Market Economy* (1998), pp. 73-79.

[31] СЗ РФ (2004), no. 31, item 3268. A similar dispute between Ingushetia and Chechnya was resolved by a boundary agreement of 26 September 2018, which led to proceedings in the Constitutional Court of the Russian Federation. In a Decree of 6 December 2018 the Constitutional Court of the Russian Federation determined that the said Agreement was not contrary to the Constitution of the Russian Federation. For the text, see СЗ РФ (2018), no. 51, item 8095.

majority of the population. In the Nenets Autonomous National Area, for example, the native population constitutes 16.5% of the total population.

The 1993 Russian Constitution (Article 65(2)) recognizes that new subjects of the Federation may be created or that existing subjects may be transformed into a new subject. On 17 December 2001 the Federal Constitutional Law on the Procedure for Admission to the Russian Federation and Formation Within its Composition of a New Subject of the Russian Federation was adopted in accordance with the Constitution to regulate the process, as amended.[32] Admission is open to a foreign State or part thereof by way of accession (a provision that one day may be used by Abkhazia or South Osetia to become part of Russia and in any event was used when Crimea became a subject of the Russian Federation). The formation of a new subject refers to a procedure under which there is a change in the composition of existing subjects of the Russian Federation which is not linked with the admission of a foreign State or part thereof.

Admission must have regard to the State interests of the Russian Federation, the principles of the structure of the Federation, the rights and freedoms of man and citizen, and the historical, economic, and cultural links of subjects of the Russian Federation and their socio-economic opportunities. Formation may involve the combining of two or more existing subjects of the Federation which border one another, including the termination of the existence of subjects of the Federation whose territories are being unified. A change of name does not constitute "formation".

In the case of admission, the initiator must be the foreign State, whereupon the President of Russia will submit the proposal to the chambers of the Federal Assembly in the procedure provided for by the 1995 Law on International Treaties, as amended. The 2001 Law sets out questions which may be addressed in a treaty with the proposing foreign State. When such a treaty is signed, the President of Russia then applies to the Constitutional Court of the Russian Federation with a request that the treaty be verified for its conformity to the Russian Constitution. If the Constitutional Court finds no non-conformities, the draft treaty is submitted to the State Duma for ratification. Following ratification, a federal constitutional law is to be adopted concerning the consequential amendment of Article 65 and the Constitution republished in a new version.

> *Crimea.* Crimea formally became part of the Russian Soviet Federated Socialist Republic (RSFSR) in October 1921. The RSFSR, in turn, by the Treaty of the Union of 30 December 1922, became a founding member of the Union of Soviet Socialist Republics (USSR) and remained such until Russia denounced the Treaty of the Union

[32] СЗ РФ (2001), no. 52(I), item 4916, as amended; transl. in W. E. Butler, *Russia & The Republics: Legal Materials* (loose-leaf service; 2006-).

on 12 December 1991.[33] Within the RSFSR, Crimea was initially an autonomous republic, downgraded in 1946 to the status of a region, and pursuant to a Decree of 5 February 1954[34] was transferred to the Ukrainian SSR by agreement between the RSFSR and the Ukrainian SSR ultimately approved by the USSR. Within the Ukrainian SSR and later Ukraine, Crimea was given the status of an autonomous republic.

Whatever the course of political and military events behind the scenes, the sequence of legal events so far as the public record discloses begins within Crimea at two levels: the level of the Republic Crimea, and the level of the cities of Sevastopol – designated in due course a city of federal significance – and Simferopol, the capital of Crimea.

On 6 March 2014 the Supreme Rada of the Autonomous Republic Crimea adopted a Decree "On an All-Crimean Referendum", to be held on 16 March 2014 in which voters would be invited to choose one of the following two questions:

1. Do you support the reunification of Crimea with Russia as a subject of the Russian Federation?

2. Do you support the restoration of the Constitution of the Republic Crimea as of 1992 and the status of Crimea as part of Ukraine?

Ukraine made it clear that holding the referendum for the purposes of changing the territorial integrity of Ukraine was contrary to the 1996 Constitution of Ukraine. On 7 March 2014 the Acting President of Ukraine in exercise of his constitutional powers suspended the operation of the Crimean Decree to hold the referendum. The Crimean referendum decree also was referred to the Constitutional Court of Ukraine for an opinion as to whether the Decree was in accordance with the Constitution of Ukraine. The Constitutional Court ruled that a change in the territorial boundaries of Ukraine could only be proposed in an all-Ukrainian referendum[35] and that only the Supreme Rada of Ukraine was empowered to call for a referendum. The Court held that the Crimean decree was unconstitutional and directed the Crimean authorities to cease financing the referendum.

On 11 March 2014 the deputies of the Supreme Rada of the Autonomous Republic Crimea and the Sevastopol City Soviet adopted a slightly curious Declaration of Independence of those two entities, curious because it is unusual to see a City declare independence. The Declaration was

[33] Translated in W. E. Butler (comp., transl. & ed.), *Basic Legal Documents of the Russian Federation* (1992), p. 53.

[34] For the RSFSR Decree of 5 February 1954, see Butler, note 32 above.

[35] Article 73 provides: "Questions concerning the change of the territory of Ukraine shall be decided exclusively by an all-Ukrainian referendum". Translated in W. E. Butler, *Constitutional Foundations of CIS Countries* (1999), p. 615.

contingent on the outcome of the referendum and declared the intention of the two entities to declare themselves to be an independent sovereign State with a republican form of government and then to seek acceptance into the Russian Federation as a subject of the Federation on the basis of an international treaty. The reference to an international treaty in this context was important because the reference was consistent with relevant Russian legislation on the acceptance of a new subject of the Federation into the Russian constitutional order, namely, the Federal Constitutional Law "On the Procedure of Acceptance into the Russian Federation and Formation Within its Composition of a New Subject of the Russian Federation", of 17 December 2001, as amended 11 October 2005.[36]

On the same day, 11 March 2014, the Ministry of Foreign Affairs of the Russian Federation took note of the Crimean Declaration, briefly summarized the substance thereof, observed in particular that the jurisprudence of the International Court of Justice in the Kosovo case had confirmed that the "unilateral announcement of independence by part of a state does not violate any provision of international law", expressed the belief that the Crimean Supreme Rada was within its rights to make the Declaration of Independence, and stipulated that Russia would "fully respect" the free will of the Crimean people in the referendum.[37]

The precise outcome of the referendum has been the subject of contradictory reports.[38] However, on 17 March 2014 the Supreme Rada of the Autonomous Republic Crimea, "proceeding from the direct expression of will of the peoples of Crimea at a referendum on 16 March 2014 which showed that the peoples of Crimea favored entry into Russia and, consequently, withdrawal from Ukraine and the creation of an independent State, being guided by the Declaration of Independence of the Republic Crimea adopted at an extraordinary plenary session of the Supreme Rada of the Autonomous Republic Crimea on 11 March 2014 and an extraordinary plenary session of the Sevastopol City Soviet on 11 March 2014", decreed to proclaim that the Republic Crimea was an independent sovereign State in which the City of Sevastopol enjoyed a special status.[39]

In accordance with the questions put to the referendum, the Declaration of Independence of 17 March 2014 contained an appeal to the Russian Federation that the Republic Crimea should be accepted into the Russian Federation as a subject of the Federation – a proposal consistent with procedures set out in the 2001 Federal Constitutional Law. The Declaration

[36] Translated in Butler, note 32 above.

[37] English text from the website of the Russian Ministry of Foreign Affairs, 11 March 2014: http://archive.mid.ru

[38] Summarized in Thomas D. Grant, *Aggression against Ukraine: Territory, Responsibility, and International Law* (2015), p. 18.

[39] Translated in Butler, note 32 above.

of Independence of 17 March 2014 addressed a number of issues of legal succession, but no reference was made to the independent Republic Crimea succeeding to any treaties, rights, duties, or obligations of Ukraine. The disposition of Ukrainian legislation was confusing as set out in the Edict, which provided in point 2:

> 2. From the day of entry of the present Decree into force the legislation of Ukraine shall not apply on the territory of the Republic Crimea and decisions of the Supreme Rada of Ukraine and other State agencies of Ukraine adopted after 21 February 2014 shall not be executed.
>
> Legislation of Ukraine, except that specified in paragraph one of the present point, shall apply on the territory of the Republic Crimea until respective normative acts of the Republic Crimea.

In paragraph one the legislation of Ukraine is in general said not to apply in Crimea, including any decisions of the Supreme Rada and other State agencies of Ukraine adopted after 21 February 2014; that is, the date on which the then President of Ukraine, Viktor Fedorovych Yanukovych, left Kyiv. Paragraph two then seems to reinstate Ukrainian legislation in Crimea until respective normative acts of Crimea are adopted. But if paragraph one is read literally, there is nothing left to reinstate.

Pursuant to points 5 and 6 of the Declaration, "all institutions, enterprises, and other organizations founded by Ukraine or with the participation thereof on the territory of Crimea shall become institutions, enterprises, and other organizations founded by the Republic Crimea". Ukrainian State property was declared to be Crimean State property: "State ownership of Ukraine situated on the day of adoption of the present Decree on the territory of the Republic Crimea shall be the State ownership of the Republic Crimea". In substance, therefore, points 5 and 6 of the Declaration purport to determine the succession of Crimea to Ukrainian State identity and ownership on Crimean territory:

Also on 17 March 2014 the State Council of the Republic Crimea adopted a Decree on the Legal Succession of the Republic Crimea which provided in point 4:

> Agencies of executive power, courts, procuracy agencies, law enforcement, and control agencies, and agencies of local self-government which operated on the territory of the Autonomous Republic Crimea before the proclamation of the Republic Crimea as an independent sovereign State shall effectuate their powers in the part not contrary to the interests of the Republic Crimea before the adoption of the Constitution of the Republic Crimea.

The 2001 Federal Constitutional Law thus distinguishes between an "acceptance" (some prefer "admission") procedure and a "formation" procedure (Article 1[1]):

> The acceptance of a new subject into the Russian Federation shall be a procedure providing for a change of the composition of subjects of the Russian Federation as a result of the accession to the Russian Federation of a foreign State or part thereof.

The 2001 Federal Constitutional Law provides in Article 2(1):

> Acceptance into the Russian Federation of a new subject shall be effectuated in accordance with the Constitution of the Russian Federation, international (inter-State) treaties of the Russian Federation, the present Federal Constitutional Law, and also federal constitutional laws concerning the acceptance of a new subject into the Russian Federation.

The "basic requirements" for acceptance in the Russian Federation and formation of a new subject within the Russian Federation are that such acceptance be on a "voluntary basis" and that the "State interests of the Russian Federation, principles of the federal system of the Russian Federation, rights and freedoms of man and citizen" are complied with and that the "historical, economic, and cultural ties" of the subject of the Russian Federation and the socio-economic possibilities thereof are taken into account (Article 3, 2001 Federal Constitutional Law).

The "conditions" of acceptance of a new State or part thereof as a subject of the Russian Federation are: (1) mutual consent of the Russian Federation and the particular foreign State: (2) expressed in an international treaty concluded by the Russian Federation and the particular foreign State; (3) with the status of a republic unless agreed otherwise between the parties to the said international treaty (Article 4), 2001 Federal Constitutional Law).

The "procedure" for acceptance is regulated in detail by the 2001 Federal Constitutional Law. The initiator of the procedure must be the particular foreign State (Article 6(1)), which proposes that the respective international treaty be concluded for this purpose. Upon receipt of such a proposal, the President of the Russian Federation informs the Soviet of the Federation, the State Duma, and the Government of the Russian Federation about the proposal and, when necessary, consults with those bodies. The actual proposal and the adoption of decisions within Russia are considered pursuant to the 1995 Federal Law "On International Treaties of the Russian Federation".[40]

[40] For the Federal Law "On International Treaties of the Russian Federation", see Butler, note 32 above.

The international treaty concerning acceptance of a foreign State or part thereof into the Russian Federation will ordinarily contain provisions that address: (1) the name and status of the new subject of the Russian Federation; (2) the procedure for the acquisition of citizenship of the Russian Federation by citizens of the foreign State and the extending to them in full of the legal status of a citizen of the Russian Federation; (3) legal succession with respect to membership of the foreign State in international organizations (which did not affect Crimea) and its property assets and liabilities; (4) the operation of legislation of the Russian Federation on the territory of the new subject of the Russian Federation; and (5) the functioning of agencies of State power and agencies of local self-government of the foreign State on the territory of the new subject of the Russian Federation (Article 7(1), 2001 Federal Constitutional Law).

The treaty may establish a transition period during which the new subject of the Russian Federation is integrated into the economic, financial, credit, and legal system of the Russian Federation, as well as within the system of agencies of State power of the Russian Federation (Article 7(2), 2001 Federal Constitutional Law). This was in fact done in Crimea.

Special protocols subject to ratification simultaneously with ratification of the international treaty may be signed by the Russian Federation and the particular foreign State. So far as the public record discloses, there were no such special protocols in the case of Crimea.

After signature of the international treaty, the President of the Russian Federation then applies to the Constitutional Court of the Russian Federation seeking clarification from the Court that the particular international treaty conforms to the Constitution of the Russian Federation. That procedure was followed with respect to Crimea, as will be discussed below; Crimea is the first example of this procedure being invoked in Russian constitutional law.

The consideration of the signed treaty by the Constitutional Court occurs before the Treaty has entered into force. If the Constitutional Court determines, as it did in the instance of the Treaty with Crimea, that the Treaty is in conformity with the Constitution of the Russian Federation, the Treaty is then submitted to the lower chamber of the Federal Assembly of the Russian Federation – the State Duma – for ratification in the procedure provided by the Federal Law "On International Treaties of the Russian Federation" together with the draft Federal Law on ratification and a draft Federal Constitutional Law on the acceptance of the new subject of the Russian Federation (Article 8, 2001 Federal Constitutional Law). The issues to be addressed in the draft Federal Constitutional Law on the acceptance of the new subject of the Russian Federation are provided for in Article 8(3), 2001 Federal Constitutional Law:

> The draft federal constitutional law on acceptance of a new subject in the Russian Federation should contain provisions determining the

name, status, and boundaries of the new subject, and also concluding and transitional provisions establishing the periods during which the new subject should be integrated into the economic, financial, credit, and legal system of the Russian Federation, and also the system of agencies of State power of the Russian Federation. The draft federal constitutional law may also contain other provisions arising from the international treaty and protocols thereto.

It will be observed that the provisions of Article 8(3) are not exhaustive; the parties to the treaty are at liberty to include other provisions and/or protocols.

The adoption of the federal law on ratification of the international treaty accepting a new subject of the Russian Federation had to conform to the voting andquorum requirements set out in Articles 105, 106, and 107 of the 1993 Russian Constitution. These requirements, without entering into detail, were satisfied. The Federal Constitutional Law accepting Crimea into the Russian Federation required, pursuant to Article 108 of the 1993 Russian Constitution, a three-quarters positive vote of the total number of members of the upper chamber of the Federal Assembly and not less than two-thirds of the total number of deputies in the lower chamber – the State Duma. These minimum requirements were achieved.

Pursuant to the 2001 Federal Constitutional Law (Article 9[3]), the enactment accepting the new subject of the Federation may not enter into force before the Treaty between the Russian Federation and the new subject enters into force.

Acceptance of Crimea into Russian Federation. On 17 March 2014 the President of the Russian Federation adopted Edict No. 147, which recognized the referendum outcome in Crimea as favoring independence and declared that the Russian Federation recognized the Republic Crimea as an independent State in which the City of Sevastopol enjoyed a special status.[41] So far as the Russian Federation was concerned, this Edict confirmed the establishment of the Republic Crimea as an independent State with international legal personality, including the legal capacity to seek affiliation with another independent State (Russia) pursuant to an international treaty.

Under both the 1993 Constitution of the Russian Federation and the 1996 Constitution of Ukraine, designated cities enjoy a special status – a practice that extended back to the 1937 constitutions of the RSFSR and Ukrainian SSR. In Russia the cities of federal significance were Moscow and St. Petersburg; in Ukraine cities enjoying a special status were and are Kyiv and Sevastopol. From the standpoint of Sevastopol, they were being

[41] СЗ РФ (2014), no. 12, item 1259.

transferred from being a special city in Ukraine to being a city of federal significance in Russia. The formulation of the Russian Presidential edict makes it clear that Sevastopol does not enjoy international legal personality as such, which was the position in Ukrainian law as well; presumably the involvement of Sevastopol in the deliberations and in the Declaration of Independence reflects the fact that historically Sevastopol has been a special entity and not merely a routine Crimean city, such as Simferopol.

Also on 17 March 2014 the President of Russia adopted a Regulation approving the text of the draft treaty between the Russian Federation and the Republic Crimea on the Acceptance of the Republic Crimea into the Russian Federation and the Formation of New Subjects of the Russian Federation and authorizing the signature thereof at the highest level.

For its part, the Supreme Rada of the Republic Crimea adopted a Decree authorizing the Chairman of the Supreme Rada and the Chairman of the Council of Ministers of the Republic Crimea to sign the "inter-State treaty" with Russia. These individuals were respectively the head of State and the head of Government of Crimea.

The Treaty was signed by the respective parties on 18 March 2014. The Treaty applied provisionally upon signature and entered into force upon completion of ratification procedures.

The Preamble to the Treaty in effect outlines the Russian legal theory of what had transpired. The Preamble recites the long-standing historical links between Russia and Crimea, refers to the principles of equality and self-determination embodied in the United Nations Charter, invokes the outcome of the Crimean referendum on 16 March 2014, and relies upon the proposal submitted by the Republic Crimea and the City of Sevastopol to be accepted into the Russian Federation as new subjects.

The date of acceptance of the Republic Crimea into the Russian Federation is 18 March 2014, the day on which the Treaty was signed. The 1993 Constitution of Russia, the 2001 Federal Constitutional Law, the Federal Constitutional Law on the Acceptance of the Republic Crimea into the Russian Federation and Formation within the Composition of the Russian Federation of New Subjects – Republic Crimea and City of Federal Significance Sevastopol (still not adopted as of 18 March 2014), and the Treaty itself are stipulated to govern the acceptance process.

Constitutional Court Proceedings. As noted above, the 2001 Federal Constitutional Law required that a treaty between the Russian Federation and a foreign State or part thereof concerning acceptance into the Russian Federation be submitted to the Constitutional Court of the Russian Federation in order to determine whether the treaty was consistent with the 1993 Russian Constitution. The President of the Russian Federation submitted an "inquiry" to the Constitutional Court in this matter, and on 19 March 2014 the Constitutional Court rendered its Decree on this matter.

For the Constitutional Court, this was the first occasion upon which it had been requested to rule on the acceptance of a foreign State as a subject of the Russian Federation. In its Decree of 19 March, the Court outlined what it considered the tasks confronting the Court under such an inquiry to be. The political advisability of entering into a treaty was not a matter for the Court. The Court (point 2):

> establishes the conformity to the Constitution of the Russian Federation of normative acts of agencies of State power and treaties between them with regard to the content of norms, form, procedure for signature, conclusion, adoption, publication, or introduction into operation from the standpoint established by the Constitution of the Russian Federation of the separation of State power into legislative, executive, and judicial, from the standpoint established by the Constitution of the Russian Federation of the delimitation of competence between federal agencies of State power, and from the standpoint of the delimitation of the subject-matter of jurisdiction and powers between agencies of State power of the Russian Federation and agencies of State power of subjects of the Russian Federation established by the Constitution of the Russian Federation and federative and other treaties concerning the delimitation of the subject-matter of jurisdiction and powers.

The Constitutional Court then proceeded to consider one by one each of the aforementioned issues of conformity. With respect to the power of the President of Russia to sign the Treaty, the Court determined that "... the signature of the considered Treaty by the President of the Russian Federation corresponds to the Constitution of the Russian Federation".

Moreover, the

> Treaty is not contrary to the Constitution of the Russian Federation also from the standpoint of the separation established by it of State power into legislative, executive, and judicial and the delimitation of competence between federal agencies of State power inasmuch as in accordance with Article 8 of the Federal Constitutional Law "On the Procedure for the Acceptance into the Russian Federation and the Formation Within the Composition Thereof of a New Subject of the Russian Federation" the question of the ratification thereof is authorized by the Federal Assembly.

Furthermore, because the

> Constitution of the Russian Federation relegates the conclusion of international treaties of the Russian Federation to the jurisdiction of the Russian Federation (Article 71(j)), the signature of the

> considered Treaty cannot generate doubts also from the standpoint of the delimitation established by the Constitution of the Russian Federation of subject-matter of jurisdiction and powers between agencies of State power of the Russian Federation and agencies of State power of subjects of the Russian Federation.

The Constitutional Court then turned to the entry into force of the treaty and its provisional application, noting that:

> *de facto* the acceptance of the Republic Crimea into the Russian Federation is provided for as an element of the application of the considered Treaty before its ratification, stipulating the introduction of treaties into operation in accordance with the law of international treaties. At the same time, the possibility of the application of international treaties before the entry thereof into force, if this is provided in the treaty or if an arrangement about this was reached with the parties who signed the treaty, arises from Article 25(1) of the Vienna Convention on the Law of Treaties of 23 May 1969, a participant of which is the Russian Federation, which in essence is reproduced in Article 23 of the Federal Law of 15 July 1995, No. 101-Ф3, "On International Treaties of the Russian Federation". The admissibility of this legal construction is affirmed by the Constitutional Court of the Russian Federation in the Decree of 27 March 2012, No. 8-П, in which it is indicated, in particular, that the provisional application of an international treaty is used by the Russian Federation in the practice of inter-State communion, as a rule, in instances when the subject-matter of the treaty represents special interest for the participants thereof, as a consequence of which they are interested that it be introduced into operation without waiting for ratification and entry into force.

With regard to the considered Treaty, the use of the possibility permitted by Russian and by international law of applying an international treaty before the entry thereof into force also meant that from the moment of signature of the considered Treaty, as follows from Articles 1, 2, and 10 thereof in connection with Article 67(1) of the Constitution of the Russian Federation, the Republic Crimea and the City of Federal Significance Sevastopol are within the Russian Federation as subjects thereof. The indication of Article 1 of the considered Treaty to the fact that from the date of signature thereof the Republic Crimea is considered to be accepted into the Russian Federation has, in essence, the character of a principled political expression of will assuming thereafter the use of the procedure for the formalization of acceptance within the Russian Federation and the formation on the basis of the territory of the Republic Crimea new subjects of the Russian Federation – the Republic Crimea and the City of Federal Significance Sevastopol.

The Court concluded on this point that the Treaty "… cannot be considered as violating the Constitution of the Russian Federation with regard to the procedure for signature provided by it, conclusion, and introduction into operation".

The Constitutional Court moved on to consider the effect of the Treaty provisions within Russian municipal law. Of particular relevance here is the Court's view on Article 9 of the Treaty addressing the operation of Russian, Crimean, and, by implication, Ukrainian normative legal acts on the territory of Crimea. The Court saw no inconsistency between the Treaty provisions and Russian law:

> Article 9 of the considered Treaty in which, in essence, the operation is determined on the territory of the Republic Crimea and the City of Federal Significance Sevastopol of legislative and other normative legal acts in connection with the acceptance of the Republic Crimea into the Russian Federation and the formation within the Russian Federation of new subjects has the purpose of their integration into the Russian legal system while ensuring maximum stability of legal regulation and the avoidance of gaps therein making difficult the realization of the rights, freedoms, and legal interests of citizens and organizations.
>
> Taking this into account, in particular, point 3 of the particular Article according to which normative legal acts of the Autonomous Republic Crimea and the City of Sevastopol, Republic Crimea, and city with special status, Sevastopol, contrary to the Constitution of the Russian Federation are not applied cannot be regarded as non-conformity – by virtue of the absence of an indication of the impossibility of the application of these acts because of their being contrary to a federal law – to the requirements of the Constitution of the Russian Federation concerning the supremacy throughout the entire territory of the Russian Federation not only the Constitution of the Russian Federation, but also federal laws (Article 4(2)) and concerning the duties of agencies of State power, agencies of local self-government, officials, citizens, and associations thereof to comply with both the Constitution of the Russian Federation and laws (Article 15(2)). By virtue of the direct operation of the Constitution of the Russian Federation with respect to compliance by all subjects of legal relations with federal laws, these requirements in any event are applicable as a general rule and the resolution of possible contradictions conditioned by the peculiarities of the transition period may be ensured both by subsequent federal legislative regulation and by judicial practice.

The ultimate conclusion of the Constitutional Court was: "To deem the international treaty which has not entered into force between the Russian

Federation and the Republic Crimea on the acceptance of the Republic Crimea into the Russian Federation and the formation of new subjects within the Russian Federation to correspond to the Constitution of the Russian Federation". The President of the Russian Federation was so advised.

Thus, the procedure followed in the Constitutional Court and subsequently was fully consistent with the requirements of the 2001 Federal Constitutional Law (Article 8): the text of the signed Treaty was submitted to the State Duma for ratification together with the draft federal constitutional law to accept Crimea as a subject of the Federation.

Ratification of Russo-Crimean Treaty. On 21 March 2014 the Russian Federation adopted Federal Law No. 36-ФЗ to ratify the Treaty between the Russian Federation and the Republic Crimea on acceptance of the Republic Crimea into the Russian Federation and the formation of new subjects with the Russian Federation, signed at Moscow on 18 March 2014.[42] The Treaty itself made no provision for ratification by both parties. Russian ratification formalities followed pursuant to the 2001 Federal Constitutional Law. There is no evidence that the Republic Crimea ratified the treaty or had provisions or requirements for ratification in place as a matter of Crimean legislation. Crimea could conceivably have applied relevant Ukrainian legislation,[43] but appears not to have done so. Unless there is evidence to the contrary, it would appear that signature on the part of the Crimean side was sufficient for the Treaty to enter into force for Crimea. However; if Crimean ratification was required or essential, that would affect the legal validity of Crimea being accepted into the Russian Federation as a matter of Russian law.

Acceptance of Crimea as Subject of Russian Federation. On 21 March 2014 the Russian Federation adopted the 2014 Federal Constitutional Law, as amended, which regulated the precise details of accepting Crimea into the Russian Federation. The effective date of acceptance of Crimea as part of the Russian Federation (and the formation of new subjects of the Russian Federation) is the date of the Treaty; that is, 18 March 2014.

The Treaty (Article 9) addressed at some length the applicability of Russian, Crimean, and, by implication, Ukrainian legislation on the territory of Crimea:

[42] СЗ РФ (2014), no. 12, item 1202. The Federal Law was adopted by the State Duma on 20 March and by the Soviet of the Federation on 21 March and signed by the President of Russia on 21 March 2014.

[43] If legislation of Ukraine continued to apply in the Republic Crimea pursuant to the Declaration of Independence of 17 March 2014, arguably that would include Ukrainian legislation on international treaties. The Law of Ukraine "On International Treaties of Ukraine" provided that treaties regulating territorial issues require ratification by the Supreme Rada of Ukraine.

> 1. Legislative and other normative acts of the Russian Federation shall operate on the territories of the Republic Crimea and City of Federal Significance Sevastopol from the day of acceptance of the Republic Crimea into the Russian Federation and the formation within the composition of the Russian Federation of new subjects, unless provided otherwise by legislation of the Russian Federation.
>
> 2. Normative legal acts of the Autonomous Republic Crimea and City of Sevastopol, Republic Crimea and City with Special Status Sevastopol, shall operate on the territories respectively of the Republic Crimea and City of Federal Significance Sevastopol until the end of the transition period or until the adoption of a respective normative legal act of the Russian Federation and/or normative legal act of the Republic Crimea, normative legal act of the Russian Federation, and/or normative legal act of the City of Federal Significance Sevastopol.
>
> 3. Normative legal acts of the Autonomous Republic Crimea and City of Sevastopol, Republic Crimea, and City with Special Status Sevastopol which are contrary to the Constitution of the Russian Federation shall not be applied.

Article 23 of the 2014 Federal Constitutional Law reproduced the language of the Treaty with respect to the interaction of Ukrainian, Crimean, and Russian normative-legal acts:

> 1. Legislative and other normative acts of the Russian Federation shall operate on the territories of the Republic Crimea and City of Federal Significance Sevastopol from the day of acceptance of the Republic Crimea into the Russian Federation and the formation within the composition of the Russian Federation of new subjects, unless provided otherwise by the present Federal Constitutional Law.
>
> 2. Normative legal acts of the Autonomous Republic Crimea and City of Sevastopol, Republic Crimea and City with Special Status Sevastopol, shall operate on the territories respectively of the Republic Crimea and City of Federal Significance Sevastopol until the end of the transition period or until the adoption of a respective normative legal act of the Russian Federation and/or normative legal act of the Republic Crimea, normative legal act of the Russian Federation, and/or normative legal act of the City of Federal Significance Sevastopol.
>
> 3. Normative legal acts of the Autonomous Republic Crimea and City of Sevastopol, Republic Crimea, and City with Special Status Sevastopol which are contrary to the Constitution of the Russian Federation shall not be applied.

It follows that from 18 March 2014 Russian legislation, including international treaties of the Russian Federation, were fully applicable on the territory of the Republic Crimea. Russia fully established administrative and judicial jurisdiction and authority over Crimea and commenced the process of integrating Crimea into Russia in accordance with Russian policies and preferences.

The adoption of the 2014 Federal Constitutional Law represented the completion of the Russian treaty and legislative framework for accepting the Republic Crimea and the City of Sevastopol into the Russian Federation. The Russian Federation considered that the Republic Crimea and Sevastopol had been accepted and each as a new subject of the Russian Federation was formed with effect from 18 March 2014, the date of the Treaty between Russia and Crimea. The relevant Russian Federation legislation regulating the acceptance of a foreign State as a subject of the Russian Federation had been fully and correctly complied with.

On the same day that Russia enacted the 2014 Federal Constitutional Law, the President of the Russian Federation took several steps to consolidate and integrate the Republic Crimea and the City of Sevastopol within the Russian Federation. By Edict No. 168 of 21 March 2014, the President of Russia formed the "Crimean Federal Area", sometimes called a "Federal District", and laid the groundwork for the appointment of a plenipotentiary, or empowered representative, of the President of the Russian Federation to the Republic Crimea and to the City of Federal Significance Sevastopol.[44] By Edict No. 169 of the same date, the Representative of the President in the Crimean Federal Area was appointed.[45]

The question arises in Russian law of the civil-legal status of a subject of the Russian Federation. Do subjects of the Federation have the same legal capacity as juridical persons; indeed, are they juridical persons, or are they a "public-law formation" which enjoys a special legal status. Russian doctrinal writings are divided on the issue.As noted above, the 1993 Constitution of the Russian Federation and other relevant Russian legislative acts define "subjects of the Federation" by example rather than by generic definition. The Civil Code of the Russian Federation does the same, referring to the "Russian Federation, subjects of Russian Federation, and municipal formations" (Article 124).[46] Accordingly, the Civil Code distinguishes among the legal status of natural persons (Chapter 3), juridical persons (Chapter 4), and the Russian Federation, subjects of the Russian Federation, and municipal formations (Chapter 5) – all of those regulated

[44] СЗ РФ (2014), no. 12, item 1265.

[45] СЗ РФ (2014), no. 12, item 1273.

[46] "In accordance with Article 124(1) of the Civil Code, there are relegated to public-law formations: the Russian Federation, subjects of the Russian Federation, and municipal formations". B. M. Gongalo, Гражданское право [Civil Law] (2016), para. 7.1. For the text of the Civil Code, see W. E. Butler (ed. & transl.), *Civil Code of the Russian Federation* (2021), I, p. 95.

by Chapter 5 being grouped together by Russian legal doctrine within the category of "public-law formations".

The difference between a "juridical person" and a "public-law formation" (including subjects of the Russian Federation) has been explained as follows:

> Russian legislation in force considers the State and State and municipal (public-law) formations to be autonomous, special subjects of law (*sui generis*) existing side by side with juridical and natural persons.[47]

Accordingly, when public-law formations enter into civil-law transactions, they do not do so as juridical persons:

> Civil-law transactions with the participation of public-law formations, on the contrary, as a general rule (in the absence of special exceptions) are subject to norms on transactions with the participation of juridical persons, although these subjects themselves are not juridical persons.[48]

The same view was emphasized by Viktor Pavlovich Mozolin (1924-2015):

> According to the provisions of Article 124(2) of the Civil Code, the Russian Federation, subjects of the Russian Federation, and municipal formations are not juridical persons …
>
> On the other hand, norms exist in civil legislation and other normative acts concerning juridical persons which are not applicable to the State or to State and municipal formations. Thus, norms of the Civil Code relating to the formation of a juridical person, its constitutive documents, reorganization of a juridical person have no relevance to the said subjects of civil law. Likewise the provision of Article 49 of the Civil Code concerning the general legal capacity of a juridical person is not applicable to them. For the State and State and municipal formations more appropriate is the concept of special legal capacity determined by the powers and functions consolidated in the Constitution, constitutions of the republics which are part of the Russian Federation, charters of territories, regions, cities of federal significance, autonomous region, autonomous national areas, and laws on local self-government.[49]

[47] E. A. Sukhanov, Гражданское право [Civil Law] (2008), para. 10.1.1.

[48] Ibid., para. 10.1.2.

[49] V. P. Mozolin, in T. E. Abova, M. M. Boguslavskii, A. Iu. Kabalkin, and A. G. Lisitsyn-Svetlanov (eds.), Постатейный комментарий к Гражданскому кодексу Российской Федерации, частей первой, второй, третьей [Article-by-Article Commentary to the Civil Code of the Russian Federation, Parts One, Two, Three] (2003), Article 124.

The Constitutional Court of the Russian Federation elaborated on the distinction between juridical persons and public-law formations when a claimant argued that the provisions establishing the special legal capacity of public-law formations were unconstitutional:

> The constitutional norms predetermine the special character of the legal capacity of public-law formations: the Russian Federation, subjects of the Russian Federation, and municipal formations participate in civil-law relations as subjects with special legal capacity which by virtue of their public-law nature does not coincide with the legal capacity of other subjects of civil law – citizens and juridical persons.
>
> Article 124 of the Civil Code of the Russian Federation, in developing the norms of Article 2(1), paragraph two, of the Code, consolidates the general provisions on the participation of the Russian Federation, subjects of the Russian Federation, and municipal formations in civil law relations and the application to them of norms of civil law. The reference contained therein to the peculiarities of public-law formations, by virtue of which provisions may not be applicable to them determining the participation of juridical persons in relations regulated by civil legislation means, especially, that there are special norms in civil legislation regulating the participation of the particular subjects in civil law relations, and also legal norms concerning juridical persons which are not applicable to the State and to State and municipal formations (for example, norms relating to the formation of a juridical person, its constitutive documents, reorganization of a juridical person, and so on) by virtue of the specific nature of the last which basically emanate from the special organization of institutions of public power.[50]

The category of "public-law formations" and the distinctions drawn in Russian legislation and legal doctrine between juridical persons and public-law formations are not unique to Russian law. Other post-Soviet legal systems draw a similar distinction, including the legal system and legal doctrine of Ukraine.[51]

ELECTORAL SYSTEM

The President of the Russian Federation and the lower chamber of the Federal Assembly – the State Duma – are directly elected; where senior

[50] Ruling of the Constitutional Court of the Russian Federation, No. 297-O, 5 July 2005. Available on Consultant Plus.

[51] See, for example, O. M. Vynnyk, "Economic Legal Means of Ensuring the Development of Relations of Public/Private Partnership", in Iu. S. Shemshuchenko (ed.), *Legal Doctrine of Ukraine*, transl. W. E. Butler (2017), IV, pp. 227-265. Although the expression public/private is used in Ukrainian legal writings, so too is the more precise version: State/private partnership.

posts are filled by appointment, commonly in Russia the appointment is made by the elective agencies of State. The same pattern applies at the middle and lowest levels of State agencies of executive power. Russian legal doctrine draws a distinction between the concept of an "electoral system" and the "right of suffrage", although it is recognized that in common usage the two terms are for all practical purposes identical. In Russia the two terms encompass five so-called subsystems:

(1) the procedure for election of the President of the Russian Federation;

(2) the procedure for election of deputies of the State Duma;

(3) the procedure for election of the heads of administration of subjects of the Russian Federation;

(4) the procedure for election of deputies of legislative agencies of subjects of the Federation; and

(5) the procedure for election of agencies of local self-government.

The right to vote is laid down in the 1993 Russian Constitution: "Citizens of the Russian Federation shall have the right to elect and to be elected to agencies of State power and agencies of local self-government, and also to participate in a referendum" (Article 32(2)). Other articles of the Constitution establish the electivity of the President of Russia and the State Duma. The detailed procedures for elections are set out in the Federal Law on the Basic Guarantees of Electoral Rights and the Right to Participate in a Referendum of Citizens of the Russian Federation, of 12 June 2002, as amended.[52] The provisions regulating elections in this Federal Law apply throughout Russia, including the subjects of the Federation. Although subjects of the Federation have their own laws on elections, their provisions may not be contrary to the Federal Law; however, additional guarantees may be established that are not found at the federal level. Each individual federal election is then addressed in separate legislation: the Federal Law on Elections of the President of the Russian Federation of 10 January 2003, as amended;[53] the Federal Law on Elections of Deputies of the State Duma of the Russian Federation of 22 February 2014, as amended;[54] and the Federal Law on Ensuring the Constitutional Rights of Citizens of the Russian Federation to Elect and Be Elected to Agencies of Local Self-Government of 26 November 1996, as amended.[55] Referendums are governed by the Federal Constitutional Law on Referendum of the Russian Federation of 28 June 2004.[56] There are in addition a number of other federal laws and

[52] СЗ РФ (2002), no. 24, item 2253.
[53] СЗ РФ (2003), no. 2, item 171, as amended.
[54] СЗ РФ (2014), no. 8, item 740, as amended. This Federal Law replaced that of same title adopted 18 May 2005. See СЗ РФ (2005), no. 21, item 1919; as amended.
[55] СЗ РФ (1996), no. 49, item 5497.
[56] СЗ РФ (2004), no. 27, item 2710, as amended.

subordinate normative acts concerned with, for example, single mandate constituencies, the procedure for forming precinct election commissions, and the regulations for campaign financing. The Central Electoral Commission itself is a considerable source of decrees, instructions, and explanations which elaborate the electoral process. As one proceeds down the administrative-territorial ladder in Russia, the constitutive documents of all the subjects of the Federation and all agencies of local self-government issue normative acts concerning elections.

Basically, Russian citizens acquire the right to vote at the age of 18 years. Depending upon the election concerned, there may be a requirement of residence in a particular area of the country in order to vote. Russian citizens abroad have the right to vote. There is no legal requirement to vote in Russia, however. Until 2007, the validity of elections commonly turned upon a stipulated percentage of the electorate turning out to vote. In the case of the President of the Russian Federation, 50% of registered voters had to take part; for elections of deputies to the State Duma the minimum turnout was 25%, and the same was true in most subjects of the Federation for elections at that level. The requirement for a minimum voter turnout was repealed by the Federal Law of 5 December 2006.[57] Russian elections are, in sum, universal, equal, direct, secret, and held periodically.

Russian law rigorously regulates the so-called "electoral process". Once that process is underway, interference is not tolerated. In November 1995 the Constitutional Court of the Russian Federation declined to examine the constitutionality of certain provisions in the 1995 version of the Federal Law on Elections of Deputies of the State Duma of the Federal Assembly of the Russian Federation because the request for review had been made two months after the election campaign had commenced, that is, after the nomination and registration of candidates had occurred. The Court held that conducting a judicial examination in the course of an election campaign immediately before voting could unjustifiably complicate the electoral process, tell negatively on the expression of will by the voters, and ultimately influence the results of the elections. Once electoral legal relations had been engaged, the Constitutional Court believed that any decision it might render could impinge upon voting rights and prejudice the basic constitutional principles of the electoral process.

Referendums may be of three types: all-Russian, subject of the Russian Federation, or local. The 1993 Russian Constitution was adopted by an all-Russian referendum. Certain questions may not be put to a referendum, amongst them changing the status of a subject of the Federation, terminating before time or prolonging the terms of office of the President of Russia or deputies of the State Duma, or members of the Soviet of the Federation,

[57] СЗ РФ (2006), no. 50, item 5303.

amnesties and pardons, or questions of limiting or abolishing generally-recognized rights and freedoms of man and citizen or the constitutional guarantees for realizing them. The 2020 amendments to the Constitution were put to a national vote, but not a referendum; under the Constitution (Article 136) the national vote was not required because they affected Chapters 3 to 8 and might be adopted in the same procedure as a Federal Constitutional Law. The national vote was therefore an embellishment on the usual procedure, given the far-reaching and comprehensive nature of the proposed changes; the Federal Assembly imposed the requirement of the national vote in its discretion.

Subjects of the Russian Federation have introduced quite diverse electoral laws with regard to their own State agencies of power. Some which have their own citizenship, for example, Buratia, limit electoral participation to individuals who have such citizenship; others have introduced minimum periods of residence on the territory of the subject of the Federation. These are accepted by federal legislation, as a rule, but residence requirements may not exceed one year. The Constitutional Court of the Russian Federation has struck down as unconstitutional legislation of subjects of the Federation which introduced formulas that in practice gave some citizens greater or more equal rights to elect than others.

Under the 2001 Federal Law on Political Parties, the duly registered political parties have an exclusive right to participate in federal and regional elections by way of nominating candidates for office. Political associations in existence were required prior to 14 July 2003 to transform themselves into political parties and register as such; not all of them were successful in making the transition.[58]

THE PRESIDENCY

In the Soviet era the Head of State was the chairman of a collegial organ, the Presidium of the Supreme Soviet, which operated in the intervals between sessions of the Supreme Soviet. This has been construed by some Russian lawyers to mean that the post of Head of State did not in fact exist.[59] The post of President of the Russian Federation was instituted by an all-people's referendum held on 12 April 1991, and elections to this post were held in the same procedure on 12 June 1991, precisely one year from the date of the Declaration of State Sovereignty of the Russian Federation, for a five-year term. The 1978 Constitution of the RSFSR was amended to introduce the Presidency, although the expression "Head of State" was not used. Instead the President was referred to as the "highest official" (Article 121^1, 1978 RSFSR Constitution) and the "head of executive power".

58 СЗ РФ (2001), no. 29, item 2950, as amended; transl. in Butler, note 32 above.

59 M. V. Baglai, note 1, p. 476.

Under the 1993 Russian Constitution the President is the Head of State (Article 80), representing the Russian Federation within the country and in international relations. There is no post of Vice President; introduced in the amendments to the 1978 RSFSR Constitution, it became such a source of political conflict and rivalry that the architects of the 1993 Constitution deliberately excluded it. The principal functions of the President, besides acting as Head of State, are to be the guarantor of the Constitution of the Russian Federation and of the rights and freedoms of man and citizen, to take measures to protect the sovereignty of the Russian Federation, its independence and State integrity, and ensure the coordinated functioning and interaction of agencies of State power, and to determine the basic orientations of internal and foreign policy of the Russian Federation in accordance with the Constitution and federal laws.

The President is elected for a term of six years (beginning in 2012; previously the term was four years) in accordance with the Russian Constitution as amended[60] and the Federal Law on Elections of the President of the Russian Federation of 10 January 2003, as amended,[61] by citizens of the Russian Federation on the basis of universal equal and direct suffrage by secret ballot. A second successive term is possible, but a third term or more may be served only if there is an interruption after the second term (a scenario which occurred after President Putin, who served two terms in office, from 2000 to 2008, acted as Prime Minister during the Presidency of Dmitrii Medvedev from 2008 to 2012, and was then re-elected to a third term in 2013 and a fourth term in 2018).[62] On 14 March 2020 the Constitution was amended to provide that the limit on terms is no more than two and would not apply to the incumbent President, V. V. Putin, who might, if he so chose, stand for re-election in 2024 and 2030 (Article 81(3^1)). Russian citizens aged 18 on election day or older may vote in the Presidential election.

The constitutional requirements for a Presidential candidate are few: a Russian citizen at least 35 years of age, permanently resident in the Russian Federation for no less than twenty-five years may run for office, provided that this person did not and does not hold the citizenship of a foreign State or a residence permit or other document confirming the right of permanent residence of a Russian citizen on the territory of a foreign State, who does

[60] The Constitution was amended to this effect by a Federal Constitutional Law of 30 December 2008, No. 6-ФКЗ; СЗ РФ (2009), no. 1, item 1, which took effect in 2012.

[61] СЗ РФ (2003), no. 2, item 171, as amended.

[62] The amendment was dictated in part because the Constitutional Court of the Russian Federation issued a Ruling on 5 November 1998 that President Eltsin, having been elected in 1991 before the 1993 Russian Constitution was adopted for a term up to 1996 and re-elected in 1996 until the year 2000 could not stand for another term in the year 2000 because the initial election preceding the 1993 Constitution must be regarded as his first term in office. The Court said: "two terms of powers in succession ... constitute the constitutional limit, exceeding which the Constitution of the Russian Federation ... does not permit". The Ruling is available on Consultant Plus.

not have a record of conviction for the commission of a grave or especially grave crime that has not been removed or canceled, and other limitations related to criminal acts. The requirement for a candidate for the office of President of the Russian Federation concerning his lacking citizenship of a foreign State does not extend to citizens of the Russian Federation who previously had citizenship of a State which was admitted or part of which was admitted to the Russian Federation in accordance with a federal constitutional law and permanently resided on the territory of the State admitted to the Russian Federation or territory of part of the State admitted to the Russian Federation. No special education or experience is required, nor is there a maximum age limit, as in the case of judges. The President of the Russian Federation is prohibited from opening or having an account (or deposits) and keeping cash monetary means and valuables in foreign banks outside Russian territory.

The winning candidate must receive a simple majority of the votes. If there are more than two candidates and no one receives a majority of the votes cast, a second election is held between the two candidates who received the most votes. The winning candidate of the second round must receive a larger number of votes than the other candidate including abstentions. In 1996 about 70% of the electorate voted in the Presidential elections; none of the ten candidates received a majority. The second ballot resulted in the winner receiving 53.7% of the votes, and the loser, 40.4%. In 2008 there were four candidates, and the winner received 70.3% of the vote cast on the first ballot. In 2018 there were eight candidates; 67.5% of registered voters took part in the election. The winner received 76.69% of the votes of those who actually voted. The elected individual takes office on the 30th day after the official announcement of the election result, swearing the oath of office set out in the Constitution (Article 82) in the presence of the Soviet of the Federation, State Duma, and judges of the Constitutional Court of the Russian Federation. From the moment of taking oath, the President is in office.

The President of the Russian Federation stands down from office upon the expiry of his term at the moment when the newly-elected President takes the oath of office. His term may be terminated before time by resignation (which happened in the case of Boris Eltsin in 1999), by becoming unable for health reasons to effectuate his power, or by impeachment. Resignation presupposes a statement or application of the President himself. Neither the Constitution nor Russian legislation offers any guidance as to procedures for determining whether the President's state of health requires that he leave office or is unable to perform his duties, although a 2014 Instruction of the Ministry of Public Health offers guidance. Impeachment requires the implementation of procedures set out in the 1993 Russian Constitution (Article 93); in practice such accusations have been brought but failed to secure the require majority in the Federal Assembly. When the President is unable to perform his duties, the Chairman of the Government temporarily performs them; the same applies if the President were to die in office[63] or became ill for an extended period. When the President of the Russian Federation had a serious operation, his powers were distributed by Edict of the President to the Chairman of the Government and others on 19 September 1996.[64] An individual serving as acting President may not dissolve the State Duma, designate referendums, or propose amendments to or revision of the Russian Constitution; the logic of these limitations is that the acting President, unlike the individual being replaced, has not received the direct mandate of the Russian voters.

At the end of his presidential term, the head of State is granted immunity: he or she may not be brought to criminal or administrative responsibility, detained, arrested, interrogated, subjected to search or personal inspection. This rule extends to dwelling and office premises, means of transport or communications, documents, baggage, and correspondence. These privileges apply to actions undertaken during the performance of presidential duties or such actions taken while not so performing. Only the Soviet of the Federation may deprive a former President of such privileges, and only if the individual is accused of treason against the State or other grave crime by the State Duma. The decision must be adopted by two-thirds of the parliamentarians in each chamber of the Federal Assembly upon the initiative of at least one-third of the deputies of the State Duma and an opinion of a special commission appointed for this purpose. The accusation must be confirmed by the Supreme Court and Constitutional Court of the Russian Federation. The Soviet of the Federation must decide the issue of whether to deprive the President of immunity within three months after the accusation is forwarded to it; otherwise the accusation is considered to be rejected – pursuant to a Federal Law of 12 February 2001, as amended.[65]

Under the Federal Law on Centers of Historical Heritage of Presidents of the Russian Federation Who Have Terminated the Performance of Their Powers, of 13 May 2008, as amended,[66] such centers may be created in the

[63] The vexsome question of when a Head of State is actually deceased has in Russia been addressed in the Instruction on the Procedure for Establishing the Diagnosis of Death of the Human Brain, confirmed by Order of the Ministry of Public Health of the Russian Federation, on 25 December 2014, No. 908-н. Available on Consultant Plus. Registered by the Minister of Justice on 12 May 2015, No. 37230. This Instruction replaced the Instruction With Regard to Stating the Death of a Person on the Basis of Diagnosis of Death of the Brain, confirmed by Order of the Ministry of Public Health of the Russian Federation on 20 December 2001, No. 460, and registered by the Ministry of Justice of the Russian Federation on 17 January 2002, No. 3170. In a Decree of 11 July 2000, No. 12-П, the Constitutional Court determined that this question should be resolved by a Federal Law, which to date has not happened.

[64] СЗ РФ (1996), no. 39, item 4533; the Edict lost force as of 06:00 hours on 6 November 1996, when the President returned to take up his duties. СЗ РФ (1996), no. 46, item 5240.

[65] СЗ РФ (2001), no. 7, item 617, as amended.

[66] СЗ РФ (2008), no. 20, item 2253, as amended.

organizational-legal form of a foundation and are subject, with certain exceptions, to the legal regime of a noncommercial organization. Such centers are conceived as a combination archive, library, and museum, may engage in publishing activity, and may carry on scientific-research work. They are the equivalent of what in the United States have come to be called presidential libraries, with a somewhat broader mandate. They may be located at a site chosen by the president concerned, or his heirs, but if not situated in Moscow, will have a branch in the City of Moscow. The decision to create a center and confirmation of the Charter of a center is undertaken by the Administration of the President of the Russian Federation. A center is not subject to reorganization and may not be deemed to be insolvent or bankrupt. The Presidential Library of President Boris Eltsin opened at St. Petersburg in 2014 and the Eltsin Presidential Center at Ekaterinburg in 2015.

Presidential power and the Federal Assembly

There is little overlap between Presidential and parliamentary powers. The President has the right to designate elections of the State Duma in accordance with the 1993 Russian Constitution and the federal law on elections, whereas the Soviet of the Federation has the right to designate elections for the President. The formation of the Soviet of the Federation proceeds without the participation of either the State Duma or the President.

The President has, and actively uses, the right of legislative initiative to submit draft laws to the State Duma, and also possesses the right of veto over laws adopted by the Federal Assembly. The veto may be overridden if the vetoed law is adopted a second time by both chambers of the Federal Assembly in separate sittings by a two-thirds vote in each chamber, in which case the President must sign the law within seven days. A refusal of the President to sign under these circumstances on the ground of irregularities in the voting was held unconstitutional by the Constitutional Court of the Russian Federation in March 1998. But as of 2020, if the President of the Russian Federation submits an query to the Constitutional Court of the Russian Federation to verify the constitutionality of a federal constitutional law, the period for the signature of this law is suspended while the Constitutional Court considers the query. If the Constitutional Court confirms the constitutionality of the said law, the President signs it within three days from the moment of the decision of the Constitutional Court. If the Constitutional Court does not confirm constitutionality, the President of the Russian Federation returns it to the State Duma without signature.

The President delivers yearly messages to the Federal Assembly on the state of the Federation, the basic orientations of domestic and foreign policy, and the like. Although the Federal Assembly is not bound in any way by the ideas expressed in these messages, the views of the President are influential and on the Federal Assembly and commonly televised to a large audience. In accordance with a federal constitutional law, the President designates the holding of a referendum.

The President may dissolve the State Duma in accordance with the Constitution, but not the Soviet of the Federation. Dissolution of the State Duma occurs if the Duma rejects three times his proposed candidacy for the Chairman of the Government, a situation avoided by the State Duma in April 1998 when on the third ballot the President's candidacy for Chairman of the Government was approved (Article 111(4), Constitution); when lack of confidence in the Government has been expressed twice by the State Duma within three months (Article 117(3), Constitution); and when the government requests the State Duma for an expression of confidence and such is refused (Article 117(4), Constitution). If the Duma is dissolved, the President designates new elections so that the newly-elected Duma may convene not later than four months after being dissolved.

Under certain circumstances the State Duma may not be dissolved by the President: within a year after the Duma is elected; from the moment of putting forward an accusation against the President until the Soviet of the Federation takes a decision; when a military or extraordinary situation has been declared throughout the entire territory of the Russian Federation; and within six months of the end of the term of powers of the President. In all instances the Soviet of the Federation remains in office, so that the country is never entirely without a legislative chamber in operation.

Presidential relations with the Federal Assembly are facilitated by the appointment of plenipotentiaries to represent the President in the chambers with regard to a particularly important or technical piece of legislation; they may also explain to the Federal Assembly the reasons a particular draft law was rejected by the President.

Presidential power and the Government

There is no question of a balance of powers between the President and the Government of the Russian Federation. The President enjoys absolute priority; he appoints the Chairman of the Government with the consent of the State Duma. Under the 2020 Law on the Government of the Russian Federation,[67] the President will appoint the Chairman of the Government himself if the State Duma three times in succession refuses to accept the candidacies proposed by the President. The President takes the decision to dismiss the Government, as was done in September 2007, even if no lack of confidence has been expressed in the Government. The President also appoints federal ministers – the heads of power ministries after consultations with the Soviet of the Federation and, upon the proposal of the

[67] СЗ РФ (2020), no. 45, item 7061.

Chairman of the Government, the deputy chairmen and federal ministers. He has the right, and in practice often has done so, to preside at sessions of the Government, leaving no doubt as to who is in charge. Moreover, within a week after being appointed and confirmed, the Chairman of the Government must submit to the President for confirmation proposals concerning the structure of federal agencies of State power.

The President exerts decisive influence on the appointment and dismissal of the chairman of the Central Bank of the Russian Federation, even though the Bank is not an agency of executive power. If the State Duma does not confirm the candidacy proposed, the President may make this candidate the acting chairman of the Bank and again submit this candidacy to the Duma. No other agency has the right of initiative in this matter except the President.

Presidential power and the Subjects of the Federation

The 1993 Constitution has little to say explicitly about Presidential powers with respect to the subjects of the Federation. Mostly these powers relate to the role of the President as the guarantor of the Constitution. In practice a key lever of Presidential power has been Article 83(j) of the Constitution enabling the President to appoint plenipotentiary representatives to an individual subject or group of subjects of the Russian Federation on the basis of a Statute confirmed by an Edict of the President of the Russian Federation of 9 July 1997, which was replaced on 13 May 2000 by another Edict dividing Russia into seven federal districts, each with a designated plenipotentiary, and in 2010 an eighth federal district was added, called the North Caucasian Federal District.[68]

These plenipotentiaries are not part of the agencies of State power of the subjects of the Federation, but rather are within the Administration of the President of the Russian Federation and accordingly independent of local and regional authorities. Plenipotentiaries may not be members of political parties or socio-political movements, nor hold office in State agencies, local government, enterprises, institutions, or organizations, nor engage in entrepreneurial activity. Their purpose is to interact with political, social, and religious associations and citizens in their respective regions, assist the President in effectuating his Presidential powers, coordinate the activities of federal services in the region, take part in the work of agencies of executive power and be present at sessions of the representative agencies of power of the relevant subjects of the Federation. Although in practice it can be a thin line to draw, the plenipotentiaries may not interfere in the

[68] See Edict of the President of the Russian Federation, 19 January 2010, No. 82. СЗ РФ (2010), no. 4, item 369, as amended. When Crimea acceded to the Russian Federation, a new Crimean Federal District was initially created, but in 2016 merged into the Southern Federal District. See СЗ РФ (2014), no. 12, item 1265; (2016), no. 31, item 4984.

operational activities of agencies, enterprises, institutions, or organizations at the regional level nor adopt decisions binding on them. The aim is to create effective liaison with the regional levels without violating their legal autonomy. If the plenipotentiary discovers that the regional authorities are violating or failing to comply with federal laws, Presidential edicts, or decisions of courts, he brings this to the attention of the Chief Control Administration of the President of the Russian Federation.

Under Article 85 of the Russian Constitution, the President does have the right to intervene in disputes between agencies of State power of the Russian Federation and agencies of State power of subjects of the Federation, using conciliation procedures to this end; if these are unsuccessful, the President may transfer the dispute for consideration to a court. Moreover, if there are election irregularities in a subject of the Federation, the President of Russia may appoint to or relieve from office the head of the respective regional administration. Under Article 78(4) of the Constitution, many Russian jurists accept that the President and the Government may act against deliberate and organized insubordination on the part of regional authorities.

It is widely said that normative legal acts adopted by subjects of the Federation frequently violate the Russian Constitution or federal laws. In the case of some subjects, the figure has been placed as high as 50% of all enactments. The President of Russia may suspend the operation of acts of agencies of executive power of subjects of the Federation if they are contrary to the Constitution, federal laws, international treaties of Russia, or violate the rights and freedoms of man and citizen. Most often the heads of regional administrations repeal the acts themselves when the violation is brought to their attention, but the President has used the power of suspension and referred the matter to a court.

Presidential power and the courts

Although the President is forbidden to interfere in judicial power, he participates in appointments or elections to the courts by nominating candidates for the Constitutional Court of the Russian Federation and the Supreme Court for consideration by the Soviet of the Federation. The President also appoints judges to the other federal courts under Article 83(f) of the Constitution.

In practice there have been occasions when the Soviet of the Federation has repeatedly rejected candidacies for the Constitutional Court of the Russian Federation.

Presidential powers and the military

The President of Russia is the Supreme Commander-in-Chief of the Armed Forces of the Russian Federation. He confirms the Military Doctrine of the Russian Federation, which takes the form of a specific document approved by the Security Council and confirmed, most recently, by Edict of the President of the Russian Federation on 25 December 2014.[69] The President appoints and dismisses the high command of the Armed Forces. Military formations in Russia exist purely at the Federation level; subjects of the Federation are not permitted their own military forces. Although the President may declare a military situation, immediately upon doing so informing the State Duma and the Soviet of the Federation, the President does not have the right to declare war.

The specific powers of the President in matters military have been elaborated in the Federal Law on the Procedure for the Granting by the Russian Federation of Military and Civilian Personnel for Participation in Activity Relating to the Maintenance or Restoration of International Peace and Security, of 23 June 1995, as amended;[70] the Federal Law on Defense, of 31 May 1996, as amended;[71] and the Federal Law on Mobilization Preparation and Mobilization in the Russian Federation, of 26 February 1997, as amended.[72]

Presidential power and security

The constitutional powers of the President in the domain of security have been clarified and supplemented by the Federal Law "On Security" of 28 December 2010, as amended.[73] The President determines the basic orientations of State policy in the field of ensuring security, which is broadly defined to include predicting, identifying, analyzing, and evaluating security threats, legal regulation in the field of ensuring security, developing and applying a complex of operational and long-term measures to identify, prevent, and eliminate security threats and to localize and neutralize their consequences, apply special economic measures (which include actions with respect to a foreign State(s) or citizen, and stateless persons, and others by suspending the realization of economic and technical assistance or military-technical cooperation, prohibiting financial or foreign-economic operations, or suspending or terminating international trade treaties, changing import or export duties, and so on),[74] developing and introducing contemporary types of weapons and technology, and similar measures. The Security Council of the Russian Federation plays a major role.

[69] Российская газета [Russian Newspaper], no. 298 (30 December 2014). The Military Doctrine confirmed on 25 December 2014 replaced that of 5 February 2010, which in turn superseded that confirmed on 21 April 2000, which in turn had replaced that formulated in an Edict of 2 November 1993. See respectively: СЗ РФ (1993), no. 45, item 4329; (2000), no. 17, item 1852; (2010), no. 7, item 724.

[70] СЗ РФ (1995), no. 26, item 2401, as amended.

[71] СЗ РФ (1996), no. 23, item 2750, as amended.

[72] СЗ РФ (1997), no. 9, item 1014, as amended.

[73] СЗ РФ (2011), no. 1, item 2, as amended.

[74] See the Federal Law on Special Economic Measures of 30 December 2006. СЗ РФ (2007), no. 1(I), item 44.

The President has anti-terrorism duties set out in the Federal Law "On Counteracting Terrorism" of 6 March 2006, as amended. These are elaborated conceptually in the Conception of Counteracting Terrorism in the Russian Federation, confirmed by Edict of the President of the Russian Federation on 5 October 2009.[75] The National Anti-Terrorist Committee was formed by Edict of the President of the Russian Federation of 15 February 2006, No. 116.[76] The Committee is headed by the Director of the Federal Security Service and prepares proposals for forming State security policy, improving legislation on the subject-matter, coordinating security activity of agencies of power, among others. The "Complex Plan for Counteracting the Ideology of Terrorism in the Russian Federation for 2019-2023" (available online) was confirmed by the President of the Russian Federation on 28 December 2018, No. Пр-2665.

Presidential power and foreign relations

In his capacity as the Head of State, the President of the Russian Federation represents Russia in international relations and directs foreign policy. Under the 1993 Constitution, the President conducts negotiations with foreign States and signs international treaties of the Russian Federation, signs instruments of ratification, and accepts credentials and letters of recall of diplomats accredited to the Russian Federation. In consultation with the relevant committees or commissions of the State Duma and Soviet of the Federation, he appoints and recalls Russian ambassadors and other diplomatic representatives of the Russian Federation to foreign States and international organizations.

On 30 November 2016, the Russian Federation issued the Conception of Foreign Policy of the Russian Federation, confirmed by Edict of the President of the Russian Federation.[77] This document superseded a Conception confirmed by Edict of the President of the Russian Federation on 2 February 2013, and in reverse chronological order, the 2013 Conception replaced versions of 12 July 2008, 28 June 2000, and 23 April 1993.[78]

Presidential power and military and extraordinary situations

In the event of aggression against the Russian Federation or a direct threat of aggression the President of Russia has the right to introduce a military situation on the territory of the Russian Federation or in individual localities

[75] Российская газета [Russian Newspaper], 20 October 2009. Available on Consultant Plus.

[76] СЗ РФ (2006), no. 8, item 897, as amended. The Edict confirmed the Statute on the National Anti-Terrorist Committee.

[77] СЗ РФ (2016), no. 49, item 6886; transl. in Butler, note 32 above. See W. E. Butler, "Foreign Policy Discourses as Part of Understanding Russia and International Law", in P. Sean Morris, *Russian Discourses on International Law: Sociological and Philosophical Phenomenon* (2018), pp. 177-196.

[78] The texts of all are available on Consultant Plus.

thereof, notifying at once the Soviet of the Federation and the State Duma thereof. The procedure and consequences of declaring a military situation, including general and partial mobilization, are set out in the Federal Constitutional Law on a Military Situation, of 30 January 2002, as amended, together with a detailed definition of what constitute acts of aggression.[79]

Under the 1993 Russian Constitution (Article 88), the President of the Russian Federation has the exclusive right by edict to introduce an extraordinary situation on the territory of the Russian Federation or in a particular locality. This power has been exercised especially when natural disasters occur, such as floods, avalanches, large forest fires. Upon doing so, he must immediately notify the Soviet of the Federation and the State Duma thereof and request confirmation of his edict by the Soviet of the Federation. The Federal Constitutional Law on an Extraordinary Situation of 30 May 2001, as amended, determines the circumstances and procedure for introducing an extraordinary situation.[80] The declaring of such a situation is a provisional measure to be introduced solely to ensure the safety of citizens and to defend the constitutional system of the Russian Federation.

An extraordinary situation introduces a special regime of administration which unavoidably impinges upon the rights and freedoms of citizens. The President must give the reasons for so acting and enumerate the extraordinary measures to be implemented not less than six hours before the situation enters into force. An exemplary list of such circumstances is given in Article 3 of the Federal Constitutional Law.

Presidential power and State awards

The President of the Russian Federation confers State awards, titles of honor, and senior military and other ranks of the Russian Federation upon recipients in accordance with Statutes on the particular award confirmed by Edict of the President issued on 2 March 1994,[81] as amended.

Presidential power and citizenship

A single Federation citizenship operates in the Russian Federation; each citizen of a republic within the Federation is simultaneously a citizen of the Russian Federation. The 1993 Constitution requires that such citizenship shall be uniform and equal irrespective of the grounds of acquisition, that

[79] СЗ РФ (2002), no. 5, item 375.

[80] СЗ РФ (2001), no. 23, item 2277, as amended. Prior to the federal constitutional law being enacted, the President acted on the basis of a Law of 17 May 1991. Ведомости СНД и ВС РСФСР (1991), no. 22, item 773. It is noteworthy that in addition to repealing the Law of 17 May 1991, the Federal Constitutional Law of 30 May 2001 (Article 42) also deemed as not prevailing and not subject to application on the territory of the Russian Federation the USSR Law of 3 April 1990 on the Legal Regime of an Extraordinary Situation. Ведомости СНД и ВС СССР (1990), no. 15, item 250.

[81] САПП РФ (1994), no. 10, item 775, as amended.

each citizen shall possess on Russian territory all the rights and freedoms and bear equal duties as provided for by the Constitution, and that a citizen may not be deprived of his citizenship or of the right to change it. The details, including the powers of the President relating to citizenship, are elaborated in the Federal Law on Citizenship of the Russian Federation of 31 May 2002, as amended,[82] adopted in furtherance of Article 6 of the Russian Constitution. International treaties modify its provisions under certain circumstances.

Amnesty, Pardon, and Asylum

Amnesties are the prerogative of the State Duma (see below); pardons and political asylum are within the discretion of the President.

Pardons are granted, under the 1993 Russian Constitution, by the President of the Russian Federation to an individually determined person in accordance with the Statute on the Procedure for Consideration of Petitions Concerning a Pardon in the Russian Federation, confirmed by Edict of 28 December 2001, as amended 14 December 2020.[83] They have been used with some frequency to commute capital punishment and less commonly to relieve from the further serving of punishment.[84] A pardon may also remove a record of conviction. The procedure for considering petitions to grant a pardon, previously centralized in a Commission attached to the President of the Russian Federation, has been partially decentralized by the creation of a network of pardon commissions set up in the subjects of the Federation. These commissions vet petitions and prepare opinions, which are then passed to the highest official of the subject of the Federation to prepare a recommendation for the President of the Russian Federation, with whom the ultimate right and power to pardon resides. Names of persons recommended for pardon are to be published in the media, together with the article of the Criminal Code under which they were convicted.

Asylum was provided for in all Soviet constitutions from 1917. The 1993 Russian Constitution speaks of "political asylum", which may be granted to foreign citizens and stateless persons "in accordance with generally-recognized norms of international law" (Article 63(1)). The Statute on the Procedure for Granting Political Asylum in the Russian Federation was confirmed by Edict of the President of the Russian Federation on 21 July 1997, as amended.[85] As regulated in 1997, political asylum required that a number of stringent requirements be satisfied. Political asylum would not

[82] СЗ РФ (2002), no. 22, item 2031, as amended; the 2002 Federal Law replaced that of 28 November 1991, as amended. Ведомости СНД и ВС РФ (1992), no. 6, item 243; (1993), no. 29, item 1112; СЗ РФ (1995), no. 7, item 496; (1996), no. 21, item 2579.

[83] СЗ РФ (2001), no. 53(II), item 5149, as amended.

[84] President Putin exercised this power to pardon Mikhail Khodorkovsky on 20 December 2013, Edict No. 922. СЗ РФ (2013), no. 51, item 6854.

[85] СЗ РФ (1997), no. 30, item 3601, as amended; transl. in Butler, note 32 above, pp. 159-162.

be granted under certain circumstances: if the person was being persecuted for actions or failure to act deemed in the Russian Federation to be a crime or was guilty of performing actions which were contrary to the purposes and principles of the United Nations, the individual seeking asylum was an accused in a criminal case or there was a conviction which had entered into legal force and was subject to being executed in the Russian Federation; the individual had entered Russia from a third country with developed and stable human rights protections; the individual arrived from a country with which Russia had a treaty on visa-free travel, without prejudice to the right of that individual to seek asylum as a refugee; the individual has citizenship of a third State where he or she is not being persecuted; of the person cannot or does not wish to return to his country of citizenship for economic reasons or usual place of residence for economic reasons or as a consequence of hunger, epidemic, or extraordinary situations of a natural of technogenic character. These formidable barriers resulted in only one case of political asylum being granted, in 1992, so far as open sources disclose: a postgraduate student at Moscow University from the Korean People's Democratic Republic.

The grounds for granting asylum changed dramatically as from 19 December 2018 in comparison with the Soviet era, when asylum was fundamentally ideological in character, and with the post-Soviet legal regime of asylum until then. Russia will grant political asylum to persons seeking protection against persecution or a real threat of becoming a victim of persecution in the country of which he is a citizen or of his usual residence by reason of his socio-political activity or convictions which are not contrary to democratic principles recognized by the international community nor to norms of international law. The persecution must be directed expressly against the person seeking asylum. Political asylum is granted by individual edict of the President of the Russian Federation, who has the right to take into account the State interests of Russia when deciding to grant asylum or not.

An individual granted asylum is assimilated to the legal regime for foreign citizens. A person may be deprived of the political asylum granted to him by the Russian Federation for considerations of State security, and also if this person engages in activity which is contrary to the purposes and principles of the United Nations or if he has committed a crime and with respect to him there is a judgment of conviction of a court which has entered into legal force and is subject to execution. The 1997 Statute also enumerates situations under which political asylum may be forfeited.

By a Decree of the Government of the Russian Federation "On Granting Temporary Asylum on the Territory of the Russian Federation", adopted

9 April 2001,[86] as amended, the concept of "temporary asylum" was introduced for foreign citizens and stateless persons who arrive temporarily in the Russian Federation. This status gives such foreigners a number of special rights and guarantees against deportation to the State of their citizenship or previous ordinary place of residence. In Russian practice temporary asylum has been granted most often to Afghans who fled the conflict unleashed there by the Taliban. In a celebrated instance the Russian Federation granted temporary asylum in 2013 to a United States citizen, Edward Snowden, initially for a period of one year.

Following the legislative changes introduced in December 2018, attributed by many specialists as a Russian response to individuals from Ukraine seeking to resettle in the Russian Federation, as of 1 January 2020, there were registered in the Russian Federation 119 refugees from Ukraine and 368 refugees from places other than Ukraine. 1,672 persons were granted temporary asylum who were not from Ukraine, and 40,274 were from Ukraine. The total number of stateless persons in the Russian Federation totaled ca. 178,000.

State Council of Russian Federation

By an Edict of 1 September 2000,[87] the President of Russia formed the State Council of the Russian Federation. Viewed by some at the time as a weakening of central authority, the State Council was in practice hardly visible. It was a consultative organ intended to assist the President in coordinating the functioning and interaction of agencies of State power. Its principal tasks were to discuss problems of especially important State significance concerning relations between the central government and the subjects of the Federation. Draft legislation, including the draft federal law on the federal budget, was routinely on the agenda. The President of Russia was the Chairman of the State Council; its members were *ex officio* the chairmen of the State Duma and Soviet of the Federation of the Federal Assembly of the Russian Federation, empowered representatives of the President of the Russian Federation in the federal districts, highest officials of the subjects of the Federation, and the leaders of factions in the State Duma of the Russian Federation. A Presidium of the State Council composed of eight members who rotate every six months dealt with operational issues of the State Council. Sessions were convened, as a rule, every three months but held more often by decision of the President, who also determined the procedure for taking decisions within the Council on the basis of discussion. Voting occurred when the President so wished, and

86 СЗ РФ (2001), no. 16, item 1603, as amended.

87 СЗ РФ (2000), no. 36, item 3633, as amended. The Edict confirmed the Statute on the State Council. It lost force and was replaced by the Edict of 21 December 2020, No. 800, "On Questions of the State Council of the Russian Federation", which confirmed the Statute on the Working Organs of the State Council and the Secretary of the State Council.

he was free to pursue consensus decisions. Decisions of the State Council were formalized by a protocol which was signed by the secretary of the State Council, but, if necessary, decisions took the form of presidential edicts, regulations, or assignments. If formal legislation was required from the Federal Assembly, proposals and drafts were submitted to the State Duma by way of presidential legislative initiative.

Under the constitutional amendments of 2020 (Article $83(3^1)(f^5)$), the remit of the State Council is considerably broader. The State Council of the Russian Federation is formed by the President of the Russian Federation "for the purposes of ensuring the coordinated functioning and interaction of agencies of public power, determination of the basic orientations of internal and foreign policy of the Russian Federation, and priority orientations of the socio-economic development of the State". Although this expansion of the powers of the State Council has been viewed in some Russian doctrinal writings as a weakening of Presidential powers, the details of the reform suggest otherwise.

According to the 2020 Federal Law "On the State Council of the Russian Federation", the purpose of the legislation is to improve the coordination of the functioning of the system of unified public power in Russia, by which is meant agencies of State power at the federal level, subjects of the Russian Federation, other State agencies, and agencies of local self-government in aggregate on the basis of organizational-legal, functional, and financial-budgetary interaction. Under the constitutional reforms, the State Council became a State agency of constitutional stature. The agency is headed by the President of the Russian Federation as Chairman and has a Presidium consisting of individuals chosen by the President. The President presides at sessions of the State Council, directs its activity, determines where and when sessions of the State Council are held, determines the work plan and agenda, appoints the secretary of the State Council from among its members, and decides other questions.

Ex officio members of the State Council include the Chairman of the Government, Chairman of the Soviet of the Federation, Chairman of the State Duma, Head of the Administration of the President of the Russian Federation, and senior officials of subjects of the Russian Federation. Representatives of political parties which have factions in the State Duma, representatives of local self-government, and others may be invited by the President to be members of the State Council. Sessions of the Council are held regularly, without precise specification of intervals; a quorum of a majority of the members is required. Extraordinary sessions are possible by decision of the President.

The State council adopts decisions, which are signed by the President of the Russian Federation. Whether they are considered to be normative or binding is not addressed by the Russian Constitution or legislation on the State Council. If the State Council considers it advisable or necessary to adopt or amend a federal constitutional law, federal law, or to make changes in or amendments to a draft federal constitutional law or draft federal law, it has the power of legislative initiative to submit a draft to the State Duma. Similarly, if the State Council believes that strategic planning documents should be prepared or existing documents changed, it may make recommendations to the Government of the Russian Federation or to a relevant subject of the Russian Federation or municipal formation.

The State Council has its own commissions, working groups, and other working organs. The commissions are created by decision of the President of the Russian Federation, as is their membership and jurisdiction. The State Council or its working organs may invite members of the Government, executives of federal agencies of executive power, other federal agencies of State power, agencies of subjects of the Russian Federation, other State agencies, agencies of local self-government, or organizations to its sessions, request and receive necessary information and materials relating to matters within its jurisdiction, and organize scientific research or studies by scholars and specialists.

Members of the State Council serve voluntarily by Presidential appointment or *ex officio* and receive no salary for their services.

Presidential Administration and Advisory Agencies

Around the President is a vast variety of aides, advisors, counselors, and assistants united in a structure called the Administration of the President, which operates on the basis of a Statute on the Administration of the President of the Russian Federation confirmed by an Edict of 6 April 2004, as amended.[88] The Administration includes the Director of the Administration, his first deputies and deputies, amongst them the Head of the Chancellery of the President, the heads of chief administrations and administrations, and the press secretary, Presidential aides, including the head of protocol, plenipotentiaries, and counselors. All are directly subordinate to the President and appointed by him. Also attached to the President are consultative and advisory agencies under various names: commissions, councils, and others. Reorganizations of these bodies occur with frequency.

THE FEDERAL ASSEMBLY

The parliament of the Russian Federation is called the Federal Assembly. It consists of two chambers: the Soviet of the Federation and the State Duma. By virtue of being named, together with the President, the Government, and the courts of the Russian Federation, as effectuating State power, not

[88] СЗ РФ (2004), no. 15, item 1395, as amended; transl. in Butler, note 32 above.

even the Federal Assembly may change its own stature in the Russian constitutional system without undergoing the complex procedures for amending the Constitution laid down in Article 135(1) of the Constitution. The parliament is independent in the sense that the Constitution prescribes no precise limits to the legislation which it may enact. It is financially autonomous, determining its own expenses in the State budget, and also determines its own internal structure and procedures, being guided only by the Constitution itself.

Nonetheless, the powers of the Federal Assembly are not unlimited. Certain laws may be adopted by referendum, bypassing the parliament, and during a military or extraordinary situation, the operation of laws may be suspended. The Constitutional Court of the Russian Federation has the right to declare laws unconstitutional, and the President may under certain circumstances dissolve the State Duma. International treaties of the Russian Federation may take precedence over laws adopted by the parliament, and certain laws on finances may be enacted only when the Government of Russia has submitted an opinion regarding them.

Although called the parliament of Russia in the Constitution (Article 94), the Federal Assembly is further characterized as the "legislative and representative" agency of the Russian Federation. Gone from the Russian Constitution is the vertical integration of legislative power which sought in the Soviet period to make all local soviets subordinate to superior legislative branches of the State. No longer is the parliament conceived as also being a control and administrative agency of State power. Russian constitutional doctrine takes the view that deputies of the Federal Assembly, once elected, whether directly by the voters in electoral districts or by subjects of the Federation, become representatives of the people at large and not merely the voters of their narrow constituency. They are not bound by imperative mandates from their electors, nor subject to recall for failure to fulfil them.

Many Russian constitutional lawyers continue to adhere to the view, notwithstanding the doctrines of separation of powers and checks and balances, that parliament adopts the enactments of the highest legal force [*lex*], which no other branch of the State may do. The emotional power of закон [*lex*] has yet to come to terms with the constitutional reality that in Russia only the Constitution itself is *lex* and that all other enactments – parliamentary, Presidential, governmental – are subordinate [подзаконный]. If this were not the case, the separation of powers would be meaningless. All branches of the State must act in conformity with the Constitution, and the Constitution must conform to Russian law: право [*jus*].

Structure of the Federal Assembly

A bicameral parliament was first introduced in Russia by way of constitutional amendments in 1990; prior thereto the highest representative agencies of the RSFSR had from 1917 been unicameral. The experience from 1990 to 1993 was not regarded as successful; mostly the chambers of the parliament sat in joint session, dominated by its presidium.

Under the Constitution neither chamber of the Federal Assembly is lower or higher; each has equal rights, albeit different powers. The burden of enacting federal laws falls principally upon the State Duma in practice, for the legislative process commences in this chamber. In the popular mind, the Soviet of the Federation is more analogous to a Senate, less politicized, less partisan, more deliberate, and more responsive to regional interests. When the chambers have differed on matters of substance, as frequently happens, the conciliation procedures for resolving them have on the whole operated effectively.

The State Duma consists of 450 deputies, whereas the Soviet of the Federation at full strength consists of two members from each subject of the Federation; these are representatives from legislative (or representative) and executive agencies of State power of subjects of the Federation pursuant to amendments to the 1993 Russian Constitution made in 2014. In addition, a President of the Russian Federation who has left office may serve for life in the Soviet of the Federation at his or her choice. No more than thirty representatives of the Russian Federation appointed by the President of the Russian Federation may serve in the Soviet of the Federation, no more than seven of whom may be appointed for life.

One person may not be simultaneously a member of both chambers. The State Duma is elected every five years (most recently on 10 September 2016), whereas the Soviet of the Federation has no stipulated term of office. Elections to the State Duma are held on the basis of the Federal Law on Elections of Deputies of the State Duma of the Federal Assembly of the Russian Federation, of 22 February 2014, as amended;[89] the Federal Law on the Procedure for Forming the Soviet of the Federation of the Federal Assembly of the Russian Federation, of 3 December 2012,[90] regulates the formation of the Soviet of the Federation. In compliance with the Concluding and Transitional Provisions of the 1993 Russian Constitution, both chambers were formed initially for a two-year term of office (1993-1995); thereafter, the State Duma was elected to a four-year term (until constitutional amendments of 2008) and thereafter a five-year term, and the Soviet of the Federation was formed on the basis of the 1995 Law.

The word "deputies" applies only to those in the State Duma; the Soviet of the Federation from 1995 has "members", from 2020 called "senators".

[89] СЗ РФ (2014), no. 8, item 740, as amended.

[90] СЗ РФ (2012), no. 40(IV), item 6952, as amended; transl. in Butler, note 32 above; the 2012 Law replaced the Federal Law of 5 August 2000. СЗ РФ (2000), no. 32, item 3336, as amended. This 2000 Federal Law replaced that of 5 December 1995. СЗ РФ (1995), no. 50, item 4869.

Under the Law of 5 August 2000, the Soviet of the Federation was no longer based upon representation by the head of the legislative or representative agency of the subject and the head of the executive agency of State power. As from 1 January 2002, the representatives from subjects of the Federation in the Soviet of the Federation were individuals appointed by the heads of executive power and legislative agency in the respective subject. It does not follow that the choices of representatives will be synchronized by the executive and legislative branches within each subject of the Federation, or that the representatives chosen will not be changed at will by the appointing body. This scheme of selection was retained in the 2012 Federal Law.

Internal organization of the Federal Assembly

The Federal Assembly is a permanently operating professional parliament, in sharp contrast to its Soviet predecessors which assembled two to four times yearly for a few days. The convocation of the Federal Assembly does not depend in any way upon the President, but rather its own initiative. The State Duma meets for its first session on the 30th day after the elections, although the President may convoke it earlier. The session of the Duma is opened by its most senior member in age; only from this moment do the powers of the previous Duma lapse (Article 99, Constitution).

The chambers sit separately. Joint sessions are held only to hear messages from the President of Russia. Accordingly, the chambers do not consider questions together or adopt joint decisions, even if they sit in joint session. The absence of a common presidium or official who would manage the two chambers further ensures that they work autonomously. The two chambers are physically located in different buildings in Moscow and have their own support personnel. Each chamber operates in accordance with its own Reglament, a change from the past when a single Reglament governed both chambers. The Reglaments share much in common but differ in details. The State Duma Reglament was adopted 22 January 1998.[91] The Soviet of the Federation adopted a new Reglament on 30 January 2002 which, as amended, prohibits political groups or factions from being created within the upper chamber. The prohibition was retained in the 2012 Federal Law (Article 1[4]) and 2020 Federal Law (Article 1[6]).[92]

The constitutional foundations for electing the leadership of each chamber are identical, the specific procedures being laid down in each Reglament. Each chamber elects its own chairman, and neither is beholden to the President for this position. The chairman of the State Duma is elected for a five-year term, although he may be removed from office at any time;

[91] Translated in Butler, note 32 above.

[92] Federal Law of 22 December 2020, No. 439-ФЗ, "On the Procedure for the Formation of the Soviet of the Federation of the Federal Assembly of the Russian Federation", which replaced the Federal Law of 3 December 2012, No 229-ФЗ.

the chairman of the Soviet of the Federation is elected without limit of term and likewise may be replaced at the pleasure of his chamber.

The Chairman of the Soviet of the Federation presides at sessions of the Soviet, signs decrees, maintains order, sends draft laws to committees and, when adopted, to the President for signature, represents the Soviet in relations with the State Duma, Government, and other agencies of State power and with parliaments of foreign States, supervises the administrative apparatus of the Soviet, and the like. In the Chairman's absence his deputy may perform many of his functions, including signing decrees of the chamber.

Just as the Soviet of the Federation, the State Duma also forms a Council consisting of the Chairman, First Deputy Chairmen, Deputy Chairmen, and the leaders of the factions. The Council is occupied with preparing in advance the organizational decisions of the State Duma: work program at the current session, calendar for considering draft laws, sending draft laws to committees, deciding whether to hold parliamentary hearings, confirming the distribution of duties among the deputy chairman, and others. The deputies are informed about all decisions taken.

The 1993 Russian Constitution requires that both chambers of the Federal Assembly form committees and commissions to prepare and give advance consideration to draft laws and hold hearings. All senators of the Soviet of the Federation and all deputies of the State Duma, except the chairmen and their deputies, must serve on at least one committee of their chamber. Each chamber determines the numerical size of committees; in the Soviet of the Federation there must be no less than eleven persons and no more than 21, whereas in the State Duma the committees vary from 12 to 35 deputies in size. Each member or deputy of the chambers is allowed to express a preference for committee assignment, the final choice being made by vote of each chamber. The State Duma elected the chairmen and deputy chairmen of the committees; in the Soviet of the Federation this is done at a session of the committee, the chairman of the committee then being confirmed by the full chamber.

Committees and commissions have the right to request documents and materials needed for their activities and to invite State officials and officials of social associations, enterprises, institutions, and organizations to their sessions, all of whom are obliged to submit the documents and materials requested. By all accounts the committees and commissions have an active role in law-making, often producing multiple drafts or rival drafts of major legislation. Their deliberations are governed by the Reglaments of the chambers and their own rules and procedures. Each chamber determines which committees to form or to abolish, and committees may themselves form subcommittees. The competence of each committee is confirmed by the Reglament. For example, the Committee of the Soviet of the Federation for Constitutional Legislation and State Construction has within its competence:

changes in the Constitution of the Russian Federation;

amendments to the Constitution of the Russian Federation;

rights and freedoms of man and citizen;

State structure of the Russian Federation;

organization of the system of State power in the Russian Federation;

State service;

legal status of citizens of the Russian Federation, foreign citizens, and stateless persons;

development of a civil society;

interaction of citizens, society, and the State;

social associations, religious organizations, political parties, trade unions;

noncommercial organizations, except for State corporations;

State migration policy;

judicial system, procuracy, investigation, justice, advokatura, notariat;

constitutional law

criminal law;

criminal procedure law

penal law;

civil law;

civil procedure law;

arbitrazh procedure law;

administrative law;

family law;

execution law;

State policy in the sphere of mass media, information technologies, and defense of information;

development of single information space of Russian Federation and creation of an information society;

information exchange, development of computer networks of common use;

information security of children;

dissemination of periodical publications, books and other printed products, audio and video products;

publishing and printing;

preliminary discussion and submission for consideration of Soviet of the Federation of candidacies for appointment to office of the Chairman of the Constitutional Court of the Russian Federation, deputy chairmen of the Constitutional Court of the Russian Federation, and judges of the Constitutional Court of the Russian Federation;

preliminary discussion and submission for consideration of the Soviet of the Federation of candidacies for appointment to office of the Chairman of the Supreme Court of the Russian Federation, deputy chairmen of the Supreme Court of the Russian Federation, members of the Presidium of the Supreme Court of the Russian Federation, and judges of the Supreme Court of the Russian Federation;

preliminary discussion and submission for consideration of the Soviet of the Federation of candidacies for appointment to the office of judge of the Economic Court of the Commonwealth of Independent States;

preliminary discussion of candidacies, forming, and submission for consideration of the Soviet of the Federation of the List of representatives of the public for appointment as members of the High Qualifications College of Judges of the Russian Federation and preliminary discussion of the question of the termination before time of the powers of members of the High Qualifications College of Judges of the Russian Federation – representatives of the public appointed by the Soviet of the Federation;

preliminary discussion and submission for consideration of the Soviet of the Federation of candidacies for appointment to office of the Procurator General of the Russian Federation, First Deputy Procurator General of the Russian Federation, deputies of the Procurator General of the Russian Federation, and questions of the relieving from office of the Procurator General of the Russian Federation, First Deputy Procurator General of the Russian Federation, and deputies of the Procurator General of the Russian Federation;

ensuring interaction of the Soviet of the Federation with the Constitutional Court of the Russian Federation;

ensuring interaction of the Soviet of the Federation with the Supreme Court of the Russian Federation, High Qualifications College of Judges of the Russian Federation, General Procuracy of the Russian Federation, Investigative Committee of the Russian Federation, Ministry of Justice of the Russian Federation, Social Chamber of the Russian Federation, and Plenipotentiary for Human Rights in the Russian Federation;

ensuring consideration at a session of the Soviet of the Federation of the annual report of the Procurator General of the Russian Federation on the state of legality and legal order in the Russian Federation and on work done with regard to the strengthening thereof, and the annual report of the Plenipotentiary for Human Rights in the Russian Federation.

In addition the Soviet of the Federation has a commission to resolve issues related to control over the use of the electronic system and associated personnel of the Apparatus of the Soviet of the Federation. This commission consists of senators appointed by the Soviet of the Federation and is a working organ of a session of the Soviet. Its chairman is allocated a special place during sessions equipped with the necessary electronic and other equipment to manage and operate the electronic system (Article 70^3, Reglament of the Soviet of the Federation). *Ad hoc* commissions are formed from time to time.

The powers of a senator are recognized, terminated, or confirmed from the moment that the full chamber adopts a respective decision. Since the Soviet of the Federation operates without a formal term of office, so too do its committees and commissions. Senators come and go from the committees as their terms of office change; a committee is quorate if more than half of the members are present. Sessions are held not less than once a month. The committees and commissions often form working groups together with representatives from State agencies, social associations, and academic institutions. They also may enlist the services of individual scholars and other specialists to assist.

The State Duma forms committees for its five-year term of office giving, insofar as possible, proportional representation on each committee. Each committee may form subcommittees. Sessions are held as needed, but not less than twice monthly. A deputy group or one-quarter of the members of a committee may demand an extraordinary session, the decision to sit being decided by a majority of those present at the meeting to resolve the issue. Committees and commissions frequently hold sessions with one another. Each committee or commission has the right to submit proposals to the Council of the State Duma regarding the session of the Duma, and the chairman of the committee or commission has the right to speak at sessions of the chamber or of other committees and commissions of the State Duma in respect of matters within the jurisdiction of his committee or commission. Working groups may be formed with membership from several committees or commissions and outside specialists or representatives of State agencies, social organizations, and academic institutions.

Inter-faction working groups may be formed with the consent of existing committees to prepare agreed proposals to improve legislation or agreed positions on other questions relegated to the State Duma. These inter-faction working groups may not exercise powers or rights provided by the Reglament of the State Duma for committees and commissions.

Commissions of the State Duma are formed from the members of committees of the chamber. They include the credentials commission, commissions to verify particular events or investigate officials, to count the results of secret ballots, to give opinions, and perform other tasks. The remit of each commission is determined by the decree of the State Duma creating it. Among the commissions of comparatively recent origin is the Commission of the State Duma for Questions of Control over the Reliability of Information on Revenues, Property, and Obligations of a Property Character Submitted by Deputies of the State Duma, Mandate Questions, and Questions of Deputy Ethics. This commission addresses alleged violations of deputy ethics and whether a deputy should be stripped of inviolability against prosecution for criminal behavior.

The so-called "deputy associations" are key units within the State Duma; they do not exist in the Soviet of the Federation. The deputy associations take the form of factions. The definition of a faction is complex, but basically amounts to an association of deputies formed on the basis of an electoral association which entered the State Duma under an all-federal electoral district and single-mandate electoral districts. Moreover, all deputies of the State Duma nominated by a political party as candidates on the federal list of candidates and all deputies nominated by this political party as candidate in single mandate electoral districts are in a faction. The factions essentially, but not exactly, are political parties or groupings and are subject to registration in the Duma. Factions duly registered have equal rights. A deputy may be a member of only one faction. Each faction organizes its own affairs. The principal factions in the State Duma as of 2020 are: "United Russia" (336 deputies), "A Just Russia" (22 deputies), "Communist Party of the Russian Federation" (41 deputies), and "Liberal-Democratic Party of Russia" (40 deputies). From time to time mergers and alliances amongst them result in new names, images, and candidacies.

Internal work procedures of the Federal Assembly

Although they share certain operational procedures in common, the two chambers of the Federal Assembly do differ in many key respects, reflecting their varying competence, the numbers of deputies and senators involved, and their constituencies. For each chamber the Reglament operates as an exceptionally detailed manual of operations setting out every stage of daily work. The Soviet of the Federation meets, in practice, less frequently than the State Duma, although both chambers operate on a permanent basis. The division of the State Duma into factions imposes requirements of discipline not needed in the Soviet of the Federation. Sheer numbers make it more difficult for a deputy of the State Duma to speak in plenary session than is the case for a senator of the Soviet of the Federation.

The opening and closing of a session of the Soviet of the Federation is marked by performing the national anthem of the Russian Federation. Sessions are quorate if more than half of the total number of senators are present, a fact which is determined by registration of senators at each morning and evening session of the Soviet. If there is to be a formal vote, an additional registration is conducted to verify the existence of a quorum. Sessions are held between 25 January and 15 July for the spring session and 16 September and 31 December for the autumn session of each calendar year.[93] Extraordinary sessions may be convoked at the request of the President of the Russian Federation, Chairman of the Soviet of the Federation, Council of the Chamber, committee of the Soviet of the Federation with regard to questions relegated to its jurisdiction, or upon the proposal of one-third of the total number of senators of the Soviet of the Federation. The proposal of a committee of the Soviet of the Federation must be supported by no less than one-fifth of the total number of senators of the Russian Federation. Formal protocols and verbatim transcripts are kept of each session, signed by the person presiding, and published in due course. Senators have access to the transcript before publication.

The structure of the agenda, the precise functions of the person presiding, the procedures for granting the floor to a senator, for putting questions to a vote, for submitting questions, the time to be allocated to types of reports from commissions and committees, for clarifying remarks or explaining votes, for reducing or extending periods of time allotted, and the like are strictly determined by the Reglament. No one may speak or yield the floor to another without the permission of the person presiding. A senator who violates this rule may be deprived of the floor by the person presiding (usually the microphone is turned off). The Reglaments require that a senator, deputy, or civil servant, when referring to issues of cost or value, use rubles as the currency unit unless Russian legislation provides otherwise.

The State Duma, as noted above, commences its first session on the thirtieth day after election unless the President of the Russian Federation convokes the session earlier. After electing its Chairman and deputy chairman, the Duma elects a counting commission, provisional commission

[93] Article 41(1), Reglament of the Soviet of the Federation of the Federal Assembly of the Russian Federation. СЗ РФ (2002), no. 7, item 635, as amended.

for control over the electronic voting system, provisional commission for the Reglament of the State Duma, provisional secretariat, and the credentials commission. The President of the Russian Federation or his plenipotentiary representative to the Federal Assembly, the Chairman, members of the Government, and plenipotentiary of the Government of the Russian Federation, members of the Constitutional Court and the Supreme Court, the Chairman, deputy chairman, and auditors of the Counting Chamber, the Plenipotentiary for human rights, the Procurator General of the Russian Federation, and the Chairman of the Central Electoral Commission of the Russian Federation have the right to be present at any open or closed session of the State Duma; others may be present at a closed session only by special invitation.

Deference to the President is expressed by allocating to him a special place in the hall, above which are placed the State Flag and Arms of the Russian Federation. Protocols and verbatim transcripts are kept and officially published, except for the transcripts of closed sessions. The State Duma assembles in spring and autumn sessions, from approximately 12 January to 20 July in spring and from early September to 31 December in autumn. Plenary sessions are held on Tuesdays and Thursdays, and the sundry committees, commission, working groups, hearings, and the like proceed throughout the entire session of the Duma.

The Council of the State Duma meets "regularly", usually on Mondays and Wednesdays. Committees and commissions schedule sessions for Mondays, Wednesdays, and Fridays. One week of every month is earmarked for deputies to work with their respective constituencies. The Reglament further stipulates that every Tuesday of the first and third week is "question time", during which not more than two members of the Government appear to answer questions.

The "question time" is highly structured by the Reglament. Deputies submit suggestions in writing to the Council of the State Duma as to who should be invited and the questions it is proposed to put to them. The decision to invite is sent to the member of the Government at least ten days before "question time". The questions are sent five days in advance. The member of Government (federal minister) has 20 minutes to reply to the question (others – five minutes; an auditor of the Counting Chamber – ten minutes). Deputies may put questions to those invited for "question time", but the duration of the question may not exceed one minute, and the reply – three minutes. Speeches are not permitted during "question time". At the end of "question time", representatives of factions have up to seven minutes to sum up the discussion. The federal minister(s) or other officials may offer a final concluding word. The State Duma adopted a decree with regard to the results of every "question time" which may contain decisions or recommendations.

A session of the State Duma commences with the registration of deputies present, which is performed by the person presiding. A quorum is a majority (226) of the total number of deputies of the chamber (450). It is a requirement that deputies be present at a session; if this is impossible for justifiable reasons the deputy must inform the chairman of the State Duma. A justifiable reason is temporary incapacity to work, being abroad as part of an official parliamentary delegation, or being sent on a business trip by instruction of the Chairman of the State Duma. For every session of a chamber missed by a member of the State Duma without a justifiable reason, a deduction of one-ninth of the monthly payment is made and appropriate notification made on the official website of the State Duma. More often than not, in practice the notification requirement is not complied with by a large number of deputies.

Sessions of the State Duma are held in accordance with a model program of draft law work for the current session, a calendar for consideration of questions by the State Duma during the current month, and the work procedure for the session of the State Duma. Deputies are notified in advance about the agenda of the session and supplied with draft laws and decrees and other necessary materials not later than three days before their consideration in a session. The daily agenda follows a general work program confirmed at the first session of the Duma, a calendar drawn up for each month by the Council of the State Duma, and a calendar for each month confirmed by the Duma as a whole by majority vote. Changes in the calendar are made by written request of a majority of the factions and deputy groups. Certain matters are considered on an urgent or priority basis: messages of the President of the Russian Federation, urgent draft laws submitted by the President or by the Government, draft federal laws on the federal budget and budget system of the Russian Federation, draft laws on the ratification of international treaties, draft laws which need to be adopted pursuant to federal constitutional laws, federal laws, or decisions of the Constitutional Court of the Russian Federation, draft laws submitted to the State Duma by the Soviet of the Federation jointly by a member of the Soviet of the Federation who is the Chairman of the Soviet of the Federation and a deputy of the State Duma who is the Chairman of the State Duma, draft laws submitted to the State Duma in execution of assignments of the Chairman of the State Duma, and other draft laws by decision of the Council of the State Duma. Other matters may be considered in priority only if a majority of the chamber so decides.

The person presiding in the State Duma enjoys substantial rights. He directs the general flow of the session, ensures compliance with the Reglament, gives the floor to deputies, fulfils the organizational decisions taken by the State Duma, puts to a vote each proposal of a deputy in the sequence in which they are received, conducts voting and announces the result, oversees the work of the apparatus of the State Duma, and keeps protocols and verbatim transcripts of the sessions. If a deputy violates the Reglament, the person presiding issues a warning; a second violation means the offender no longer has the floor, although a flagrant first violation will result in the same sanction. If legislation of the Russian Federation or the Reglament of the chamber is violated, the person presiding is obliged to point this out, and also to rectify factual errors made in speeches by deputies. He may order removed from the hall any invited persons who obstruct the work of the State Duma. However, the person presiding may not express his own personal view on matters being discussed, nor comment on the speeches of deputies, nor characterize those who have spoken. When voting is open without the use of electronic equipment, the person presiding votes last. If the person presiding himself violates the Reglament, the chamber may appoint another person to preside before adopting a decision on the question under discussion.

Deputies speak in the State Duma from the lectern or in the hall from a positioned microphone. The Reglament requires that deputies wear business attire consistent with the official character of the activity of the State Duma. As in the Soviet of the Federation, speeches, reports, and other addresses to the Duma are strictly timed. The person presiding gives a warning of time expiring and then withdraws the floor from those who exceed their limit. It is common practice for the person presiding to establish with the assent of a majority of deputies present a total time limit for discussion a particular matter on the agenda, including questions and answers, or to extend a time limit previously set. No one may speak without the permission of the person presiding; deputies who do not have an opportunity to speak because of insufficient time may attach the written texts of their intended remarks to the verbatim transcript of the Duma session.

The Reglaments of both chambers of the Federal Assembly lay down a special work procedure for considering questions relegated to the jurisdiction of the chambers, most especially for the adoption or approval of laws.

Voting in the Federal Assembly

Decisions of the Soviet of the Federation are adopted by open or by secret ballot. Several methods are used: electronic equipment, ballots. When the electronic system is used, three methods are available: quantitative, rating, or alternative. Quantitative voting requires that a member vote "yes"', "no"', or "abstain". The votes are counted and the results announced in absolute figures and in percentage of votes cast if the question is substantive, but if the question is procedural, only absolute figures are given. A vote by rating constitutes a series of consecutive quantitative votes in which each member of the Soviet may take part with respect to each question put. The results are announced in absolute and percentage figures only after the entire sequence of votes has been cast. Alternative voting is to vote for only one of several variants of a question, the results being disclosed in absolute and percentage figures for all variants of the question simultaneously.

A decision is considered to be adopted when more than half of the total number of members of the Soviet of the Federation has voted in favor unless the Constitution of the Russian Federation or the Reglament of the Soviet provide otherwise. Procedural questions – whether to have a break in the session, carry over a session, or adjourn, terminate speeches relating to the agenda, and the like – are adopted by a majority of members present at a session. Voting is considered to be constituted if the number of members of the Soviet of the Federation present at a session is not less than the number of members needed to adopt a decision. If a quorum is not present, the person presiding has the right to designate a time for voting on a question, the discussion of which has been completed.

Open voting may be conducted with or without the use of electronic equipment, as the chamber may determine. Once voting has commenced it may not be interrupted except by a point of order. Secret voting is carried out with the use of the electronic system or by ballot, the ballot being deposited in a special box sealed by the Counting Commission. The results of a secret ballot are formalized by a decree of the Soviet of the Federation.

The State Duma also uses both open and secret ballots. When open voting is conducted with the electronic system, each deputy has the right to receive the results with a full list of those who voted and how they voted. In the case of a secret ballot, the list of individual names is not entered in the electronic memory. Decrees of the State Duma are adopted by a majority (226) of the total number of deputies, except with regard to procedural matters, where a majority of those present is sufficient. A deputy who is absent during the voting may not cast his vote once the period allocated for voting has elapsed. When multiple candidacies or matters are put to the State Duma, the Duma may decide to proceed by rounds of voting. If in the second round none of the variants or candidacies has received the minimum number of votes required, the question is removed from further consideration. It is for the State Duma to decide in each instance whether to use electronic voting or not. When the electronic system is not used, the Counting Commission is responsible for counting the ballots. The person presiding announces the results. As in the case of the Soviet of the Federation, voting, once commenced, may not be interrupted except by a point of order. Secret ballots are conducted by the Counting Commission, which issues a protocol and a report concerning the results; on the basis of these the person presiding announces the result. Both chambers have created special groups of members to oversee the electronic voting system and ensure that it performs as it should.

Parliamentary hearings of the Federal Assembly

In accordance with Article 101(3) of the Russian Constitution, both chambers of the Federal Assembly hold hearings on matters within their jurisdiction. Hearings may be open or closed and may be conducted by commissions or committees of both chambers jointly. Hearings result not in decisions, but in recommendations. Each committee which organizes hearings also decides who shall be invited to take part. Hearings may concern draft laws, international treaties submitted for ratification, the federal budget, or other major issues of domestic or foreign policy. Most hearings are open to the press and the general public. Closed hearings discuss, as a rule, issues involving State security or secrecy. The duration of hearings is determined by the committee or commission holding them.

Recommendations emanating from hearings held at the State Duma are adopted by a majority of the deputies taking part therein and may be published in the press. The materials of closed hearings are submitted to the deputies, the President of the Russian Federation, the Government of the Russian Federation, and to State agencies whose representatives took part in the hearings. If the Soviet of the Federation held closed hearings, the materials are circulated to the senators and the State agencies whose representatives took part in the hearings.

Competence of the Federal Assembly

The subject-matter jurisdiction of the Federal Assembly has not been determined precisely by the 1993 Constitution of the Russian Federation. In some measure the matters within the exclusive and joint jurisdiction of the Russian Federation (Articles 71 and 72, Russian Constitution) affect the competence of the Federal Assembly, but that enumeration is much broader, including the competence of the President and the Government, and other federal agencies of State power. However, those Articles of the Constitution which expressly call for a federal law do determine in part the competence of the Federal Assembly. Nonetheless, the competence of the two chambers is not identical even in this respect. The Soviet of the Federation is required to consider laws adopted by the State Duma only with respect to the budget, taxes, war and peace, and others listed in Article 106 of the Constitution. Whether the Soviet of the Federation bothers to consider other laws passed by the State Duma is purely a matter of its discretion. If the Soviet fails to consider them within a stipulated period, the State Duma may pass them along to the President for signature and promulgation (Article 105(4), Constitution).

Each chamber of the Federal Assembly also has special competence expressly provided for by the Russian Constitution. The division of special competence is in part a reflection of the principle of checks-and-balances within the parliament.

Special competence of Soviet of the Federation

Set out principally in Article 102 of the Constitution, but also in others, the Soviet of the Federation has the following areas of special competence.

(1) *Confirmation of changes of boundaries between subjects of Federation.* The Soviet of the Federation considers this matter by mutual consent of the subjects of the Federation whose boundaries are to be changed. The text of the agreement to change the boundaries confirmed by the legislative agencies of State power of each of the subjects concerned, a reasoned case for the change endorsed by each subject, and a map of the locality are submitted to the Soviet of the Federation. The matter is first referred to a committee of the Soviet, whose opinion is submitted to the plenary session. Representatives of the legislative and executive agencies of State power of subjects of the Federation whose boundaries are being changed by the Federal Service for State Registration, Cadastre, and Cartography are invited to the plenary session, together with representatives of the Government of the Russian Federation. The decision to confirm the change of boundaries is adopted by a majority of the total number of senators of the Soviet of the Federation and is formalized in the form of a decree. The decree is final, and is sent to the relevant agencies of the respective subjects of the Federation and to federal agencies of executive power. It will be noted that neither the State Duma nor the President are involved in this matter, and that no federal law is adopted. The decree is the conclusive document.

(2) *Confirmation of edicts of President of Russian Federation on introducing military and extraordinary situations.* When the President of the Russian Federation issues an edict introducing a military or extraordinary situation in a certain locality or throughout the Russian Federation, the edict, together with the consent of the subject of the Federation if such a situation is declared in a subject of the Federation, is sent immediately to the Soviet of the Federation, which must consider the matter within 72 hours of receipt. Whether the Soviet of the Federation confirms the edict, the decision is formalized in the form of a decree. If the edict is not confirmed, the Soviet of the Federation may propose to the President that a joint conciliation commission be formed to resolve existing disagreements. If the unwillingness to confirm the edict is final, the operation of the edict terminates from the moment that the Soviet of the Federation adopts such a decree.

(3) *Possible use of Armed Forces of Russian Federation beyond limits of territory thereof.* This matter is dealt with on the basis of the Federal Law on the Procedure for the Granting by the Russian Federation of Military and Civilian Personnel for Participation in Activity Relating to the Maintenance or Restoration of Peace and Security of 23 June 1995. The Soviet of the Federation assembles to consider the request of the President of the Russian Federation within not more than five days after receiving it. The President

of Russia, the Chairman of the Government, the Minister of Defense, the Head of the General Staff of the Russian Armed Forces, the Minister of Internal Affairs, the Minister of Foreign Affairs, the Head of the Federal Security Service, and the Head of the Federal Foreign Intelligence Service are all invited to the session. A positive decision requires the votes of more than half of the members of the Soviet of the Federation and is formalized as a Decree which, if adopted, is sent to the President within two days of being adopted. By Decree of 31 January 1997, for example, the Soviet of the Federation approved a military contingent of 1,600 persons for peace-keeping operations in Bosnia and Herzogovina. There have been a number of other instances since then. The State Duma plays no role in this matter, and the decree adopted does not require the signature of the President of the Russian Federation.

(4) *Designation of elections of President of Russian Federation.* The grounds for such a decision would be expiry of the Presidential term or termination of Presidential powers in accordance with Article 92(2) of the Russian Constitution. The decision to hold new elections must be taken by the Soviet of the Federation within a week from the moment of the termination of powers, except in the case of impeachment, when the date of election must be announced on the day that the decision to impeach is adopted.

(5) *Impeachment and Removal of Inviolability of President of Russian Federation.* Impeachment of the President may occur only on the basis of an accusation put forward by the State Duma of treason or the commission of another grave crime, the said accusation being confirmed by an opinion of the Supreme Court of the Russian Federation that the acts of the President contain the indicia of a crime and an opinion of the Constitutional Court of the Russian Federation that the established procedure for putting the accusation forward has been complied with. In addition to these documents, the Soviet of the Federation must have the opinion of a special State Duma commission formed to evaluate the well-foundedness of the accusation against the President and a transcript of the session of the State Duma which considered the accusation against the President. These are then referred to a committee of the Soviet of the Federation for consideration and the Chairman of the Soviet requests the Constitutional Court for the aforementioned opinion regarding procedural compliance.

Once the opinion of the Constitutional Court has been received, the Soviet of the Federation must assemble within 72 hours. The date of the session to consider the accusation must be notified to the President and a lengthy list of other senior State officials and judges. The Chairman of the State Duma opens the session by setting out the substance of the accusation, followed by the Chairman of the Constitutional Court to disclose that Court's view on compliance with procedures. Next the Chairman of the Supreme Court speaks to address the substance of the accusation. The opinion is then heard of the Committee of the Soviet of the Federation Regarding Constitutional

Legislation and State Construction. The President of the Russian Federation or his representative may be granted the floor at their wish.

The draft decree to impeach the President is then put to secret ballot without using the electronic system. Not less than two-thirds of the total number of senators of the Soviet must vote in favor. If the requisite majority is not achieved, the case is terminated, which also is formalized by a decree. The decision of the Soviet of the Federation must be adopted not later than three months after the State Duma puts forward the accusation against the President.

Under additions introduced in 2020 to the 1993 Russian Constitution, a President of the Russian Federation whose term of office has been completed, or who has resigned, or who for reasons of health is unable to complete the term of office is guaranteed inviolability (Article 92[1], Constitution). The inviolability may be removed only on the basis of an accusation put forward by the State Duma of treason to the State or commission of another grave crime confirmed by an opinion of the Supreme Court of the Russian Federation concerning the existence in the actions of the President of the Russian Federation whose term of office has ended of the indicia of a crime and opinion of the Constitutional Court of the Russian Federation concerning compliance with the established procedure for putting forward the accusation (Article 93, Constitution).

The decision of the State Duma to put forward an accusation and the decision of the Soviet of the Federation to remove the President of the Russian Federation from office, or to deprive the President of inviolability, must be adopted by two-thirds of the votes of the total number, respectively, of the senators of the Russian Federation and deputies of the State Duma at the initiative of no less than one-third of the deputies of the State Duma, having obtained an opinion supporting such actions of a special commission formed by the State Duma.

The decision of the Soviet of the Federation to remove the President of the Russian Federation from office or deprive the President of inviolability must be adopted within a three-month period after the State Duma put forward the accusation against the President. If the Soviet of the Federation has not adopted a decision within this period, the accusation is considered to be rejected

(6) *Appointment to and Removal from Office of judges of Constitutional Court and Supreme Court*. The President of the Russian Federation recommends to the Soviet of the Federation the appointment of the Chairman, deputy chairman, and judges of the Constitutional Court of the Russian Federation, Chairman, deputy chairmen, and judges of the Supreme Court of the Russian Federation. The decision to appoint lies with the Soviet of the Federation.

Other judges are appointed by the President of the Russian Federation without the involvement of the Soviet of the Federation. The 1992 Agreement on the Status of the Economic Court of the Commonwealth of Independent States, which confirmed the Statute on the said court, provides (point 7, Statute) that the Russian judge on the court shall be appointed in the procedure established for the appointment of judges to the Supreme Court of the Russian Federation.

Dismissal from judicial office is another matter. In this instance the President of the Russian Federation submits to the Soviet of the Federation a recommendation to terminate the powers of the Chairman, Deputy Chairman, or judges of the Constitutional Court of the Russian Federation, the Chairman, deputy chairmen, and judges of the Supreme Court of the Russian Federation, or the chairmen, deputy chairmen, and judges of cassational and appellate courts if they commit an offense disgracing the honor and dignity of a judge or making the exercise of the powers of the judge impossible.

(7) *Appointment to and removal from office of Procurators.* The 1993 Constitution as amended in 2020 provided that the President of the Russian Federation appoints the Procurator General, deputy procurators general of the Russian Federation, procurators of subjects of the Russian Federation, military procurators, and procurators of other specialized procuracies to office "after consultations with the Soviet of the Federation". The Soviet of the Federation is to respond within a week and inform the President of the result of their deliberations in written form. The President of the Russian Federation also appoints to and relieves from office other procurators for whom such procedure of appointment and relieving from office has been established by a federal law.

Dismissal from office requires the same process of consultation between the President of the Russian Federation and the Soviet of the Federation.

(8) *Appointment to office of Chairman and Members of Chamber of Accounts of Russian Federation.* The President of the Russian Federation submits to the Soviet of the Federation candidacies for appointment to the office of Chairman of the Chamber of Accounts and half of the total number of auditors of the Chamber of Accounts. To the State Duma the President of the Russian Federation submits candidacies for appointment to the office of deputy chairman of the Chamber of Accounts and half of the total number of auditors of the Chamber of Accounts.

(9) *Appointment of Central Electoral Commission.* Under the Federal Law on Basic Guarantees of Electoral Rights of Citizens of the Russian Federation (Article 12), the Soviet of the Federation appoints five members of the Central Electoral Commission of the Russian Federation from candidacies proposed by the legislative and executive agencies of State power of subjects of the Federation and highest officials of subjects of the Russian Federation.

The appointment is by secret ballot and is formalized by a decree of the Soviet.

(10) *Recourse to Constitutional Court of Russian Federation.* The Russian Constitution (Article 125) empowers the Soviet of the Federation to request the Constitutional Court for an opinion about the constitutionality of federal laws, normative acts of the President, the State Duma, the Government, other legal acts, treaties between agencies of State power of the Russian Federation and agencies of State power of subjects of the Russian Federation, treaties between agencies of State power of subjects of the Russian Federation, and international treaties of the Russian Federation which have not entered into legal force. However, the Soviet of the Federation may not request the Constitutional Court to rule on a matter with respect to which a previous decree of the said Court remains in force.

The Soviet of the Federation adopts a decree referring the matter or petition to the Constitutional Court and also appoints an official representative(s) to represent the Soviet when the Court considers the matter. It is possible that one-fifth of the members of the Soviet of the Federation may refer a matter to the Constitutional Court, in which case the request is signed by the individual members and does not take the form of a decree.

Special competence of State Duma

Although dispersed in several articles of the Constitution, the special competence of the State Duma is concentrated principally in Article 103 and in certain federal laws. A special procedure for considering each matter of special competence is laid down by the Reglament of the State Duma.

(1) *Confirmation of appointment of Chairman, Deputy Chairmen, and Ministers of Government of Russian Federation.* In the case of the Prime Minister, the Duma must consider a candidacy proposed by the President of the Russian Federation within a week from submission of the candidacy. The candidate addresses the State Duma, setting out the basic orientations of his Government's future activity and answers questions of deputies. At the end of the question period, the representatives of factions indicate whether they support the candidate or not. The decision to confirm the appointment is taken at the Duma's discretion by secret voting either by using the electronic system or by ballot. A majority of the Duma is required for confirmation, and a decree is adopted with regard to the results of the vote. If the candidacy is rejected, a new candidacy (which may be the same person) is submitted within a week, and if rejected again, a third candidacy may be proposed within a week (which also may be the same person).

The amendments to the Constitution of 2020 add to the confirmation process the positions of deputy chairmen of the Government and federal ministers, excluding those ministers of so-called "power ministries" enumerated in Article 83(e[1]) of the Constitution.

(2) *Lack of confidence in Government.* Under Article 117(3) of the Constitution, the State Duma may express lack of confidence in the Government of the Russian Federation. One-fifth of the deputies of the Duma may submit a proposal to this effect, which must be considered by the plenary session within a week of submission as a priority matter. Open voting is practiced. Adoption of the decree requires a majority of all deputies of the Duma. If the President of the Russian Federation does not agree with the decision of the Duma, a second vote on the same proposal may be held within three months; the Chairman of the Government himself may request a vote of confidence. In the latter instance the vote of confidence must attract the votes of a majority of the deputies; a failure to do so means the State Duma has expressed no confidence in the Government, and either the Government falls or new elections are called.

(3) *Appointment to and relieving from office of Plenipotentiary for Human Rights.* Candidacies for this post may be proposed by the President or by the Soviet of the Federation or by deputies or deputy associations of the State Duma. The appointment is for a term of five years, which may be renewed once. The candidate addresses the State Duma setting out briefly an action program. Questions may be put by deputies to the candidate and opinions expressed for and against the appointment. If the candidacy is rejected, the same person or another individual may be proposed. A majority of deputies of the Duma is required for appointment to or removal from office, and a decree formalizes the position.

In 2017 the State Duma amended its Reglament to make special provision for interaction with the Plenipotentiary for Human Rights in the form of (a) consideration by the State Duma of the annual Report and special reports of the Plenipotentiary; (b) addresses of the Plenipotentiary at sessions of the State Duma in the event of a flagrant or mass violation of human rights; (b) consideration of a request by the Plenipotentiary for parliamentary hearings concerning violations of human rights; (d) consideration of proposals by the Plenipotentiary received in accordance with the Federal Constitutional Law on the plenipotentiary.

In 2020 constitutional amendments required that the Plenipotentiary for Human Rights be a citizen of the Russian Federation permanently residing in the Russian Federation, not having the citizenship of a foreign State or residence permit or other document confirming the right to permanent residence of a citizen of the Russian Federation on the territory of a foreign State. The Plenipotentiary for Human Rights is prohibited from opening and having accounts (or deposits) and keeping cash monetary means and valuables in foreign banks located beyond the limits of the territory of the Russian Federation.

(4) *Appointment to and relieving from office the Deputy Chairman of Chamber of Accounts and half of auditors thereof.* Candidacies for the office of Deputy Chairman of the Chamber of Accounts and auditors thereof, and removal from such office, are proposed by the President of the Russian Federation. The appointment is for six years and requires a majority vote by all deputies of the Duma for each position, formalized by a decree.

(5) *Appointment to and relieving from office of Chairman of Central Bank.* The President of the Russian Federation proposes the candidate for chairman of the Central Bank of Russia. The candidacy is first considered by the Committee for the Budget and Financial Market, whose opinion is submitted to the Duma. The candidate addresses the Duma, setting out briefly a proposed program. A majority of all deputies is required to approve the appointment. If the appointment is rejected, a new candidacy (including the same person) is considered immediately after submission by the President. Removal from office follows the same procedure. Under constitutional amendments of 2020, the State Duma hears the annual reports of the Central Bank.

(6) *Accusation against President or Former President of Russian Federation.* A proposal to impeach the President of the Russian Federation or to strip a former President of his immunity against prosecution may be made at the initiative of at least one-third of the deputies of the State Duma. It must contain specific indication of the elements of the alleged crime and substantiate his involvement in the crime. The proposal is first referred for the opinion of a special commission formed by the Duma so as to determine whether the procedural rules have been complied with and there is factual substantiation for the accusation, and at the same time to the Supreme Court of the Russian Federation for an opinion as to whether the actions of the President contain the indicia of a crime. The special commission of the Duma is elected and consists of a Chairman, deputy chairman, and 13 deputies. The Chairman is chosen by open ballot and must receive a majority of the votes of the total number of deputies in the Duma. The commission members are elected by the chamber upon the recommendation of factions and deputy groups from a common list, the same majority being required. The commission should contain equal representation from the factions. The commission verifies whether the accusation is substantiated, compliance with quorum requirements, whether votes were counted properly, and the like. The commission hears the testimony of individuals concerning the facts underlying the accusation, examines relevant documents, and hears the representative of the President of the Russian Federation. By a majority vote of its members, the commission adopts an opinion as to whether there are factual circumstances underlying the accusation or not and whether procedural requirements have been observed.

The opinion of the commission is considered by the State Duma, in a closed session if the Duma so votes. In addition to the deputies, experts and others whose evaluation of the evidence is significant may take part. The decree to put forward the accusation against the President requires a two-thirds vote of all deputies of the State Duma. Decrees are adopted by secret vote with the use of ballots or by an open vote with the use of inscribed ballots. The decision on which voting method to use is adopted by a majority vote of the total number of deputies of the State Duma. If adopted, the decree is sent within five days to the Soviet of the Federation; if the required majority is not obtained, the Duma adopts a decree refusing to accuse the President; this decree is final and subject to official publication. It also must be sent to the Soviet of the Federation and to the President.

(7) *Declaration of amnesty*. The State Duma introduces an amnesty in the form of a decree, which also sets out the procedure for implementing it. The decree is submitted and considered in the same procedure as a draft federal law. The signature or endorsement of the President of the Russian Federation is not required. The decree is subject to official publication within three days after adoption and enters into force immediately. The State Duma exercises its right of amnesty from time to time, for example, in December 2013 in connection with the twentieth anniversary of the adoption of the 1993 Russian Constitution.[94]

The amnesty for Victory Day happens every five years. In 2015 about 232,000 individuals were released, among which ca. 34,000 from colonies, in celebration of the seventieth anniversary of the victory in the Second World War. The amnesty was postponed in 2020 by reason of Covid-19. Sometimes the media use the term "amnesty" less strictly and accurately. On 15 June 2020, for example, the President of the Russian Federation amended an Edict regulating the registration of foreigners and stateless persons on Russian territory in connection with COVID-19 to liberalize the registration requirements. This was labelled an "amnesty".

(8) *Recourse to Constitutional Court of Russian Federation*. Under the 1993 Constitution the State Duma has the right to petition the Constitutional Court of the Russian Federation to settle cases regarding the constitutionality of normative acts and international treaties as stipulated in the Article. This right has been exercised on numerous occasions by the State Duma, which may also seek a formal interpretation from the Constitutional Court on other matters relegated to the jurisdiction of the State Duma by Article 125

[94] See the Decree of the State Duma, 18 December 2013, No. 3500-6 ГД, "On the Announcement of an Amnesty in Connection with the 20th Anniversary of the Adoption of the Constitution of the Russian Federation". СЗ РФ (2013), no. 51, item 6820. This Decree resulted in the amnestied release of more than 30,000 inmates, including those accused in connection with the Greenpeace incident in Russian Arctic waters. In this instance the Decree on the Procedure for applying the amnesty document was adopted on the same date in a separate enactment. No. 3505-6 ГД.

of the 1993 Constitution. However, such an inquiry may not be sent with regard to questions already under proceedings in the Constitutional Court.

Within the State Duma the proposal to apply to the Constitutional Court with an inquiry may originate with a faction, committee of the State Duma, or a group of deputies consisting of no less than one-fifth of the total number of deputies (90) with respect to questions provided by Article 125(2) of the 1993 Constitution of the Russian Federation. A majority vote of the deputies is sufficient to forward an inquiry; however, more formal procedures must be complied with to petition the Court to rule on the constitutionality of normative acts.

Budgetary powers of Federal Assembly

Of all the legislation before the Federal Assembly, the draft federal law on the annual budget generates the greatest controversy and requires the greatest investment of time by the deputies and members. The jurisdiction of the Federal Assembly over the budget originates in Article 71 of the 1993 Constitution, which refers to the right of the Federal Assembly to adopt laws on the federal budget. The budgetary process itself is regulated in great detail by the Budget Code of the Russian Federation[95] and various federal laws which address how agencies of State power are to draw up, consider, and execute the budget. These are augmented by the annual law on the budget itself which also sets out budgetary procedures.

Unlike other federal laws, which can undergo as many as three readings in the State Duma, the draft law on the budget routinely goes through four readings. If the law is not adopted in final form before 1 January of the relevant financial year, State agencies operate on the basis pro rata of the last quarter of the preceding financial year or, as may also happen, the State Duma adopts a special federal law to cover the interim period.

The State Duma adopts other federal laws: taxation, and the budgets of the Pension Fund, Federal Fund for Obligatory Medical Insurance, Employment Fund, Social Insurance Fund.

Defense and security powers

Most important of the powers in this domain is the traditional right to declare war and conclude peace. In fact, the 1993 Constitution is silent as to which branch of State exercises this right. Arguably, on the basis of Article 71(j) and 106(f) of the 1993 Constitution, this right is within the competence of the two chambers of the Federal Assembly. On that reasoning the State Duma would adopt a federal law subject to obligatory consideration by the Soviet of the Federation. Presidential signature also would be required.

[95] СЗ РФ (1998), no. 31, item 3823, as amended.

However, it is the President who has the right to declare a general or partial mobilization if aggression or a direct threat thereof were committed against the Russian Federation, declare a military situation on Russian territory or parts thereof, and in his capacity as Supreme Commander-in-Chief issue orders to undertake military actions. Russian law therefore distinguishes between conducting military actions, introducing a military situation, and formally declaring war. This view finds support in Article 87(2) of the 1993 Russian Constitution and in the Federal Law on Defense of 31 May 1996, as amended. The Law on Defense expressly stipulates that military actions on the part of the Russian Federation may commence only in the event of aggression, a direct threat, or armed conflicts directed against Russia. Legally speaking, a declaration of war is confined to a defensive situation.

Concluding peace in the form of negotiations falls within the jurisdiction of the Government, but any agreement reached would acquire full legal force only after ratification of the treaty by the Federal Assembly in the form of a federal law and signature by the President.

The legal regime of a military situation is defined in the Federal Constitutional Law on the Military Situation of 30 January 2002, as amended, as a "special legal regime introduced on the territory of the Russian Federation or in individual localities thereof in accordance with the Constitution of the Russian Federation by the President of the Russian Federation in the event of aggression against the Russian Federation or the direct threat of aggression" (Article 1).[96] Such a situation may be introduced by edict of the President of the Russian Federation. The general powers of the Federal Assembly in the domain of defense and security have been clarified and considerably enlarged in the 1996 Federal Law on Defense, which expressly provided that the Federal Assembly shall consider defense expenditures to be included in the federal budget, all federal laws relating to defense, confirm edicts of the President of the Russian Federation introducing a military situation or involving the Armed Forces of the Russian Federation, other forces, and military formations and agencies to perform tasks not within their usual purpose, and decide the question of using Russian forces beyond the limits of the territory of the Russian Federation.[97] There are no constitutional limitations on the types of laws that the Federal Assembly may adopt in the sphere of defense.

[96] СЗ РФ (2002), no. 5, item 375, as amended. Aggression is defined, "in accordance with generally-recognized principles and norms of international law" as the "application of armed force by a foreign State (or group of States) against the sovereignty, political independence, and territorial integrity of the Russian Federation or any other way incompatible with the United Nations Charter" (Article 3).

[97] On the use of armed forces outside Russia, see the Federal Law on the Procedure for the Granting by the Russian Federation of Military and Civilian Personnel to Participate in Activity Relating to the Maintenance or Restoration of International Peace and Security, of 23

The Federal Assembly has the right to adopt federal laws regulating the State boundaries.

Foreign policy and international relations

The Federal Assembly necessarily plays a lesser role in this domain given the extensive powers accorded to the President of the Russian Federation (Article 86, Russian Constitution). Under its Reglament, the State Duma may consider foreign policy issues at its own initiative or at the request of the President of the Russian Federation. The most important power in this domain is the ratification of international treaties of the Russian Federation.[98] These are submitted by the President or the Government of the Russian Federation to the State Duma together with a draft federal law to ratify, an explanatory memorandum, and other necessary documents and materials. The Chairman of the State Duma must notify deputies about the impending ratification, and the Council of the State Duma, depending upon the subject matter of the treaty, assigns it to a committee to consider the matter. The treaty and accompanying materials are sent routinely to the Committee for International Affairs or to the Committee for CIS Affairs. The Council may designate other committees of the chamber to consider the treaty as well. The committees may request additional information or seek the views of independent experts on the draft treaty, and independently may ask other committees of the State Duma to become involved. Parliamentary hearings may be held.

The plenipotentiary of the President or of the Government to the State Duma or other empowered individual will be heard at a committee session. When these deliberations are completed, the committee prepares a formal Opinion and makes a recommendation to ratify or not, with or without possible declarations, statements, or reservations. A majority vote of all members of the committee is sufficient for adoption of the Opinion. The Opinion is then forwarded to the State Duma, where the Council of the Duma places the question on the agenda as a priority item. The procedure for considering a draft law to ratify a treaty is the same as for other federal laws. A simple majority of all deputies is sufficient for adoption. If the State Duma decides to postpone ratification, it must be reasoned. If an inquiry has been sent to the Constitutional Court of the Russian Federation concerning the constitutionality of the treaty, the State Duma will not consider the question of ratification until a reply is received from the Court.

Appointments and recalls of diplomatic representatives of the Russian Federation to foreign States and international organizations are made by the President of the Russian Federation after consultations with committees and commissions of the chambers of the Federal Assembly. The detailed

June 1995. СЗ РФ (1995), no. 26, item 2401, as amended.

98 See for details W. E. Butler, *International Law in the Russian Legal System* (2020), pp. 66-90.

provisions regulating these consultations are set out in the Reglament of the Federal Assembly.

Stages of the legislative process

The enactment of a federal law requires the completion of several consecutive stages: it is considered to be adopted and to have entered into legal force once it has been submitted, considered, and adopted by both chambers of the Federal Assembly, and then been signed and promulgated by the President, in accordance with the procedure established by the 1993 Constitution. It is therefore technically incorrect to speak of the 'adoption' of a federal law, for that word is used only to characterize the final result of processes within the State Duma, although the Constitution unfortunately also used the term for the entire legislative process (Article 105(1)). The Constitutional Court of the Russian Federation introduced a certain clarity when it observed that the expression "adopted federal law" in Article 107(1) of the Constitution refers to the entire legislative process and should be distinguished from the concept of a "federal law adopted by the State Duma" (Articles 105 and 106, Constitution).

The Russian legislative process may be divided into eight stages, although some have sub-stages associated with them:

(1) legislative initiative and preliminary consideration;

(2) consideration of draft laws and adoption of laws by State Duma;

(3) consideration by Soviet of Federation of laws adopted by State Duma;

(4) consideration of laws in conciliation commission when disagreements between the chambers arise;

(5) second consideration by State Duma of laws rejected by Soviet of Federation;

(6) second consideration by State Duma of laws rejected by President of Russian Federation;

(7) second consideration by Soviet of Federation of laws rejected by President of Russian Federation;

(8) signature and promulgation of laws by President of Russian Federation.

We consider each of these in succession.

Legislative initiative and preliminary consideration

Under Article 104(1) of the Russian Constitution, the President of the Russian Federation, Soviet of the Federation, senators of the Soviet of the Federation, deputies of the State Duma, Government of the Russian

Federation, legislative or representative agencies of subjects of the Federation, the Constitutional Court and the Supreme Court of the Russian Federation all enjoy the right of legislative initiative, the respective courts being confined to legislative initiative on questions within their jurisdiction. All draft laws must originate in the State Duma, including those initiated by the Soviet of the Federation; they may be laws having an integral subject matter, amendments to existing laws, proposals to draft new laws or deem existing laws to have lost force, or laws to change the Constitution of Russia, and others. A draft law must be accompanied by certain materials: the text of the draft, a substantiation of the need to adopt it and prediction of likely consequences if the text is adopted, a list of other laws and normative acts which must be changed, amended, repealed, or added to if the proposed new law is enacted, among others. The draft also enumerates by name those deputies who have initiated the draft Law and the State agencies, social organizations, institutions, and organizations and individual persons who helped to prepare it. The draft must include provisions concerning the periods and procedure for its entry into force, the repeal or change of other laws, and the routine proposal to the President and to the Russian Government to bring their legal acts into conformity with the newly adopted law.

Draft laws submitted to the State Duma are subject to registration by the Duma, which supervises this process through the Committee for Control and Reglament of the State Duma. If the requirements of form are not complied with, the Council of the State Duma may return the draft to the initiators to make necessary adjustments. If the draft falls within the purview of several committees, the Council of the Duma determines which committee shall be the lead committee. Working groups may be created, and a deadline may be assigned for producing a revised draft.

If a draft law falls within the joint jurisdiction of the Russian Federation and subjects of the Federation, the draft is circulated to the subjects of the Federation for comments and proposals. They may also be circulated to the Government of Russia, ministries, departments, or to State and social organizations.

Consideration of drafts and adoption of laws by State Duma

Excluding the law on the budget, laws undergo three readings in the State Duma unless the chamber decides otherwise with respect to a particular draft. During the first reading, the basic provisions of the draft law are discussed, whether it should be enacted or not, and the general assessment of the concept of the draft. The initiator of the draft commences the discussion by presenting a report, followed by a report from the committee which considered the draft. Comments and suggestions are received from factions, the plenipotentiary of the President, representatives of the Government or subjects of the Federation, and others. The Duma will either adopt the law at first reading and establish a time for the second reading, reject the draft, or, rarely, adopt it in final form at first reading. A majority of the total number of deputies is required to adopt a draft at first reading, the decision to do so being formalized in the form of a decree.

Amendments to a draft at first reading are sent to the committee of the State Duma responsible for the draft. Amendments may also be submitted by the President, Soviet of the Federation, members of the Soviet of the Federation, deputies of the State Duma, and others who have the right of legislative initiative, except the courts, who may suggest amendments only in respect of matters within their jurisdiction. The committee responsible will consider all of the proposed amendments; the sources of the amendments have the right to clarify them. The revised draft is then submitted to the State Duma for second reading, accompanied by a table of proposed amendments which the committee recommended be rejected and a second table which the committee believes should be accepted. The tables also are circulated to the President of the Russian Federation and to the initiator of the draft law.

At the second reading, the chairman of the committee responsible reports on its deliberation, on the amendments proposed, and on those recommended. He is followed by the plenipotentiary of the President of the Russian Federation and representatives of those who proposed the draft law. The person presiding then determines whether the factions object to the proposed amendments. If there are objections, debate is opened on these and the rapporteur replies to the objections raised. Voting on the amendments then ensues by deciding first whether the original draft law may be used as the basis for the amendments. If that vote is affirmative, voting proceeds on the amendments, and then whether to adopt the draft law as amended at second reading. There are a variety of technical variations on these procedures which are governed by the Reglament of the State Duma.

The version of the draft law adopted at second reading is then sent to the committee responsible which, together with the Legal Administration of the Apparatus of the State Duma, edits the draft to eliminate internal contradictions and correct style, punctuation, and editorial adjustments. When this task is completed, the draft law is sent within seven days to the Council of the State Duma for inclusion on the agenda.

At third reading the draft law cannot be returned for further amendments or discussion as a whole except in the most unusual circumstances when deputy associations representing a majority of deputies so decide. A majority of votes of the total number of members of the State Duma is required to adopt a federal law, and a two-thirds majority if a federal constitutional law is being adopted. After being adopted a third reading, the draft is sent on the basis of a decree of the State Duma to the Soviet of the Federation for consideration.

The phrase "a majority of votes of the total number of deputies of the State Duma" has been variously interpreted. If, for example, the number of deputies actually elected to office were less than the established size of the chamber, as has occurred, the majority required to adopt a law would differ from the number required if the majority had to be of deputy places. To clarify the problem, the State Duma requested an interpretation of the 1993 Russian Constitution from the Constitutional Court of the Russian Federation, which on 12 April 1995 ruled that this phrase can only mean a majority of the constitutionally-established number of seats in each chamber.[99] In the State Duma the minimum majority required will be 226 votes.

Consideration by Soviet of Federation of laws adopted by State Duma

Laws adopted by the State Duma and sent within five days to the Soviet of the Federation, as provided by Article 105(3) of the 1993 Russian Constitution, are directed to the relevant committee(s) of the Soviet of the Federation for consideration. If the materials forwarded by the State Duma do not include the Opinion of the Government of the Russian Federation, the Soviet of the Federation may immediately reject the federal law if it concerns the introduction or repeal of taxes, issue of State loans, change of State financial obligations, or otherwise engages expenditures to be covered from the federal budget.

Article 105(4) of the 1993 Russian Constitution established a 14-day period within which the Soviet of the Federation must consider certain federal laws. The period commences from the day following the date on which the law was registered for consideration in the Soviet of the Federation. The Constitution further stipulates (Article 106) that federal laws relating to the federal budget, federal taxes and charges, financial, currency, credit, and customs regulation, monetary emission, ratification and denunciation of international treaties, the status and defense of the State boundary of Russia, and war and peace must be considered by the Soviet of the Federation. In practice the Soviet of the Federation has found it impossible always to comply with the 14-day period, raising therefore the question of whether the federal laws enumerated in Article 106 of the Constitution fell under the 14-day requirement of Article 105(4). The question was put to the Constitutional Court of the Russian Federation, which on 23 March 1995 ruled that the 14-day period referred only to the commencement of consideration by the Soviet of the Federation. It was not mandatory that consideration be completed within that period. Questions

[99] СЗ РФ (1995), no. 16, item 1451.

carried over, however, are subject to obligatory consideration at the next regular session.

A law not subject to obligatory consideration and not considered within the 14-day period is sent to the President for signature and promulgation. If a law is considered and does not receive the required majority, the rejection is formalized by a decree of the chamber. The decree may contain a list of articles, sections, chapters, or other provisions which the chamber considers should be discussed with the State Duma or by a conciliation commission between the two chambers. The decree recording the rejection of a federal law is sent to the State Duma within five days. If the State Duma adopts the law a second time taking into account all of the proposals of the Soviet of the Federation, it is returned to the respective committee of the Soviet, which confirms acceptance of the proposals and recommends approval of the law without further plenary discussion. If the State Duma accepts only some of the proposals, or introduces new provisions, or removes previous provisions, the law returned by the State Duma is reconsidered as though it were an entirely newly adopted text.

Conciliation commissions

When a law is adopted by the State Duma and rejected by the Soviet of the Federation, a conciliation commission is formed from representatives of each chamber on a parity basis elected by the respective chambers. Either chamber may take the initiative to form the commission. The commission considers only those provisions of the law which were the subject of disagreement and seeks to work out agreed provisions in the form of a unified text. The co-chairmen of the commission conduct separate voting within each delegation, and a decision is adopted if both deputations vote for the agreed text. The matter is then referred back to the State Duma, which may or may not accept the result of the conciliation commission. If the result is rejected, the State Duma may propose that the conciliation commission continue its work, and the Soviet of the Federation may either agree or refuse to participate. If the conciliation commission cannot overcome the differences between the two chambers, the law is sent back to each chamber, in which case the Soviet of the Federation has the right to approve the text in any form which it chooses, or to change its delegation to the conciliation commission, or to refuse to continue to take part in the work of the commission. Whatever decrees are adopted are sent to the State Duma within five days.

Second consideration by State Duma of laws rejected by Soviet of Federation

When the conciliation commission refers the results of its deliberations to the State Duma, the latter chamber places the federal law on the calendar for discussion. Only proposals contained in the protocol of the conciliation commission are discussed; no amendments going beyond those proposals are considered. If even one of the conciliation proposals are rejected, the State Duma may suggest that the commission continue its work having regard to the amendments approved and that the commission within ten days submit new proposals, which, when submitted, are considered by the State Duma in the same procedure. Each proposal of the conciliation commission is voted upon individually by the State Duma, and each must obtain the majority of the total number of deputies of the chamber. The law adopted in the version of the conciliation commission is then sent to the Soviet of the Federation.

If the Soviet of the Federation rejects the law at second consideration, or the State Duma did not accept the proposals of the conciliation commission and disagreed with the decision of the Soviet of the Federation to reject the law, the law is put to a vote in the State Duma in its original form before the conciliation procedures. If not less than two-thirds of the deputies voted in favor of the law, it is considered to be adopted and sent within five days to the President of the Russian Federation for signature.

Second consideration by State Duma of laws rejected by President of Russia

Under the Constitution, if the President of the Russian Federation within 14 days of receiving a federal law for signature rejects it, the State Duma gives second consideration to the law. The Council of the Duma refers the law to the committee responsible or to a specially-created commission, which considers the law within ten days. The committee or commission may recommend that the State Duma approve the law in the version proposed by the President, or agree with the President that such a law should not be adopted, or approve the law again in its original version.

Reconsideration of the law is a priority item on the agenda. The plenipotentiary of the President addresses the chamber, followed by the opinion of the committee or commission. If the President proposes that such a law is not required, this may be put to a vote, a majority of the total number of deputies being required. If the chamber votes to open discussion, only representatives of the factions may take part. At the end of the discussion, the question first put to a vote is whether to approve the law in the version proposed by the President; this requires a simple majority of the total number of deputies. If that proposal is rejected by the Duma, the next question is whether to approve the law in the version originally adopted by the Duma, that is, whether to override the Presidential veto. This requires a two-thirds majority of the total number of deputies. Whichever decision is adopted, the law is sent on the same day to the Soviet of the Federation.

If neither decision is adopted, the State Duma proceeds to vote again on the Presidential version, in this case voting separately on each section, chapter, article, paragraph, and point, the vote required being a simple majority of the total number of deputies. Further consideration is then deferred to the next session of the chamber, during which interval the committee or commission prepares a new version of the law incorporating those proposals of the President which were adopted. This version is then submitted as a whole to the State Duma and requires a simple majority of the total number of deputies for adoption. If adopted, the normal legislative process resumes.

Second consideration by Soviet of Federation of laws rejected by President of Russian Federation

The Soviet of the Federation receives from the State Duma the text of the law and the decree of the Duma concerning the second consideration, together with the text of the President's letter to the Duma. The procedure for overriding the Presidential veto begins with the committee which previously reported on the law reconsidering the text in light of the President's comments together with the version of the law adopted at second consideration by the State Duma. When considering the text in plenary session, the Soviet of the Federation may vote either to approve the text or to open discussion. If not less than two-thirds of the members voted in favor of the version originally adopted, the law is adopted. Approval of the law vetoed by the President is sent in the form of a decree to the President, who is obliged to sign and promulgate it within seven days.

If the President of the Russian Federation requests the Constitutional Court of the Russian Federation to verify the constitutionality of the federal law, the seven-day period for signature is suspended while the Constitutional Court considers the query. If the Constitutional Court confirms the constitutionality of the federal law, the President of the Russian Federation signs it within a three-day period from the moment the Constitutional Court renders the respective decision. If the Constitutional Court does not confirm the constitutionality of the federal law, the President of the Russian Federation returns the said law to the State Duma without signature.

The President and the legislative process

Under Article 107(2) of the 1993 Russian Constitution, the President is required to sign a federal law unless within 14 days from the moment of receiving it he vetoes the law. Moreover, if the Federal Assembly overrides his veto, he must also sign the law within seven days of receiving the decrees of the chambers of the Federal Assembly approving the law in its original version. In 1998 the Constitutional Court held that the law must be signed notwithstanding reservations held by the President about voting irregularities in the chambers. In practice the veto has been used rather frequently by the President, and it is rarely overridden.

The President is actively involved in the legislative process at a number of stages. He frequently exercises his right of legislative initiative, gives opinions on draft laws adopted by the State Duma at first and second readings, and through his plenipotentiary makes his views known to the chambers and may ask the Constitutional Court to verify the constitutionality of a federal law submitted for signature. These actions have become accepted routines on the basis of the Statute on the Procedure for the Interaction of the President of the Russian Federation with Chambers in the Federal Assembly of the Russian Federation in the Law-Formation Process, confirmed by an Edict of the President of the Russian Federation on 13 April 1996, as amended.[100] The Statute sets out specific actions to be taken by plenipotentiaries of the President at all stages of the legislative process, the role of the administration of the President, the veto of laws, the submission of opinions on draft laws, and other matters.

Legal status of deputies and senators of the Federal Assembly

The status of deputies of the State Duma and senators of the Soviet of the Federation is regulated principally by the 1993 Russian Constitution and the Federal Law on the Status of a Deputy of the Soviet of the Federation and Status of a Deputy of the State Duma of the Federal Assembly of the Russian Federation of 8 May 1994, in the version of 5 July 1999 as amended.[101] The expression "deputy of the Soviet of the Federation" (originally used in the 1994 Law and reflecting an era when the Soviet of the Federation was directly elected, 1991-1994), has been changed to "member" and then in the 2020 amendments to the Constitution was changed to "senator".

Deputies of the Duma represent the people as a whole, being directly elected, work on a permanent professional basis, may not be a civil servant nor engage in other paid activity except teaching, scientific, or creative. Senators of the Soviet of the Federation are not full-time, in some cases represent their respective subjects of the Federation, and do hold State office elsewhere.

The Russian Constitution is silent as to whether deputies and senators of the Federal Assembly have an "imperative" or a "free" mandate from their constituencies. In Russian constitutional doctrine the distinction is crucial, for in the late Soviet era the imperative mandate dominated, that is, the powers of a deputy emanated from his electors and he was obliged to fulfil their directions and be responsible to them for his actions. If a deputy did not perform his pre-electoral promises or generally does not perform his duties satisfactorily, he was subject to recall. Under this approach the deputy is not free to vote in the parliament as he believes is in the best interest of his country, but must serve his narrow constituency. The prevailing

[100] СЗ РФ (1996), no. 16, item 1842, as amended.

[101] СЗ РФ (1994), no. 2, item 74, as amended; transl. in Butler, note 32 above, pp. 249-274.

view in Russian constitutional doctrine is that the imperative mandate no longer operates. The right of recall has been abolished, and there is no legal requirement that a deputy follow the instructions of his constituents, or political party, or other outside source of discipline, although to be sure a deputy will be likely to be guided by his pre-electoral platform and the rights and interests of his constituents and of his political affiliation.

The State Duma is elected for a term of five years, so that the term of office of a deputy of the State Duma commences from the day of election and terminates from the moment that the next newly-elected Duma commences work, subject to certain exceptions provided for by legislation. In the case of a senator, the term of office commences from the day the decision of the respective agency of State power of a subject of the Russian Federation endowing the individual with the powers of a senator enters into force and terminates from the day when the respective subject of the Russian Federation endows a new senator with the powers of office as a representative of the respective agency of State power of the subject of the Russian Federation.

Under the Russian Constitution (Article 98), deputies and senators of the Federal Assembly enjoy inviolability throughout their term of office. More than one candidate for office in the State Duma with a criminal accusation pending has used election to the Duma to postpone reckoning or engage the period of limitations. They may not be detained, arrested, subjected to search (unless detained at the site of a crime), nor subjected to personal inspection unless provided otherwise by a federal law. The inviolability extends to their dwelling, official premises, correspondence, communications, and documents belonging to them. They may refuse to give witness testimony in civil and criminal cases regarding circumstances which became known to them in connection with the performance of their duties. Whether immunity should be waived or not is decided by the respective chamber of the Federal Assembly upon the recommendation of the Procurator General of the Russian Federation; in practice, such immunity has been waived in the State Duma, but waiver has been refused several times. On 30 January 2019 the Soviet of the Federation decreed to deprive Senator Rauf Arashukov of immunity and consent to his detention, accusation, search of his dwelling, and confinement under guard in connection with an investigation of contract killings. The Decree was sent to the Procurator General of the Russian Federation and entered into force from the moment of adoption.[102]

The 1994 Federal Law on the status of deputies significantly expanded the enumeration of instances when parliamentary immunity may be invoked, in comparison with the enumeration in the 1993 Russian

[102] СЗ РФ (2019), no. 6, item 481.

Constitution. In a decree of 20 February 1996 the Constitutional Court of the Russian Federation confirmed the constitutionality of the Law, but rejected an expansive interpretation of the Law and abbreviated the list of activities enjoying immunity not connected with deputy activity.

Deputies receive a salary, free life and health insurance equal to the yearly salary of a federal minister, exemption from military service, right to reinstatement in their former job or equivalent thereto, a lump-sum benefit for the remainder of the parliamentary term if the State Duma is dissolved, free travel to and from their place of residence if the Duma is dissolved and free carriage of personal belongings up to ten tons in weight, inclusion of service in the Federal Assembly as part of labor experience, with the right to receive a State pension earlier, if desired. All deputies receive an identical salary, except that the Chairman of the State Duma receives the equivalent of the Prime Minister of the Government. An expense allowance exists to cover expenses associated with living away from the permanent place of residence. Annual paid leave of 42 work days per year is granted. Each deputy has the right to a furnished office and communications, including governmental, and all types of postal and telegraph expenses connected with official matters are paid for. On the territory of Russia deputies and members of the Federal Assembly may use air, railway, motor vehicle, and water transport, including urban and suburban transport, free of charge, excluding taxis. State and municipal hotels must provide deputies and members with a separate hotel room within an hour; deputies from outside Moscow are also provided with living accommodation, which must be vacated within a month after their term of office ends. Each deputy and member may have up to five aides, with the total number per chamber to be determined by each chamber.

The Criminal Code of the Russian Federation and other legislation provide sanctions for obstructing a deputy or member of the Federal Assembly in his duties, failure to provide information requested or for providing false information, unlawfully attempting to influence such persons, insulting a deputy or member, and others.

THE GOVERNMENT

The word "Government" [правительство] is a narrow and precise term in Russian constitutional law, as it is in England but not necessarily in the United States. It refers to a particular branch of the State and cannot under any circumstances refer to the State at large. Confusion between the two is usually caused by mistranslating the term 'State' [государство] as "Government", for which there is no foundation in Russian (or Soviet) law and constitutes malpractice as both legal and translation error.

The legal status of the Government is regulated principally by the 1993 Constitution of the Russian Federation (Chapter 6) and the Federal

Constitutional Law on the Government of the Russian Federation of 17 December 1997, as amended,[103] replaced by Federal Constitutional Law on the Government of the Russian Federation of 6 November 2020, as amended. The Government is an agency of State power of the Russian Federation and effectuates executive power under the general guidance of the President of the Russian Federation; it is a collegial organ under the chairmanship of the Chairman of the Government of the Russian Federation and heads the unified system of executive power in Russia. It consists of its Chairman, deputy chairmen, and federal ministers. The Government of the Russian Federation is not a juridical person and enjoys no autonomous legal capacity.

The Chairman of the Government is appointed by the President of the Russian Federation after confirmation of the candidacy by the State Duma. The President submits the name of a candidate within two weeks after being newly elected, or after the Government has resigned, or within a week from the State Duma rejecting a previous candidacy, or the President of the Russian Federation has dismissed the Chairman of the Government from office, or the Chairman of the Government has resigned.

A candidate for Chairman of the Government, Deputy Chairman of the Government, federal minister, or other executive of a federal agency of executive power must have Russian citizenship, not be a citizen of a foreign State, and not have a residence permit or other document confirming the right of a Russian citizen to permanently reside on the territory of a foreign State, and be at least 30 years of age. The candidate is prohibited from opening or having an account or deposit of money or valuables in foreign banks located outside the Russian Federation and to possess and/or use foreign financial instruments. This prohibition extends to the spouse and minor children of a member of the Government of the Russian Federation.

In practice the State Duma has rejected many candidacies for the post of Chairman of the Government. The State Duma must consider a candidacy within a week of the President making the proposal. If the State Duma rejects candidacies submitted three times, the President appoints the Chairman of the Government himself and has the right to dissolve the State Duma and designate new elections for the Duma. The Chairman is relieved from office if he resigns or if he can no longer perform his duties.

Once in office, the Chairman of the Government no later than a week after appointment makes proposals to the President of the Russian Federation concerning the structure of federal agencies of executive power, except when the President of the Russian Federation dismissed the previous Chairman of the Government. The Chairman of the Government then submits to the State Duma for confirmation the candidacies for Deputy

[103] СЗ РФ (1997), no. 51, item 5712, as amended; transl. in Butler, note 32 above.

Chairman of the Government and federal ministers (except for the so-called power ministries). Within no later than a week, the State Duma adopts a decision with regard to the candidacies submitted.

In the interests of eliminating conflicts of interest and undue influence from outsider sources the Chairman and deputy chairmen of the Government and federal ministers and heads of federal services and agencies are required upon appointment to office and thereafter annually to submit information to tax agencies of the Russian Federation about revenues, securities, and property belonging to them by right of ownership which are objects of taxation. This information is sent to the President of the Russian Federation and to the Federal Assembly by the tax agencies. Such information may be published.

There are in addition certain limitations imposed on those who hold any of these offices: among them are prohibitions against being a senator of the Soviet of the Federation or deputy of the State Duma or of other legislative or representative agencies of State power of subjects of the Russian Federation or deputies of elective agencies of State power of subjects of the Russian Federation or deputies of elective agencies of local self-government or in social associations; or engaging in entrepreneurial activity personally or through entrusted persons, including participation in the management of an economic subject irrespective of its organizational-legal form. Members of the Government are, moreover, required to transfer participatory shares or blocs of stock in the charter capital of commercial organizations in their ownership to trust management under guarantee of the State. Any other paid activity is prohibited except teaching, scholarly, and other creative activity. Nor may they act as attorneys or representatives of third persons in agencies of State power, or receive royalties for publications or speaking as a member of the Government, nor receive loans, gifts, monetary or other remuneration, including services or payment for attractions and leisure from natural or juridical persons not provided for by federal legislation, nor receive honorary and special titles, awards, or other marks of distinction of foreign States, nor make business trips outside Russia at the expense of natural or juridical persons except those effectuated in accordance with Russian Federation legislation, international treaties of the Russian Federation, or on a mutually agreed basis between federal agencies of State power and the State agencies of foreign states or of international and foreign organizations.[104]

[104] The State officials who are required to comply with these reporting standards are enumerated in the Edict of the President of the Russian Federation of 15 May 1997, No. 484, as amended, "On the Submission by Persons Holding State Offices of the Russian Federation and by Persons Holding State Offices of State Service and Offices in Agencies of Local Self-Government of Information Concerning Revenues and Property". СЗ РФ (1997), no. 20, item 2239, as amended. This Edict was replaced by five more stringent Edicts of 18 May 2009, Nos. 427 and 557-560. See СЗ РФ (2009), no. 21, items 2542, 2543, 2544, 2545, and 2546,

Standards for State officials and other civil servants of this nature are without precedent in Russia. During the Soviet era, it was commonplace for Party and State officials to combine offices in Party and State institutions or for State officials to hold more than one office, or for individuals to serve in both the legislative and executive branches of the State.

The 1993 Constitution of the Russian Federation says relatively little about precisely what the Government is to do. Article 114 provides, without characterizing these as duties or functions, that the Government is to work out and submit to the State Duma the federal budget and ensure its execution and submit a report to the State Duma concerning execution of the budget, ensure that unified financial, credit, monetary, cultural, science, education, public health, social security, and ecology policies are implemented in the Russian Federation, effectuate the administration of federal ownership and measures related to ensuring the defense of Russia and State security, the realization of Russian foreign policy, measures to ensure legality, the rights and freedoms of citizens, protection of ownership and public order, the struggle against criminality, and, under a general powers formulation, effectuate "other powers placed on it by the Constitution", federal laws, and edicts of the President of the Russian Federation.

The 2020 constitutional amendments and the 2020 Federal Constitutional Law on the Government added several items to the activities of the Government: to ensure the implementation in the Russian Federation of a unified socially-oriented State policy in the domain of culture, science, education, public health, social security, support for, strengthening, and defense of the family, preservation of traditional family values, and also in the domain of protection of the natural environment; ensure State support for scientific-technological development of the Russian Federation, and the preservation and development of its scientific potential; ensure the functioning of the system of social defense of disabled persons based on the full and equal effectuated by them of rights and freedoms of man and citizen, their social integration without any discrimination, and the creation of an accessible milieu for disabled persons and improvement of the quality of their life; effectuate measures for the support of institutions of a civil society, including non-commercial organizations, and ensure their participation in working out and implementing State policy; effectuate measures for the support of voluntary activity; promote the development of

as amended. The last Edict was repealed and replaced by the Edict of the President of the Russian Federation "Questions of Counteracting Corruption", which confirmed the Statute on the Placement of Information concerning Revenues, Expenses, Property, and Obligations of a Property Character of Individual Categories of Persons and Members of Their Families on Official Sites of Federal State Agencies, Agencies of State Power of Subjects of the Russian Federation, and Organizations, and the Provision of this Information to All-Russian Mass Media for Publication, adopted 8 July 2013, No. 613. СЗ РФ (2013), no. 28, item 3813, as amended.

entrepreneurship and private initiative; ensure the realization of principles of social partnership in the sphere of the regulation of labor and other relations directly linked with them; effectuate measures directed towards the creation of favorable conditions for the vital activity of the population, reduction of the negative impact of economic and other activity on the environment, preservation of unique natural and biological diversity of the country, and forming in society of a responsible attitude towards fauna; and create the conditions for development of a system of ecological education of citizens and nurturing of an ecological culture.

On the basis of this language, the Law on the Government devotes numerous lengthy articles to defining the "powers" of the Government. Some are classified as "general powers", some as "powers", and the remainder as "other powers". Compared with most constitutions of the Anglo-American family of legal systems, which have no "law" on the "Government", the enumeration of powers is vast and the terminology used to describe those powers is sweeping in scope. In practice the limitation on governmental powers originates more in the status of the Government *vis-à-vis* other agencies of State power and administration than it does in the special nature of the legal capacity which the Government possesses by virtue of the Constitution. With respect to adopting normative acts, this is expressed in Article 115(3) of the 1993 Russian Constitution, which provides that decrees and regulations of the Government may, if they fail to conform to the Constitution, federal laws, or edicts and regulations of the President of the Russian Federation, be repealed by the President of the Russian Federation.

The Federal Constitutional Law on the Government addresses the internal procedures for adopting certain types of decisions and the allocations of duties among the Chairman, deputy chairmen, and federal ministers. Sessions of the Government must be held not less than once a month. Certain persons who are not members of the Government have the right to participate in sessions, for example, the chairmen of the chambers of the Federal Assembly, the chairmen of the Constitutional Court and the Supreme Court, the Procurator General, the Central Bank, and others. Individual matters may be considered at closed sessions. There is a list of questions which may be decided solely at sessions of the Government, for example, the decision to submit the federal budget to the State Duma, or to conclude international treaties of the Russian Federation which are subject to ratification. The Government also has the right of legislative initiative in the Federal Assembly and may submit amendments to draft laws being considered by the State Duma.

The Government has the right to form a Presidium in order to deal with operational issues. The Presidium meets as required and operates by majority vote. Its decisions cannot be contrary to acts adopted at sessions of the Government and are subject to repeal by the Government. The

Government adopted its own Reglament to help with deciding internal procedural questions and a Statute on the Apparatus of the Government of the Russian Federation of 1 June 2004, as amended.[105]

Two provisions of the Reglament have been found to be unconstitutional by the Russian courts. Point 100 of the Reglament had provided that:

> A draft law received for an opinion in the Government without a financial-economic substantiation and other necessary materials shall be returned by the Apparatus of the Government to the subject of legislative initiative with communication of the reasons for which it is impossible to submit the opinion.

The Constitutional Court of the Russian Federation held that this provision interfered with the separation of powers between legislative, executive, and judicial branches of the State, for in effect the submission of a draft law to the State Duma by way of legislative initiative would depend upon the will of the apparatus of the Government and not the subject of the Russian Federation granted the right of legislative initiative.[106]

An analogous issue arose under Point 108, paragraph three, of the Reglament, which provided:

> A deputy inquiry and recourse of a member of the Soviet of the Federation or deputy of the State Duma to the Government, Chairman of the Government, or deputy chairman of the Government shall be sent by the Apparatus of the Government for reply to federal agencies of executive power, the direction of whose activity the President of the Russian Federation or Government effectuates. The reply shall be given by the respective executive of the federal agency of executive power or his deputy in written form not later than within a 30-day period from the date of receipt of the deputy inquiry and recourse to the Government.

The Supreme Court of the Russian Federation held this paragraph to be unconstitutional because it in effect enabled the Apparatus of the Government to serve as the exclusive channel for communication between a deputy or member of the Federal Assembly and deprived these persons of their right to receive a reply signed by the specific officials to whom the inquiry or recourse was directed. The Supreme Court, in resolving the issue of constitutionality, relied upon the Code of Civil Procedure (Article 253), which enables a court of ordinary jurisdiction to deem invalid a normative legal act or part thereof which is contrary to a federal law or other normative

105 C3 PΦ (2004), no. 23, item 2313, as amended; transl. in Butler, note 32 above.

106 See the Decree of the Constitutional Court of the Russian Federation, 29 November 2006, "Re Verification of the Constitutionality of Point 100 of the Reglament of the Government of the Russian Federation". C3 PΦ (2006), no. 50, item 5371.

legal act having greater legal force. The Constitution was deemed to be such an act of greater legal force.[107]

When a new President of the Russian Federation is elected, the existing Government resigns as of the day when the President takes office. At any other time the Government also may offer to resign, and the President is at liberty to accept or reject such offer. The President may require the Government to resign, and may do so irrespective of whether such decision reflects a lack of confidence expressed by the State Duma or represents the President's own decision. If the State Duma has expressed a lack of confidence and the President does not concur with the State Duma, the Government remains in office; however, if within three months of the first vote of no confidence the State Duma again expresses its lack of confidence in the Government, the President of Russia must either declare the resignation of the Government or dissolve the State Duma for new elections. If the Chairman of the Government himself places the question of confidence in the Government before the State Duma and the latter refuses confidence, the President must within seven days accept the resignation of the Government or dissolve the State Duma and designate new elections. When the Government does resign or lay down its powers, it nonetheless continues to operate until a new Government is formed. There is consequently no vacuum of Government as a result of the exercise of no-confidence options.

The stability of government is reinforced by the constitutional requirement that the State Duma may not express no confidence in a Government and the Chairman of the Government may not place the question of confidence in the Government before the State Duma in the situations provided by Article 109(3)-(5) of the Russian Constitution or when, under Article 111(4) of the Constitution, the President of the Russian Federation has appointed a Chairman of the Government in the face of three refusals of the State Duma to make such appointment. In this last event, the President may call new elections.

The Government is not subordinate to the President but is decidedly inferior to the President. The President of the Russian Federation ensures that the Government and other agencies of State power function and interact on a coordinated basis. The President at any time may preside at sessions of the Government or of its Presidium. Although federal agencies of executive power are part of the Government of Russia, the activity of certain of them is directed by the President and not by the Chairman of the Government; such activity concerns questions of defense, security, internal affairs, foreign affairs, and the prevention of extraordinary situations and liquidation of their consequences. In these instances it is the President who confirms the

[107] See Decision of the Supreme Court of the Russian Federation, 15 February 2007; by Ruling of the Supreme Court of May 2007, No. KAC07-151, the decision was left without change. Available on Consultant Plus.

Statutes on these agencies upon the recommendation of the Chairman of the Government and who appoints their heads. The Government then coordinates the activities of these federal agencies of executive power in accordance with the Constitution, federal constitutional laws, federal laws, and the edicts and regulations of the President of the Russian Federation.

In matters of joint jurisdiction with subjects of the Russian Federation, the Government of the Russian Federation coordinates the exercise of executive power by agencies of executive power of the subjects of the Federation. The Government therefore acts as the channel by which agencies of executive power of the subjects of the Federation communicate with and make proposals to other agencies of the Russian State. Time limits are laid down (not exceeding one month) for the consideration of proposals emanating from subjects of the Federation, and the Government likewise must send its own draft decisions to all relevant subjects of the Federation which appertain to matters of joint jurisdiction. The responses of the subjects of the Federation regarding such draft decisions must be considered by the Government. However, the powers of the Government in this domain go beyond coordination. The Government of Russia is also empowered to effectuate control over the activity of federal agencies of executive power generally. It may settle disputes and disagreements between federal agencies of executive power and those equivalent agencies of subjects of the Federation by forming conciliation commissions for this purpose. The ultimate sanction is that the Government of Russia may propose to the President of the Russian Federation that acts of agencies of executive power of subjects of the Federation be suspended if they are contrary to the Constitution of the Russian Federation, federal constitutional laws or federal laws, international obligations of the Russian Federation, or a violation of the rights and freedoms of man and citizen.

As regards the Russian judiciary, the Government of Russia is obliged to finance the courts only from the federal budget and to ensure that the courts are fully independent to perform their functions; the Government is also to ensure the enforcement of judicial decisions.

LOCAL SELF-GOVERNMENT

In the Russian Federation local self-government refers to those administrative-territorial entities which are below the subjects of the Russian Federation in hierarchical stature. The 1993 Russian Constitution refers to them laconically as a system created by citizens autonomously to resolve questions of local significance and the possession, use, and disposition of municipal ownership (Article 130). Although a separate Chapter 8 is allotted in the Constitution to local self-government (Articles 130 to 133), other provisions of the Constitution touch upon the subject (Articles 8, 9, 15, 24, 32, 33, 40, 41, 43, 46, and 68).

The basic constitutional position is that local self-government is autonomous within the limits of its powers, is not part of the system of agencies of State power, decides questions of local significance and the possession, use, and disposition of municipal ownership, uses referendums, elections, and other means to determine the expression of will of the local populace, and has boundaries which cannot be changed without taking into account the views of the local populace. Autonomy in this context means the right to manage municipal ownership, form, confirm, and execute the local budget, establish local taxes and charges, protect public order, ensure access to medical care within its competence provided by a federal law, and the like. Under the Constitution local self-government may have recourse to the courts if its rights are infringed and has the right to compensation for additional expenses which arise for it as a result of decisions taken by agencies of State power.

Nonetheless, although agencies of local self-government are not part of the system of agencies of State power, under 2020 amendments to the Constitution they are conceived of as being within a "unified system of public power in the Russian Federation" and are required to interact in order to achieve the most effective resolution of their tasks in the interests of the population on the respective territory of the agency of local self-government (Article 132(3)). Article 133 was also changed in favor of local communities: their additional expenses will be compensated if they arise as a result of the performance of public functions by agencies of local self-government in interaction with the agencies of State power (not only as a result of decisions taken by the agencies of State power as in the previous version).

The law of local self-government, often called "municipal law" in doctrinal writings, rests, in addition to the Russian Constitution, upon the Federal Law on the General Principles of the Organization Local Self-Government in the Russian Federation, of 6 October 2003, as amended,[108] and upon the charters or statutes adopted by each "municipal formation". The last expression is a neutral one embracing a city or rural settlement, or several settlements combining a common territory, or part of a settlement within whose limits local self-government is exercised – all of the foregoing having their own charter, municipal ownership, a local budget, and elective agencies of self-government. The municipal charter is subject to State registration in the procedure established by the respective subject of the Russian Federation in which the municipal formation is situated; registration may be refused if the charter is contrary to the Russian Constitution.

Municipal charters vary considerably, but contain as a rule the boundaries and composition of the territory of the municipal formation, its

[108] C3 PФ (2003), no. 40, item 3822, as amended, which replaced a Federal Law of 28 August 1995, as amended. See C3 PФ (1995), no. 35, item 3506, as amended.

jurisdiction, the structure and procedure for forming local self-government agencies, the term of powers of deputies elected, other elective posts, and the procedure for the adoption and entry into force of normative acts of local self-government. In some subjects of the Federation, although local self-government is autonomous and not part of the system of agencies of State power, local agencies of State power have been created side-by-side with local self-government (e.g. Iakutia, Komi, Bashkortostan) which are directly subordinate to the "center". In some areas the local self-government has been determined to be simultaneously an agency of State power. The procedure for choosing the chief executive officer, and his stature, also varies. In Tver Region the head of the administration of a city, district, settlement, or rural national area is the head of the superior administration, whereas in other areas the same scheme is augmented by the requirement of the consent of the respective representative agencies of local self-government to be obtained, for example, in Arkhangelsk Region. On two occasions the Constitutional Court has struck down attempts of subjects of the Federation to interfere in the formation or transformation of local self-government in the Chita Region[109] and Udmurt Republic.[110]

Issues of local significance are decided rather frequently by local referendums, including boundary issues. The procedure for holding referendums is regulated by the charter of the municipal formation in accordance with legislation of the respective subject of the Russian Federation. The same applies to municipal elections for representative organs, except that agencies of State power of the Russian Federation and of the relevant subject of the Federation are required to ensure that local elections do take place. If the municipal formation does not have its own electoral legislation, as happens, the elections are held on the basis of the Federal Law on Ensuring the Constitutional Rights of Citizens of the Russian Federation to Elect and to Be Elected to Agencies of Local Self-Government, of 26 November 1996, as amended.[111]

Reversion to the ancient tradition of "assemblies of citizens" may be authorized in municipal formations, provided that the procedure for convoking and conducting them, adopting and changing decisions, and their precise competence must be determined in the charter of the municipal formation in accordance with legislation of the relevant subject of the Federation. A form of popular legislative initiative exists, called

[109] Decree of the Constitutional Court of the Russian Federation "Re Verification of the Constitutionality of a Number of Provisions of the Charter – Basic Law of Chita Region", 1 February 1996. C3 PΦ (1996), no. 7, item 700.

[110] Decree of the Constitutional Court of the Russian Federation "Re Verification of the Constitutionality of the Law of the Udmurt Republic of 17 April 1996 "'On the System of Agencies of State Power in the Udmurt Republic'", 24 January 1997. C3 PΦ (1997), no. 5, item 708.

[111] C3 PΦ (1996), no. 49, item 5497, as amended.

the "people's law-creation initiative", whereby in accordance with the municipal charter the general public may put forward draft legal acts on questions of local significance. These must be considered by the local self-government in open session and the results of the consideration officially published. Municipal charters may also provide for "territorial social self-government", pursuant to which citizens organize themselves at their place of residence and assume responsibility for certain questions of self-government.

Municipal ownership consists of the means of the local budget, municipal extra-budgetary funds, the property of agencies of local self-government, municipal land and other natural resources, municipal enterprises and organizations, municipal banks and other credit institutions, educational, public health, culture and sport institutions, stockholdings or other equity in juridical persons, and other moveable and immoveable property. In large cities the total asset-base can be very substantial and has been successfully used as security to achieve project financing to back the issue of securities. Under the Russian Civil Code municipal agencies of self-government have legal personality and legal capacity and may transfer, lease out, or alienate their property or conclude other transactions with the property in their ownership. The privatization of municipal property is resolved at the local level, and revenues from privatization go to the local budget. It has been common practice when major State enterprises are transformed into joint-stock societies to transfer the so-called social infrastructure (housing, clubs, cinemas, children's nurseries, and the like) to the balance sheet of the municipal formation.

Municipal formations may and often do invest in entrepreneurial enterprises, and have the right to engage in foreign economic activity.

CONSTITUTIONAL AMENDMENTS

The Russian Constitution is not easily amended or revised. Chapters 1 (Foundations of the Constitutional System), 2 (Rights and Freedoms of Man and Citizen), and 9 (Constitutional Amendments and Revision of the Constitution) cannot be amended by the Federal Assembly. If a proposal to amend or revise any of those three chapters is supported by the votes of three-fifths of the total number of members of the Soviet of the Federation and the State Duma, a Constitutional Assembly must be convoked in accordance with a federal constitutional law. Amendments to Chapters 3 to 8 of the Constitution may be adopted by the Federal Assembly in the same procedure as is used to adopt a federal constitutional law, but they enter into force only after approval by the agencies of legislative power of not less than two-thirds of the subjects of the Russian Federation (Article 136, Constitution). This procedure was followed when amending the Constitution in 2013-2014. All 83 (then) subjects of the Federation voted in favor of the amendments.

In 2020 this procedure was augmented by a decision, although not required by the Constitution, to put the amendments as a package to a national vote. 67.88% of registered voters took part in the voting: 78.66% voted in favor of the amendments. 84 of the 85 subjects of the Russian Federation supported the amendments, the Nenets Autonomous National Area being the exception.

If a Constitutional Assembly is convoked, it either confirms the Constitution in its existing form or prepares the draft of a new Constitution. The new draft must be adopted by two-thirds of the total number of delegates at the Assembly or be submitted to an all-people's referendum. If a referendum is held, at least half of the electors must take part for there to be a valid referendum, and a simple majority of the electors must vote in favor of the new Constitution.

Article 65 of the Constitution is subject to yet another procedure for amendment. If a new subject of the Federation is formed, including by way of accession to the Federation, or if there is a change in the constitutional legal status of an existing subject, the consequential changes in the Constitution are set out in the federal constitutional law on the admission of a new subject or changing the status of an existing subject of the Federation. If a subject of the Federation simply changes its name, as already has happened, the new name is subject to inclusion in Article 65 of the Constitution; in practice this occurs on the basis of an edict of the President of the Russian Federation.

The constitutional provisions governing amendments to the Constitution have been elaborated in the Federal Law on the Procedure for the Adoption and Entry into Force of Amendments to the Constitution of the Russian Federation, of 4 March 1998.[112] An '"amendment" with respect to Chapters 3 to 8 of the Constitution means "any change of the text of Chapters 3 to 8 of the Constitution of the Russian Federation: exclusion, addition, new version, or any provision of the said chapters". Interconnected changes of several titles may be incorporated in a single law introducing the amendments, including consequential changes arising out of the proposed amendment. If a section, chapter, or article is to be eliminated from the Constitution, the resulting official text must specify by which law it was excluded, the date, and the number of the law, the original numbering of the text being preserved. The draft law proposing the amendment must also set out the reasons for the amendment and include a full list of federal constitutional laws and federal laws which must be repealed, changed, added to, or adopted as a result of the amendment.

The proposal to amend the Constitution is first referred to the State Duma, which considers the draft in committee and then subjects the draft law to three readings. A two-thirds vote in the State Duma of all members is

112 СЗ РФ (1998), no. 10, item 1146.

required for adoption. Within five days the adopted law is sent to the Soviet of the Federation for obligatory consideration (in this case the Soviet of the Federation cannot fail to take up the law). A three-quarters majority of all members of the Soviet of the Federation must support the draft law; if the law is defeated, the Soviet of the Federation has the right to propose to the State Duma that a conciliation commission be created to discuss the matter. If the Soviet of the Federation approves the law on the amendment, it must be published within five days for general information and also be sent to the subjects of the Federation for consideration.

The subjects of the Federation have one year from the date of adoption by the Soviet of the Federation to consider the law on the amendment to the Constitution; each subject itself determines the procedure for considering the matter. Once they take a decision on the matter, their decree must be sent within 14 days to the Soviet of the Federation, which keeps a record of how many subjects consider the question and when. At its next regular session after the year's period has elapsed for subjects of the Federation to consider the matter, the Soviet of the Federation determines the results of the consideration in the procedure laid down in its Reglament. Within seven days after the results are determined, the President of the Russian Federation or any subject of the Federation may appeal the decree to the Supreme Court of the Russian Federation, which considers the case in accordance with the Code of Civil Procedure of the Russian Federation. If no appeal is filed within the seven-day period, the Chairman of the Soviet of the Federation sends the law for signature to the President of the Russian Federation and official publication. Should the Supreme Court of the Russian Federation satisfy the appeal against the decree of the Soviet of the Federation, the Soviet reconsiders the matter at its next regular session.

The President of the Russian Federation has 14 days to sign and officially publish the law on the amendment to the Constitution. Within a month after the law enters into force, the President of the Russian Federation must arrange for the new official publication of the Constitution incorporating the amendment.

If the law on the amendment failed to obtain the necessary approval of two-thirds of the subjects of the Federation within one year, the amendment may not be resubmitted to the State Duma until a year has elapsed since the results of the consideration were established by the Soviet of the Federation.

POLITICAL PARTIES

One of the major steps taken during the *perestroika* era in transforming Russia into a democratic society was the abolition of the constitutionally enshrined stature of the Communist Party of the Soviet Union as the sole political party (Article 6, 1977 USSR Constitution). The 1993 Russian Constitution provides that "political diversity and a multi-party system" are recognized in the Russian Federation (Article 13). This provision served as the occasion for the adoption of the Federal Law on Political Parties of 11 July 2001, as amended.[113] Russian citizens also enjoy a constitutional right to association, or not to associate (Article 30), and the freedom of social associations is guaranteed.

The true place of political parties in the Russian political and legal systems remains ambiguous and ambivalent. Literally hundreds of political parties were organized and registered as such in Russia after the Soviet Union was dissolved. Many were purely the creation of a handful of individuals and enjoyed neither broad support nor a national base. Most did not command deep allegiance from their membership, and split and merged with bewildering rapidity. In the State Duma affiliation to a political party does influence the internal organization of work the distribution of committee assignments, and sometimes voting patterns. Yet the President of the Russian Federation is, as a matter of law, not expected to remain a member of a political party while in office.

Legally speaking, a political party is a "social association" created for the participation of Russian citizens in the political life of society by means of forming and expressing their political will, participating in social and political actions, elections, and referendums, and to represent their interests in agencies of State power and agencies of local self-government. A political party must satisfy certain requirements: (1) it must have regional divisions in more than half of the subjects of the Russian Federation and may have only one regional division per subject of the Federation; (2) the political party has at least 500 members, a citizen of Russia being a member of only one political party in a single regional division of this political party at his place of permanent or preferred residence; (3) and the executive and other organs of the political party, its regional divisions, and other structural subdivisions all must be situated on the territory of the Russian Federation. These minimum requirements are as provided in amendments of 2 April 2012 to the Federal Law on Political Parties.

Each political party must have a charter and a program. The newspaper Российская газета or other all-Russian printed periodical publications are required by the Law on Political Parties (Article 14) to publish notice of the place and date for a political party to hold its constitutive congress within two weeks of submission of the information for publication. The Law on Political Parties introduced a clean-slate policy, requiring all parties to register anew under the Law in order to continue to have the status of a political party. Those who registered were then required to meet the new requirements introduced in December 2004.

[113] СЗ РФ (2001), no. 29, item 2950, as amended; transl. in Butler, note 32 above. Prior to the enactment of this Law, Articles 6 and 9 of the USSR Law on Social Associations were in force with regard to Russian political parties. Ведомости СНД и ВС СССР (1990), no. 42, item 839.

The creation of a political party is prohibited whose purposes or actions are directed towards a forcible change of the foundations of the constitutional system and a violation of the integrity of the Russian Federation, subversion of State security, creation of armed or militarized formations, or the incitement of social, racial, nationality, or religious enmity. Political programs which favor social justness, however, are not to be regarded as inciting social enmity. Nor are political parties permitted which are based on professional, racial, nationality, or religious affiliation, by which is understood an indication in the party charter or program that the aim is to defend professional, racial, nationality, or religious interests. Nor may a political party consist of persons from a single profession. Moreover, political parties must be organized territorially and may not have structural subdivisions within agencies of State power, agencies of local self-government, the Armed Forces, law enforcement and other State agencies or in State and non-State organizations (excluding representative, or parliamentary, agencies at all levels). Political parties are further prohibited from interfering in the instructional process of educational institutions. Political parties, or structural subdivisions thereof, of foreign States may not be created or operated on the territory of the Russian Federation.

The creation of a political party must meet the legal criteria laid down in the Federal Law on Political Parties. As noted above, there must be a constitutive congress. No authorizations of agencies of State power are required for such congresses. The founders of a political party are the delegates who attend the constitutive congress. Preparations for the Congress are made by an organizing committee consisting of at least ten persons; the organizing committee notifies in written form the federal agency of executive power empowered to register political parties of its intention to create a political party and indicates the proposed name of the party, together with the submission of other information documents. The registering agency issues a formal receipt of the submission, which then serves as the basis for approaching the media about publication of the time and place of the constitutive congress. A constitutive congress is quorate if delegates representing no less than half of the subjects of the Russian Federation and residing primarily in those subjects of the Russian Federation have taken part on the congress.

Registration may be refused to a political party whose charter is contrary to the Constitution of Russia, federal constitutional laws, the Law on Political Parties, and other federal laws; whose name or symbols do not meet the requirements of the Law on Political Parties; which failed to submit the documents necessary for State registration, or whose submitted documents do not contain the information required by the Law on Political Parties, or which has not submitted the required documents in a timely manner.

Membership of political parties is voluntary and individual, open to citizens who have reached 18 years of age. Foreign citizens and stateless persons, and Russian citizens who have been deemed by a court to lack dispositive legal capacity, may not join political parties, and a Russian citizen may join only one political party, and in that event must be associated with a particular regional subdivision at his place of permanent or preferred residence. It is prohibited to ask whether a citizen is a member of a political party or not (a sharp change of practice of the Soviet era, when, for example, even in a criminal proceeding a defendant was asked whether he was a Party member or not).

Political parties enjoy special legal capacity. They are juridical persons and may have in ownership any property needed for their activity as provided by the Law on Political Parties and their own charter. The party as a whole is the owner of the party's property, including the property of its regional divisions and other structural subdivisions. Regional divisions and other registered structural subdivisions have the right of operative management over property consolidated to them by the owner, together with an autonomous balance sheet or estimate. Party members have no rights with respect to the party's property, and the property may be used only to realize the purposes and tasks provided for by the party charter and program. Regional divisions and other registered structural subdivisions are liable for their obligations with the property at their disposition, and if such property is insufficient to meet obligations, the political party as a whole bears responsibility for them.

Against the background of reported widespread abuses in campaign financing, the Law on Political Parties provides a number of requirements intended to reduce the incidence of such abuses. Political parties may receive money from entry and membership dues, if the Party charter so provides, means of the federal budget provided in accordance with the Law on Political Parties, donations, proceeds from measures conducted by the political party or divisions and structural subdivisions, revenues from entrepreneurial activity and civil-law transactions, and other proceeds not prohibited by law. A political party may have only one settlement account for the party itself and for its regional divisions and other registered structural subdivisions and such accounts must be in credit institutions registered on the territory of Russia. Any donations from natural and juridical persons must have documentary confirmation and the source of revenues must be specified. A political party and its regional divisions (unless established otherwise by the charter of the political party) have the right the enter into contracts of loan with natural and juridical persons or to conclude credit contracts with juridical persons.

There is an extensive list of prohibited donors to political parties: foreign States, foreign juridical persons, foreign citizens, stateless persons, citizens of Russia under 18 years of age, Russian juridical persons with foreign participation if the foreign equity share exceeds 30% on the day of drawing up the list of persons who have the right to take part in the yearly general meeting of stockholders, international organizations and international social movements, agencies of State power, other State agencies, and agencies of local self-government, State and municipal institutions and State and municipal unitary enterprises, juridical persons having charter capital in which there is State or municipal ownership exceeding 30%, organizations founded by State agencies and/or agencies of local self-government (subject to certain exceptions), military units, military organizations, law enforcement agencies, philanthropic organizations and religious associations or institutions and organizations thereof, anonymous donors, juridical persons registered for less than one year before the donation was made, and certain non-commercial organizations, including those performing the functions of a foreign agent (Russian non-commerecial organization which receives money or other property from foreign States, State agencies thereof, international and foreign organizations, foreign citizens, stateless persons, or persons empowered by them, and/or from Russian juridical persons receiving money or other property from the said sources (except for open joint-stock societies with State participation and subsidiaries thereof) and which take part, including in the interests of foreign sources, in political activity on the territory of the Russian Federation).

Donations in the prohibited category must be returned to the donor within a month, and if that is impossible, they go to the revenue of the Russian Federation. Limited State financing is available to political parties from the federal budget provided that the party meets certain criteria laid down in the Law on Political Parties.

SOCIAL CHAMBER OF RUSSIAN FEDERATION

By a Federal Law of 4 April 2005, as amended, introduced at the initiative of the President of the Russian Federation, the Social Chamber of the Russian Federation (sometimes called the Public Chamber or the Civic Chamber)[114] was created as a unique body established by the State but not part of the State to further the objective of creating a civil society in Russia.[115] The aim of the Social Chamber is to be achieved by encouraging interaction and dialogue between citizens of Russia and State agencies and their officials at all levels of the Russian Federation. A number of subjects of the Federation have formed analogous chambers; however, there is no hierarchy or other

[114] This is a good example of the use of the Russian word общественная, which can be translated as "social" or as "public" and is obscure in both versions here; the website of the body prefers "civic" chamber, which is not a translation, but a description. On the origins of the Social Chamber, see Jane E. Henderson, *The Constitution of the Russian Federation: A Contextual Analysis* (2011), pp. 145-148.

[115] СЗ РФ (2005), no. 15, item 1277, as amended.

relationship between the Social Chamber of the Russian Federation and those at lower levels.[116] The activity of the Social Chamber also is regulated by the Federal Law "On Social Control over Ensuring Human Rights in Places of Compulsory Confinement and Assistance to Persons in Places of Compulsory Confinement", of 10 June 2008,[117] and by the Federal Law on the Fundamental Principles of Social Control of 21 July 2014.[118]

Legally speaking, the Social Chamber is an advisory and consultative body whose functions are determined by the Federal Law which created it. The Chamber is not a juridical person and has no right to take part in legal relations as a juridical person. It operates through its apparatus, which is analogous to that of a State institution, and is financed from the federal budget. It does not exercise State powers; its decisions are not binding on officials, State agencies, juridical persons, or citizens. Any document adopted is purely of a recommendatory nature.

It may request information from agencies of State power and agencies of local self-government on matters within its jurisdiction, subject draft laws and other normative legal acts to expert evaluation from a citizen's viewpoint, offer opinions on violations of legislation by agencies of State power and send its opinion in this respect to competent State agencies, agencies of local self-government, or officials, and take the initiative in making proposals with regard to social issues. Neither the State nor any other persons or organizations have the right to interfere in its activities.

The Social Chamber operates on the basis of a Reglament, which it confirmed on 21 December 2015, replacing the Reglament of 22 January 2006.[119] The Reglament determines the procedure for the participation of members of the Chamber in its activity, the periods and procedure for holding plenary sessions of the Chamber, the membership, powers, and procedure for activity of the Council and the Secretary, First Deputy Secretary, deputy secretaries, commissions, and working groups of the Social Chamber, the formation and activities of the apparatus of the Chamber, and procedure for adopting decisions, the ways of working with social associations who are not represented in the Social Chamber, and the procedure for preparing and publishing the annual report of the Social Chamber on the State of a Civil Society in the Russian Federation.

The membership of the Social Chamber comprises 40 citizens of Russia confirmed by the President of the Russian Federation, 43 representatives

116 The individual efforts of some subjects of the Russian Federation have been reinforced and unified by the enactment of the Federal Law on General Principles for the Organization and Activity of Social Chambers of Subjects of the Russian Federation of 23 June 2016. СЗ РФ (2016), no. 26(I), item 3852, as amended.

117 СЗ РФ (2008), no. 24, item 2789, as amended.

118 СЗ РФ (2014), no. 30(I), item 4213, as amended.

119 Both are available on Consultant Plus.

of All-Russian social associations and other non-commercial organizations, and 85 representatives of social chambers of subjects of the Russian Federation. Political parties and extremist associations are not permitted to nominate members. A Russian citizen who has reached 18 years of age may be a member, subject to a number of exclusions which mostly consist of State officials, judges, and others of similar employment. A member of the Social Chamber is required to suspend his membership in any political party during his term of office. Members are reimbursed for expenses and a per diem rate for each day of work lost while attending meetings or sessions connected with the Social Chamber. Members serve for three years from the day of the first plenary session of the Social Chamber; there is no prohibition against reappointment.

Members are required to comply with a Code of Ethics, which, *inter alia,* requires that they be guided in their duties by high social interests, perform their duties with honor, reason, and good faith and refrain in public discussion from gross and incorrect expressions, respect the State symbols of the Russian Federation and the Russian language, be guided by principles of legality, impartiality, and justness, not allow any forms of public support for political parties, and display respect for the convictions, traditions, and cultures of ethnic and social groups, religious confessions and further inter-nationality and inter-confessional peace and harmony.[120]

[120] The Code of Ethics was confirmed at the Second Plenary Session of the Social Chamber on 14 April 2006. See A. S. Avtonomov and S. A. Popov, Постатейный комментарий к Федеральному закону «Об Общественной палате Российской Федерации» [Article-by-Article Commentary on the Federal Law "On the Social Chamber of the Russian Federation"] (2007), p. 42.

9

FURTHER READING

The references below are to additional materials, mostly recent, that may interest readers of this book or contain detailed information about works cited in the footnotes. For a more extensive list, see W. E. Butler, *Russian Law* (3d ed.; Oxford, Oxford University Press, 2009), Chapter 21. My own publications, including the more than 4,000 translations of Soviet, Russian, and other doctrinal writings, legislation, and treaties, are recorded in *International and Comparative Law: A Bibliography with Annotations and Notes of the Publishing Writings and Reports of William E. Butler* (2d ed.; London, Wildy, Simmonds & Hill, 2015).

Documents, Casebooks, and Dictionaries

Butler, W. E. (comp., transl., & ed.), *Basic Legal Documents of the Russian Federation* (Dobbs Ferry, New York, Oceana Publications, 1992).

Butler, W. E. (transl. & ed.), *Civil Code of the Russian Federation* (London, Wildy, Simmonds & Hill Publishing, 2016).

Butler, W. E. (transl. & intro.), *Russian Civil and Arbitrazh Procedure* (London, Wildy, Simmonds and Hill Publishing, 2012).

Butler, W. E. (transl. & intro.), *Russian Criminal Law and Procedure* (London, Wildy, Simmonds and Hill Publishing, 2011).

Butler, W. E., *Russian Law and Legal Institutions* (London, Wildy, Simmonds & Hill, 2014).

Butler, W. E., *Russian-English Legal Dictionary and Bibliographic Sources for Russian Law in English* (Ardsley, New York, Transnational Publishers Inc./ London, Wildy, Simmonds & Hill, 2001).

Butler, W. E., *Russian Public Law: The Foundations of a Rule-of-Law State: Legislation and Documents* (3d ed.; London, Wildy, Simmonds & Hill Publishers, 2013; 2d ed., 2009; 1st ed.; 2005).

Butler, W. E., Tomsinov, V. A. (eds.), *The Nakaz of Catherine the Great: Collected Texts* (Clark, New Jersey, Lawbook Exchange Ltd., 2010).

Dewey, H. W. (comp., transl. & ed.), *Muscovite Judicial Texts: 1488-1556* (Ann Arbor, Michigan, Department of Slavic Languages and Literatures, 1966) (Michigan Slavic Materials, No. 7).

Dewey, H. W., Kleimola, A. M. (transl. & ed.), *Russian Private Law: XIV-XVII Centuries* (Ann Arbor, Michigan, Department of Slavic Languages and Literatures, 1973) (Michigan Slavic Materials, No. 9).

Griffiths, D., Munro, G. E. (transl. & ed.), *Catherine II's Charters to the Nobility and Towns of 1785* (Idyllwild, California, Charles Schlacks, Publisher, 1991).

Hellie, R. (transl. & ed.), *The Muscovite Law Code (Ulozhenie) of 1649* (Idyllwild, California, Charles Schlacks, Publisher, 1988).

Kaiser, D. (transl. & ed.), *The Laws of Rus' – Tenth to Fifteenth Centuries* (Idyllwild, California, Charles Schlacks, Publisher, 1992).

Kivelson, V. A., Worobec, C. D. (eds.), *Witchcraft in Russia and Ukraine, 1000-1900. A Sourcebook* (DeKalb, Illinois, Northern Illinois University Press, 2020).

Maggs, Peter B., Schwartz, Olga, Burnham, William, *Law and Legal System of the Russian Federation* (7th ed.; Huntingdon, New York, Juris Publishers Inc., 2020). 1084 p.

Pollard, Alan P. (transl. & ed.), *The Laws of February 18-19, 1861 on the Emancipation of the Russian Peasants* (Idyllwild, California, Charles Schlacks, Publisher, 2008).

Pushkarev, S. G. (comp.), *Dictionary of Russian Historical Terms from the Eleventh Century to 1917*, ed. G. Vernadsky and R. T. Fisher, Jr. (New Haven, Yale University Press, 1970).

Vernadsky G. V. (transl. & intro.), *Medieval Russian Laws* (New York, Columbia University Press, 1947).

Looseleaf Service

Butler, W. E., *Russia & The Republics: Legal Materials* (Huntingdon, New York, Juris Publishers Inc., 2006-). 6 supplements annually.

Legal History and Theory

Adams, Bruce F., *The Politics of Punishment: Prison Reform in Russia, 1863-1917* (DeKalb, Illinois, Northern Illinois University Press, 1996).

Antonov, Sergei, *Bankrupts and Usurers of Imperial Russia: Debt, Property, and the Law in the Age of Dostoyevsky and Tolstoi* (Cambridge, Harvard University Press, 2016).

Avrutin, Eugene M., *The Velizh Affair: Blood Libel in a Russian Town* (Oxford, Oxford University Press, 2018).

Becker, Elisa M., *Medicine, Law and the State in Imperial Russia* (Budapest-New York, Central European University Press, 2011).

Berest, Julia, *The Emergence of Russian Liberalism: Alexander Kunitsyn in Context, 1783-1840* (New York, Palgrave Macmillan, 2011).

Berman, H. J., *Justice in the U.S.S.R.* (Cambridge, Mass., Harvard University Press, 1963).

Butler, W. E., *Russia and the Law of Nations in Historical Perspective: Collected Essays* (London, Wildy, Simmonds & Hill, 2009.

Butler, W. E. (ed.), *Russian Law: Historical and Political Perspectives* (Leyden, A. W. Sijthoff, 1977).

Butler, W. E., *Soviet Law* (London, Butterworths, 1982; 2d ed.; 1988).

Butler, W. E., Tomsinov, V. A. (eds.), *Russian Legal Biography* (London, Wildy, Simmonds & Hill Publishing, 2007). Vol. 1.

Cassiday, Julie A., *The Enemy of Trial: Early Soviet Courts on Stage and Screen* (DeKalb, Illinois, Northern Illinois University Press, 2000).

Daly, Jonathan W., *Autocracy under Siege: Security Police and Opposition in Russia, 1866-1905* (DeKalb, Illinois, Northern Illinois University Press, 1998).

Daly, Jonathan W., *The Watchful State: Security Police and Opposition in Russia, 1906-1917* (DeKalb, Illinois, Northern Illinois University Press, 2004).

Dennison, Tracy K., *The Institutional Framework of Russian Serfdom* (Cambridge, England, Cambridge University Press, 2011).

Feldbrugge, F. J. M., *A History of Russian Law: From Ancient Times to the Council Code (Ulozhenie) of Tsar Aleksei Mikhailovich of 1649* (Leiden, Brill/ Nijhoff, 2017).

Feldbrugge, F. J. M., *Law in Medieval Russia* (Leiden, Martinus Nijhoff Publishers, 2009).

Feldbrugge, F. J. M., *Russian Law: The End of the Soviet System* (Dordrecht, Martinus Nijhoff Publishers, 1993).

Franklin, Simon, *The Russian Graphosphere, 1450-1850* (Cambridge, Cambridge University Press, 2019).

Galmarini-Kabala, Maria C., *The Right to be Helped: Deviance, Entitlement, and the Soviet Moral Order* (DeKalb, Illinois, Northern Illinois University Press, 2016).

Glebov, Sergey, *From Empire to Eurasia: Politics, Scholarship, and Ideology in Russian Eurasianism, 1920s-1930s* (DeKalb, Illinois, Northern Illinois University Press, 2017).

Gorshkov, Boris B., *Russia's Factory Children: State, Society, and Law, 1800-1917* (Pittsburg, Pennsylvania, Pittsburgh University Press, 2009).

Hamburg, G. M. (ed. & transl.), *Liberty, Equality, and the Market: Essays by B. N. Chicherin* (New Haven and London, Yale University Press, 1998).

Hamburg, G. M., *Russia's Path toward Enlightenment: Faith, Politics and Reason, 1500-1801* (New Haven, Yale University Press, 2016).

Hansen, Julie, Rogachevskii, Andrei (eds.), *Punishment as a Crime? Perspectives on Prison Experience in Russian Culture* (Uppsala, Uppsala University Press, 2014).

Hazard, John N., *Managing Change in the USSR: The Politico-Legal Role of the Soviet Jurist* (Cambridge, England, Cambridge University Press, 1983).

Hazard, John N., *Settling Disputes in Soviet Society: The Formative Years of Legal Institutions* (New York, Columbia University Press, 1960).

Healey, Dan, *Bolshevik Sexual Forensics: Diagnosing Disorder in the Clinic and Courtroom, 1917-1939* (DeKalb, Illinois, Northern Illinois University Press, 2009).

Healey, Dan, *Homosexual Desire in Revolutionary Russia: The Regulation of Sexual and Gender Dissent* (Chicago, Illinois, University of Chicago Press, 2001).

Heinzen, James, *The Art of the Bribe: Corruption Under Stalin, 1943-1953* (New Haven, Yale University Press, 2016).

Heuman, Susan, *Kistiakovsky: The Struggle for National and Constitutional Rights in the Last Years of Tsardom* (Cambridge, Massachusetts, Harvard Ukrainian Research Institute, 1998).

Hudson, Hugh G., Jr., *Peasants, Political Police, and the Early Soviet State: Surveillance and Accommodation under the New Economic Policy* (New York, Palgrave Macmillan, 2012).

Huskey, Eugene, *Russian Lawyers and the Soviet State: The Origins and Development of the Soviet Bar, 1917-1939* (Princeton, New Jersey, Princeton University Press, 1986).

Il'in, Ivan Aleksandrovich, *On the Essence of Legal Consciousness*, ed. and transl. W. E. Butler, P. T. Grier, and V. A. Tomsinov (London, Wildy, Simmonds and Hill, 2014).

Jaworskyj, Michael (transl. & ed.), *Soviet Political Thought: An Anthology* (Baltimore, Maryland, Johns Hopkins Press, 1967).

Kirmse, Stefan B., *The Lawful Empire: Legal Change and Cultural Diversity in Late Tsarist Russia* (Cambridge, Cambridge University Press, 2019).

Kivelson, Valerie, *Desperate Magic: The Moral Economy of Witchcraft in Seventeenth Century Russia* (Ithaca, New York, Cornell University Press, 2013).

Kollmann, Nancy, *Crime and Punishment in Early Modern Russia* (Cambridge, England, Cambridge University Press, 2012).

Kowalsky, Sharon, *Deviant Women: Female Crime and Criminology in Revolutionary Russia, 1880-1930* (DeKalb, Illinois, Northern Illinois University Press, 2002).

Lampert, N., *Whistleblowing in the Soviet Union: Complaints and Abuses under State Socialism* (New York, Schocken Books, 1985).

LaPierre, Brian, *Hooligans in Khrushchev's Russia: Defining, Policing, and Producing Deviance during the Thaw* (Madison, University of Wisconsin Press, 2012).

LeDonne, John P., *Forging a Unitary State: Russia's Management of the Eurasian Space 1650-1850* (Toronto, Canada, Toronto University Press, 2020).

Loewe, Karl von, *The Lithuanian Statute of 1529* (Leiden, E. J. Brill, 1976).

McReynolds, Louise, *Murder Most Russian: True Crime and Punishment in Late Imperial Russia* (Ithaca, New York, Cornell University Press, 2012).

Moon, David, *Russian Peasants and Tsarist Legislation on the Eve of Reform* (Basingstoke, Macmillan Press Ltd., 1992).

Nordlander, Ingegerd, *Real Estate Transfer Deeds in Novgorod: Text and Commentary* (Stockholm, Sweden, Almqvist & Wiksell International, 1987).

Pallot, Judith, Katz, Elena, *Waiting at the Prison Gate: Women, Identity, and the Russian Penal System* (London, I. B. Tauris, 2017).

Pozdnakova, Alla (ed.), *Russian Revolutions of 1917: Scandinavian Perspectives* (London, Wildy, Simmonds & Hill Publishing, 2019).

Pravilova, Ekaterina, *A Public Empire: Property and the Quest for the Common Good in Imperial Russia* (Princeton, Princeton University Press, 2014).

Ronner, Amy D., *Dostoyevsky and the Law* (Durham, Carolina Academic Press, 2015).

Rowland, Daniel B., *God, Tsar, and People: The Political Culture of Early Modern Russia* (DeKalb, Illinois, Northern Illinois University Press, 2020).

Schrader, Abby M., *Languages of the Lash: Corporal Punishment and Identity in Imperial Russia* (DeKalb, Illinois, Northern Illinois University Press, 2002).

Shelley, Louise I., *Lawyers in Soviet Work Life* (New Brunswick, New Jersey, Rutgers University Press, 1984).

Solomon, P. H., *Soviet Criminal Justice under Stalin* (Cambridge, England, Cambridge University Press, 1996).

Unger, A. L., *Constitutional Development in the USSR: a Guide to the Soviet Constitutions* (London, Methuen, 1981).

Utechin, S. V., *Russian Political Thought: A Concise History* (New York, Frederick A. Praeger, 1963).

Walicki, A., *Legal Philosophies of Russian Liberalism* (Oxford, Clarendon Press, 1987).

Walkin, Jacob, *The Rise of Democracy in Pre-Revolutionary Russia: Political and Social Institutions under the Last Three Czars* (New York, Frederick A. Praeger, 1962).

Weickhardt, George G., *Early Russian Law* (Idyllwild, California, Charles Schlacks, Publisher, 2008).

Weinberg, Robert, *Blood Libel in Late Imperial Russia: The Ritual Murder Trial of Mendel Beilis* (Bloomington, Indiana University Press, 2013).

Williams, Stephen F., *Liberal Reform in an Illiberal Regime: The Creation of Private Property in Russia, 1906-1915* (Stanford, California, Hoover Institution Press, 2006).

Williams, Stephen F., *The Reformer: How One Liberal Fought to Preempt the Russian Revolution* (New York/London: Encounter Books, 2017).

Wirtschafter, Elise K., *Structures of Society: Imperial Russia's 'People of Various Ranks'* (DeKalb, Illinois, Northern Illinois University Press, 1994).

Wood, Elizabeth, *Performing Justice: Agitation Trials in Early Soviet Russia* (Ithaca, New York, Cornell University Press, 2005).

Wortman, R. S., *The Development of a Russian Legal Consciousness* (Chicago, Illinois, University of Chicago Press, 1976).

Wortman, R. S., *The Power of Language and Rhetoric in Russian Political History: Charismatic Words from the 18th to the 21st Centuries* (London, Bloomsbury, 2018).

Wortman, R. S., *Russian Monarchy: Representation and Rule: Collected Articles* (Brighton, Academic Studies Press, 2013).

Wozniuk, V. (ed. & transl.), *Politics, Law & Morality: Essays by V. S. Soloviev* (New Haven, Yale University Press, 2000).

Post-Soviet Russian Law

Abdeih, R. B., *Russia's Constitutional Revolution: Legal Consciousness and the Transition to Democracy 1985-1996* (University Park, Pennsylvania, Penn State Press, 1997).

Borisova, T. Iu., Simons, W. B. (eds.), *The Legal Dimension in Cold-War Interactions: Some Notes from the Field* (Leiden, Martinus Nijhoff Publishers, 2012).

Burkov, A. L., *The Impact of the European Convention on Human Rights on Russian Law* (Stuttgart, ibidem-Verlag, 2007).

Burnham, W., Maggs, P. G., Danilenko, G. M., *Law and Legal System of the Russian Federation* (5th ed.; Huntington, New York, Juris Publishing, 2012).

Butler, W. E., *Narcotics & HIV/AIDS in Russia: Harm Reduction Policies Under Russian Law* (London, Wildy, Simmonds & Hill Publishing, 2004).

Butler, W. E., *Russian Family Law* (London, Wildy, Simmonds & Hill Publishing, 2015).

Butler, W. E., *Russian Foreign Relations and Investment Law* (Oxford, Oxford University Press, 2006).

Butler, W. E., *Russian Inheritance Law* (London, Wildy, Simmonds & Hill Publishing, 2014).

Butler, W. E., *Russian Law* (3d ed.; Oxford, Oxford University Press, 2009; 2d ed.; 2003; 1st ed., 1999).

Butler, W. E., *The Russian Legal Practitioner* (The Hague, Eleven Publishing, 2011).

Henderson, Jane E., *The Constitution of the Russian Federation: A Contextual Analysis* (Oxford, Hart Publishing, 2011) (Constitutional Systems of the World).

Hendley, Kathryn, *Everyday Law in Russia* (Ithaca, Cornell University Press, 2017).

Kahn, J., *Federalism, Democratization, and the Rule of Law in Russia* (Oxford, Oxford University Press, 2002).

Kurkchiyan, Marina, Kubal, A. (eds.), *Sociology of Justice in Russia* (Cambridge, Cambridge University Press, 2018).

Martens, John A., *Secret Patenting in the U. S. S. R. and Russia* (Sante Fe, New Mexico, Deep North Press, 2010).

McCarthy, Lauren A., *Trafficking Justice: How Russian Police Enforce New Laws, from Crime to Courtroom* (Ithaca, Cornell University Press, 2015).

Mozolin, V. P., Masliaev, A. I. (eds.), *Russian Civil and Commercial Law*, ed. & transl. W. E. Butler (London, Wildy, Simmonds & Hill, 2009-2012). 2 vols.

Muravyeva, Marianna (ed.), *The Foundations of Russian Law* (London, Hart Publishing, 2018).

Pomeranz, William E., *Law and the Russian State: Russia's Legal Evolution from Peter the Great to Vladimir Putin* (London/New York, Bloomsbury Academic, 2019).

Trochev, A. M., *Judging Russia: Constitutional Court in Russian Politics, 1990-2006* (Cambridge, England, Cambridge University Press, 2008).

Vereshchagin, A. N., *Judicial Law-Making in Post-Soviet Russia* (Abingdon, Routledge-Cavendish, 2007).

Comparative Law

Butler, W. E., *International Civil Procedure in Post-Soviet Space: The Participation of Foreigners* (London, Wildy, Simmonds & Hill Publishing, 2020).

Butler, W. E. (ed.), *International Law in Comparative Perspective* (Alphen aan den Rijn, Netherlands, Sijthoff & Noordhoff, 1980).

Butler, W. E., Kresin, O. V. (eds.), *The Interaction of Legal Systems: Post-Soviet Approaches* (London, Wildy, Simmonds & Hill Publishing, 2015).

Butler, W. E., Kresin, O. V., Shemshuchenko, Iu. S. (eds.), *Foundations of Comparative Law: Methods and Typologies* (London, Wildy, Simmonds & Hill Publishing, 2011).

Erpyleva, N. Iu., Gashi-Butler, Maryann E. (eds.), *"The Best in the West": Educator, Jurist, Arbitrator. Liber Amicorum in Honour of Professor William Butler* (London, Wildy, Simmonds & Hill Publishing, 2014).

Kresin, O. V., *Comparative Legal Studies: 1750 to 1835. Approaches to Conceptualization* (London, Wildy, Simmonds & Hill Publishing, 2019). 2 vols.

Lebedev, V. M., Khabrieva, T. Y. (eds.), *Justice in the Modern World*, transl. M. E. Gashi-Butler; ed. W. E. Butler (The Hague, Eleven International Publishing, 2014).

Quigley, John B., Jr., *Soviet Legal Innovation and the Law of the Western World* (Cambridge, Cambridge University Press, 2007).

Saidov, A. Kh., *Comparative Law*, ed. & transl. W. E. Butler (London, Wildy, Simmonds & Hill Publishing, 2003).

International Law

Butler, W. E., *Foreign Investment Law in the Commonwealth of Independent States* (London, Simmonds & Hill Publishing Ltd., 2002).

Butler, W. E., *International Law in the Russian Legal System* (Oxford, Oxford University Press, 2020).

Butler, W. E., *The Law of Treaties in Russia and the Commonwealth of Independent States: Text and Commentary* (Cambridge, England, Cambridge University Press, 2002).

Butler, W. E., *Northeast Arctic Passage* (Alphen aan den Rijn, Netherlands, Sijthoff & Noordhoff, 1978) (International Straits of the World, ed. G. J. Mangone).

Butler, W. E. (ed.), *Perestroika and International Law* (Dordrecht, Martinus Nijhoff Publishers, 1990).

Butler, W. E. (ed. & comp.), *Russia and the International Legal System: A Bibliography of Writings by Russian Jurists on Public and Private International Law to 1917 with References to Publications in Emigration* (London, Wildy, Simmonds & Hill, 2006).

Butler, W. E. and Tunkin, V. G. (eds.), *The Tunkin Diary and Lectures* (The Hague, Eleven International Publishing, 2011).

Grabar, V. E., *The History of International Law in Russia 1647-1917: A Bio-Bibliographical Study*, transl. W. E. Butler (Oxford, Clarendon Press, 1990).

Kolodkin, A. L., Gutsuliak, V. N., Bobrova, Iu. V., *The World Ocean: International Legal Regime*, ed. & transl. W. E. Butler (The Hague, Netherlands, Eleven International Publishing, 2010).

Kolodkin, R. A., Punzhin, S. M. (eds.), *International Law of the Sea: Essays in Memory of A. L. Kolodkin* (Moscow, Statut, 2014).

Kovalev, A. A., *Contemporary Issues of the Law of the Sea: Modern Russian Approaches*, ed. & transl. W. E. Butler (The Hague, Netherlands, Eleven International Publishing, 2004).

Kuznetsov, V. I., Tuzmukhamedov, B. R. (eds.), *International Law: A Russian Introduction*, ed. & transl. W. E. Butler (The Hague, Netherlands, Eleven International Publishing, 2009).

Långström, Tarja, *Transformation in Russia and International Law* (Leiden, Martinus Nijhoff Publishers, 2003).

Mälksoo, Lauri (ed.), *Russia and European Human-Rights Law: The Rise of the Civilizational Argument* (Leiden, Brill Nijhoff, 2014).

Mälksoo, Lauri, *Russian Approaches to International Law* (Oxford, Oxford University Press, 2015).

Tunkin, G. I., *Theory of International Law*, transl. & ed. W. E. Butler (Cambridge, Massachusetts, Harvard University Press, 1974; 2d ed.; London, Wildy, Simmonds & Hill Publishing, 2003).

Vylegzhanin, A. N., Zilanov, V. K., *Spitzbergen: Legal Regime of Adjacent Marine Areas* (The Hague, Netherlands, Eleven International Publishing, 2007).

CONSTITUTION
OF THE
RUSSIAN FEDERATION

Translated by
William E. Butler

[Adopted by Referendum, 12 December 1993, as amended by Edicts of the President of the Russian Federation, 9 January 1996, No. 20; 10 February 1996, No. 173; 9 June 2001, No. 679; 25 July 2003, No 841; Federal Constitutional Law, 25 March 2004, No 1-ФКЗ; Federal Constitutional Law, 14 October 2005, No 6-ФКЗ; Federal Constitutional Law, 12 July 2006, No 2-ФКЗ; Federal Constitutional Law, 30 December 2006, No 6-ФКЗ; Federal Constitutional Law, 21 July 2007, No 5-ФКЗ; Federal Constitutional Laws, 30 December 2008, Nos. 6-ФКЗ and 7-ФКЗ; Federal Constitutional Law, 5 February 2014, No. 2-ФКЗ; Federal Constitutional Law, 21 March 2014, No. 6-ФКЗ; Federal Constitutional Law, 21 July 2014, No. 11-ФКЗ; Federal Constitutional Law, 14 March 2020, No. 1-ФКЗ. *Российская газета* [Russian Newspaper], 25 December 1993; СЗ РФ (1996), no 3, item 152; no 7, item 676; (2001), no 24, item 2421; (2003), no 30, item 3051; (2004) no 13, item 1110; (2005), no 42, item 4212; (2006), no 29, item 3119; (2007), no 1(I), item 1; no 30, item 3745; (2009), no. 1, items 1 and 2; (2014), no. 6, item 548; no. 12, item 1201; no. 30(I), item 4204; (2020), no. 11, item 1416]

We, the multinational people of the Russian Federation,
united by a common fate on our land,
affirming the rights and freedoms of man and civil peace and harmony,
retaining the historically-formed State unity,
proceeding from generally-recognized principles of equality and self-determination of peoples,
honoring the memory of ancestors who transmitted to us love and respect for the Fatherland and faith in good and justness,
renewing the sovereign Statehood of Russia and affirming the inviolability of its democratic foundations,
endeavoring to ensure the well-being and prosperity of Russia,
proceeding from a responsibility for the Motherland to the present and future generations,
aware of being part of the world community,
adopt the Constitution of the Russian Federation.

SECTION ONE

Chapter 1. Foundations of the Constitutional System

Article 1

1. The Russian Federation – Russia is a democratic federated rule-of-law State with a republic form of government.

2. The names Russian Federation and Russia are of equal significance.

Article 2

Man, his rights and freedoms are the highest value. Recognition of, compliance with, and defense of the rights and freedoms of man and citizen shall be the duty of the State.

Article 3

1. The bearer of sovereignty and the sole source of power in the Russian Federation shall be its multinational people.

2. The people shall effectuate their power directly and also through agencies of State power and agencies of local self-government.

3. The highest direct expression of the power of the people shall be the referendum and free elections.

4. No one may appropriate power in the Russian Federation. The seizure of power or the appropriation of the powers of rule shall be prosecuted according to a federal law.

Article 4

1. The sovereignty of the Russian Federation shall extend to all of its territory.

2. The Constitution of the Russian Federation and federal laws shall have supremacy throughout the entire territory of the Russian Federation.

3. The Russian Federation shall ensure the integrity and inviolability of its territory.

Article 5

1. The Russian Federation shall consist of republics, territories, regions, cities of federal significance, autonomous region, autonomous national areas – which shall be equal subjects of the Russian Federation.

2. A republic (State) shall have its own constitution and legislation. A territory, region, city of federal significance, autonomous region, or autonomous national area shall have its own charter and legislation.

3. The federated structure of the Russian Federation shall be based on its State integrity, unity of the system of State power, delimitation of the subjects of jurisdiction and powers among the agencies of State power of the Russian Federation and agencies of State power of the subjects of the Russian Federation and the equality and self-determination of peoples in the Russian Federation.

4. All subjects of the Russian Federation shall be equal between themselves in mutual relations with federal agencies of State power.

Article 6

1. Citizenship of the Russian Federation shall be acquired and shall terminate in accordance with a federal law and shall be uniform and equal irrespective of the grounds of acquisition.

2. Each citizen of the Russian Federation shall possess on its territory all the rights and freedoms and bear equal duties provided for by the Constitution of the Russian Federation.

3. A citizen of the Russian Federation may not be deprived of his citizenship or the right to change it.

Article 7

1. The Russian Federation shall be a social State whose policy is directed towards the creation of conditions ensuring a life of dignity and the free development of man.

2. Labor and human health shall be protected in the Russian Federation, a guaranteed minimum amount of payment for labor shall be established, State support of the family, motherhood, fatherhood, childhood, disabled persons, and aged citizens shall be ensured, the system of social services shall be developed, and State pensions, benefits, and other guarantees of social defense shall be established.

Article 8

1. The unity of economic space, free movement of goods, services, and financial assets, support of competition, and freedom of economic activity shall be guaranteed in the Russian Federation.

2. Private, State, municipal, and other forms of ownership shall be equally recognized and defended in the Russian Federation.

Article 9

1. Land and other natural resources shall be used and protected in the Russian Federation as the basis of the life and activity of peoples residing on the respective territory.

2. Land and other natural resources may be in private, State, municipal, and other forms of ownership.

Article 10

State power in the Russian Federation shall be effectuated on the basis of separation into legislative, executive, and judicial. Agencies of legislative, executive, and judicial power shall be autonomous.

Article 11

1. State power in the Russian Federation shall be effectuated by the President of the Russian Federation, the Federal Assembly (Soviet of the Federation and the State Duma), the Government of the Russian Federation, and the courts of the Russian Federation.

2. State power in the subjects of the Russian Federation shall be effectuated by agencies of State power formed by them.

3. Delimitation of the subjects of jurisdiction and powers among the agencies of State power of the Russian Federation and agencies of State power of the subjects of the Russian Federation shall be effectuated by the present Constitution, by the Treaty of the Federation, and by other treaties on the delimitation of the subjects of jurisdiction and powers.

Article 12

Local self-government shall be recognized and guaranteed in the Russian Federation. Local self-government within the limits of its powers shall be autonomous. Agencies of local self-government shall not be within the system of agencies of State power.

Article 13

1. Ideological diversity shall be recognized in the Russian Federation.

2. No ideology may be established as State or obligatory.

3. Political diversity and a multi-party system shall be recognized in the Russian Federation.

4. Social associations shall be equal before the law.

5. The creation and activity of social associations whose purposes or actions are directed towards the forcible change of the foundations of the constitutional system and a violation of the integrity of the Russian Federation, subverting the security of the State, the creation of armed formations, incitement of social, racial, nationality, and religious enmity shall be prohibited.

Article 14

1. The Russian Federation is a secular State. No religion may be established as State or obligatory.

2. Religious associations shall be separate from the State and equal before the law.

Article 15

1. The Constitution of the Russian Federation shall have the highest legal force, direct effect, and be applied throughout the entire territory of the Russian Federation. Laws and other legal acts applicable in the Russian Federation must not be contrary to the Constitution of the Russian Federation.

2. Agencies of State power, agencies of local self-government, officials, citizens, and their associations shall be obliged to comply with the Constitution of the Russian Federation and laws.

3. Laws shall be subject to official publication. Unpublished laws shall not be applied. Any normative legal acts affecting the rights, freedoms, and duties of man and citizen may not be applied if they have not been published officially for general information.

4. Generally-recognized principles and norms of international law and international treaties of the Russian Federation shall be an integral part of its legal system. If other rules have been established by an international treaty of the Russian Federation than provided for by a law, the rules of the international treaty shall apply.

Article 16

1. The provisions of the present Chapter of the Constitution shall comprise the foundations of the constitutional system of the Russian Federation and may not be changed other than in the procedure established by the present Constitution.

2. No other provisions of the present Constitution may be contrary to the foundations of the constitutional system of the Russian Federation.

Chapter 2. Rights and Freedoms of Man and Citizen

Article 17

1. The rights and freedoms of man and citizen according to generally-recognized principles and norms of international law and in accordance with the present Constitution shall be recognized and guaranteed in the Russian Federation.

2. The basic rights and freedoms of man shall be inalienable and shall belong to each from birth.

3. The effectuation of the rights and freedoms of man and citizen must not violate the rights and freedoms of other persons.

Article 18

The rights and freedoms of man and citizen shall be of direct effect. They shall determine the sense, content, and application of laws and the activity of legislative and executive power and local self-government and shall be ensured by justice.

Article 19

1. All shall be equal before law and court.

2. The State shall guarantee the equality of rights and freedoms of man and citizen irrespective of sex, race, nationality, language, origin, property and official position, place of residence, attitude towards religion, convictions, affiliation to social associations, and also other circumstances. Any forms of the limitation of the rights of citizens according to indicia of social, racial, nationality, language, or religious affiliation shall be prohibited.

3. Man and woman shall have equal rights and freedoms and equal opportunities for the realization thereof.

Article 20

1. Each shall have the right to life.

2. The death penalty may until the abolition thereof be established by a federal law as an exceptional measure of punishment for especially grave crimes against life while granting to the accused the right to consideration of his case by a court with the participation of jurors.

Article 21

1. The dignity of the person shall be protected by the State. Nothing may be grounds for demeaning it.

2. No one may be subjected to tortures, force, or other cruel treatment or punishment humiliating human dignity. No one may be subjected without voluntary consent to medical, scientific, or other experiments.

Article 22

1. Each shall have the right to freedom and personal inviolability.

2. Arrest, confinement under guard, and maintenance under guard shall be permitted only according to a judicial decision. Before a judicial decision

a person may not be subjected to detention for a period of more than 48 hours.

Article 23

1. Each shall have the right to inviolability of private life, personal and family secrecy, and defense of his honor and good name.

2. Each shall have the right to secrecy of correspondence, telephone conversations, postal, telegraph, and other communications. Limitation of this right shall be permitted only on the basis of a judicial decision.

Article 24

1. The collection, keeping, use, and dissemination of information concerning the private life of a person without his consent shall not be permitted.

2. Agencies of State power and agencies of local self-government and their officials shall be obliged to ensure to each the opportunity to familiarize himself with documents and material directly affecting his rights and freedoms unless provided otherwise by a law.

Article 25

A dwelling shall be inviolable. No one shall have the right to penetrate into a dwelling against the will of the persons residing therein other than in the instances established by a federal law or on the basis of a judicial decision.

Article 26

1. Each shall have the right to determine and specify his nationality affiliation. No one may be forced to determine and specify his nationality affiliation.

2. Each shall have the right to use his native language and to the free choice of language for communion, nurturing, study, and creativity.

Article 27

1. Each who is legally on the territory of the Russian Federation shall have the right to freely move about and choose a place of sojourn and residence.

2. Each may freely depart from the limits of the Russian Federation. A citizen of the Russian Federation shall have the right without hindrance to return to the Russian Federation.

Article 28

Each shall be guaranteed the freedom of conscience, freedom of religious belief, including the right to propagate any religion individually or jointly with others, or not to propagate, freely choose, have, and disseminate religious and other convictions and to act in accordance with them.

Article 29

1. Freedom of thought and speech shall be guaranteed to each.

2. Propaganda or agitation inciting social, racial, nationality, or religious enmity and hatred shall not be permitted. Propaganda of social, racial, nationality, religious, or linguistic supremacy shall be prohibited.

3. No one may be forced to express his opinions and convictions or to renounce them.

4. Each shall have the right to freely seek, receive, transmit, produce, and disseminate information by any legal means. A list of information constituting a State secret shall be determined by a federal law.

5. The freedom of mass information shall be guaranteed. Censorship shall be prohibited.

Article 30

1. Each shall have the right to association, including the right to create trade unions in order to defend their interests. The freedom of activity of social associations shall be guaranteed.

2. No one may be forced to join any association or to be therein.

Article 31

Citizens of the Russian Federation shall have the right to assemble peacefully without weapons, hold assemblies, meetings, and demonstrations, processions, and picketing.

Article 32

1. Citizens of Russian Federation shall have the right to participate in the administration of affairs of the State both directly and through their representatives.

2. Citizens of the Russian Federation shall have the right to elect and to be elected to agencies of State power and agencies of local self-government, and also to participate in a referendum.

3. Citizens deemed by a court to lack dispositive legal capacity, and also maintained in places of deprivation of freedom by judgment of a court, shall not have the right to elect and to be elected.

4. Citizens of the Russian Federation shall have equal access to State service.

5. Citizens of the Russian Federation shall have the right to participate in the dispensing of justice.

Article 33

Citizens of the Russian Federation shall have the right to have recourse personally, and also to send individual and collective appeals to State agencies and to agencies of local self-government.

Article 34

1. Each shall have the right to free use of his abilities and property for entrepreneurial and other economic activity not prohibited by a law.

2. Economic activity directed towards monopolization and unfair competition shall not be permitted.

Article 35

1. The right of private ownership shall be protected by a law.

2. Each shall have the right to have property in ownership, possess, use, and dispose of it both as one person and jointly with other persons.

3. No one may be deprived of his property other than by decision of a court. The compulsory alienation of property for State needs may be done only on condition of advance and fair compensation.

4. The right of inheritance shall be guaranteed.

Article 36

1. Citizens and their associations shall have the right to have land in private ownership.

2. The possession, use, and disposition of land and other natural resources shall be effectuated by their owners freely unless this brings damage to the environment and does not violate the rights and legal interests of other persons.

3. The conditions and procedure for the use of land shall be determined on the basis of a federal law.

Article 37

1. Labor shall be free. Each shall have the right to freely dispose of his capabilities to labor and to choose the nature of activity and profession.

2. Forced labor shall be prohibited.

3. Each shall have the right to labor in conditions which meet the requirements of safety and hygiene, to remuneration for labor without any discrimination whatever, and to the minimum amount of payment

for labor established by a federal law, and also the right to defense against unemployment.

4. The right to individual and collective labor disputes with the use of means established by a federal law for the settlement thereof, including the right to strike.

5. Each shall have the right to leisure. The duration of work time, days off and holidays, and paid annual leave established by a federal law shall be guaranteed to a person working under a labor contract.

Article 38

1. Motherhood and childhood and the family shall be under the defense of the State.

2. Concern for children and their nurturing shall be the equal right and duty of the parents.

3. Children capable of labor who have attained 18 years of age must be concerned for parents who are not capable of labor.

Article 39

1. To each shall be guaranteed social security for age, illness, disability, loss of breadwinner, nurturing children, and in other instances established by a law.

2. State pensions and social benefits shall be established by a law.

3. Voluntary social insurance and the creation of additional forms of social security and philanthropy shall be encouraged.

Article 40

1. Each shall have the right to housing. No one may be arbitrarily deprived of housing.

2. Agencies of State power and agencies of local self-government shall encourage housing construction and create conditions for the effectuation of the right to housing.

3. Indigent and other citizens specified in a law who need housing shall be granted such free of charge or for affordable payment from State, municipal, and other housing funds in accordance with norms established by a law.

Article 41

1. Each shall have the right to health protection and medical assistance. Medical assistance in State and municipal public health institutions shall be rendered to citizens free of charge at the expense of assets of the respective budget, insurance contributions, and other proceeds.

2. Federal programs for the protection and strengthening of health of the populace shall be financed in the Russian Federation, measures shall be taken for the development of State, municipal, and private public health systems, activity shall be encouraged which promotes the strengthening of the health of man, the development of physical culture and sport, and ecological and sanitary-epidemiological well-being.

3. The concealment by officials of facts and circumstances threatening human life and health shall entail responsibility in accordance with a federal law.

Article 42

Each shall have the right to a favorable environment, reliable information concerning the state thereof, and compensation for damage caused to his health or property by an ecological violation.

Article 43

1. Each shall have the right to education.

2. The general accessibility of and free preschool, basic general and secondary vocational education in State or municipal educational institutions and at enterprises shall be guaranteed.

3. Each shall have the right on a competitive basis to receive higher education free of charge in a State or municipal educational institution or at an enterprise.

4. Basic general education shall be obligatory. Parents or persons replacing them shall ensure the receipt of basic general education by children.

5. The Russian Federation shall establish federal State educational standards and shall support various forms of education and self-education.

Article 44

1. To each shall be guaranteed the freedom of literary, artistic, scientific, technical, and other types of creativity and teaching. Intellectual property shall be protected by a law.

2. Each shall have the right to participation in cultural life and the use of institutions of culture and of access to cultural valuables.

3. Each shall be obliged to be concerned for the preservation of the historical and cultural heritage and to care for monuments of history and culture.

Article 45

1. The State defense of the rights and freedoms of man and citizen shall be guaranteed in the Russian Federation.

2. Each shall have the right to defend his rights and freedoms by all means not prohibited by a law.

Article 46

1. To each shall be guaranteed the judicial defense of his rights and freedoms.

2. Decisions and actions (or omissions to act) of agencies of State power, agencies of local self-government, social associations, and officials may be appealed to a court.

3. Each shall have the right in accordance with international treaties of the Russian Federation to apply to inter-State agencies for the defense of the rights and freedoms of man if all available intra-State means of legal defense have been exhausted.

Article 47

1. No one may be deprived of the right to consideration of a case in that court and by those judges to whose jurisdiction it has been relegated by a law.

2. A person accused of committing a crime shall have the right to consideration of his case with the participation of jurors in the instances provided for by a federal law.

Article 48

1. To each shall be guaranteed the right to receive qualified legal assistance. In the instances provided for by a law, legal assistance shall be rendered free of charge.

2. Each person detained, confined under guard, or accused of committing a crime shall have the right to take advantage of the assistance of an advocate (or defender) from the moment respectively of the detention, confinement under guard, or presentation of the accusation.

Article 49

1. Each person accused of committing a crime shall be considered to be innocent until his guilt is proved in the procedure provided for by a federal law and established by the judgment of a court which has entered into legal force.

2. An accused person shall not be obliged to prove his innocence.

3. Ineradicable doubts of the guilt of a person shall be interpreted to the benefit of the accused person.

Article 50

1. No one may be convicted a second time for one and the same crime.

2. When effectuating justice, the use of evidence obtained in violation of a federal law shall not be permitted.

3. Each person convicted for a crime shall have the right to a review of the judgment by a superior court in the procedure established by a federal law, and also the right to request a pardon or mitigation of punishment.

Article 51

1. No one may be obliged to testify against himself, his spouse, or near relatives, the group of which shall be determined by a federal law.

2. Other instances of being relieved from the duty to give witness testimony may be established by a federal law.

Article 52

The rights of victims of crimes and abuses of power shall be protected by a law. The State shall ensure the victim access to justice and contributory compensation for damage caused.

Article 53

Each shall have the right to compensation by the State for harm caused by the illegal actions (or omissions to act) of agencies of State power or their officials.

Article 54

1. A law establishing or aggravating responsibility shall not have retroactive force.

2. No one may bear responsibility for an act which at the moment of its commission was not deemed to be a violation of law. If after the commission of a violation of law responsibility therefor has been eliminated or mitigated, the new law shall be applied.

Article 55

1. The enumeration in the Constitution of the Russian Federation of the basic rights and freedoms must not be interpreted as a denial or diminution of other generally-recognized rights and freedoms of man and citizen.

2. Laws abolishing or diminishing the rights and freedoms of man and citizen must not be issued in the Russian Federation.

3. The rights and freedoms of man and citizen may be limited by a federal law only in the extent to which this is necessary for the purposes of defense of the foundations of the constitutional system, morality, health, rights, and legal interests of other persons and ensuring the defense of the country and security of the State.

Article 56

1. Under conditions of an extraordinary situation in order to ensure the safety of citizens and defense of the constitutional system individual limitations of the rights and freedoms may be established by a federal constitutional law, specifying the limits and the period of their operation.

2. An extraordinary situation throughout the entire territory of the Russian Federation and individual localities thereof may be introduced when the circumstances are present and in the procedure established by a federal constitutional law.

3. The rights and freedoms provided for by Articles 20, 21, 23 (paragraph 1), 24, 28, 34 (paragraph 1), 40 (paragraph 1), 46-54 of the Constitution of the Russian Federation shall not be subject to limitation.

Article 57

Each shall be obliged to pay legally established taxes and charges. Laws establishing new taxes or worsening the position of taxpayers shall not have retroactive force.

Article 58

Each shall be obliged to preserve nature and the environment and to care for that relegated to natural wealth.

Article 59

1. Defense of the Fatherland shall be the obligation and duty of a citizen of the Russian Federation.

2. A citizen of the Russian Federation shall bear military service in accordance with a federal law.

3. A citizen of the Russian Federation shall, in the event his convictions or religious belief is contrary to bearing military service, and also in other instances established by a federal law, have the right to replace it with alternative civilian service.

Article 60

A citizen of the Russian Federation may autonomously effectuate his rights and duties in full from 18 years of age.

Article 61

1. A citizen of the Russian Federation may not be deported beyond the limits of the Russian Federation or extradited to another State.

2. The Russian Federation shall guarantee to its citizens defense and protection beyond its limits.

Article 62

1. A citizen of the Russian Federation may have the citizenship of a foreign State (dual citizenship) in accordance with a federal law or international treaty of the Russian Federation.

2. That a citizen of the Russian Federation has the citizenship of a foreign State shall not diminish his rights and freedoms nor relieve him from duties arising from Russian citizenship unless provided otherwise by a federal law or by an international treaty of the Russian Federation.

3. Foreign citizens and stateless persons shall enjoy in the Russian Federation the rights and bear the duties equally with citizens of the Russian Federation except for instances established by a federal law or by an international treaty of the Russian Federation.

Article 63

1. The Russian Federation shall grant political asylum to foreign citizens and stateless persons in accordance with generally-recognized norms of international law.

2. The extradition to other States of persons being persecuted for political convictions, and also for actions (or omission to act) which are not deemed to be a crime in the Russian Federation, shall not be permitted in the Russian Federation. The extradition of persons accused of committing a crime, and also the transfer of convicted persons to serve punishment in other States, shall be effectuated on the basis of a federal law or international treaty of the Russian Federation.

Article 64

The provisions of the present Chapter shall constitute the foundations of the legal status of the person in the Russian Federation and may not be changed other than in the procedure established by the present Constitution.

Chapter 3. Federated Structure

Article 65

1. There shall be subjects within the Russian Federation:

Republic Adygeia (Adygeia), Republic Altai, Republic Bashkortostan, Republic Buriatiia, Republic Dagestan, Republic Ingushetia, Kabardino-

Balkarian Republic, Republic Kalmykiia, Karachaevo-Cherkessy Republic, Republic Karelia, Republic Komi, Republic Crimea, Republic Marii El, Republic Mordovia, Republic Sakha (Iakutia), Republic Northern Osetia-Alania, Republic Tatarstan (Tatarstan), Republic Tyva, Udmurt Republic, Republic Khakasiia, Chechen Republic, Chuvash Republic-Chavashia [as amended by Edicts of the President of the Russian Federation, 9 January 1996, 10 February 1996, 9 June 2001, and Federal Constitutional Law, 21 March 2014, No. 6-ФКЗ];

Altai Territory, Trans-Baikal Territory, Kamchatka Territory, Krasnodar Territory, Krasnoiarsk Territory, Perm Territory, Maritime Territory, Stavropol Territory, Khabarovsk Territory [as amended by Federal Constitutional Law of 25 March 2004 and 21 July 2007];

Amur Region, Arkhangel Region, Astrakhan Region, Belgorod Region, Briansk Region, Vladimir Region, Volgograd Region, Vologda Region, Voronezh Region, Ivanovo Region, Irkutsk Region, Kaliningrad Region, Kaluga Region, Kemerovo Region, Kirov Region, Kostroma Region, Kurgan Region, Kursk Region, Leningrad Region, Lipetsk Region, Magadan Region, Moscow Region, Murmansk Region, Nizhegorod Region, Novgorod Region, Novosibirsk Region, Omsk Region, Orenburg Region, Orlov Region, Penza Region, Pskov Region, Rostov Region, Riazan Region, Samara Region, Saratov Region, Sakhalin Region, Sverdlovsk Region, Smolensk Region, Tambov Region, Tver Region, Tomsk Region, Tula Region, Tiumen Region, Ulianovsk Region, Cheliabinsk Region, Iaroslavl Region;

Moscow, St. Petersburg, Sevastopol – cities of federal significance [as amended by Federal Constitutional Law, 21 March 2014, No. 6-ФКЗ];

Jewish Autonomous Region;

Nenets Autonomous National Area, Khanty-Mansiisk Autonomous National Area-Iurga, Chukotsk Autonomous National Area, Iamalo-Nenets Autonomous National Area [as amended by Edict of the President of the Russian Federation, 25 July 2003, and by Federal Constitutional Laws of 25 March 2004, 14 October 2005, 30 December 2006, and 21 July 2007].

2. The admission to the Russian Federation and the formation within it of a new subject shall be effectuated in the procedure established by a federal constitutional law.

Article 66

1. The status of a republic shall be determined by the Constitution of the Russian Federation and the constitution of the republic.

2. The status of a territory, region, city of federal significance, autonomous region, or autonomous national area shall be determined by the Constitution of the Russian Federation and by the charter of the territory, region, city of federal significance, autonomous region, or autonomous

national area adopted by the legislative (or representative) agency of the respective subject of the Russian Federation.

3. Upon the recommendation of legislative and executive agencies of an autonomous region or autonomous national area, a federal law on the autonomous region or autonomous national area may be adopted.

4. The relations of autonomous national areas within a territory or region may be regulated by a federal law and by a treaty between the agencies of State power of the autonomous region and, respectively, the agencies of State power of the territory or region.

5. The status of a subject of the Russian Federation may be changed by mutual consent of the Russian Federation and the subject of the Russian Federation in accordance with a federal constitutional law.

Article 67

1. The territory of the Russian Federation shall include the territories of its subjects, internal waters, and the territorial sea, and superjacent airspace. Federal territories may be created on the territory of the Russian Federation in accordance with a federal law. The organization of public power on federal territories shall be established by the said federal law [as amended by Federal Constitutional Law, 14 March 2020, No. 1-ФКЗ].

2. The Russian Federation shall possess sovereign rights and effectuate jurisdiction on the continental shelf and in the exclusive economic zone of the Russian Federation in the procedure determined by a federal law and norms of international law.

2^1. The Russian Federation shall ensure the defense of its sovereignty and territorial integrity. Actions (except for delimitation, demarcation, and re-demarcation of the State boundary of the Russian Federation with neighboring States) directed towards the alienation of part of the territory of the Russian Federation, and also appeals for such actions, shall not be permitted [added by Federal Constitutional Law, 14 March 2020, No. 1-ФКЗ].

3. The boundaries between subjects of the Russian Federation may be changed with their mutual consent.

Article 67^1

[added by Federal Constitutional Law, 14 March 2020, No. 1-ФКЗ]

1. The Russian Federation shall be the legal successor of the USSR on its territory, and also the legal successor (or legal continuer) of the USSR with respect to membership in international organizations, organs thereof, participation in international treaties, and also with respect to obligations and assets of the USSR provided for by international treaties beyond the limits of the territory of the Russian Federation.

2. The Russian Federation, united by a thousand-year history, preserving the memory of ancestors and the ideals and faith in God passed on to us, and also succession in the development of the Russian State, shall be deemed a historically-formed State unity.

3. The Russian Federation shall honor the defenders of the Fatherland and ensure the defense of the historical truth. Disparagement of the significance of the exploit of the people during the defense of the Fatherland shall not be permitted.

4. Children shall be the most important priority of State policy of Russia. The State shall create conditions furthering the comprehensive spiritual, moral, intellectual, and physical development of children, the nurturing of patriotism in them, civic spirit, and respect for elders. The State, in ensuring the priority of family nurturing, shall assume the duty of parents with respect to children left without care.

Article 68

1. The Russian language shall, as the language of the State-forming people within the multinational union of equal peoples of the Russian Federation, be the State language of the Russian Federation throughout all of its territory [as amended by Federal Constitutional Law, 14 March 2020, No. 1-ФКЗ].

2. Republics shall have the right to establish their own State languages. They shall be used, together with the State language of the Russian Federation, in agencies of State power, agencies of local self-government, and State institutions of the Republic.

3. The Russian Federation shall guarantee to all of its peoples the right to preservation of the native language and the creation of conditions for its study and development.

4. Culture in the Russian Federation shall be the unique heritage of its multinational people. Culture shall be supported and protected by the State [added by Federal Constitutional Law, 14 March 2020, No. 1-ФКЗ].

Article 69

1. The Russian Federation shall guarantee the rights of native small peoples in accordance with generally-recognized principles and norms of international law and international treaties of the Russian Federation.

2. The State shall defend the cultural uniqueness of all peoples and ethnic communities of the Russian Federation and guarantee the preservation of ethno-cultural and linguistic diversity [added by Federal Constitutional Law, 14 March 2020, No. 1-ФКЗ].

3. The Russian Federation shall render support to compatriots residing abroad in the exercise of their rights, ensuring the defense of their interests,

and preservation of all-Russian cultural identity [added by Federal Constitutional Law, 14 March 2020, No. 1-ФКЗ].

Article 70

1. The State flag, arms, and anthem of the Russian Federation, the description thereof, and the procedure for the official use shall be established by a federal constitutional law.

2. The capital of the Russian Federation shall be the city of Moscow. The status of the capital shall be established by a federal law. The site of permanent sojourn of individual federal agencies of State power may be another city determined by a federal constitutional law [as amended by Federal Constitutional Law, 14 March 2020, No. 1-ФКЗ].

Article 71

There shall be within the jurisdiction of the Russian Federation:

(a) the adoption and change of the Constitution of the Russian Federation and federal laws, and control over compliance therewith;

(b) the federated structure and territory of the Russian Federation;

(c) the regulation and defense of the rights and freedoms of man and citizen; citizenship in the Russian Federation; regulation and defense of the rights of national minorities;

(d) the organization of public power, establishment of the system of federal agencies of legislative, executive, and judicial power, the procedure for their organization and activity; and the formation of federal agencies of State power [as amended by Federal Constitutional Law, 14 March 2020, No. 1-ФКЗ];

(e) federal State ownership and the administration thereof;

(f) the establishment of the fundamental principles of federal policy and federal programs in the domain of State, economic, ecological, scientific-technological, social, cultural, and nationality development of the Russian Federation; the establishment of unified legal foundations of the system of public health, system of nurturing and education, including uninterrupted education [as amended by Federal Constitutional Law, 14 March 2020, No. 1-ФКЗ];

(g) the establishment of the legal foundations of a single market; financial, currency, credit, and customs regulations, monetary emission, foundations of price policy; federal economic services, including federal banks;

(h) federal budget; federal taxes and charges; federal regional development funds;

(i) federal electric power system, nuclear power, fissionable materials; federal transport, railways, information, information technologies and communications; activity in outer space [as amended by Federal Constitutional Law, 14 March 2020, No. 1-ФКЗ];

(j) foreign policy and international relations of the Russian Federation, international treaties of the Russian Federation; questions of war and peace;

(k) foreign economic relations of the Russian Federation;

(l) defense and security; defense production; determination of the procedure for the sale and purchase of weapons, ammunition, combat technology, and other military property; production of poisonous substances, narcotic means, and the procedure for the use thereof; ensuring the security of the person, society, and the State when applying information technologies and turnover of digital data [as amended by Federal Constitutional Law, 14 March 2020, No. 1-ФКЗ];

(m) determination of the status and defense of the State boundary, territorial sea, airspace, exclusive economic zone, and continental shelf of the Russian Federation;

(n) court organization; procuracy; criminal and penal legislation; amnesty and pardon; civil legislation; procedural legislation; legal regulation of intellectual property [as amended by Federal Constitutional Law, 5 February 2014, No. 2-ФКЗ];

(o) federal conflicts of law;

(p) metrological service, standards, metric system, and calculation of time; geodesy and cartography; names of geographic objects; meteorological service; official statistical and bookkeeping records [as amended by Federal Constitutional Law, 14 March 2020, No. 1-ФКЗ];

(q) State awards and titles of honor of the Russian Federation;

(r) federal State service; establishment of limitations for filing State and municipal offices, offices of State and municipal service, including limitations connected with the existence of citizenship of a foreign State or residence permit or other document confirming the right to permanent residence of a citizen of the Russian Federation on the territory of a foreign State, and also limitations connected with the opening and existence of accounts (or deposits) and keeping of cash monetary means and valuables in foreign banks located beyond the limits of the territory of the Russian Federation [as amended by Federal Constitutional Law, 14 March 2020, No. 1-ФКЗ].

Article 72

1. There shall be within the joint jurisdiction of the Russian Federation and the subjects of the Russian Federation:

(a) ensuring the conformity of the constitutions and laws of the republics and the charters, laws, and other normative legal acts of territories, regions, cities of federal significance, autonomous region, and autonomous national areas to the Constitution of the Russian Federation and to federal laws;

(b) defense of the rights and freedoms of man and citizen; defense of the rights of national minorities; ensuring legality, legal order, and public security; the regime of border zones;

(c) questions of the possession, use, and disposition of land, subsoil, water, and other natural resources;

(d) delimitation of State ownership;

(e) nature use; agriculture; protection of the natural environment and ensuring ecological security; specially protected nature territories; protection of monuments of history and culture [as amended by Federal Constitutional Law, 14 March 2020, No. 1-ФКЗ];

(f) general questions of nurturing, education, science, culture, physical culture and sport, youth policy [as amended by Federal Constitutional Law, 14 March 2020, No. 1-ФКЗ];

(g) coordination of questions of public health, including the ensuring of the rendering of accessible and qualitative medical care; preservation and strengthening of public health; creation of conditions for conducting a healthy way of life; forming of a culture of a responsible attitude of citizens to their health; social defense, including social security [as amended by Federal Constitutional Law, 14 March 2020, No. 1-ФКЗ];

(g^1) defense of the family, motherhood, fatherhood, and childhood; defense in the institution of marriage as a union of a man and woman; creation of conditions for the worthy nurturing of children in the family, and also for the effectuation by children who have reached majority of the duty to care for their parents [added by Federal Constitutional Law, 14 March 2020, No. 1-ФКЗ];

(h) effectuation of measures relating to the struggle against catastrophes, natural disasters, epidemics, and liquidation of their consequences;

(i) establishment of general principles of taxation and charges in the Russian Federation;

(j) administrative, administrative procedure, labor, family, housing, land, water, and forest legislation, legislation on the subsoil and on environmental protection;

(k) personnel of judicial and law enforcement agencies; advokatura, notariat;

(l) defense of the natural habitat and traditional way of life of small ethnic communities;

(m) establishment of general principles for the organization of the system of agencies of State power and local self-government;

(n) coordination of international and foreign economic relations of subjects of the Russian Federation, and the fulfillment of international treaties of the Russian Federation.

2. The provisions of the present Article shall in equal measure extend to the republics, territories, regions, cities of federal significance, autonomous region, and autonomous national areas.

Article 73

Beyond the limits of jurisdiction of the Russian Federation and powers of the Russian Federation relating to subject-matter of joint jurisdiction of the Russian Federation and subjects of the Russian Federation, the subjects of the Russian Federation shall possess the entire plenitude of State power.

Article 74

1. The establishment of customs boundaries, duties, charges, and any other hindrances to the free movement of goods, services, and financial means shall not be permitted on the territory of the Russian Federation.

2. Limitations on the movement of goods and services may be introduced in accordance with a federal law if this is necessary in order to ensure security, defense of human life and health, protection of nature, and cultural valuables.

Article 75

1. The monetary unit in the Russian Federation shall be the ruble. Monetary emission shall be effectuated exclusively by the Central Bank of the Russian Federation. The introduction and emission of other monies in the Russian Federation shall not be permitted.

2. The defense of and ensuring the stability of the ruble shall be the principal function of the Central Bank of the Russian Federation, which it shall effectuate independently from other agencies of State power.

3. The system of taxes to be recovered to the federal budget and the general principles of taxation and charges in the Russian Federation shall be established by a federal law.

4. State loans shall be issued in the procedure determined by a federal law and shall be placed on a voluntary basis.

5. The Russian Federation shall respect the labor of citizens and ensure the defense of their rights. A minimum payment for labor no less than the

amount of the living minimum for the able-bodied population as a whole in the Russian Federation shall be guaranteed by the State [added by Federal Constitutional Law, 14 March 2020, No. 1-ФКЗ].

6. A system of pension security for citizens shall be formed in the Russian Federation on the basis of the principles of universality, justness, and solidarity of generations and the effective functioning thereof shall be supported, and also the indexation of pensions shall be effectuated no less frequently than once a year in the procedure established by a federal law [added by Federal Constitutional Law, 14 March 2020, No. 1-ФКЗ].

7. Obligatory social insurance and addressed social support of citizens and indexation of social benefits and other social payments shall be guaranteed in the Russian Federation in accordance with a federal law [added by Federal Constitutional Law, 14 March 2020, No. 1-ФКЗ].

Article 75[1]

[added by Federal Constitutional Law, 14 March 2020, No. 1-ФКЗ]

Conditions shall be created in the Russian Federation for the stable economic growth of the country and enhancing the well-being of citizens and for mutual confidence of the State and society, the defense of the dignity of citizens and respect for a person of labor shall be guaranteed, the balancing of the rights and duties of a citizen, social partnership, and economic, political, and social solidarity shall be ensured.

Article 76

1. Federal constitutional laws and federal laws having direct effect throughout the entire territory of the Russian Federation shall be adopted with regard to the subject-matter of jurisdiction of the Russian Federation.

2. Federal laws and laws and other normative legal acts of subjects of the Russian Federation adopted in accordance therewith shall be issued with regard to the subject-matter of joint jurisdiction of the Russian Federation and subjects of the Russian Federation.

3. Federal laws may not be contrary to federal constitutional laws.

4. Beyond the limits of the jurisdiction of the Russian Federation and the joint jurisdiction of the Russian Federation and subjects of the Russian Federation, the republics, territories, regions, cities of federal significance, autonomous region, and autonomous national areas shall effectuate own legal regulation, including the adoption of laws and other normative legal acts.

5. Laws and other normative legal acts of subjects of the Russian Federation may not be contrary to federal laws adopted in accordance with paragraphs one and two of the present Article. In the event of a contradiction

between a federal law and another act issued in the Russian Federation, the federal law shall operate.

6. In the event of a contradiction between a federal law and a normative legal act of a subject of the Russian Federation issued in accordance with paragraph four of the present Article, the normative legal act of the subject of the Russian Federation shall operate.

Article 77

1. The system of agencies of State power of republics, territories, regions, cities of federal significance, autonomous region, and autonomous national areas shall be established by the subjects of the Russian Federation autonomously in accordance with the foundations of the constitutional system of the Russian Federation and the general principles for organizing representative and executive agencies of State power established by a federal law.

2. Within the limits of the jurisdiction of the Russian Federation and powers of the Russian Federation with regard to the subject-matter of joint jurisdiction of the Russian Federation and the subjects of the Russian Federation, federal agencies of executive power and agencies of executive power of the subjects of the Russian Federation shall form a unified system of executive power in the Russian Federation.

3. A citizen of the Russian Federation who has attained 30 years of age, permanently residing in the Russian Federation, not having the citizenship of a foreign State or residence permit or other document confirming the right to permanent residence of a citizen of the Russian Federation on the territory of a foreign State may be a high official of a subject of the Russian Federation (or executive of a high executive agency of State power of a subject of the Russian Federation). A high official of a subject of the Russian Federation (or executive of a high executive agency of State power of a subject of the Russian Federation) in the procedure established by a federal law shall be prohibited from opening and having accounts (or deposits) and to keep cash monetary means and valuables in foreign banks located beyond the limits of the territory of the Russian Federation. Additional requirements may be established by a federal law for a high official of a subject of the Russian Federation (or executive of a high executive agency of State power of a subject of the Russian Federation) [point 3 added by Federal Constitutional Law, 14 March 2020, No. 1-ФКЗ].

Article 78

1. Federal agencies of executive power may, in order to effectuate their powers, create their territorial agencies and appoint the respective officials.

2. Federal agencies of executive power by agreement with agencies of executive power of subjects of the Russian Federation may transfer to

them the effectuation of part of their powers if this is not contrary to the Constitution of the Russian Federation and federal laws.

3. Agencies of executive power of subjects of the Russian Federation by agreement with federal agencies of executive power may transfer to them the effectuation of part of their powers.

4. The President of the Russian Federation and the Government of the Russian Federation shall ensure in accordance with the Constitution of the Russian Federation the effectuation of the powers of federal State power throughout the entire territory of the Russian Federation.

5. A citizen of the Russian Federation who has attained 30 years of age, not having citizenship of a foreign State or residence permit or other document confirming the right to permanent residence of a citizen of the Russian Federation on the territory of a foreign State may be an executive of a federal State agency. The executive of a federal State agency in the procedure established by a federal law shall be prohibited from opening and having an accounts (or deposits) and to keep cash monetary means and valuables in foreign banks located beyond the limits of the territory of the Russian Federation [point 5 added by Federal Constitutional Law, 14 March 2020, No. 1-ФК3].

Article 79

The Russian Federation may participate in inter-State associations and transfer to them part of its powers in accordance with international treaties of the Russian Federation if this does not entail a limitation of the rights and freedoms of man and citizen and is not contrary to the foundations of the constitutional system of the Russian Federation. Decisions of inter-State agencies adopted on the basis of provisions of international treaties of the Russian Federation in a construction thereof contrary to the Constitution of the Russian Federation shall not be subject to execution in the Russian Federation [as amended by Federal Constitutional Law, 14 March 2020, No. 1-ФК3].

Article 79[1]

[added by Federal Constitutional Law, 14 March 2020, No. 1-ФК3]

The Russian Federation shall take measures relating to the maintenance and strengthening of international peace and security, ensuring of the peaceful coexistence of States and peoples, and not permitting interference in the internal affairs of States.

Chapter 4. President of the Russian Federation

Article 80

1. The President of the Russian Federation shall be the head of State.

2. The President of the Russian Federation shall be the guarantor of the Constitution of the Russian Federation and the rights and freedoms of man and citizen. In the procedure established by the Constitution of the Russian Federation he shall take measures to protect the sovereignty of the Russian Federation, its independence and State integrity, maintain civil peace and amity in the country, and ensure the coordinated functioning and interaction of agencies within the unified system of public power [as amended by Federal Constitutional Law, 14 March 2020, No. 1-ФКЗ].

3. The President of the Russian Federation shall in accordance with the Constitution of the Russian Federation and federal laws determine the basic orientations of internal and foreign policy of the State.

4. The President of the Russian Federation as the head of State shall represent the Russian Federation within the country and in international relations.

Article 81

1. The President of the Russian Federation shall be elected for a term of six years by citizens of the Russian Federation on the basis of universal, equal, and direct suffrage by secret ballot [as amended by Federal Constitutional Law, 30 December 2008, No. 6-ФКЗ].

2. A citizen of the Russian Federation not younger than 35 years and permanently residing in the Russian Federation for no less than 25 years, not having and did not have previously the citizenship of a foreign State or residence permit or other document confirming the right to permanent residence of a citizen of the Russian Federation on the territory of a foreign State may be elected President of the Russian Federation. The requirement for a candidate for the office of President of the Russian Federation concerning his lacking citizenship of a foreign State shall not extend to citizens of the Russian Federation who previously had citizenship of a State which was admitted or part of which was admitted to the Russian Federation in accordance with a federal constitutional law and permanently resided on the territory of the State admitted to the Russian Federation or territory of part of the State admitted to the Russian Federation. The President of the Russian Federation in the procedure established by a federal law shall be prohibited from opening or having an account (or deposits) and to keep cash monetary means and valuables in foreign banks located beyond the territory of the Russian Federation [as amended by Federal Constitutional Law, 14 March 2020, No. 1-ФКЗ].

3. One and the same person may not occupy the office of President of the Russian Federation for more than two terms [as amended by Federal Constitutional Law, 14 March 2020, No. 1-ФКЗ].

3[1]. The provision of Article 81(3) of the Constitution of the Russian Federation limiting the number of terms which one and the same person may hold the office of President of the Russian Federation shall apply to the person who held and/or holds the office of President of the Russian Federation without taking into account the number of terms during which he held and/or holds this office at the moment of entry into force of amendments to the Constitution of the Russian Federation which introduced the respective limitation and shall not exclude for him the possibility to hold the office of President of the Russian Federation during the terms permitted by the said provision [added by Federal Constitutional Law, 14 March 2020, No. 1-ФК3].

4. The procedure for elections of the President of the Russian Federation shall be determined by a federal law.

Article 82

1. When taking up the office, the President of the Russian Federation shall take the following oath to the people:

"I swear when effectuating the powers of President of the Russian Federation to respect and protect the rights and freedoms of man and citizen, to comply with and defend the Constitution of the Russian Federation, to defend the sovereignty and independence, security, and integrity of the State, and to loyally serve the people."

2. The oath shall be taken in a solemn ceremony in the presence of senators of the Russian Federation, deputies of the State Duma, and judges of the Constitutional Court of the Russian Federation [as amended by Federal Constitutional Law, 14 March 2020, No. 1-ФК3].

Article 83

The President of the Russian Federation shall:

(a) appoint the Chairman of the Government of the Russian Federation, whose candidacy is confirmed by the State Duma upon the recommendation of the President of the Russian Federation and relieved the Chairman of the Government of the Russian Federation from office [as amended by Federal Constitutional Law, 14 March 2020, No. 1-ФК3];

(b) effectuate general guidance of the government of the Russian Federation; have the right to preside at sessions of the Government of the Russian Federation [as amended by Federal Constitutional Law, 14 March 2020, No. 1-ФК3];

(b[1]) confirm upon the proposal of the Chairman of the Government of the Russian Federation the structure of federal agencies of executive power and make changes therein; determine agencies in the structure of federal agencies of executive power, direction of whose activity the President of the Russian Federation effectuates, and agencies, the direction of whose activity the Government of the Russian Federation effectuates. If the Chairman of the Government of the Russian Federation is relieved by the President of the Russian Federation from office, the newly-appointed Chairman of the Government of the Russian Federation shall not submit to the President of the Russian Federation proposals concerning the structure of federal agencies of executive power [added by Federal Constitutional Law, 14 March 2020, No. 1-ФКЗ];

(c) take the decision concerning the resignation of the Government of the Russian Federation;

(c^1) accept the resignation of the Chairman of the Government of the Russian Federation, deputy chairmen of the Government of the Russian Federation, federal ministers, and also executives of federal agencies of executive power, the direction of whose activity the President of the Russian Federation effectuates [added by Federal Constitutional Law, 14 March 2020, No. 1-ФКЗ];

(d) submit to the State Duma a candidacy for appointment to the office of Chairman of the Central Bank of the Russian Federation; place before the State Duma the question of relieving from office the Chairman of the Central Bank of the Russian Federation;

(e) appoint to and relieve from office the deputy chairmen of the Government of the Russian Federation and federal ministers whose candidacies have been confirmed by the State Duma (except federal ministers specified in point (e^1) of the present Article) [as amended by Federal Constitutional Law, 14 March 2020, No. 1-ФКЗ];

(e^1) appoint to and relieve from office after consultations with the Soviet of the Federation the executives of federal agencies of executive power (including federal ministers) having jurisdiction over questions of defense, security of the State, internal affairs, justice, foreign affairs, prevention of extraordinary situations, and elimination of the consequences of natural disasters, and public security [added by Federal Constitutional Law, 14 March 2020, No. 1-ФКЗ];

(f) submit to the Soviet of the Federation candidacies for appointment to the office of Chairman of the Constitutional Court of the Russian Federation, Deputy Chairman of the Constitutional Court of the Russian Federation, and judges of the Constitutional Court of the Russian Federation, and Chairman of the Supreme Court of the Russian Federation, Deputy Chairmen of the Supreme Court of the Russian Federation, and judges of the Supreme Court of the Russian Federation; appoint chairmen, deputy chairmen, and judges of other federal courts [as amended Federal Constitutional Law, 21 March 2014, No. 6-ФКЗ, and Federal Constitutional Law, 14 March 2020, No. 1-ФКЗ];

(f^1) appoint to and relieve from office, after consultations with the Soviet of the Federation, the Procurator General of the Russian Federation, deputies of the Procurator General of the Russian Federation, procurators of subjects of the Russian Federation, procurators of military and other specialized procuracies equated to procurators of subjects of the Russian Federation; appoint to and relieve from office other procurators for whom such procedure of appointment and relieving from office has been established by a federal law [added by Federal Constitutional Law, 21 March 2014, No. 6-ФКЗ, as amended by Federal Constitutional Law, 14 March 2020, No. 1-ФКЗ];

(f^2) appoint and relieve representatives of the Russian Federation to the Soviet of the Federation [added by Federal Constitutional Law, 21 July 2014, No. 11-ФКЗ];

(f^3) submit to the Soviet of the Federation a recommendation concerning the termination in accordance with a federal constitutional law the powers of the Chairman of the Constitutional Court of the Russian Federation, deputy chairman of the Constitutional Court of the Russian Federation, and judges of the Constitutional Court of the Russian Federation, Chairman of the Supreme Court of the Russian Federation, deputy chairmen of the Supreme Court of the Russian Federation, and judges of the Supreme Court of the Russian Federation, chairmen, deputy chairmen, and judges of cassational and appellate courts in the event of the commission by them of an offense disgracing the honor and dignity of a judge, and also in other instances provided by a federal constitutional law testifying to the impossibility of the effectuation by a judge of his powers [added by Federal Constitutional Law, 14 March 2020, No. 1-ФКЗ];

(f^4) submit to the Soviet of the Federation candidacies for appointment to the office of Chairman of the Chamber of Accounts and half of the total number of auditors of the Chamber of Accounts; submit to the State Duma candidacies for appointment to the office of deputy chairman of the Chamber of Accounts and half of the total number of auditors of the Chamber of Accounts [added by Federal Constitutional Law, 14 March 2020, No. 1-ФКЗ];

(f^5) form the State Council of the Russian Federation for the purposes of ensuring the coordinated functioning and interaction of agencies of public power, determination of the basic orientations of internal and foreign policy of the Russian Federation, and priority orientations of the socio-economic development of the State; the status of the State Council of the Russian Federation shall be determined by a federal law [added by Federal Constitutional Law, 14 March 2020, No. 1-ФКЗ];

(g) form the Security Council of the Russian Federation for the purposes of assisting the Head of State in the realization of his powers with regard to questions of ensuring the national interests and security of the person, society, and the State, and also maintain civic peace and amity in the country, protection of the sovereignty of the Russian Federation, the independence and State integrity thereof, prevention of internal and external threats; head the Security Council of the Russian Federation. The status of the Security

Council of the Russian Federation shall be determined by a federal law [as amended by Federal Constitutional Law, 14 March 2020, No. 1-ФКЗ];

(h) confirm the military doctrine of the Russian Federation;

(i) form the Administration of the President of the Russian Federation for the purposes of ensuring the realization of his powers [as amended by Federal Constitutional Law, 14 March 2020, No. 1-ФКЗ];

(j) appoint and relieve plenipotentiary representatives of the President of the Russian Federation;

(k) appoint and relieve the high command of the Armed Forces of the Russian Federation;

(l) appoint and recall after consultations with the respective committees or commissions of the chambers of the Federal Assembly diplomatic representatives of the Russian Federation to foreign States and international organizations.

Article 84

The President of the Russian Federation shall:

(a) designate elections of the State Duma in accordance with the Constitution of the Russian Federation and a federal law;

(b) dissolve the State Duma in the instances and procedure provided for by the Constitution of the Russian Federation;

(c) designate a referendum in the procedure established by a federal constitutional law;

(d) submit draft laws to the State Duma;

(e) sign and promulgate federal laws;

(f) address the Federal Assembly with annual messages on the situation in the country and the basic orientations of internal and foreign policy of the State.

Article 85

1. The President of the Russian Federation may use conciliation procedures in order to settle disagreements between agencies of State power of the Russian Federation and agencies of State power of subjects of the Russian Federation, and also between agencies of State power of subjects of the Russian Federation. In the event of the failure to reach an agreed decision, he may transfer settlement of the dispute for consideration of the respective court.

2. The President of the Russian Federation shall have the right to suspend the operation of acts of agencies of executive power of subjects of the

Russian Federation in the event these acts are contrary to the Constitution of the Russian Federation and federal laws or international obligations of the Russian Federation or violate the rights and freedoms of man and citizen until this question is decided by the respective court.

Article 86

The President of the Russian Federation shall:

(a) effectuate guidance over the foreign policy of the Russian Federation;

(b) conduct negotiations and sign international treaties of the Russian Federation;

(c) sign instruments of ratification;

(d) accept credentials and letters of recall of diplomatic representatives accredited to him.

Article 87

1. The President of the Russian Federation shall be the Supreme Commander-in-Chief of the Armed Forces of the Russian Federation.

2. In the event of aggression against the Russian Federation or a direct threat of aggression the President of the Russian Federation shall introduce a military situation on the territory of the Russian Federation or in individual localities thereof, immediately notifying the Soviet of the Federation and the State Duma thereof.

3. The regime of a military situation shall be determined by a federal constitutional law.

Article 88

The President of the Russian Federation shall, under the circumstances and in the procedure provided for by a federal constitutional law, introduce on the territory of the Russian Federation or in individual localities thereof an extraordinary situation, immediately notifying the Soviet Federation and the State Duma thereof.

Article 89

The President of the Russian Federation shall:

(a) decide questions of citizenship of the Russian Federation and grant political asylum;

(b) award State awards of the Russian Federation, confer titles of honor of the Russian Federation and the highest military and highest special ranks;

(c) effectuate a pardon.

Article 90

1. The President of the Russian Federation shall issue edicts and regulations.

2. Edicts and regulations of the President of the Russian Federation shall be binding for execution throughout the entire territory of the Russian Federation.

3. Edicts and regulations of the President of the Russian Federation must not be contrary to the Constitution of the Russian Federation and federal laws.

Article 91

The President of the Russian Federation shall possess inviolability.

Article 92

1. The President of the Russian Federation shall embark upon the performance of powers from the moment of taking the oath and shall terminate the performance thereof with the expiry of the period of his sojourn in office from the moment of the newly elected President of the Russian Federation taking the oath.

2. The President of the Russian Federation shall terminate the performance of powers before time in the event of his resignation, becoming unable by reason of state of health to effectuate the powers belonging to him, or impeachment. In so doing elections of the President of the Russian Federation must take place not later than three months from the moment of the termination of the performance of powers before time.

3. In all instances when the President of the Russian Federation is not in a state to fulfill his duties, the Chairman of the Government of the Russian Federation shall perform them. The person performing the duties of the President of the Russian Federation shall not have the right to dissolve the State Duma, designate a referendum, nor make proposals concerning amendments to and the revision of provisions of the Constitution of the Russian Federation.

Article 92^1

[added by Federal Constitutional Law, 14 March 2020, No. 1-ФКЗ]

1. The President of the Russian Federation who has terminated the execution of powers in connection with the expiration of the term of sojourn in office or before time in the event of his resignation or stable inability for reasons of state of health to effectuate the powers belonging to him shall possess inviolability.

2. Other guarantees to the President of the Russian Federation who has terminated the execution of powers in connection with the expiration of the

term of his sojourn in office or before time in the event of his resignation or stable inability for reasons of health to effectuate the powers belonging to him shall be established by a federal law.

3. The President of the Russian Federation who has terminated the execution of his powers may be deprived of inviolability in the procedure provided by Article 93 of the Constitution of the Russian Federation.

Article 93

1. The President of the Russian Federation may be removed from office, and a President of the Russian Federation who has terminated the execution of his powers and deprived of inviolability by the Soviet of the Federation only on the basis of an accusation put forward by the State Duma of treason to the State or commission of another grave crime confirmed by an opinion of the Supreme Court of the Russian Federation concerning the existence in the actions of the President of the Russian Federation, both acting and who has terminated the execution of his powers, of the indicia of a crime and opinion of the Constitutional Court of the Russian Federation concerning compliance with the established procedure for putting forward the accusation [as amended by Federal Constitutional Law, 14 March 2020, No. 1-ФКЗ].

2. The decision of the State Duma to put forward an accusation and the decision of the Soviet of the Federation to remove the President of the Russian Federation from office, or the deprivation of inviolability of a President of the Russian Federation who has terminated the execution of his powers, must be adopted by two-thirds of the votes of the total number, respectively, of the senators of the Russian Federation and deputies of the State Duma at the initiative of no less than one-third of the deputies of the State Duma and in the presence of an opinion of a special commission formed by the State Duma [as amended by Federal Constitutional Law, 14 March 2020, No. 1-ФКЗ].

3. The decision of the Soviet of the Federation to remove the President of the Russian Federation from office or the deprivation of inviolability of the President of the Russian Federation who has terminated the execution of his powers, must be adopted no later than within a three-month period after the State Duma put forward the accusation against the President of the Russian Federation. If within this period the decision of the Soviet of the Federation is not adopted, the accusation against the President of the Russian Federation or the President of the Russian Federation who has terminated the execution of his powers shall be considered to be rejected [as amended by Federal Constitutional Law, 14 March 2020, No. 1-ФКЗ].

Chapter 5. The Federal Assembly

Article 94

The Federal Assembly – the parliament of the Russian Federation – shall be the representative and legislative agency of the Russian Federation.

Article 95

1. The Federal Assembly shall consist of two chambers – the Soviet of the Federation and the State Duma.

2. The Soviet of the Federation shall consist of senators of the Russian Federation [as amended by Federal Constitutional Law, 14 March 2020, No. 1-ФКЗ].

In the Soviet of the Federation shall be:

(a) two representatives from each subject of the Russian Federation: one each from the legislative (representative) and executive agencies of State power – for the term of powers of the respective agency [as amended by Federal Constitutional Law, 14 March 2020, No. 1-ФКЗ];

(b) the President of the Russian Federation who has terminated the execution of his powers in connection with the expiration of the term of his sojourn in office or before time in the event of his resignation – for life. A President of the Russian Federation who has terminated the execution of his powers in connection with the expiration of the term of his sojourn in office or before time in the event of his resignation shall have the right to renounce the powers of a senator of the Russian Federation [added by Federal Constitutional Law, 14 March 2020, No. 1-ФКЗ];

(c) no more than 30 representatives of the Russian Federation to be appointed by the President of the Russian Federation, of which no more than seven may be appointed for life [as amended by Federal Constitutional Law, 21 July 2014, No. 11-ФКЗ, and by Federal Constitutional Law, 14 March 2020, No. 1-ФКЗ].

3. The total number of senators of the Russian Federation shall be determined by proceeding from the number of representatives from subjects of the Russian Federation enumerated in Article 65 of the Constitution of the Russian Federation and the number of persons effectuating the powers of senators of the Russian Federation specified in point 2(b) and (c) of the present Article [added by Federal Constitutional Law, 21 July 2014, No. 11-ФКЗ, as amended by Federal Constitutional Law, 14 March 2014, No. 1-ФКЗ].

4. A citizen of the Russian Federation who has attained 30 years of age, permanently residing in the Russian Federation, not having the citizenship of a foreign State or residence permit or other document confirming the right to permanent residence of a citizen of the Russian Federation on the territory of a foreign State may be a senator of the Russian Federation.

Senators of the Russian Federation in the procedure established by a federal law shall be prohibited from opening and having accounts (or deposits) and keeping cash monetary means and valuables in foreign banks located beyond the limits of the territory of the Russian Federation [added by Federal Constitutional Law, 14 March 2020, No. 1-ФКЗ].

5. Citizens having outstanding services to the country in the sphere of State and social activity may be appointed as representatives of the Russian Federation to the Soviet of the Federation effectuating the powers of senators of the Russian Federation for life [added by Federal Constitutional Law, 14 March 2020, No. 1-ФКЗ].

6. Representatives of the Russian Federation in the Soviet of the Federation, except for representatives of the Russian Federation effectuating the powers of senators of the Russian Federation for life, shall be appointed for a term of six years [added by Federal Constitutional Law, 21 July 2014, No. 11-ФКЗ; as renumbered and amended by Federal Constitutional Law, 14 March 2020, No. 1-ФКЗ].

7. The State Duma shall consist of 450 deputies [renumbered by Federal Constitutional Law, 14 March 2020, No. 1-ФКЗ].

Article 96

1. The State Duma shall be elected for a term of five years [as amended by Federal Constitutional Law, 30 December 2008, No. 6-ФКЗ].

2. The procedure for the formation of the Soviet of the Federation and the procedure for elections of the State Duma shall be established by federal laws.

Article 97

1. A citizen of the Russian Federation who has attained 21 years of age and has the right to participate in elections, permanently residing in the Russian Federation, not having the citizenship of a foreign State or residence permit or other document confirming the right to permanent residence of a citizen of the Russian Federation on the territory of a foreign State, may be elected a deputy of the State Duma. Deputies of the State Duma in the procedure established by a federal law shall be prohibited from opening and having accounts (or deposits) or keeping cash monetary means and valuables in foreign banks located beyond the limits of the territory of the Russian Federation [as amended by Federal Constitutional Law, 14 March 2020, No. 1-ФКЗ].

2. One and the same person may not be simultaneously a senator of the Soviet of the Federation and a deputy of the State Duma. A deputy of the State Duma may not be a deputy of other representative agencies of State power and agencies of local self-government [as amended by Federal Constitutional Law, 14 March 2020, No. 1-ФКЗ].

3. Deputies of the State Duma shall work on a professional permanent basis. Deputies of the State Duma may not be in State service and engage in other paid activity, except for teaching, scientific, and other creative activity.

Article 98

1. Senators of the Russian Federation and deputies of the State Duma shall possess inviolability throughout the entire term of their powers. They may not be detained, arrested, subjected to search, except for instances of detention at the site of a crime, and also subjected to personal inspection, except for instances when this has been provided for by a federal law in order to ensure the safety of other people [as amended by Federal Constitutional Law, 14 March 2020, No. 1-ФКЗ].

2. The question of deprivation of inviolability shall be decided upon the recommendation of the Procurator General of the Russian Federation by the respective chamber of the Federal Assembly.

Article 99

1. The Federal Assembly shall be a permanently operating agency.

2. The State Duma shall assemble for the first session on the thirtieth day after election. The President of the Russian Federation may convoke a session of the State Duma earlier than this period.

3. The first session of the State Duma shall be opened by the deputy most senior in age.

4. From the moment of the commencement of work of the State Duma, new convocation, the powers of the State Duma of the previous convocation shall terminate.

Article 100

1. The Soviet of the Federation and the State Duma shall sit separately.

2. Sessions of the Soviet of the Federation and the State Duma shall be open. In the instances provided for by the Reglament of the chamber, it shall have the right to hold closed sessions.

3. The chambers may assemble jointly in order to hear messages of the President of the Russian Federation [point 3 as amended by Federal Constitutional Law, 14 March 2020, No. 1-ФКЗ].

Article 101

1. The Soviet of the Federation shall elect from its membership the Chairman of the Soviet of the Federation and his deputies. The State Duma shall elect from its membership the Chairman of the State Duma and his deputies.

2. The Chairman of the Soviet of the Federation and his deputies and the Chairman of the State Duma and his deputies shall conduct sessions and the internal order of the chamber.

3. The Soviet of the Federation and the State Duma shall form committees and commissions and hold parliamentary hearings regarding questions within their jurisdiction.

4. Each chamber shall adopt its own Reglament and decide questions of internal order of its activity.

5. In order to effectuate control over the execution of the federal budget the Soviet of the Federation and the State Duma shall form the Chamber of Accounts, the membership and procedure for the activity of which shall be determined by a federal law.

Article 102

1. There shall be relegated to the jurisdiction of the Soviet of the Federation:

(a) confirmation of changes of boundaries between subjects of the Russian Federation;

(b) confirmation of an edict of the President of the Russian Federation concerning the introduction of a military situation;

(c) confirmation of an edict of the President of the Russian Federation concerning the introduction of an extraordinary situation;

(d) deciding of the question of the possibility of the use of the Armed Forces of the Russian Federation beyond the limits of the territory of the Russian Federation;

(e) designation of elections of the President of the Russian Federation;

(f) removal of the President of the Russian Federation from office; deprivation of inviolability of the President of the Russian Federation who has terminated the execution of his powers [as amended by Federal Constitutional Law, 14 March 2020, No. 1-ФК3];

(g) appointment to office upon the recommendation of the President of the Russian Federation of the chairman of the Constitutional Court of the Russian Federation, Deputy Chairman of the Constitutional Court of the Russian Federation, and judges of the Constitutional Court of the Russian Federation, Chairman of the Supreme Court of the Russian Federation, deputy chairmen of the Supreme Court of the Russian Federation, and judges of the Supreme Court of the Russian Federation [as amended by Federal Constitutional Law, 5 February 2014, and Federal Constitutional Law, 14 March 2020, No. 1-ФК3];

(h) hold consultations with regard to proposals by the President of the Russian Federation for candidacies for the office of the Procurator General of the Russian Federation, deputies of the Procurator General of the Russian Federation, procurators of subjects of the Russian Federation, procurators of military and other specialized procuracies equated to procurators of subjects of the Russian Federation [as amended by Federal Constitutional Law, 5 February 2014, and Federal Constitutional Law, 14 March 2020, No. 1-ФКЗ];

(i) appointment to and relieving from office of the Chairman of the Chamber of Accounts and half of the total number of auditors of the Chamber of Accounts, upon the recommendation of the President of the Russian Federation [as amended by Federal Constitutional Law, 14 March 2020, No. 1-ФКЗ];

(j) hold consultations with regard to proposals by the President of the Russian Federation for candidacies for the office of executives of federal agencies of executive power (including federal ministries) having jurisdiction over questions of defense, security of the State, internal affairs, justice, foreign affairs, prevention of extraordinary situations and elimination of the consequences of natural calamities, and public security [added by Federal Constitutional Law, 14 March 2020, No. 1-ФКЗ];

(k) termination upon the recommendation of the President of the Russian Federation in accordance with a federal constitutional law of the powers of the Chairman of the Constitutional Court of the Russian Federation, Deputy Chairman of the Constitutional Court of the Russian Federation, and judges of the Constitutional Court of the Russian Federation, Chairman of the Supreme Court of the Russian Federation, Deputy Chairmen of the Supreme Court of the Russian Federation, and judges of the Supreme Court of the Russian Federation, chairmen, deputy chairmen, and judges of cassational and appellate courts in the event of the commission by them of an offense disparaging the honor and dignity of a judge, and also in other instances provided by a federal constitutional law testifying to the impossibility of the effectuation by judges of their powers [added by Federal Constitutional Law, 14 March 2020, No. 1-ФКЗ];

(l) hearing annual reports of the Procurator General of the Russian Federation on the state of legality and legal order in the Russian Federation [added by Federal Constitutional Law, 14 March 2020, No. 1-ФКЗ].

2. The Soviet of the Federation shall adopt decrees regarding questions relegated to its jurisdiction by the Constitution of the Russian Federation.

3. Decrees of the Soviet of the Federation shall be adopted by a majority of votes of the total number of senators of the Soviet of the Federation unless another procedure for the adoption of decisions has been provided

for by the Constitution of the Russian Federation [as amended by Federal Constitutional Law, 14 March 2020, No. 1-ФКЗ].

Article 103

1. There shall be relegated to the jurisdiction of the State Duma:

(a) confirmation upon the recommendation of the President of the Russian Federation of the candidacy of the Chairman of the Government of the Russian Federation [as amended by Federal Constitutional Law, 14 March 2020, No. 1-ФКЗ];

(a^1) confirmation upon the recommendation of the Chairman of the Government of the Russian Federation of candidacies for Deputy Chairmen of the Government of the Russian Federation and federal ministers, except for federal ministers specified in Article 83(e^1) of the Constitution of the Russian Federation [added by Federal Constitutional Law, 14 March 2020, No. 1-ФКЗ];

(b) deciding the question of confidence in the Government of the Russian Federation;

(c) hearing annual reports of the Government of the Russian Federation on the results of its activity, including questions put by the State Duma [added and renumbered by Federal Constitutional Law, 30 December 2008, No. 7-ФКЗ];

(d) appointing to and relieving from office the Chairman of the Central Bank of the Russian Federation;

(d^1) hearing annual reports of the Central Bank of the Russian Federation [added by Federal Constitutional Law, 14 March 2020, No. 1-ФКЗ];

(e) appointment to and relieving from office the Deputy Chairman of the Chamber of Accounts and half of the total number of auditors of the Chamber of Accounts upon the recommendation of the President of the Russian Federation [as amended by Federal Constitutional Law, 14 March 2020, No. 1-ФКЗ];

(f) appointment to and relieving from office the Plenipotentiary for Human Rights acting in accordance with a federal constitutional law. A citizen of the Russian Federation permanently residing in the Russian Federation, not having the citizenship of a foreign State or residence permit or other document confirming the right to permanent residence of a citizen of the Russian Federation on the territory of a foreign State, may be the Plenipotentiary for Human Rights. The Plenipotentiary for Human Rights in the procedure established by a federal law shall be prohibited from opening and having accounts (or deposits) and keeping cash monetary means and valuables in foreign banks located beyond the limits of the territory of the

Russian Federation [as amended by Federal Constitutional Law, 14 March 2020, No. 1-ФКЗ];

(g) declaration of an amnesty;

(h) putting forward an accusation against the President of the Russian Federation for the purposes of removing him from office or against a President of the Russian Federation who has terminated the execution of his powers for the purposes of depriving him of inviolability [as amended by Federal Constitutional Law, 14 March 2020, No. 1-ФКЗ].

2. The State Duma shall adopt decrees regarding questions relegated to its jurisdiction by the Constitution of the Russian Federation.

3. Decrees of the State Duma shall be adopted by a majority of the votes of the total number of deputies of the State Duma unless another procedure has been provided to adopt decisions by the Constitution of the Russian Federation.

Article 103[1]

[added by Federal Constitutional Law, 14 March 2020, No. 1-ФКЗ]

The Soviet of the Federation and the State Duma shall have the right to effectuate parliamentary control, including to send parliamentary queries to executives of State agencies and agencies of local self-government with regard to questions within the competence of these agencies and officials. The procedure for the effectuation of parliamentary control shall be determined by federal laws and reglaments of chambers of the Federal Assembly.

Article 104

1. The right of legislative initiative shall belong to the President of the Russian Federation, the Soviet of the Federation, senators of the Russian Federation, deputies of the State Duma, the Government of the Russian Federation, and legislative (or representative) agencies of subjects of the Russian Federation. The right of legislative initiative shall also belong to the Constitutional Court of the Russian Federation and the Supreme Court of the Russian Federation with regard to questions of their jurisdiction [as amended by Federal Constitutional Law, 5 February 2014, No. 2-ФКЗ, and by Federal Constitutional Law, 14 March 2020, No. 1-ФКЗ].

2. Draft laws shall be submitted to the State Duma.

3. Draft laws concerning the introduction or abolition of taxes, exemption from the payment thereof, the issuance of State loans, change of financial obligations of the State, and other draft laws providing for expenses to be covered at the expense of the federal budget may be submitted only when there is an opinion of the Government of the Russian Federation.

Article 105

1. Federal laws shall be adopted by the State Duma.

2. Federal laws shall be adopted by a majority vote of the total number of deputies of the State Duma unless provided otherwise by the Constitution of the Russian Federation.

3. Federal laws adopted by the State Duma shall be transferred within five days for consideration by the Soviet of the Federation.

4. A federal law shall be considered to be approved by the Soviet of the Federation if more than half of the total number of members of this chamber has voted for it or if within fourteen days it was not considered by the Soviet of the Federation. In the event of the rejection of a federal law by the Soviet of the Federation, the chambers may create a conciliation commission in order to overcome disagreements which have arisen, after which the federal law shall be subject to consideration a second time by the State Duma.

5. In the event that the State Duma fails to agree with the decision of the Soviet of the Federation, a federal law shall be considered to be adopted if during the second vote not less than two thirds of the total number of deputies of the State Duma have voted for it.

Article 106

Federal laws adopted by the State Duma shall be subject to obligatory consideration in the Soviet of the Federation with regard to questions of:

(a) the federal budget;

(b) federal taxes and charges;

(c) financial, currency, credit, customs regulation, monetary emission;

(d) ratification and denunciation of international treaties of the Russian Federation;

(e) status and defense of the State boundary of the Russian Federation;

(f) war and peace.

Article 107

1. A federal law adopted shall be sent within five days to the President of the Russian Federation for signature and promulgation.

2. The President of the Russian Federation shall sign the federal law within fourteen days and promulgate it.

3. If the President of the Russian Federation within fourteen days from the moment of receipt of a federal law rejects it, the State Duma and the Soviet of the Federation shall in the procedure established by the Constitution

of the Russian Federation consider the said law anew. If during a second consideration a federal law is approved in the version previously adopted by a majority of no less than two-thirds of the votes of the total number of senators of the Russian Federation and deputies of the State Duma, it shall be subject to signature by the President of the Russian Federation within seven days and to promulgation. If the President of the Russian Federation within the said period applies to the Constitutional Court of the Russian Federation with a query concerning verification of the constitutionality of the federal law, the period for the signature of such law shall be suspended during the consideration of the query by the Constitutional Court of the Russian Federation. If the Constitutional Court of the Russian Federation confirms the constitutionality of the federal law, the President of the Russian Federation shall sign it within a three-day period from the moment of the Constitutional Court of the Russian Federation rendering the respective decision. Unless the Constitutional Court of the Russian Federation confirms the constitutionality of the federal law, the President of the Russian Federation shall return it to the State Duma without signature [as amended by Federal Constitutional Law, 14 March 2020, No. 1-ФКЗ].

Article 108

1. Federal constitutional laws shall be adopted with regard to questions provided for by the Constitution of the Russian Federation.

2. A federal constitutional law shall be considered to be adopted if it was approved by a majority of no less than three-quarters of the votes of the total number of senators of the Russian Federation and no less than two-thirds of the votes of the total number of deputies of the State Duma. A federal constitutional law adopted shall be subject to signature within fourteen days by the President of the Russian Federation and to promulgation. If the President of the Russian Federation within the said period applies to the Constitutional Court of the Russian Federation with a query concerning verification of the constitutionality of the federal constitutional law, the period for the signature of such law shall be suspended during the consideration of the query by the Constitutional Court of the Russian Federation. If the Constitutional Court of the Russian Federation confirms the constitutionality of the federal constitutional law, the President of the Russian Federation shall sign it within a three-day period from the moment of rendering by the Constitutional Court of the Russian Federation of the respective decision. If the Constitutional Court of the Russian Federation does not confirm the constitutionality of the federal constitutional law, the President of the Russian Federation shall return it to the State Duma without signature [as amended by Federal Constitutional Law, 14 March 2020, No. 1-ФКЗ].

Article 109

1. The State Duma may be dissolved by the President of the Russian Federation in the instances provided for by Articles 111, 112, and 117 of the Constitution of the Russian Federation [as amended by Federal Constitutional Law, 14 March 2020, No. 1-ФКЗ].

2. In the event of the dissolution of the State Duma the President of the Russian Federation shall designate the date of elections so that the newly elected State Duma shall assemble not later than within four months from the moment of dissolution.

3. The State Duma may not be dissolved on the grounds provided for by Article 117 of the Constitution of the Russian Federation within a year after its election.

4. The State Duma may not be dissolved from the moment of putting forward an accusation against the President of the Russian Federation until the adoption of a respective decision by the Soviet of the Federation.

5. The State Duma may not be dissolved during the period of the operation throughout the territory of the Russian Federation of a military or extraordinary situation, and also within six months before the ending of the term of powers of the President of the Russian Federation.

Chapter 6. Government of the Russian Federation

Article 110

1. The Government of the Russian Federation shall, under the general guidance of the President of the Russian Federation, effectuate executive power of the Russian Federation [as amended by Federal Constitutional Law, 14 March 2020, No. 1-ФКЗ].

2. The Government of the Russian Federation shall consist of the Chairman of the Government of the Russian Federation, the deputy chairmen of the Government of the Russian Federation, and federal ministers.

3. The Government of the Russian Federation shall direct the activity of federal agencies of executive power, except for federal agencies of executive power, the direction of whose activity the President of the Russian Federation effectuates [added by Federal Constitutional Law, 14 March 2020, No. 1-ФКЗ].

4. A citizen of the Russian Federation who has attained 30 years of age, not having the citizenship of a foreign State or residence permit or other document confirming the right to permanent residence of a citizen of the Russian Federation on the territory of a foreign State, may be the Chairman of the Government of the Russian Federation, Deputy Chairman of the Government of the Russian Federation, federal minister, or other executive

of a federal agency of executive power. The Chairman of the Government of the Russian Federation, Deputy Chairmen of the Government of the Russian Federation, federal ministers, or other executives of federal agencies of executive power in the procedure established by a federal law shall be prohibited from opening and having accounts (or deposits) and to keep cash monetary means and valuables in foreign banks located beyond the limits of the territory of the Russian Federation [added by Federal Constitutional Law, 14 March 2020, No. 1-ФКЗ].

Article 111

1. The Chairman of the Government of the Russian Federation shall be appointed by the President of the Russian Federation after confirmation of his candidacy by the State Duma [as amended by Federal Constitutional Law, 14 March 2020, No. 1-ФКЗ].

2. A recommendation with regard to the candidacy of the Chairman of the Government of the Russian Federation shall be submitted to the State Duma by the President of the Russian Federation no later than within two weeks after the newly elected President of the Russian Federation takes office or after the resignation of the Government of the Russian Federation or within a week from the date of the State Duma rejecting the candidacy of the Chairman of the Government of the Russian Federation or the relieving by the President of the Russian Federation from office or resignation of the Chairman of the Government of the Russian Federation [as amended by Federal Constitutional Law, 14 March 2020, No. 1-ФКЗ].

3. The State Duma shall consider the candidacy recommended by the President of the Russian Federation for Chairman of the Government of the Russian Federation within a week from the day of submitting the recommendation [as amended by Federal Constitutional Law, 14 March 2020, No. 1-ФКЗ].

4. After the State Duma rejecting three times the candidacies recommended for Chairman of the Government of the Russian Federation, the President of the Russian Federation shall appoint the Chairman of the Government of the Russian Federation. In this event the President of the Russian Federation shall have the right to dissolve the State Duma and designate new elections [as amended by Federal Constitutional Law, 14 March 2020, No. 1-ФКЗ].

Article 112

1. The Chairman of the Government of the Russian Federation shall no later than a week after appointment submit to the President of the Russian Federation proposals concerning the structure of the federal agencies of executive power, except for an instance when the preceding Chairman of the Government of the Russian Federation is relieved from office by the

President of the Russian Federation [as amended by Federal Constitutional Law, 14 March 2020, No. 1-ФКЗ].

2. The Chairman of the Government of the Russian Federation shall submit to the State Duma candidacies for deputy chairmen of the Government of the Russian Federation and federal ministers (except for federal ministers specified in Article 83(e[1]) of the Constitution of the Russian Federation). The State Duma within no later than a week shall adopt a decision with regard to the recommended candidacies [as amended by Federal Constitutional Law, 14 March 2020, No. 1-ФКЗ].

3. The deputy chairmen of the Government of the Russian Federation and federal ministers whose candidacies have been confirmed by the State Duma shall be appointed to office by the President of the Russian Federation. The President of the Russian Federation shall not have the right to refuse to appoint to office the deputy chairmen of the Government of the Russian Federation and federal ministers whose candidacies have been confirmed by the State Duma [added by Federal Constitutional Law, 14 March 2020, No. 1-ФКЗ].

4. After the State Duma rejecting three times the candidacies submitted in accordance with point 2 of the present Article for deputy chairmen of the Government of the Russian Federation and federal ministers, the President of the Russian Federation shall have the right to appoint the deputy chairmen of the Government of the Russian Federation and federal ministers from among the candidacies submitted by the Chairman of the Government of the Russian Federation. If after the State Duma rejecting three times the candidacies submitted in accordance with point 2 of the present Article more than one-third of the offices of members of the Government of the Russian Federation (except for the offices of federal ministers specified in Article 83(e[1]) of the Constitution of the Russian Federation) remain vacant, the President of the Russian Federation shall have the right to dissolve the State Duma and designate new elections [added by Federal Constitutional Law, 14 March 2020, No. 1-ФКЗ].

5. In the event provided by Article 111(4) of the Constitution of the Russian Federation, and also in the event of the dissolution of the State Duma in accordance with the Constitution of the Russian Federation, the President of the Russian Federation shall appoint the deputy chairmen of the Government of the Russian Federation and federal ministers (except for federal ministers specified in Article 83(e[1]) of the Constitution of the Russian Federation) upon the recommendation of the Chairman of the Government of the Russian Federation [added by Federal Constitutional Law, 14 March 2020, No. 1-ФКЗ].

Article 113

The Chairman of the Government of the Russian Federation shall in accordance with the Constitution of the Russian Federation and federal laws and edicts, regulations, and assignments of the President of the Russian Federation organize the work of the Government of the Russian Federation. The Chairman of the Government of the Russian Federation shall bear personal responsibility to the President of the Russian Federation for the effectuation of powers placed on the Government of the Russian Federation [as amended by Federal Constitutional Law, 14 March 2020, No. 1-ФК3].

Article 114

1. The Government of the Russian Federation shall:

(a) work out and submit to the State Duma the federal budget and ensure its execution; submit to the State Duma the report concerning execution of the federal budget; submit to the State Duma reports concerning the results of its activity, including on questions put by the State Duma [as amended by Federal Constitutional Law, 30 December 2008, No. 7-ФК3];

(b) ensure the implementation in the Russian Federation of a unified financial, credit, and monetary policy;

(c) ensure the implementation in the Russian Federation of a unified socially-oriented State policy in the domain of culture, science, education, public health, social security, support for, strengthening, and defense of the family, preservation of traditional family values, and also in the domain of protection of the natural environment [as amended by Federal Constitutional Law, 14 March 2020, No. 1-ФК3];

(c^1) ensure State support for scientific-technological development of the Russian Federation, and the preservation and development of its scientific potential [added by Federal Constitutional Law, 14 March 2020, No. 1-ФК3];

(c^2) ensure the functioning of the system of social defense of disabled persons based on the full and equal effectuated by them of rights and freedoms of man and citizen, their social integration without any discrimination, and the creation of an accessible milieu for disabled persons and improvement of the quality of their life [added by Federal Constitutional Law, 14 March 2020, No. 1-ФК3];

(d) effectuate the administration of federal ownership;

(e) effectuate measures relating to ensuring the defense of the country, State security, and the realization of the foreign policy of the Russian Federation;

(f) effectuate measures relating to ensuring legality, the rights and freedoms of citizens, protection of ownership and public order, and the struggle against criminality;

(f^1) effectuate measures for the support of institutions of a civil society, including non-commercial organizations, and ensure their participation in working out and implementing State policy [added by Federal Constitutional Law, 14 March 2020, No. 1-ФКЗ];

(f^2) effectuate measures for the support of voluntary activity [added by Federal Constitutional Law, 14 March 2020, No. 1-ФКЗ];

(f^3) promote the development of entrepreneurship and private initiative [added by Federal Constitutional Law, 14 March 2020, No. 1-ФКЗ];

(f^4) ensure the realization of principles of social partnership in the sphere of the regulation of labor and other relations directly linked with them [added by Federal Constitutional Law, 14 March 2020, No. 1-ФКЗ];

(f^5) effectuate measures directed towards the creation of favorable conditions for the vital activity of the population, reduction of the negative impact of economic and other activity on the environment, preservation of unique natural and biological diversity of the country, and forming in society of a responsible attitude towards fauna [added by Federal Constitutional Law, 14 March 2020, No. 1-ФКЗ];

(f^6) create the conditions for development of a system of ecological education of citizens and nurturing of an ecological culture [added by Federal Constitutional Law, 14 March 2020, No. 1-ФКЗ];

(g) effectuate other powers placed on it by the Constitution of the Russian Federation, federal laws, and edicts of the President of the Russian Federation.

2. The procedure for the activity of the Government of the Russian Federation shall be determined by a federal constitutional law.

Article 115

1. On the basis of and in execution of the Constitution of the Russian Federation, federal laws, edicts, regulations, and assignments of the President of the Russian Federation, the Government of the Russian Federation shall issue decrees and regulations and ensure their execution [as amended by Federal Constitutional Law, 14 March 2020, No. 1-ФКЗ].

2. Decrees and regulations of the Government of the Russian Federation shall be binding for execution in the Russian Federation.

3. Decrees and regulations of the Government of the Russian Federation may in the event of their contradiction to the Constitution of the Russian Federation, federal laws, and edicts and regulations of the President of the

Russian Federation be repealed by the President of the Russian Federation [as amended by Federal Constitutional Law, 14 March 2020, No. 1-ФКЗ].

Article 116

The Government of the Russian Federation shall lay down its powers to a newly elected President of the Russian Federation.

Article 117

1. The Government of the Russian Federation may offer to resign, which may be accepted or rejected by the President of the Russian Federation.

2. The President of the Russian Federation may adopt a decision concerning the resignation of the Government of the Russian Federation.

3. The State Duma may express lack of confidence in the Government of the Russian Federation. The decree concerning lack of confidence in the Government of the Russian Federation shall be adopted by a majority vote of the total number of deputies of the State Duma. After the expression by the State Duma of lack of confidence in the Government of the Russian Federation, the President of the Russian Federation shall have the right to declare the resignation of the Government of the Russian Federation or not to agree with the decision of the State Duma. If the State Duma within three months expresses its lack of confidence a second time in the Government of the Russian Federation the President of the Russian Federation shall declare the resignation of the Government of the Russian Federation or dissolve the State Duma and designate new elections [as amended by Federal Constitutional Law, 14 March 2020, No. 1-ФКЗ].

4. The Chairman of the Government of the Russian Federation shall have the right to place before the State Duma the question of confidence in the Government of the Russian Federation, which shall be subject to consideration with seven days. If the State Duma refuses confidence in the Government of the Russian Federation, the President of the Russian Federation shall within seven days have the right to adopt a decision concerning the resignation of the Government of the Russian Federation or dissolution of the State Duma and the designation of new elections. If the Government of the Russian Federation within three months places a second time before the State Duma the question concerning confidence, and the State Duma refuses confidence in the Government of the Russian Federation, the President of the Russian Federation shall adopt a decision concerning the resignation of the Government of the Russian Federation or dissolution of the State Duma and the designation of new elections [as amended by Federal Constitutional Law, 14 March 2020, No. 1-ФКЗ]

4[1]. The Chairman of the Government of the Russian Federation, Deputy Chairman of the Government of the Russian Federation, and federal minister shall have the right to resign, which shall be adopted or rejected by the President of the Russian Federation [added by Federal Constitutional Law, 14 March 2020, No. 1-ФКЗ].

5. In the event of resignation or laying down powers, the Government of the Russian Federation shall on behalf of the President of the Russian Federation continue to operate until the formation of a new Government of the Russian Federation. In the event of being relieved from office by the President of the Russian Federation or resignation of the Chairman of the Government of the Russian Federation, Deputy Chairman of the Government of the Russian Federation, or federal minister, the President of the Russian Federation shall have the right to assign this person to continue to perform duties *ex officio* or place their execution on another person until the respective appointment [as amended by Federal Constitutional Law, 14 March 2020, No. 1-ФКЗ].

6. The State Duma may not express no confidence in the Government of the Russian Federation, and the Chairman of the Government of the Russian Federation may not place before the State Duma the question of confidence in the Government of the Russian Federation in instances provided by Article 109(3)-(5) of the Constitution of the Russian Federation, and also within a year after the appointment of the Chairman of the Government of the Russian Federation in accordance with Article 111(4) of the Constitution of the Russian Federation [added by Federal Constitutional Law, 14 March 2020, No. 1-ФКЗ].

Chapter 7. Judicial Power and the Procuracy

[as amended by Federal Constitutional Law, 5 February 2014, No. 2-ФКЗ]

Article 118

1. Justice in the Russian Federation shall be effectuated only by a court.

2. Judicial power shall be effectuated by means of constitutional, civil, arbitrazh, administrative, and criminal procedure [as amended by Federal Constitutional Law, 14 March 2020, No. 1-ФКЗ].

3. The judicial system of the Russian Federation shall be established by the Constitution of the Russian Federation and by a federal constitutional law. The Constitutional Court of the Russian Federation, Supreme Court of the Russian Federation, federal courts of general jurisdiction, arbitrazh courts, and justices of the peace of subjects of the Russian Federation shall comprise the judicial system of the Russian Federation. The creation of extraordinary courts shall not be permitted [as amended by Federal Constitutional Law, 14 March 2020, No. 1-ФКЗ].

Article 119

Citizens of the Russian Federation who have attained 25 years of age have a higher legal education and work experience in the legal profession of no less than five years, permanently reside in the Russian Federation, do not have the citizenship of a foreign State or residence permit or other document confirming the right to permanent residence of a citizen of the Russian federation on the territory of a foreign State, may be judges. Judges of courts of the Russian Federation in the procedure established by a federal law shall be prohibited to open and to have accounts (or deposits) and to keep cash monetary means and valuables in foreign banks located beyond the territory of the Russian Federation. Additional requirements for judges of courts of the Russian Federation may be established by a federal law [as amended by Federal Constitutional Law, 14 March 2020, No. 1-ФКЗ].

Article 120

1. Judges shall be independent and subordinate only to the Constitution of the Russian Federation and to a federal law.

2. A court, having established when considering a case the failure of an act of a State or other agency to conform to a law, shall adopt a decision in accordance with the law.

Article 121

1. Judges shall not be removable.

2. The powers of a judge may be terminated or suspended not other than in the procedure and on the grounds established by a federal law.

Article 122

1. Judges shall be inviolable.

2. A judge may not be brought to criminal responsibility other than in the procedure determined by a federal law.

Article 123

1. The examination of cases in all courts shall be open. The hearing of cases in closed session shall be permitted in the instances provided for by a federal law.

2. The examination of criminal cases in courts in absentia shall not be permitted except for instances provided for by a federal law.

3. Court procedure shall be effectuated on the basis of contentiousness and equality of the parties.

4. In the instances provided for by a federal law court procedure shall be effectuated with the participation of jurors.

Article 124

The financing of the courts shall be only from the federal budget and must ensure the full and independent effectuation of justice in accordance with a federal law.

Article 125

1. The Constitutional Court of the Russian Federation shall be the high judicial agency of constitutional control in the Russian Federation effectuating judicial power by means of constitutional adjudication for the purposes of the defense of the constitutional system, fundamental rights and freedoms of man and citizen, ensuring the supremacy and direct operation of the Constitution of the Russian Federation throughout the entire territory of the Russian Federation. The Constitutional Court of the Russian Federation shall consist of 11 judges, including the Chairman of the Constitutional Court of the Russian Federation and the deputy thereof [as amended by Federal Constitutional Law, 14 March 2020, No. 1-ФКЗ].

2. The Constitutional Court of the Russian Federation shall, with regard to queries of the President of the Russian Federation, Soviet of the Federation, State Duma, one-fifth of the senators of the Russian Federation or deputies of the State Duma, Government of the Russian Federation, Supreme Court of the Russian Federation, and agencies of legislative and executive power of subjects of the Russian Federation, settle cases concerning the conformity to the Russian Constitution of [as amended by Federal Constitutional Law, 5 February 2014, No. 2-ФКЗ, and by Federal Constitutional Law, 14 March 2020, No. 1-ФКЗ]:

(a) federal constitutional laws, federal laws, normative acts of the President of the Russian Federation, Soviet of the Federation, State Duma, and Government of the Russian Federation [as amended by Federal Constitutional Law, 14 March 2020, No. 1-ФКЗ];

(b) constitutions of the republics, charters, and also laws and other normative acts of subjects of the Russian Federation issued with regard to questions relegated to the jurisdiction of agencies of State power of the Russian Federation and the joint jurisdiction of agencies of State power of the Russian Federation and agencies of State power of subjects of the Russian Federation;

(c) treaties between agencies of State power of the Russian Federation and agencies of State power of subjects of the Russian Federation, and treaties between agencies of State power of subjects of the Russian Federation;

(d) international treaties of the Russian Federation which have not entered into legal force.

3. The Constitutional Court of the Russian Federation shall settle disputes concerning the competence:

(a) between federal agencies of State power;

(b) between agencies of State power of the Russian Federation and agencies of State power of subjects of the Russian Federation;

(c) between the highest State agencies of subjects of the Russian Federation.

4. The Constitutional Court of the Russian Federation shall verify in the procedure established by a federal constitutional law [as amended by Federal Constitutional Law, 14 March 2020, No. 1-ΦΚ3]:

(a) with regard to appeals against a violation of the constitutional rights and freedoms of citizens – the constitutionality of laws and other normative acts specified in point 2(a) and (b) of the present Article being applied in a concrete case if all other municipal means of judicial defense have been exhausted [as amended by Federal Constitutional Law, 14 March 2020, No. 1-ΦΚ3];

(b) with regard to queries of courts – the constitutionality of laws and other normative acts specified in point 2(a) and (b) of the present Article which are subject to application in a concrete case [as amended by Federal Constitutional Law, 14 March 2020, No. 1-ΦΚ3].

5. The Constitutional Court of the Russian Federation shall at the requests of the President of the Russian Federation, Soviet of the Federation, State Duma, Government of the Russian Federation, and agencies of legislative power of subjects of the Russian Federation give an interpretation of the Constitution of the Russian Federation.

5^1. The Constitutional Court of the Russian Federation shall [added by Federal Constitutional Law, 14 March 2020, No. 1-ΦΚ3]:

(a) with regard to a query of the President of the Russian Federation verify the constitutionality of draft laws of the Russian Federation concerning an amendment to the Constitution of the Russian Federation, draft federal constitutional laws and federal laws, and also laws before their signature by the President of the Russian Federation to be adopted in the procedure provided by Article 107(2) and (3) and Article 108(2) of the Constitution of the Russian Federation [added by Federal Constitutional Law, 14 March 2020, No. 1-ΦΚ3];

(b) in the procedure established by a federal constitutional law, settle the question concerning the possibility of the execution of decisions of inter-State agencies adopted on the basis of provisions of international treaties of the Russian Federation in a construing thereof which is contrary to the Constitution of the Russian Federation, and also the possibility of the execution of the decision of a foreign or international (or inter-State) court or foreign or international arbitration court imposing duties on the Russian Federation if this decision is contrary to the fundamental principles of public policy of the Russian Federation [added by Federal Constitutional Law, 14 March 2020, No. 1-ФКЗ];

(c) with regard to a query of the President of the Russian Federation in the procedure established by a federal constitutional law, verify the constitutionality of laws of subjects of the Russian Federation before their promulgation by the high official of a subject of the Russian Federation (or executive of the high executive agency of State power of a subject of the Russian Federation) [added by Federal Constitutional Law, 14 March 2020, No. 1-ФКЗ].

6. Acts or individual provisions thereof deemed to be unconstitutional shall lose force; international treaties of the Russian Federation which do not conform to the Constitution of the Russian Federation shall not be subject to introduction into operation and application. Acts or individual provisions thereof deemed to be unconstitutional in a construing given by the Constitutional Court of the Russian Federation shall not be subject to application in another construing [as amended by Federal Constitutional Law, 14 March 2020, No. 1-ФКЗ].

7. The Constitutional Court of the Russian Federation with regard to a query of the Soviet of the Federation shall give an opinion concerning the compliance with the established procedure of the putting forward of an accusation against the President of the Russian Federation or President of the Russian Federation who has terminated the execution of his powers of treason against the State or commission of another grave crime [as amended by Federal Constitutional Law, 14 March 2020, No. 1-ФКЗ].

8. The Constitutional Court of the Russian Federation shall effectuate other powers established by a federal constitutional law [added by Federal Constitutional Law, 14 March 2020, No. 1-ФКЗ].

Article 126

The Supreme Court of the Russian Federation shall be the high judicial agency with regard to civil cases, settlement of economic disputes, criminal, administrative and other cases within the jurisdiction of the courts of general jurisdiction and arbitrazh courts formed in accordance with a federal constitutional law and effectuating judicial power by means of civil, arbitrazh, administrative, and criminal adjudication. The Supreme Court of the Russian Federation shall effectuate judicial supervision over the activity of courts of general jurisdiction and arbitrazh courts in the procedural forms provided for by a federal law and give explanations regarding questions of judicial practice [as amended by Federal Constitutional Law, 5 February 2014, No. 2-ФКЗ, and by Federal Constitutional Law, 14 March 2020, No. 1-ФКЗ].

Article 127

[repealed by Amendment to the Constitution of the Russian Federation (Law of the Russian Federation on the Amendment to the Constitution of the Russian Federation "On the Supreme Court of the Russian Federation and Procuracy of the Russian Federation")].

Article 128

1. The Chairman of the Constitutional Court of the Russian Federation, Deputy Chairman of the Constitutional Court of the Constitutional Court of the Russian Federation, and judges of the Constitutional Court of the Russian Federation, Chairman of the Supreme Court of the Russian Federation, deputy chairmen of the Supreme Court of the Russian Federation, and judges of the Supreme Court of the Russian Federation shall be appointed by the Soviet of the Federation upon the recommendation of the President of the Russian Federation [as amended by Federal Constitutional Law, 5 February 2014, No. 2-ФКЗ, and by Federal Constitutional Law, 14 March 2020, No. 1-ФКЗ].

2. The chairmen, deputy chairmen, and judges of other federal courts shall be appointed by the President of the Russian Federation in the procedure established by a federal law [as amended by Federal Constitutional Law, 14 March 2020, No. 1-ФКЗ].

3. The powers, procedure for the formation, and activity of the Constitutional Court of the Russian Federation, Supreme Court of the Russian Federation, and other federal courts shall be established by the Constitution of the Russian Federation and a federal constitutional law. The procedure for the effectuation of civil, arbitrazh, administrative, and criminal adjudication shall be regulated also by respective procedural legislation [as amended by Federal Constitutional Law, 5 February 2014, No. 2-ФКЗ, and by Federal Constitutional Law, 14 March 2020, No. 1-ФКЗ].

Article 129

1. The Procuracy of the Russian Federation shall be a unified federal centralized system of agencies effectuating supervision over compliance with the Constitution of the Russian Federation and execution of laws, supervision over compliance with the rights and freedoms of man and citizen, criminal prosecution in accordance with its powers, and also fulfilling other functions. The powers and functions of the Procuracy of the Russian Federation, and the organization and procedure for the activity thereof, shall be determined by a federal law [as amended by Federal Constitutional Law, 5 February 2014, No. 2-ФКЗ, and by Federal Constitutional Law, 14 March 2020, No. 1-ФКЗ].

2. Citizens of the Russian Federation not having the citizenship of a foreign State or residence permit or other document confirming the right to

permanent residence of a citizen of the Russian Federation on the territory of a foreign State, may be procurators. Procurators in the procedure established by a federal law shall be prohibited from opening and having accounts (or deposits) and keeping cash monetary means and valuables in foreign banks located beyond the limits of the territory of the Russian Federation [added by Federal Constitutional Law, 14 March 2020, No. 1-ФК3].

3. The Procurator General of the Russian Federation and deputies of the Procurator General shall be appointed to office after consultations with the Soviet of the Federation and shall be relieved from office by the President of the Russian Federation [as amended by Federal Constitutional Law, 5 February 2014, No. 2-ФК3, and by Federal Constitutional Law, 14 March 2020, No. 1-ФК3].

4. The procurators of subjects of the Russian Federation and procurators of military and other specialized procuracies equated to procurators of subjects of the Russian Federation shall be appointed to office after consultations with the Soviet of the Federation and shall be relieved from office by the President of the Russian Federation [as amended by Federal Constitutional Law, 5 February 2014, No. 2-ФК3, and by Federal Constitutional Law, 14 March 2020, No. 1-ФК3].

4. Other procurators may be appointed to and relieved from office by the President of the Russian Federation if such procedure for appointment to and relieving from office has been established by a federal law [as amended by Federal Constitutional Law, 5 February 2014, No. 2-ФК3, and by Federal Constitutional Law, 14 March 2020, No. 1-ФК3].

6. Unless provided otherwise by a federal law, the procurators of cities, districts, and procurators equated thereto shall be appointed to and relieved from office by the Procurator General of the Russian Federation [as amended by Federal Constitutional Law, 5 February 2014, No. 2-ФК3, and by Federal Constitutional Law, 14 March 2020, No. 1-ФК3].

Chapter 8. Local Self-Government

Article 130

1. Local self-government in the Russian Federation shall ensure the autonomous deciding by the populace of questions of local significance and the possession, use, and disposition of municipal ownership.

2. Local self-government shall be effectuated by citizens through referendums, elections, and other forms of the direct expression of will and through elective and other agencies of local self-government.

Article 131

1. Local self-government shall be effectuated in municipal formations, the types of which shall be established by a federal law. The territories of municipal formations shall be determined by taking into account historical and other local traditions. The structure of agencies of local self-government shall be determined by the population autonomously in accordance with the general principles for the organization of local self-government in the Russian Federation established by a federal law [as amended by Federal Constitutional Law, 14 March 2020, No. 1-ФКЗ].

1^1. Agencies of State power may participate in the forming of agencies of local self-government, appoint and remove officials of local self-government to and from office in the procedure and instances established by a federal law [added by Federal Constitutional Law, 14 March 2020, No. 1-ФКЗ].

2. A change of the boundaries of the territories within whose limits local self-government is effectuated shall be permitted by taking into account the opinion of the populace of the respective territories in the procedure established by a federal law [as amended by Federal Constitutional Law, 14 March 2020, No. 1-ФКЗ].

3. The peculiarities of the effectuation of public power on the territories of cities of federal significance, administrative centers (or capitals) of subjects of the Russian Federation, and other territories may be established by a federal law [added by Federal Constitutional Law, 14 March 2020, No. 1-ФКЗ].

Article 132

1. Agencies of local self-government autonomously shall administer municipal ownership, form, confirm, and execute the local budget, introduce local taxes and charges, decide other questions of local significance, and also in accordance with a federal law ensure accessibility to medical care within the limits of its competence [as amended by Federal Constitutional Law, 14 March 2020, No. 1-ФКЗ].

2. Agencies of local self-government may be endowed by a federal law or law of a subject of the Russian Federation with individual State powers on condition of the transfer to them of necessary material and financial means for the effectuation of such powers. The realization of the powers transferred shall be under the control of the State [as amended by Federal Constitutional Law, 14 March 2020, No. 1-ФКЗ].

3. Agencies of local self-government and agencies of State power shall be within a unified system of public power in the Russian Federation and interact for the most effective resolution of tasks in the interests of the population residing on the respective territory [added by Federal Constitutional Law, 14 March 2020, No. 1-ФКЗ].

Article 133

Local self-government in the Russian Federation shall be guaranteed by the right to judicial defense, contributory compensation of additional expenses which arose as a result of the fulfillment of public functions by agencies of local self-government in interaction with agencies of State power, and also the prohibition against the limitation of the rights of local self-government established by the Constitution of the Russian Federation and by federal laws [as amended by Federal Constitutional Law, 14 March 2020, No. 1-ФКЗ].

Chapter 9. Constitutional Amendments and Revision of the Constitution

Article 134

Proposals concerning amendments to and revision of provisions of the Constitution of the Russian Federation may be submitted by the President of the Russian Federation, Soviet of the Federation, State Duma, Government of the Russian Federation, legislative (or representative) agencies of subjects of the Russian Federation, and also groups numbering not less than one-fifth of the members of the Soviet of the Federation or deputies of the State Duma.

Article 135

1. The provisions of Chapters 1, 2, and 9 of the Constitution of the Russian Federation may not be revised by the Federal Assembly.

2. If a proposal concerning a revision of the provisions of Chapters 1, 2, and 9 of the Constitution of the Russian Federation is supported by three-fifths of the votes of the total number of members of the Soviet of the Federation and deputies of the State Duma, then in accordance with a federal constitutional law a Constitutional Assembly shall be convoked.

3. A Constitutional Assembly either shall confirm the immutability of the Constitution of the Russian Federation or work out a draft new Constitution of the Russian Federation, which shall be adopted by the Constitutional Assembly by two-thirds of the votes of the total number of its members or shall be submitted to an all-people's referendum. When an all-people's referendum is held the Constitution of the Russian Federation shall be considered to be adopted if more than half of the electors who took part in the voting voted for it on condition that more than half of the electors have taken part in it.

Article 136

Amendments to Chapters 3-8 of the Constitution of the Russian Federation shall be adopted in the procedure provided for the adoption of a federal constitutional law and shall enter into force after their approval by agencies of legislative power of not less than two-thirds of the subjects of the Russian Federation.

Article 137

1. Changes in Article 65 of the Constitution of the Russian Federation determining the composition of the Russian Federation shall be made on the basis of a federal constitutional law concerning the admission to the Russian Federation and formation within it of a new subject of the Russian Federation and on changing the constitutional law status of a subject of the Russian Federation.

2. In the event of a change of name of a republic, territory, region, city of federal significance, autonomous region, or autonomous national area, the new name of a subject of the Russian Federation shall be subject to inclusion in Article 65 of the Constitution of the Russian Federation.

SECTION TWO

Concluding and Transitional Provisions

1. The Constitution of the Russian Federation shall enter into force from the day of its official publication according to the results of the all-people's vote.

The day of the all-people's vote on 12 December 1993 shall be considered to be the date of adoption of the Constitution of the Russian Federation.

The operation of the Constitution (Basic Law) of the Russian Federation-Russia adopted 12 April 1978, with subsequent changes and additions, shall terminate simultaneously.

In the event of the failure of the provisions of the Constitution of the Russian Federation to conform to the provisions of the Treaty of the Federation – the Treaty of the Delimitation of the Subjects of Jurisdiction and Powers Between Federal Agencies of State Power of the Russian Federation and Agencies of State Power of the Sovereign Republics within the Russian Federation, the Treaty on the Delimitation of the Subject of Jurisdiction and Powers Between Federal Agencies of State Power of the Russian Federation and Agencies of State Power of Territories, Regions, and the Cities of Moscow and St. Petersburg of the Russian Federation, the Treaty on the Delimitation of Subjects of Jurisdiction and Powers Between the Federal Agencies of State Power of the Russian Federation and the Agencies of State Power of the Autonomous Region and Autonomous National Areas within the Russian Federation, and also other treaties between federal agencies of State power of the Russian Federation and agencies of State power of subjects of the Russian Federation and treaties between agencies of State power of subjects of the Russian Federation – the provisions of the Constitution of the Russian Federation shall operate.

2. Laws and other legal acts which have operated on the territory of the Russian Federation before the entry into force of the present Constitution shall be applied in that part which is not contrary to the Constitution of the Russian Federation.

3. The President of the Russian Federation elected in accordance with the Constitution (Basic Law) of the Russian Federation-Russia shall from the date of entry into force of the present Constitution effectuate the powers established by it until the expiry of the term for which he was elected.

4. The Council of Ministers-Government of the Russian Federation shall from the date of entry into force of the present Constitution acquire the rights, duties, and responsibility of the Government of the Russian Federation established by the Constitution of the Russian Federation and thenceforth shall be named – the Government of the Russian Federation.

5. The courts in the Russian Federation shall effectuate justice in accordance with their powers established by the present Constitution.

After the entry into force of the Constitution the judges of all courts of the Russian Federation shall retain their powers until the expiry of the term for which they were elected. Vacant posts shall be filled in the procedure established by the present Constitution.

6. Until the introduction into operation of a federal law established the procedure for the consideration of cases by a court with the participation of jurors, the previous procedure for the judicial consideration of the respective cases shall be retained.

Until criminal procedure legislation of the Russian Federation is brought into conformity with the provisions of the present Constitution the previous procedure for arrest, confinement under guard, and detention of persons suspected of committing a crime shall be retained.

7. The Soviet of the Federation, first convocation, and the State Duma, first convocation, shall be elected for a term of two years.

8. The Soviet of the Federation shall assemble for its first session on the thirtieth day after the election. The first session of the Soviet of the Federation shall be opened by the President of the Russian Federation.

9. A deputy of the State Duma, first convocation, may simultaneously be a member of the Government of the Russian Federation. The provisions of the present Constitution concerning the inviolability of deputies with respect to responsibility for actions (or omissions to act) connected with the fulfillment of employment duties shall not extend to deputies of the State Duma who are members of the Government of the Russian Federation.

Deputies of the Soviet of the Federation, first convocation, shall effectuate their powers on a nonpermanent basis.

INDEX OF NAMES

www.ingramcontent.com/pod-product-compliance
Lightning Source LLC
LaVergne TN
LVHW091522200926
848483LV00002B/280
9781616196486